The Python Standard Library by Example

Developer's Library Series

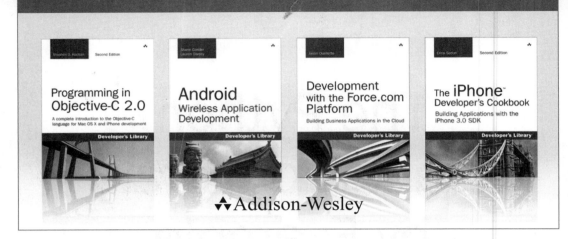

Visit **developers-library.com** for a complete list of available products

---

The **Developer's Library Series** from Addison-Wesley provides practicing programmers with unique, high-quality references and tutorials on the latest programming languages and technologies they use in their daily work. All books in the Developer's Library are written by expert technology practitioners who are exceptionally skilled at organizing and presenting information in a way that's useful for other programmers.

Developer's Library books cover a wide range of topics, from open-source programming languages and databases, Linux programming, Microsoft, and Java, to Web development, social networking platforms, Mac/iPhone programming, and Android programming.

PEARSON

✦Addison-Wesley   **Cisco Press**   EXAM/**CRAM**   **IBM** Press.   QUE   ‡‡ PRENTICE HALL   **S/AMS** | Safari Books Online

The Python Standard Library by Example

Doug Hellmann

✦ Addison-Wesley

Upper Saddle River, NJ • Boston • Indianapolis • San Francisco
New York • Toronto • Montreal • London • Munich • Paris • Madrid
Capetown • Sydney • Tokyo • Singapore • Mexico City

The publisher offers excellent discounts on this book when ordered in quantity for bulk purchases or special sales, which may include electronic versions and/or custom covers and content particular to your business, training goals, marketing focus, and branding interests. For more information, please contact:

U.S. Corporate and Government Sales
(800) 382-3419
corpsales@pearsontechgroup.com

For sales outside the United States, please contact:

International Sales
international@pearsoned.com

Visit us on the Web: informit.com/aw

Library of Congress Cataloging-in-Publication Data

Hellmann, Doug.

The Python standard library by example / Doug Hellmann.

p. cm.

Includes index.

ISBN 978-0-321-76734-9 (pbk. : alk. paper)

1. Python (Computer program language) I. Title.

QA76.73.P98H446 2011

005.13'3—dc22

2011006256

ISBN-13: 978-0-321-76734-9
ISBN-10:   0-321-76734-9

Text printed in the United States on recycled paper at Edwards Brothers in Ann Arbor, Michigan.
First printing, May 2011

This book is dedicated to my wife, Theresa,
for everything she has done for me.

CONTENTS AT A GLANCE

CONTENTS

TABLES

FOREWORD

It's Thanksgiving Day, 2010. For those outside of the United States, and for many of those within it, it might just seem like a holiday where people eat a ton of food, watch some football, and otherwise hang out.

For me, and many others, it's a time to take a look back and think about the things that have enriched our lives and give thanks for them. Sure, we should be doing that every day, but having a single day that's focused on just saying thanks sometimes makes us think a bit more broadly and a bit more deeply.

I'm sitting here writing the foreward to this book, something I'm very thankful for having the opportunity to do—but I'm not just thinking about the content of the book, or the author, who is a fantastic community member. I'm thinking about the subject matter itself—Python—and specifically, its standard library.

Every version of Python shipped today contains hundreds of modules spanning many years, many developers, many subjects, and many tasks. It contains modules for everything from sending and receiving email, to GUI development, to a built-in HTTP server. By itself, the standard library is a massive work. Without the people who have maintained it throughout the years, and the hundreds of people who have submitted patches, documentation, and feedback, it would not be what it is today.

It's an astounding accomplishment, and something that has been the critical component in the rise of Python's popularity as a language and ecosystem. Without the standard library, without the "batteries included" motto of the core team and others, Python would never have come as far. It has been downloaded by hundreds of thousands of people and companies, and has been installed on millions of servers, desktops, and other devices.

Without the standard library, Python would still be a fantastic language, built on solid concepts of teaching, learning, and readability. It might have gotten far enough on its own, based on those merits. But the standard library turns it from an interesting experiment into a powerful and effective tool.

Every day, developers across the world build tools and entire applications based on nothing but the core language and the standard library. You not only get the ability to conceptualize what a car is (the language), but you also get enough parts and tools to put together a basic car yourself. It might not be the perfect car, but it gets you from A to B, and that's incredibly empowering and rewarding. Time and time again, I speak to people who look at me proudly and say, "Look what I built with nothing except what came with Python!"

It is not, however, a *fait accompli*. The standard library has its warts. Given its size and breadth, and its age, it's no real surprise that some of the modules have varying levels of quality, API clarity, and coverage. Some of the modules have suffered "feature creep," or have failed to keep up with modern advances in the areas they cover. Python continues to evolve, grow, and improve over time through the help and hard work of many, many unpaid volunteers.

Some argue, though, that due to the shortcomings and because the standard library doesn't necessarily comprise the "best of breed" solutions for the areas its modules cover ("best of" is a continually moving and adapting target, after all), that it should be killed or sent out to pasture, despite continual improvement. These people miss the fact that not only is the standard library a critical piece of what makes Python continually successful, but also, despite its warts, it is still an excellent resource.

But I've intentionally ignored one giant area: documentation. The standard library's documentation is good and is constantly improving and evolving. Given the size and breadth of the standard library, the documentation is amazing for what it is. It's awesome that we have hundreds of pages of documentation contributed by hundreds of developers and users. The documentation is used every single day by hundreds of thousands of people to create things—things as simple as one-off scripts and as complex as the software that controls giant robotic arms.

The documentation is why we are here, though. All good documentation and code starts with an idea—a kernel of a concept about what something is, or will be. Outward from that kernel come the characters (the APIs) and the storyline (the modules). In the case of code, sometimes it starts with a simple idea: "I want to parse a string and look for a date." But when you reach the end—when you're looking at the few hundred unit tests, functions, and other bits you've made—you sit back and realize you've built something much, much more vast than originally intended. The same goes for documentation, especially the documentation of code.

The examples are the most critical component in the documentation of code, in my estimation. You can write a narrative about a piece of an API until it spans entire books, and you can describe the loosely coupled interface with pretty words and thoughtful use cases. But it all falls flat if a user approaching it for the first time can't glue those pretty words, thoughtful use cases, and API signatures together into something that makes sense and solves their problems.

Examples are the gateway by which people make the critical connections—those logical jumps from an abstract concept into something concrete. It's one thing to "know" the ideas and API; it's another to see it used. It helps jump the void when you're not only trying to learn something, but also trying to improve existing things.

Which brings us back to Python. Doug Hellmann, the author of this book, started a blog in 2007 called the *Python Module of the Week*. In the blog, he walked through various modules of the standard library, taking an example-first approach to showing how each one worked and why. From the first day I read it, it had a place right next to the core Python documentation. His writing has become an indispensable resource for me and many other people in the Python community.

Doug's writings fill a critical gap in the Python documentation I see today: the need for examples. Showing how and why something works in a functional, simple manner is no easy task. And, as we've seen, it's a critical and valuable body of work that helps people every single day. People send me emails with alarming regularity saying things like, "Did you see this post by Doug? This is awesome!" or "Why isn't this in the core documentation? It helped me understand how things really work!"

When I heard Doug was going to take the time to further flesh out his existing work, to turn it into a book I could keep on my desk to dog-ear and wear out from near constant use, I was more than a little excited. Doug is a fantastic technical writer with a great eye for detail. Having an entire book dedicated to real examples of how over a hundred modules in the standard library work, written by him, blows my mind.

You see, I'm thankful for Python. I'm thankful for the standard library—warts and all. I'm thankful for the massive, vibrant, yet sometimes dysfunctional community we have. I'm thankful for the tireless work of the core development team, past, present and future. I'm thankful for the resources, the time, and the effort so many community members—of which Doug Hellmann is an exemplary example—have put into making this community and ecosystem such an amazing place.

Lastly, I'm thankful for this book. Its author will continue to be well respected and the book well used in the years to come.

— Jesse Noller
  Python Core Developer
  PSF Board Member
  Principal Engineer, Nasuni Corporation

ACKNOWLEDGMENTS

This book would not have come into being without the contributions and support of many people.

I was first introduced to Python around 1997 by Dick Wall, while we were working together on GIS software at ERDAS. I remember being simultaneously happy that I had found a new tool language that was so easy to use, and sad that the company did not let us use it for "real work." I have used Python extensively at all of my subsequent jobs, and I have Dick to thank for the many happy hours I have spent working on software since then.

The Python core development team has created a robust ecosystem of language, tools, and libraries that continue to grow in popularity and find new application areas. Without the amazing investment in time and resources they have given us, we would all still be spending our time reinventing wheel after wheel.

As described in the Introduction, the material in this book started out as a series of blog posts. Each of those posts has been reviewed and commented on by members of the Python community, with corrections, suggestions, and questions that led to changes in the version you find here. Thank you all for reading along week after week, and contributing your time and attention.

The technical reviewers for the book—Matt Culbreth, Katie Cunningham, Jeff McNeil, and Keyton Weissinger—spent many hours looking for issues with the example code and accompanying explanations. The result is stronger than I could have produced on my own. I also received advice from Jesse Noller on the multiprocessing module and Brett Cannon on creating custom importers.

A special thanks goes to the editors and production staff at Pearson for all their hard work and assistance in helping me realize my vision for this book.

Finally, I want to thank my wife, Theresa Flynn, who has always given me excellent writing advice and was a constant source of encouragement throughout the entire process of creating this book. I doubt she knew what she was getting herself into when she told me, "You know, at some point, you have to sit down and start writing it." It's your turn.

ABOUT THE AUTHOR

Doug Hellmann is currently a senior developer with Racemi, Inc., and communications director of the Python Software Foundation. He has been programming in Python since version 1.4 and has worked on a variety of UNIX and non-UNIX platforms for projects in fields such as mapping, medical news publishing, banking, and data center automation. After a year as a regular columnist for *Python Magazine*, he served as editor-in-chief from 2008–2009. Since 2007, Doug has published the popular *Python Module of the Week* series on his blog. He lives in Athens, Georgia.

INTRODUCTION

Distributed with every copy of Python, the standard library contains hundreds of modules that provide tools for interacting with the operating system, interpreter, and Internet. All of them are tested and ready to be used to jump start the development of your applications. This book presents selected examples demonstrating how to use the most commonly used features of the modules that give Python its "batteries included" slogan, taken from the popular *Python Module of the Week* (PyMOTW) blog series.

This Book's Target Audience

The audience for this book is an intermediate Python programmer, so although all the source code is presented with discussion, only a few cases include line-by-line explanations. Every section focuses on the features of the modules, illustrated by the source code and output from fully independent example programs. Each feature is presented as concisely as possible, so the reader can focus on the module or function being demonstrated without being distracted by the supporting code.

An experienced programmer familiar with other languages may be able to learn Python from this book, but it is not intended to be an introduction to the language. Some prior experience writing Python programs will be useful when studying the examples.

Several sections, such as the description of network programming with sockets or hmac encryption, require domain-specific knowledge. The basic information needed to explain the examples is included here, but the range of topics covered by the modules in the standard library makes it impossible to cover every topic comprehensively in a single volume. The discussion of each module is followed by a list of suggested sources for more information and further reading. These include online resources, RFC standards documents, and related books.

Although the current transition to Python 3 is well underway, Python 2 is still likely to be the primary version of Python used in production environments for years to come because of the large amount of legacy Python 2 source code available and the slow transition rate to Python 3. All the source code for the examples has been updated from the original online versions and tested with Python 2.7, the final release of the 2.x series. Many of the example programs can be readily adapted to work with Python 3, but others cover modules that have been renamed or deprecated.

How This Book Is Organized

The modules are grouped into chapters to make it easy to find an individual module for reference and browse by subject for more leisurely exploration. The book supplements the comprehensive reference guide available on http://docs.python.org, providing fully functional example programs to demonstrate the features described there.

Downloading the Example Code

The original versions of the articles, errata for the book, and the sample code are available on the author's web site (http://www.doughellmann.com/books/byexample).

Chapter 1

TEXT

The `string` class is the most obvious text-processing tool available to Python programmers, but plenty of other tools in the standard library are available to make advanced text manipulation simple.

Older code, written before Python 2.0, uses functions from the `string` module, instead of methods of `string` objects. There is an equivalent method for each function from the module, and use of the functions is deprecated for new code.

Programs using Python 2.4 or later may use `string.Template` as a simple way to parameterize strings beyond the features of the `string` or `unicode` classes. While not as feature-rich as templates defined by many of the Web frameworks or extension modules available from the Python Package Index, `string.Template` is a good middle ground for user-modifiable templates where dynamic values need to be inserted into otherwise static text.

The `textwrap` module includes tools for formatting text taken from paragraphs by limiting the width of output, adding indentation, and inserting line breaks to wrap lines consistently.

The standard library includes two modules related to comparing text values beyond the built-in equality and sort comparison supported by string objects. `re` provides a complete regular expression library, implemented in C for speed. Regular expressions are well-suited to finding substrings within a larger data set, comparing strings against a pattern more complex than another fixed string, and performing mild parsing.

`difflib`, on the other hand, computes the actual differences between sequences of text in terms of the parts added, removed, or changed. The output of the comparison functions in `difflib` can be used to provide more detailed feedback to users about where changes occur in two inputs, how a document has changed over time, etc.

1.1 string—Text Constants and Templates

> **Purpose** Contains constants and classes for working with text.
> **Python Version** 1.4 and later

The `string` module dates from the earliest versions of Python. In version 2.0, many of the functions previously implemented only in the module were moved to methods of `str` and `unicode` objects. Legacy versions of those functions are still available, but their use is deprecated and they will be dropped in Python 3.0. The `string` module retains several useful constants and classes for working with `string` and `unicode` objects, and this discussion will concentrate on them.

1.1.1 Functions

The two functions `capwords()` and `maketrans()` are not moving from the string module. `capwords()` capitalizes all words in a string.

```
import string

s = 'The quick brown fox jumped over the lazy dog.'

print s
print string.capwords(s)
```

The results are the same as calling `split()`, capitalizing the words in the resulting list, and then calling `join()` to combine the results.

```
$ python string_capwords.py

The quick brown fox jumped over the lazy dog.
The Quick Brown Fox Jumped Over The Lazy Dog.
```

The `maketrans()` function creates translation tables that can be used with the `translate()` method to change one set of characters to another more efficiently than with repeated calls to `replace()`.

```
import string

leet = string.maketrans('abegiloprstz', '463611092572')
```

```
s = 'The quick brown fox jumped over the lazy dog.'

print s
print s.translate(leet)
```

In this example, some letters are replaced by their l33t number alternatives.

```
$ python string_maketrans.py

The quick brown fox jumped over the lazy dog.
Th3 qu1ck 620wn f0x jum93d 0v32 7h3 142y d06.
```

1.1.2   Templates

String templates were added in Python 2.4 as part of PEP 292 and are intended as an alternative to the built-in interpolation syntax. With `string.Template` interpolation, variables are identified by prefixing the name with `$` (e.g., `$var`) or, if necessary to set them off from surrounding text, they can also be wrapped with curly braces (e.g., `${var}`).

This example compares a simple template with a similar string interpolation using the `%` operator.

```
import string

values = { 'var':'foo' }

t = string.Template("""
Variable         : $var
Escape           : $$
Variable in text: ${var}iable
""")

print 'TEMPLATE:', t.substitute(values)

s = """
Variable         : %(var)s
Escape           : %%
Variable in text: %(var)siable
"""

print 'INTERPOLATION:', s % values
```

In both cases, the trigger character ($ or %) is escaped by repeating it twice.

```
$ python string_template.py

TEMPLATE:
Variable        : foo
Escape          : $
Variable in text: fooiable

INTERPOLATION:
Variable        : foo
Escape          : %
Variable in text: fooiable
```

One key difference between templates and standard string interpolation is that the argument type is not considered. The values are converted to strings, and the strings are inserted into the result. No formatting options are available. For example, there is no way to control the number of digits used to represent a floating-point value.

A benefit, though, is that by using the `safe_substitute()` method, it is possible to avoid exceptions if not all values the template needs are provided as arguments.

```
import string

values = { 'var':'foo' }

t = string.Template("$var is here but $missing is not provided")

try:
    print 'substitute()      :', t.substitute(values)
except KeyError, err:
    print 'ERROR:', str(err)

print 'safe_substitute():', t.safe_substitute(values)
```

Since there is no value for *missing* in the values dictionary, a `KeyError` is raised by `substitute()`. Instead of raising the error, `safe_substitute()` catches it and leaves the variable expression alone in the text.

```
$ python string_template_missing.py
```

```
substitute()      : ERROR: 'missing'
safe_substitute(): foo is here but $missing is not provided
```

1.1.3   Advanced Templates

The default syntax for string.Template can be changed by adjusting the regular expression patterns it uses to find the variable names in the template body. A simple way to do that is to change the delimiter and idpattern class attributes.

```
import string

template_text = '''
  Delimiter : %%
  Replaced  : %with_underscore
  Ignored   : %notunderscored
'''

d = { 'with_underscore':'replaced',
      'notunderscored':'not replaced',
      }

class MyTemplate(string.Template):
    delimiter = '%'
    idpattern = '[a-z]+_[a-z]+'

t = MyTemplate(template_text)
print 'Modified ID pattern:'
print t.safe_substitute(d)
```

In this example, the substitution rules are changed so that the delimiter is % instead of $ and variable names must include an underscore. The pattern %notunderscored is not replaced by anything because it does not include an underscore character.

```
$ python string_template_advanced.py

Modified ID pattern:

  Delimiter : %
  Replaced  : replaced
  Ignored   : %notunderscored
```

For more complex changes, override the `pattern` attribute and define an entirely new regular expression. The pattern provided must contain four named groups for capturing the escaped delimiter, the named variable, a braced version of the variable name, and any invalid delimiter patterns.

```
import string

t = string.Template('$var')
print t.pattern.pattern
```

The value of `t.pattern` is a compiled regular expression, but the original string is available via its `pattern` attribute.

```
\$(?:
  (?P<escaped>\$) |                    # two delimiters
  (?P<named>[_a-z][_a-z0-9]*)      | # identifier
  {(?P<braced>[_a-z][_a-z0-9]*)} | # braced identifier
  (?P<invalid>)                       # ill-formed delimiter exprs
)
```

This example defines a new pattern to create a new type of template using `{{var}}` as the variable syntax.

```
import re
import string

class MyTemplate(string.Template):
    delimiter = '{{'
    pattern = r'''
    \{\{(?:
    (?P<escaped>\{\{)|
    (?P<named>[_a-z][_a-z0-9]*)\}\}|
    (?P<braced>[_a-z][_a-z0-9]*)\}\}|
    (?P<invalid>)
    )
    '''

t = MyTemplate('''
{{{{
{{var}}
''')
```

```
print 'MATCHES:', t.pattern.findall(t.template)
print 'SUBSTITUTED:', t.safe_substitute(var='replacement')
```

Both the `named` and `braced` patterns must be provided separately, even though they are the same. Running the sample program generates:

```
$ python string_template_newsyntax.py

MATCHES: [('{{', '', '', ''), ('', 'var', '', '')]
SUBSTITUTED:
{{
replacement
```

See Also:

string (http://docs.python.org/lib/module-string.html) Standard library documentation for this module.

String Methods (http://docs.python.org/lib/string-methods.html#string-methods) Methods of `str` objects that replace the deprecated functions in `string`.

PEP 292 (www.python.org/dev/peps/pep-0292) A proposal for a simpler string substitution syntax.

l33t (http://en.wikipedia.org/wiki/Leet) "Leetspeak" alternative alphabet.

1.2   textwrap—Formatting Text Paragraphs

> **Purpose** Formatting text by adjusting where line breaks occur in a paragraph.
> **Python Version** 2.5 and later

The `textwrap` module can be used to format text for output when pretty-printing is desired. It offers programmatic functionality similar to the paragraph wrapping or filling features found in many text editors and word processors.

1.2.1   Example Data

The examples in this section use the module `textwrap_example.py`, which contains a string `sample_text`.

```
sample_text = '''
    The textwrap module can be used to format text for output in
    situations where pretty-printing is desired.  It offers
```

```
    programmatic functionality similar to the paragraph wrapping
    or filling features found in many text editors.
    '''
```

1.2.2   Filling Paragraphs

The fill() function takes text as input and produces formatted text as output.

```
import textwrap
from textwrap_example import sample_text

print 'No dedent:\n'
print textwrap.fill(sample_text, width=50)
```

The results are something less than desirable. The text is now left justified, but the first line retains its indent and the spaces from the front of each subsequent line are embedded in the paragraph.

```
$ python textwrap_fill.py

No dedent:

    The textwrap module can be used to format
text for output in     situations where pretty-
printing is desired.   It offers    programmatic
functionality similar to the paragraph wrapping
or filling features found in many text editors.
```

1.2.3   Removing Existing Indentation

The previous example has embedded tabs and extra spaces mixed into the output, so it is not formatted very cleanly. Removing the common whitespace prefix from all lines in the sample text produces better results and allows the use of docstrings or embedded multiline strings straight from Python code while removing the code formatting itself. The sample string has an artificial indent level introduced for illustrating this feature.

```
import textwrap
from textwrap_example import sample_text

dedented_text = textwrap.dedent(sample_text)
print 'Dedented:'
print dedented_text
```

The results are starting to look better:

```
$ python textwrap_dedent.py

Dedented:

The textwrap module can be used to format text for output in
situations where pretty-printing is desired.  It offers
programmatic functionality similar to the paragraph wrapping
or filling features found in many text editors.
```

Since "dedent" is the opposite of "indent," the result is a block of text with the common initial whitespace from each line removed. If one line is already indented more than another, some of the whitespace will not be removed.

Input like

```
␣Line one.
␣␣␣Line two.
␣Line three.
```

becomes

```
Line one.
␣␣Line two.
Line three.
```

1.2.4   Combining Dedent and Fill

Next, the dedented text can be passed through `fill()` with a few different *width* values.

```
import textwrap
from textwrap_example import sample_text

dedented_text = textwrap.dedent(sample_text).strip()
for width in [ 45, 70 ]:
        print '%d Columns:\n' % width
        print textwrap.fill(dedented_text, width=width)
        print
```

This produces outputs in the specified widths.

```
$ python textwrap_fill_width.py

45 Columns:

The textwrap module can be used to format
text for output in situations where pretty-
printing is desired.  It offers programmatic
functionality similar to the paragraph
wrapping or filling features found in many
text editors.

70 Columns:

The textwrap module can be used to format text for output in
situations where pretty-printing is desired.  It offers programmatic
functionality similar to the paragraph wrapping or filling features
found in many text editors.
```

1.2.5   Hanging Indents

Just as the width of the output can be set, the indent of the first line can be controlled independently of subsequent lines.

```
import textwrap
from textwrap_example import sample_text

dedented_text = textwrap.dedent(sample_text).strip()
print textwrap.fill(dedented_text,
                    initial_indent='',
                    subsequent_indent=' ' * 4,
                    width=50,
                    )
```

This makes it possible to produce a hanging indent, where the first line is indented less than the other lines.

```
$ python textwrap_hanging_indent.py

The textwrap module can be used to format text for
    output in situations where pretty-printing is
    desired.  It offers programmatic functionality
```

```
similar to the paragraph wrapping or filling
features found in many text editors.
```

The indent values can include nonwhitespace characters, too. The hanging indent can be prefixed with `*` to produce bullet points, etc.

See Also:
textwrap (http://docs.python.org/lib/module-textwrap.html) Standard library documentation for this module.

1.3   re—Regular Expressions

Purpose Searching within and changing text using formal patterns.
Python Version 1.5 and later

Regular expressions are text-matching patterns described with a formal syntax. The patterns are interpreted as a set of instructions, which are then executed with a string as input to produce a matching subset or modified version of the original. The term "regular expressions" is frequently shortened to "regex" or "regexp" in conversation. Expressions can include literal text matching, repetition, pattern composition, branching, and other sophisticated rules. Many parsing problems are easier to solve using a regular expression than by creating a special-purpose lexer and parser.

Regular expressions are typically used in applications that involve a lot of text processing. For example, they are commonly used as search patterns in text-editing programs used by developers, including vi, emacs, and modern IDEs. They are also an integral part of UNIX command line utilities, such as sed, grep, and awk. Many programming languages include support for regular expressions in the language syntax (Perl, Ruby, Awk, and Tcl). Other languages, such as C, C++, and Python, support regular expressions through extension libraries.

There are multiple open source implementations of regular expressions, each sharing a common core syntax but having different extensions or modifications to their advanced features. The syntax used in Python's `re` module is based on the syntax used for regular expressions in Perl, with a few Python-specific enhancements.

Note: Although the formal definition of "regular expression" is limited to expressions that describe regular languages, some of the extensions supported by `re` go beyond describing regular languages. The term "regular expression" is used here in a more general sense to mean any expression that can be evaluated by Python's `re` module.

1.3.1   Finding Patterns in Text

The most common use for `re` is to search for patterns in text. The `search()` function takes the pattern and text to scan, and returns a `Match` object when the pattern is found. If the pattern is not found, `search()` returns `None`.

Each `Match` object holds information about the nature of the match, including the original input string, the regular expression used, and the location within the original string where the pattern occurs.

```
import re

pattern = 'this'
text = 'Does this text match the pattern?'

match = re.search(pattern, text)

s = match.start()
e = match.end()

print 'Found "%s"\nin "%s"\nfrom %d to %d ("%s")' % \
    (match.re.pattern, match.string, s, e, text[s:e])
```

The `start()` and `end()` methods give the indexes into the string showing where the text matched by the pattern occurs.

```
$ python re_simple_match.py

Found "this"
in "Does this text match the pattern?"
from 5 to 9 ("this")
```

1.3.2   Compiling Expressions

`re` includes module-level functions for working with regular expressions as text strings, but it is more efficient to *compile* the expressions a program uses frequently. The `compile()` function converts an expression string into a `RegexObject`.

```
import re

# Precompile the patterns
regexes = [ re.compile(p)
```

```
            for p in [ 'this', 'that' ]
            ]
text = 'Does this text match the pattern?'

print 'Text: %r\n' % text

for regex in regexes:
    print 'Seeking "%s" ->' % regex.pattern,

    if regex.search(text):
        print 'match!'
    else:
        print 'no match'
```

The module-level functions maintain a cache of compiled expressions. However, the size of the cache is limited, and using compiled expressions directly avoids the cache lookup overhead. Another advantage of using compiled expressions is that by precompiling all expressions when the module is loaded, the compilation work is shifted to application start time, instead of to a point when the program may be responding to a user action.

```
$ python re_simple_compiled.py

Text: 'Does this text match the pattern?'

Seeking "this" -> match!
Seeking "that" -> no match
```

1.3.3   Multiple Matches

So far, the example patterns have all used `search()` to look for single instances of literal text strings. The `findall()` function returns all substrings of the input that match the pattern without overlapping.

```
import re

text = 'abbaaabbbbaaaaa'

pattern = 'ab'

for match in re.findall(pattern, text):
    print 'Found "%s"' % match
```

There are two instances of `ab` in the input string.

```
$ python re_findall.py

Found "ab"
Found "ab"
```

`finditer()` returns an iterator that produces `Match` instances instead of the strings returned by `findall()`.

```
import re

text = 'abbaaabbbbaaaaa'

pattern = 'ab'

for match in re.finditer(pattern, text):
    s = match.start()
    e = match.end()
    print 'Found "%s" at %d:%d' % (text[s:e], s, e)
```

This example finds the same two occurrences of `ab`, and the `Match` instance shows where they are in the original input.

```
$ python re_finditer.py

Found "ab" at 0:2
Found "ab" at 5:7
```

1.3.4   Pattern Syntax

Regular expressions support more powerful patterns than simple literal text strings. Patterns can repeat, can be anchored to different logical locations within the input, and can be expressed in compact forms that do not require every literal character to be present in the pattern. All of these features are used by combining literal text values with *metacharacters* that are part of the regular expression pattern syntax implemented by `re`.

```
import re

def test_patterns(text, patterns=[]):
```

```
    """Given source text and a list of patterns, look for
    matches for each pattern within the text and print
    them to stdout.
    """
    # Look for each pattern in the text and print the results
    for pattern, desc in patterns:
        print 'Pattern %r (%s)\n' % (pattern, desc)
        print '  %r' % text
        for match in re.finditer(pattern, text):
            s = match.start()
            e = match.end()
            substr = text[s:e]
            n_backslashes = text[:s].count('\\')
            prefix = '.' * (s + n_backslashes)
            print '  %s%r' % (prefix, substr)
        print
    return


if __name__ == '__main__':
    test_patterns('abbaaabbbbaaaaa',
                  [('ab', "'a' followed by 'b'"),
                  ])
```

The following examples will use `test_patterns()` to explore how variations in patterns change the way they match the same input text. The output shows the input text and the substring range from each portion of the input that matches the pattern.

```
$ python re_test_patterns.py

Pattern 'ab' ('a' followed by 'b')

  'abbaaabbbbaaaaa'
  'ab'
  .....'ab'
```

Repetition

There are five ways to express repetition in a pattern. A pattern followed by the metacharacter `*` is repeated zero or more times. (Allowing a pattern to repeat zero times means it does not need to appear at all to match.) Replace the `*` with `+` and the pattern must appear at least once. Using `?` means the pattern appears zero times or one time. For a specific number of occurrences, use `{m}` after the pattern, where *m* is the number of times the pattern should repeat. And, finally, to allow a variable but limited number of repetitions, use {m, n} where *m* is the minimum number of repetitions and *n* is the maximum. Leaving out *n* ({m, }) means the value appears at least *m* times, with no maximum.

```
from re_test_patterns import test_patterns
```

```
test_patterns(
    'abbaabbba',
    [ ('ab*',     'a followed by zero or more b'),
      ('ab+',     'a followed by one or more b'),
      ('ab?',     'a followed by zero or one b'),
      ('ab{3}',   'a followed by three b'),
      ('ab{2,3}', 'a followed by two to three b'),
      ])
```

There are more matches for ab* and ab? than ab+.

```
$ python re_repetition.py

Pattern 'ab*' (a followed by zero or more b)

  'abbaabbba'
  'abb'
  ...'a'
  ....'abbb'
  ........'a'

Pattern 'ab+' (a followed by one or more b)

  'abbaabbba'
  'abb'
  ....'abbb'

Pattern 'ab?' (a followed by zero or one b)

  'abbaabbba'
  'ab'
  ...'a'
  ....'ab'
  ........'a'
```

```
Pattern 'ab{3}' (a followed by three b)

  'abbaabbba'
  ....'abbb'

Pattern 'ab{2,3}' (a followed by two to three b)

  'abbaabbba'
  'abb'
  ....'abbb'
```

Normally, when processing a repetition instruction, re will consume as much of the input as possible while matching the pattern. This so-called *greedy* behavior may result in fewer individual matches, or the matches may include more of the input text than intended. Greediness can be turned off by following the repetition instruction with ?.

from re_test_patterns import test_patterns

```
test_patterns(
    'abbaabbba',
    [ ('ab*?',     'a followed by zero or more b'),
      ('ab+?',     'a followed by one or more b'),
      ('ab??',     'a followed by zero or one b'),
      ('ab{3}?',   'a followed by three b'),
      ('ab{2,3}?', 'a followed by two to three b'),
    ])
```

Disabling greedy consumption of the input for any patterns where zero occurrences of b are allowed means the matched substring does not include any b characters.

```
$ python re_repetition_non_greedy.py

Pattern 'ab*?' (a followed by zero or more b)

  'abbaabbba'
  'a'
  ...'a'
  ....'a'
  ........'a'
```

```
Pattern 'ab+?' (a followed by one or more b)

  'abbaabbba'
  'ab'
  ....'ab'

Pattern 'ab??' (a followed by zero or one b)

  'abbaabbba'
  'a'
  ...'a'
  ....'a'
  ........'a'

Pattern 'ab{3}?' (a followed by three b)

  'abbaabbba'
  ....'abbb'

Pattern 'ab{2,3}?' (a followed by two to three b)

  'abbaabbba'
  'abb'
  ....'abb'
```

Character Sets

A *character set* is a group of characters, any one of which can match at that point in the pattern. For example, [ab] would match either a or b.

```
from re_test_patterns import test_patterns

test_patterns(
    'abbaabbba',
    [ ('[ab]',     'either a or b'),
      ('a[ab]+',   'a followed by 1 or more a or b'),
      ('a[ab]+?', 'a followed by 1 or more a or b, not greedy'),
      ])
```

The greedy form of the expression (a[ab]+) consumes the entire string because the first letter is a and every subsequent character is either a or b.

```
$ python re_charset.py

Pattern '[ab]' (either a or b)

  'abbaabbba'
  'a'
 .'b'
 ..'b'
 ...'a'
 ....'a'
 .....'b'
 ......'b'
 .......'b'
 ........'a'

Pattern 'a[ab]+' (a followed by 1 or more a or b)

  'abbaabbba'
  'abbaabbba'

Pattern 'a[ab]+?' (a followed by 1 or more a or b, not greedy)

  'abbaabbba'
  'ab'
 ...'aa'
```

A character set can also be used to exclude specific characters. The carat (^) means to look for characters not in the set following.

```
from re_test_patterns import test_patterns

test_patterns(
    'This is some text -- with punctuation.',
    [ ('[^-. ]+', 'sequences without -, ., or space'),
      ])
```

This pattern finds all the substrings that do not contain the characters -, ., or a space.

```
$ python re_charset_exclude.py

Pattern '[^-. ]+' (sequences without -, ., or space)
```

```
'This is some text -- with punctuation.'
'This'
.....'is'
........'some'
............'text'
....................'with'
........................'punctuation'
```

As character sets grow larger, typing every character that should (or should not) match becomes tedious. A more compact format using *character ranges* can be used to define a character set to include all contiguous characters between a start point and a stop point.

```
from re_test_patterns import test_patterns

test_patterns(
    'This is some text -- with punctuation.',
    [ ('[a-z]+', 'sequences of lowercase letters'),
      ('[A-Z]+', 'sequences of uppercase letters'),
      ('[a-zA-Z]+', 'sequences of lowercase or uppercase letters'),
      ('[A-Z][a-z]+', 'one uppercase followed by lowercase'),
      ])
```

Here the range a-z includes the lowercase ASCII letters, and the range A-Z includes the uppercase ASCII letters. The ranges can also be combined into a single character set.

```
$ python re_charset_ranges.py

Pattern '[a-z]+' (sequences of lowercase letters)

  'This is some text -- with punctuation.'
  .'his'
  .....'is'
  ........'some'
  ............'text'
  ....................'with'
  ........................'punctuation'

Pattern '[A-Z]+' (sequences of uppercase letters)

  'This is some text -- with punctuation.'
  'T'
```

Pattern '[a-zA-Z]+' (sequences of lowercase or uppercase letters)

```
'This is some text -- with punctuation.'
'This'
.....'is'
........'some'
............'text'
...................'with'
........................'punctuation'
```

Pattern '[A-Z][a-z]+' (one uppercase followed by lowercase)

```
'This is some text -- with punctuation.'
'This'
```

As a special case of a character set, the metacharacter dot, or period (.), indicates that the pattern should match any single character in that position.

from re_test_patterns import test_patterns

```
test_patterns(
    'abbaabbba',
    [ ('a.',    'a followed by any one character'),
      ('b.',    'b followed by any one character'),
      ('a.*b',  'a followed by anything, ending in b'),
      ('a.*?b', 'a followed by anything, ending in b'),
    ])
```

Combining a dot with repetition can result in very long matches, unless the non-greedy form is used.

```
$ python re_charset_dot.py
```

Pattern 'a.' (a followed by any one character)

```
'abbaabbba'
'ab'
...'aa'
```

Pattern 'b.' (b followed by any one character)

```
'abbaabbba'
.'bb'
.....'bb'
.......'ba'
```

Pattern 'a.*b' (a followed by anything, ending in b)

```
'abbaabbba'
'abbaabbb'
```

Pattern 'a.*?b' (a followed by anything, ending in b)

```
'abbaabbba'
'ab'
...'aab'
```

Escape Codes

An even more compact representation uses escape codes for several predefined character sets. The escape codes recognized by re are listed in Table 1.1.

Table 1.1. Regular Expression Escape Codes

Code	Meaning
\d	A digit
\D	A nondigit
\s	Whitespace (tab, space, newline, etc.)
\S	Nonwhitespace
\w	Alphanumeric
\W	Nonalphanumeric

Note: Escapes are indicated by prefixing the character with a backslash (\). Unfortunately, a backslash must itself be escaped in normal Python strings, and that results in expressions that are difficult to read. Using *raw* strings, created by prefixing the literal value with r, eliminates this problem and maintains readability.

```
from re_test_patterns import test_patterns

test_patterns(
    'A prime #1 example!',
```

```
[ (r'\d+', 'sequence of digits'),
  (r'\D+', 'sequence of nondigits'),
  (r'\s+', 'sequence of whitespace'),
  (r'\S+', 'sequence of nonwhitespace'),
  (r'\w+', 'alphanumeric characters'),
  (r'\W+', 'nonalphanumeric'),
  ])
```

These sample expressions combine escape codes with repetition to find sequences of like characters in the input string.

```
$ python re_escape_codes.py

Pattern '\\d+' (sequence of digits)

  'A prime #1 example!'
  .........'1'

Pattern '\\D+' (sequence of nondigits)

  'A prime #1 example!'
  'A prime #'
  .........' example!'

Pattern '\\s+' (sequence of whitespace)

  'A prime #1 example!'
  .' '
  .......' '
  .........' '

Pattern '\\S+' (sequence of nonwhitespace)

  'A prime #1 example!'
  'A'
  ..'prime'
  ........'#1'
  ..........'example!'

Pattern '\\w+' (alphanumeric characters)

  'A prime #1 example!'
  'A'
```

```
..'prime'
.........'1'
..........'example'
```

```
Pattern '\\W+' (nonalphanumeric)
```

```
'A prime #1 example!'
.' '
.......' #'
..........' '
.................'!'
```

To match the characters that are part of the regular expression syntax, escape the characters in the search pattern.

from re_test_patterns import test_patterns

```
test_patterns(
    r'\d+ \D+ \s+',
    [ (r'\\.\+', 'escape code'),
      ])
```

The pattern in this example escapes the backslash and plus characters, since, as metacharacters, both have special meaning in a regular expression.

```
$ python re_escape_escapes.py
```

```
Pattern '\\\\.\\+' (escape code)
```

```
'\\d+ \\D+ \\s+'
'\\d+'
.....'\\D+'
..........'\\s+'
```

Anchoring

In addition to describing the content of a pattern to match, the relative location can be specified in the input text where the pattern should appear by using *anchoring* instructions. Table 1.2 lists valid anchoring codes.

Table 1.2. Regular Expression Anchoring Codes

Code	Meaning
^	Start of string, or line
$	End of string, or line
\A	Start of string
\Z	End of string
\b	Empty string at the beginning or end of a word
\B	Empty string not at the beginning or end of a word

```
from re_test_patterns import test_patterns

test_patterns(
    'This is some text -- with punctuation.',
    [ (r'^\w+',      'word at start of string'),
      (r'\A\w+',     'word at start of string'),
      (r'\w+\S*$',   'word near end of string, skip punctuation'),
      (r'\w+\S*\Z',  'word near end of string, skip punctuation'),
      (r'\w*t\w*',   'word containing t'),
      (r'\bt\w+',    't at start of word'),
      (r'\w+t\b',    't at end of word'),
      (r'\Bt\B',     't, not start or end of word'),
    ])
```

The patterns in the example for matching words at the beginning and end of the string are different because the word at the end of the string is followed by punctuation to terminate the sentence. The pattern \w+$ would not match, since . is not considered an alphanumeric character.

```
$ python re_anchoring.py

Pattern '^\\w+' (word at start of string)

  'This is some text -- with punctuation.'
  'This'

Pattern '\\A\\w+' (word at start of string)

  'This is some text -- with punctuation.'
  'This'

Pattern '\\w+\\S*$' (word near end of string, skip punctuation)
```

```
'This is some text -- with punctuation.'
.........................'punctuation.'
```

Pattern '\\w+\\S*\\Z' (word near end of string, skip punctuation)

```
'This is some text -- with punctuation.'
.........................'punctuation.'
```

Pattern '\\w*t\\w*' (word containing t)

```
'This is some text -- with punctuation.'
.............'text'
....................'with'
........................'punctuation'
```

Pattern '\\bt\\w+' (t at start of word)

```
'This is some text -- with punctuation.'
.............'text'
```

Pattern '\\w+t\\b' (t at end of word)

```
'This is some text -- with punctuation.'
.............'text'
```

Pattern '\\Bt\\B' (t, not start or end of word)

```
'This is some text -- with punctuation.'
......................'t'
..............................'t'
...............................'t'
```

1.3.5 Constraining the Search

If it is known in advance that only a subset of the full input should be searched, the regular expression match can be further constrained by telling re to limit the search range. For example, if the pattern must appear at the front of the input, then using match() instead of search() will anchor the search without having to explicitly include an anchor in the search pattern.

```
import re

text = 'This is some text -- with punctuation.'
pattern = 'is'
```

```
print 'Text     :', text
print 'Pattern:', pattern

m = re.match(pattern, text)
print 'Match  :', m
s = re.search(pattern, text)
print 'Search :', s
```

Since the literal text `is` does not appear at the start of the input text, it is not found using `match()`. The sequence appears two other times in the text, though, so `search()` finds it.

```
$ python re_match.py

Text    : This is some text -- with punctuation.
Pattern: is
Match   : None
Search  : <_sre.SRE_Match object at 0x100d2bed0>
```

The `search()` method of a compiled regular expression accepts optional *start* and *end* position parameters to limit the search to a substring of the input.

```
import re

text = 'This is some text -- with punctuation.'
pattern = re.compile(r'\b\w*is\w*\b')

print 'Text:', text
print

pos = 0
while True:
    match = pattern.search(text, pos)
    if not match:
        break
    s = match.start()
    e = match.end()
    print '  %2d : %2d = "%s"' % \
        (s, e-1, text[s:e])
    # Move forward in text for the next search
    pos = e
```

This example implements a less efficient form of `iterall()`. Each time a match is found, the end position of that match is used for the next search.

```
$ python re_search_substring.py

Text: This is some text -- with punctuation.

  0 :  3 = "This"
  5 :  6 = "is"
```

1.3.6   Dissecting Matches with Groups

Searching for pattern matches is the basis of the powerful capabilities provided by regular expressions. Adding *groups* to a pattern isolates parts of the matching text, expanding those capabilities to create a parser. Groups are defined by enclosing patterns in parentheses ((and)).

```
from re_test_patterns import test_patterns

test_patterns(
    'abbaaabbbbaaaaa',
    [ ('a(ab)',      'a followed by literal ab'),
      ('a(a*b*)',    'a followed by 0-n a and 0-n b'),
      ('a(ab)*',     'a followed by 0-n ab'),
      ('a(ab)+',     'a followed by 1-n ab'),
    ])
```

Any complete regular expression can be converted to a group and nested within a larger expression. All repetition modifiers can be applied to a group as a whole, requiring the entire group pattern to repeat.

```
$ python re_groups.py

Pattern 'a(ab)' (a followed by literal ab)

  'abbaaabbbbaaaaa'
  ....'aab'

Pattern 'a(a*b*)' (a followed by 0-n a and 0-n b)

  'abbaaabbbbaaaaa'
```

```
'abb'
...'aaabbbb'
..........'aaaaa'
```

Pattern 'a(ab)*' (a followed by 0-n ab)

```
'abbaaabbbbaaaaa'
'a'
...'a'
....'aab'
..........'a'
...........'a'
............'a'
.............'a'
..............'a'
```

Pattern 'a(ab)+' (a followed by 1-n ab)

```
'abbaaabbbbaaaaa'
....'aab'
```

To access the substrings matched by the individual groups within a pattern, use the groups() method of the Match object.

```
import re

text = 'This is some text -- with punctuation.'

print text
print

patterns = [
    (r'^(\w+)', 'word at start of string'),
    (r'(\w+)\S*$', 'word at end, with optional punctuation'),
    (r'(\bt\w+)\W+(\w+)', 'word starting with t, another word'),
    (r'(\w+t)\b', 'word ending with t'),
    ]

for pattern, desc in patterns:
    regex = re.compile(pattern)
    match = regex.search(text)
    print 'Pattern %r (%s)\n' % (pattern, desc)
```

```
print '   ', match.groups()
print
```

`Match.groups()` returns a sequence of strings in the order of the groups within the expression that matches the string.

```
$ python re_groups_match.py

This is some text -- with punctuation.

Pattern '^(\\w+)' (word at start of string)

    ('This',)

Pattern '(\\w+)\\S*$' (word at end, with optional punctuation)

    ('punctuation',)

Pattern '(\\bt\\w+)\\W+(\\w+)' (word starting with t, another word)

    ('text', 'with')

Pattern '(\\w+t)\\b' (word ending with t)

    ('text',)
```

Ask for the match of a single group with `group()`. This is useful when grouping is being used to find parts of the string, but some parts matched by groups are not needed in the results.

```
import re

text = 'This is some text -- with punctuation.'

print 'Input text                 :', text

# word starting with 't' then another word
regex = re.compile(r'(\bt\w+)\W+(\w+)')
print 'Pattern                    :', regex.pattern

match = regex.search(text)
print 'Entire match               :', match.group(0)
```

```
print 'Word starting with "t":', match.group(1)
print 'Word after "t" word    :', match.group(2)
```

Group 0 represents the string matched by the entire expression, and subgroups are numbered starting with 1 in the order their left parenthesis appears in the expression.

```
$ python re_groups_individual.py

Input text                : This is some text -- with punctuation.
Pattern                   : (\bt\w+)\W+(\w+)
Entire match              : text -- with
Word starting with "t": text
Word after "t" word       : with
```

Python extends the basic grouping syntax to add *named groups*. Using names to refer to groups makes it easier to modify the pattern over time, without having to also modify the code using the match results. To set the name of a group, use the syntax (?P<name>pattern).

```
import re

text = 'This is some text -- with punctuation.'

print text
print

for pattern in [ r'^(?P<first_word>\w+)',
                 r'(?P<last_word>\w+)\S*$',
                 r'(?P<t_word>\bt\w+)\W+(?P<other_word>\w+)',
                 r'(?P<ends_with_t>\w+t)\b',
                 ]:
    regex = re.compile(pattern)
    match = regex.search(text)
    print 'Matching "%s"' % pattern
    print '  ', match.groups()
    print '  ', match.groupdict()
    print
```

Use groupdict() to retrieve the dictionary that maps group names to substrings from the match. Named patterns also are included in the ordered sequence returned by groups().

```
$ python re_groups_named.py

This is some text -- with punctuation.

Matching "^(?P<first_word>\w+)"
   ('This',)
   {'first_word': 'This'}

Matching "(?P<last_word>\w+)\S*$"
   ('punctuation',)
   {'last_word': 'punctuation'}

Matching "(?P<t_word>\bt\w+)\W+(?P<other_word>\w+)"
   ('text', 'with')
   {'other_word': 'with', 't_word': 'text'}

Matching "(?P<ends_with_t>\w+t)\b"
   ('text',)
   {'ends_with_t': 'text'}
```

An updated version of `test_patterns()` that shows the numbered and named groups matched by a pattern will make the following examples easier to follow.

```
import re

def test_patterns(text, patterns=[]):
    """Given source text and a list of patterns, look for
    matches for each pattern within the text and print
    them to stdout.
    """
    # Look for each pattern in the text and print the results
    for pattern, desc in patterns:
        print 'Pattern %r (%s)\n' % (pattern, desc)
        print '  %r' % text
        for match in re.finditer(pattern, text):
            s = match.start()
            e = match.end()
            prefix = ' ' * (s)
            print '  %s%r%s ' % (prefix, text[s:e], ' '*(len(text)-e)),
            print match.groups()
            if match.groupdict():
                print '%s%s' % (' ' * (len(text)-s), match.groupdict())
        print
    return
```

Since a group is itself a complete regular expression, groups can be nested within other groups to build even more complicated expressions.

```
from re_test_patterns_groups import test_patterns

test_patterns(
    'abbaabbba',
    [ (r'a((a*)(b*))', 'a followed by 0-n a and 0-n b'),
    ])
```

In this case, the group `(a*)` matches an empty string, so the return value from `groups()` includes that empty string as the matched value.

```
$ python re_groups_nested.py

Pattern 'a((a*)(b*))' (a followed by 0-n a and 0-n b)

  'abbaabbba'
  'abb'            ('bb', '', 'bb')
     'aabbb'       ('abbb', 'a', 'bbb')
          'a'      ('', '', '')
```

Groups are also useful for specifying alternative patterns. Use the pipe symbol (|) to indicate that one pattern or another should match. Consider the placement of the pipe carefully, though. The first expression in this example matches a sequence of a followed by a sequence consisting entirely of a single letter, a or b. The second pattern matches a followed by a sequence that may include *either* a or b. The patterns are similar, but the resulting matches are completely different.

```
from re_test_patterns_groups import test_patterns

test_patterns(
    'abbaabbba',
    [ (r'a((a+)|(b+))', 'a then seq. of a or seq. of b'),
      (r'a((a|b)+)', 'a then seq. of [ab]'),
    ])
```

When an alternative group is not matched but the entire pattern does match, the return value of `groups()` includes a `None` value at the point in the sequence where the alternative group should appear.

```
$ python re_groups_alternative.py

Pattern 'a((a+)|(b+))'  (a then seq. of a or seq. of b)

  'abbaabbba'
  'abb'            ('bb', None, 'bb')
     'aa'          ('a', 'a', None)

Pattern 'a((a|b)+)'  (a then seq. of [ab])

  'abbaabbba'
  'abbaabbba'      ('bbaabbba', 'a')
```

Defining a group containing a subpattern is also useful when the string matching the subpattern is not part of what should be extracted from the full text. These groups are called *noncapturing*. Noncapturing groups can be used to describe repetition patterns or alternatives, without isolating the matching portion of the string in the value returned. To create a noncapturing group, use the syntax (?:pattern).

```
from re_test_patterns_groups import test_patterns

test_patterns(
    'abbaabbba',
    [ (r'a((a+)|(b+))',      'capturing form'),
      (r'a((?:a+)|(?:b+))',  'noncapturing'),
    ])
```

Compare the groups returned for the capturing and noncapturing forms of a pattern that match the same results.

```
$ python re_groups_noncapturing.py

Pattern 'a((a+)|(b+))'  (capturing form)

  'abbaabbba'
  'abb'            ('bb', None, 'bb')
     'aa'          ('a', 'a', None)

Pattern 'a((?:a+)|(?:b+))'  (noncapturing)

  'abbaabbba'
```

```
'abb'          ('bb',)
  'aa'         ('a',)
```

1.3.7 Search Options

The way the matching engine processes an expression can be changed using option flags. The flags can be combined using a bitwise OR operation, then passed to `compile()`, `search()`, `match()`, and other functions that accept a pattern for searching.

Case-Insensitive Matching

`IGNORECASE` causes literal characters and character ranges in the pattern to match both uppercase and lowercase characters.

```python
import re

text = 'This is some text -- with punctuation.'
pattern = r'\bT\w+'
with_case = re.compile(pattern)
without_case = re.compile(pattern, re.IGNORECASE)

print 'Text:\n  %r' % text
print 'Pattern:\n  %s' % pattern
print 'Case-sensitive:'
for match in with_case.findall(text):
    print '  %r' % match
print 'Case-insensitive:'
for match in without_case.findall(text):
    print '  %r' % match
```

Since the pattern includes the literal T, without setting `IGNORECASE`, the only match is the word `This`. When case is ignored, `text` also matches.

```
$ python re_flags_ignorecase.py

Text:
  'This is some text -- with punctuation.'
Pattern:
  \bT\w+
Case-sensitive:
  'This'
```

```
Case-insensitive:
  'This'
  'text'
```

Input with Multiple Lines

Two flags affect how searching in multiline input works: MULTILINE and DOTALL. The MULTILINE flag controls how the pattern-matching code processes anchoring instructions for text containing newline characters. When multiline mode is turned on, the anchor rules for ^ and $ apply at the beginning and end of each line, in addition to the entire string.

```
import re

text = 'This is some text -- with punctuation.\nA second line.'
pattern = r'(^\w+)|(\w+\S*$)'
single_line = re.compile(pattern)
multiline = re.compile(pattern, re.MULTILINE)

print 'Text:\n  %r' % text
print 'Pattern:\n  %s' % pattern
print 'Single Line :'
for match in single_line.findall(text):
    print '  %r' % (match,)
print 'Multiline   :'
for match in multiline.findall(text):
    print '  %r' % (match,)
```

The pattern in the example matches the first or last word of the input. It matches line. at the end of the string, even though there is no newline.

```
$ python re_flags_multiline.py

Text:
  'This is some text -- with punctuation.\nA second line.'
Pattern:
  (^\w+)|(\w+\S*$)
Single Line :
  ('This', '')
  ('', 'line.')
Multiline   :
  ('This', '')
  ('', 'punctuation.')
```

```
('A', '')
('', 'line.')
```

DOTALL is the other flag related to multiline text. Normally, the dot character (.) matches everything in the input text except a newline character. The flag allows dot to match newlines as well.

```
import re

text = 'This is some text -- with punctuation.\nA second line.'
pattern = r'.+'
no_newlines = re.compile(pattern)
dotall = re.compile(pattern, re.DOTALL)

print 'Text:\n  %r' % text
print 'Pattern:\n  %s' % pattern
print 'No newlines :'
for match in no_newlines.findall(text):
    print '  %r' % match
print 'Dotall       :'
for match in dotall.findall(text):
    print '  %r' % match
```

Without the flag, each line of the input text matches the pattern separately. Adding the flag causes the entire string to be consumed.

```
$ python re_flags_dotall.py

Text:
  'This is some text -- with punctuation.\nA second line.'
Pattern:
  .+
No newlines :
  'This is some text -- with punctuation.'
  'A second line.'
Dotall      :
  'This is some text -- with punctuation.\nA second line.'
```

Unicode

Under Python 2, str objects use the ASCII character set, and regular expression processing assumes that the pattern and input text are both ASCII. The escape codes described earlier are defined in terms of ASCII by default. Those assumptions mean that the pattern \w+ will match the word "French" but not the word "Français," since the ç is not part of the ASCII character set. To enable Unicode matching in Python 2, add the UNICODE flag when compiling the pattern or when calling the module-level functions search() and match().

```
import re
import codecs
import sys

# Set standard output encoding to UTF-8.
sys.stdout = codecs.getwriter('UTF-8')(sys.stdout)

text = u'Français złoty Österreich'
pattern = ur'\w+'
ascii_pattern = re.compile(pattern)
unicode_pattern = re.compile(pattern, re.UNICODE)

print 'Text     :', text
print 'Pattern :', pattern
print 'ASCII    :', u', '.join(ascii_pattern.findall(text))
print 'Unicode :', u', '.join(unicode_pattern.findall(text))
```

The other escape sequences (\W, \b, \B, \d, \D, \s, and \S) are also processed differently for Unicode text. Instead of assuming what members of the character set are identified by the escape sequence, the regular expression engine consults the Unicode database to find the properties of each character.

```
$ python re_flags_unicode.py

Text     : Français złoty Österreich
Pattern : \w+
ASCII    : Fran, ais, z, oty, sterreich
Unicode : Français, złoty, Österreich
```

> **Note:** Python 3 uses Unicode for all strings by default, so the flag is not necessary.

Verbose Expression Syntax

The compact format of regular expression syntax can become a hindrance as expressions grow more complicated. As the number of groups in an expression increases, it will be more work to keep track of why each element is needed and how exactly the parts of the expression interact. Using named groups helps mitigate these issues, but a better solution is to use *verbose mode* expressions, which allow comments and extra whitespace to be embedded in the pattern.

A pattern to validate email addresses will illustrate how verbose mode makes working with regular expressions easier. The first version recognizes addresses that end in one of three top-level domains: `.com`, `.org`, and `.edu`.

```
import re

address = re.compile('[\w\d.+-]+@([\w\d.]+\.)+(com|org|edu)',
                     re.UNICODE)

candidates = [
    u'first.last@example.com',
    u'first.last+category@gmail.com',
    u'valid-address@mail.example.com',
    u'not-valid@example.foo',
    ]

for candidate in candidates:
    match = address.search(candidate)
    print '%-30s  %s' % (candidate, 'Matches' if match else 'No match')
```

This expression is already complex. There are several character classes, groups, and repetition expressions.

```
$ python re_email_compact.py

first.last@example.com            Matches
first.last+category@gmail.com     Matches
valid-address@mail.example.com    Matches
not-valid@example.foo             No match
```

Converting the expression to a more verbose format will make it easier to extend.

```
import re

address = re.compile(
    '''
    [\w\d.+-]+          # username
    @
    ''')
```

```
    ([\w\d.]+\.)+     # domain name prefix
    (com|org|edu)     # TODO: support more top-level domains
    ''',
    re.UNICODE | re.VERBOSE)

candidates = [
    u'first.last@example.com',
    u'first.last+category@gmail.com',
    u'valid-address@mail.example.com',
    u'not-valid@example.foo',
    ]

for candidate in candidates:
    match = address.search(candidate)
    print '%-30s  %s' % (candidate, 'Matches' if match else 'No match')
```

The expression matches the same inputs, but in this extended format, it is easier to read. The comments also help identify different parts of the pattern so that it can be expanded to match more inputs.

```
$ python re_email_verbose.py

first.last@example.com              Matches
first.last+category@gmail.com       Matches
valid-address@mail.example.com      Matches
not-valid@example.foo               No match
```

This expanded version parses inputs that include a person's name and email address, as might appear in an email header. The name comes first and stands on its own, and the email address follows surrounded by angle brackets (< and >).

```
import re

address = re.compile(
    '''

    # A name is made up of letters, and may include "."
    # for title abbreviations and middle initials.
    ((?P<name>
      ([\w.,]+\s+)*[\w.,]+)
      \s*
      # Email addresses are wrapped in angle
```

```
            # brackets: < > but only if a name is
            # found, so keep the start bracket in this
            # group.
            <
        )? # the entire name is optional

        # The address itself: username@domain.tld
        (?P<email>
            [\w\d.+-]+       # username
            @
            ([\w\d.]+\.)+    # domain name prefix
            (com|org|edu)    # limit the allowed top-level domains
        )

        >? # optional closing angle bracket
        ''',
        re.UNICODE | re.VERBOSE)

candidates = [
    u'first.last@example.com',
    u'first.last+category@gmail.com',
    u'valid-address@mail.example.com',
    u'not-valid@example.foo',
    u'First Last <first.last@example.com>',
    u'No Brackets first.last@example.com',
    u'First Last',
    u'First Middle Last <first.last@example.com>',
    u'First M. Last <first.last@example.com>',
    u'<first.last@example.com>',
    ]

for candidate in candidates:
    print 'Candidate:', candidate
    match = address.search(candidate)
    if match:
        print '  Name :', match.groupdict()['name']
        print '  Email:', match.groupdict()['email']
    else:
        print '  No match'
```

As with other programming languages, the ability to insert comments into verbose regular expressions helps with their maintainability. This final version includes implementation notes to future maintainers and whitespace to separate the groups from each other and highlight their nesting level.

```
$ python re_email_with_name.py

Candidate: first.last@example.com
  Name : None
  Email: first.last@example.com
Candidate: first.last+category@gmail.com
  Name : None
  Email: first.last+category@gmail.com
Candidate: valid-address@mail.example.com
  Name : None
  Email: valid-address@mail.example.com
Candidate: not-valid@example.foo
  No match
Candidate: First Last <first.last@example.com>
  Name : First Last
  Email: first.last@example.com
Candidate: No Brackets first.last@example.com
  Name : None
  Email: first.last@example.com
Candidate: First Last
  No match
Candidate: First Middle Last <first.last@example.com>
  Name : First Middle Last
  Email: first.last@example.com
Candidate: First M. Last <first.last@example.com>
  Name : First M. Last
  Email: first.last@example.com
Candidate: <first.last@example.com>
  Name : None
  Email: first.last@example.com
```

Embedding Flags in Patterns

If flags cannot be added when compiling an expression, such as when a pattern is passed as an argument to a library function that will compile it later, the flags can be embedded inside the expression string itself. For example, to turn case-insensitive matching on, add (?i) to the beginning of the expression.

```
import re

text = 'This is some text -- with punctuation.'
pattern = r'(?i)\bT\w+'
regex = re.compile(pattern)

print 'Text       :', text
print 'Pattern    :', pattern
print 'Matches    :', regex.findall(text)
```

Because the options control the way the entire expression is evaluated or parsed, they should always come at the beginning of the expression.

```
$ python re_flags_embedded.py

Text       : This is some text -- with punctuation.
Pattern    : (?i)\bT\w+
Matches    : ['This', 'text']
```

The abbreviations for all flags are listed in Table 1.3.

Table 1.3. Regular Expression Flag Abbreviations

Flag	Abbreviation
IGNORECASE	i
MULTILINE	m
DOTALL	s
UNICODE	u
VERBOSE	x

Embedded flags can be combined by placing them within the same group. For example, (?imu) turns on case-insensitive matching for multiline Unicode strings.

1.3.8   Looking Ahead or Behind

In many cases, it is useful to match a part of a pattern only if some other part will also match. For example, in the email parsing expression, the angle brackets were each marked as optional. Really, though, the brackets should be paired, and the expression should only match if both are present or neither is. This modified version of the expression uses a *positive look-ahead* assertion to match the pair. The look-ahead assertion syntax is `(?=pattern)`.

```
import re

address = re.compile(
    '''
    # A name is made up of letters, and may include "."
    # for title abbreviations and middle initials.
    ((?P<name>
        ([\w.,]+\s+)*[\w.,]+
     )
     \s+
    ) # name is no longer optional

    # LOOKAHEAD
    # Email addresses are wrapped in angle brackets, but only
    # if they are both present or neither is.
    (?= (<.*>$)       # remainder wrapped in angle brackets
        |
        ([^<].*[^>]$) # remainder *not* wrapped in angle brackets
     )

    <? # optional opening angle bracket

    # The address itself: username@domain.tld
    (?P<email>
      [\w\d.+-]+       # username
      @
      ([\w\d.]+\.)+    # domain name prefix
      (com|org|edu)    # limit the allowed top-level domains
    )

    >? # optional closing angle bracket
    ''',
    re.UNICODE | re.VERBOSE)

candidates = [
    u'First Last <first.last@example.com>',
    u'No Brackets first.last@example.com',
    u'Open Bracket <first.last@example.com',
    u'Close Bracket first.last@example.com>',
    ]
```

```
for candidate in candidates:
    print 'Candidate:', candidate
    match = address.search(candidate)
    if match:
        print '  Name :', match.groupdict()['name']
        print '  Email:', match.groupdict()['email']
    else:
        print '  No match'
```

Several important changes occur in this version of the expression. First, the name portion is no longer optional. That means stand-alone addresses do not match, but it also prevents improperly formatted name/address combinations from matching. The positive look-ahead rule after the "name" group asserts that the remainder of the string is either wrapped with a pair of angle brackets or there is not a mismatched bracket; the brackets are either both present or neither is. The look-ahead is expressed as a group, but the match for a look-ahead group does not consume any of the input text. The rest of the pattern picks up from the same spot after the look-ahead matches.

```
$ python re_look_ahead.py

Candidate: First Last <first.last@example.com>
  Name : First Last
  Email: first.last@example.com
Candidate: No Brackets first.last@example.com
  Name : No Brackets
  Email: first.last@example.com
Candidate: Open Bracket <first.last@example.com
  No match
Candidate: Close Bracket first.last@example.com>
  No match
```

A *negative look-ahead* assertion (`(?!pattern)`) says that the pattern does not match the text following the current point. For example, the email recognition pattern could be modified to ignore `noreply` mailing addresses automated systems commonly use.

```
import re

address = re.compile(
    '''
    ^
```

```
        # An address: username@domain.tld

        # Ignore noreply addresses
        (?!noreply@.*$)

        [\w\d.+-]+        # username
        @
        ([\w\d.]+\.)+     # domain name prefix
        (com|org|edu)     # limit the allowed top-level domains

        $
        ''',
        re.UNICODE | re.VERBOSE)

candidates = [
    u'first.last@example.com',
    u'noreply@example.com',
    ]

for candidate in candidates:
    print 'Candidate:', candidate
    match = address.search(candidate)
    if match:
        print '  Match:', candidate[match.start():match.end()]
    else:
        print '  No match'
```

The address starting with `noreply` does not match the pattern, since the look-ahead assertion fails.

```
$ python re_negative_look_ahead.py

Candidate: first.last@example.com
  Match: first.last@example.com
Candidate: noreply@example.com
  No match
```

Instead of looking ahead for `noreply` in the username portion of the email address, the pattern can also be written using a *negative look-behind* assertion after the username is matched using the syntax (`?<!pattern`).

```
import re

address = re.compile(
```

```
    '''
    ^

    # An address: username@domain.tld

    [\w\d.+-]+          # username

    # Ignore noreply addresses
    (?<!noreply)

    @
    ([\w\d.]+\.)+      # domain name prefix
    (com|org|edu)       # limit the allowed top-level domains

    $
    ''',
    re.UNICODE | re.VERBOSE)

candidates = [
    u'first.last@example.com',
    u'noreply@example.com',
    ]

for candidate in candidates:
    print 'Candidate:', candidate
    match = address.search(candidate)
    if match:
        print '  Match:', candidate[match.start():match.end()]
    else:
        print '  No match'
```

Looking backward works a little differently than looking ahead, in that the expression must use a fixed-length pattern. Repetitions are allowed, as long as there is a fixed number (no wildcards or ranges).

```
$ python re_negative_look_behind.py

Candidate: first.last@example.com
  Match: first.last@example.com
Candidate: noreply@example.com
  No match
```

A *positive look-behind* assertion can be used to find text following a pattern using the syntax (?<=pattern). For example, this expression finds Twitter handles.

```
import re

twitter = re.compile(
    '''
    # A twitter handle: @username
    (?<=@)
    ([\w\d_]+)           # username
    ''',
    re.UNICODE | re.VERBOSE)

text = '''This text includes two Twitter handles.
One for @ThePSF, and one for the author, @doughellmann.
'''

print text
for match in twitter.findall(text):
    print 'Handle:', match
```

The pattern matches sequences of characters that can make up a Twitter handle, as long as they are preceded by an @.

```
$ python re_look_behind.py

This text includes two Twitter handles.
One for @ThePSF, and one for the author, @doughellmann.

Handle: ThePSF
Handle: doughellmann
```

1.3.9   Self-Referencing Expressions

Matched values can be used in later parts of an expression. For example, the email example can be updated to match only addresses composed of the first and last name of the person by including back-references to those groups. The easiest way to achieve this is by referring to the previously matched group by id number, using \num.

```
import re

address = re.compile(
    r'''

    # The regular name
```

```
    (\w+)                   # first name
    \s+
    (([\w.]+)\s+)?          # optional middle name or initial
    (\w+)                   # last name

    \s+

    <

    # The address: first_name.last_name@domain.tld
    (?P<email>
      \1                    # first name
      \.
      \4                    # last name
      @
      ([\w\d.]+\.)+         # domain name prefix
      (com|org|edu)         # limit the allowed top-level domains
    )

    >
    ''',
    re.UNICODE | re.VERBOSE | re.IGNORECASE)

candidates = [
    u'First Last <first.last@example.com>',
    u'Different Name <first.last@example.com>',
    u'First Middle Last <first.last@example.com>',
    u'First M. Last <first.last@example.com>',
    ]


for candidate in candidates:
    print 'Candidate:', candidate
    match = address.search(candidate)
    if match:
        print '  Match name :', match.group(1), match.group(4)
        print '  Match email:', match.group(5)
    else:
        print '  No match'
```

Although the syntax is simple, creating back-references by numerical id has a couple of disadvantages. From a practical standpoint, as the expression changes, the groups must be counted again and every reference may need to be updated. The other disadvantage is that only 99 references can be made this way, because if the id number is three digits long, it will be interpreted as an octal character value instead of a group reference. On the other hand, if an expression has more than 99 groups, more serious maintenance challenges will arise than not being able to refer to some groups in the expression.

```
$ python re_refer_to_group.py

Candidate: First Last <first.last@example.com>
  Match name : First Last
  Match email: first.last@example.com
Candidate: Different Name <first.last@example.com>
  No match
Candidate: First Middle Last <first.last@example.com>
  Match name : First Last
  Match email: first.last@example.com
Candidate: First M. Last <first.last@example.com>
  Match name : First Last
  Match email: first.last@example.com
```

Python's expression parser includes an extension that uses `(?P=name)` to refer to the value of a named group matched earlier in the expression.

```
import re

address = re.compile(
    '''

    # The regular name
    (?P<first_name>\w+)
    \s+
    (([\w.]+)\s+)?          # optional middle name or initial
    (?P<last_name>\w+)

    \s+

    <

    # The address: first_name.last_name@domain.tld
    (?P<email>
      (?P=first_name)
      \.
      (?P=last_name)
```

```
        @
        ([\w\d.]+\.)+      # domain name prefix
        (com|org|edu)      # limit the allowed top-level domains
    )

    >
    ''',
    re.UNICODE | re.VERBOSE | re.IGNORECASE)

candidates = [
    u'First Last <first.last@example.com>',
    u'Different Name <first.last@example.com>',
    u'First Middle Last <first.last@example.com>',
    u'First M. Last <first.last@example.com>',
    ]

for candidate in candidates:
    print 'Candidate:', candidate
    match = address.search(candidate)
    if match:
        print '  Match name :', match.groupdict()['first_name'],
        print match.groupdict()['last_name']
        print '  Match email:', match.groupdict()['email']
    else:
        print '  No match'
```

The address expression is compiled with the IGNORECASE flag on, since proper names are normally capitalized but email addresses are not.

```
$ python re_refer_to_named_group.py

Candidate: First Last <first.last@example.com>
  Match name : First Last
  Match email: first.last@example.com
Candidate: Different Name <first.last@example.com>
  No match
Candidate: First Middle Last <first.last@example.com>
  Match name : First Last
  Match email: first.last@example.com
Candidate: First M. Last <first.last@example.com>
  Match name : First Last
  Match email: first.last@example.com
```

The other mechanism for using back-references in expressions chooses a different pattern based on whether a previous group matched. The email pattern can be corrected so that the angle brackets are required if a name is present, but not if the email address is by itself. The syntax for testing to see if a group has matched is `(?(id)yes-expression|no-expression)`, where *id* is the group name or number, *yes-expression* is the pattern to use if the group has a value, and *no-expression* is the pattern to use otherwise.

```
import re

address = re.compile(
    '''
    ^

    # A name is made up of letters, and may include "."
    # for title abbreviations and middle initials.
    (?P<name>
       ([\w.]+\s+)*[\w.]+
     )?
    \s*

    # Email addresses are wrapped in angle brackets, but
    # only if a name is found.
    (?(name)
      # remainder wrapped in angle brackets because
      # there is a name
      (?P<brackets>(?=(<.*>$)))
      |
      # remainder does not include angle brackets without name
      (?=([^<].*[^>]$))
     )

    # Only look for a bracket if the look-ahead assertion
    # found both of them.
    (?(brackets)<|\s*)

    # The address itself: username@domain.tld
    (?P<email>
      [\w\d.+-]+       # username
      @
      ([\w\d.]+\.)+    # domain name prefix
      (com|org|edu)    # limit the allowed top-level domains
```

```
    )

    # Only look for a bracket if the look-ahead assertion
    # found both of them.
    (?(brackets)>|\s*)

    $
    ''',
    re.UNICODE | re.VERBOSE)

candidates = [
    u'First Last <first.last@example.com>',
    u'No Brackets first.last@example.com',
    u'Open Bracket <first.last@example.com',
    u'Close Bracket first.last@example.com>',
    u'no.brackets@example.com',
    ]

for candidate in candidates:
    print 'Candidate:', candidate
    match = address.search(candidate)
    if match:
        print '  Match name :', match.groupdict()['name']
        print '  Match email:', match.groupdict()['email']
    else:
        print '  No match'
```

This version of the email address parser uses two tests. If the name group matches, then the look-ahead assertion requires both angle brackets and sets up the brackets group. If name is not matched, the assertion requires that the rest of the text not have angle brackets around it. Later, if the brackets group is set, the actual pattern-matching code consumes the brackets in the input using literal patterns; otherwise, it consumes any blank space.

```
$ python re_id.py

Candidate: First Last <first.last@example.com>
  Match name : First Last
  Match email: first.last@example.com
Candidate: No Brackets first.last@example.com
  No match
Candidate: Open Bracket <first.last@example.com
```

```
  No match
Candidate: Close Bracket first.last@example.com>
  No match
Candidate: no.brackets@example.com
  Match name  : None
  Match email: no.brackets@example.com
```

1.3.10 Modifying Strings with Patterns

In addition to searching through text, re also supports modifying text using regular expressions as the search mechanism, and the replacements can reference groups matched in the regex as part of the substitution text. Use sub() to replace all occurrences of a pattern with another string.

```
import re

bold = re.compile(r'\*{2}(.*?)\*{2}')

text = 'Make this **bold**.  This **too**.'

print 'Text:', text
print 'Bold:', bold.sub(r'<b>\1</b>', text)
```

References to the text matched by the pattern can be inserted using the \num syntax used for back-references.

```
$ python re_sub.py

Text: Make this **bold**.  This **too**.
Bold: Make this <b>bold</b>.  This <b>too</b>.
```

To use named groups in the substitution, use the syntax \g<name>.

```
import re

bold = re.compile(r'\*{2}(?P<bold_text>.*?)\*{2}', re.UNICODE)

text = 'Make this **bold**.  This **too**.'

print 'Text:', text
print 'Bold:', bold.sub(r'<b>\g<bold_text></b>', text)
```

The \g<name> syntax also works with numbered references, and using it eliminates any ambiguity between group numbers and surrounding literal digits.

```
$ python re_sub_named_groups.py

Text: Make this **bold**.  This **too**.
Bold: Make this <b>bold</b>.  This <b>too</b>.
```

Pass a value to *count* to limit the number of substitutions performed.

```
import re

bold = re.compile(r'\*{2}(.*?)\*{2}', re.UNICODE)

text = 'Make this **bold**.  This **too**.'

print 'Text:', text
print 'Bold:', bold.sub(r'<b>\1</b>', text, count=1)
```

Only the first substitution is made because *count* is 1.

```
$ python re_sub_count.py

Text: Make this **bold**.  This **too**.
Bold: Make this <b>bold</b>.  This **too**.
```

subn() works just like sub(), except that it returns both the modified string and
the count of substitutions made.

```
import re

bold = re.compile(r'\*{2}(.*?)\*{2}', re.UNICODE)

text = 'Make this **bold**.  This **too**.'

print 'Text:', text
print 'Bold:', bold.subn(r'<b>\1</b>', text)
```

The search pattern matches twice in the example.

```
$ python re_subn.py
```

```
Text: Make this **bold**.  This **too**.
Bold: ('Make this <b>bold</b>.  This <b>too</b>.', 2)
```

1.3.11   Splitting with Patterns

`str.split()` is one of the most frequently used methods for breaking apart strings to parse them. It only supports using literal values as separators, though, and sometimes a regular expression is necessary if the input is not consistently formatted. For example, many plain-text markup languages define paragraph separators as two or more newline (\n) characters. In this case, `str.split()` cannot be used because of the "or more" part of the definition.

A strategy for identifying paragraphs using `findall()` would use a pattern like `(.+?)\n{2,}`.

```
import re

text = '''Paragraph one
on two lines.

Paragraph two.


Paragraph three.'''

for num, para in enumerate(re.findall(r'(.+?)\n{2,}',
                                      text,
                                      flags=re.DOTALL)
                            ):
    print num, repr(para)
    print
```

That pattern fails for paragraphs at the end of the input text, as illustrated by the fact that "Paragraph three." is not part of the output.

```
$ python re_paragraphs_findall.py

0 'Paragraph one\non two lines.'

1 'Paragraph two.'
```

Extending the pattern to say that a paragraph ends with two or more newlines or the end of input fixes the problem, but makes the pattern more complicated. Converting to `re.split()` instead of `re.findall()` handles the boundary condition automatically and keeps the pattern simpler.

```python
import re

text = '''Paragraph one
on two lines.

Paragraph two.


Paragraph three.'''

print 'With findall:'
for num, para in enumerate(re.findall(r'(.+?)(\n{2,}|$)',
                                      text,
                                      flags=re.DOTALL)):
    print num, repr(para)
    print

print
print 'With split:'
for num, para in enumerate(re.split(r'\n{2,}', text)):
    print num, repr(para)
    print
```

The pattern argument to `split()` expresses the markup specification more precisely: Two or more newline characters mark a separator point between paragraphs in the input string.

```
$ python re_split.py

With findall:
0 ('Paragraph one\non two lines.', '\n\n')

1 ('Paragraph two.', '\n\n\n')

2 ('Paragraph three.', '')
```

```
With split:
0 'Paragraph one\non two lines.'

1 'Paragraph two.'

2 'Paragraph three.'
```

Enclosing the expression in parentheses to define a group causes split() to work more like str.partition(), so it returns the separator values as well as the other parts of the string.

```
import re

text = '''Paragraph one
on two lines.

Paragraph two.


Paragraph three.'''

print 'With split:'
for num, para in enumerate(re.split(r'(\n{2,})', text)):
    print num, repr(para)
    print
```

The output now includes each paragraph, as well as the sequence of newlines separating them.

```
$ python re_split_groups.py

With split:
0 'Paragraph one\non two lines.'

1 '\n\n'

2 'Paragraph two.'

3 '\n\n\n'

4 'Paragraph three.'
```

See Also:

re (http://docs.python.org/library/re.html) The standard library documentation for this module.

Regular Expression HOWTO (http://docs.python.org/howto/regex.html) Andrew Kuchling's introduction to regular expressions for Python developers.

Kodos (http://kodos.sourceforge.net/) An interactive tool for testing regular expressions, created by Phil Schwartz.

Python Regular Expression Testing Tool (http://www.pythonregex.com/) A Web-based tool for testing regular expressions created by David Naffziger at Brand Verity.com and inspired by Kodos.

Regular expression (http://en.wikipedia.org/wiki/Regular_expressions) Wikipedia article that provides a general introduction to regular expression concepts and techniques.

`locale` **(page 909)** Use the `locale` module to set the language configuration when working with Unicode text.

`unicodedata` **(docs.python.org/library/unicodedata.html)** Programmatic access to the Unicode character property database.

1.4 difflib—Compare Sequences

Purpose Compare sequences, especially lines of text.
Python Version 2.1 and later

The `difflib` module contains tools for computing and working with differences between sequences. It is especially useful for comparing text and includes functions that produce reports using several common difference formats.

The examples in this section will all use this common test data in the `difflib_data.py` module:

```
text1 = """Lorem ipsum dolor sit amet, consectetuer adipiscing
elit. Integer eu lacus accumsan arcu fermentum euismod. Donec
pulvinar porttitor tellus. Aliquam venenatis. Donec facilisis
pharetra tortor.  In nec mauris eget magna consequat
convallis. Nam sed sem vitae odio pellentesque interdum. Sed
consequat viverra nisl. Suspendisse arcu metus, blandit quis,
rhoncus ac, pharetra eget, velit. Mauris urna. Morbi nonummy
molestie orci. Praesent nisi elit, fringilla ac, suscipit non,
tristique vel, mauris. Curabitur vel lorem id nisl porta
adipiscing. Suspendisse eu lectus. In nunc. Duis vulputate
tristique enim. Donec quis lectus a justo imperdiet tempus."""
```

```
text1_lines = text1.splitlines()

text2 = """Lorem ipsum dolor sit amet, consectetuer adipiscing
elit. Integer eu lacus accumsan arcu fermentum euismod. Donec
pulvinar, porttitor tellus. Aliquam venenatis. Donec facilisis
pharetra tortor. In nec mauris eget magna consequat
convallis. Nam cras vitae mi vitae odio pellentesque interdum. Sed
consequat viverra nisl. Suspendisse arcu metus, blandit quis,
rhoncus ac, pharetra eget, velit. Mauris urna. Morbi nonummy
molestie orci. Praesent nisi elit, fringilla ac, suscipit non,
tristique vel, mauris. Curabitur vel lorem id nisl porta
adipiscing. Duis vulputate tristique enim. Donec quis lectus a
justo imperdiet tempus.  Suspendisse eu lectus. In nunc."""

text2_lines = text2.splitlines()
```

1.4.1 Comparing Bodies of Text

The `Differ` class works on sequences of text lines and produces human-readable *deltas*, or change instructions, including differences within individual lines. The default output produced by `Differ` is similar to the **diff** command line tool under UNIX. It includes the original input values from both lists, including common values, and markup data to indicate what changes were made.

- Lines prefixed with – indicate that they were in the first sequence, but not the second.
- Lines prefixed with + were in the second sequence, but not the first.
- If a line has an incremental difference between versions, an extra line prefixed with ? is used to highlight the change within the new version.
- If a line has not changed, it is printed with an extra blank space on the left column so that it is aligned with the other output, which may have differences.

Breaking up the text into a sequence of individual lines before passing it to `compare()` produces more readable output than passing it in large strings.

```
import difflib
from difflib_data import *

d = difflib.Differ()
diff = d.compare(text1_lines, text2_lines)
print '\n'.join(diff)
```

The beginning of both text segments in the sample data is the same, so the first line prints without any extra annotation.

```
Lorem ipsum dolor sit amet, consectetuer adipiscing
elit. Integer eu lacus accumsan arcu fermentum euismod. Donec
```

The third line of the data changes to include a comma in the modified text. Both versions of the line print, with the extra information on line five showing the column where the text is modified, including the fact that the , character is added.

```
- pulvinar porttitor tellus. Aliquam venenatis. Donec facilisis
+ pulvinar, porttitor tellus. Aliquam venenatis. Donec facilisis
?         +
```

The next few lines of the output show that an extra space is removed.

```
- pharetra tortor.  In nec mauris eget magna consequat
?                 -
+ pharetra tortor. In nec mauris eget magna consequat
```

Next, a more complex change is made, replacing several words in a phrase.

```
- convallis. Nam sed sem vitae odio pellentesque interdum. Sed
?               -  --
+ convallis. Nam cras vitae mi vitae odio pellentesque interdum. Sed
?               +++ +++++    +
```

The last sentence in the paragraph is changed significantly, so the difference is represented by removing the old version and adding the new.

```
  consequat viverra nisl. Suspendisse arcu metus, blandit quis,
  rhoncus ac, pharetra eget, velit. Mauris urna. Morbi nonummy
  molestie orci. Praesent nisi elit, fringilla ac, suscipit non,
  tristique vel, mauris. Curabitur vel lorem id nisl porta
- adipiscing. Suspendisse eu lectus. In nunc. Duis vulputate
- tristique enim. Donec quis lectus a justo imperdiet tempus.
+ adipiscing. Duis vulputate tristique enim. Donec quis lectus a
+ justo imperdiet tempus.  Suspendisse eu lectus. In nunc.
```

The `ndiff()` function produces essentially the same output. The processing is specifically tailored for working with text data and eliminating *noise* in the input.

Other Output Formats

While the `Differ` class shows all input lines, a *unified diff* includes only modified lines and a bit of context. In Python 2.3, the `unified_diff()` function was added to produce this sort of output.

```
import difflib
from difflib_data import *

diff = difflib.unified_diff(text1_lines,
                            text2_lines,
                            lineterm='',
                            )
print '\n'.join(list(diff))
```

The *lineterm* argument is used to tell `unified_diff()` to skip appending newlines to the control lines it returns because the input lines do not include them. Newlines are added to all lines when they are printed. The output should look familiar to users of subversion or other version control tools.

```
$ python difflib_unified.py

---
+++
@@ -1,11 +1,11 @@
 Lorem ipsum dolor sit amet, consectetuer adipiscing
 elit. Integer eu lacus accumsan arcu fermentum euismod. Donec
-pulvinar porttitor tellus. Aliquam venenatis. Donec facilisis
-pharetra tortor.  In nec mauris eget magna consequat
-convallis. Nam sed sem vitae odio pellentesque interdum. Sed
+pulvinar, porttitor tellus. Aliquam venenatis. Donec facilisis
+pharetra tortor. In nec mauris eget magna consequat
+convallis. Nam cras vitae mi vitae odio pellentesque interdum. Sed
 consequat viverra nisl. Suspendisse arcu metus, blandit quis,
 rhoncus ac, pharetra eget, velit. Mauris urna. Morbi nonummy
 molestie orci. Praesent nisi elit, fringilla ac, suscipit non,
 tristique vel, mauris. Curabitur vel lorem id nisl porta
-adipiscing. Suspendisse eu lectus. In nunc. Duis vulputate
-tristique enim. Donec quis lectus a justo imperdiet tempus.
```

```
+adipiscing. Duis vulputate tristique enim. Donec quis lectus a
+justo imperdiet tempus.  Suspendisse eu lectus. In nunc.
```

Using `context_diff()` produces similar readable output.

1.4.2   Junk Data

All functions that produce difference sequences accept arguments to indicate which lines should be ignored and which characters within a line should be ignored. These parameters can be used to skip over markup or whitespace changes in two versions of a file, for example.

```
# This example is adapted from the source for difflib.py.

from difflib import SequenceMatcher

def show_results(s):
    i, j, k = s.find_longest_match(0, 5, 0, 9)
    print '  i = %d' % i
    print '  j = %d' % j
    print '  k = %d' % k
    print '  A[i:i+k] = %r' % A[i:i+k]
    print '  B[j:j+k] = %r' % B[j:j+k]

A = " abcd"
B = "abcd abcd"

print 'A = %r' % A
print 'B = %r' % B

print '\nWithout junk detection:'
show_results(SequenceMatcher(None, A, B))

print '\nTreat spaces as junk:'
show_results(SequenceMatcher(lambda x: x==" ", A, B))
```

The default for `Differ` is to not ignore any lines or characters explicitly, but to rely on the ability of `SequenceMatcher` to detect noise. The default for `ndiff()` is to ignore space and tab characters.

```
$ python difflib_junk.py
```

```
A = ' abcd'
B = 'abcd abcd'

Without junk detection:
  i = 0
  j = 4
  k = 5
  A[i:i+k] = ' abcd'
  B[j:j+k] = ' abcd'

Treat spaces as junk:
  i = 1
  j = 0
  k = 4
  A[i:i+k] = 'abcd'
  B[j:j+k] = 'abcd'
```

1.4.3 Comparing Arbitrary Types

The `SequenceMatcher` class compares two sequences of any type, as long as the values are hashable. It uses an algorithm to identify the longest contiguous matching blocks from the sequences, eliminating *junk* values that do not contribute to the real data.

```
import difflib
from difflib_data import *

s1 = [ 1, 2, 3, 5, 6, 4 ]
s2 = [ 2, 3, 5, 4, 6, 1 ]

print 'Initial data:'
print 's1 =', s1
print 's2 =', s2
print 's1 == s2:', s1==s2
print

matcher = difflib.SequenceMatcher(None, s1, s2)
for tag, i1, i2, j1, j2 in reversed(matcher.get_opcodes()):

    if tag == 'delete':
        print 'Remove %s from positions [%d:%d]' % \
            (s1[i1:i2], i1, i2)
        del s1[i1:i2]
```

```
    elif tag == 'equal':
        print 's1[%d:%d] and s2[%d:%d] are the same' % \
            (i1, i2, j1, j2)

    elif tag == 'insert':
        print 'Insert %s from s2[%d:%d] into s1 at %d' % \
            (s2[j1:j2], j1, j2, i1)
        s1[i1:i2] = s2[j1:j2]

    elif tag == 'replace':
        print 'Replace %s from s1[%d:%d] with %s from s2[%d:%d]' % (
            s1[i1:i2], i1, i2, s2[j1:j2], j1, j2)
        s1[i1:i2] = s2[j1:j2]

    print '  s1 =', s1

print 's1 == s2:', s1==s2
```

This example compares two lists of integers and uses `get_opcodes()` to derive the instructions for converting the original list into the newer version. The modifications are applied in reverse order so that the list indexes remain accurate after items are added and removed.

```
$ python difflib_seq.py

Initial data:
s1 = [1, 2, 3, 5, 6, 4]
s2 = [2, 3, 5, 4, 6, 1]
s1 == s2: False

Replace [4] from s1[5:6] with [1] from s2[5:6]
  s1 = [1, 2, 3, 5, 6, 1]
s1[4:5] and s2[4:5] are the same
  s1 = [1, 2, 3, 5, 6, 1]
Insert [4] from s2[3:4] into s1 at 4
  s1 = [1, 2, 3, 5, 4, 6, 1]
s1[1:4] and s2[0:3] are the same
  s1 = [1, 2, 3, 5, 4, 6, 1]
Remove [1] from positions [0:1]
  s1 = [2, 3, 5, 4, 6, 1]
s1 == s2: True
```

`SequenceMatcher` works with custom classes, as well as built-in types, as long as they are hashable.

See Also:

difflib (http://docs.python.org/library/difflib.html) The standard library documentation for this module.

Pattern Matching: The Gestalt Approach (http://www.ddj.com/documents/s=1103/ddj8807c/) Discussion of a similar algorithm by John W. Ratcliff and D. E. Metzener, published in Dr. Dobb's Journal in July 1988.

Chapter 2

DATA STRUCTURES

Python includes several standard programming data structures, such as `list`, `tuple`, `dict`, and `set`, as part of its built-in types. Many applications do not require other structures, but when they do, the standard library provides powerful and well-tested versions that are ready to use.

The `collections` module includes implementations of several data structures that extend those found in other modules. For example, `Deque` is a double-ended queue that allows the addition or removal of items from either end. The `defaultdict` is a dictionary that responds with a default value if a key is missing, while `OrderedDict` remembers the sequence in which items are added to it. And `namedtuple` extends the normal `tuple` to give each member item an attribute name in addition to a numeric index.

For large amounts of data, an `array` may make more efficient use of memory than a `list`. Since the `array` is limited to a single data type, it can use a more compact memory representation than a general purpose `list`. At the same time, `arrays` can be manipulated using many of the same methods as a `list`, so it may be possible to replace `lists` with `arrays` in an application without a lot of other changes.

Sorting items in a sequence is a fundamental aspect of data manipulation. Python's `list` includes a `sort()` method, but sometimes it is more efficient to maintain a list in sorted order without resorting it each time its contents are changed. The functions in `heapq` modify the contents of a list while preserving the sort order of the list with low overhead.

Another option for building sorted lists or arrays is `bisect`. It uses a binary search to find the insertion point for new items and is an alternative to repeatedly sorting a list that changes frequently.

Although the built-in `list` can simulate a queue using the `insert()` and `pop()` methods, it is not thread-safe. For true ordered communication between threads, use the `Queue` module. `multiprocessing` includes a version of a `Queue` that works between processes, making it easier to convert a multithreaded program to use processes instead.

`struct` is useful for decoding data from another application, perhaps coming from a binary file or stream of data, into Python's native types for easier manipulation.

This chapter covers two modules related to memory management. For highly interconnected data structures, such as graphs and trees, use `weakref` to maintain references while still allowing the garbage collector to clean up objects after they are no longer needed. The functions in `copy` are used for duplicating data structures and their contents, including recursive copies with `deepcopy()`.

Debugging data structures can be time consuming, especially when wading through printed output of large sequences or dictionaries. Use `pprint` to create easy-to-read representations that can be printed to the console or written to a log file for easier debugging.

And, finally, if the available types do not meet the requirements, subclass one of the native types and customize it, or build a new container type using one of the abstract base classes defined in `collections` as a starting point.

2.1 collections—Container Data Types

Purpose Container data types.
Python Version 2.4 and later

The `collections` module includes container data types beyond the built-in types `list`, `dict`, and `tuple`.

2.1.1 Counter

A `Counter` is a container that tracks how many times equivalent values are added. It can be used to implement the same algorithms for which other languages commonly use bag or multiset data structures.

Initializing

`Counter` supports three forms of initialization. Its constructor can be called with a sequence of items, a dictionary containing keys and counts, or using keyword arguments mapping string names to counts.

```
import collections

print collections.Counter(['a', 'b', 'c', 'a', 'b', 'b'])
print collections.Counter({'a':2, 'b':3, 'c':1})
print collections.Counter(a=2, b=3, c=1)
```

The results of all three forms of initialization are the same.

```
$ python collections_counter_init.py

Counter({'b': 3, 'a': 2, 'c': 1})
Counter({'b': 3, 'a': 2, 'c': 1})
Counter({'b': 3, 'a': 2, 'c': 1})
```

An empty `Counter` can be constructed with no arguments and populated via the `update()` method.

```
import collections

c = collections.Counter()
print 'Initial :', c

c.update('abcdaab')
print 'Sequence:', c

c.update({'a':1, 'd':5})
print 'Dict    :', c
```

The count values are increased based on the new data, rather than replaced. In this example, the count for a goes from 3 to 4.

```
$ python collections_counter_update.py

Initial : Counter()
Sequence: Counter({'a': 3, 'b': 2, 'c': 1, 'd': 1})
Dict    : Counter({'d': 6, 'a': 4, 'b': 2, 'c': 1})
```

Accessing Counts

Once a `Counter` is populated, its values can be retrieved using the dictionary API.

```
import collections

c = collections.Counter('abcdaab')

for letter in 'abcde':
    print '%s : %d' % (letter, c[letter])
```

Counter does not raise KeyError for unknown items. If a value has not been seen in the input (as with e in this example), its count is 0.

```
$ python collections_counter_get_values.py

a : 3
b : 2
c : 1
d : 1
e : 0
```

The elements() method returns an iterator that produces all items known to the Counter.

```
import collections

c = collections.Counter('extremely')
c['z'] = 0
print c
print list(c.elements())
```

The order of elements is not guaranteed, and items with counts less than or equal to zero are not included.

```
$ python collections_counter_elements.py

Counter({'e': 3, 'm': 1, 'l': 1, 'r': 1, 't': 1, 'y': 1, 'x': 1,
'z': 0})
['e', 'e', 'e', 'm', 'l', 'r', 't', 'y', 'x']
```

Use most_common() to produce a sequence of the *n* most frequently encountered input values and their respective counts.

```
import collections

c = collections.Counter()
with open('/usr/share/dict/words', 'rt') as f:
    for line in f:
        c.update(line.rstrip().lower())

print 'Most common:'
for letter, count in c.most_common(3):
    print '%s: %7d' % (letter, count)
```

This example counts the letters appearing in all words in the system dictionary to produce a frequency distribution, and then prints the three most common letters. Leaving out the argument to `most_common()` produces a list of all the items, in order of frequency.

```
$ python collections_counter_most_common.py

Most common:
e:   234803
i:   200613
a:   198938
```

Arithmetic

`Counter` instances support arithmetic and set operations for aggregating results.

```
import collections

c1 = collections.Counter(['a', 'b', 'c', 'a', 'b', 'b'])
c2 = collections.Counter('alphabet')

print 'C1:', c1
print 'C2:', c2

print '\nCombined counts:'
print c1 + c2

print '\nSubtraction:'
print c1 - c2
```

```
print '\nIntersection (taking positive minimums):'
print c1 & c2

print '\nUnion (taking maximums):'
print c1 | c2
```

Each time a new `Counter` is produced through an operation, any items with zero or negative counts are discarded. The count for `a` is the same in `c1` and `c2`, so subtraction leaves it at zero.

```
$ python collections_counter_arithmetic.py

C1: Counter({'b': 3, 'a': 2, 'c': 1})
C2: Counter({'a': 2, 'b': 1, 'e': 1, 'h': 1, 'l': 1, 'p': 1, 't': 1})

Combined counts:
Counter({'a': 4, 'b': 4, 'c': 1, 'e': 1, 'h': 1, 'l': 1, 'p': 1,
        't': 1})

Subtraction:
Counter({'b': 2, 'c': 1})

Intersection (taking positive minimums):
Counter({'a': 2, 'b': 1})

Union (taking maximums):
Counter({'b': 3, 'a': 2, 'c': 1, 'e': 1, 'h': 1, 'l': 1, 'p': 1,
        't': 1})
```

2.1.2   defaultdict

The standard dictionary includes the method `setdefault()` for retrieving a value and establishing a default if the value does not exist. By contrast, `defaultdict` lets the caller specify the default up front when the container is initialized.

```
import collections

def default_factory():
    return 'default value'

d = collections.defaultdict(default_factory, foo='bar')
print 'd:', d
```

```
print 'foo =>', d['foo']
print 'bar =>', d['bar']
```

This method works well, as long as it is appropriate for all keys to have the same default. It can be especially useful if the default is a type used for aggregating or accumulating values, such as a `list`, `set`, or even `int`. The standard library documentation includes several examples of using `defaultdict` this way.

```
$ python collections_defaultdict.py

d: defaultdict(<function default_factory
    at 0x100d9ba28>, {'foo': 'bar'})
foo => bar
bar => default value
```

See Also:
defaultdict examples (http://docs.python.org/lib/defaultdict-examples.html)
     Examples of using `defaultdict` from the standard library documentation.
Evolution of Default Dictionaries in Python
     (http://jtauber.com/blog/2008/02/27/evolution_of_default_dictionaries_in_
     python/) Discussion from James Tauber of how `defaultdict` relates to other
     means of initializing dictionaries.

2.1.3   Deque

A double-ended queue, or `deque`, supports adding and removing elements from either end. The more commonly used structures, stacks, and queues are degenerate forms of deques where the inputs and outputs are restricted to a single end.

```
import collections

d = collections.deque('abcdefg')
print 'Deque:', d
print 'Length:', len(d)
print 'Left end:', d[0]
print 'Right end:', d[-1]

d.remove('c')
print 'remove(c):', d
```

Since deques are a type of sequence container, they support some of the same operations as `list`, such as examining the contents with __getitem__ (), determining length, and removing elements from the middle by matching identity.

```
$ python collections_deque.py

Deque: deque(['a', 'b', 'c', 'd', 'e', 'f', 'g'])
Length: 7
Left end: a
Right end: g
remove(c): deque(['a', 'b', 'd', 'e', 'f', 'g'])
```

Populating

A `deque` can be populated from either end, termed "left" and "right" in the Python implementation.

```
import collections

# Add to the right
d1 = collections.deque()
d1.extend('abcdefg')
print 'extend    :', d1
d1.append('h')
print 'append    :', d1

# Add to the left
d2 = collections.deque()
d2.extendleft(xrange(6))
print 'extendleft:', d2
d2.appendleft(6)
print 'appendleft:', d2
```

The `extendleft()` function iterates over its input and performs the equivalent of an `appendleft()` for each item. The end result is that the `deque` contains the input sequence in reverse order.

```
$ python collections_deque_populating.py

extend    : deque(['a', 'b', 'c', 'd', 'e', 'f', 'g'])
append    : deque(['a', 'b', 'c', 'd', 'e', 'f', 'g', 'h'])
```

```
extendleft: deque([5, 4, 3, 2, 1, 0])
appendleft: deque([6, 5, 4, 3, 2, 1, 0])
```

Consuming

Similarly, the elements of the `deque` can be consumed from both ends or either end, depending on the algorithm being applied.

```
import collections

print 'From the right:'
d = collections.deque('abcdefg')
while True:
    try:
        print d.pop(),
    except IndexError:
        break
print

print '\nFrom the left:'
d = collections.deque(xrange(6))
while True:
    try:
        print d.popleft(),
    except IndexError:
        break
print
```

Use `pop()` to remove an item from the right end of the `deque` and `popleft()` to take from the left end.

```
$ python collections_deque_consuming.py

From the right:
g f e d c b a

From the left:
0 1 2 3 4 5
```

Since deques are thread-safe, the contents can even be consumed from both ends at the same time from separate threads.

```
import collections
import threading
import time

candle = collections.deque(xrange(5))

def burn(direction, nextSource):
    while True:
        try:
            next = nextSource()
        except IndexError:
            break
        else:
            print '%8s: %s' % (direction, next)
            time.sleep(0.1)
    print '%8s done' % direction
    return

left = threading.Thread(target=burn, args=('Left', candle.popleft))
right = threading.Thread(target=burn, args=('Right', candle.pop))

left.start()
right.start()

left.join()
right.join()
```

The threads in this example alternate between each end, removing items until the deque is empty.

```
$ python collections_deque_both_ends.py

 Left: 0
Right: 4
Right: 3
 Left: 1
Right: 2
 Left done
Right done
```

Rotating

Another useful capability of the deque is to rotate it in either direction, to skip over some items.

```
import collections

d = collections.deque(xrange(10))
print 'Normal          :', d

d = collections.deque(xrange(10))
d.rotate(2)
print 'Right rotation:', d

d = collections.deque(xrange(10))
d.rotate(-2)
print 'Left rotation :', d
```

Rotating the `deque` to the right (using a positive rotation) takes items from the right end and moves them to the left end. Rotating to the left (with a negative value) takes items from the left end and moves them to the right end. It may help to visualize the items in the `deque` as being engraved along the edge of a dial.

```
$ python collections_deque_rotate.py

Normal         : deque([0, 1, 2, 3, 4, 5, 6, 7, 8, 9])
Right rotation: deque([8, 9, 0, 1, 2, 3, 4, 5, 6, 7])
Left rotation : deque([2, 3, 4, 5, 6, 7, 8, 9, 0, 1])
```

See Also:

Deque (http://en.wikipedia.org/wiki/Deque) Wikipedia article that provides a discussion of the deque data structure.

Deque Recipes (http://docs.python.org/lib/deque-recipes.html) Examples of using deques in algorithms from the standard library documentation.

2.1.4   namedtuple

The standard `tuple` uses numerical indexes to access its members.

```
bob = ('Bob', 30, 'male')
print 'Representation:', bob

jane = ('Jane', 29, 'female')
print '\nField by index:', jane[0]

print '\nFields by index:'
for p in [ bob, jane ]:
    print '%s is a %d year old %s' % p
```

This makes `tuples` convenient containers for simple uses.

```
$ python collections_tuple.py

Representation: ('Bob', 30, 'male')

Field by index: Jane

Fields by index:
Bob is a 30 year old male
Jane is a 29 year old female
```

On the other hand, remembering which index should be used for each value can lead to errors, especially if the `tuple` has a lot of fields and is constructed far from where it is used. A `namedtuple` assigns names, as well as the numerical index, to each member.

Defining

`namedtuple` instances are just as memory efficient as regular tuples because they do not have per-instance dictionaries. Each kind of `namedtuple` is represented by its own class, created by using the `namedtuple()` factory function. The arguments are the name of the new class and a string containing the names of the elements.

```
import collections

Person = collections.namedtuple('Person', 'name age gender')

print 'Type of Person:', type(Person)

bob = Person(name='Bob', age=30, gender='male')
print '\nRepresentation:', bob

jane = Person(name='Jane', age=29, gender='female')
print '\nField by name:', jane.name

print '\nFields by index:'
for p in [ bob, jane ]:
    print '%s is a %d year old %s' % p
```

As the example illustrates, it is possible to access the fields of the `namedtuple` by name using dotted notation (`obj.attr`) as well as using the positional indexes of standard tuples.

```
$ python collections_namedtuple_person.py

Type of Person: <type 'type'>

Representation: Person(name='Bob', age=30, gender='male')

Field by name: Jane

Fields by index:
Bob is a 30 year old male
Jane is a 29 year old female
```

Invalid Field Names

Field names are invalid if they are repeated or conflict with Python keywords.

```
import collections

try:
    collections.namedtuple('Person', 'name class age gender')
except ValueError, err:
    print err

try:
    collections.namedtuple('Person', 'name age gender age')
except ValueError, err:
    print err
```

As the field names are parsed, invalid values cause `ValueError` exceptions.

```
$ python collections_namedtuple_bad_fields.py

Type names and field names cannot be a keyword: 'class'
Encountered duplicate field name: 'age'
```

If a `namedtuple` is being created based on values outside of the control of the program (such as to represent the rows returned by a database query, where the schema is not known in advance), set the *rename* option to `True` so the invalid fields are renamed.

```
import collections

with_class = collections.namedtuple(
    'Person', 'name class age gender',
    rename=True)
```

```
print with_class._fields

two_ages = collections.namedtuple(
    'Person', 'name age gender age',
    rename=True)
print two_ages._fields
```

The new names for renamed fields depend on their index in the `tuple`, so the field with name `class` becomes `_1` and the duplicate `age` field is changed to `_3`.

```
$ python collections_namedtuple_rename.py

('name', '_1', 'age', 'gender')
('name', 'age', 'gender', '_3')
```

2.1.5 OrderedDict

An `OrderedDict` is a dictionary subclass that remembers the order in which its contents are added.

```
import collections

print 'Regular dictionary:'
d = {}
d['a'] = 'A'
d['b'] = 'B'
d['c'] = 'C'

for k, v in d.items():
    print k, v

print '\nOrderedDict:'
d = collections.OrderedDict()
d['a'] = 'A'
d['b'] = 'B'
d['c'] = 'C'

for k, v in d.items():
    print k, v
```

A regular `dict` does not track the insertion order, and iterating over it produces the values in order based on how the keys are stored in the hash table. In an `OrderedDict`, by contrast, the order in which the items are inserted is remembered and used when creating an iterator.

```
$ python collections_ordereddict_iter.py

Regular dictionary:
a A
c C
b B

OrderedDict:
a A
b B
c C
```

Equality

A regular `dict` looks at its contents when testing for equality. An `OrderedDict` also considers the order the items were added.

```
import collections

print 'dict          :',
d1 = {}
d1['a'] = 'A'
d1['b'] = 'B'
d1['c'] = 'C'

d2 = {}
d2['c'] = 'C'
d2['b'] = 'B'
d2['a'] = 'A'

print d1 == d2

print 'OrderedDict:',

d1 = collections.OrderedDict()
d1['a'] = 'A'
d1['b'] = 'B'
d1['c'] = 'C'
```

```
d2 = collections.OrderedDict()
d2['c'] = 'C'
d2['b'] = 'B'
d2['a'] = 'A'

print d1 == d2
```

In this case, since the two ordered dictionaries are created from values in a different order, they are considered to be different.

```
$ python collections_ordereddict_equality.py

dict       : True
OrderedDict: False
```

See Also:
collections (http://docs.python.org/library/collections.html) The standard library documentation for this module.

2.2   array—Sequence of Fixed-Type Data

> **Purpose** Manage sequences of fixed-type numerical data efficiently.
> **Python Version** 1.4 and later

The `array` module defines a sequence data structure that looks very much like a `list`, except that all members have to be of the same primitive type. Refer to the standard library documentation for `array` for a complete list of the types supported.

2.2.1   Initialization

An `array` is instantiated with an argument describing the type of data to be allowed, and possibly an initial sequence of data to store in the array.

```
import array
import binascii

s = 'This is the array.'
a = array.array('c', s)

print 'As string:', s
print 'As array :', a
print 'As hex   :', binascii.hexlify(a)
```

In this example, the array is configured to hold a sequence of bytes and is initialized with a simple string.

```
$ python array_string.py

As string: This is the array.
As array : array('c', 'This is the array.')
As hex   : 54686973206973207468652061727261792e
```

2.2.2 Manipulating Arrays

An array can be extended and otherwise manipulated in the same ways as other Python sequences.

```
import array
import pprint

a = array.array('i', xrange(3))
print 'Initial :', a

a.extend(xrange(3))
print 'Extended:', a

print 'Slice    :', a[2:5]

print 'Iterator:'
print list(enumerate(a))
```

The supported operations include slicing, iterating, and adding elements to the end.

```
$ python array_sequence.py

Initial : array('i', [0, 1, 2])
Extended: array('i', [0, 1, 2, 0, 1, 2])
Slice   : array('i', [2, 0, 1])
Iterator:
[(0, 0), (1, 1), (2, 2), (3, 0), (4, 1), (5, 2)]
```

2.2.3 Arrays and Files

The contents of an array can be written to and read from files using built-in methods coded efficiently for that purpose.

```
import array
import binascii
import tempfile

a = array.array('i', xrange(5))
print 'A1:', a

# Write the array of numbers to a temporary file
output = tempfile.NamedTemporaryFile()
a.tofile(output.file) # must pass an *actual* file
output.flush()

# Read the raw data
with open(output.name, 'rb') as input:
    raw_data = input.read()
    print 'Raw Contents:', binascii.hexlify(raw_data)

    # Read the data into an array
    input.seek(0)
    a2 = array.array('i')
    a2.fromfile(input, len(a))
    print 'A2:', a2
```

This example illustrates reading the data raw, directly from the binary file, versus reading it into a new array and converting the bytes to the appropriate types.

```
$ python array_file.py

A1: array('i', [0, 1, 2, 3, 4])
Raw Contents: 0000000001000000020000000300000004000000
A2: array('i', [0, 1, 2, 3, 4])
```

2.2.4 Alternate Byte Ordering

If the data in the array is not in the native byte order, or needs to be swapped before being sent to a system with a different byte order (or over the network), it is possible to convert the entire array without iterating over the elements from Python.

```
import array
import binascii

def to_hex(a):
    chars_per_item = a.itemsize * 2 # 2 hex digits
```

```python
    hex_version = binascii.hexlify(a)
    num_chunks = len(hex_version) / chars_per_item
    for i in xrange(num_chunks):
        start = i*chars_per_item
        end = start + chars_per_item
        yield hex_version[start:end]

a1 = array.array('i', xrange(5))
a2 = array.array('i', xrange(5))
a2.byteswap()

fmt = '%10s %10s %10s %10s'
print fmt % ('A1 hex', 'A1', 'A2 hex', 'A2')
print fmt % (('-' * 10,) * 4)
for values in zip(to_hex(a1), a1, to_hex(a2), a2):
    print fmt % values
```

The `byteswap()` method switches the byte order of the items in the array from within C, so it is much more efficient than looping over the data in Python.

```
$ python array_byteswap.py

   A1 hex         A1    A2 hex          A2
---------- ---------- ---------- ----------
 00000000          0  00000000           0
 01000000          1  00000001    16777216
 02000000          2  00000002    33554432
 03000000          3  00000003    50331648
 04000000          4  00000004    67108864
```

See Also:
array (http://docs.python.org/library/array.html) The standard library documentation for this module.
struct (page 102) The `struct` module.
Numerical Python (www.scipy.org) NumPy is a Python library for working with large data sets efficiently.

2.3 heapq—Heap Sort Algorithm

Purpose The `heapq` module implements a min-heap sort algorithm suitable for use with Python's lists.
Python Version New in 2.3 with additions in 2.5

A *heap* is a tree-like data structure where the child nodes have a sort-order relationship with the parents. *Binary heaps* can be represented using a list or an array organized so that the children of element N are at positions 2*N+1 and 2*N+2 (for zero-based indexes). This layout makes it possible to rearrange heaps in place, so it is not necessary to reallocate as much memory when adding or removing items.

A max-heap ensures that the parent is larger than or equal to both of its children. A min-heap requires that the parent be less than or equal to its children. Python's `heapq` module implements a min-heap.

2.3.1   Example Data

The examples in this section use the data in `heapq_heapdata.py`.

```
# This data was generated with the random module.

data = [19, 9, 4, 10, 11]
```

The heap output is printed using `heapq_showtree.py`.

```
import math
from cStringIO import StringIO

def show_tree(tree, total_width=36, fill=' '):
    """Pretty-print a tree."""
    output = StringIO()
    last_row = -1
    for i, n in enumerate(tree):
        if i:
            row = int(math.floor(math.log(i+1, 2)))
        else:
            row = 0
        if row != last_row:
            output.write('\n')
        columns = 2**row
        col_width = int(math.floor((total_width * 1.0) / columns))
        output.write(str(n).center(col_width, fill))
        last_row = row
    print output.getvalue()
    print '-' * total_width
    print
    return
```

2.3.2   Creating a Heap

There are two basic ways to create a heap: `heappush()` and `heapify()`.

```
import heapq
from heapq_showtree import show_tree
from heapq_heapdata import data

heap = []
print 'random :', data
print

for n in data:
    print 'add %3d:' % n
    heapq.heappush(heap, n)
    show_tree(heap)
```

Using `heappush()`, the heap sort order of the elements is maintained as new items are added from a data source.

```
$ python heapq_heappush.py

random : [19, 9, 4, 10, 11]

add  19:

                    19
------------------------------------

add   9:

                    9
          19
------------------------------------

add   4:

                    4
          19                 9
------------------------------------

add  10:

                    4
```

```
        10                    9
    19
------------------------------------

add  11:

                    4
        10                    9
    19          11
------------------------------------
```

If the data is already in memory, it is more efficient to use `heapify()` to rearrange the items of the list in place.

```
import heapq
from heapq_showtree import show_tree
from heapq_heapdata import data

print 'random    :', data
heapq.heapify(data)
print 'heapified :'
show_tree(data)
```

The result of building a list in heap order one item at a time is the same as building it unordered and then calling `heapify()`.

```
$ python heapq_heapify.py

random    : [19, 9, 4, 10, 11]
heapified :

                    4
        9                    19
    10          11
------------------------------------
```

2.3.3   Accessing Contents of a Heap

Once the heap is organized correctly, use `heappop()` to remove the element with the lowest value.

```
import heapq
from heapq_showtree import show_tree
from heapq_heapdata import data
```

```
print 'random      :', data
heapq.heapify(data)
print 'heapified :'
show_tree(data)
print

for i in xrange(2):
    smallest = heapq.heappop(data)
    print 'pop      %3d:' % smallest
    show_tree(data)
```

In this example, adapted from the stdlib documentation, `heapify()` and `heappop()` are used to sort a list of numbers.

```
$ python heapq_heappop.py

random    : [19, 9, 4, 10, 11]
heapified :

                    4
          9                   19
      10        11
-----------------------------------


pop      4:

                    9
          10                  19
      11
-----------------------------------


pop      9:

                    10
          11                  19
-----------------------------------
```

To remove existing elements and replace them with new values in a single operation, use `heapreplace()`.

```
import heapq
from heapq_showtree import show_tree
from heapq_heapdata import data
```

```
heapq.heapify(data)
print 'start:'
show_tree(data)

for n in [0, 13]:
    smallest = heapq.heapreplace(data, n)
    print 'replace %2d with %2d:' % (smallest, n)
    show_tree(data)
```

Replacing elements in place makes it possible to maintain a fixed-size heap, such as a queue of jobs ordered by priority.

```
$ python heapq_heapreplace.py

start:

                    4
          9                   19
      10        11
-----------------------------------

replace  4 with  0:

                    0
          9                   19
      10        11
-----------------------------------

replace  0 with 13:

                    9
          10                  19
      13        11
-----------------------------------
```

2.3.4   Data Extremes from a Heap

heapq also includes two functions to examine an iterable to find a range of the largest or smallest values it contains.

```
import heapq
from heapq_heapdata import data
```

```
print 'all         :', data
print '3 largest :', heapq.nlargest(3, data)
print 'from sort :', list(reversed(sorted(data)[-3:]))
print '3 smallest:', heapq.nsmallest(3, data)
print 'from sort :', sorted(data)[:3]
```

Using `nlargest()` and `nsmallest()` is only efficient for relatively small values of $n > 1$, but can still come in handy in a few cases.

```
$ python heapq_extremes.py

all       : [19, 9, 4, 10, 11]
3 largest : [19, 11, 10]
from sort : [19, 11, 10]
3 smallest: [4, 9, 10]
from sort : [4, 9, 10]
```

See Also:

heapq (http://docs.python.org/library/heapq.html) The standard library documentation for this module.

Heap (data structure) (http://en.wikipedia.org/wiki/Heap_(data_structure))
Wikipedia article that provides a general description of heap data structures.

Priority Queue **(page 98)** A priority queue implementation from `Queue` (page 96) in the standard library.

2.4   bisect—Maintain Lists in Sorted Order

Purpose Maintains a list in sorted order without having to call sort each time an item is added to the list.

Python Version 1.4 and later

The `bisect` module implements an algorithm for inserting elements into a list while maintaining the list in sorted order. For some cases, this is more efficient than repeatedly sorting a list or explicitly sorting a large list after it is constructed.

2.4.1   Inserting in Sorted Order

Here is a simple example using `insert()` to insert items into a list in sorted order.

```
import bisect
import random

# Use a constant seed to ensure that
# the same pseudo-random numbers
# are used each time the loop is run.
random.seed(1)

print 'New  Pos  Contents'
print '---  ---  --------'

# Generate random numbers and
# insert them into a list in sorted
# order.
l = []
for i in range(1, 15):
    r = random.randint(1, 100)
    position = bisect.bisect(l, r)
    bisect.insort(l, r)
    print '%3d  %3d' % (r, position), l
```

The first column of the output shows the new random number. The second column shows the position where the number will be inserted into the list. The remainder of each line is the current sorted list.

```
$ python bisect_example.py

New  Pos  Contents
---  ---  --------
 14    0 [14]
 85    1 [14, 85]
 77    1 [14, 77, 85]
 26    1 [14, 26, 77, 85]
 50    2 [14, 26, 50, 77, 85]
 45    2 [14, 26, 45, 50, 77, 85]
 66    4 [14, 26, 45, 50, 66, 77, 85]
 79    6 [14, 26, 45, 50, 66, 77, 79, 85]
 10    0 [10, 14, 26, 45, 50, 66, 77, 79, 85]
  3    0 [3, 10, 14, 26, 45, 50, 66, 77, 79, 85]
 84    9 [3, 10, 14, 26, 45, 50, 66, 77, 79, 84, 85]
 44    4 [3, 10, 14, 26, 44, 45, 50, 66, 77, 79, 84, 85]
 77    9 [3, 10, 14, 26, 44, 45, 50, 66, 77, 77, 79, 84, 85]
  1    0 [1, 3, 10, 14, 26, 44, 45, 50, 66, 77, 77, 79, 84, 85]
```

This is a simple example, and for the amount of data being manipulated, it might be faster to simply build the list and then sort it once. But for long lists, significant time and memory savings can be achieved using an insertion sort algorithm such as this one.

2.4.2   Handling Duplicates

The result set shown previously includes a repeated value, 77. The bisect module provides two ways to handle repeats. New values can be inserted to the left of existing values or to the right. The insert() function is actually an alias for insort_right(), which inserts after the existing value. The corresponding function insort_left() inserts before the existing value.

```
import bisect
import random

# Reset the seed
random.seed(1)

print 'New  Pos  Contents'
print '---  ---  --------'

# Use bisect_left and insort_left.
l = []
for i in range(1, 15):
    r = random.randint(1, 100)
    position = bisect.bisect_left(l, r)
    bisect.insort_left(l, r)
    print '%3d  %3d' % (r, position), l
```

When the same data is manipulated using bisect_left() and insort_left(), the results are the same sorted list, but the insert positions are different for the duplicate values.

```
$ python bisect_example2.py

New  Pos  Contents
---  ---  --------
 14    0 [14]
 85    1 [14, 85]
 77    1 [14, 77, 85]
 26    1 [14, 26, 77, 85]
 50    2 [14, 26, 50, 77, 85]
 45    2 [14, 26, 45, 50, 77, 85]
```

```
66    4 [14, 26, 45, 50, 66, 77, 85]
79    6 [14, 26, 45, 50, 66, 77, 79, 85]
10    0 [10, 14, 26, 45, 50, 66, 77, 79, 85]
 3    0 [3, 10, 14, 26, 45, 50, 66, 77, 79, 85]
84    9 [3, 10, 14, 26, 45, 50, 66, 77, 79, 84, 85]
44    4 [3, 10, 14, 26, 44, 45, 50, 66, 77, 79, 84, 85]
77    8 [3, 10, 14, 26, 44, 45, 50, 66, 77, 77, 79, 84, 85]
 1    0 [1, 3, 10, 14, 26, 44, 45, 50, 66, 77, 77, 79, 84, 85]
```

In addition to the Python implementation, a faster C implementation is available. If the C version is present, that implementation automatically overrides the pure Python implementation when `bisect` is imported.

See Also:
bisect (http://docs.python.org/library/bisect.html) The standard library documentation for this module.
Insertion Sort (http://en.wikipedia.org/wiki/Insertion_sort) Wikipedia article that provides a description of the insertion sort algorithm.

2.5 Queue—Thread-Safe FIFO Implementation

Purpose Provides a thread-safe FIFO implementation.
Python Version At least 1.4

The `Queue` module provides a first-in, first-out (FIFO) data structure suitable for multithreaded programming. It can be used to pass messages or other data safely between producer and consumer threads. Locking is handled for the caller, so many threads can work with the same `Queue` instance safely. The size of a `Queue` (the number of elements it contains) may be restricted to throttle memory usage or processing.

Note: This discussion assumes you already understand the general nature of a queue. If you do not, you may want to read some of the references before continuing.

2.5.1 Basic FIFO Queue

The `Queue` class implements a basic first-in, first-out container. Elements are added to one end of the sequence using `put()`, and removed from the other end using `get()`.

```
import Queue

q = Queue.Queue()

for i in range(5):
    q.put(i)

while not q.empty():
    print q.get(),
print
```

This example uses a single thread to illustrate that elements are removed from the queue in the same order they are inserted.

```
$ python Queue_fifo.py

0 1 2 3 4
```

2.5.2   LIFO Queue

In contrast to the standard FIFO implementation of Queue, the LifoQueue uses last-in, first-out (LIFO) ordering (normally associated with a stack data structure).

```
import Queue

q = Queue.LifoQueue()

for i in range(5):
    q.put(i)

while not q.empty():
    print q.get(),
print
```

The item most recently put into the queue is removed by get.

```
$ python Queue_lifo.py

4 3 2 1 0
```

2.5.3   Priority Queue

Sometimes, the processing order of the items in a queue needs to be based on characteristics of those items, rather than just on the order in which they are created or added to the queue. For example, print jobs from the payroll department may take precedence over a code listing printed by a developer. `PriorityQueue` uses the sort order of the contents of the queue to decide which to retrieve.

```python
import Queue
import threading

class Job(object):
    def __init__(self, priority, description):
        self.priority = priority
        self.description = description
        print 'New job:', description
        return
    def __cmp__(self, other):
        return cmp(self.priority, other.priority)

q = Queue.PriorityQueue()

q.put( Job(3, 'Mid-level job') )
q.put( Job(10, 'Low-level job') )
q.put( Job(1, 'Important job') )

def process_job(q):
    while True:
        next_job = q.get()
        print 'Processing job:', next_job.description
        q.task_done()

workers = [ threading.Thread(target=process_job, args=(q,)),
            threading.Thread(target=process_job, args=(q,)),
            ]
for w in workers:
    w.setDaemon(True)
    w.start()

q.join()
```

This example has multiple threads consuming the jobs, which are to be processed based on the priority of items in the queue at the time `get()` was called. The order of processing for items added to the queue while the consumer threads are running depends on thread context switching.

```
$ python Queue_priority.py

New job: Mid-level job
New job: Low-level job
New job: Important job
Processing job: Important job
Processing job: Mid-level job
Processing job: Low-level job
```

2.5.4 Building a Threaded Podcast Client

The source code for the podcasting client in this section demonstrates how to use the Queue class with multiple threads. The program reads one or more RSS feeds, queues up the enclosures for the five most recent episodes to be downloaded, and processes several downloads in parallel using threads. It does not have enough error handling for production use, but the skeleton implementation provides an example of how to use the Queue module.

First, some operating parameters are established. Normally, these would come from user inputs (preferences, a database, etc.). The example uses hard-coded values for the number of threads and a list of URLs to fetch.

```python
from Queue import Queue
from threading import Thread
import time
import urllib
import urlparse

import feedparser

# Set up some global variables
num_fetch_threads = 2
enclosure_queue = Queue()

# A real app wouldn't use hard-coded data...
feed_urls = [ 'http://advocacy.python.org/podcasts/littlebit.rss',
            ]
```

The function downloadEnclosures() will run in the worker thread and process the downloads using urllib.

```
def downloadEnclosures(i, q):
    """This is the worker thread function.
    It processes items in the queue one after
    another.  These daemon threads go into an
    infinite loop, and only exit when
    the main thread ends.
    """
    while True:
        print '%s: Looking for the next enclosure' % i
        url = q.get()
        parsed_url = urlparse.urlparse(url)
        print '%s: Downloading:' % i, parsed_url.path
        response = urllib.urlopen(url)
        data = response.read()
        # Save the downloaded file to the current directory
        outfile_name = url.rpartition('/')[-1]
        with open(outfile_name, 'wb') as outfile:
            outfile.write(data)
        q.task_done()
```

Once the threads' target function is defined, the worker threads can be started. When `downloadEnclosures()` processes the statement `url = q.get()`, it blocks and waits until the queue has something to return. That means it is safe to start the threads before there is anything in the queue.

```
# Set up some threads to fetch the enclosures
for i in range(num_fetch_threads):
    worker = Thread(target=downloadEnclosures,
                    args=(i, enclosure_queue,))
    worker.setDaemon(True)
    worker.start()
```

The next step is to retrieve the feed contents using Mark Pilgrim's `feedparser` module (www.feedparser.org) and enqueue the URLs of the enclosures. As soon as the first URL is added to the queue, one of the worker threads picks it up and starts downloading it. The loop will continue to add items until the feed is exhausted, and the worker threads will take turns dequeuing URLs to download them.

```
# Download the feed(s) and put the enclosure URLs into
# the queue.
for url in feed_urls:
    response = feedparser.parse(url, agent='fetch_podcasts.py')
```

```
for entry in response['entries'][-5:]:
    for enclosure in entry.get('enclosures', []):
        parsed_url = urlparse.urlparse(enclosure['url'])
        print 'Queuing:', parsed_url.path
        enclosure_queue.put(enclosure['url'])
```

The only thing left to do is wait for the queue to empty out again, using `join()`.

```
# Now wait for the queue to be empty, indicating that we have
# processed all the downloads.
print '*** Main thread waiting'
enclosure_queue.join()
print '*** Done'
```

Running the sample script produces the following.

```
$ python fetch_podcasts.py

0: Looking for the next enclosure
1: Looking for the next enclosure
Queuing: /podcasts/littlebit/2010-04-18.mp3
Queuing: /podcasts/littlebit/2010-05-22.mp3
Queuing: /podcasts/littlebit/2010-06-06.mp3
Queuing: /podcasts/littlebit/2010-07-26.mp3
Queuing: /podcasts/littlebit/2010-11-25.mp3
*** Main thread waiting
0: Downloading: /podcasts/littlebit/2010-04-18.mp3
0: Looking for the next enclosure
0: Downloading: /podcasts/littlebit/2010-05-22.mp3
0: Looking for the next enclosure
0: Downloading: /podcasts/littlebit/2010-06-06.mp3
0: Looking for the next enclosure
0: Downloading: /podcasts/littlebit/2010-07-26.mp3
0: Looking for the next enclosure
0: Downloading: /podcasts/littlebit/2010-11-25.mp3
0: Looking for the next enclosure
*** Done
```

The actual output will depend on the contents of the RSS feed used.

See Also:

Queue (http://docs.python.org/lib/module-Queue.html) Standard library documentation for this module.

Deque **(page 75) from** `collections` **(page 70)** The `collections` module includes
a `deque` (double-ended queue) class.

Queue data structures (http://en.wikipedia.org/wiki/Queue_(data_structure))
Wikipedia article explaining queues.

FIFO (http://en.wikipedia.org/wiki/FIFO) Wikipedia article explaining first-in,
first-out data structures.

2.6 struct—Binary Data Structures

Purpose Convert between strings and binary data.
Python Version 1.4 and later

The `struct` module includes functions for converting between strings of bytes and
native Python data types, such as numbers and strings.

2.6.1 Functions vs. Struct Class

There is a set of module-level functions for working with structured values, and there
is also the `Struct` class. Format specifiers are converted from their string format to a
compiled representation, similar to the way regular expressions are handled. The conversion takes some resources, so it is typically more efficient to do it once when creating
a `Struct` instance and call methods on the instance, instead of using the module-level
functions. The following examples all use the `Struct` class.

2.6.2 Packing and Unpacking

Structs support *packing* data into strings and *unpacking* data from strings using format specifiers made up of characters representing the data type and optional count and
endianness indicators. Refer to the standard library documentation for a complete list
of the supported format specifiers.

In this example, the specifier calls for an integer or long value, a two-character
string, and a floating-point number. The spaces in the format specifier are included to
separate the type indicators and are ignored when the format is compiled.

```
import struct
import binascii

values = (1, 'ab', 2.7)
s = struct.Struct('I 2s f')
packed_data = s.pack(*values)
```

```
print 'Original values:', values
print 'Format string  :', s.format
print 'Uses           :', s.size, 'bytes'
print 'Packed Value   :', binascii.hexlify(packed_data)
```

The example converts the packed value to a sequence of hex bytes for printing with `binascii.hexlify()`, since some characters are nulls.

```
$ python struct_pack.py

Original values: (1, 'ab', 2.7)
Format string  : I 2s f
Uses           : 12 bytes
Packed Value   : 0100000061620000cdcc2c40
```

Use `unpack()` to extract data from its packed representation.

```
import struct
import binascii

packed_data = binascii.unhexlify('0100000061620000cdcc2c40')

s = struct.Struct('I 2s f')
unpacked_data = s.unpack(packed_data)
print 'Unpacked Values:', unpacked_data
```

Passing the packed value to `unpack()` gives basically the same values back (note the discrepancy in the floating-point value).

```
$ python struct_unpack.py

Unpacked Values: (1, 'ab', 2.700000047683716)
```

2.6.3 Endianness

By default, values are encoded using the native C library notion of *endianness*. It is easy to override that choice by providing an explicit endianness directive in the format string.

```
import struct
import binascii
```

```
values = (1, 'ab', 2.7)
print 'Original values:', values
endianness = [
    ('@', 'native, native'),
    ('=', 'native, standard'),
    ('<', 'little-endian'),
    ('>', 'big-endian'),
    ('!', 'network'),
    ]

for code, name in endianness:
    s = struct.Struct(code + ' I 2s f')
    packed_data = s.pack(*values)
    print
    print 'Format string  :', s.format, 'for', name
    print 'Uses           :', s.size, 'bytes'
    print 'Packed Value   :', binascii.hexlify(packed_data)
    print 'Unpacked Value :', s.unpack(packed_data)
```

Table 2.1 lists the byte order specifiers used by struct.

Table 2.1. Byte Order Specifiers for struct

Code	Meaning
@	Native order
=	Native standard
<	Little-endian
>	Big-endian
!	Network order

```
$ python struct_endianness.py

Original values: (1, 'ab', 2.7)

Format string  : @ I 2s f for native, native
Uses           : 12 bytes
Packed Value   : 0100000061620000cdcc2c40
Unpacked Value : (1, 'ab', 2.700000047683716)

Format string  : = I 2s f for native, standard
Uses           : 10 bytes
Packed Value   : 010000006162cdcc2c40
```

```
Unpacked Value : (1, 'ab', 2.700000047683716)

Format string : < I 2s f for little-endian
Uses          : 10 bytes
Packed Value   : 010000006162cdcc2c40
Unpacked Value : (1, 'ab', 2.700000047683716)

Format string : > I 2s f for big-endian
Uses          : 10 bytes
Packed Value   : 000000016162402ccccd
Unpacked Value : (1, 'ab', 2.700000047683716)

Format string : ! I 2s f for network
Uses          : 10 bytes
Packed Value   : 000000016162402ccccd
Unpacked Value : (1, 'ab', 2.700000047683716)
```

2.6.4 Buffers

Working with binary packed data is typically reserved for performance-sensitive situations or when passing data into and out of extension modules. These cases can be optimized by avoiding the overhead of allocating a new buffer for each packed structure. The `pack_into()` and `unpack_from()` methods support writing to preallocated buffers directly.

```
import struct
import binascii

s = struct.Struct('I 2s f')
values = (1, 'ab', 2.7)
print 'Original:', values

print
print 'ctypes string buffer'

import ctypes
b = ctypes.create_string_buffer(s.size)
print 'Before  :', binascii.hexlify(b.raw)
s.pack_into(b, 0, *values)
print 'After   :', binascii.hexlify(b.raw)
print 'Unpacked:', s.unpack_from(b, 0)
```

```
print
print 'array'

import array
a = array.array('c', '\0' * s.size)
print 'Before  :', binascii.hexlify(a)
s.pack_into(a, 0, *values)
print 'After   :', binascii.hexlify(a)
print 'Unpacked:', s.unpack_from(a, 0)
```

The *size* attribute of the `Struct` tells us how big the buffer needs to be.

```
$ python struct_buffers.py

Original: (1, 'ab', 2.7)

ctypes string buffer
Before  : 000000000000000000000000
After   : 0100000061620000cdcc2c40
Unpacked: (1, 'ab', 2.700000047683716)

array
Before  : 000000000000000000000000
After   : 0100000061620000cdcc2c40
Unpacked: (1, 'ab', 2.700000047683716)
```

See Also:

struct (http://docs.python.org/library/struct.html) The standard library documentation for this module.

array (page 84) The `array` module, for working with sequences of fixed-type values.

binascii (http://docs.python.org/library/binascii.html) The `binascii` module, for producing ASCII representations of binary data.

Endianness (http://en.wikipedia.org/wiki/Endianness) Wikipedia article that provides an explanation of byte order and endianness in encoding.

2.7 weakref—Impermanent References to Objects

Purpose Refer to an "expensive" object, but allow its memory to be reclaimed by the garbage collector if there are no other nonweak references.

Python Version 2.1 and later

The `weakref` module supports weak references to objects. A normal reference increments the reference count on the object and prevents it from being garbage collected. This is not always desirable, either when a circular reference might be present or when building a cache of objects that should be deleted when memory is needed. A weak reference is a handle to an object that does not keep it from being cleaned up automatically.

2.7.1   References

Weak references to objects are managed through the `ref` class. To retrieve the original object, call the reference object.

```python
import weakref

class ExpensiveObject(object):
    def __del__(self):
        print '(Deleting %s)' % self

obj = ExpensiveObject()
r = weakref.ref(obj)

print 'obj:', obj
print 'ref:', r
print 'r():', r()

print 'deleting obj'
del obj
print 'r():', r()
```

In this case, since `obj` is deleted before the second call to the reference, the `ref` returns `None`.

```
$ python weakref_ref.py

obj: <__main__.ExpensiveObject object at 0x100da5750>
ref: <weakref at 0x100d99b50; to 'ExpensiveObject' at 0x100da5750>
r(): <__main__.ExpensiveObject object at 0x100da5750>
deleting obj
(Deleting <__main__.ExpensiveObject object at 0x100da5750>)
r(): None
```

2.7.2   Reference Callbacks

The `ref` constructor accepts an optional callback function to invoke when the referenced object is deleted.

```
import weakref

class ExpensiveObject(object):
    def __del__(self):
        print '(Deleting %s)' % self

def callback(reference):
    """Invoked when referenced object is deleted"""
    print 'callback(', reference, ')'

obj = ExpensiveObject()
r = weakref.ref(obj, callback)

print 'obj:', obj
print 'ref:', r
print 'r():', r()

print 'deleting obj'
del obj
print 'r():', r()
```

The callback receives the reference object as an argument after the reference is "dead" and no longer refers to the original object. One use for this feature is to remove the weak reference object from a cache.

```
$ python weakref_ref_callback.py

obj: <__main__.ExpensiveObject object at 0x100da1950>
ref: <weakref at 0x100d99ba8; to 'ExpensiveObject' at 0x100da1950>
r(): <__main__.ExpensiveObject object at 0x100da1950>
deleting obj
callback( <weakref at 0x100d99ba8; dead> )
(Deleting <__main__.ExpensiveObject object at 0x100da1950>)
r(): None
```

2.7.3   Proxies

It is sometimes more convenient to use a proxy, rather than a weak reference. Proxies can be used as though they were the original object and do not need to be called before the object is accessible. That means they can be passed to a library that does not know it is receiving a reference instead of the real object.

```
import weakref

class ExpensiveObject(object):
    def __init__(self, name):
        self.name = name
    def __del__(self):
        print '(Deleting %s)' % self

obj = ExpensiveObject('My Object')
r = weakref.ref(obj)
p = weakref.proxy(obj)

print 'via obj:', obj.name
print 'via ref:', r().name
print 'via proxy:', p.name
del obj
print 'via proxy:', p.name
```

If the proxy is accessed after the referent object is removed, a `ReferenceError` exception is raised.

```
$ python weakref_proxy.py

via obj: My Object
via ref: My Object
via proxy: My Object
(Deleting <__main__.ExpensiveObject object at 0x100da27d0>)
via proxy:
Traceback (most recent call last):
  File "weakref_proxy.py", line 26, in <module>
    print 'via proxy:', p.name
ReferenceError: weakly-referenced object no longer exists
```

2.7.4   Cyclic References

One use for weak references is to allow cyclic references without preventing garbage collection. This example illustrates the difference between using regular objects and proxies when a graph includes a cycle.

The `Graph` class in `weakref_graph.py` accepts any object given to it as the "next" node in the sequence. For the sake of brevity, this implementation supports a single outgoing reference from each node, which is of limited use generally, but makes it easy to create cycles for these examples. The function `demo()` is a utility function to exercise the `Graph` class by creating a cycle and then removing various references.

```python
import gc
from pprint import pprint
import weakref

class Graph(object):
    def __init__(self, name):
        self.name = name
        self.other = None
    def set_next(self, other):
        print '%s.set_next(%r)' % (self.name, other)
        self.other = other
    def all_nodes(self):
        "Generate the nodes in the graph sequence."
        yield self
        n = self.other
        while n and n.name != self.name:
            yield n
            n = n.other
        if n is self:
            yield n
        return
    def __str__(self):
        return '->'.join(n.name for n in self.all_nodes())
    def __repr__(self):
        return '<%s at 0x%x name=%s>' % (self.__class__.__name__,
                                         id(self), self.name)
    def __del__(self):
        print '(Deleting %s)' % self.name
        self.set_next(None)

def collect_and_show_garbage():
    "Show what garbage is present."
    print 'Collecting...'
    n = gc.collect()
    print 'Unreachable objects:', n
    print 'Garbage:',
    pprint(gc.garbage)
```

```
def demo(graph_factory):
    print 'Set up graph:'
    one = graph_factory('one')
    two = graph_factory('two')
    three = graph_factory('three')
    one.set_next(two)
    two.set_next(three)
    three.set_next(one)

    print
    print 'Graph:'
    print str(one)
    collect_and_show_garbage()

    print
    three = None
    two = None
    print 'After 2 references removed:'
    print str(one)
    collect_and_show_garbage()

    print
    print 'Removing last reference:'
    one = None
    collect_and_show_garbage()
```

This example uses the `gc` module to help debug the leak. The DEBUG_LEAK flag causes `gc` to print information about objects that cannot be seen, other than through the reference the garbage collector has to them.

```
import gc
from pprint import pprint
import weakref

from weakref_graph import Graph, demo, collect_and_show_garbage

gc.set_debug(gc.DEBUG_LEAK)

print 'Setting up the cycle'
print
demo(Graph)
```

```
print
print 'Breaking the cycle and cleaning up garbage'
print
gc.garbage[0].set_next(None)
while gc.garbage:
    del gc.garbage[0]
print
collect_and_show_garbage()
```

Even after deleting the local references to the `Graph` instances in `demo()`, the graphs all show up in the garbage list and cannot be collected. Several dictionaries are also found in the garbage list. They are the `__dict__` values from the `Graph` instances and contain the attributes for those objects. The graphs can be forcibly deleted, since the program knows what they are. Enabling unbuffered I/O by passing the `-u` option to the interpreter ensures that the output from the **print** statements in this example program (written to standard output) and the debug output from `gc` (written to standard error) are interleaved correctly.

```
$ python -u weakref_cycle.py

Setting up the cycle

Set up graph:
one.set_next(<Graph at 0x100db7590 name=two>)
two.set_next(<Graph at 0x100db75d0 name=three>)
three.set_next(<Graph at 0x100db7550 name=one>)

Graph:
one->two->three->one
Collecting...
Unreachable objects: 0
Garbage:[]

After 2 references removed:
one->two->three->one
Collecting...
Unreachable objects: 0
Garbage:[]

Removing last reference:
Collecting...
gc: uncollectable <Graph 0x100db7550>
gc: uncollectable <Graph 0x100db7590>
```

```
gc: uncollectable <Graph 0x100db75d0>
gc: uncollectable <dict 0x100c63c30>
gc: uncollectable <dict 0x100c5e150>
gc: uncollectable <dict 0x100c63810>
Unreachable objects: 6
Garbage:[<Graph at 0x100db7550 name=one>,
 <Graph at 0x100db7590 name=two>,
 <Graph at 0x100db75d0 name=three>,
 {'name': 'one', 'other': <Graph at 0x100db7590 name=two>},
 {'name': 'two', 'other': <Graph at 0x100db75d0 name=three>},
 {'name': 'three', 'other': <Graph at 0x100db7550 name=one>}]

Breaking the cycle and cleaning up garbage

one.set_next(None)
(Deleting two)
two.set_next(None)
(Deleting three)
three.set_next(None)
(Deleting one)
one.set_next(None)

Collecting...
Unreachable objects: 0
Garbage:[]
```

The next step is to create a more intelligent `WeakGraph` class that knows how to avoid creating cycles with regular references by using weak references when a cycle is detected.

```python
import gc
from pprint import pprint
import weakref

from weakref_graph import Graph, demo

class WeakGraph(Graph):
    def set_next(self, other):
        if other is not None:
            # See if we should replace the reference
            # to other with a weakref.
            if self in other.all_nodes():
                other = weakref.proxy(other)
```

```
        super(WeakGraph, self).set_next(other)
        return

demo(WeakGraph)
```

Since the `WeakGraph` instances use proxies to refer to objects that have already been seen, as `demo()` removes all local references to the objects, the cycle is broken and the garbage collector can delete the objects.

```
$ python weakref_weakgraph.py

Set up graph:
one.set_next(<WeakGraph at 0x100db4790 name=two>)
two.set_next(<WeakGraph at 0x100db47d0 name=three>)
three.set_next(<weakproxy at 0x100dac6d8 to WeakGraph at 0x100db4750>
)

Graph:
one->two->three
Collecting...
Unreachable objects: 0
Garbage:[]

After 2 references removed:
one->two->three
Collecting...
Unreachable objects: 0
Garbage:[]

Removing last reference:
(Deleting one)
one.set_next(None)
(Deleting two)
two.set_next(None)
(Deleting three)
three.set_next(None)
Collecting...
Unreachable objects: 0
Garbage:[]
```

2.7.5   Caching Objects

The `ref` and `proxy` classes are considered "low level." While they are useful for maintaining weak references to individual objects and allowing cycles to be garbage collected, the `WeakKeyDictionary` and `WeakValueDictionary` provide a more appropriate API for creating a cache of several objects.

The `WeakValueDictionary` uses weak references to the values it holds, allowing them to be garbage collected when other code is not actually using them. Using explicit calls to the garbage collector illustrates the difference between memory handling with a regular dictionary and `WeakValueDictionary`.

```python
import gc
from pprint import pprint
import weakref

gc.set_debug(gc.DEBUG_LEAK)

class ExpensiveObject(object):
    def __init__(self, name):
        self.name = name
    def __repr__(self):
        return 'ExpensiveObject(%s)' % self.name
    def __del__(self):
        print '    (Deleting %s)' % self


def demo(cache_factory):
    # hold objects so any weak references
    # are not removed immediately
    all_refs = {}
    # create the cache using the factory
    print 'CACHE TYPE:', cache_factory
    cache = cache_factory()
    for name in [ 'one', 'two', 'three' ]:
        o = ExpensiveObject(name)
        cache[name] = o
        all_refs[name] = o
        del o # decref

    print '  all_refs =',
    pprint(all_refs)
    print '\n  Before, cache contains:', cache.keys()
    for name, value in cache.items():
        print '    %s = %s' % (name, value)
        del value # decref

    # Remove all references to the objects except the cache
    print '\n  Cleanup:'
```

```
    del all_refs
    gc.collect()

    print '\n  After, cache contains:', cache.keys()
    for name, value in cache.items():
        print '    %s = %s' % (name, value)
    print '  demo returning'
    return

demo(dict)
print

demo(weakref.WeakValueDictionary)
```

Any loop variables that refer to the values being cached must be cleared explicitly so the reference count of the object is decremented. Otherwise, the garbage collector would not remove the objects, and they would remain in the cache. Similarly, the *all_refs* variable is used to hold references to prevent them from being garbage collected prematurely.

```
$ python weakref_valuedict.py

CACHE TYPE: <type 'dict'>
  all_refs ={'one': ExpensiveObject(one),
 'three': ExpensiveObject(three),
 'two': ExpensiveObject(two)}

  Before, cache contains: ['three', 'two', 'one']
    three = ExpensiveObject(three)
    two = ExpensiveObject(two)
    one = ExpensiveObject(one)

  Cleanup:

  After, cache contains: ['three', 'two', 'one']
    three = ExpensiveObject(three)
    two = ExpensiveObject(two)
    one = ExpensiveObject(one)
  demo returning
    (Deleting ExpensiveObject(three))
    (Deleting ExpensiveObject(two))
    (Deleting ExpensiveObject(one))
```

```
CACHE TYPE: weakref.WeakValueDictionary
  all_refs ={'one': ExpensiveObject(one),
 'three': ExpensiveObject(three),
 'two': ExpensiveObject(two)}

 Before, cache contains: ['three', 'two', 'one']
   three = ExpensiveObject(three)
   two = ExpensiveObject(two)
   one = ExpensiveObject(one)

 Cleanup:
   (Deleting ExpensiveObject(three))
   (Deleting ExpensiveObject(two))
   (Deleting ExpensiveObject(one))

 After, cache contains: []
 demo returning
```

The `WeakKeyDictionary` works similarly, but it uses weak references for the keys instead of the values in the dictionary.

Warning: The library documentation for `weakref` contains this warning:
Caution: Because a `WeakValueDictionary` is built on top of a Python dictionary, it must not change size when iterating over it. This can be difficult to ensure for a `WeakValueDictionary` because actions performed by the program during iteration may cause items in the dictionary to vanish "by magic" (as a side effect of garbage collection).

See Also:

weakref (http://docs.python.org/lib/module-weakref.html) Standard library documentation for this module.

gc (page 1138) The `gc` module is the interface to the interpreter's garbage collector.

2.8 copy—Duplicate Objects

> **Purpose** Provides functions for duplicating objects using shallow or deep copy semantics.
>
> **Python Version** 1.4 and later

The copy module includes two functions, copy() and deepcopy(), for duplicating existing objects.

2.8.1 Shallow Copies

The *shallow copy* created by copy() is a new container populated with references to the contents of the original object. When making a shallow copy of a list object, a new list is constructed and the elements of the original object are appended to it.

```python
import copy

class MyClass:
    def __init__(self, name):
        self.name = name
    def __cmp__(self, other):
        return cmp(self.name, other.name)

a = MyClass('a')
my_list = [ a ]
dup = copy.copy(my_list)

print '                      my_list:', my_list
print '                          dup:', dup
print '          dup is my_list:', (dup is my_list)
print '          dup == my_list:', (dup == my_list)
print 'dup[0] is my_list[0]:', (dup[0] is my_list[0])
print 'dup[0] == my_list[0]:', (dup[0] == my_list[0])
```

For a shallow copy, the MyClass instance is not duplicated, so the reference in the dup list is to the same object that is in my_list.

```
$ python copy_shallow.py

              my_list: [<__main__.MyClass instance at 0x100dadc68>]
                  dup: [<__main__.MyClass instance at 0x100dadc68>]
        dup is my_list: False
        dup == my_list: True
dup[0] is my_list[0]: True
dup[0] == my_list[0]: True
```

2.8.2 Deep Copies

The *deep copy* created by deepcopy() is a new container populated with copies of the contents of the original object. To make a deep copy of a list, a new list is constructed, the elements of the original list are copied, and then those copies are appended to the new list.

Replacing the call to copy() with deepcopy() makes the difference in the output apparent.

```
dup = copy.deepcopy(my_list)
```

The first element of the list is no longer the same object reference, but when the two objects are compared, they still evaluate as being equal.

```
$ python copy_deep.py

              my_list: [<__main__.MyClass instance at 0x100dadc68>]
                  dup: [<__main__.MyClass instance at 0x100dadc20>]
        dup is my_list: False
        dup == my_list: True
   dup[0] is my_list[0]: False
   dup[0] == my_list[0]: True
```

2.8.3 Customizing Copy Behavior

It is possible to control how copies are made using the __copy__() and __deepcopy__() special methods.

- __copy__() is called without any arguments and should return a shallow copy of the object.
- __deepcopy__() is called with a memo dictionary and should return a deep copy of the object. Any member attributes that need to be deep-copied should be passed to copy.deepcopy(), along with the memo dictionary, to control for recursion. (The memo dictionary is explained in more detail later.)

This example illustrates how the methods are called.

```
import copy

class MyClass:
    def __init__(self, name):
        self.name = name
    def __cmp__(self, other):
        return cmp(self.name, other.name)
```

```
    def __copy__(self):
        print '__copy__()'
        return MyClass(self.name)
    def __deepcopy__(self, memo):
        print '__deepcopy__(%s)' % str(memo)
        return MyClass(copy.deepcopy(self.name, memo))

a = MyClass('a')

sc = copy.copy(a)
dc = copy.deepcopy(a)
```

The memo dictionary is used to keep track of the values that have been copied already, to avoid infinite recursion.

```
$ python copy_hooks.py

__copy__()
__deepcopy__({})
```

2.8.4   Recursion in Deep Copy

To avoid problems with duplicating recursive data structures, deepcopy() uses a dictionary to track objects that have already been copied. This dictionary is passed to the __deepcopy__() method so it can be examined there as well.

This example shows how an interconnected data structure, such as a directed graph, can assist with protecting against recursion by implementing a __deepcopy__() method.

```
import copy
import pprint

class Graph:

    def __init__(self, name, connections):
        self.name = name
        self.connections = connections

    def add_connection(self, other):
        self.connections.append(other)

    def __repr__(self):
        return 'Graph(name=%s, id=%s)' % (self.name, id(self))
```

```
def __deepcopy__(self, memo):
    print '\nCalling __deepcopy__ for %r' % self
    if self in memo:
        existing = memo.get(self)
        print '  Already copied to %r' % existing
        return existing
    print '  Memo dictionary:'
    pprint.pprint(memo, indent=4, width=40)
    dup = Graph(copy.deepcopy(self.name, memo), [])
    print '  Copying to new object %s' % dup
    memo[self] = dup
    for c in self.connections:
        dup.add_connection(copy.deepcopy(c, memo))
    return dup

root = Graph('root', [])
a = Graph('a', [root])
b = Graph('b', [a, root])
root.add_connection(a)
root.add_connection(b)

dup = copy.deepcopy(root)
```

The `Graph` class includes a few basic directed-graph methods. An instance can be initialized with a name and a list of existing nodes to which it is connected. The `add_connection()` method is used to set up bidirectional connections. It is also used by the `deepcopy` operator.

The `__deepcopy__()` method prints messages to show how it is called and manages the memo dictionary contents, as needed. Instead of copying the connection list wholesale, it creates a new list and appends copies of the individual connections to it. That ensures that the memo dictionary is updated as each new node is duplicated and avoids recursion issues or extra copies of nodes. As before, it returns the copied object when it is done.

There are several cycles in the graph shown in Figure 2.1, but handling the recursion with the memo dictionary prevents the traversal from causing a stack overflow error. When the *root* node is copied, the output is as follows.

```
$ python copy_recursion.py

Calling __deepcopy__ for Graph(name=root, id=4309347072)
  Memo dictionary:
{    }
```

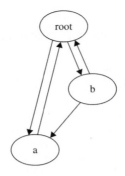

Figure 2.1. Deepcopy for an object graph with cycles

```
Copying to new object Graph(name=root, id=4309347360)

Calling __deepcopy__ for Graph(name=a, id=4309347144)
  Memo dictionary:
{   Graph(name=root, id=4309347072): Graph(name=root, id=4309347360),
    4307936896: ['root'],
    4309253504: 'root'}
  Copying to new object Graph(name=a, id=4309347504)

Calling __deepcopy__ for Graph(name=root, id=4309347072)
  Already copied to Graph(name=root, id=4309347360)

Calling __deepcopy__ for Graph(name=b, id=4309347216)
  Memo dictionary:
{   Graph(name=root, id=4309347072): Graph(name=root, id=4309347360),
    Graph(name=a, id=4309347144): Graph(name=a, id=4309347504),
    4307936896: [   'root',
                    'a',
                    Graph(name=root, id=4309347072),
                    Graph(name=a, id=4309347144)],
    4308678136: 'a',
    4309253504: 'root',
    4309347072: Graph(name=root, id=4309347360),
    4309347144: Graph(name=a, id=4309347504)}
  Copying to new object Graph(name=b, id=4309347864)
```

The second time the *root* node is encountered, while the *a* node is being copied, __deepcopy__() detects the recursion and reuses the existing value from the memo dictionary instead of creating a new object.

See Also:
copy (http://docs.python.org/library/copy.html) The standard library documentation for this module.

2.9   pprint—Pretty-Print Data Structures

> **Purpose** Pretty-print data structures.
> **Python Version** 1.4 and later

pprint contains a "pretty printer" for producing aesthetically pleasing views of data structures. The formatter produces representations of data structures that can be parsed correctly by the interpreter and are also easy for a human to read. The output is kept on a single line, if possible, and indented when split across multiple lines.

The examples in this section all depend on pprint_data.py, which contains the following.

```
data = [ (1, { 'a':'A', 'b':'B', 'c':'C', 'd':'D' }),
         (2, { 'e':'E', 'f':'F', 'g':'G', 'h':'H',
               'i':'I', 'j':'J', 'k':'K', 'l':'L',
               }),
       ]
```

2.9.1   Printing

The simplest way to use the module is through the pprint() function.

```
from pprint import pprint

from pprint_data import data

print 'PRINT:'
print data
print
print 'PPRINT:'
pprint(data)
```

pprint() formats an object and writes it to the data stream passed as argument (or sys.stdout by default).

```
$ python pprint_pprint.py
```

```
PRINT:
[(1, {'a': 'A', 'c': 'C', 'b': 'B', 'd': 'D'}), (2, {'e': 'E', 'g':
'G', 'f': 'F', 'i': 'I', 'h': 'H', 'k': 'K', 'j': 'J', 'l': 'L'})]

PPRINT:
[(1, {'a': 'A', 'b': 'B', 'c': 'C', 'd': 'D'}),
 (2,
  {'e': 'E',
   'f': 'F',
   'g': 'G',
   'h': 'H',
   'i': 'I',
   'j': 'J',
   'k': 'K',
   'l': 'L'})]
```

2.9.2 Formatting

To format a data structure without writing it directly to a stream (i.e., for logging), use
pformat() to build a string representation.

```
import logging
from pprint import pformat
from pprint_data import data

logging.basicConfig(level=logging.DEBUG,
                    format='%(levelname)-8s %(message)s',
                    )

logging.debug('Logging pformatted data')
formatted = pformat(data)
for line in formatted.splitlines():
    logging.debug(line.rstrip())
```

The formatted string can then be printed or logged independently.

```
$ python pprint_pformat.py

DEBUG    Logging pformatted data
DEBUG    [(1, {'a': 'A', 'b': 'B', 'c': 'C', 'd': 'D'}),
DEBUG     (2,
DEBUG      {'e': 'E',
DEBUG       'f': 'F',
```

```
DEBUG        'g': 'G',
DEBUG        'h': 'H',
DEBUG        'i': 'I',
DEBUG        'j': 'J',
DEBUG        'k': 'K',
DEBUG        'l': 'L'})]
```

2.9.3   Arbitrary Classes

The `PrettyPrinter` class used by `pprint()` can also work with custom classes, if they define a __repr__() method.

```
from pprint import pprint

class node(object):
    def __init__(self, name, contents=[]):
        self.name = name
        self.contents = contents[:]
    def __repr__(self):
        return ( 'node(' + repr(self.name) + ', ' +
                    repr(self.contents) + ')'
                    )

trees = [ node('node-1'),
          node('node-2', [ node('node-2-1')]),
          node('node-3', [ node('node-3-1')]),
          ]
pprint(trees)
```

The representations of the nested objects are combined by the `PrettyPrinter` to return the full string representation.

```
$ python pprint_arbitrary_object.py

[node('node-1', []),
 node('node-2', [node('node-2-1', [])]),
 node('node-3', [node('node-3-1', [])])]
```

2.9.4   Recursion

Recursive data structures are represented with a reference to the original source of the data, with the form `<Recursion on typename with id=number>`.

```
from pprint import pprint

local_data = [ 'a', 'b', 1, 2 ]
local_data.append(local_data)

print 'id(local_data) =>', id(local_data)
pprint(local_data)
```

In this example, the list `local_data` is added to itself, creating a recursive reference.

```
$ python pprint_recursion.py

id(local_data) => 4309215280
['a', 'b', 1, 2, <Recursion on list with id=4309215280>]
```

2.9.5   Limiting Nested Output

For very deep data structures, it may not be desirable for the output to include all details. The data may not format properly, the formatted text might be too large to manage, or some of the data may be extraneous.

```
from pprint import pprint

from pprint_data import data

pprint(data, depth=1)
```

Use the *depth* argument to control how far down into the nested data structure the pretty printer recurses. Levels not included in the output are represented by an ellipsis.

```
$ python pprint_depth.py

[(...), (...)]
```

2.9.6   Controlling Output Width

The default output width for the formatted text is 80 columns. To adjust that width, use the *width* argument to `pprint()`.

```
from pprint import pprint
```

```
from pprint_data import data

for width in [ 80, 5 ]:
    print 'WIDTH =', width
    pprint(data, width=width)
    print
```

When the width is too low to accommodate the formatted data structure, the lines are not truncated or wrapped if that would introduce invalid syntax.

```
$ python pprint_width.py

WIDTH = 80
[(1, {'a': 'A', 'b': 'B', 'c': 'C', 'd': 'D'}),
 (2,
  {'e': 'E',
   'f': 'F',
   'g': 'G',
   'h': 'H',
   'i': 'I',
   'j': 'J',
   'k': 'K',
   'l': 'L'})]

WIDTH = 5
[(1,
  {'a': 'A',
   'b': 'B',
   'c': 'C',
   'd': 'D'}),
 (2,
  {'e': 'E',
   'f': 'F',
   'g': 'G',
   'h': 'H',
   'i': 'I',
   'j': 'J',
   'k': 'K',
   'l': 'L'})]
```

See Also:

pprint (http://docs.python.org/lib/module-pprint.html) Standard library documentation for this module.

Chapter 3

ALGORITHMS

Python includes several modules for implementing algorithms elegantly and concisely using whatever style is most appropriate for the task. It supports purely procedural, object-oriented, and functional styles. All three styles are frequently mixed within different parts of the same program.

`functools` includes functions for creating function decorators, enabling aspect-oriented programming and code reuse beyond what a traditional object-oriented approach supports. It also provides a class decorator for implementing all rich comparison APIs using a shortcut and `partial` objects for creating references to functions with their arguments included.

The `itertools` module includes functions for creating and working with iterators and generators used in functional programming. The `operator` module eliminates the need for many trivial lambda functions when using a functional programming style by providing function-based interfaces to built-in operations, such as arithmetic or item lookup.

`contextlib` makes resource management easier, more reliable, and more concise for all programming styles. Combining context managers and the **with** statement reduces the number of **try:finally** blocks and indentation levels needed, while ensuring that files, sockets, database transactions, and other resources are closed and released at the right time.

3.1 functools—Tools for Manipulating Functions

Purpose Functions that operate on other functions.
Python Version 2.5 and later

The `functools` module provides tools for adapting or extending functions and other callable objects, without completely rewriting them.

3.1.1 Decorators

The primary tool supplied by the `functools` module is the class `partial`, which can be used to "wrap" a callable object with default arguments. The resulting object is itself callable and can be treated as though it is the original function. It takes all the same arguments as the original, and it can be invoked with extra positional or named arguments as well. A `partial` can be used instead of a **lambda** to provide default arguments to a function, while leaving some arguments unspecified.

Partial Objects

This example shows two simple `partial` objects for the function `myfunc()`. The output of `show_details()` includes the `func`, `args`, and `keywords` attributes of the partial object.

```python
import functools


def myfunc(a, b=2):
    """Docstring for myfunc()."""
    print '   called myfunc with:', (a, b)
    return


def show_details(name, f, is_partial=False):
    """Show details of a callable object."""
    print '%s:' % name
    print '  object:', f
    if not is_partial:
        print '  __name__:', f.__name__
    if is_partial:
        print '  func:', f.func
        print '  args:', f.args
        print '  keywords:', f.keywords
    return


show_details('myfunc', myfunc)
myfunc('a', 3)
print

# Set a different default value for 'b', but require
# the caller to provide 'a'.
p1 = functools.partial(myfunc, b=4)
show_details('partial with named default', p1, True)
```

```
p1('passing a')
p1('override b', b=5)
print

# Set default values for both 'a' and 'b'.
p2 = functools.partial(myfunc, 'default a', b=99)
show_details('partial with defaults', p2, True)
p2()
p2(b='override b')
print

print 'Insufficient arguments:'
p1()
```

At the end of the example, the first `partial` created is invoked without passing a value for *a*, causing an exception.

```
$ python functools_partial.py

myfunc:
    object: <function myfunc at 0x100d9bf50>
    __name__: myfunc
    called myfunc with: ('a', 3)

partial with named default:
    object: <functools.partial object at 0x100d993c0>
    func: <function myfunc at 0x100d9bf50>
    args: ()
    keywords: {'b': 4}
    called myfunc with: ('passing a', 4)
    called myfunc with: ('override b', 5)

partial with defaults:
    object: <functools.partial object at 0x100d99418>
    func: <function myfunc at 0x100d9bf50>
    args: ('default a',)
    keywords: {'b': 99}
    called myfunc with: ('default a', 99)
    called myfunc with: ('default a', 'override b')

Insufficient arguments:
Traceback (most recent call last):
```

```
  File "functools_partial.py", line 51, in <module>
    p1()
TypeError: myfunc() takes at least 1 argument (1 given)
```

Acquiring Function Properties

The `partial` object does not have `__name__` or `__doc__` attributes by default, and without those attributes, decorated functions are more difficult to debug. Using `update_wrapper()` copies or adds attributes from the original function to the `partial` object.

```python
import functools

def myfunc(a, b=2):
    """Docstring for myfunc()."""
    print '  called myfunc with:', (a, b)
    return

def show_details(name, f):
    """Show details of a callable object."""
    print '%s:' % name
    print '  object:', f
    print '  __name__:',
    try:
        print f.__name__
    except AttributeError:
        print '(no __name__)'
    print '  __doc__', repr(f.__doc__)
    print
    return

show_details('myfunc', myfunc)

p1 = functools.partial(myfunc, b=4)
show_details('raw wrapper', p1)

print 'Updating wrapper:'
print '  assign:', functools.WRAPPER_ASSIGNMENTS
print '  update:', functools.WRAPPER_UPDATES
print

functools.update_wrapper(p1, myfunc)
show_details('updated wrapper', p1)
```

The attributes added to the wrapper are defined in WRAPPER_ASSIGNMENTS, while WRAPPER_UPDATES lists values to be modified.

```
$ python functools_update_wrapper.py

myfunc:
  object: <function myfunc at 0x100da2050>
  __name__: myfunc
  __doc__ 'Docstring for myfunc().'

raw wrapper:
  object: <functools.partial object at 0x100d993c0>
  __name__: (no __name__)
  __doc__ 'partial(func, *args, **keywords) - new function with parti
al application\n    of the given arguments and keywords.\n'

Updating wrapper:
  assign: ('__module__', '__name__', '__doc__')
  update: ('__dict__',)

updated wrapper:
  object: <functools.partial object at 0x100d993c0>
  __name__: myfunc
  __doc__ 'Docstring for myfunc().'
```

Other Callables

Partials work with any callable object, not just with stand-alone functions.

```
import functools


class MyClass(object):
    """Demonstration class for functools"""

    def method1(self, a, b=2):
        """Docstring for method1()."""
        print '  called method1 with:', (self, a, b)
        return

    def method2(self, c, d=5):
        """Docstring for method2"""
        print '  called method2 with:', (self, c, d)
        return
```

```
        wrapped_method2 = functools.partial(method2, 'wrapped c')
        functools.update_wrapper(wrapped_method2, method2)

    def __call__(self, e, f=6):
        """Docstring for MyClass.__call__"""
        print '  called object with:', (self, e, f)
        return

def show_details(name, f):
    """Show details of a callable object."""
    print '%s:' % name
    print '  object:', f
    print '  __name__:',
    try:
        print f.__name__
    except AttributeError:
        print '(no __name__)'
    print '  __doc__', repr(f.__doc__)
    return


o = MyClass()

show_details('method1 straight', o.method1)
o.method1('no default for a', b=3)
print


p1 = functools.partial(o.method1, b=4)
functools.update_wrapper(p1, o.method1)
show_details('method1 wrapper', p1)
p1('a goes here')
print


show_details('method2', o.method2)
o.method2('no default for c', d=6)
print


show_details('wrapped method2', o.wrapped_method2)
o.wrapped_method2('no default for c', d=6)
print


show_details('instance', o)
o('no default for e')
print
```

```
p2 = functools.partial(o,  f=7)
show_details('instance wrapper', p2)
p2('e goes here')
```

This example creates partials from an instance and methods of an instance.

```
$ python functools_method.py

method1 straight:
  object: <bound method MyClass.method1 of <__main__.MyClass object
at 0x100da3550>>
  __name__: method1
  __doc__ 'Docstring for method1().'
  called method1 with: (<__main__.MyClass object at 0x100da3550>, 'n
o default for a', 3)

method1 wrapper:
  object: <functools.partial object at 0x100d99470>
  __name__: method1
  __doc__ 'Docstring for method1().'
  called method1 with: (<__main__.MyClass object at 0x100da3550>, 'a
 goes here', 4)

method2:
  object: <bound method MyClass.method2 of <__main__.MyClass object
at 0x100da3550>>
  __name__: method2
  __doc__ 'Docstring for method2'
  called method2 with: (<__main__.MyClass object at 0x100da3550>, 'n
o default for c', 6)

wrapped method2:
  object: <functools.partial object at 0x100d993c0>
  __name__: method2
  __doc__ 'Docstring for method2'
  called method2 with: ('wrapped c', 'no default for c', 6)

 instance:
  object: <__main__.MyClass object at 0x100da3550>
  __name__: (no __name__)
  __doc__ 'Demonstration class for functools'
  called object with: (<__main__.MyClass object at 0x100da3550>, 'no
```

```
 default for e', 6)
instance wrapper:
  object: <functools.partial object at 0x100d994c8>
  __name__: (no __name__)
  __doc__ 'partial(func, *args, **keywords) - new function with part
ial application\n    of the given arguments and keywords.\n'
  called object with: (<__main__.MyClass object at 0x100da3550>, 'e
goes here', 7)
```

Acquiring Function Properties for Decorators

Updating the properties of a wrapped callable is especially useful when used in a decorator, since the transformed function ends up with properties of the original "bare" function.

```python
import functools

def show_details(name, f):
    """Show details of a callable object."""
    print '%s:' % name
    print '  object:', f
    print '  __name__:',
    try:
        print f.__name__
    except AttributeError:
        print '(no __name__)'
    print '  __doc__', repr(f.__doc__)
    print
    return

def simple_decorator(f):
    @functools.wraps(f)
    def decorated(a='decorated defaults', b=1):
        print '  decorated:', (a, b)
        print '  ',
        f(a, b=b)
        return
    return decorated

def myfunc(a, b=2):
    "myfunc() is not complicated"
    print '  myfunc:', (a,b)
    return
```

```
# The raw function
show_details('myfunc', myfunc)
myfunc('unwrapped, default b')
myfunc('unwrapped, passing b', 3)
print

# Wrap explicitly
wrapped_myfunc = simple_decorator(myfunc)
show_details('wrapped_myfunc', wrapped_myfunc)
wrapped_myfunc()
wrapped_myfunc('args to wrapped', 4)
print

# Wrap with decorator syntax
@simple_decorator
def decorated_myfunc(a, b):
    myfunc(a, b)
    return

show_details('decorated_myfunc', decorated_myfunc)
decorated_myfunc()
decorated_myfunc('args to decorated', 4)
```

functools provides a decorator, `wraps()`, that applies `update_wrapper()` to the decorated function.

```
$ python functools_wraps.py

myfunc:
  object: <function myfunc at 0x100da3488>
  __name__: myfunc
  __doc__ 'myfunc() is not complicated'

  myfunc: ('unwrapped, default b', 2)
  myfunc: ('unwrapped, passing b', 3)

wrapped_myfunc:
  object: <function myfunc at 0x100da3500>
  __name__: myfunc
  __doc__ 'myfunc() is not complicated'

  decorated: ('decorated defaults', 1)
    myfunc: ('decorated defaults', 1)
```

```
decorated: ('args to wrapped', 4)
   myfunc: ('args to wrapped', 4)

decorated_myfunc:
  object: <function decorated_myfunc at 0x100da35f0>
  __name__: decorated_myfunc
  __doc__ None

decorated: ('decorated defaults', 1)
   myfunc: ('decorated defaults', 1)
decorated: ('args to decorated', 4)
   myfunc: ('args to decorated', 4)
```

3.1.2 Comparison

Under Python 2, classes can define a __cmp__() method that returns −1, 0, or 1 based on whether the object is less than, equal to, or greater than the item being compared. Python 2.1 introduces the *rich comparison* methods API (__lt__(), __le__(), __eq__(), __ne__(), __gt__(), and __ge__()), which perform a single comparison operation and return a Boolean value. Python 3 deprecated __cmp__() in favor of these new methods, so functools provides tools to make it easier to write Python 2 classes that comply with the new comparison requirements in Python 3.

Rich Comparison

The rich comparison API is designed to allow classes with complex comparisons to implement each test in the most efficient way possible. However, for classes where comparison is relatively simple, there is no point in manually creating each of the rich comparison methods. The total_ordering() class decorator takes a class that provides some of the methods and adds the rest of them.

```python
import functools
import inspect
from pprint import pprint

@functools.total_ordering
class MyObject(object):
    def __init__(self, val):
        self.val = val
    def __eq__(self, other):
        print ' testing __eq__(%s, %s)' % (self.val, other.val)
        return self.val == other.val
```

```
    def __gt__(self, other):
        print ' testing __gt__(%s, %s)' % (self.val, other.val)
        return self.val > other.val

print 'Methods:\n'
pprint(inspect.getmembers(MyObject, inspect.ismethod))

a = MyObject(1)
b = MyObject(2)

print '\nComparisons:'
for expr in [ 'a < b', 'a <= b', 'a == b', 'a >= b', 'a > b' ]:
    print '\n%-6s:' % expr
    result = eval(expr)
    print ' result of %s: %s' % (expr, result)
```

The class must provide implementation of __eq__() and one other rich comparison method. The decorator adds implementations of the rest of the methods that work by using the comparisons provided.

```
$ python functools_total_ordering.py

Methods:

[('__eq__', <unbound method MyObject.__eq__>),
 ('__ge__', <unbound method MyObject.__ge__>),
 ('__gt__', <unbound method MyObject.__gt__>),
 ('__init__', <unbound method MyObject.__init__>),
 ('__le__', <unbound method MyObject.__le__>),
 ('__lt__', <unbound method MyObject.__lt__>)]

Comparisons:

a < b :
  testing __gt__(2, 1)
  result of a < b: True

a <= b:
  testing __gt__(1, 2)
  result of a <= b: True

a == b:
  testing __eq__(1, 2)
  result of a == b: False
```

```
a >= b:
  testing __gt__(2, 1)
  result of a >= b: False

a > b :
  testing __gt__(1, 2)
  result of a > b: False
```

Collation Order

Since old-style comparison functions are deprecated in Python 3, the `cmp` argument to functions like `sort()` is also no longer supported. Python 2 programs that use comparison functions can use `cmp_to_key()` to convert them to a function that returns a *collation key*, which is used to determine the position in the final sequence.

```python
import functools

class MyObject(object):
    def __init__(self, val):
        self.val = val
    def __str__(self):
        return 'MyObject(%s)' % self.val

def compare_obj(a, b):
    """Old-style comparison function.
    """
    print 'comparing %s and %s' % (a, b)
    return cmp(a.val, b.val)

# Make a key function using cmp_to_key()
get_key = functools.cmp_to_key(compare_obj)

def get_key_wrapper(o):
    """Wrapper function for get_key to allow for print statements.
    """
    new_key = get_key(o)
    print 'key_wrapper(%s) -> %s' % (o, new_key)
    return new_key
objs = [ MyObject(x) for x in xrange(5, 0, -1) ]

for o in sorted(objs, key=get_key_wrapper):
    print o
```

Normally, `cmp_to_key()` would be used directly, but in this example, an extra wrapper function is introduced to print out more information as the key function is being called.

The output shows that `sorted()` starts by calling `get_key_wrapper()` for each item in the sequence to produce a key. The keys returned by `cmp_to_key()` are instances of a class defined in `functools` that implements the rich comparison API using the old-style comparison function passed in. After all keys are created, the sequence is sorted by comparing the keys.

```
$ python functools_cmp_to_key.py

key_wrapper(MyObject(5)) -> <functools.K object at 0x100da2a50>
key_wrapper(MyObject(4)) -> <functools.K object at 0x100da2a90>
key_wrapper(MyObject(3)) -> <functools.K object at 0x100da2ad0>
key_wrapper(MyObject(2)) -> <functools.K object at 0x100da2b10>
key_wrapper(MyObject(1)) -> <functools.K object at 0x100da2b50>
comparing MyObject(4) and MyObject(5)
comparing MyObject(3) and MyObject(4)
comparing MyObject(2) and MyObject(3)
comparing MyObject(1) and MyObject(2)
MyObject(1)
MyObject(2)
MyObject(3)
MyObject(4)
MyObject(5)
```

See Also:

functools (http://docs.python.org/library/functools.html) The standard library documentation for this module.

Rich comparison methods (http://docs.python.org/reference/datamodel.html#object.__lt__) Description of the rich comparison methods from the Python Reference Guide.

inspect (page 1200) Introspection API for live objects.

3.2   itertools—Iterator Functions

Purpose The itertools module includes a set of functions for working with sequence data sets.

Python Version 2.3 and later

The functions provided by `itertools` are inspired by similar features of functional programming languages such as Clojure and Haskell. They are intended to be fast and use memory efficiently, and also to be hooked together to express more complicated iteration-based algorithms.

Iterator-based code offers better memory consumption characteristics than code that uses lists. Since data is not produced from the iterator until it is needed, all data does not need to be stored in memory at the same time. This "lazy" processing model uses less memory, which can reduce swapping and other side effects of large data sets, improving performance.

3.2.1   Merging and Splitting Iterators

The `chain()` function takes several iterators as arguments and returns a single iterator that produces the contents of all of them as though they came from a single iterator.

```
from itertools import *

for i in chain([1, 2, 3], ['a', 'b', 'c']):
    print i,
print
```

`chain()` makes it easy to process several sequences without constructing one large list.

```
$ python itertools_chain.py

1 2 3 a b c
```

`izip()` returns an iterator that combines the elements of several iterators into tuples.

```
from itertools import *

for i in izip([1, 2, 3], ['a', 'b', 'c']):
    print i
```

It works like the built-in function `zip()`, except that it returns an iterator instead of a list.

```
$ python itertools_izip.py

(1, 'a')
(2, 'b')
(3, 'c')
```

The `islice()` function returns an iterator that returns selected items from the input iterator, by index.

```
from itertools import *

print 'Stop at 5:'
for i in islice(count(), 5):
    print i,
print '\n'

print 'Start at 5, Stop at 10:'
for i in islice(count(), 5, 10):
    print i,
print '\n'

print 'By tens to 100:'
for i in islice(count(), 0, 100, 10):
    print i,
print '\n'
```

`islice()` takes the same arguments as the slice operator for lists: *start*, *stop*, and *step*. The start and step arguments are optional.

```
$ python itertools_islice.py

Stop at 5:
0 1 2 3 4

Start at 5, Stop at 10:
5 6 7 8 9

By tens to 100:
0 10 20 30 40 50 60 70 80 90
```

The `tee()` function returns several independent iterators (defaults to 2) based on a single original input.

```
from itertools import *

r = islice(count(), 5)
i1, i2 = tee(r)

print 'i1:', list(i1)
print 'i2:', list(i2)
```

`tee()` has semantics similar to the UNIX **tee** utility, which repeats the values it reads from its input and writes them to a named file and standard output. The iterators returned by `tee()` can be used to feed the same set of data into multiple algorithms to be processed in parallel.

```
$ python itertools_tee.py

i1: [0, 1, 2, 3, 4]
i2: [0, 1, 2, 3, 4]
```

The new iterators created by `tee()` share their input, so the original iterator should not be used once the new ones are created.

```
from itertools import *

r = islice(count(), 5)
i1, i2 = tee(r)

print 'r:',
for i in r:
    print i,
    if i > 1:
        break
print

print 'i1:', list(i1)
print 'i2:', list(i2)
```

If values are consumed from the original input, the new iterators will not produce those values:

```
$ python itertools_tee_error.py

r: 0 1 2
i1: [3, 4]
i2: [3, 4]
```

3.2.2 Converting Inputs

The `imap()` function returns an iterator that calls a function on the values in the input iterators and returns the results. It works like the built-in `map()`, except that it stops when any input iterator is exhausted (instead of inserting `None` values to completely consume all inputs).

```
from itertools import *

print 'Doubles:'
for i in imap(lambda x:2*x, xrange(5)):
    print i

print 'Multiples:'
for i in imap(lambda x,y:(x, y, x*y), xrange(5), xrange(5,10)):
    print '%d * %d = %d' % i
```

In the first example, the lambda function multiplies the input values by 2. In the second example, the lambda function multiplies two arguments, taken from separate iterators, and returns a `tuple` with the original arguments and the computed value.

```
$ python itertools_imap.py

Doubles:
0
2
4
6
8
Multiples:
0 * 5 = 0
1 * 6 = 6
2 * 7 = 14
3 * 8 = 24
4 * 9 = 36
```

The `starmap()` function is similar to `imap()`, but instead of constructing a `tuple` from multiple iterators, it splits up the items in a single iterator as arguments to the mapping function using the `*` syntax.

```
from itertools import *

values = [(0, 5), (1, 6), (2, 7), (3, 8), (4, 9)]
for i in starmap(lambda x,y:(x, y, x*y), values):
    print '%d * %d = %d' % i
```

Where the mapping function to `imap()` is called `f(i1, i2)`, the mapping function passed to `starmap()` is called `f(*i)`.

```
$ python itertools_starmap.py

0 * 5 = 0
1 * 6 = 6
2 * 7 = 14
3 * 8 = 24
4 * 9 = 36
```

3.2.3 Producing New Values

The `count()` function returns an iterator that produces consecutive integers, indefinitely. The first number can be passed as an argument (the default is zero). There is no upper bound argument [see the built-in `xrange()` for more control over the result set].

```
from itertools import *

for i in izip(count(1), ['a', 'b', 'c']):
    print i
```

This example stops because the list argument is consumed.

```
$ python itertools_count.py

(1, 'a')
(2, 'b')
(3, 'c')
```

The `cycle()` function returns an iterator that indefinitely repeats the contents of the arguments it is given. Since it has to remember the entire contents of the input iterator, it may consume quite a bit of memory if the iterator is long.

```
from itertools import *

for i, item in izip(xrange(7), cycle(['a', 'b', 'c'])):
    print (i, item)
```

A counter variable is used to break out of the loop after a few cycles in this example.

```
$ python itertools_cycle.py

(0, 'a')
(1, 'b')
(2, 'c')
(3, 'a')
(4, 'b')
(5, 'c')
(6, 'a')
```

The `repeat()` function returns an iterator that produces the same value each time it is accessed.

```
from itertools import *

for i in repeat('over-and-over', 5):
    print i
```

The iterator returned by `repeat()` keeps returning data forever, unless the optional *times* argument is provided to limit it.

```
$ python itertools_repeat.py

over-and-over
over-and-over
over-and-over
over-and-over
over-and-over
```

It is useful to combine `repeat()` with `izip()` or `imap()` when invariant values need to be included with the values from the other iterators.

```
from itertools import *

for i, s in izip(count(), repeat('over-and-over', 5)):
    print i, s
```

A counter value is combined with the constant returned by `repeat()` in this example.

```
$ python itertools_repeat_izip.py

0 over-and-over
1 over-and-over
2 over-and-over
3 over-and-over
4 over-and-over
```

This example uses `imap()` to multiply the numbers in the range 0 through 4 by 2.

```
from itertools import *

for i in imap(lambda x,y:(x, y, x*y), repeat(2), xrange(5)):
    print '%d * %d = %d' % i
```

The `repeat()` iterator does not need to be explicitly limited, since `imap()` stops processing when any of its inputs ends, and the `xrange()` returns only five elements.

```
$ python itertools_repeat_imap.py

2 * 0 = 0
2 * 1 = 2
2 * 2 = 4
2 * 3 = 6
2 * 4 = 8
```

3.2.4 Filtering

The `dropwhile()` function returns an iterator that produces elements of the input iterator after a condition becomes false for the first time.

```
from itertools import *

def should_drop(x):
    print 'Testing:', x
    return (x<1)

for i in dropwhile(should_drop, [ -1, 0, 1, 2, -2 ]):
    print 'Yielding:', i
```

dropwhile() does not filter every item of the input; after the condition is false the first time, all remaining items in the input are returned.

```
$ python itertools_dropwhile.py

Testing: -1
Testing: 0
Testing: 1
Yielding: 1
Yielding: 2
Yielding: -2
```

The opposite of dropwhile() is takewhile(). It returns an iterator that returns items from the input iterator, as long as the test function returns true.

```
from itertools import *

def should_take(x):
    print 'Testing:', x
    return (x<2)

for i in takewhile(should_take, [ -1, 0, 1, 2, -2 ]):
    print 'Yielding:', i
```

As soon as should_take() returns False, takewhile() stops processing the input.

```
$ python itertools_takewhile.py

Testing: -1
Yielding: -1
Testing: 0
```

```
Yielding: 0
Testing: 1
Yielding: 1
Testing: 2
```

ifilter() returns an iterator that works like the built-in filter() does for lists, including only items for which the test function returns true.

```
from itertools import *

def check_item(x):
    print 'Testing:', x
    return (x<1)

for i in ifilter(check_item, [ -1, 0, 1, 2, -2 ]):
    print 'Yielding:', i
```

ifilter() is different from dropwhile() in that every item is tested before it is returned.

```
$ python itertools_ifilter.py

Testing: -1
Yielding: -1
Testing: 0
Yielding: 0
Testing: 1
Testing: 2
Testing: -2
Yielding: -2
```

ifilterfalse() returns an iterator that includes only items where the test function returns false.

```
from itertools import *

def check_item(x):
    print 'Testing:', x
    return (x<1)

for i in ifilterfalse(check_item, [ -1, 0, 1, 2, -2 ]):
    print 'Yielding:', i
```

The test expression in `check_item()` is the same, so the results in this example with `ifilterfalse()` are the opposite of the results from the previous example.

```
$ python itertools_ifilterfalse.py

Testing: -1
Testing: 0
Testing: 1
Yielding: 1
Testing: 2
Yielding: 2
Testing: -2
```

3.2.5   Grouping Data

The `groupby()` function returns an iterator that produces sets of values organized by a common key. This example illustrates grouping related values based on an attribute.

```python
from itertools import *
import operator
import pprint


class Point:
    def __init__(self, x, y):
        self.x = x
        self.y = y
    def __repr__(self):
        return '(%s, %s)' % (self.x, self.y)
    def __cmp__(self, other):
        return cmp((self.x, self.y), (other.x, other.y))


# Create a dataset of Point instances
data = list(imap(Point,
                 cycle(islice(count(), 3)),
                 islice(count(), 7),
                 )
            )
print 'Data:'
pprint.pprint(data, width=69)
print


# Try to group the unsorted data based on X values
print 'Grouped, unsorted:'
```

```
for k, g in groupby(data, operator.attrgetter('x')):
    print k, list(g)
print

# Sort the data
data.sort()
print 'Sorted:'
pprint.pprint(data, width=69)
print

# Group the sorted data based on X values
print 'Grouped, sorted:'
for k, g in groupby(data, operator.attrgetter('x')):
    print k, list(g)
print
```

The input sequence needs to be sorted on the key value in order for the groupings to work out as expected.

```
$ python itertools_groupby_seq.py

Data:
[(0, 0),
 (1, 1),
 (2, 2),
 (0, 3),
 (1, 4),
 (2, 5),
 (0, 6),
 (1, 7),
 (2, 8),
 (0, 9)]

Grouped, unsorted:
0 [(0, 0)]
1 [(1, 1)]
2 [(2, 2)]
0 [(0, 3)]
1 [(1, 4)]
2 [(2, 5)]
0 [(0, 6)]
1 [(1, 7)]
```

```
2 [(2, 8)]
0 [(0, 9)]

Sorted:
[(0, 0),
 (0, 3),
 (0, 6),
 (0, 9),
 (1, 1),
 (1, 4),
 (1, 7),
 (2, 2),
 (2, 5),
 (2, 8)]

Grouped, sorted:
0 [(0, 0), (0, 3), (0, 6), (0, 9)]
1 [(1, 1), (1, 4), (1, 7)]
2 [(2, 2), (2, 5), (2, 8)]
```

See Also:

itertools (http://docs.python.org/library/itertools.html) The standard library documentation for this module.

The Standard ML Basis Library (www.standardml.org/Basis/) The library for SML.

Definition of Haskell and the Standard Libraries (www.haskell.org/definition/) Standard library specification for the functional language Haskell.

Clojure (http://clojure.org/) Clojure is a dynamic functional language that runs on the Java Virtual Machine.

tee (http://unixhelp.ed.ac.uk/CGI/man-cgi?tee) UNIX command line tool for splitting one input into multiple identical output streams.

3.3 operator—Functional Interface to Built-in Operators

Purpose Functional interface to built-in operators.

Python Version 1.4 and later

Programming with iterators occasionally requires creating small functions for simple expressions. Sometimes, these can be implemented as **lambda** functions, but for some operations, new functions are not needed at all. The `operator` module defines functions that correspond to built-in operations for arithmetic and comparison.

3.3.1 Logical Operations

There are functions for determining the Boolean equivalent for a value, negating it to create the opposite Boolean value, and comparing objects to see if they are identical.

```
from operator import *

a = -1
b = 5

print 'a =', a
print 'b =', b
print

print 'not_(a)      :', not_(a)
print 'truth(a)     :', truth(a)
print 'is_(a, b)    :', is_(a,b)
print 'is_not(a, b):', is_not(a,b)
```

`not_()` includes the trailing underscore because **not** is a Python keyword. `truth()` applies the same logic used when testing an expression in an **if** statement. `is_()` implements the same check used by the **is** keyword, and `is_not()` does the same test and returns the opposite answer.

```
$ python operator_boolean.py

a = -1
b = 5

not_(a)      : False
truth(a)     : True
is_(a, b)    : False
is_not(a, b): True
```

3.3.2 Comparison Operators

All rich comparison operators are supported.

```
from operator import *

a = 1
b = 5.0
```

```
print 'a =', a
print 'b =', b
for func in (lt, le, eq, ne, ge, gt):
    print '%s(a, b):' % func.__name__, func(a, b)
```

The functions are equivalent to the expression syntax using <, <=, ==, >=, and >.

```
$ python operator_comparisons.py

a = 1
b = 5.0
lt(a, b): True
le(a, b): True
eq(a, b): False
ne(a, b): True
ge(a, b): False
gt(a, b): False
```

3.3.3 Arithmetic Operators

The arithmetic operators for manipulating numerical values are also supported.

```
from operator import *

a = -1
b = 5.0
c = 2
d = 6

print 'a =', a
print 'b =', b
print 'c =', c
print 'd =', d

print '\nPositive/Negative:'
print 'abs(a):', abs(a)
print 'neg(a):', neg(a)
print 'neg(b):', neg(b)
print 'pos(a):', pos(a)
print 'pos(b):', pos(b)
```

```
print '\nArithmetic:'
print 'add(a, b)      :', add(a, b)
print 'div(a, b)      :', div(a, b)
print 'div(d, c)      :', div(d, c)
print 'floordiv(a, b):', floordiv(a, b)
print 'floordiv(d, c):', floordiv(d, c)
print 'mod(a, b)      :', mod(a, b)
print 'mul(a, b)      :', mul(a, b)
print 'pow(c, d)      :', pow(c, d)
print 'sub(b, a)      :', sub(b, a)
print 'truediv(a, b) :', truediv(a, b)
print 'truediv(d, c) :', truediv(d, c)

print '\nBitwise:'
print 'and_(c, d)   :', and_(c, d)
print 'invert(c)    :', invert(c)
print 'lshift(c, d):', lshift(c, d)
print 'or_(c, d)    :', or_(c, d)
print 'rshift(d, c):', rshift(d, c)
print 'xor(c, d)    :', xor(c, d)
```

There are two separate division operators: `floordiv()` (integer division as implemented in Python before version 3.0) and `truediv()` (floating-point division).

```
$ python operator_math.py

a = -1
b = 5.0
c = 2
d = 6

Positive/Negative:
abs(a): 1
neg(a): 1
neg(b): -5.0
pos(a): -1
pos(b): 5.0

Arithmetic:
add(a, b)      : 4.0
div(a, b)      : -0.2
div(d, c)      : 3
floordiv(a, b): -1.0
floordiv(d, c): 3
mod(a, b)      : 4.0
```

```
mul(a, b)      : -5.0
pow(c, d)      : 64
sub(b, a)      : 6.0
truediv(a, b) : -0.2
truediv(d, c) : 3.0

Bitwise:
and_(c, d)   : 2
invert(c)    : -3
lshift(c, d): 128
or_(c, d)    : 6
rshift(d, c): 1
xor(c, d)    : 4
```

3.3.4   Sequence Operators

The operators for working with sequences can be divided into four groups: building up sequences, searching for items, accessing contents, and removing items from sequences.

```
from operator import *

a = [ 1, 2, 3 ]
b = [ 'a', 'b', 'c' ]

print 'a =', a
print 'b =', b

print '\nConstructive:'
print '  concat(a, b):', concat(a, b)
print '  repeat(a, 3):', repeat(a, 3)

print '\nSearching:'
print '  contains(a, 1)   :', contains(a, 1)
print '  contains(b, "d"):', contains(b, "d")
print '  countOf(a, 1)    :', countOf(a, 1)
print '  countOf(b, "d") :', countOf(b, "d")
print '  indexOf(a, 5)    :', indexOf(a, 1)

print '\nAccess Items:'
print '  getitem(b, 1)              :', getitem(b, 1)
print '  getslice(a, 1, 3)          :', getslice(a, 1, 3)
print '  setitem(b, 1, "d")         :', setitem(b, 1, "d"),
print ', after b =', b
```

```
print '  setslice(a, 1, 3, [4, 5]):', setslice(a, 1, 3, [4, 5]),
print ', after a =', a

print '\nDestructive:'
print '  delitem(b, 1)    :', delitem(b, 1), ', after b =', b
print '  delslice(a, 1, 3):', delslice(a, 1, 3), ', after a =', a
```

Some of these operations, such as `setitem()` and `delitem()`, modify the sequence in place and do not return a value.

```
$ python operator_sequences.py

a = [1, 2, 3]
b = ['a', 'b', 'c']

Constructive:
  concat(a, b): [1, 2, 3, 'a', 'b', 'c']
  repeat(a, 3): [1, 2, 3, 1, 2, 3, 1, 2, 3]

Searching:
  contains(a, 1)  : True
  contains(b, "d"): False
  countOf(a, 1)   : 1
  countOf(b, "d") : 0
  indexOf(a, 5)   : 0

Access Items:
  getitem(b, 1)              : b
  getslice(a, 1, 3)          : [2, 3]
  setitem(b, 1, "d")         : None , after b = ['a', 'd', 'c']
  setslice(a, 1, 3, [4, 5]): None , after a = [1, 4, 5]

Destructive:
  delitem(b, 1)      : None , after b = ['a', 'c']
  delslice(a, 1, 3): None , after a = [1]
```

3.3.5 In-Place Operators

In addition to the standard operators, many types of objects support "in-place" modification through special operators such as +=. There are equivalent functions for in-place modifications, too.

```
from operator import *

a = -1
b = 5.0
c = [ 1, 2, 3 ]
d = [ 'a', 'b', 'c']
print 'a =', a
print 'b =', b
print 'c =', c
print 'd =', d
print

a = iadd(a, b)
print 'a = iadd(a, b) =>', a
print

c = iconcat(c, d)
print 'c = iconcat(c, d) =>', c
```

These examples demonstrate only a few of the functions. Refer to the standard library documentation for complete details.

```
$ python operator_inplace.py

a = -1
b = 5.0
c = [1, 2, 3]
d = ['a', 'b', 'c']

a = iadd(a, b)  => 4.0

c = iconcat(c, d)  => [1, 2, 3, 'a', 'b', 'c']
```

3.3.6 Attribute and Item "Getters"

One of the most unusual features of the operator module is the concept of *getters*. These are callable objects constructed at runtime to retrieve attributes of objects or contents from sequences. Getters are especially useful when working with iterators or generator sequences, where they are intended to incur less overhead than a **lambda** or Python function.

```python
from operator import *

class MyObj(object):
    """example class for attrgetter"""
    def __init__(self, arg):
        super(MyObj, self).__init__()
        self.arg = arg
    def __repr__(self):
        return 'MyObj(%s)' % self.arg

l = [ MyObj(i) for i in xrange(5) ]
print 'objects   :', l

# Extract the 'arg' value from each object
g = attrgetter('arg')
vals = [ g(i) for i in l ]
print 'arg values:', vals

# Sort using arg
l.reverse()
print 'reversed :', l
print 'sorted   :', sorted(l, key=g)
```

Attribute getters work like `lambda x, n='attrname': getattr(x, n)`:

```
$ python operator_attrgetter.py

objects   : [MyObj(0), MyObj(1), MyObj(2), MyObj(3), MyObj(4)]
arg values: [0, 1, 2, 3, 4]
reversed  : [MyObj(4), MyObj(3), MyObj(2), MyObj(1), MyObj(0)]
sorted    : [MyObj(0), MyObj(1), MyObj(2), MyObj(3), MyObj(4)]
```

Item getters work like `lambda x, y=5: x[y]`:

```python
from operator import *

l = [ dict(val=-1 * i) for i in xrange(4) ]
print 'Dictionaries:', l
g = itemgetter('val')
vals = [ g(i) for i in l ]
print '    values:', vals
print '    sorted:', sorted(l, key=g)
```

```
print
l = [ (i, i*-2) for i in xrange(4) ]
print 'Tuples       :', l
g = itemgetter(1)
vals = [ g(i) for i in l ]
print '        values:', vals
print '        sorted:', sorted(l, key=g)
```

Item getters work with mappings as well as sequences.

```
$ python operator_itemgetter.py

Dictionaries: [{'val': 0}, {'val': -1}, {'val': -2}, {'val': -3}]
      values: [0, -1, -2, -3]
      sorted: [{'val': -3}, {'val': -2}, {'val': -1}, {'val': 0}]

Tuples      : [(0, 0), (1, -2), (2, -4), (3, -6)]
      values: [0, -2, -4, -6]
      sorted: [(3, -6), (2, -4), (1, -2), (0, 0)]
```

3.3.7   Combining Operators and Custom Classes

The functions in the `operator` module work via the standard Python interfaces for their operations, so they work with user-defined classes as well as the built-in types.

```
from operator import *

class MyObj(object):
    """Example for operator overloading"""
    def __init__(self, val):
        super(MyObj, self).__init__()
        self.val = val
        return
    def __str__(self):
        return 'MyObj(%s)' % self.val
    def __lt__(self, other):
        """compare for less-than"""
        print 'Testing %s < %s' % (self, other)
        return self.val < other.val
    def __add__(self, other):
        """add values"""
```

```
        print 'Adding %s + %s' % (self, other)
        return MyObj(self.val + other.val)
a = MyObj(1)
b = MyObj(2)

print 'Comparison:'
print lt(a, b)

print '\nArithmetic:'
print add(a, b)
```

Refer to the Python reference guide for a complete list of the special methods each operator uses.

```
$ python operator_classes.py

Comparison:
Testing MyObj(1) < MyObj(2)
True

Arithmetic:
Adding MyObj(1) + MyObj(2)
MyObj(3)
```

3.3.8 Type Checking

The `operator` module also includes functions for testing API compliance for mapping, number, and sequence types.

```
from operator import *

class NoType(object):
    """Supports none of the type APIs"""

class MultiType(object):
    """Supports multiple type APIs"""
    def __len__(self):
        return 0
    def __getitem__(self, name):
        return 'mapping'
    def __int__(self):
        return 0
```

```
o = NoType()
t = MultiType()

for func in (isMappingType, isNumberType, isSequenceType):
    print '%s(o):' % func.__name__, func(o)
    print '%s(t):' % func.__name__, func(t)
```

The tests are not perfect, since the interfaces are not strictly defined, but they do provide some idea of what is supported.

```
$ python operator_typechecking.py

isMappingType(o): False
isMappingType(t): True
isNumberType(o): False
isNumberType(t): True
isSequenceType(o): False
isSequenceType(t): True
```

See Also:
operator (http://docs.python.org/lib/module-operator.html) Standard library documentation for this module.
functools (page 129) Functional programming tools, including the `total_ordering()` decorator for adding rich comparison methods to a class.
itertools (page 141) Iterator operations.
abc (page 1178) The `abc` module includes *abstract base classes* that define the APIs for collection types.

3.4 contextlib—Context Manager Utilities

Purpose Utilities for creating and working with context managers.
Python Version 2.5 and later

The `contextlib` module contains utilities for working with context managers and the **with** statement.

Note: Context managers are tied to the **with** statement. Since **with** is officially part of Python 2.6, import it from __future__ before using `contextlib` in Python 2.5.

3.4.1 Context Manager API

A *context manager* is responsible for a resource within a code block, possibly creating it when the block is entered and then cleaning it up after the block is exited. For example, files support the context manager API to make it easy to ensure they are closed after all reading or writing is done.

```
with open('/tmp/pymotw.txt', 'wt') as f:
    f.write('contents go here')
# file is automatically closed
```

A context manager is enabled by the **with** statement, and the API involves two methods. The __enter__() method is run when execution flow enters the code block inside the **with**. It returns an object to be used within the context. When execution flow leaves the **with** block, the __exit__() method of the context manager is called to clean up any resources being used.

```
class Context(object):
    def __init__(self):
        print '__init__()'
    def __enter__(self):
        print '__enter__()'
        return self
    def __exit__(self, exc_type, exc_val, exc_tb):
        print '__exit__()'

with Context():
    print 'Doing work in the context'
```

Combining a context manager and the **with** statement is a more compact way of writing a **try:finally** block, since the context manager's __exit__() method is always called, even if an exception is raised.

```
$ python contextlib_api.py

__init__()
__enter__()
Doing work in the context
__exit__()
```

The __enter__() method can return any object to be associated with a name specified in the **as** clause of the **with** statement. In this example, the Context returns an object that uses the open context.

```
class WithinContext(object):
    def __init__(self, context):
        print 'WithinContext.__init__(%s)' % context
    def do_something(self):
        print 'WithinContext.do_something()'
    def __del__(self):
        print 'WithinContext.__del__'


class Context(object):
    def __init__(self):
        print 'Context.__init__()'
    def __enter__(self):
        print 'Context.__enter__()'
        return WithinContext(self)
    def __exit__(self, exc_type, exc_val, exc_tb):
        print 'Context.__exit__()'


with Context() as c:
    c.do_something()
```

The value associated with the variable c is the object returned by __enter__(), which is not necessarily the Context instance created in the **with** statement.

```
$ python contextlib_api_other_object.py

Context.__init__()
Context.__enter__()
WithinContext.__init__(<__main__.Context object at 0x100d98a10>)
WithinContext.do_something()
Context.__exit__()
WithinContext.__del__
```

The __exit__() method receives arguments containing details of any exception raised in the **with** block.

```
class Context(object):
    def __init__(self, handle_error):
        print '__init__(%s)' % handle_error
        self.handle_error = handle_error
    def __enter__(self):
        print '__enter__()'
        return self
    def __exit__(self, exc_type, exc_val, exc_tb):
        print '__exit__()'
        print '  exc_type =', exc_type
        print '  exc_val  =', exc_val
        print '  exc_tb   =', exc_tb
        return self.handle_error


with Context(True):
    raise RuntimeError('error message handled')

print

with Context(False):
    raise RuntimeError('error message propagated')
```

If the context manager can handle the exception, __exit__() should return a true value to indicate that the exception does not need to be propagated. Returning false causes the exception to be reraised after __exit__() returns.

```
$ python contextlib_api_error.py

__init__(True)
__enter__()
__exit__()
  exc_type = <type 'exceptions.RuntimeError'>
  exc_val  = error message handled
  exc_tb   = <traceback object at 0x100da52d8>

__init__(False)
__enter__()
__exit__()
  exc_type = <type 'exceptions.RuntimeError'>
  exc_val  = error message propagated
  exc_tb   = <traceback object at 0x100da5368>
```

```
Traceback (most recent call last):
  File "contextlib_api_error.py", line 33, in <module>
    raise RuntimeError('error message propagated')
RuntimeError: error message propagated
```

3.4.2 From Generator to Context Manager

Creating context managers the traditional way, by writing a class with __enter__()
and __exit__() methods, is not difficult. But sometimes, writing everything out
fully is extra overhead for a trivial bit of context. In those sorts of situations, use the
contextmanager() decorator to convert a generator function into a context manager.

```
import contextlib

@contextlib.contextmanager
def make_context():
    print '  entering'
    try:
        yield {}
    except RuntimeError, err:
        print '  ERROR:', err
    finally:
        print '  exiting'

print 'Normal:'
with make_context() as value:
    print '  inside with statement:', value

print '\nHandled error:'
with make_context() as value:
    raise RuntimeError('showing example of handling an error')

print '\nUnhandled error:'
with make_context() as value:
    raise ValueError('this exception is not handled')
```

The generator should initialize the context, yield exactly one time, and then clean
up the context. The value yielded, if any, is bound to the variable in the **as** clause of the
with statement. Exceptions from within the **with** block are reraised inside the generator,
so they can be handled there.

```
$ python contextlib_contextmanager.py

Normal:
  entering
  inside with statement: {}
  exiting

Handled error:
  entering
  ERROR: showing example of handling an error
  exiting

Unhandled error:
  entering
  exiting
Traceback (most recent call last):
  File "contextlib_contextmanager.py", line 34, in <module>
    raise ValueError('this exception is not handled')
ValueError: this exception is not handled
```

3.4.3 Nesting Contexts

At times, it is necessary to manage multiple contexts simultaneously (such as when copying data between input and output file handles, for example). It is possible to nest **with** statements one inside another, but if the outer contexts do not need their own separate block, this adds to the indention level without giving any real benefit. Using nested() nests the contexts using a single **with** statement.

```
import contextlib

@contextlib.contextmanager
def make_context(name):
    print 'entering:', name
    yield name
    print 'exiting :', name

with contextlib.nested(make_context('A'),
                       make_context('B')) as (A, B):
    print 'inside with statement:', A, B
```

Program execution leaves the contexts in the reverse order in which they are entered.

```
$ python contextlib_nested.py

entering: A
entering: B
inside with statement: A B
exiting : B
exiting : A
```

In Python 2.7 and later, `nested()` is deprecated because the **with** statement supports nesting directly.

```python
import contextlib

@contextlib.contextmanager
def make_context(name):
    print 'entering:', name
    yield name
    print 'exiting :', name

with make_context('A') as A, make_context('B') as B:
    print 'inside with statement:', A, B
```

Each context manager and optional **as** clause are separated by a comma (`,`). The effect is similar to using `nested()`, but avoids some of the edge-cases around error handling that `nested()` could not implement correctly.

```
$ python contextlib_nested_with.py

entering: A
entering: B
inside with statement: A B
exiting : B
exiting : A
```

3.4.4   Closing Open Handles

The `file` class supports the context manager API directly, but some other objects that represent open handles do not. The example given in the standard library documentation for `contextlib` is the object returned from `urllib.urlopen()`. There are other legacy classes that use a `close()` method but do not support the context manager API. To ensure that a handle is closed, use `closing()` to create a context manager for it.

```python
import contextlib

class Door(object):
    def __init__(self):
        print ' __init__()'
    def close(self):
        print ' close()'

print 'Normal Example:'
with contextlib.closing(Door()) as door:
    print ' inside with statement'

print '\nError handling example:'
try:
    with contextlib.closing(Door()) as door:
        print ' raising from inside with statement'
        raise RuntimeError('error message')
except Exception, err:
    print ' Had an error:', err
```

The handle is closed whether there is an error in the **with** block or not.

```
$ python contextlib_closing.py

Normal Example:
  __init__()
  inside with statement
  close()

Error handling example:
  __init__()
  raising from inside with statement
  close()
  Had an error: error message
```

See Also:

contextlib (http://docs.python.org/library/contextlib.html) The standard library documentation for this module.

PEP 343 (http://www.python.org/dev/peps/pep-0343) The **with** statement.

Context Manager Types (**http://docs.python.org/library/stdtypes.html#type contextmanager**) Description of the context manager API from the standard library documentation.

With Statement Context Managers
(**http://docs.python.org/reference/datamodel.html#context-managers**) Description of the context manager API from the Python Reference Guide.

Chapter 4

DATES AND TIMES

Python does not include native types for dates and times as it does for int, float, and str, but there are three modules for manipulating date and time values in several representations.

- The time module exposes the time-related functions from the underlying C library. It includes functions for retrieving the clock time and the processor runtime, as well as basic parsing and string-formatting tools.
- The datetime module provides a higher-level interface for date, time, and combined values. The classes in datetime support arithmetic, comparison, and time zone configuration.
- The calendar module creates formatted representations of weeks, months, and years. It can also be used to compute recurring events, the day of the week for a given date, and other calendar-based values.

4.1 time—Clock Time

Purpose Functions for manipulating clock time.
Python Version 1.4 and later

The time module exposes C library functions for manipulating dates and times. Since it is tied to the underlying C implementation, some details (such as the start of the epoch and the maximum date value supported) are platform specific. Refer to the library documentation for complete details.

4.1.1   Wall Clock Time

One of the core functions of the `time` module is `time()`, which returns the number of seconds since the start of the epoch as a floating-point value.

```
import time

print 'The time is:', time.time()
```

Although the value is always a float, actual precision is platform dependent.

```
$ python time_time.py

The time is: 1291499267.33
```

The float representation is useful when storing or comparing dates, but it is not as useful for producing human-readable representations. For logging or printing time, `ctime()` can be more useful.

```
import time

print 'The time is       :', time.ctime()
later = time.time() + 15
print '15 secs from now :', time.ctime(later)
```

The second **print** statement in this example shows how to use `ctime()` to format a time value other than the current time.

```
$ python time_ctime.py

The time is       : Sat Dec  4 16:47:47 2010
15 secs from now : Sat Dec  4 16:48:02 2010
```

4.1.2   Processor Clock Time

While `time()` returns a wall clock time, `clock()` returns processor clock time. The values returned from `clock()` should be used for performance testing, benchmarking, etc., since they reflect the actual time the program uses and can be more precise than the values from `time()`.

```
import hashlib
import time

# Data to use to calculate md5 checksums
data = open(__file__, 'rt').read()

for i in range(5):
    h = hashlib.sha1()
    print time.ctime(), ': %0.3f %0.3f' % (time.time(), time.clock())
    for i in range(300000):
        h.update(data)
    cksum = h.digest()
```

In this example, the formatted ctime() is printed along with the floating-point values from time() and clock() for each iteration through the loop.

> **Note:** If you want to run the example on your system, you may have to add more cycles to the inner loop or work with a larger amount of data to actually see a difference in the times.

```
$ python time_clock.py

Sat Dec  4 16:47:47 2010 : 1291499267.446 0.028
Sat Dec  4 16:47:48 2010 : 1291499268.844 1.413
Sat Dec  4 16:47:50 2010 : 1291499270.247 2.794
Sat Dec  4 16:47:51 2010 : 1291499271.658 4.171
Sat Dec  4 16:47:53 2010 : 1291499273.128 5.549
```

Typically, the processor clock does not tick if a program is not doing anything.

```
import time

for i in range(6, 1, -1):
    print '%s %0.2f %0.2f' % (time.ctime(),
                              time.time(),
                              time.clock())
    print 'Sleeping', i
    time.sleep(i)
```

In this example, the loop does very little work by going to sleep after each iteration. The `time()` value increases even while the application is asleep, but the `clock()` value does not.

```
$ python time_clock_sleep.py

Sat Dec  4 16:47:54 2010 1291499274.65 0.03
Sleeping 6
Sat Dec  4 16:48:00 2010 1291499280.65 0.03
Sleeping 5
Sat Dec  4 16:48:05 2010 1291499285.65 0.03
Sleeping 4
Sat Dec  4 16:48:09 2010 1291499289.66 0.03
Sleeping 3
Sat Dec  4 16:48:12 2010 1291499292.66 0.03
Sleeping 2
```

Calling `sleep()` yields control from the current thread and asks it to wait for the system to wake it back up. If a program has only one thread, this effectively blocks the app and it does no work.

4.1.3   Time Components

Storing times as elapsed seconds is useful in some situations, but there are times when a program needs to have access to the individual fields of a date (year, month, etc.). The `time` module defines `struct_time` for holding date and time values with components broken out so they are easy to access. Several functions work with `struct_time` values instead of floats.

```
import time

def show_struct(s):
    print '  tm_year :', s.tm_year
    print '  tm_mon  :', s.tm_mon
    print '  tm_mday :', s.tm_mday
    print '  tm_hour :', s.tm_hour
    print '  tm_min  :', s.tm_min
    print '  tm_sec  :', s.tm_sec
    print '  tm_wday :', s.tm_wday
    print '  tm_yday :', s.tm_yday
    print '  tm_isdst:', s.tm_isdst
```

```
print 'gmtime:'
show_struct(time.gmtime())
print '\nlocaltime:'
show_struct(time.localtime())
print '\nmktime:', time.mktime(time.localtime())
```

The gmtime() function returns the current time in UTC. localtime() returns the current time with the current time zone applied. mktime() takes a struct_time instance and converts it to the floating-point representation.

```
$ python time_struct.py

gmtime:
  tm_year : 2010
  tm_mon  : 12
  tm_mday : 4
  tm_hour : 21
  tm_min  : 48
  tm_sec  : 14
  tm_wday : 5
  tm_yday : 338
  tm_isdst: 0

localtime:
  tm_year : 2010
  tm_mon  : 12
  tm_mday : 4
  tm_hour : 16
  tm_min  : 48
  tm_sec  : 14
  tm_wday : 5
  tm_yday : 338
  tm_isdst: 0

mktime: 1291499294.0
```

4.1.4 Working with Time Zones

The functions for determining the current time depend on having the time zone set, either by the program or by using a default time zone set for the system. Changing the time zone does not change the actual time, just the way it is represented.

To change the time zone, set the environment variable TZ, and then call tzset(). The time zone can be specified with a lot of detail, right down to the start and stop times for daylight savings time. It is usually easier to use the time zone name and let the underlying libraries derive the other information, though.

This example program changes the time zone to a few different values and shows how the changes affect other settings in the time module.

```
import time
import os

def show_zone_info():
    print '  TZ    :', os.environ.get('TZ', '(not set)')
    print '  tzname:', time.tzname
    print '  Zone  : %d (%d)' % (time.timezone,
                                 (time.timezone / 3600))
    print '  DST   :', time.daylight
    print '  Time  :', time.ctime()
    print

print 'Default :'
show_zone_info()

ZONES = [ 'GMT',
          'Europe/Amsterdam',
          ]

for zone in ZONES:
    os.environ['TZ'] = zone
    time.tzset()
    print zone, ':'
    show_zone_info()
```

The default time zone on the system used to prepare the examples is US/Eastern. The other zones in the example change the tzname, daylight flag, and timezone offset value.

```
$ python time_timezone.py

Default :
  TZ    : (not set)
  tzname: ('EST', 'EDT')
  Zone  : 18000 (5)
```

```
 DST    : 1
 Time   : Sat Dec   4 16:48:14 2010

GMT :
 TZ      : GMT
 tzname: ('GMT', 'GMT')
 Zone   : 0 (0)
 DST    : 0
 Time   : Sat Dec   4 21:48:14 2010

Europe/Amsterdam :
 TZ      : Europe/Amsterdam
 tzname: ('CET', 'CEST')
 Zone   : -3600 (-1)
 DST    : 1
 Time   : Sat Dec   4 22:48:15 2010
```

4.1.5 Parsing and Formatting Times

The two functions `strptime()` and `strftime()` convert between `struct_time` and string representations of time values. A long list of formatting instructions is available to support input and output in different styles. The complete list is documented in the library documentation for the `time` module.

This example converts the current time from a string to a `struct_time` instance and back to a string.

```python
import time

def show_struct(s):
    print '  tm_year :', s.tm_year
    print '  tm_mon  :', s.tm_mon
    print '  tm_mday :', s.tm_mday
    print '  tm_hour :', s.tm_hour
    print '  tm_min  :', s.tm_min
    print '  tm_sec  :', s.tm_sec
    print '  tm_wday :', s.tm_wday
    print '  tm_yday :', s.tm_yday
    print '  tm_isdst:', s.tm_isdst

now = time.ctime()
print 'Now:', now
```

```
parsed = time.strptime(now)
print '\nParsed:'
show_struct(parsed)

print '\nFormatted:', time.strftime("%a %b %d %H:%M:%S %Y", parsed)
```

The output string is not exactly like the input, since the day of the month is prefixed with a zero.

```
$ python time_strptime.py

Now: Sat Dec  4 16:48:14 2010

Parsed:
  tm_year : 2010
  tm_mon  : 12
  tm_mday : 4
  tm_hour : 16
  tm_min  : 48
  tm_sec  : 14
  tm_wday : 5
  tm_yday : 338
  tm_isdst: -1

Formatted: Sat Dec 04 16:48:14 2010
```

See Also:

time (http://docs.python.org/lib/module-time.html) Standard library documentation for this module.

datetime (page 180) The datetime module includes other classes for doing calculations with dates and times.

calendar (page 191) Work with higher-level date functions to produce calendars or calculate recurring events.

4.2 datetime—Date and Time Value Manipulation

Purpose The datetime module includes functions and classes for doing date and time parsing, formatting, and arithmetic.

Python Version 2.3 and later

datetime contains functions and classes for working with dates and times, separately and together.

4.2.1   Times

Time values are represented with the `time` class. A `time` instance has attributes for `hour`, `minute`, `second`, and `microsecond` and can also include time zone information.

```
import datetime

t = datetime.time(1, 2, 3)
print t
print 'hour        :', t.hour
print 'minute      :', t.minute
print 'second      :', t.second
print 'microsecond:', t.microsecond
print 'tzinfo      :', t.tzinfo
```

The arguments to initialize a `time` instance are optional, but the default of 0 is unlikely to be correct.

```
$ python datetime_time.py

01:02:03
hour        : 1
minute      : 2
second      : 3
microsecond: 0
tzinfo      : None
```

A `time` instance only holds values of time, and not a date associated with the time.

```
import datetime

print 'Earliest   :', datetime.time.min
print 'Latest     :', datetime.time.max
print 'Resolution:', datetime.time.resolution
```

The `min` and `max` class attributes reflect the valid range of times in a single day.

```
$ python datetime_time_minmax.py

Earliest   : 00:00:00
Latest     : 23:59:59.999999
Resolution: 0:00:00.000001
```

The resolution for `time` is limited to whole microseconds.

```
import datetime

for m in [ 1, 0, 0.1, 0.6 ]:
    try:
        print '%02.1f :' % m, datetime.time(0, 0, 0, microsecond=m)
    except TypeError, err:
        print 'ERROR:', err
```

The way floating-point values are treated depends on the version of Python. Version 2.7 raises a `TypeError`, while earlier versions produce a `DeprecationWarning` and convert the floating-point number to an integer.

```
$ python2.7 datetime_time_resolution.py

1.0 : 00:00:00.000001
0.0 : 00:00:00
0.1 : ERROR: integer argument expected, got float
0.6 : ERROR: integer argument expected, got float

$ python2.6 datetime_time_resolution.py

1.0 : 00:00:00.000001
0.0 : 00:00:00
datetime_time_resolution.py:16: DeprecationWarning: integer argument
expected, got float
  print '%02.1f :' % m, datetime.time(0, 0, 0, microsecond=m)
0.1 : 00:00:00
0.6 : 00:00:00
```

4.2.2 Dates

Calendar date values are represented with the `date` class. Instances have attributes for `year`, `month`, and `day`. It is easy to create a date representing the current date using the `today()` class method.

```
import datetime

today = datetime.date.today()
print today
print 'ctime  :', today.ctime()
tt = today.timetuple()
print 'tuple  : tm_year =', tt.tm_year
```

```
print '            tm_mon   =', tt.tm_mon
print '            tm_mday  =', tt.tm_mday
print '            tm_hour  =', tt.tm_hour
print '            tm_min   =', tt.tm_min
print '            tm_sec   =', tt.tm_sec
print '            tm_wday  =', tt.tm_wday
print '            tm_yday  =', tt.tm_yday
print '            tm_isdst =', tt.tm_isdst
print 'ordinal:', today.toordinal()
print 'Year    :', today.year
print 'Mon     :', today.month
print 'Day     :', today.day
```

This example prints the current date in several formats.

```
$ python datetime_date.py

2010-11-27
ctime   : Sat Nov 27 00:00:00 2010
tuple   : tm_year  = 2010
          tm_mon   = 11
          tm_mday  = 27
          tm_hour  = 0
          tm_min   = 0
          tm_sec   = 0
          tm_wday  = 5
          tm_yday  = 331
          tm_isdst = -1
ordinal: 734103
Year    : 2010
Mon     : 11
Day     : 27
```

There are also class methods for creating instances from POSIX timestamps or integers representing date values from the Gregorian calendar, where January 1 of the year 1 is 1 and each subsequent day increments the value by 1.

```
import datetime
import time

o = 733114
print 'o               :', o
```

```
print 'fromordinal(o)   :', datetime.date.fromordinal(o)

t = time.time()
print 't                :', t
print 'fromtimestamp(t):', datetime.date.fromtimestamp(t)
```

This example illustrates the different value types used by fromordinal() and fromtimestamp().

```
$ python datetime_date_fromordinal.py

o                 : 733114
fromordinal(o)    : 2008-03-13
t                 : 1290874810.14
fromtimestamp(t): 2010-11-27
```

As with time, the range of date values supported can be determined using the min and max attributes.

```
import datetime

print 'Earliest   :', datetime.date.min
print 'Latest     :', datetime.date.max
print 'Resolution:', datetime.date.resolution
```

The resolution for dates is whole days.

```
$ python datetime_date_minmax.py

Earliest   : 0001-01-01
Latest     : 9999-12-31
Resolution: 1 day, 0:00:00
```

Another way to create new date instances uses the replace() method of an existing date.

```
import datetime

d1 = datetime.date(2008, 3, 29)
print 'd1:', d1.ctime()
```

```
d2 = d1.replace(year=2009)
print 'd2:', d2.ctime()
```

This example changes the year, leaving the day and month unmodified.

```
$ python datetime_date_replace.py

d1: Sat Mar 29 00:00:00 2008
d2: Sun Mar 29 00:00:00 2009
```

4.2.3 timedeltas

Future and past dates can be calculated using basic arithmetic on two `datetime` objects, or by combining a `datetime` with a `timedelta`. Subtracting dates produces a `timedelta`, and a `timedelta` can be added or subtracted from a date to produce another date. The internal values for a `timedelta` are stored in days, seconds, and microseconds.

```
import datetime

print "microseconds:", datetime.timedelta(microseconds=1)
print "milliseconds:", datetime.timedelta(milliseconds=1)
print "seconds      :", datetime.timedelta(seconds=1)
print "minutes      :", datetime.timedelta(minutes=1)
print "hours        :", datetime.timedelta(hours=1)
print "days         :", datetime.timedelta(days=1)
print "weeks        :", datetime.timedelta(weeks=1)
```

Intermediate level values passed to the constructor are converted into days, seconds, and microseconds.

```
$ python datetime_timedelta.py

microseconds: 0:00:00.000001
milliseconds: 0:00:00.001000
seconds      : 0:00:01
minutes      : 0:01:00
hours        : 1:00:00
days         : 1 day, 0:00:00
weeks        : 7 days, 0:00:00
```

The full duration of a `timedelta` can be retrieved as a number of seconds using `total_seconds()`.

```python
import datetime

for delta in [datetime.timedelta(microseconds=1),
              datetime.timedelta(milliseconds=1),
              datetime.timedelta(seconds=1),
              datetime.timedelta(minutes=1),
              datetime.timedelta(hours=1),
              datetime.timedelta(days=1),
              datetime.timedelta(weeks=1),
              ]:
    print '%15s = %s seconds' % (delta, delta.total_seconds())
```

The return value is a floating-point number, to accommodate subsecond durations.

```
$ python datetime_timedelta_total_seconds.py

 0:00:00.000001 = 1e-06 seconds
 0:00:00.001000 = 0.001 seconds
        0:00:01 = 1.0 seconds
        0:01:00 = 60.0 seconds
        1:00:00 = 3600.0 seconds
 1 day, 0:00:00 = 86400.0 seconds
7 days, 0:00:00 = 604800.0 seconds
```

4.2.4 Date Arithmetic

Date math uses the standard arithmetic operators.

```python
import datetime

today = datetime.date.today()
print 'Today    :', today

one_day = datetime.timedelta(days=1)
print 'One day  :', one_day

yesterday = today - one_day
print 'Yesterday:', yesterday
```

```
tomorrow = today + one_day
print 'Tomorrow :', tomorrow

print
print 'tomorrow - yesterday:', tomorrow - yesterday
print 'yesterday - tomorrow:', yesterday - tomorrow
```

This example with date objects illustrates using `timedelta` objects to compute new dates, and subtracting date instances to produce timedeltas (including a negative delta value).

```
$ python datetime_date_math.py

Today     : 2010-11-27
One day   : 1 day, 0:00:00
Yesterday: 2010-11-26
Tomorrow  : 2010-11-28

tomorrow - yesterday: 2 days, 0:00:00
yesterday - tomorrow: -2 days, 0:00:00
```

4.2.5   Comparing Values

Both date and time values can be compared using the standard comparison operators to determine which is earlier or later.

```
import datetime
import time

print 'Times:'
t1 = datetime.time(12, 55, 0)
print '  t1:', t1
t2 = datetime.time(13, 5, 0)
print '  t2:', t2
print '  t1 < t2:', t1 < t2

print
print 'Dates:'
d1 = datetime.date.today()
print '  d1:', d1
d2 = datetime.date.today() + datetime.timedelta(days=1)
```

```
print '   d2:', d2
print '   d1 > d2:', d1 > d2
```

All comparison operators are supported.

```
$ python datetime_comparing.py

Times:
  t1: 12:55:00
  t2: 13:05:00
  t1 < t2: True

Dates:
  d1: 2010-11-27
  d2: 2010-11-28
  d1 > d2: False
```

4.2.6 Combining Dates and Times

Use the `datetime` class to hold values consisting of both date and time components.
As with `date`, there are several convenient class methods to create `datetime` instances
from other common values.

```
import datetime

print 'Now    :', datetime.datetime.now()
print 'Today  :', datetime.datetime.today()
print 'UTC Now:', datetime.datetime.utcnow()
print

FIELDS = [ 'year', 'month', 'day',
           'hour', 'minute', 'second', 'microsecond',
           ]

d = datetime.datetime.now()
for attr in FIELDS:
    print '%15s: %s' % (attr, getattr(d, attr))
```

As might be expected, the `datetime` instance has all attributes of both a `date`
and a `time` object.

```
$ python datetime_datetime.py

Now    : 2010-11-27 11:20:10.479880
Today  : 2010-11-27 11:20:10.481494
UTC Now: 2010-11-27 16:20:10.481521

         year: 2010
        month: 11
          day: 27
         hour: 11
       minute: 20
       second: 10
  microsecond: 481752
```

Just as with `date`, `datetime` provides convenient class methods for creating new instances. It also includes `fromordinal()` and `fromtimestamp()`.

```
import datetime

t = datetime.time(1, 2, 3)
print 't :', t

d = datetime.date.today()
print 'd :', d

dt = datetime.datetime.combine(d, t)
print 'dt:', dt
```

`combine()` creates `datetime` instances from one `date` and one `time` instance.

```
$ python datetime_datetime_combine.py

t : 01:02:03
d : 2010-11-27
dt: 2010-11-27 01:02:03
```

4.2.7 Formatting and Parsing

The default string representation of a `datetime` object uses the ISO-8601 format (YYYY-MM-DDTHH:MM:SS.mmmmmm). Alternate formats can be generated using `strftime()`.

```
import datetime

format = "%a %b %d %H:%M:%S %Y"

today = datetime.datetime.today()
print 'ISO      :', today

s = today.strftime(format)
print 'strftime:', s

d = datetime.datetime.strptime(s, format)
print 'strptime:', d.strftime(format)
```

Use `datetime.strptime()` to convert formatted strings to `datetime` instances.

```
$ python datetime_datetime_strptime.py

ISO      : 2010-11-27 11:20:10.571582
strftime: Sat Nov 27 11:20:10 2010
strptime: Sat Nov 27 11:20:10 2010
```

4.2.8 Time Zones

Within `datetime`, time zones are represented by subclasses of `tzinfo`. Since `tzinfo` is an abstract base class, applications need to define a subclass and provide appropriate implementations for a few methods to make it useful. Unfortunately, `datetime` does not include any actual ready-to-use implementations, although the documentation does provide a few sample implementations. Refer to the standard library documentation page for examples using fixed offsets, as well as a DST-aware class and more details about creating custom time zone classes. `pytz` is also a good source for time zone implementation details.

See Also:

datetime (http://docs.python.org/lib/module-datetime.html) The standard library documentation for this module.

calendar (page 191) The `calendar` module.

time (page 173) The `time` module.

dateutil (http://labix.org/python-dateutil) `dateutil` from Labix extends the `datetime` module with additional features.

WikiPedia: Proleptic Gregorian calendar (http://en.wikipedia.org/wiki/Proleptic_Gregorian_calendar) A description of the Gregorian calendar system.

pytz (http://pytz.sourceforge.net/) World Time Zone database.

ISO 8601 (http://www.iso.org/iso/support/faqs/faqs_widely_used_standards/ widely_used_standards_other/date_and_time_format.htm) The standard for numeric representation of dates and time.

4.3   calendar—Work with Dates

> **Purpose** The `calendar` module implements classes for working with dates to manage year-, month-, and week-oriented values.
>
> **Python Version** 1.4, with updates in 2.5

The `calendar` module defines the `Calendar` class, which encapsulates calculations for values such as the dates of the weeks in a given month or year. In addition, the `TextCalendar` and `HTMLCalendar` classes can produce preformatted output.

4.3.1   Formatting Examples

The `prmonth()` method is a simple function that produces the formatted text output for a month.

```
import calendar

c = calendar.TextCalendar(calendar.SUNDAY)
c.prmonth(2011, 7)
```

The example configures `TextCalendar` to start weeks on Sunday, following the American convention. The default is to use the European convention of starting a week on Monday.

Here is what the output looks like.

```
$ python calendar_textcalendar.py

     July 2011
Su Mo Tu We Th Fr Sa
                1  2
 3  4  5  6  7  8  9
10 11 12 13 14 15 16
17 18 19 20 21 22 23
24 25 26 27 28 29 30
31
```

A similar HTML table can be produced with HTMLCalendar and formatmonth(). The rendered output looks roughly the same as the plain-text version, but is wrapped with HTML tags. Each table cell has a class attribute corresponding to the day of the week so the HTML can be styled through CSS.

To produce output in a format other than one of the available defaults, use calendar to calculate the dates and organize the values into week and month ranges, and then iterate over the result. The weekheader(), monthcalendar(), and yeardays2calendar() methods of Calendar are especially useful for that.

Calling yeardays2calendar() produces a sequence of "month row" lists. Each list includes the months as another list of weeks. The weeks are lists of tuples made up of day number (1–31) and weekday number (0–6). Days that fall outside of the month have a day number of 0.

```
import calendar
import pprint

cal = calendar.Calendar(calendar.SUNDAY)

cal_data = cal.yeardays2calendar(2011, 3)
print 'len(cal_data)          :', len(cal_data)

top_months = cal_data[0]
print 'len(top_months)        :', len(top_months)

first_month = top_months[0]
print 'len(first_month)       :', len(first_month)

print 'first_month:'
pprint.pprint(first_month)
```

Calling yeardays2calendar(2011, 3) returns data for 2011, organized with three months per row.

```
$ python calendar_yeardays2calendar.py

len(cal_data)      : 4
len(top_months)    : 3
len(first_month)   : 6
first_month:
[[(0, 6), (0, 0), (0, 1), (0, 2), (0, 3), (0, 4), (1, 5)],
 [(2, 6), (3, 0), (4, 1), (5, 2), (6, 3), (7, 4), (8, 5)],
```

```
[(9, 6), (10, 0), (11, 1), (12, 2), (13, 3), (14, 4), (15, 5)],
[(16, 6), (17, 0), (18, 1), (19, 2), (20, 3), (21, 4), (22, 5)],
[(23, 6), (24, 0), (25, 1), (26, 2), (27, 3), (28, 4), (29, 5)],
[(30, 6), (31, 0), (0, 1), (0, 2), (0, 3), (0, 4), (0, 5)]]
```

This is equivalent to the data used by `formatyear()`.

import calendar

```
cal = calendar.TextCalendar(calendar.SUNDAY)
print cal.formatyear(2011, 2, 1, 1, 3)
```

For the same arguments, `formatyear()` produces this output.

```
$ python calendar_formatyear.py

                              2011

         January                 February                 March
Su Mo Tu We Th Fr Sa    Su Mo Tu We Th Fr Sa    Su Mo Tu We Th Fr Sa
                   1        1  2  3  4  5              1  2  3  4  5
 2  3  4  5  6  7  8     6  7  8  9 10 11 12     6  7  8  9 10 11 12
 9 10 11 12 13 14 15    13 14 15 16 17 18 19    13 14 15 16 17 18 19
16 17 18 19 20 21 22    20 21 22 23 24 25 26    20 21 22 23 24 25 26
23 24 25 26 27 28 29    27 28                   27 28 29 30 31
30 31

          April                    May                     June
Su Mo Tu We Th Fr Sa    Su Mo Tu We Th Fr Sa    Su Mo Tu We Th Fr Sa
                1  2     1  2  3  4  5  6  7              1  2  3  4
 3  4  5  6  7  8  9     8  9 10 11 12 13 14     5  6  7  8  9 10 11
10 11 12 13 14 15 16    15 16 17 18 19 20 21    12 13 14 15 16 17 18
17 18 19 20 21 22 23    22 23 24 25 26 27 28    19 20 21 22 23 24 25
24 25 26 27 28 29 30    29 30 31                26 27 28 29 30

          July                   August                 September
Su Mo Tu We Th Fr Sa    Su Mo Tu We Th Fr Sa    Su Mo Tu We Th Fr Sa
                1  2        1  2  3  4  5  6              1  2  3
 3  4  5  6  7  8  9     7  8  9 10 11 12 13     4  5  6  7  8  9 10
10 11 12 13 14 15 16    14 15 16 17 18 19 20    11 12 13 14 15 16 17
17 18 19 20 21 22 23    21 22 23 24 25 26 27    18 19 20 21 22 23 24
24 25 26 27 28 29 30    28 29 30 31             25 26 27 28 29 30
31
```

```
        October                 November                December
Su Mo Tu We Th Fr Sa     Su Mo Tu We Th Fr Sa     Su Mo Tu We Th Fr Sa
                  1                  1  2  3  4  5                  1  2  3
 2  3  4  5  6  7  8      6  7  8  9 10 11 12      4  5  6  7  8  9 10
 9 10 11 12 13 14 15     13 14 15 16 17 18 19     11 12 13 14 15 16 17
16 17 18 19 20 21 22     20 21 22 23 24 25 26     18 19 20 21 22 23 24
23 24 25 26 27 28 29     27 28 29 30              25 26 27 28 29 30 31
30 31
```

The `day_name`, `day_abbr`, `month_name`, and `month_abbr` module attributes are useful for producing custom-formatted output (e.g., to include links in the HTML output). They are automatically configured correctly for the current locale.

4.3.2 Calculating Dates

Although the `calendar` module focuses mostly on printing full calendars in various formats, it also provides functions useful for working with dates in other ways, such as calculating dates for a recurring event. For example, the Python Atlanta Users Group meets on the second Thursday of every month. To calculate the meeting dates for a year, use the return value of `monthcalendar()`.

```
import calendar
import pprint

pprint.pprint(calendar.monthcalendar(2011, 7))
```

Some days have a 0 value. Those are days of the week that overlap with the given month, but that are part of another month.

```
$ python calendar_monthcalendar.py

[[0, 0, 0, 0, 1, 2, 3],
 [4, 5, 6, 7, 8, 9, 10],
 [11, 12, 13, 14, 15, 16, 17],
 [18, 19, 20, 21, 22, 23, 24],
 [25, 26, 27, 28, 29, 30, 31]]
```

The first day of the week defaults to Monday. It is possible to change that setting by calling `setfirstweekday()`, but since the `calendar` module includes constants for indexing into the date ranges returned by `monthcalendar()`, it is more convenient to skip that step in this case.

To calculate the group meeting dates for 2011, assuming the second Thursday of every month, the 0 values indicate whether the Thursday of the first week is included in the month (or if the month starts, for example, on a Friday).

```
import calendar

# Show every month
for month in range(1, 13):

    # Compute the dates for each week that overlaps the month
    c = calendar.monthcalendar(2011, month)
    first_week = c[0]
    second_week = c[1]
    third_week = c[2]

    # If there is a Thursday in the first week, the second Thursday
    # is in the second week.  Otherwise, the second Thursday must
    # be in the third week.
    if first_week[calendar.THURSDAY]:
        meeting_date = second_week[calendar.THURSDAY]
    else:
        meeting_date = third_week[calendar.THURSDAY]

    print '%3s: %2s' % (calendar.month_abbr[month], meeting_date)
```

So, the meeting schedule for this year is

```
$ python calendar_secondthursday.py

Jan: 13
Feb: 10
Mar: 10
Apr: 14
May: 12
Jun:  9
Jul: 14
Aug: 11
Sep:  8
Oct: 13
Nov: 10
Dec:  8
```

See Also:

calendar (http://docs.python.org/library/calendar.html) The standard library documentation for this module.

time (page 173) Lower-level time functions.

datetime (page 180) Manipulate date values, including timestamps and time zones.

Chapter 5

MATHEMATICS

As a general-purpose programming language, Python is frequently used to solve mathematical problems. It includes built-in types for managing integers and floating-point numbers, which are suitable for the basic math that might appear in an average application. The standard library includes modules for more advanced needs.

Python's built-in floating-point numbers use the underlying `double` representation. They are sufficiently precise for most programs with mathematical requirements, but when more accurate representations of noninteger values are needed, the `decimal` and `fractions` modules will be useful. Arithmetic with decimal and fractional values retains precision, but it is not as fast as the native `float`.

The `random` module includes a uniform distribution pseudorandom number generator, as well as functions for simulating many common nonuniform distributions.

The `math` module contains fast implementations of advanced mathematical functions, such as logarithms and trigonometric functions. The full complement of IEEE functions usually found in the native platform C libraries is available through the module.

5.1 decimal—Fixed and Floating-Point Math

Purpose Decimal arithmetic using fixed and floating-point numbers.
Python Version 2.4 and later

The `decimal` module implements fixed and floating-point arithmetic using the model familiar to most people, rather than the IEEE floating-point version implemented by most computer hardware and familiar to programmers. A `Decimal` instance can represent any number exactly, round it up or down, and apply a limit to the number of significant digits.

5.1.1   Decimal

Decimal values are represented as instances of the `Decimal` class. The constructor takes as argument one integer or string. Floating-point numbers can be converted to a string before being used to create a `Decimal`, letting the caller explicitly deal with the number of digits for values that cannot be expressed exactly using hardware floating-point representations. Alternately, the class method `from_float()` converts to the exact decimal representation.

```
import decimal

fmt = '{0:<25} {1:<25}'
print fmt.format('Input', 'Output')
print fmt.format('-' * 25, '-' * 25)

# Integer
print fmt.format(5, decimal.Decimal(5))

# String
print fmt.format('3.14', decimal.Decimal('3.14'))

# Float
f = 0.1
print fmt.format(repr(f), decimal.Decimal(str(f)))
print fmt.format('%.23g' % f,
                 str(decimal.Decimal.from_float(f))[:25])
```

The floating-point value of `0.1` is not represented as an exact value in binary, so the representation as a `float` is different from the `Decimal` value. It is truncated to 25 characters in this output.

```
$ python decimal_create.py

Input                     Output
------------------------- -------------------------
5                         5
3.14                      3.14
0.1                       0.1
0.1000000000000000055112  0.1000000000000000055111
```

`Decimal`s can also be created from tuples containing a sign flag (0 for positive, 1 for negative), a `tuple` of digits, and an integer exponent.

```
import decimal

# Tuple
t = (1, (1, 1), -2)
print 'Input    :', t
print 'Decimal:', decimal.Decimal(t)
```

The tuple-based representation is less convenient to create, but it does offer a portable way of exporting decimal values without losing precision. The `tuple` form can be transmitted through the network or stored in a database that does not support accurate decimal values, and then turned back into a `Decimal` instance later.

```
$ python decimal_tuple.py

Input    : (1, (1, 1), -2)
Decimal: -0.11
```

5.1.2 Arithmetic

`Decimal` overloads the simple arithmetic operators so instances can be manipulated in much the same way as the built-in numeric types.

```
import decimal

a = decimal.Decimal('5.1')
b = decimal.Decimal('3.14')
c = 4
d = 3.14

print 'a        =', repr(a)
print 'b        =', repr(b)
print 'c        =', repr(c)
print 'd        =', repr(d)
print

print 'a + b =', a + b
print 'a - b =', a - b
print 'a * b =', a * b
print 'a / b =', a / b
print

print 'a + c =', a + c
print 'a - c =', a - c
```

```
print 'a * c =', a * c
print 'a / c =', a / c
print

print 'a + d =',
try:
    print a + d
except TypeError, e:
    print e
```

Decimal operators also accept integer arguments, but floating-point values must be converted to Decimal instances.

```
$ python decimal_operators.py

a       = Decimal('5.1')
b       = Decimal('3.14')
c       = 4
d       = 3.14

a + b = 8.24
a - b = 1.96
a * b = 16.014
a / b = 1.6242038216560509955414012739

a + c = 9.1
a - c = 1.1
a * c = 20.4
a / c = 1.275

a + d = unsupported operand type(s) for +: 'Decimal' and 'float'
```

Beyond basic arithmetic, Decimal includes the methods to find the base 10 and natural logarithms. The return values from log10() and ln() are Decimal instances, so they can be used directly in formulas with other values.

5.1.3 Special Values

In addition to the expected numerical values, Decimal can represent several special values, including positive and negative values for infinity, "not a number," and zero.

```
import decimal

for value in [ 'Infinity', 'NaN', '0' ]:
```

```
        print decimal.Decimal(value), decimal.Decimal('-' + value)
print

# Math with infinity
print 'Infinity + 1:', (decimal.Decimal('Infinity') + 1)
print '-Infinity + 1:', (decimal.Decimal('-Infinity') + 1)

# Print comparing NaN
print decimal.Decimal('NaN') == decimal.Decimal('Infinity')
print decimal.Decimal('NaN') != decimal.Decimal(1)
```

Adding to infinite values returns another infinite value. Comparing for equality with NaN always returns false, and comparing for inequality always returns true. Comparing for sort order against NaN is undefined and results in an error.

```
$ python decimal_special.py

Infinity -Infinity
NaN -NaN
0 -0

Infinity + 1: Infinity
-Infinity + 1: -Infinity
False
True
```

5.1.4 Context

So far, the examples all have used the default behaviors of the decimal module. It is possible to override settings such as the precision maintained, how rounding is performed, error handling, etc., by using a *context*. Contexts can be applied for all Decimal instances in a thread or locally within a small code region.

Current Context

To retrieve the current global context, use getcontext().

```
import decimal
import pprint

context = decimal.getcontext()

print 'Emax      =', context.Emax
print 'Emin      =', context.Emin
```

```
print 'capitals =', context.capitals
print 'prec     =', context.prec
print 'rounding =', context.rounding
print 'flags    ='
pprint.pprint(context.flags)
print 'traps    ='
pprint.pprint(context.traps)
```

This example script shows the public properties of a `Context`.

```
$ python decimal_getcontext.py

Emax       = 999999999
Emin       = -999999999
capitals = 1
prec       = 28
rounding = ROUND_HALF_EVEN
flags      =
{<class 'decimal.Clamped'>: 0,
 <class 'decimal.InvalidOperation'>: 0,
 <class 'decimal.DivisionByZero'>: 0,
 <class 'decimal.Inexact'>: 0,
 <class 'decimal.Rounded'>: 0,
 <class 'decimal.Subnormal'>: 0,
 <class 'decimal.Overflow'>: 0,
 <class 'decimal.Underflow'>: 0}
traps      =
{<class 'decimal.Clamped'>: 0,
 <class 'decimal.InvalidOperation'>: 1,
 <class 'decimal.DivisionByZero'>: 1,
 <class 'decimal.Inexact'>: 0,
 <class 'decimal.Rounded'>: 0,
 <class 'decimal.Subnormal'>: 0,
 <class 'decimal.Overflow'>: 1,
 <class 'decimal.Underflow'>: 0}
```

Precision

The `prec` attribute of the context controls the precision maintained for new values created as a result of arithmetic. Literal values are maintained as described.

```
import decimal

d = decimal.Decimal('0.123456')
for i in range(4):
```

```
decimal.getcontext().prec = i
print i, ':', d, d * 1
```

To change the precision, assign a new value directly to the attribute.

```
$ python decimal_precision.py

0 : 0.123456 0
1 : 0.123456 0.1
2 : 0.123456 0.12
3 : 0.123456 0.123
```

Rounding

There are several options for rounding to keep values within the desired precision.

ROUND_CEILING Always round upward toward infinity.

ROUND_DOWN Always round toward zero.

ROUND_FLOOR Always round down toward negative infinity.

ROUND_HALF_DOWN Round away from zero if the last significant digit is greater than or equal to 5; otherwise, round toward zero.

ROUND_HALF_EVEN Like ROUND_HALF_DOWN, except that if the value is 5, then the preceding digit is examined. Even values cause the result to be rounded down, and odd digits cause the result to be rounded up.

ROUND_HALF_UP Like ROUND_HALF_DOWN, except if the last significant digit is 5, the value is rounded away from zero.

ROUND_UP Round away from zero.

ROUND_05UP Round away from zero if the last digit is 0 or 5; otherwise, round toward zero.

```
import decimal

context = decimal.getcontext()

ROUNDING_MODES = [
    'ROUND_CEILING',
    'ROUND_DOWN',
    'ROUND_FLOOR',
    'ROUND_HALF_DOWN',
    'ROUND_HALF_EVEN',
    'ROUND_HALF_UP',
    'ROUND_UP',
    'ROUND_05UP',
    ]
header_fmt = '{:10} ' + ' '.join(['{:^8}'] * 6)
```

```
print header_fmt.format(' ',
                        '1/8 (1)', '-1/8 (1)',
                        '1/8 (2)', '-1/8 (2)',
                        '1/8 (3)', '-1/8 (3)',
                        )
for rounding_mode in ROUNDING_MODES:
    print '{0:10}'.format(rounding_mode.partition('_')[-1]),
    for precision in [ 1, 2, 3 ]:
        context.prec = precision
        context.rounding = getattr(decimal, rounding_mode)
        value = decimal.Decimal(1) / decimal.Decimal(8)
        print '{0:^8}'.format(value),
        value = decimal.Decimal(-1) / decimal.Decimal(8)
        print '{0:^8}'.format(value),
    print
```

This program shows the effect of rounding the same value to different levels of precision using the different algorithms.

```
$ python decimal_rounding.py
```

	1/8 (1)	-1/8 (1)	1/8 (2)	-1/8 (2)	1/8 (3)	-1/8 (3)
CEILING	0.2	-0.1	0.13	-0.12	0.125	-0.125
DOWN	0.1	-0.1	0.12	-0.12	0.125	-0.125
FLOOR	0.1	-0.2	0.12	-0.13	0.125	-0.125
HALF_DOWN	0.1	-0.1	0.12	-0.12	0.125	-0.125
HALF_EVEN	0.1	-0.1	0.12	-0.12	0.125	-0.125
HALF_UP	0.1	-0.1	0.13	-0.13	0.125	-0.125
UP	0.2	-0.2	0.13	-0.13	0.125	-0.125
05UP	0.1	-0.1	0.12	-0.12	0.125	-0.125

Local Context

Using Python 2.5 or later, the context can be applied to a block of code using the **with** statement.

```
import decimal

with decimal.localcontext() as c:
    c.prec = 2
    print 'Local precision:', c.prec
    print '3.14 / 3 =', (decimal.Decimal('3.14') / 3)
```

```
print
print 'Default precision:', decimal.getcontext().prec
print '3.14 / 3 =', (decimal.Decimal('3.14') / 3)
```

The `Context` supports the context manager API used by **with**, so the settings only apply within the block.

```
$ python decimal_context_manager.py

Local precision: 2
3.14 / 3 = 1.0

Default precision: 28
3.14 / 3 = 1.0466666666666666666666666667
```

Per-Instance Context

Contexts also can be used to construct `Decimal` instances, which then inherit from the context the precision and rounding arguments to the conversion.

```
import decimal

# Set up a context with limited precision
c = decimal.getcontext().copy()
c.prec = 3

# Create our constant
pi = c.create_decimal('3.1415')

# The constant value is rounded off
print 'PI    :', pi

# The result of using the constant uses the global context
print 'RESULT:', decimal.Decimal('2.01') * pi
```

This lets an application select the precision of constant values separately from the precision of user data, for example.

```
$ python decimal_instance_context.py

PI    : 3.14
RESULT: 6.3114
```

Threads

The "global" context is actually thread-local, so each thread can potentially be configured using different values.

```python
import decimal
import threading
from Queue import PriorityQueue

class Multiplier(threading.Thread):
    def __init__(self, a, b, prec, q):
        self.a = a
        self.b = b
        self.prec = prec
        self.q = q
        threading.Thread.__init__(self)
    def run(self):
        c = decimal.getcontext().copy()
        c.prec = self.prec
        decimal.setcontext(c)
        self.q.put( (self.prec, a * b) )
        return

a = decimal.Decimal('3.14')
b = decimal.Decimal('1.234')
# A PriorityQueue will return values sorted by precision, no matter
# what order the threads finish.
q = PriorityQueue()
threads = [ Multiplier(a, b, i, q) for i in range(1, 6) ]
for t in threads:
    t.start()

for t in threads:
    t.join()

for i in range(5):
    prec, value = q.get()
    print prec, '\t', value
```

This example creates a new context using the specified value, and then installs it within each thread.

```
$ python decimal_thread_context.py

1       4
2       3.9
3       3.87
4       3.875
5       3.8748
```

See Also:

decimal (http://docs.python.org/library/decimal.html) The standard library documentation for this module.

Floating Point (http://en.wikipedia.org/wiki/Floating_point) Wikipedia article on floating-point representations and arithmetic.

Floating Point Arithmetic: Issues and Limitations
   (http://docs.python.org/tutorial/floatingpoint.html) Article from the Python tutorial describing floating-point math representation issues.

5.2   fractions—Rational Numbers

Purpose Implements a class for working with rational numbers.
Python Version 2.6 and later

The `Fraction` class implements numerical operations for rational numbers based on the API defined by `Rational` in the `numbers` module.

5.2.1   Creating Fraction Instances

As with the `decimal` module, new values can be created in several ways. One easy way is to create them from separate numerator and denominator values, as follows.

```
import fractions

for n, d in [ (1, 2), (2, 4), (3, 6) ]:
    f = fractions.Fraction(n, d)
    print '%s/%s = %s' % (n, d, f)
```

The lowest common denominator is maintained as new values are computed.

```
$ python fractions_create_integers.py

1/2 = 1/2
2/4 = 1/2
3/6 = 1/2
```

Another way to create a Fraction is to use a string representation of <numerator> / <denominator>:

```
import fractions

for s in [ '1/2', '2/4', '3/6' ]:
    f = fractions.Fraction(s)
    print '%s = %s' % (s, f)
```

The string is parsed to find the numerator and denominator values.

```
$ python fractions_create_strings.py

1/2 = 1/2
2/4 = 1/2
3/6 = 1/2
```

Strings can also use the more usual decimal or floating-point notation of a series of digits separated by a period.

```
import fractions

for s in [ '0.5', '1.5', '2.0' ]:
    f = fractions.Fraction(s)
    print '%s = %s' % (s, f)
```

The numerator and denominator values represented by the floating-point value are computed automatically.

```
$ python fractions_create_strings_floats.py

0.5 = 1/2
1.5 = 3/2
2.0 = 2
```

There are also class methods for creating `Fraction` instances directly from other representations of rational values, such as `float` or `Decimal`.

```
import fractions

for v in [ 0.1, 0.5, 1.5, 2.0 ]:
    print '%s = %s' % (v, fractions.Fraction.from_float(v))
```

Floating-point values that cannot be expressed exactly may yield unexpected results.

```
$ python fractions_from_float.py

0.1 = 3602879701896397/36028797018963968
0.5 = 1/2
1.5 = 3/2
2.0 = 2
```

Using `decimal` representations of the values gives the expected results.

```
import decimal
import fractions

for v in [ decimal.Decimal('0.1'),
           decimal.Decimal('0.5'),
           decimal.Decimal('1.5'),
           decimal.Decimal('2.0'),
           ]:
    print '%s = %s' % (v, fractions.Fraction.from_decimal(v))
```

The internal implementation of the `decimal` does not suffer from the precision errors of the standard floating-point representation.

```
$ python fractions_from_decimal.py

0.1 = 1/10
0.5 = 1/2
1.5 = 3/2
2.0 = 2
```

5.2.2 Arithmetic

Once the fractions are instantiated, they can be used in mathematical expressions.

```
import fractions

f1 = fractions.Fraction(1, 2)
f2 = fractions.Fraction(3, 4)

print '%s + %s = %s' % (f1, f2, f1 + f2)
print '%s - %s = %s' % (f1, f2, f1 - f2)
print '%s * %s = %s' % (f1, f2, f1 * f2)
print '%s / %s = %s' % (f1, f2, f1 / f2)
```

All standard operators are supported.

```
$ python fractions_arithmetic.py

1/2 + 3/4 = 5/4
1/2 - 3/4 = -1/4
1/2 * 3/4 = 3/8
1/2 / 3/4 = 2/3
```

5.2.3 Approximating Values

A useful feature of Fraction is the ability to convert a floating-point number to an approximate rational value.

```
import fractions
import math

print 'PI       =', math.pi

f_pi = fractions.Fraction(str(math.pi))
print 'No limit =', f_pi

for i in [ 1, 6, 11, 60, 70, 90, 100 ]:
    limited = f_pi.limit_denominator(i)
    print '{0:8} = {1}'.format(i, limited)
```

The value of the fraction can be controlled by limiting the denominator size.

```
$ python fractions_limit_denominator.py

PI        = 3.14159265359
No limit  = 314159265359/100000000000
       1  = 3
       6  = 19/6
      11  = 22/7
      60  = 179/57
      70  = 201/64
      90  = 267/85
     100  = 311/99
```

See Also:

fractions (http://docs.python.org/library/fractions.html) The standard library documentation for this module.

decimal (page 197) The `decimal` module provides an API for fixed and floating-point math.

numbers (http://docs.python.org/library/numbers.html) Numeric abstract base classes.

5.3   random—Pseudorandom Number Generators

Purpose Implements several types of pseudorandom number generators.
Python Version 1.4 and later

The `random` module provides a fast pseudorandom number generator based on the *Mersenne Twister* algorithm. Originally developed to produce inputs for Monte Carlo simulations, Mersenne Twister generates numbers with nearly uniform distribution and a large period, making it suited for a wide range of applications.

5.3.1   Generating Random Numbers

The `random()` function returns the next random floating-point value from the generated sequence. All return values fall within the range $0 <= n < 1.0$.

```
import random

for i in xrange(5):
    print '%04.3f' % random.random(),
print
```

Running the program repeatedly produces different sequences of numbers.

```
$ python random_random.py

0.809 0.485 0.521 0.800 0.247

$ python random_random.py

0.614 0.551 0.705 0.479 0.659
```

To generate numbers in a specific numerical range, use `uniform()` instead.

```
import random

for i in xrange(5):
    print '%04.3f' % random.uniform(1, 100),
print
```

Pass minimum and maximum values, and `uniform()` adjusts the return values from `random()` using the formula `min + (max - min) * random()`.

```
$ python random_uniform.py

78.558 96.734 74.521 52.386 98.499
```

5.3.2   Seeding

`random()` produces different values each time it is called and has a very large period before it repeats any numbers. This is useful for producing unique values or variations, but there are times when having the same data set available to be processed in different ways is useful. One technique is to use a program to generate random values and save them to be processed by a separate step. That may not be practical for large amounts of data, though, so `random` includes the `seed()` function for initializing the pseudorandom generator so that it produces an expected set of values.

```
import random

random.seed(1)

for i in xrange(5):
    print '%04.3f' % random.random(),
print
```

The seed value controls the first value produced by the formula used to produce pseudorandom numbers, and since the formula is deterministic, it also sets the full sequence produced after the seed is changed. The argument to `seed()` can be any hashable object. The default is to use a platform-specific source of randomness, if one is available. Otherwise, the current time is used.

```
$ python random_seed.py

0.134 0.847 0.764 0.255 0.495

$ python random_seed.py

0.134 0.847 0.764 0.255 0.495
```

5.3.3 Saving State

The internal state of the pseudorandom algorithm used by `random()` can be saved and used to control the numbers produced in subsequent runs. Restoring the previous state before continuing reduces the likelihood of repeating values or sequences of values from the earlier input. The `getstate()` function returns data that can be used to reinitialize the random number generator later with `setstate()`.

```python
import random
import os
import cPickle as pickle

if os.path.exists('state.dat'):
    # Restore the previously saved state
    print 'Found state.dat, initializing random module'
    with open('state.dat', 'rb') as f:
        state = pickle.load(f)
    random.setstate(state)
else:
    # Use a well-known start state
    print 'No state.dat, seeding'
    random.seed(1)

# Produce random values
for i in xrange(3):
    print '%04.3f' % random.random(),
print
```

```
# Save state for next time
with open('state.dat', 'wb') as f:
    pickle.dump(random.getstate(), f)

# Produce more random values
print '\nAfter saving state:'
for i in xrange(3):
    print '%04.3f' % random.random(),
print
```

The data returned by getstate() is an implementation detail, so this example saves the data to a file with pickle, but otherwise treats it as a black box. If the file exists when the program starts, it loads the old state and continues. Each run produces a few numbers before and after saving the state to show that restoring the state causes the generator to produce the same values again.

```
$ python random_state.py

No state.dat, seeding
0.134 0.847 0.764

After saving state:
0.255 0.495 0.449

$ python random_state.py

Found state.dat, initializing random module
0.255 0.495 0.449

After saving state:
0.652 0.789 0.094
```

5.3.4 Random Integers

random() generates floating-point numbers. It is possible to convert the results to integers, but using randint() to generate integers directly is more convenient.

```
import random

print '[1, 100]:',
```

```
for i in xrange(3):
    print random.randint(1, 100),

print '\n[-5, 5]:',
for i in xrange(3):
    print random.randint(-5, 5),
print
```

The arguments to `randint()` are the ends of the inclusive range for the values. The numbers can be positive or negative, but the first value should be less than the second.

```
$ python random_randint.py

[1, 100]: 91 77 67
[-5, 5]: -5 -3 3
```

`randrange()` is a more general form of selecting values from a range.

```
import random

for i in xrange(3):
    print random.randrange(0, 101, 5),
print
```

`randrange()` supports a *step* argument, in addition to start and stop values, so it is fully equivalent to selecting a random value from `range(start, stop, step)`. It is more efficient, because the range is not actually constructed.

```
$ python random_randrange.py

50 10 60
```

5.3.5 Picking Random Items

One common use for random number generators is to select a random item from a sequence of enumerated values, even if those values are not numbers. `random` includes the `choice()` function for making a random selection from a sequence. This example simulates flipping a coin 10,000 times to count how many times it comes up heads and how many times it comes up tails.

```python
import random
import itertools

outcomes = { 'heads':0,
             'tails':0,
             }
sides = outcomes.keys()

for i in range(10000):
    outcomes[ random.choice(sides) ] += 1

print 'Heads:', outcomes['heads']
print 'Tails:', outcomes['tails']
```

Only two outcomes are allowed, so rather than use numbers and convert them, the words "heads" and "tails" are used with `choice()`. The results are tabulated in a dictionary using the outcome names as keys.

```
$ python random_choice.py

Heads: 5038
Tails: 4962
```

5.3.6 Permutations

A simulation of a card game needs to mix up the deck of cards and then deal the cards to the players, without using the same card more than once. Using `choice()` could result in the same card being dealt twice, so instead, the deck can be mixed up with `shuffle()` and then individual cards removed as they are dealt.

```python
import random
import itertools

FACE_CARDS = ('J', 'Q', 'K', 'A')
SUITS = ('H', 'D', 'C', 'S')

def new_deck():
    return list(itertools.product(
            itertools.chain(xrange(2, 11), FACE_CARDS),
            SUITS,
            ))
```

```
def show_deck(deck):
    p_deck = deck[:]
    while p_deck:
        row = p_deck[:13]
        p_deck = p_deck[13:]
        for j in row:
            print '%2s%s' % j,
        print

# Make a new deck, with the cards in order
deck = new_deck()
print 'Initial deck:'
show_deck(deck)

# Shuffle the deck to randomize the order
random.shuffle(deck)
print '\nShuffled deck:'
show_deck(deck)

# Deal 4 hands of 5 cards each
hands = [ [], [], [], [] ]

for i in xrange(5):
    for h in hands:
        h.append(deck.pop())

# Show the hands
print '\nHands:'
for n, h in enumerate(hands):
    print '%d:' % (n+1),
    for c in h:
        print '%2s%s' % c,
    print

# Show the remaining deck
print '\nRemaining deck:'
show_deck(deck)
```

The cards are represented as tuples with the face value and a letter indicating the suit. The dealt "hands" are created by adding one card at a time to each of four lists and then removing it from the deck so it cannot be dealt again.

```
$ python random_shuffle.py
```

Initial deck:

2H	2D	2C	2S	3H	3D	3C	3S	4H	4D	4C	4S	5H
5D	5C	5S	6H	6D	6C	6S	7H	7D	7C	7S	8H	8D
8C	8S	9H	9D	9C	9S	10H	10D	10C	10S	JH	JD	JC
JS	QH	QD	QC	QS	KH	KD	KC	KS	AH	AD	AC	AS

Shuffled deck:

3C	KH	QH	6H	JD	AC	7S	5D	3S	10S	7H	QC	2C
5C	7C	4H	6S	9D	10H	4D	2H	3D	7D	5S	10D	9H
2S	9C	KC	5H	6C	8S	3H	10C	JS	2D	AH	KD	AD
4C	QS	8D	8C	JC	8H	4S	JH	QD	9S	AS	KS	6D

Hands:
```
1:  6D   QD   JC   4C   2D
2:  KS   JH   8C   AD   JS
3:  AS   4S   8D   KD   10C
4:  9S   8H   QS   AH   3H
```

Remaining deck:

3C	KH	QH	6H	JD	AC	7S	5D	3S	10S	7H	QC	2C
5C	7C	4H	6S	9D	10H	4D	2H	3D	7D	5S	10D	9H
2S	9C	KC	5H	6C	8S							

5.3.7 Sampling

Many simulations need random samples from a population of input values. The `sample()` function generates samples without repeating values and without modifying the input sequence. This example prints a random sample of words from the system dictionary.

```python
import random

with open('/usr/share/dict/words', 'rt') as f:
    words = f.readlines()
words = [ w.rstrip() for w in words ]

for w in random.sample(words, 5):
    print w
```

The algorithm for producing the result set takes into account the sizes of the input and the sample requested to produce the result as efficiently as possible.

```
$ python random_sample.py

pleasureman
consequency
docibility
youdendrift
Ituraean

$ python random_sample.py

jigamaree
readingdom
sporidium
pansylike
foraminiferan
```

5.3.8   Multiple Simultaneous Generators

In addition to module-level functions, random includes a Random class to manage the internal state for several random number generators. All of the functions described earlier are available as methods of the Random instances, and each instance can be initialized and used separately, without interfering with the values returned by other instances.

```
import random
import time

print 'Default initializiation:\n'

r1 = random.Random()
r2 = random.Random()

for i in xrange(3):
    print '%04.3f   %04.3f' % (r1.random(), r2.random())

print '\nSame seed:\n'

seed = time.time()
r1 = random.Random(seed)
r2 = random.Random(seed)

for i in xrange(3):
    print '%04.3f   %04.3f' % (r1.random(), r2.random())
```

On a system with good native random-value seeding, the instances start out in unique states. However, if there is no good platform random-value generator, the instances are likely to have been seeded with the current time, and therefore, produce the same values.

```
$ python random_random_class.py

Default initializiation:

0.370   0.303
0.437   0.142
0.323   0.088

Same seed:

0.684   0.684
0.060   0.060
0.977   0.977
```

To ensure that the generators produce values from different parts of the random period, use `jumpahead()` to shift one of them away from its initial state.

```
import random
import time

r1 = random.Random()
r2 = random.Random()

# Force r2 to a different part of the random period than r1.
r2.setstate(r1.getstate())
r2.jumpahead(1024)

for i in xrange(3):
    print '%04.3f   %04.3f' % (r1.random(), r2.random())
```

The argument to `jumpahead()` should be a nonnegative integer based the number of values needed from each generator. The internal state of the generator is scrambled based on the input value, but not simply by incrementing it by the number of steps given.

```
$ python random_jumpahead.py
```

```
0.858   0.093
0.510   0.707
0.444   0.556
```

5.3.9   SystemRandom

Some operating systems provide a random number generator that has access to more sources of entropy that can be introduced into the generator. `random` exposes this feature through the `SystemRandom` class, which has the same API as `Random` but uses `os.urandom()` to generate the values that form the basis of all other algorithms.

```python
import random
import time

print 'Default initializiation:\n'

r1 = random.SystemRandom()
r2 = random.SystemRandom()

for i in xrange(3):
    print '%04.3f   %04.3f' % (r1.random(), r2.random())

print '\nSame seed:\n'

seed = time.time()
r1 = random.SystemRandom(seed)
r2 = random.SystemRandom(seed)

for i in xrange(3):
    print '%04.3f   %04.3f' % (r1.random(), r2.random())
```

Sequences produced by `SystemRandom` are not reproducible because the randomness is coming from the system, rather than from the software state (in fact, `seed()` and `setstate()` have no effect at all).

```
$ python random_system_random.py

Default initializiation:

0.551   0.873
0.643   0.975
0.106   0.268
```

```
Same seed:

0.211   0.985
0.101   0.852
0.887   0.344
```

5.3.10   Nonuniform Distributions

While the uniform distribution of the values produced by `random()` is useful for a lot of purposes, other distributions more accurately model specific situations. The `random` module includes functions to produce values in those distributions, too. They are listed here, but not covered in detail because their uses tend to be specialized and require more complex examples.

Normal

The *normal* distribution is commonly used for nonuniform continuous values, such as grades, heights, weights, etc. The curve produced by the distribution has a distinctive shape that has lead to it being nicknamed a "bell curve." `random` includes two functions for generating values with a normal distribution, `normalvariate()` and the slightly faster `gauss()`. (The normal distribution is also called the Gaussian distribution.)

The related function, `lognormvariate()`, produces pseudorandom values where the logarithm of the values is distributed normally. Log-normal distributions are useful for values that are the product of several random variables that do not interact.

Approximation

The *triangular* distribution is used as an approximate distribution for small sample sizes. The "curve" of a triangular distribution has low points at known minimum and maximum values, and a high point at the mode, which is estimated based on a "most likely" outcome (reflected by the mode argument to `triangular()`).

Exponential

`expovariate()` produces an exponential distribution useful for simulating arrival or interval time values for use in homogeneous Poisson processes, such as the rate of radioactive decay or requests coming into a Web server.

The Pareto, or power law, distribution matches many observable phenomena and was popularized by *The Long Tail*, by Chris Anderson. The `paretovariate()` function is useful for simulating allocation of resources to individuals (wealth to people, demand for musicians, attention to blogs, etc.).

Angular

The von Mises, or circular normal, distribution (produced by `vonmisesvariate()`) is used for computing probabilities of cyclic values, such as angles, calendar days, and times.

Sizes

`betavariate()` generates values with the Beta distribution, which is commonly used in Bayesian statistics and applications such as task duration modeling.

The Gamma distribution produced by `gammavariate()` is used for modeling the sizes of things, such as waiting times, rainfall, and computational errors.

The Weibull distribution computed by `weibullvariate()` is used in failure analysis, industrial engineering, and weather forecasting. It describes the distribution of sizes of particles or other discrete objects.

See Also:

random (http://docs.python.org/library/random.html) The standard library documentation for this module.

Mersenne Twister: A 623-dimensionally equidistributed uniform pseudorandom number generator Article by M. Matsumoto and T. Nishimura from *ACM Transactions on Modeling and Computer Simulation*, Vol. 8, No. 1, January pp. 3–30 1998.

Mersenne Twister (http://en.wikipedia.org/wiki/Mersenne_twister) Wikipedia article about the pseudorandom generator algorithm used by Python.

Uniform distribution [http://en.wikipedia.org/wiki/Uniform_distribution_ (continuous)] Wikipedia article about continuous uniform distributions in statistics.

5.4   math—Mathematical Functions

Purpose Provides functions for specialized mathematical operations.

Python Version 1.4 and later

The `math` module implements many of the IEEE functions that would normally be found in the native platform C libraries for complex mathematical operations using floating-point values, including logarithms and trigonometric operations.

5.4.1   Special Constants

Many math operations depend on special constants. `math` includes values for π (pi) and *e*.

```
import math

print 'π: %.30f' % math.pi
print 'e: %.30f' % math.e
```

Both values are limited in precision only by the platform's floating-point C library.

```
$ python math_constants.py

π: 3.141592653589793115997963468544
e: 2.718281828459045090795598298428
```

5.4.2   Testing for Exceptional Values

Floating-point calculations can result in two types of exceptional values. The first of these, INF (infinity), appears when the *double* used to hold a floating-point value over-flows from a value with a large absolute value.

```
import math

print '{:^3}  {:6}  {:6}  {:6}'.format('e', 'x', 'x**2', 'isinf')
print '{:-^3}  {:-^6}  {:-^6}  {:-^6}'.format('', '', '', '')

for e in range(0, 201, 20):
    x = 10.0 ** e
    y = x*x
    print '{:3d}  {!s:6}  {!s:6}  {!s:6}'.format(e, x, y,
                                                 math.isinf(y),
                                                 )
```

When the exponent in this example grows large enough, the square of *x* no longer fits inside a *double*, and the value is recorded as infinite.

```
$ python math_isinf.py

  e    x        x**2      isinf
 ---  ------   ------    ------
   0  1.0      1.0       False
  20  1e+20    1e+40     False
  40  1e+40    1e+80     False
  60  1e+60    1e+120    False
  80  1e+80    1e+160    False
```

```
100   1e+100   1e+200   False
120   1e+120   1e+240   False
140   1e+140   1e+280   False
160   1e+160   inf      True
180   1e+180   inf      True
200   1e+200   inf      True
```

Not all floating-point overflows result in `INF` values, however. Calculating an exponent with floating-point values, in particular, raises `OverflowError` instead of preserving the `INF` result.

```
x = 10.0 ** 200

print 'x     =', x
print 'x*x   =', x*x
try:
    print 'x**2 =', x**2
except OverflowError, err:
    print err
```

This discrepancy is caused by an implementation difference in the library used by C Python.

```
$ python math_overflow.py

x     = 1e+200
x*x   = inf
x**2 = (34, 'Result too large')
```

Division operations using infinite values are undefined. The result of dividing a number by infinity is `NaN` (not a number).

```
import math

x = (10.0 ** 200) * (10.0 ** 200)
y = x/x

print 'x =', x
print 'isnan(x) =', math.isnan(x)
print 'y = x / x =', x/x
print 'y == nan =', y == float('nan')
print 'isnan(y) =', math.isnan(y)
```

NaN does not compare as equal to any value, even itself, so to check for NaN, use
`isnan()`.

```
$ python math_isnan.py

x = inf
isnan(x)  = False
y = x / x = nan
y == nan = False
isnan(y)  = True
```

5.4.3 Converting to Integers

The `math` module includes three functions for converting floating-point values to whole numbers. Each takes a different approach and will be useful in different circumstances.

The simplest is `trunc()`, which truncates the digits following the decimal, leaving only the significant digits making up the whole-number portion of the value. `floor()` converts its input to the largest preceding integer, and `ceil()` (ceiling) produces the largest integer following sequentially after the input value.

```
import math

HEADINGS = ('i', 'int', 'trunk', 'floor', 'ceil')
print '{:^5}  {:^5}  {:^5}  {:^5}  {:^5}'.format(*HEADINGS)
print '{:-^5}  {:-^5}  {:-^5}  {:-^5}  {:-^5}'.format(
    '', '', '', '', '',
    )

fmt = '  '.join(['{:5.1f}'] * 5)

TEST_VALUES = [ -1.5,
                -0.8,
                -0.5,
                -0.2,
                0,
                0.2,
                0.5,
                0.8,
                1,
                ]
```

```
for i in TEST_VALUES:
    print fmt.format(i,
                     int(i),
                     math.trunc(i),
                     math.floor(i),
                     math.ceil(i))
```

trunc() is equivalent to converting to int directly.

```
$ python math_integers.py
```

i	int	trunk	floor	ceil
-1.5	-1.0	-1.0	-2.0	-1.0
-0.8	0.0	0.0	-1.0	-0.0
-0.5	0.0	0.0	-1.0	-0.0
-0.2	0.0	0.0	-1.0	-0.0
0.0	0.0	0.0	0.0	0.0
0.2	0.0	0.0	0.0	1.0
0.5	0.0	0.0	0.0	1.0
0.8	0.0	0.0	0.0	1.0
1.0	1.0	1.0	1.0	1.0

5.4.4 Alternate Representations

modf() takes a single floating-point number and returns a tuple containing the fractional and whole-number parts of the input value.

```
import math

for i in range(6):
    print '{}/2 = {}'.format(i, math.modf(i/2.0))
```

Both numbers in the return value are floats.

```
$ python math_modf.py

0/2 = (0.0, 0.0)
1/2 = (0.5, 0.0)
2/2 = (0.0, 1.0)
3/2 = (0.5, 1.0)
4/2 = (0.0, 2.0)
5/2 = (0.5, 2.0)
```

`frexp()` returns the mantissa and exponent of a floating-point number, and can be used to create a more portable representation of the value.

```
import math

print '{:^7}   {:^7}   {:^7}'.format('x', 'm', 'e')
print '{:-^7}   {:-^7}   {:-^7}'.format('', '', '')

for x in [ 0.1, 0.5, 4.0 ]:
    m, e = math.frexp(x)
    print '{:7.2f}   {:7.2f}   {:7d}'.format(x, m, e)
```

`frexp()` uses the formula x = m * 2**e, and returns the values *m* and *e*.

```
$ python math_frexp.py

   x          m          e
-------    -------    -------
  0.10       0.80         -3
  0.50       0.50          0
  4.00       0.50          3
```

`ldexp()` is the inverse of `frexp()`.

```
import math

print '{:^7}   {:^7}   {:^7}'.format('m', 'e', 'x')
print '{:-^7}   {:-^7}   {:-^7}'.format('', '', '')

for m, e in [ (0.8, -3),
              (0.5,  0),
              (0.5,  3),
            ]:
    x = math.ldexp(m, e)
    print '{:7.2f}   {:7d}   {:7.2f}'.format(m, e, x)
```

Using the same formula as `frexp()`, `ldexp()` takes the mantissa and exponent values as arguments and returns a floating-point number.

```
$ python math_ldexp.py

   m          e          x
-------    -------    -------
   0.80        -3       0.10
   0.50         0       0.50
   0.50         3       4.00
```

5.4.5   Positive and Negative Signs

The absolute value of a number is its value without a sign. Use `fabs()` to calculate the absolute value of a floating-point number.

```
import math

print math.fabs(-1.1)
print math.fabs(-0.0)
print math.fabs(0.0)
print math.fabs(1.1)
```

In practical terms, the absolute value of a `float` is represented as a positive value.

```
$ python math_fabs.py

1.1
0.0
0.0
1.1
```

To determine the sign of a value, either to give a set of values the same sign or to compare two values, use `copysign()` to set the sign of a known good value.

```
import math

HEADINGS = ('f', 's', '< 0', '> 0', '= 0')
print '{:^5} {:^5} {:^5} {:^5} {:^5}'.format(*HEADINGS)
print '{:-^5} {:-^5} {:-^5} {:-^5} {:-^5}'.format(
    '', '', '', '', '',
    )

for f in [ -1.0,
           0.0,
           1.0,
```

```
                float('-inf'),
                float('inf'),
                float('-nan'),
                float('nan'),
                ]:
    s = int(math.copysign(1, f))
    print '{:5.1f}  {:5d}  {!s:5}  {!s:5}  {!s:5}'.format(
        f, s, f < 0, f > 0, f==0,
        )
```

An extra function like `copysign()` is needed because comparing NaN and −NaN directly with other values does not work.

```
$ python math_copysign.py

    f       s     < 0    > 0    = 0
  -----   -----  -----  -----  -----
  -1.0     -1    True   False  False
   0.0      1    False  False  True
   1.0      1    False  True   False
  -inf     -1    True   False  False
   inf      1    False  True   False
   nan     -1    False  False  False
   nan      1    False  False  False
```

5.4.6 Commonly Used Calculations

Representing precise values in binary floating-point memory is challenging. Some values cannot be represented exactly, and the more often a value is manipulated through repeated calculations, the more likely a representation error will be introduced. `math` includes a function for computing the sum of a series of floating-point numbers using an efficient algorithm that minimizes such errors.

```
import math

values = [ 0.1 ] * 10

print 'Input values:', values

print 'sum()        : {:.20f}'.format(sum(values))

s = 0.0
```

```
for i in values:
    s += i
print 'for-loop     : {:.20f}'.format(s)

print 'math.fsum() : {:.20f}'.format(math.fsum(values))
```

Given a sequence of ten values, each equal to 0.1, the expected value for the sum of the sequence is 1.0. Since 0.1 cannot be represented exactly as a floating-point value, however, errors are introduced into the sum unless it is calculated with fsum().

```
$ python math_fsum.py

Input values: [0.1, 0.1, 0.1, 0.1, 0.1, 0.1, 0.1, 0.1, 0.1, 0.1]
sum()        : 0.99999999999999988898
for-loop     : 0.99999999999999988898
math.fsum()  : 1.00000000000000000000
```

factorial() is commonly used to calculate the number of permutations and combinations of a series of objects. The factorial of a positive integer n, expressed $n!$, is defined recursively as $(n-1)!*n$ and stops with $0!==1$.

```
import math

for i in [ 0, 1.0, 2.0, 3.0, 4.0, 5.0, 6.1 ]:
    try:
        print '{:2.0f}  {:6.0f}'.format(i, math.factorial(i))
    except ValueError, err:
        print 'Error computing factorial(%s):' % i, err
```

factorial() only works with whole numbers, but it does accept float arguments as long as they can be converted to an integer without losing value.

```
$ python math_factorial.py

 0       1
 1       1
 2       2
 3       6
 4      24
 5     120
Error computing factorial(6.1): factorial() only accepts integral
  values
```

`gamma()` is like `factorial()`, except that it works with real numbers and the value is shifted down by one (gamma is equal to $(n - 1)!$).

```python
import math

for i in [ 0, 1.1, 2.2, 3.3, 4.4, 5.5, 6.6 ]:
    try:
        print '{:2.1f}  {:6.2f}'.format(i, math.gamma(i))
    except ValueError, err:
        print 'Error computing gamma(%s):' % i, err
```

Since zero causes the start value to be negative, it is not allowed.

```
$ python math_gamma.py

Error computing gamma(0): math domain error
1.1     0.95
2.2     1.10
3.3     2.68
4.4    10.14
5.5    52.34
6.6   344.70
```

`lgamma()` returns the natural logarithm of the absolute value of gamma for the input value.

```python
import math

for i in [ 0, 1.1, 2.2, 3.3, 4.4, 5.5, 6.6 ]:
    try:
        print '{:2.1f}  {:.20f}  {:.20f}'.format(
            i,
            math.lgamma(i),
            math.log(math.gamma(i)),
            )
    except ValueError, err:
        print 'Error computing lgamma(%s):' % i, err
```

Using `lgamma()` retains more precision than calculating the logarithm separately using the results of `gamma()`.

```
$ python math_lgamma.py

Error computing lgamma(0): math domain error
1.1   -0.04987244125984036103   -0.04987244125983997245
2.2    0.09694746679063825923    0.09694746679063866168
3.3    0.98709857789473387513    0.98709857789473409717
4.4    2.31610349142485727469    2.31610349142485727469
5.5    3.95781396761871651080    3.95781396761871606671
6.6    5.84268005527463252236    5.84268005527463252236
```

The modulo operator (%) computes the remainder of a division expression (e.g., 5 % 2 = 1). The operator built into the language works well with integers, but, as with so many other floating-point operations, intermediate calculations cause representational issues that result in a loss of data. fmod() provides a more accurate implementation for floating-point values.

```
import math

print '{:^4}  {:^4}  {:^5}  {:^5}'.format('x', 'y', '%', 'fmod')
print '----  ----  -----  -----'

for x, y in [ (5, 2),
              (5, -2),
              (-5, 2),
              ]:
    print '{:4.1f}  {:4.1f}  {:5.2f}  {:5.2f}'.format(
        x,
        y,
        x % y,
        math.fmod(x, y),
        )
```

A potentially more frequent source of confusion is the fact that the algorithm used by fmod() for computing modulo is also different from that used by %, so the sign of the result is different.

```
$ python math_fmod.py

  x     y      %     fmod
----  ----  -----  -----
 5.0   2.0   1.00   1.00
 5.0  -2.0  -1.00   1.00
-5.0   2.0   1.00  -1.00
```

5.4.7   Exponents and Logarithms

Exponential growth curves appear in economics, physics, and other sciences. Python has a built-in exponentiation operator (" ** "), but pow() can be useful when a callable function is needed as an argument to another function.

```python
import math

for x, y in [
    # Typical uses
    (2, 3),
    (2.1, 3.2),

    # Always 1
    (1.0, 5),
    (2.0, 0),

    # Not-a-number
    (2, float('nan')),

    # Roots
    (9.0, 0.5),
    (27.0, 1.0/3),
    ]:
    print '{:5.1f} ** {:5.3f} = {:6.3f}'.format(x, y, math.pow(x, y))
```

Raising 1 to any power always returns 1.0, as does raising any value to a power of 0.0. Most operations on the not-a-number value nan return nan. If the exponent is less than 1, pow() computes a root.

```
$ python math_pow.py

 2.0 ** 3.000 =  8.000
 2.1 ** 3.200 = 10.742
 1.0 ** 5.000 =  1.000
 2.0 ** 0.000 =  1.000
 2.0 **   nan =    nan
 9.0 ** 0.500 =  3.000
27.0 ** 0.333 =  3.000
```

Since square roots (exponent of $\frac{1}{2}$) are used so frequently, there is a separate function for computing them.

```
import math

print math.sqrt(9.0)
print math.sqrt(3)
try:
    print math.sqrt(-1)
except ValueError, err:
    print 'Cannot compute sqrt(-1):', err
```

Computing the square roots of negative numbers requires *complex numbers*, which are not handled by math. Any attempt to calculate a square root of a negative value results in a ValueError.

```
$ python math_sqrt.py

3.0
1.73205080757
Cannot compute sqrt(-1): math domain error
```

The logarithm function finds *y* where $x = b \text{ ** } y$. By default, log() computes the natural logarithm (the base is *e*). If a second argument is provided, that value is used as the base.

```
import math

print math.log(8)
print math.log(8, 2)
print math.log(0.5, 2)
```

Logarithms where *x* is less than one yield negative results.

```
$ python math_log.py

2.07944154168
3.0
-1.0
```

There are two variations of log(). Given floating-point representation and rounding errors, the computed value produced by log(x, b) has limited accuracy, especially for some bases. log10() computes log(x, 10), using a more accurate algorithm than log().

```
import math

print '{:2}  {:^12}  {:^10}  {:^20}  {:8}'.format(
    'i', 'x', 'accurate', 'inaccurate', 'mismatch',
    )
print '{:-^2}  {:-^12}  {:-^10}  {:-^20}  {:-^8}'.format(
    '', '', '', '', '',
    )

for i in range(0, 10):
    x = math.pow(10, i)
    accurate = math.log10(x)
    inaccurate = math.log(x, 10)
    match = '' if int(inaccurate) == i else '*'
    print '{:2d}  {:12.1f}  {:10.8f}  {:20.18f}  {:^5}'.format(
        i, x, accurate, inaccurate, match,
        )
```

The lines in the output with trailing * highlight the inaccurate values.

```
$ python math_log10.py

i        x           accurate        inaccurate          mismatch
--  ------------  ----------  --------------------  --------
0            1.0  0.00000000  0.000000000000000000
1           10.0  1.00000000  1.000000000000000000
2          100.0  2.00000000  2.000000000000000000
3         1000.0  3.00000000  2.999999999999999556     *
4        10000.0  4.00000000  4.000000000000000000
5       100000.0  5.00000000  5.000000000000000000
6      1000000.0  6.00000000  5.999999999999999112     *
7     10000000.0  7.00000000  7.000000000000000000
8    100000000.0  8.00000000  8.000000000000000000
9   1000000000.0  9.00000000  8.999999999999998224     *
```

log1p() calculates the Newton-Mercator series (the natural logarithm of 1+x).

```
import math

x = 0.0000000000000000000000001
print 'x      :', x
print '1 + x  :', 1+x
```

```
print 'log(1+x):', math.log(1+x)
print 'log1p(x):', math.log1p(x)
```

log1p() is more accurate for values of *x* very close to zero because it uses an algorithm that compensates for round-off errors from the initial addition.

```
$ python math_log1p.py

x         : 1e-25
1 + x     : 1.0
log(1+x)  : 0.0
log1p(x)  : 1e-25
```

exp() computes the exponential function ($e**x$).

```
import math

x = 2

fmt = '%.20f'
print fmt % (math.e ** 2)
print fmt % math.pow(math.e, 2)
print fmt % math.exp(2)
```

As with other special-case functions, it uses an algorithm that produces more accurate results than the general-purpose equivalent `math.pow(math.e, x)`.

```
$ python math_exp.py

7.38905609893064951876
7.38905609893064951876
7.38905609893065040694
```

expm1() is the inverse of log1p() and calculates $e**x - 1$.

```
import math

x = 0.0000000000000000000000001
```

```
print x
print math.exp(x) - 1
print math.expm1(x)
```

Small values of *x* lose precision when the subtraction is performed separately, like with `log1p()`.

```
$ python math_expm1.py

1e-25
0.0
1e-25
```

5.4.8 Angles

Although degrees are more commonly used in everyday discussions of angles, radians are the standard unit of angular measure in science and math. A radian is the angle created by two lines intersecting at the center of a circle, with their ends on the circumference of the circle spaced one radius apart.

The circumference is calculated as $2\pi r$, so there is a relationship between radians and π, a value that shows up frequently in trigonometric calculations. That relationship leads to radians being used in trigonometry and calculus, because they result in more compact formulas.

To convert from degrees to radians, use `radians()`.

```
import math

print '{:^7}  {:^7}  {:^7}'.format('Degrees', 'Radians', 'Expected')
print '{:-^7}  {:-^7}  {:-^7}'.format('', '', '')

for deg, expected in [ (  0,   0),
                       ( 30,   math.pi/6),
                       ( 45,   math.pi/4),
                       ( 60,   math.pi/3),
                       ( 90,   math.pi/2),
                       (180,   math.pi),
                       (270,   3/2.0 * math.pi),
                       (360,   2 * math.pi),
                       ]:
```

```
print '{:7d}    {:7.2f}    {:7.2f}'.format(deg,
                                           math.radians(deg),
                                           expected,
                                           )
```

The formula for the conversion is `rad = deg * π / 180`.

```
$ python math_radians.py

Degrees  Radians  Expected
-------  -------  -------
      0     0.00     0.00
     30     0.52     0.52
     45     0.79     0.79
     60     1.05     1.05
     90     1.57     1.57
    180     3.14     3.14
    270     4.71     4.71
    360     6.28     6.28
```

To convert from radians to degrees, use `degrees()`.

```
import math

print '{:^8}    {:^8}    {:^8}'.format('Radians', 'Degrees', 'Expected')
print '{:-^8}    {:-^8}    {:-^8}'.format('', '', '')
for rad, expected in [ (0,                   0),
                       (math.pi/6,          30),
                       (math.pi/4,          45),
                       (math.pi/3,          60),
                       (math.pi/2,          90),
                       (math.pi,           180),
                       (3 * math.pi / 2,   270),
                       (2 * math.pi,       360),
                       ]:
    print '{:8.2f}    {:8.2f}    {:8.2f}'.format(rad,
                                                 math.degrees(rad),
                                                 expected,
                                                 )
```

The formula is `deg = rad * 180 / π`.

```
$ python math_degrees.py

Radians   Degrees   Expected
--------  --------  --------
   0.00      0.00      0.00
   0.52     30.00     30.00
   0.79     45.00     45.00
   1.05     60.00     60.00
   1.57     90.00     90.00
   3.14    180.00    180.00
   4.71    270.00    270.00
   6.28    360.00    360.00
```

5.4.9 Trigonometry

Trigonometric functions relate angles in a triangle to the lengths of its sides. They show up in formulas with periodic properties such as harmonics or circular motion, or when dealing with angles. All trigonometric functions in the standard library take angles expressed as radians.

Given an angle in a right triangle, the *sine* is the ratio of the length of the side opposite the angle to the hypotenuse (sin A = opposite/hypotenuse). The *cosine* is the ratio of the length of the adjacent side to the hypotenuse (cos A = adjacent/hypotenuse). And the *tangent* is the ratio of the opposite side to the adjacent side (tan A = opposite/adjacent).

```
import math

print 'Degrees   Radians   Sine      Cosine     Tangent'
print '-------   -------   -------   --------   -------'

fmt = '   '.join(['%7.2f'] * 5)

for deg in range(0, 361, 30):
    rad = math.radians(deg)
    if deg in (90, 270):
        t = float('inf')
    else:
        t = math.tan(rad)
    print fmt % (deg, rad, math.sin(rad), math.cos(rad), t)
```

The tangent can also be defined as the ratio of the sine of the angle to its cosine, and since the cosine is 0 for $\pi/2$ and $3\pi/2$ radians, the tangent is infinite.

```
$ python math_trig.py
```

Degrees	Radians	Sine	Cosine	Tangent
0.00	0.00	0.00	1.00	0.00
30.00	0.52	0.50	0.87	0.58
60.00	1.05	0.87	0.50	1.73
90.00	1.57	1.00	0.00	inf
120.00	2.09	0.87	-0.50	-1.73
150.00	2.62	0.50	-0.87	-0.58
180.00	3.14	0.00	-1.00	-0.00
210.00	3.67	-0.50	-0.87	0.58
240.00	4.19	-0.87	-0.50	1.73
270.00	4.71	-1.00	-0.00	inf
300.00	5.24	-0.87	0.50	-1.73
330.00	5.76	-0.50	0.87	-0.58
360.00	6.28	-0.00	1.00	-0.00

Given a point (x, y), the length of the hypotenuse for the triangle between the points $[(0, 0), (x, 0), (x, y)]$ is $(x**2 + y**2) ** 1/2$, and can be computed with hypot().

```
import math

print '{:^7}  {:^7}  {:^10}'.format('X', 'Y', 'Hypotenuse')
print '{:-^7}  {:-^7}  {:-^10}'.format('', '', '')

for x, y in [ # simple points
              (1, 1),
              (-1, -1),
              (math.sqrt(2), math.sqrt(2)),
              (3, 4), # 3-4-5 triangle
              # on the circle
              (math.sqrt(2)/2, math.sqrt(2)/2), # pi/4 rads
              (0.5, math.sqrt(3)/2), # pi/3 rads
              ]:
    h = math.hypot(x, y)
    print '{:7.2f}  {:7.2f}  {:7.2f}'.format(x, y, h)
```

Points on the circle always have hypotenuse == 1.

```
$ python math_hypot.py

    X           Y       Hypotenuse
 -------     -------    ----------
    1.00        1.00       1.41
   -1.00       -1.00       1.41
    1.41        1.41       2.00
    3.00        4.00       5.00
    0.71        0.71       1.00
    0.50        0.87       1.00
```

The same function can be used to find the distance between two points.

```
import math

print '{:^8}  {:^8}  {:^8}  {:^8}  {:^8}'.format(
    'X1', 'Y1', 'X2', 'Y2', 'Distance',
    )
print '{:-^8}  {:-^8}  {:-^8}  {:-^8}  {:-^8}'.format(
    '', '', '', '', '',
    )


for (x1, y1), (x2, y2) in [ ((5, 5), (6, 6)),
                            ((-6, -6), (-5, -5)),
                            ((0, 0), (3, 4)), # 3-4-5 triangle
                            ((-1, -1), (2, 3)), # 3-4-5 triangle
                            ]:
    x = x1 - x2
    y = y1 - y2
    h = math.hypot(x, y)
    print '{:8.2f}  {:8.2f}  {:8.2f}  {:8.2f}  {:8.2f}'.format(
        x1, y1, x2, y2, h,
        )
```

Use the difference in the *x* and *y* values to move one endpoint to the origin, and then pass the results to hypot().

```
$ python math_distance_2_points.py
```

X1	Y1	X2	Y2	Distance
5.00	5.00	6.00	6.00	1.41
-6.00	-6.00	-5.00	-5.00	1.41
0.00	0.00	3.00	4.00	5.00
-1.00	-1.00	2.00	3.00	5.00

`math` also defines inverse trigonometric functions.

```
import math

for r in [ 0, 0.5, 1 ]:
    print 'arcsine(%.1f)    = %5.2f' % (r, math.asin(r))
    print 'arccosine(%.1f)  = %5.2f' % (r, math.acos(r))
    print 'arctangent(%.1f) = %5.2f' % (r, math.atan(r))
    print
```

`1.57` is roughly equal to $\pi/2$, or 90 degrees, the angle at which the sine is 1 and the cosine is 0.

```
$ python math_inverse_trig.py

arcsine(0.0)    =  0.00
arccosine(0.0)  =  1.57
arctangent(0.0) =  0.00

arcsine(0.5)    =  0.52
arccosine(0.5)  =  1.05
arctangent(0.5) =  0.46

arcsine(1.0)    =  1.57
arccosine(1.0)  =  0.00
arctangent(1.0) =  0.79
```

5.4.10 Hyperbolic Functions

Hyperbolic functions appear in linear differential equations and are used when working with electromagnetic fields, fluid dynamics, special relativity, and other advanced physics and mathematics.

```
import math

print '{:^6}  {:^6}  {:^6}  {:^6}'.format(
    'X', 'sinh', 'cosh', 'tanh',
    )
print '{:-^6}  {:-^6}  {:-^6}  {:-^6}'.format('', '', '', '')

fmt = '  '.join(['{:6.4f}'] * 4)

for i in range(0, 11, 2):
    x = i/10.0
    print fmt.format(x, math.sinh(x), math.cosh(x), math.tanh(x))
```

Whereas the cosine and sine functions enscribe a circle, the hyperbolic cosine and hyperbolic sine form half of a hyperbola.

```
$ python math_hyperbolic.py

   X       sinh    cosh    tanh
------  ------  ------  ------
0.0000  0.0000  1.0000  0.0000
0.2000  0.2013  1.0201  0.1974
0.4000  0.4108  1.0811  0.3799
0.6000  0.6367  1.1855  0.5370
0.8000  0.8881  1.3374  0.6640
1.0000  1.1752  1.5431  0.7616
```

Inverse hyperbolic functions `acosh()`, `asinh()`, and `atanh()` are also available.

5.4.11   Special Functions

The Gauss Error function is used in statistics.

```
import math

print '{:^5}  {:7}'.format('x', 'erf(x)')
print '{:-^5}  {:-^7}'.format('', '')

for x in [ -3, -2, -1, -0.5, -0.25, 0, 0.25, 0.5, 1, 2, 3 ]:
    print '{:5.2f}  {:7.4f}'.format(x, math.erf(x))
```

For the error function, `erf(-x)  ==  -erf(x)`.

```
$ python math_erf.py

  x      erf(x)
-----    -------
-3.00   -1.0000
-2.00   -0.9953
-1.00   -0.8427
-0.50   -0.5205
-0.25   -0.2763
 0.00    0.0000
 0.25    0.2763
 0.50    0.5205
 1.00    0.8427
 2.00    0.9953
 3.00    1.0000
```

The complimentary error function is `1 - erf(x)`.

```python
import math

print '{:^5}    {:7}'.format('x', 'erfc(x)')
print '{:-^5}    {:-^7}'.format('', '')

for x in [ -3, -2, -1, -0.5, -0.25, 0, 0.25, 0.5, 1, 2, 3 ]:
    print '{:5.2f}    {:7.4f}'.format(x, math.erfc(x))
```

The implementation of `erfc()` avoids precision errors for small values of *x* when subtracting from 1.

```
$ python math_erfc.py

  x      erfc(x)
-----    -------
-3.00    2.0000
-2.00    1.9953
-1.00    1.8427
-0.50    1.5205
-0.25    1.2763
 0.00    1.0000
 0.25    0.7237
 0.50    0.4795
 1.00    0.1573
 2.00    0.0047
 3.00    0.0000
```

See Also:

math (http://docs.python.org/library/math.html) The standard library documentation for this module.

IEEE floating-point arithmetic in Python
(http://www.johndcook.com/blog/2009/07/21/ieee-arithmetic-python/) Blog post by John Cook about how special values arise and are dealt with when doing math in Python.

SciPy (http://scipy.org/) Open source libraries for scientific and mathematical calculations in Python.

Chapter 6

THE FILE SYSTEM

Python's standard library includes a large range of tools for working with files on the file system, building and parsing filenames, and examining file contents.

The first step in working with files is to determine the name of the file on which to work. Python represents filenames as simple strings, but provides tools for building them from standard, platform-independent components in `os.path`. List the contents of a directory with `listdir()` from `os`, or use `glob` to build a list of filenames from a pattern.

The filename pattern matching used by `glob` is also exposed directly through `fnmatch`, so it can be used in other contexts.

`dircache` provides an efficient way to scan and process the contents of a directory on the file system, and it is useful when processing files in situations where the names are not known in advance.

After the name of the file is identified, other characteristics, such as permissions or the file size, can be checked using `os.stat()` and the constants in `stat`.

When an application needs random access to files, `linecache` makes it easy to read lines by their line number. The contents of the file are maintained in a cache, so be careful of memory consumption.

`tempfile` is useful for cases that need to create scratch files to hold data temporarily, or before moving it to a permanent location. It provides classes to create temporary files and directories safely and securely. Names are guaranteed to be unique and include random components so they are not easily guessable.

Frequently, programs need to work on files as a whole, without regard to their content. The `shutil` module includes high-level file operations, such as copying files and directories, and setting permissions.

The `filecmp` module compares files and directories by looking at the bytes they contain, but without any special knowledge about their format.

The built-in `file` class can be used to read and write files visible on local file systems. A program's performance can suffer when it accesses large files through the `read()` and `write()` interfaces, though, since they both involve copying the data multiple times as it is moved from the disk to memory the application can see. Using `mmap` tells the operating system to use its virtual memory subsystem to map a file's contents directly into memory accessible by a program, avoiding a copy step between the operating system and the internal buffer for the `file` object.

Text data using characters not available in ASCII is usually saved in a Unicode data format. Since the standard `file` handle assumes each byte of a text file represents one character, reading Unicode text with multibyte encodings requires extra processing. The `codecs` module handles the encoding and decoding automatically, so that in many cases, a non-ASCII file can be used without any other changes.

For testing code that depends on reading or writing data from files, `StringIO` provides an in-memory stream object that behaves like a file, but that does not reside on disk.

6.1 os.path—Platform-Independent Manipulation of Filenames

> **Purpose** Parse, build, test, and otherwise work on filenames and paths.
> **Python Version** 1.4 and later

Writing code to work with files on multiple platforms is easy using the functions included in the `os.path` module. Even programs not intended to be ported between platforms should use `os.path` for reliable filename parsing.

6.1.1 Parsing Paths

The first set of functions in `os.path` can be used to parse strings representing filenames into their component parts. It is important to realize that these functions do not depend on the paths actually existing; they operate solely on the strings.

Path parsing depends on a few variables defined in `os`:

- `os.sep`—The separator between portions of the path (e.g., "/" or "\").
- `os.extsep`—The separator between a filename and the file "extension" (e.g., ".").
- `os.pardir`—The path component that means traverse the directory tree up one level (e.g., "..").
- `os.curdir`—The path component that refers to the current directory (e.g., ".").

The `split()` function breaks the path into two separate parts and returns a `tuple` with the results. The second element of the `tuple` is the last component of the path, and the first element is everything that comes before it.

```
import os.path

for path in [ '/one/two/three',
              '/one/two/three/',
              '/',
              '.',
              '']:
    print '%15s : %s' % (path, os.path.split(path))
```

When the input argument ends in `os.sep`, the "last element" of the path is an empty string.

```
$ python ospath_split.py

 /one/two/three : ('/one/two', 'three')
/one/two/three/ : ('/one/two/three', '')
              / : ('/', '')
              . : ('', '.')
                : ('', '')
```

The `basename()` function returns a value equivalent to the second part of the `split()` value.

```
import os.path

for path in [ '/one/two/three',
              '/one/two/three/',
              '/',
              '.',
              '']:
    print '%15s : %s' % (path, os.path.basename(path))
```

The full path is stripped down to the last element, whether that refers to a file or directory. If the path ends in the directory separator (`os.sep`), the base portion is considered to be empty.

```
$ python ospath_basename.py

 /one/two/three : three
/one/two/three/ :
              / :
              . : .
                :
```

The `dirname()` function returns the first part of the split path:

```
import os.path

for path in [ '/one/two/three',
              '/one/two/three/',
              '/',
              '.',
              '']:
    print '%15s : %s' % (path, os.path.dirname(path))
```

Combining the results of `basename()` with `dirname()` gives the original path.

```
$ python ospath_dirname.py

 /one/two/three : /one/two
/one/two/three/ : /one/two/three
              / : /
              . :
                :
```

`splitext()` works like `split()`, but divides the path on the extension separator, rather than the directory separator.

```
import os.path

for path in [ 'filename.txt',
              'filename',
              '/path/to/filename.txt',
              '/',
              '',
              'my-archive.tar.gz',
              'no-extension.',
              ]:
    print '%21s :' % path, os.path.splitext(path)
```

Only the last occurrence of `os.extsep` is used when looking for the extension, so if a filename has multiple extensions, the results of splitting it leaves part of the extension on the prefix.

```
$ python ospath_splitext.py

       filename.txt : ('filename', '.txt')
           filename : ('filename', '')
/path/to/filename.txt : ('/path/to/filename', '.txt')
                  / : ('/', '')
                    : ('', '')
   my-archive.tar.gz : ('my-archive.tar', '.gz')
       no-extension. : ('no-extension', '.')
```

`commonprefix()` takes a list of paths as an argument and returns a single string that represents a common prefix present in all paths. The value may represent a path that does not actually exist, and the path separator is not included in the consideration, so the prefix might not stop on a separator boundary.

```
import os.path

paths = ['/one/two/three/four',
         '/one/two/threefold',
         '/one/two/three/',
         ]
for path in paths:
    print 'PATH:', path

print
print 'PREFIX:', os.path.commonprefix(paths)
```

In this example, the common prefix string is `/one/two/three`, even though one path does not include a directory named `three`.

```
$ python ospath_commonprefix.py

PATH: /one/two/three/four
PATH: /one/two/threefold
PATH: /one/two/three/

PREFIX: /one/two/three
```

6.1.2 Building Paths

Besides taking existing paths apart, it is frequently necessary to build paths from other strings. To combine several path components into a single value, use `join()`.

```
import os.path

for parts in [ ('one', 'two', 'three'),
               ('/', 'one', 'two', 'three'),
               ('/one', '/two', '/three'),
             ]:
    print parts, ':', os.path.join(*parts)
```

If any argument to join begins with `os.sep`, all previous arguments are discarded and the new one becomes the beginning of the return value.

```
$ python ospath_join.py

('one', 'two', 'three') : one/two/three
('/', 'one', 'two', 'three') : /one/two/three
('/one', '/two', '/three') : /three
```

It is also possible to work with paths that include "variable" components that can be expanded automatically. For example, `expanduser()` converts the tilde (~) character to the name of a user's home directory.

```
import os.path

for user in [ '', 'dhellmann', 'postgresql' ]:
    lookup = '~' + user
    print '%12s : %s' % (lookup, os.path.expanduser(lookup))
```

If the user's home directory cannot be found, the string is returned unchanged, as with ~postgresql in this example.

```
$ python ospath_expanduser.py

          ~ : /Users/dhellmann
 ~dhellmann : /Users/dhellmann
~postgresql : ~postgresql
```

`expandvars()` is more general, and expands any shell environment variables present in the path.

```
import os.path
import os

os.environ['MYVAR'] = 'VALUE'

print os.path.expandvars('/path/to/$MYVAR')
```

No validation is performed to ensure that the variable value results in the name of a file that already exists.

```
$ python ospath_expandvars.py

/path/to/VALUE
```

6.1.3   Normalizing Paths

Paths assembled from separate strings using `join()` or with embedded variables might end up with extra separators or relative path components. Use `normpath()` to clean them up.

```
import os.path

for path in [ 'one//two//three',
              'one/./two/./three',
              'one/../alt/two/three',
              ]:
    print '%20s : %s' % (path, os.path.normpath(path))
```

Path segments made up of `os.curdir` and `os.pardir` are evaluated and collapsed.

```
$ python ospath_normpath.py

     one//two//three : one/two/three
   one/./two/./three : one/two/three
one/../alt/two/three : alt/two/three
```

To convert a relative path to an absolute filename, use `abspath()`.

```
import os
import os.path

os.chdir('/tmp')

for path in [ '.',
              '..',
              './one/two/three',
              '../one/two/three',
              ]:
    print '%17s : "%s"' % (path, os.path.abspath(path))
```

The result is a complete path, starting at the top of the file system tree.

```
$ python ospath_abspath.py

               . : "/private/tmp"
              .. : "/private"
./one/two/three : "/private/tmp/one/two/three"
../one/two/three : "/private/one/two/three"
```

6.1.4   File Times

Besides working with paths, `os.path` includes functions for retrieving file properties, similar to the ones returned by `os.stat()`.

```
import os.path
import time

print 'File          :', __file__
print 'Access time   :', time.ctime(os.path.getatime(__file__))
print 'Modified time:', time.ctime(os.path.getmtime(__file__))
print 'Change time   :', time.ctime(os.path.getctime(__file__))
print 'Size          :', os.path.getsize(__file__)
```

`os.path.getatime()` returns the access time, `os.path.getmtime()` returns the modification time, and `os.path.getctime()` returns the creation time. `os.path.getsize()` returns the amount of data in the file, represented in bytes.

```
$ python ospath_properties.py

File         : ospath_properties.py
Access time  : Sat Nov 27 12:19:50 2010
Modified time: Sun Nov 14 09:40:36 2010
Change time  : Tue Nov 16 08:07:32 2010
Size         : 495
```

6.1.5   Testing Files

When a program encounters a path name, it often needs to know whether the path refers to a file, a directory, or a symlink and whether it exists. os.path includes functions for testing all these conditions.

```python
import os.path

FILENAMES = [ __file__,
              os.path.dirname(__file__),
              '/',
              './broken_link',
              ]

for file in FILENAMES:
    print 'File          :', file
    print 'Absolute      :', os.path.isabs(file)
    print 'Is File?      :', os.path.isfile(file)
    print 'Is Dir?       :', os.path.isdir(file)
    print 'Is Link?      :', os.path.islink(file)
    print 'Mountpoint?   :', os.path.ismount(file)
    print 'Exists?       :', os.path.exists(file)
    print 'Link Exists?:', os.path.lexists(file)
    print
```

All test functions return Boolean values.

```
$ ln -s /does/not/exist broken_link
$ python ospath_tests.py

File          : ospath_tests.py
Absolute      : False
Is File?      : True
Is Dir?       : False
Is Link?      : False
```

```
Mountpoint? : False
Exists?     : True
Link Exists?: True

File        :
Absolute    : False
Is File?    : False
Is Dir?     : False
Is Link?    : False
Mountpoint? : False
Exists?     : False
Link Exists?: False

File        : /
Absolute    : True
Is File?    : False
Is Dir?     : True
Is Link?    : False
Mountpoint? : True
Exists?     : True
Link Exists?: True

File        : ./broken_link
Absolute    : False
Is File?    : False
Is Dir?     : False
Is Link?    : True
Mountpoint? : False
Exists?     : False
Link Exists?: True
```

6.1.6   Traversing a Directory Tree

os.path.walk() traverses all directories in a tree and calls a provided function, passing to it as arguments the directory name and the names of the contents of that directory.

```python
import os
import os.path
import pprint

def visit(arg, dirname, names):
    print dirname, arg
    for name in names:
```

```
        subname = os.path.join(dirname, name)
        if os.path.isdir(subname):
            print '  %s/' % name
        else:
            print '  %s' % name
    print

if not os.path.exists('example'):
    os.mkdir('example')
if not os.path.exists('example/one'):
    os.mkdir('example/one')

with open('example/one/file.txt', 'wt') as f:
    f.write('contents')
with open('example/two.txt', 'wt') as f:
    f.write('contents')

os.path.walk('example', visit, '(User data)')
```

This example produces a recursive directory listing, ignoring `.svn` directories.

```
$ python ospath_walk.py

example (User data)
  one/
  two.txt

example/one (User data)
  file.txt
```

See Also:
os.path (http://docs.python.org/lib/module-os.path.html) Standard library documentation for this module.
os (page 1108) The `os` module is a parent of `os.path`.
time (page 173) The `time` module includes functions to convert between the representation used by the time property functions in `os.path` and easy-to-read strings.

6.2   glob—Filename Pattern Matching

Purpose Use UNIX shell rules to find filenames matching a pattern.
Python Version 1.4 and later

Even though the `glob` API is small, the module packs a lot of power. It is useful in any situation where a program needs to look for a list of files on the file system with names matching a pattern. To create a list of filenames that all have a certain extension, prefix, or any common string in the middle, use `glob` instead of writing custom code to scan the directory contents.

The pattern rules for `glob` are not the same as the regular expressions used by the `re` module. Instead, they follow standard UNIX path expansion rules. There are only a few special characters used to implement two different wildcards and character ranges. The patterns rules are applied to segments of the filename (stopping at the path separator, /). Paths in the pattern can be relative or absolute. Shell variable names and tilde (~) are not expanded.

6.2.1   Example Data

The examples in this section assume the following test files are present in the current working directory.

```
$ python glob_maketestdata.py

dir
dir/file.txt
dir/file1.txt
dir/file2.txt
dir/filea.txt
dir/fileb.txt
dir/subdir
dir/subdir/subfile.txt
```

If these files do not exist, use `glob_maketestdata.py` in the sample code to create them before running the following examples.

6.2.2   Wildcards

An asterisk (*) matches zero or more characters in a segment of a name. For example, `dir/*`.

```
import glob
for name in glob.glob('dir/*'):
    print name
```

The pattern matches every path name (file or directory) in the directory "dir," without recursing further into subdirectories.

```
$ python glob_asterisk.py

dir/file.txt
dir/file1.txt
dir/file2.txt
dir/filea.txt
dir/fileb.txt
dir/subdir
```

To list files in a subdirectory, the subdirectory must be included in the pattern.

```
import glob

print 'Named explicitly:'
for name in glob.glob('dir/subdir/*'):
    print '\t', name

print 'Named with wildcard:'
for name in glob.glob('dir/*/*'):
    print '\t', name
```

The first case shown earlier lists the subdirectory name explicitly, while the second case depends on a wildcard to find the directory.

```
$ python glob_subdir.py

Named explicitly:
        dir/subdir/subfile.txt
Named with wildcard:
        dir/subdir/subfile.txt
```

The results, in this case, are the same. If there was another subdirectory, the wildcard would match both subdirectories and include the filenames from both.

6.2.3 Single Character Wildcard

A question mark (?) is another wildcard character. It matches any single character in that position in the name.

```
import glob

for name in glob.glob('dir/file?.txt'):
    print name
```

The previous example matches all filenames that begin with `file`, have one more character of any type, and then end with `.txt`.

```
$ python glob_question.py

dir/file1.txt
dir/file2.txt
dir/filea.txt
dir/fileb.txt
```

6.2.4 Character Ranges

Use a character range (`[a-z]`) instead of a question mark to match one of several characters. This example finds all files with a digit in the name before the extension.

```
import glob
for name in glob.glob('dir/*[0-9].*'):
    print name
```

The character range `[0-9]` matches any single digit. The range is ordered based on the character code for each letter/digit, and the dash indicates an unbroken range of sequential characters. The same range value could be written as `[0123456789]`.

```
$ python glob_charrange.py

dir/file1.txt
dir/file2.txt
```

See Also:

glob (http://docs.python.org/library/glob.html) The standard library documentation for this module.

Pattern Matching Notation
(http://www.opengroup.org/onlinepubs/000095399/utilities/xcu_chap02.html#tag_02_13) An explanation of globbing from The Open Group's Shell Command Language specification.

fnmatch (page 315) Filename-matching implementation.

6.3   linecache—Read Text Files Efficiently

Purpose Retrieve lines of text from files or imported Python modules, holding a cache of the results to make reading many lines from the same file more efficient.

Python Version 1.4 and later

The `linecache` module is used within other parts of the Python standard library when dealing with Python source files. The implementation of the cache holds the contents of files, parsed into separate lines, in memory. The API returns the requested line(s) by indexing into a `list`, and saves time over repeatedly reading the file and parsing lines to find the one desired. This method is especially useful when looking for multiple lines from the same file, such as when producing a traceback for an error report.

6.3.1   Test Data

This text produced by a Lorem Ipsum generator is used as sample input.

```python
import os
import tempfile

lorem = '''Lorem ipsum dolor sit amet, consectetuer
adipiscing elit.  Vivamus eget elit. In posuere mi non
risus. Mauris id quam posuere lectus sollicitudin
varius. Praesent at mi. Nunc eu velit. Sed augue massa,
fermentum id, nonummy a, nonummy sit amet, ligula. Curabitur
eros pede, egestas at, ultricies ac, apellentesque eu,
tellus.

Sed sed odio sed mi luctus mollis. Integer et nulla ac augue
convallis accumsan. Ut felis. Donec lectus sapien, elementum
nec, condimentum ac, interdum non, tellus. Aenean viverra,
mauris vehicula semper porttitor, ipsum odio consectetuer
lorem, ac imperdiet eros odio a sapien. Nulla mauris tellus,
aliquam non, egestas a, nonummy et, erat. Vivamus sagittis
porttitor eros.'''

def make_tempfile():
    fd, temp_file_name = tempfile.mkstemp()
    os.close(fd)
    f = open(temp_file_name, 'wt')
```

```
    try:
        f.write(lorem)
    finally:
        f.close()
    return temp_file_name

def cleanup(filename):
    os.unlink(filename)
```

6.3.2   Reading Specific Lines

The line numbers of files read by the linecache module start with 1, but normally lists start indexing the array from 0.

```
import linecache
from linecache_data import *

filename = make_tempfile()

# Pick out the same line from source and cache.
# (Notice that linecache counts from 1)
print 'SOURCE:'
print '%r' % lorem.split('\n')[4]
print
print 'CACHE:'
print '%r' % linecache.getline(filename, 5)

cleanup(filename)
```

Each line returned includes a trailing newline.

```
$ python linecache_getline.py

SOURCE:
'fermentum id, nonummy a, nonummy sit amet, ligula. Curabitur'

CACHE:
'fermentum id, nonummy a, nonummy sit amet, ligula. Curabitur\n'
```

6.3.3   Handling Blank Lines

The return value always includes the newline at the end of the line, so if the line is empty, the return value is just the newline.

```
import linecache
from linecache_data import *

filename = make_tempfile()

# Blank lines include the newline
print 'BLANK : %r' % linecache.getline(filename, 8)

cleanup(filename)
```

Line eight of the input file contains no text.

```
$ python linecache_empty_line.py

BLANK : '\n'
```

6.3.4   Error Handling

If the requested line number falls out of the range of valid lines in the file, `getline()` returns an empty string.

```
import linecache
from linecache_data import *

filename = make_tempfile()

# The cache always returns a string, and uses
# an empty string to indicate a line which does
# not exist.
not_there = linecache.getline(filename, 500)
print 'NOT THERE: %r includes %d characters' % \
    (not_there, len(not_there))

cleanup(filename)
```

The input file only has 12 lines, so requesting line 500 is like trying to read past the end of the file.

```
$ python linecache_out_of_range.py

NOT THERE: '' includes 0 characters
```

Reading from a file that does not exist is handled in the same way.

```python
import linecache

# Errors are even hidden if linecache cannot find the file
no_such_file = linecache.getline('this_file_does_not_exist.txt', 1)
print 'NO FILE: %r' % no_such_file
```

The module never raises an exception when the caller tries to read data.

```
$ python linecache_missing_file.py

NO FILE: ''
```

6.3.5 Reading Python Source Files

Since linecache is used so heavily when producing tracebacks, one of its key features is the ability to find Python source modules in the import path by specifying the base name of the module.

```python
import linecache
import os

# Look for the linecache module, using
# the built in sys.path search.
module_line = linecache.getline('linecache.py', 3)
print 'MODULE:'
print repr(module_line)

# Look at the linecache module source directly.
file_src = linecache.__file__
if file_src.endswith('.pyc'):
    file_src = file_src[:-1]
print '\nFILE:'
```

```
with open(file_src, 'r') as f:
    file_line = f.readlines()[2]
print repr(file_line)
```

The cache population code in `linecache` searches `sys.path` for the named module if it cannot find a file with that name in the current directory. This example looks for `linecache.py`. Since there is no copy in the current directory, the file from the standard library is found instead.

```
$ python linecache_path_search.py

MODULE:
'This is intended to read lines from modules imported -- hence if a
filename\n'

FILE:
'This is intended to read lines from modules imported -- hence if a
filename\n'
```

See Also:
linecache (http://docs.python.org/library/linecache.html) The standard library documentation for this module.
http://www.ipsum.com/ Lorem Ipsum generator.

6.4   tempfile—Temporary File System Objects

Purpose Create temporary file system objects.
Python Version 1.4 and later

Creating temporary files with unique names securely, so they cannot be guessed by someone wanting to break the application or steal the data, is challenging. The `tempfile` module provides several functions for creating temporary file system resources securely. `TemporaryFile()` opens and returns an unnamed file, `NamedTemporaryFile()` opens and returns a named file, and `mkdtemp()` creates a temporary directory and returns its name.

6.4.1   Temporary Files

Applications that need temporary files to store data, without needing to share those files with other programs, should use the `TemporaryFile()` function to create the files.

The function creates a file, and on platforms where it is possible, unlinks it immediately. This makes it impossible for another program to find or open the file, since there is no reference to it in the file system table. The file created by `TemporaryFile()` is removed automatically when it is closed, whether by calling `close()` or by using the context manager API and `with` statement.

```python
import os
import tempfile

print 'Building a filename with PID:'
filename = '/tmp/guess_my_name.%s.txt' % os.getpid()
temp = open(filename, 'w+b')
try:
    print 'temp:'
    print '  ', temp
    print 'temp.name:'
    print '  ', temp.name
finally:
    temp.close()
    # Clean up the temporary file yourself
    os.remove(filename)

print
print 'TemporaryFile:'
temp = tempfile.TemporaryFile()
try:
    print 'temp:'
    print '  ', temp
    print 'temp.name:'
    print '  ', temp.name
finally:
    # Automatically cleans up the file
    temp.close()
```

This example illustrates the difference in creating a temporary file using a common pattern for making up a name, versus using the `TemporaryFile()` function. The file returned by `TemporaryFile()` has no name.

```
$ python tempfile_TemporaryFile.py

Building a filename with PID:
temp:
```

```
    <open file '/tmp/guess_my_name.1074.txt', mode 'w+b' at
 0x100d881e0>
temp.name:
    /tmp/guess_my_name.1074.txt

TemporaryFile:
temp:
    <open file '<fdopen>', mode 'w+b' at 0x100d88780>
temp.name:
    <fdopen>
```

By default, the file handle is created with mode `'w+b'` so it behaves consistently on all platforms, and the caller can write to it and read from it.

```python
import os
import tempfile

with tempfile.TemporaryFile() as temp:
    temp.write('Some data')
    temp.seek(0)

    print temp.read()
```

After writing, the file handle must be "rewound" using `seek()` in order to read the data back from it.

```
$ python tempfile_TemporaryFile_binary.py

Some data
```

To open the file in text mode, set *mode* to `'w+t'` when the file is created.

```python
import tempfile

with tempfile.TemporaryFile(mode='w+t') as f:
    f.writelines(['first\n', 'second\n'])
    f.seek(0)

    for line in f:
        print line.rstrip()
```

The file handle treats the data as text.

```
$ python tempfile_TemporaryFile_text.py

first
second
```

6.4.2   Named Files

There are situations where having a named temporary file is important. For applications spanning multiple processes, or even hosts, naming the file is the simplest way to pass it between parts of the application. The `NamedTemporaryFile()` function creates a file without unlinking it, so the file retains its name (accessed with the `name` attribute).

```python
import os
import tempfile

with tempfile.NamedTemporaryFile() as temp:
    print 'temp:'
    print '  ', temp
    print 'temp.name:'
    print '  ', temp.name

print 'Exists after close:', os.path.exists(temp.name)
```

The file is removed after the handle is closed.

```
$ python tempfile_NamedTemporaryFile.py

temp:
    <open file '<fdopen>', mode 'w+b' at 0x100d881e0>
temp.name:
    /var/folders/9R/9R1t+tR02Raxzk+F71Q50U+++Uw/-Tmp-/tmp926BkT
Exists after close: False
```

6.4.3   Temporary Directories

When several temporary files are needed, it may be more convenient to create a single temporary directory with `mkdtemp()` and open all the files in that directory.

```
import os
import tempfile

directory_name = tempfile.mkdtemp()
print directory_name
# Clean up the directory
os.removedirs(directory_name)
```

Since the directory is not "opened" per se, it must be removed explicitly when it is no longer needed.

```
$ python tempfile_mkdtemp.py

/var/folders/9R/9R1t+tR02Raxzk+F71Q50U+++Uw/-Tmp-/tmpA7DKtP
```

6.4.4 Predicting Names

While less secure than strictly anonymous temporary files, including a predictable portion in the name makes it possible to find the file and examine it for debugging purposes. All functions described so far take three arguments to control the filenames to some degree. Names are generated using the following formula.

```
dir + prefix + random + suffix
```

All values except *random* can be passed as arguments to `TemporaryFile()`, `NamedTemporaryFile()`, and `mkdtemp()`. For example:

```
import tempfile

with tempfile.NamedTemporaryFile(
    suffix='_suffix', prefix='prefix_', dir='/tmp',
    ) as temp:
    print 'temp:'
    print '  ', temp
    print 'temp.name:'
    print '  ', temp.name
```

The *prefix* and *suffix* arguments are combined with a random string of characters to build the filename, and the *dir* argument is taken as is and used as the location of the new file.

```
$ python tempfile_NamedTemporaryFile_args.py
```

```
temp:
   <open file '<fdopen>', mode 'w+b' at 0x100d881e0>
temp.name:
   /tmp/prefix_kjvHYS_suffix
```

6.4.5 Temporary File Location

If an explicit destination is not given using the *dir* argument, the path used for the temporary files will vary based on the current platform and settings. The tempfile module includes two functions for querying the settings being used at runtime.

```
import tempfile
```

```
print 'gettempdir():', tempfile.gettempdir()
print 'gettempprefix():', tempfile.gettempprefix()
```

gettempdir() returns the default directory that will hold all temporary files and gettempprefix() returns the string prefix for new file and directory names.

```
$ python tempfile_settings.py
```

```
gettempdir(): /var/folders/9R/9R1t+tR02Raxzk+F71Q50U+++Uw/-Tmp-
gettempprefix(): tmp
```

The value returned by gettempdir() is set based on a straightforward algorithm of looking through five locations for the first place the current process can create a file. This is the search list.

1. The environment variable TMPDIR
2. The environment variable TEMP
3. The environment variable TMP
4. A fallback, based on the platform. (RiscOS uses Wimp$ScrapDir. Windows uses the first available of C:\TEMP, C:\TMP, \TEMP, or \TMP. Other platforms use /tmp, /var/tmp, or /usr/tmp.)
5. If no other directory can be found, the current working directory is used.

```
import tempfile
```

```
tempfile.tempdir = '/I/changed/this/path'
print 'gettempdir():', tempfile.gettempdir()
```

Programs that need to use a global location for all temporary files without using any of these environment variables should set `tempfile.tempdir` directly by assigning a value to the variable.

```
$ python tempfile_tempdir.py

gettempdir(): /I/changed/this/path
```

See Also:
tempfile (http://docs.python.org/lib/module-tempfile.html) Standard library documentation for this module.

6.5 shutil—High-Level File Operations

> **Purpose** High-level file operations.
> **Python Version** 1.4 and later

The `shutil` module includes high-level file operations such as copying and setting permissions.

6.5.1 Copying Files

`copyfile()` copies the contents of the source to the destination and raises `IOError` if it does not have permission to write to the destination file.

```
from shutil import *
from glob import glob

print 'BEFORE:', glob('shutil_copyfile.*')
copyfile('shutil_copyfile.py', 'shutil_copyfile.py.copy')
print 'AFTER:', glob('shutil_copyfile.*')
```

Because the function opens the input file for reading, regardless of its type, special files (such as UNIX device nodes) cannot be copied as new special files with `copyfile()`.

```
$ python shutil_copyfile.py

BEFORE: ['shutil_copyfile.py']
AFTER: ['shutil_copyfile.py', 'shutil_copyfile.py.copy']
```

The implementation of copyfile() uses the lower-level function copy-fileobj(). While the arguments to copyfile() are filenames, the arguments to copyfileobj() are open file handles. The optional third argument is a buffer length to use for reading in blocks.

```python
from shutil import *
import os
from StringIO import StringIO
import sys

class VerboseStringIO(StringIO):
    def read(self, n=-1):
        next = StringIO.read(self, n)
        print 'read(%d) bytes' % n
        return next

lorem_ipsum = '''Lorem ipsum dolor sit amet, consectetuer adipiscing
elit.  Vestibulum aliquam mollis dolor. Donec vulputate nunc ut diam.
Ut rutrum mi vel sem. Vestibulum ante ipsum.'''

print 'Default:'
input = VerboseStringIO(lorem_ipsum)
output = StringIO()
copyfileobj(input, output)

print

print 'All at once:'
input = VerboseStringIO(lorem_ipsum)
output = StringIO()
copyfileobj(input, output, -1)

print

print 'Blocks of 256:'
input = VerboseStringIO(lorem_ipsum)
output = StringIO()
copyfileobj(input, output, 256)
```

The default behavior is to read using large blocks. Use -1 to read all the input at one time, or use another positive integer to set a specific block size. This example uses several different block sizes to show the effect.

```
$ python shutil_copyfileobj.py

Default:
read(16384) bytes
read(16384) bytes

All at once:
read(-1) bytes
read(-1) bytes

Blocks of 256:
read(256) bytes
read(256) bytes
```

The `copy()` function interprets the output name like the UNIX command line tool `cp`. If the named destination refers to a directory instead of a file, a new file is created in the directory using the base name of the source.

```
from shutil import *
import os

os.mkdir('example')
print 'BEFORE:', os.listdir('example')
copy('shutil_copy.py', 'example')
print 'AFTER:', os.listdir('example')
```

The permissions of the file are copied along with the contents.

```
$ python shutil_copy.py

BEFORE: []
AFTER: ['shutil_copy.py']
```

`copy2()` works like `copy()`, but includes the access and modification times in the metadata copied to the new file.

```
from shutil import *
import os
import time
```

```
def show_file_info(filename):
    stat_info = os.stat(filename)
    print '\tMode    :', stat_info.st_mode
    print '\tCreated :', time.ctime(stat_info.st_ctime)
    print '\tAccessed:', time.ctime(stat_info.st_atime)
    print '\tModified:', time.ctime(stat_info.st_mtime)

os.mkdir('example')
print 'SOURCE:'
show_file_info('shutil_copy2.py')
copy2('shutil_copy2.py', 'example')
print 'DEST:'
show_file_info('example/shutil_copy2.py')
```

The new file has all the same characteristics as the old version.

```
$ python shutil_copy2.py

SOURCE:
        Mode    : 33188
        Created : Sat Dec  4 10:41:32 2010
        Accessed: Sat Dec  4 17:41:01 2010
        Modified: Sun Nov 14 09:40:36 2010
DEST:
        Mode    : 33188
        Created : Sat Dec  4 17:41:01 2010
        Accessed: Sat Dec  4 17:41:01 2010
        Modified: Sun Nov 14 09:40:36 2010
```

6.5.2 Copying File Metadata

By default when a new file is created under UNIX, it receives permissions based on the umask of the current user. To copy the permissions from one file to another, use copymode().

```
from shutil import *
from commands import *
import os

with open('file_to_change.txt', 'wt') as f:
    f.write('content')
os.chmod('file_to_change.txt', 0444)
```

```
print 'BEFORE:'
print getstatus('file_to_change.txt')
copymode('shutil_copymode.py', 'file_to_change.txt')
print 'AFTER :'
print getstatus('file_to_change.txt')
```

First, create a file to be modified.

```
#!/bin/sh
# Set up file needed by shutil_copymode.py
touch file_to_change.txt
chmod ugo+w file_to_change.txt
```

Then, run the example script to change the permissions.

```
$ python shutil_copymode.py

BEFORE:
-r--r--r--  1 dhellmann   dhellmann   7 Dec   4 17:41 file_to_change.txt
AFTER :
-rw-r--r--  1 dhellmann   dhellmann   7 Dec   4 17:41 file_to_change.txt
```

To copy other metadata about the file use copystat().

```
from shutil import *
import os
import time

def show_file_info(filename):
    stat_info = os.stat(filename)
    print '\tMode    :', stat_info.st_mode
    print '\tCreated :', time.ctime(stat_info.st_ctime)
    print '\tAccessed:', time.ctime(stat_info.st_atime)
    print '\tModified:', time.ctime(stat_info.st_mtime)

with open('file_to_change.txt', 'wt') as f:
    f.write('content')
os.chmod('file_to_change.txt', 0444)

print 'BEFORE:'
show_file_info('file_to_change.txt')
copystat('shutil_copystat.py', 'file_to_change.txt')
```

```
print 'AFTER:'
show_file_info('file_to_change.txt')
```

Only the permissions and dates associated with the file are duplicated with `copystat()`.

```
$ python shutil_copystat.py

BEFORE:
        Mode    : 33060
        Created : Sat Dec  4 17:41:01 2010
        Accessed: Sat Dec  4 17:41:01 2010
        Modified: Sat Dec  4 17:41:01 2010
AFTER:
        Mode    : 33188
        Created : Sat Dec  4 17:41:01 2010
        Accessed: Sat Dec  4 17:41:01 2010
        Modified: Sun Nov 14 09:45:12 2010
```

6.5.3   Working with Directory Trees

`shutil` includes three functions for working with directory trees. To copy a directory from one place to another, use `copytree()`. It recurses through the source directory tree, copying files to the destination. The destination directory must not exist in advance.

> **Note:** The documentation for `copytree()` says it should be considered a sample implementation, rather than a tool. Consider starting with the current implementation and making it more robust, or adding features like a progress meter, before using it.

```
from shutil import *
from commands import *

print 'BEFORE:'
print getoutput('ls -rlast /tmp/example')
copytree('../shutil', '/tmp/example')
print '\nAFTER:'
print getoutput('ls -rlast /tmp/example')
```

The *symlinks* argument controls whether symbolic links are copied as links or as files. The default is to copy the contents to new files. If the option is true, new symlinks are created within the destination tree.

```
$ python shutil_copytree.py

BEFORE:
ls: /tmp/example: No such file or directory

AFTER:
total 136
 8 -rwxr-xr-x   1 dhellmann   wheel    109 Oct 28 07:33 shutil_copymode.sh
 8 -rw-r--r--   1 dhellmann   wheel   1313 Nov 14 09:39 shutil_rmtree.py
 8 -rw-r--r--   1 dhellmann   wheel   1300 Nov 14 09:39 shutil_copyfile.py
 8 -rw-r--r--   1 dhellmann   wheel   1276 Nov 14 09:39 shutil_copy.py
 8 -rw-r--r--   1 dhellmann   wheel   1140 Nov 14 09:39 __init__.py
 8 -rw-r--r--   1 dhellmann   wheel   1595 Nov 14 09:40 shutil_copy2.py
 8 -rw-r--r--   1 dhellmann   wheel   1729 Nov 14 09:45 shutil_copystat.py
 8 -rw-r--r--   1 dhellmann   wheel      7 Nov 14 09:45 file_to_change.txt
 8 -rw-r--r--   1 dhellmann   wheel   1324 Nov 14 09:45 shutil_move.py
 8 -rw-r--r--   1 dhellmann   wheel    419 Nov 27 12:49 shutil_copymode.py
 8 -rw-r--r--   1 dhellmann   wheel   1331 Dec  1 21:51 shutil_copytree.py
 8 -rw-r--r--   1 dhellmann   wheel    816 Dec  4 17:39 shutil_copyfileobj.py
 8 -rw-r--r--   1 dhellmann   wheel      8 Dec  4 17:39 example.out
24 -rw-r--r--   1 dhellmann   wheel   9767 Dec  4 17:40 index.rst
 8 -rw-r--r--   1 dhellmann   wheel   1300 Dec  4 17:41 shutil_copyfile.py.copy
 0 drwxr-xr-x   3 dhellmann   wheel    102 Dec  4 17:41 example
 0 drwxrwxrwt  18 root        wheel    612 Dec  4 17:41 ..
 0 drwxr-xr-x  18 dhellmann   wheel    612 Dec  4 17:41 .
```

To remove a directory and its contents, use `rmtree()`.

```
from shutil import *
from commands import *

print 'BEFORE:'
print getoutput('ls -rlast /tmp/example')
rmtree('/tmp/example')
print 'AFTER:'
print getoutput('ls -rlast /tmp/example')
```

Errors are raised as exceptions by default, but can be ignored if the second argument is true. A special error-handler function can be provided in the third argument.

```
$ python shutil_rmtree.py

BEFORE:
total 136
 8 -rwxr-xr-x   1 dhellmann   wheel    109 Oct 28 07:33 shutil_copymode.sh
```

```
 8 -rw-r--r--   1 dhellmann   wheel   1313 Nov 14 09:39 shutil_rmtree.py
 8 -rw-r--r--   1 dhellmann   wheel   1300 Nov 14 09:39 shutil_copyfile.py
 8 -rw-r--r--   1 dhellmann   wheel   1276 Nov 14 09:39 shutil_copy.py
 8 -rw-r--r--   1 dhellmann   wheel   1140 Nov 14 09:39 __init__.py
 8 -rw-r--r--   1 dhellmann   wheel   1595 Nov 14 09:40 shutil_copy2.py
 8 -rw-r--r--   1 dhellmann   wheel   1729 Nov 14 09:45 shutil_copystat.py
 8 -rw-r--r--   1 dhellmann   wheel      7 Nov 14 09:45 file_to_change.txt
 8 -rw-r--r--   1 dhellmann   wheel   1324 Nov 14 09:45 shutil_move.py
 8 -rw-r--r--   1 dhellmann   wheel    419 Nov 27 12:49 shutil_copymode.py
 8 -rw-r--r--   1 dhellmann   wheel   1331 Dec  1 21:51 shutil_copytree.py
 8 -rw-r--r--   1 dhellmann   wheel    816 Dec  4 17:39 shutil_copyfileobj.py
 8 -rw-r--r--   1 dhellmann   wheel      8 Dec  4 17:39 example.out
24 -rw-r--r--   1 dhellmann   wheel   9767 Dec  4 17:40 index.rst
 8 -rw-r--r--   1 dhellmann   wheel   1300 Dec  4 17:41 shutil_copyfile.py.copy
 0 drwxr-xr-x   3 dhellmann   wheel    102 Dec  4 17:41 example
 0 drwxrwxrwt  18 root        wheel    612 Dec  4 17:41 ..
 0 drwxr-xr-x  18 dhellmann   wheel    612 Dec  4 17:41 .
AFTER:
ls: /tmp/example: No such file or directory
```

To move a file or directory from one place to another, use `move()`.

```
from shutil import *
from glob import glob

with open('example.txt', 'wt') as f:
    f.write('contents')

print 'BEFORE: ', glob('example*')
move('example.txt', 'example.out')
print 'AFTER : ', glob('example*')
```

The semantics are similar to those of the UNIX command **mv**. If the source and destination are within the same file system, the source is renamed. Otherwise, the source is copied to the destination and then the source is removed.

```
$ python shutil_move.py

BEFORE:  ['example.txt']
AFTER :  ['example.out']
```

See Also:

shutil (http://docs.python.org/lib/module-shutil.html) Standard library documentation for this module.

6.6   mmap—Memory-Map Files

Purpose Memory-map files instead of reading the contents directly.
Python Version 2.1 and later

Memory-mapping a file uses the operating system virtual memory system to access the data on the file system directly, instead of using normal I/O functions. Memory-mapping typically improves I/O performance because it does not involve a separate system call for each access and it does not require copying data between buffers—the memory is accessed directly by both the kernel and the user application.

Memory-mapped files can be treated as mutable strings or file-like objects, depending on the need. A mapped file supports the expected file API methods, such as `close()`, `flush()`, `read()`, `readline()`, `seek()`, `tell()`, and `write()`. It also supports the string API, with features such as slicing and methods like `find()`.

All the examples use the text file `lorem.txt`, containing a bit of Lorem Ipsum. For reference, the text of the file follows.

```
Lorem ipsum dolor sit amet, consectetuer adipiscing elit. Donec
egestas, enim et consectetuer ullamcorper, lectus ligula rutrum leo,
a elementum elit tortor eu quam. Duis tincidunt nisi ut ante. Nulla
facilisi. Sed tristique eros eu libero. Pellentesque vel
arcu. Vivamus purus orci, iaculis ac, suscipit sit amet, pulvinar eu,
lacus. Praesent placerat tortor sed nisl. Nunc blandit diam egestas
dui. Pellentesque habitant morbi tristique senectus et netus et
malesuada fames ac turpis egestas. Aliquam viverra fringilla
leo. Nulla feugiat augue eleifend nulla. Vivamus mauris. Vivamus sed
mauris in nibh placerat egestas. Suspendisse potenti. Mauris
massa. Ut eget velit auctor tortor blandit sollicitudin. Suspendisse
imperdiet justo.
```

> **Note:** There are differences in the arguments and behaviors for `mmap()` between UNIX and Windows. These differences are not fully discussed here. For more details, refer to the standard library documentation.

6.6.1   Reading

Use the `mmap()` function to create a memory-mapped file. The first argument is a file descriptor, either from the `fileno()` method of a `file` object or from `os.open()`. The caller is responsible for opening the file before invoking `mmap()` and closing it after it is no longer needed.

The second argument to mmap() is a size in bytes for the portion of the file to map. If the value is 0, the entire file is mapped. If the size is larger than the current size of the file, the file is extended.

> **Note:** Windows does not support creating a zero-length mapping.

An optional keyword argument, *access*, is supported by both platforms. Use ACCESS_READ for read-only access, ACCESS_WRITE for write-through (assignments to memory go directly to the file), or ACCESS_COPY for copy-on-write (assignments to memory are not written to the file).

```
import mmap
import contextlib

with open('lorem.txt', 'r') as f:
    with contextlib.closing(mmap.mmap(f.fileno(), 0,
                                      access=mmap.ACCESS_READ)
                            ) as m:
        print 'First 10 bytes via read :', m.read(10)
        print 'First 10 bytes via slice:', m[:10]
        print '2nd   10 bytes via read :', m.read(10)
```

The file pointer tracks the last byte accessed through a slice operation. In this example, the pointer moves ahead 10 bytes after the first read. It is then reset to the beginning of the file by the slice operation and moved ahead 10 bytes again by the slice. After the slice operation, calling read() again gives bytes 11–20 in the file.

```
$ python mmap_read.py

First 10 bytes via read : Lorem ipsu
First 10 bytes via slice: Lorem ipsu
2nd   10 bytes via read : m dolor si
```

6.6.2 Writing

To set up the memory-mapped file to receive updates, start by opening it for appending with mode 'r+' (not 'w') before mapping it. Then use any of the API methods that change the data (write(), assignment to a slice, etc.).

The next example uses the default access mode of ACCESS_WRITE and assigns to a slice to modify part of a line in place.

```python
import mmap
import shutil
import contextlib

# Copy the example file
shutil.copyfile('lorem.txt', 'lorem_copy.txt')

word = 'consectetuer'
reversed = word[::-1]
print 'Looking for     :', word
print 'Replacing with :', reversed

with open('lorem_copy.txt', 'r+') as f:
    with contextlib.closing(mmap.mmap(f.fileno(), 0)) as m:
        print 'Before:'
        print m.readline().rstrip()
        m.seek(0)  # rewind

        loc = m.find(word)
        m[loc:loc+len(word)] = reversed
        m.flush()

        m.seek(0)  # rewind
        print 'After :'
        print m.readline().rstrip()

        f.seek(0)  # rewind
        print 'File  :'
        print f.readline().rstrip()
```

The word "consectetuer" is replaced in the middle of the first line in memory and in the file.

```
$ python mmap_write_slice.py

Looking for     : consectetuer
Replacing with : reutetcesnoc
```

```
Before:
Lorem ipsum dolor sit amet, consectetuer adipiscing elit. Donec
After :
Lorem ipsum dolor sit amet, reutetcesnoc adipiscing elit. Donec
File  :
Lorem ipsum dolor sit amet, reutetcesnoc adipiscing elit. Donec
```

Copy Mode

Using the access setting ACCESS_COPY does not write changes to the file on disk.

```python
import mmap
import shutil
import contextlib

# Copy the example file
shutil.copyfile('lorem.txt', 'lorem_copy.txt')

word = 'consectetuer'
reversed = word[::-1]

with open('lorem_copy.txt', 'r+') as f:
    with contextlib.closing(mmap.mmap(f.fileno(), 0,
                                      access=mmap.ACCESS_COPY)
                            ) as m:
        print 'Memory Before:'
        print m.readline().rstrip()
        print 'File Before  :'
        print f.readline().rstrip()
        print

        m.seek(0)  # rewind
        loc = m.find(word)
        m[loc:loc+len(word)] = reversed

        m.seek(0)  # rewind
        print 'Memory After :'
        print m.readline().rstrip()

        f.seek(0)
        print 'File After   :'
        print f.readline().rstrip()
```

It is necessary to rewind the file handle in this example separately from the mmap handle, because the internal state of the two objects is maintained separately.

```
$ python mmap_write_copy.py

Memory Before:
Lorem ipsum dolor sit amet, consectetuer adipiscing elit. Donec
File Before  :
Lorem ipsum dolor sit amet, consectetuer adipiscing elit. Donec

Memory After :
Lorem ipsum dolor sit amet, reutetcesnoc adipiscing elit. Donec
File After   :
Lorem ipsum dolor sit amet, consectetuer adipiscing elit. Donec
```

6.6.3   Regular Expressions

Since a memory-mapped file can act like a string, it can be used with other modules that operate on strings, such as regular expressions. This example finds all sentences with "nulla" in them.

```
import mmap
import re
import contextlib

pattern = re.compile(r'(\.\W+)?([^.]?nulla[^.]*?\.)',
                     re.DOTALL | re.IGNORECASE | re.MULTILINE)

with open('lorem.txt', 'r') as f:
    with contextlib.closing(mmap.mmap(f.fileno(), 0,
                                      access=mmap.ACCESS_READ)
                            ) as m:
        for match in pattern.findall(m):
            print match[1].replace('\n', ' ')
```

Because the pattern includes two groups, the return value from findall() is a sequence of tuples. The **print** statement pulls out the matching sentence and replaces newlines with spaces so each result prints on a single line.

```
$ python mmap_regex.py

Nulla facilisi.
Nulla feugiat augue eleifend nulla.
```

See Also:

mmap (http://docs.python.org/lib/module-mmap.html) Standard library documentation for this module.

os (page 1108) The os module.

contextlib (page 163) Use the closing() function to create a context manager for a memory-mapped file.

re (page 13) Regular expressions.

6.7 codecs—String Encoding and Decoding

Purpose Encoders and decoders for converting text between different representations.
Python Version 2.1 and later

The codecs module provides stream interfaces and file interfaces for transcoding data. It is most commonly used to work with Unicode text, but other encodings are also available for other purposes.

6.7.1 Unicode Primer

CPython 2.x supports two types of strings for working with text data. Old-style str instances use a single 8-bit byte to represent each character of the string using its ASCII code. In contrast, unicode strings are managed internally as a sequence of Unicode *code points*. The code-point values are saved as a sequence of two or four bytes each, depending on the options given when Python is compiled. Both unicode and str are derived from a common base class and support a similar API.

When unicode strings are output, they are encoded using one of several standard schemes so that the sequence of bytes can be reconstructed as the same text string later. The bytes of the encoded value are not necessarily the same as the code-point values, and the encoding defines a way to translate between the two value sets. Reading Unicode data also requires knowing the encoding so that the incoming bytes can be converted to the internal representation used by the unicode class.

The most common encodings for Western languages are UTF-8 and UTF-16, which use sequences of one- and two-byte values, respectively, to represent each code point. Other encodings can be more efficient for storing languages where most of the characters are represented by code points that do not fit into two bytes.

See Also:
For more introductory information about Unicode, refer to the list of references at the end of this section. The *Python Unicode HOWTO* is especially helpful.

Encodings

The best way to understand encodings is to look at the different series of bytes produced by encoding the same string in different ways. The following examples use this function to format the byte string to make it easier to read.

```
import binascii

def to_hex(t, nbytes):
    """Format text t as a sequence of nbyte long values
    separated by spaces.
    """
    chars_per_item = nbytes * 2
    hex_version = binascii.hexlify(t)
    return ' '.join(
        hex_version[start:start + chars_per_item]
        for start in xrange(0, len(hex_version), chars_per_item)
        )

if __name__ == '__main__':
    print to_hex('abcdef', 1)
    print to_hex('abcdef', 2)
```

The function uses `binascii` to get a hexadecimal representation of the input byte string and then insert a space between every *nbytes* bytes before returning the value.

```
$ python codecs_to_hex.py

61 62 63 64 65 66
6162 6364 6566
```

The first encoding example begins by printing the text `'pi: π'` using the raw representation of the `unicode` class. The π character is replaced with the expression for its Unicode code point, \u03c0. The next two lines encode the string as UTF-8 and UTF-16, respectively, and show the hexadecimal values resulting from the encoding.

```
from codecs_to_hex import to_hex

text = u'pi: π'

print 'Raw    :', repr(text)
print 'UTF-8 :', to_hex(text.encode('utf-8'), 1)
print 'UTF-16:', to_hex(text.encode('utf-16'), 2)
```

The result of encoding a unicode string is a str object.

```
$ python codecs_encodings.py

Raw    : u'pi: \u03c0'
UTF-8 : 70 69 3a 20 cf 80
UTF-16: fffe 7000 6900 3a00 2000 c003
```

Given a sequence of encoded bytes as a str instance, the decode() method translates them to code points and returns the sequence as a unicode instance.

```
from codecs_to_hex import to_hex

text = u'pi: π'
encoded = text.encode('utf-8')
decoded = encoded.decode('utf-8')

print 'Original :', repr(text)
print 'Encoded  :', to_hex(encoded, 1), type(encoded)
print 'Decoded  :', repr(decoded), type(decoded)
```

The choice of encoding used does not change the output type.

```
$ python codecs_decode.py

Original : u'pi: \u03c0'
Encoded  : 70 69 3a 20 cf 80 <type 'str'>
Decoded  : u'pi: \u03c0' <type 'unicode'>
```

> **Note:** The default encoding is set during the interpreter start-up process, when `site` is loaded. Refer to the *Unicode Defaults* section from the discussion of `sys` for a description of the default encoding settings.

6.7.2   Working with Files

Encoding and decoding strings is especially important when dealing with I/O operations. Whether writing to a file, a socket, or another stream, the data must use the proper encoding. In general, all text data needs to be decoded from its byte representation as it is read and encoded from the internal values to a specific representation as it is written. A program can explicitly encode and decode data, but depending on the encoding used, it can be nontrivial to determine whether enough bytes have been read in order to fully decode the data. `codecs` provides classes that manage the data encoding and decoding, so applications do not have to do that work.

The simplest interface provided by `codecs` is a replacement for the built-in `open()` function. The new version works just like the built-in function, but adds two new arguments to specify the encoding and desired error-handling technique.

```
from codecs_to_hex import to_hex

import codecs
import sys

encoding = sys.argv[1]
filename = encoding + '.txt'

print 'Writing to', filename
with codecs.open(filename, mode='wt', encoding=encoding) as f:
    f.write(u'pi: \u03c0')

# Determine the byte grouping to use for to_hex()
nbytes = { 'utf-8':1,
           'utf-16':2,
           'utf-32':4,
           }.get(encoding, 1)

# Show the raw bytes in the file
print 'File contents:'
with open(filename, mode='rt') as f:
    print to_hex(f.read(), nbytes)
```

This example starts with a `unicode` string with the code point for π and saves the text to a file using an encoding specified on the command line.

```
$ python codecs_open_write.py utf-8

Writing to utf-8.txt
File contents:
70 69 3a 20 cf 80

$ python codecs_open_write.py utf-16

Writing to utf-16.txt
File contents:
fffe 7000 6900 3a00 2000 c003

$ python codecs_open_write.py utf-32

Writing to utf-32.txt
File contents:
fffe0000 70000000 69000000 3a000000 20000000 c0030000
```

Reading the data with `open()` is straightforward, with one catch: the encoding must be known in advance, in order to set up the decoder correctly. Some data formats, such as XML, specify the encoding as part of the file, but usually it is up to the application to manage. `codecs` simply takes the encoding as an argument and assumes it is correct.

```
import codecs
import sys

encoding = sys.argv[1]
filename = encoding + '.txt'

print 'Reading from', filename
with codecs.open(filename, mode='rt', encoding=encoding) as f:
    print repr(f.read())
```

This example reads the files created by the previous program and prints the representation of the resulting `unicode` object to the console.

```
$ python codecs_open_read.py utf-8

Reading from utf-8.txt
u'pi: \u03c0'
```

```
$ python codecs_open_read.py utf-16

Reading from utf-16.txt
u'pi: \u03c0'

$ python codecs_open_read.py utf-32

Reading from utf-32.txt
u'pi: \u03c0'
```

6.7.3 Byte Order

Multibyte encodings, such as UTF-16 and UTF-32, pose a problem when transferring data between different computer systems, either by copying a file directly or using network communication. Different systems use different ordering of the high- and low-order bytes. This characteristic of the data, known as its *endianness*, depends on factors such as the hardware architecture and choices made by the operating system and application developer. There is not always a way to know in advance what byte order to use for a given set of data, so the multibyte encodings include a *byte-order marker* (BOM) as the first few bytes of encoded output. For example, UTF-16 is defined in such a way that 0xFFFE and 0xFEFF are not valid characters and can be used to indicate the byte-order. codecs defines constants for the byte-order markers used by UTF-16 and UTF-32.

```
import codecs
from codecs_to_hex import to_hex

for name in [ 'BOM', 'BOM_BE', 'BOM_LE',
              'BOM_UTF8',
              'BOM_UTF16', 'BOM_UTF16_BE', 'BOM_UTF16_LE',
              'BOM_UTF32', 'BOM_UTF32_BE', 'BOM_UTF32_LE',
              ]:
    print '{:12} : {}'.format(name, to_hex(getattr(codecs, name), 2))
```

BOM, BOM_UTF16, and BOM_UTF32 are automatically set to the appropriate big-endian or little-endian values, depending on the current system's native byte order.

```
$ python codecs_bom.py

BOM            : fffe
```

```
BOM_BE          : feff
BOM_LE          : fffe
BOM_UTF8        : efbb bf
BOM_UTF16       : fffe
BOM_UTF16_BE    : feff
BOM_UTF16_LE    : fffe
BOM_UTF32       : fffe 0000
BOM_UTF32_BE    : 0000 feff
BOM_UTF32_LE    : fffe 0000
```

Byte ordering is detected and handled automatically by the decoders in `codecs`, but an explicit ordering can be specified when encoding.

```python
import codecs
from codecs_to_hex import to_hex

# Pick the nonnative version of UTF-16 encoding
if codecs.BOM_UTF16 == codecs.BOM_UTF16_BE:
    bom = codecs.BOM_UTF16_LE
    encoding = 'utf_16_le'
else:
    bom = codecs.BOM_UTF16_BE
    encoding = 'utf_16_be'

print 'Native order  :', to_hex(codecs.BOM_UTF16, 2)
print 'Selected order:', to_hex(bom, 2)

# Encode the text.
encoded_text = u'pi: \u03c0'.encode(encoding)
print '{:14}: {}'.format(encoding, to_hex(encoded_text, 2))

with open('nonnative-encoded.txt', mode='wb') as f:
    # Write the selected byte-order marker.  It is not included
    # in the encoded text because the byte order was given
    # explicitly when selecting the encoding.
    f.write(bom)
    # Write the byte string for the encoded text.
    f.write(encoded_text)
```

`codecs_bom_create_file.py` figures out the native byte ordering and then uses the alternate form explicitly so the next example can demonstrate auto-detection while reading.

```
$ python codecs_bom_create_file.py

Native order  : fffe
Selected order: feff
utf_16_be     : 0070 0069 003a 0020 03c0
```

`codecs_bom_detection.py` does not specify a byte order when opening the file, so the decoder uses the BOM value in the first two bytes of the file to determine it.

```
import codecs
from codecs_to_hex import to_hex

# Look at the raw data
with open('nonnative-encoded.txt', mode='rb') as f:
    raw_bytes = f.read()

print 'Raw     :', to_hex(raw_bytes, 2)

# Reopen the file and let codecs detect the BOM
with codecs.open('nonnative-encoded.txt',
                 mode='rt',
                 encoding='utf-16',
                 ) as f:
    decoded_text = f.read()

print 'Decoded:', repr(decoded_text)
```

Since the first two bytes of the file are used for byte-order detection, they are not included in the data returned by `read()`.

```
$ python codecs_bom_detection.py

Raw    : feff 0070 0069 003a 0020 03c0
Decoded: u'pi: \u03c0'
```

6.7.4   Error Handling

The previous sections pointed out the need to know the encoding being used when reading and writing Unicode files. Setting the encoding correctly is important for two reasons. If the encoding is configured incorrectly while reading from a file, the data will be interpreted incorrectly and may be corrupted or simply fail to decode. Not all Unicode characters can be represented in all encodings, so if the wrong encoding is used while writing, then an error will be generated and data may be lost.

codecs uses the same five error-handling options that are provided by the encode() method of unicode and the decode() method of str, listed in Table 6.1.

Table 6.1. Codec Error-Handling Modes

Error Mode	Description
strict	Raises an exception if the data cannot be converted
replace	Substitutes a special marker character for data that cannot be encoded
ignore	Skips the data
xmlcharrefreplace	XML character (encoding only)
backslashreplace	Escape sequence (encoding only)

Encoding Errors

The most common error condition is receiving a UnicodeEncodeError when writing Unicode data to an ASCII output stream, such as a regular file or sys.stdout. This sample program can be used to experiment with the different error-handling modes.

```
import codecs
import sys

error_handling = sys.argv[1]

text = u'pi: \u03c0'

try:
    # Save the data, encoded as ASCII, using the error
    # handling mode specified on the command line.
    with codecs.open('encode_error.txt', 'w',
                     encoding='ascii',
                     errors=error_handling) as f:
        f.write(text)

except UnicodeEncodeError, err:
    print 'ERROR:', err
```

```
else:
    # If there was no error writing to the file,
    # show what it contains.
    with open('encode_error.txt', 'rb') as f:
        print 'File contents:', repr(f.read())
```

While `strict` mode is safest for ensuring an application explicitly sets the correct encoding for all I/O operations, it can lead to program crashes when an exception is raised.

```
$ python codecs_encode_error.py strict

ERROR: 'ascii' codec can't encode character u'\u03c0' in position 4:
ordinal not in range(128)
```

Some of the other error modes are more flexible. For example, `replace` ensures that no error is raised, at the expense of possibly losing data that cannot be converted to the requested encoding. The Unicode character for pi (π) still cannot be encoded in ASCII, but instead of raising an exception, the character is replaced with ? in the output.

```
$ python codecs_encode_error.py replace

File contents: 'pi: ?'
```

To skip over problem data entirely, use `ignore`. Any data that cannot be encoded will be discarded.

```
$ python codecs_encode_error.py ignore

File contents: 'pi: '
```

There are two lossless error-handling options, both of which replace the character with an alternate representation defined by a standard separate from the encoding. `xmlcharrefreplace` uses an XML character reference as a substitute (the list of character references is specified in the W3C document, *XML Entity Definitions for Characters*).

```
$ python codecs_encode_error.py xmlcharrefreplace

File contents: 'pi: &#960;'
```

The other lossless error-handling scheme is `backslashreplace`, which produces an output format like the value returned when `repr()` of a `unicode` object is printed. Unicode characters are replaced with \u followed by the hexadecimal value of the code point.

```
$ python codecs_encode_error.py backslashreplace

File contents: 'pi: \\u03c0'
```

Decoding Errors

It is also possible to see errors when decoding data, especially if the wrong encoding is used.

```python
import codecs
import sys

from codecs_to_hex import to_hex

error_handling = sys.argv[1]

text = u'pi: \u03c0'
print 'Original       :', repr(text)

# Save the data with one encoding
with codecs.open('decode_error.txt', 'w', encoding='utf-16') as f:
    f.write(text)

# Dump the bytes from the file
with open('decode_error.txt', 'rb') as f:
    print 'File contents:', to_hex(f.read(), 1)

# Try to read the data with the wrong encoding
with codecs.open('decode_error.txt', 'r',
                 encoding='utf-8',
                 errors=error_handling) as f:
    try:
        data = f.read()
    except UnicodeDecodeError, err:
        print 'ERROR:', err
    else:
        print 'Read          :', repr(data)
```

As with encoding, `strict` error-handling mode raises an exception if the byte stream cannot be properly decoded. In this case, a `UnicodeDecodeError` results from trying to convert part of the UTF-16 BOM to a character using the UTF-8 decoder.

```
$ python codecs_decode_error.py strict

Original      : u'pi: \u03c0'
File contents: ff fe 70 00 69 00 3a 00 20 00 c0 03
ERROR: 'utf8' codec can't decode byte 0xff in position 0: invalid
start byte
```

Switching to `ignore` causes the decoder to skip over the invalid bytes. The result is still not quite what is expected, though, since it includes embedded null bytes.

```
$ python codecs_decode_error.py ignore

Original      : u'pi: \u03c0'
File contents: ff fe 70 00 69 00 3a 00 20 00 c0 03
Read          : u'p\x00i\x00:\x00 \x00\x03'
```

In `replace` mode, invalid bytes are replaced with `\uFFFD`, the official Unicode replacement character, which looks like a diamond with a black background containing a white question mark.

```
$ python codecs_decode_error.py replace

Original      : u'pi: \u03c0'
File contents: ff fe 70 00 69 00 3a 00 20 00 c0 03
Read          : u'\ufffd\ufffdp\x00i\x00:\x00 \x00\ufffd\x03'
```

6.7.5 Standard Input and Output Streams

The most common cause of `UnicodeEncodeError` exceptions is code that tries to print `unicode` data to the console or a UNIX pipeline when `sys.stdout` is not configured with an encoding.

```
import codecs
import sys

text = u'pi: π'
```

```
# Printing to stdout may cause an encoding error
print 'Default encoding:', sys.stdout.encoding
print 'TTY:', sys.stdout.isatty()
print text
```

Problems with the default encoding of the standard I/O channels can be difficult to debug. This is because the program frequently works as expected when the output goes to the console, but it causes an encoding error when it is used as part of a pipeline and the output includes Unicode characters outside of the ASCII range. This difference in behavior is caused by Python's initialization code, which sets the default encoding for each standard I/O channel *only if* the channel is connected to a terminal (isatty() returns True). If there is no terminal, Python assumes the program will configure the encoding explicitly and leaves the I/O channel alone.

```
$ python codecs_stdout.py

Default encoding: utf-8
TTY: True
pi: π

$ python codecs_stdout.py | cat -

Default encoding: None
TTY: False
Traceback (most recent call last):
  File "codecs_stdout.py", line 18, in <module>
    print text
UnicodeEncodeError: 'ascii' codec can't encode character
u'\u03c0' in position 4: ordinal not in range(128)
```

To explicitly set the encoding on the standard output channel, use getwriter() to get a stream encoder class for a specific encoding. Instantiate the class, passing sys.stdout as the only argument.

```
import codecs
import sys

text = u'pi: π'

# Wrap sys.stdout with a writer that knows how to handle encoding
# Unicode data.
```

```
wrapped_stdout = codecs.getwriter('UTF-8')(sys.stdout)
wrapped_stdout.write(u'Via write: ' + text + '\n')

# Replace sys.stdout with a writer
sys.stdout = wrapped_stdout

print u'Via print:', text
```

Writing to the wrapped version of `sys.stdout` passes the Unicode text through an encoder before sending the encoded bytes to `stdout`. Replacing `sys.stdout` means that any code used by an application that prints to standard output will be able to take advantage of the encoding writer.

```
$ python codecs_stdout_wrapped.py

Via write: pi: π
Via print: pi: π
```

The next problem to solve is how to know which encoding should be used. The proper encoding varies based on location, language, and user or system configuration, so hard-coding a fixed value is not a good idea. It would also be annoying for a user to need to pass explicit arguments to every program by setting the input and output encodings. Fortunately, there is a global way to get a reasonable default encoding using `locale`.

```
import codecs
import locale
import sys

text = u'pi: π'

# Configure locale from the user's environment settings.
locale.setlocale(locale.LC_ALL, '')

# Wrap stdout with an encoding-aware writer.
lang, encoding = locale.getdefaultlocale()
print 'Locale encoding    :', encoding
sys.stdout = codecs.getwriter(encoding)(sys.stdout)

print 'With wrapped stdout:', text
```

The function `locale.getdefaultlocale()` returns the language and preferred encoding based on the system and user configuration settings in a form that can be used with `getwriter()`.

```
$ python codecs_stdout_locale.py

Locale encoding    : UTF8
With wrapped stdout: pi: π
```

The encoding also needs to be set up when working with `sys.stdin`. Use `getreader()` to get a reader capable of decoding the input bytes.

```
import codecs
import locale
import sys

# Configure locale from the user's environment settings.
locale.setlocale(locale.LC_ALL, '')

# Wrap stdin with an encoding-aware reader.
lang, encoding = locale.getdefaultlocale()
sys.stdin = codecs.getreader(encoding)(sys.stdin)

print 'From stdin:'
print repr(sys.stdin.read())
```

Reading from the wrapped handle returns `unicode` objects instead of `str` instances.

```
$ python codecs_stdout_locale.py | python codecs_stdin.py

From stdin:
u'Locale encoding    : UTF8\nWith wrapped stdout: pi: \u03c0\n'
```

6.7.6   Encoding Translation

Although most applications will work with `unicode` data internally, decoding or encoding it as part of an I/O operation, there are times when changing a file's encoding without holding on to that intermediate data format is useful. `EncodedFile()` takes an open file handle using one encoding and wraps it with a class that translates the data to another encoding as the I/O occurs.

```
from codecs_to_hex import to_hex

import codecs
from cStringIO import StringIO

# Raw version of the original data.
data = u'pi: \u03c0'

# Manually encode it as UTF-8.
utf8 = data.encode('utf-8')
print 'Start as UTF-8    :', to_hex(utf8, 1)

# Set up an output buffer, then wrap it as an EncodedFile.
output = StringIO()
encoded_file = codecs.EncodedFile(output, data_encoding='utf-8',
                                  file_encoding='utf-16')
encoded_file.write(utf8)

# Fetch the buffer contents as a UTF-16 encoded byte string
utf16 = output.getvalue()
print 'Encoded to UTF-16:', to_hex(utf16, 2)

# Set up another buffer with the UTF-16 data for reading,
# and wrap it with another EncodedFile.
buffer = StringIO(utf16)
encoded_file = codecs.EncodedFile(buffer, data_encoding='utf-8',
                                  file_encoding='utf-16')

# Read the UTF-8 encoded version of the data.
recoded = encoded_file.read()
print 'Back to UTF-8    :', to_hex(recoded, 1)
```

This example shows reading from and writing to separate handles returned by EncodedFile(). No matter whether the handle is used for reading or writing, the *file_encoding* always refers to the encoding in use by the open file handle passed as the first argument, and the *data_encoding* value refers to the encoding in use by the data passing through the read() and write() calls.

```
$ python codecs_encodedfile.py

Start as UTF-8    : 70 69 3a 20 cf 80
```

```
Encoded to UTF-16:  fffe 7000 6900 3a00 2000 c003
Back to UTF-8     :  70 69 3a 20 cf 80
```

6.7.7 Non-Unicode Encodings

Although most of the earlier examples use Unicode encodings, `codecs` can be used for many other data translations. For example, Python includes `codecs` for working with base-64, bzip2, ROT-13, ZIP, and other data formats.

```python
import codecs
from cStringIO import StringIO

buffer = StringIO()
stream = codecs.getwriter('rot_13')(buffer)

text = 'abcdefghijklmnopqrstuvwxyz'

stream.write(text)
stream.flush()

print 'Original:', text
print 'ROT-13  :', buffer.getvalue()
```

Any transformation that can be expressed as a function taking a single input argument and returning a byte or Unicode string can be registered as a codec.

```
$ python codecs_rot13.py

Original: abcdefghijklmnopqrstuvwxyz
ROT-13  : nopqrstuvwxyzabcdefghijklm
```

Using `codecs` to wrap a data stream provides a simpler interface than working directly with `zlib`.

```python
import codecs
from cStringIO import StringIO

from codecs_to_hex import to_hex

buffer = StringIO()
stream = codecs.getwriter('zlib')(buffer)
```

```
text = 'abcdefghijklmnopqrstuvwxyz\n' * 50

stream.write(text)
stream.flush()

print 'Original length :', len(text)
compressed_data = buffer.getvalue()
print 'ZIP compressed  :', len(compressed_data)

buffer = StringIO(compressed_data)
stream = codecs.getreader('zlib')(buffer)

first_line = stream.readline()
print 'Read first line :', repr(first_line)

uncompressed_data = first_line + stream.read()
print 'Uncompressed     :', len(uncompressed_data)
print 'Same             :', text == uncompressed_data
```

Not all compression or encoding systems support reading a portion of the data through the stream interface using `readline()` or `read()` because they need to find the end of a compressed segment to expand it. If a program cannot hold the entire uncompressed data set in memory, use the incremental access features of the compression library, instead of `codecs`.

```
$ python codecs_zlib.py

Original length : 1350
ZIP compressed  : 48
Read first line : 'abcdefghijklmnopqrstuvwxyz\n'
Uncompressed    : 1350
Same            : True
```

6.7.8 Incremental Encoding

Some of the encodings provided, especially `bz2` and `zlib`, may dramatically change the length of the data stream as they work on it. For large data sets, these encodings operate better incrementally, working on one small chunk of data at a time. The `IncrementalEncoder` and `IncrementalDecoder` API is designed for this purpose.

```
import codecs
import sys
```

```python
from codecs_to_hex import to_hex

text = 'abcdefghijklmnopqrstuvwxyz\n'
repetitions = 50

print 'Text length :', len(text)
print 'Repetitions :', repetitions
print 'Expected len:', len(text) * repetitions

# Encode the text several times to build up a large amount of data
encoder = codecs.getincrementalencoder('bz2')()
encoded = []

print
print 'Encoding:',
for i in range(repetitions):
    en_c = encoder.encode(text, final = (i==repetitions-1))
    if en_c:
        print '\nEncoded : {} bytes'.format(len(en_c))
        encoded.append(en_c)
    else:
        sys.stdout.write('.')

bytes = ''.join(encoded)
print
print 'Total encoded length:', len(bytes)
print

# Decode the byte string one byte at a time
decoder = codecs.getincrementaldecoder('bz2')()
decoded = []

print 'Decoding:',
for i, b in enumerate(bytes):
    final= (i+1) == len(text)
    c = decoder.decode(b, final)
    if c:
        print '\nDecoded : {} characters'.format(len(c))
        print 'Decoding:',
        decoded.append(c)
    else:
        sys.stdout.write('.')
print
```

```
restored = u''.join(decoded)
```

print
print '*Total uncompressed length:*', len(restored)

Each time data is passed to the encoder or the decoder, its internal state is updated. When the state is consistent (as defined by the codec), data is returned and the state resets. Until that point, calls to encode() or decode() will not return any data. When the last bit of data is passed in, the argument *final* should be set to True so the codec knows to flush any remaining buffered data.

```
$ python codecs_incremental_bz2.py

Text length : 27
Repetitions : 50
Expected len: 1350

Encoding:.....................................................
Encoded : 99 bytes

Total encoded length: 99

Decoding:.......................................................
...........................
Decoded : 1350 characters
Decoding:.........

Total uncompressed length: 1350
```

6.7.9   Unicode Data and Network Communication

Like the standard input and output file descriptors, network sockets are also byte streams, and so Unicode data must be encoded into bytes before it is written to a socket. This server echos data it receives back to the sender.

```
import sys
import SocketServer


class Echo(SocketServer.BaseRequestHandler):
```

```
    def handle(self):
        # Get some bytes and echo them back to the client.
        data = self.request.recv(1024)
        self.request.send(data)
        return


if __name__ == '__main__':
    import codecs
    import socket
    import threading

    address = ('localhost', 0) # let the kernel assign a port
    server = SocketServer.TCPServer(address, Echo)
    ip, port = server.server_address # what port was assigned?

    t = threading.Thread(target=server.serve_forever)
    t.setDaemon(True) # don't hang on exit
    t.start()

    # Connect to the server
    s = socket.socket(socket.AF_INET, socket.SOCK_STREAM)
    s.connect((ip, port))

    # Send the data
    # WRONG: Not encoded first!
    text = u'pi: π'
    len_sent = s.send(text)

    # Receive a response
    response = s.recv(len_sent)
    print repr(response)

    # Clean up
    s.close()
    server.socket.close()
```

The data could be encoded explicitly before each call to send(), but missing one call to send() would result in an encoding error.

```
$ python codecs_socket_fail.py
Traceback (most recent call last):
File "codecs_socket_fail.py", line 43, in <module>
```

```
len_sent = s.send(text)
UnicodeEncodeError: 'ascii' codec can't encode character
u'\u03c0' in position 4: ordinal not in range(128)
```

Using `makefile()` to get a file-like handle for the socket, and then wrapping that handle with a stream-based reader or writer, means Unicode strings will be encoded on the way into and out of the socket.

```python
import sys
import SocketServer


class Echo(SocketServer.BaseRequestHandler):

    def handle(self):
        # Get some bytes and echo them back to the client.  There is
        # no need to decode them, since they are not used.
        data = self.request.recv(1024)
        self.request.send(data)
        return


class PassThrough(object):

    def __init__(self, other):
        self.other = other

    def write(self, data):
        print 'Writing :', repr(data)
        return self.other.write(data)

    def read(self, size=-1):
        print 'Reading :',
        data = self.other.read(size)
        print repr(data)
        return data

    def flush(self):
        return self.other.flush()

    def close(self):
        return self.other.close()
```

```
if __name__ == '__main__':
    import codecs
    import socket
    import threading

    address = ('localhost', 0) # let the kernel assign a port
    server = SocketServer.TCPServer(address, Echo)
    ip, port = server.server_address # what port was assigned?

    t = threading.Thread(target=server.serve_forever)
    t.setDaemon(True) # don't hang on exit
    t.start()

    # Connect to the server
    s = socket.socket(socket.AF_INET, socket.SOCK_STREAM)
    s.connect((ip, port))

    # Wrap the socket with a reader and writer.
    read_file = s.makefile('r')
    incoming = codecs.getreader('utf-8')(PassThrough(read_file))
    write_file = s.makefile('w')
    outgoing = codecs.getwriter('utf-8')(PassThrough(write_file))

    # Send the data
    text = u'pi: π'
    print 'Sending :', repr(text)
    outgoing.write(text)
    outgoing.flush()

    # Receive a response
    response = incoming.read()
    print 'Received:', repr(response)

    # Clean up
    s.close()
    server.socket.close()
```

This example uses `PassThrough` to show that the data is encoded before being sent and the response is decoded after it is received in the client.

```
$ python codecs_socket.py

Sending : u'pi: \u03c0'
```

```
Writing : 'pi: \xcf\x80'
Reading : 'pi: \xcf\x80'
Received: u'pi: \u03c0'
```

6.7.10   Defining a Custom Encoding

Since Python comes with a large number of standard codecs already, it is unlikely that an application will need to define a custom encoder or decoder. When it is necessary, though, there are several base classes in `codecs` to make the process easier.

The first step is to understand the nature of the transformation described by the encoding. These examples will use an "invertcaps" encoding, which converts uppercase letters to lowercase and lowercase letters to uppercase. Here is a simple definition of an encoding function that performs this transformation on an input string:

```
import string

def invertcaps(text):
    """Return new string with the case of all letters switched.
    """
    return ''.join( c.upper() if c in string.ascii_lowercase
                    else c.lower() if c in string.ascii_uppercase
                    else c
                    for c in text
                    )

if __name__ == '__main__':
    print invertcaps('ABC.def')
    print invertcaps('abc.DEF')
```

In this case, the encoder and decoder are the same function (as with `ROT-13`).

```
$ python codecs_invertcaps.py

abc.DEF
ABC.def
```

Although it is easy to understand, this implementation is not efficient, especially for very large text strings. Fortunately, `codecs` includes helper functions for creating codecs based on *character maps*, like invertcaps. A character map encoding is made up of two dictionaries. The *encoding map* converts character values from the input string to byte values in the output, and the *decoding map* goes the other way. Create the decoding map first, and then use `make_encoding_map()` to convert it to an encoding map. The C functions `charmap_encode()` and `charmap_decode()` use the maps to convert their input data efficiently.

```python
import codecs
import string

# Map every character to itself
decoding_map = codecs.make_identity_dict(range(256))

# Make a list of pairs of ordinal values for the lower and uppercase
# letters
pairs = zip([ ord(c) for c in string.ascii_lowercase],
            [ ord(c) for c in string.ascii_uppercase])

# Modify the mapping to convert upper to lower and lower to upper.
decoding_map.update( dict( (upper, lower)
                           for (lower, upper)
                           in pairs
                           )
                    )
decoding_map.update( dict( (lower, upper)
                           for (lower, upper)
                           in pairs
                           )
                    )

# Create a separate encoding map.
encoding_map = codecs.make_encoding_map(decoding_map)

if __name__ == '__main__':
    print codecs.charmap_encode('abc.DEF', 'strict', encoding_map)
    print codecs.charmap_decode('abc.DEF', 'strict', decoding_map)
    print encoding_map == decoding_map
```

Although the encoding and decoding maps for invertcaps are the same, that may not always be the case. `make_encoding_map()` detects situations where more than one input character is encoded to the same output byte and replaces the encoding value with `None` to mark the encoding as undefined.

```
$ python codecs_invertcaps_charmap.py

('ABC.def', 7)
```

```
(u'ABC.def', 7)
True
```

The character map encoder and decoder support all standard error-handling methods described earlier, so no extra work is needed to comply with that part of the API.

```
import codecs
from codecs_invertcaps_charmap import encoding_map

text = u'pi: π'

for error in [ 'ignore', 'replace', 'strict' ]:
    try:
        encoded = codecs.charmap_encode(text, error, encoding_map)
    except UnicodeEncodeError, err:
        encoded = str(err)
    print '{:7}: {}'.format(error, encoded)
```

Because the Unicode code point for π is not in the encoding map, the strict error-handling mode raises an exception.

```
$ python codecs_invertcaps_error.py

ignore : ('PI: ', 5)
replace: ('PI: ?', 5)
strict : 'charmap' codec can't encode character u'\u03c0' in position
 4: character maps to <undefined>
```

After the encoding and decoding maps are defined, a few additional classes need to be set up, and the encoding should be registered. `register()` adds a search function to the registry so that when a user wants to use the encoding, `codecs` can locate it. The search function must take a single string argument with the name of the encoding and return a `CodecInfo` object if it knows the encoding, or `None` if it does not.

```
import codecs
import encodings

def search1(encoding):
    print 'search1: Searching for:', encoding
    return None
```

```
def search2(encoding):
    print 'search2: Searching for:', encoding
    return None

codecs.register(search1)
codecs.register(search2)

utf8 = codecs.lookup('utf-8')
print 'UTF-8:', utf8

try:
    unknown = codecs.lookup('no-such-encoding')
except LookupError, err:
    print 'ERROR:', err
```

Multiple search functions can be registered, and each will be called in turn until one returns a `CodecInfo` or the list is exhausted. The internal search function registered by `codecs` knows how to load the standard codecs, such as UTF-8 from `encodings`, so those names will never be passed to custom search functions.

```
$ python codecs_register.py

UTF-8: <codecs.CodecInfo object for encoding utf-8 at 0x100d0f530>
search1: Searching for: no-such-encoding
search2: Searching for: no-such-encoding
ERROR: unknown encoding: no-such-encoding
```

The `CodecInfo` instance returned by the search function tells `codecs` how to encode and decode using all the different mechanisms supported: stateless, incremental, and stream. `codecs` includes base classes to help with setting up a character map encoding. This example puts all the pieces together to register a search function that returns a `CodecInfo` instance configured for the invertcaps codec.

```
import codecs

from codecs_invertcaps_charmap import encoding_map, decoding_map

# Stateless encoder/decoder

class InvertCapsCodec(codecs.Codec):
    def encode(self, input, errors='strict'):
        return codecs.charmap_encode(input, errors, encoding_map)
```

```
    def decode(self, input, errors='strict'):
        return codecs.charmap_decode(input, errors, decoding_map)

# Incremental forms

class InvertCapsIncrementalEncoder(codecs.IncrementalEncoder):
    def encode(self, input, final=False):
        data, nbytes = codecs.charmap_encode(input,
                                             self.errors,
                                             encoding_map)
        return data

class InvertCapsIncrementalDecoder(codecs.IncrementalDecoder):
    def decode(self, input, final=False):
        data, nbytes = codecs.charmap_decode(input,
                                             self.errors,
                                             decoding_map)
        return data

# Stream reader and writer

class InvertCapsStreamReader(InvertCapsCodec, codecs.StreamReader):
    pass

class InvertCapsStreamWriter(InvertCapsCodec, codecs.StreamWriter):
    pass

# Register the codec search function

def find_invertcaps(encoding):
    """Return the codec for 'invertcaps'.
    """
    if encoding == 'invertcaps':
        return codecs.CodecInfo(
            name='invertcaps',
            encode=InvertCapsCodec().encode,
            decode=InvertCapsCodec().decode,
            incrementalencoder=InvertCapsIncrementalEncoder,
            incrementaldecoder=InvertCapsIncrementalDecoder,
            streamreader=InvertCapsStreamReader,
            streamwriter=InvertCapsStreamWriter,
            )
    return None
```

```
codecs.register(find_invertcaps)

if __name__ == '__main__':

    # Stateless encoder/decoder
    encoder = codecs.getencoder('invertcaps')
    text = 'abc.DEF'
    encoded_text, consumed = encoder(text)
    print 'Encoded "{}" to "{}", consuming {} characters'.format(
        text, encoded_text, consumed)

    # Stream writer
    import sys
    writer = codecs.getwriter('invertcaps')(sys.stdout)
    print 'StreamWriter for stdout: ',
    writer.write('abc.DEF')
    print

    # Incremental decoder
    decoder_factory = codecs.getincrementaldecoder('invertcaps')
    decoder = decoder_factory()
    decoded_text_parts = []
    for c in encoded_text:
        decoded_text_parts.append(decoder.decode(c, final=False))
    decoded_text_parts.append(decoder.decode('', final=True))
    decoded_text = ''.join(decoded_text_parts)
    print 'IncrementalDecoder converted "{}" to "{}"'.format(
        encoded_text, decoded_text)
```

The stateless encoder/decoder base class is `Codec`. Override `encode()` and `decode()` with the new implementation (in this case, calling `charmap_encode()` and `charmap_decode()`, respectively). Each method must return a `tuple` containing the transformed data and the number of the input bytes or characters consumed. Conveniently, `charmap_encode()` and `charmap_decode()` already return that information.

`IncrementalEncoder` and `IncrementalDecoder` serve as base classes for the incremental interfaces. The `encode()` and `decode()` methods of the incremental classes are defined in such a way that they only return the actual transformed data. Any information about buffering is maintained as internal state. The invertcaps encoding does not need to buffer data (it uses a one-to-one mapping). For encodings that produce a different amount of output depending on the data being processed, such as compression algorithms, `BufferedIncrementalEncoder` and `BufferedIncrementalDecoder` are more appropriate base classes, since they manage the unprocessed portion of the input.

`StreamReader` and `StreamWriter` need `encode()` and `decode()` methods, too, and since they are expected to return the same value as the version from `Codec`, multiple inheritance can be used for the implementation.

```
$ python codecs_invertcaps_register.py

Encoded "abc.DEF" to "ABC.def", consuming 7 characters
StreamWriter for stdout: ABC.def
IncrementalDecoder converted "ABC.def" to "abc.DEF"
```

See Also:

codecs (http://docs.python.org/library/codecs.html) The standard library documentation for this module.

`locale` **(page 909)** Accessing and managing the localization-based configuration settings and behaviors.

`io` **(http://docs.python.org/library/io.html)** The `io` module includes file and stream wrappers that handle encoding and decoding, too.

`SocketServer` **(page 609)** For a more detailed example of an echo server, see the `SocketServer` module.

`encodings` Package in the standard library containing the encoder/decoder implementations provided by Python.

PEP 100 (www.python.org/dev/peps/pep-0100) Python Unicode Integration PEP.

Unicode HOWTO (http://docs.python.org/howto/unicode) The official guide for using Unicode with Python 2.x.

Python Unicode Objects (http://effbot.org/zone/unicode-objects.htm) Fredrik Lundh's article about using non-ASCII character sets in Python 2.0.

How to Use UTF-8 with Python (http://evanjones.ca/python-utf8.html) Evan Jones' quick guide to working with Unicode, including XML data and the Byte-Order Marker.

On the Goodness of Unicode (www.tbray.org/ongoing/When/200x/2003/04/06/Unicode) Introduction to internationalization and Unicode by Tim Bray.

On Character Strings (www.tbray.org/ongoing/When/200x/2003/04/13/Strings) A look at the history of string processing in programming languages, by Tim Bray.

Characters vs. Bytes (www.tbray.org/ongoing/When/200x/2003/04/26/UTF) Part one of Tim Bray's "essay on modern character string processing for computer programmers." This installment covers in-memory representation of text in formats other than ASCII bytes.

Endianness (http://en.wikipedia.org/wiki/Endianness) Explanation of endianness in Wikipedia.

W3C XML Entity Definitions for Characters (www.w3.org/TR/xml-entity-names/) Specification for XML representations of character references that cannot be represented in an encoding.

6.8 StringIO—Text Buffers with a File-like API

Purpose Work with text buffers using a file-like API.
Python Version 1.4 and later

StringIO provides a convenient means of working with text in memory using the file API (read(), write(), etc.). There are two separate implementations. The cStringIO version is written in C for speed, while StringIO is written in Python for portability. Using cStringIO to build large strings can offer performance savings over some other string concatenation techniques.

6.8.1 Examples

Here are a few standard examples of using StringIO buffers:

```python
# Find the best implementation available on this platform
try:
    from cStringIO import StringIO
except:
    from StringIO import StringIO

# Writing to a buffer
output = StringIO()
output.write('This goes into the buffer. ')
print >>output, 'And so does this.'

# Retrieve the value written
print output.getvalue()

output.close()  # discard buffer memory

# Initialize a read buffer
input = StringIO('Inital value for read buffer')
```

```
# Read from the buffer
print input.read()
```

This example uses read(), but the readline() and readlines() methods are also available. The StringIO class also provides a seek() method for jumping around in a buffer while reading, which can be useful for rewinding if a look-ahead parsing algorithm is being used.

```
$ python stringio_examples.py

This goes into the buffer. And so does this.

Inital value for read buffer
```

See Also:

StringIO (http://docs.python.org/lib/module-StringIO.html) Standard library documentation for this module.

The StringIO module ::: www.effbot.org (http://effbot.org/librarybook/stringio .htm) effbot's examples with StringIO.

Efficient String Concatenation in Python (www.skymind.com/%7Eocrow/python_ string/) Examines various methods of combining strings and their relative merits.

6.9 fnmatch—UNIX-Style Glob Pattern Matching

Purpose Handle UNIX-style filename comparisons.
Python Version 1.4 and later.

The fnmatch module is used to compare filenames against glob-style patterns such as used by UNIX shells.

6.9.1 Simple Matching

fnmatch() compares a single filename against a pattern and returns a Boolean, indicating whether or not they match. The comparison is case sensitive when the operating system uses a case-sensitive file system.

```
import fnmatch
import os
```

```
pattern = 'fnmatch_*.py'
print 'Pattern :', pattern
print

files = os.listdir('.')
for name in files:
    print 'Filename: %-25s %s' % \
        (name, fnmatch.fnmatch(name, pattern))
```

In this example, the pattern matches all files starting with 'fnmatch_' and ending in '.py'.

```
$ python fnmatch_fnmatch.py

Pattern : fnmatch_*.py

Filename: __init__.py               False
Filename: fnmatch_filter.py         True
Filename: fnmatch_fnmatch.py        True
Filename: fnmatch_fnmatchcase.py    True
Filename: fnmatch_translate.py      True
Filename: index.rst                 False
```

To force a case-sensitive comparison, regardless of the file system and operating system settings, use fnmatchcase().

```
import fnmatch
import os

pattern = 'FNMATCH_*.PY'
print 'Pattern :', pattern
print

files = os.listdir('.')

for name in files:
    print 'Filename: %-25s %s' % \
        (name, fnmatch.fnmatchcase(name, pattern))
```

Since the OS X system used to test this program uses a case-sensitive file system, no files match the modified pattern.

```
$ python fnmatch_fnmatchcase.py

Pattern : FNMATCH_*.PY

Filename: __init__.py          False
Filename: fnmatch_filter.py    False
Filename: fnmatch_fnmatch.py   False
Filename: fnmatch_fnmatchcase.py  False
Filename: fnmatch_translate.py  False
Filename: index.rst            False
```

6.9.2 Filtering

To test a sequence of filenames, use `filter()`, which returns a list of the names that match the pattern argument.

```python
import fnmatch
import os
import pprint

pattern = 'fnmatch_*.py'
print 'Pattern :', pattern

files = os.listdir('.')

print
print 'Files   :'
pprint.pprint(files)

print
print 'Matches :'
pprint.pprint(fnmatch.filter(files, pattern))
```

In this example, `filter()` returns the list of names of the example source files associated with this section.

```
$ python fnmatch_filter.py

Pattern : fnmatch_*.py

Files   :
['__init__.py',
```

```
'fnmatch_filter.py',
'fnmatch_fnmatch.py',
'fnmatch_fnmatchcase.py',
'fnmatch_translate.py',
'index.rst']

Matches :
['fnmatch_filter.py',
 'fnmatch_fnmatch.py',
 'fnmatch_fnmatchcase.py',
 'fnmatch_translate.py']
```

6.9.3   Translating Patterns

Internally, fnmatch converts the glob pattern to a regular expression and uses the re
module to compare the name and pattern. The translate() function is the public API
for converting glob patterns to regular expressions.

```
import fnmatch

pattern = 'fnmatch_*.py'
print 'Pattern :', pattern
print 'Regex   :', fnmatch.translate(pattern)
```

Some of the characters are escaped to make a valid expression.

```
$ python fnmatch_translate.py

Pattern : fnmatch_*.py
Regex   : fnmatch\_.*\.py\Z(?ms)
```

See Also:

fnmatch (http://docs.python.org/library/fnmatch.html) The standard library docu-
    mentation for this module.

glob (page 257) The   glob   module   combines   fnmatch   matching   with
    os.listdir() to produce lists of files and directories matching patterns.

re (page 13) Regular expression pattern matching.

6.10   dircache—Cache Directory Listings

Purpose Cache directory listings, updating when the modification time of
a directory changes.
Python Version 1.4 and later

The `dircache` module reads directory listings from the file system and holds them in
memory.

6.10.1   Listing Directory Contents

The main function in the `dircache` API is `listdir()`, which is a wrapper around
`os.listdir()`. Each time it is called with a given path, `dircache.listdir()`
returns the same `list` object, unless the modification date of the directory changes.

```
import dircache

path = '.'
first = dircache.listdir(path)
second = dircache.listdir(path)

print 'Contents :'
for name in first:
    print '   ', name

print
print 'Identical:', first is second
print 'Equal    :', first == second
```

It is important to recognize that the exact same `list` is returned each time, so it
should not be modified in place.

```
$ python dircache_listdir.py

Contents :
    __init__.py
    dircache_annotate.py
    dircache_listdir.py
```

```
dircache_listdir_file_added.py
dircache_reset.py
index.rst
```

```
Identical: True
Equal    : True
```

If the contents of the directory changes, it is rescanned.

```
import dircache
import os

path = '/tmp'
file_to_create = os.path.join(path, 'pymotw_tmp.txt')

# Look at the directory contents
first = dircache.listdir(path)

# Create the new file
open(file_to_create, 'wt').close()

# Rescan the directory
second = dircache.listdir(path)

# Remove the file we created
os.unlink(file_to_create)

print 'Identical :', first is second
print 'Equal     :', first == second
print 'Difference:', list(set(second) - set(first))
```

In this case, the new file causes a new `list` to be constructed.

```
$ python dircache_listdir_file_added.py

Identical : False
Equal     : False
Difference: ['pymotw_tmp.txt']
```

It is also possible to reset the entire cache, discarding its contents so that each path will be rechecked.

```
import dircache

path = '/tmp'
first = dircache.listdir(path)
dircache.reset()
second = dircache.listdir(path)

print 'Identical :', first is second
print 'Equal     :', first == second
print 'Difference:', list(set(second) - set(first))
```

After resetting, a new `list` instance is returned.

```
$ python dircache_reset.py

Identical : False
Equal     : True
Difference: []
```

6.10.2   Annotated Listings

Another interesting function provided by the `dircache` module is `annotate()`, which modifies a `list()`, such as is returned by `listdir()`, by adding a `'/'` to the end of the names that represent directories.

```
import dircache
from pprint import pprint
import os

path = '../..'

contents = dircache.listdir(path)

annotated = contents[:]
dircache.annotate(path, annotated)

fmt = '%25s\t%25s'

print fmt % ('ORIGINAL', 'ANNOTATED')
print fmt % (('-' * 25,)*2)
```

```
for o, a in zip(contents, annotated):
    print fmt % (o, a)
```

Unfortunately for Windows users, although `annotate()` uses `os.path.join()` to construct names to test, it always appends a `'/'`, not `os.sep`.

```
$ python dircache_annotate.py

              ORIGINAL                           ANNOTATED
-------------------------          -------------------------
             .DS_Store                           .DS_Store
                   .hg                                .hg/
             .hgignore                           .hgignore
               .hgtags                             .hgtags
           LICENSE.txt                         LICENSE.txt
           MANIFEST.in                         MANIFEST.in
                PyMOTW                             PyMOTW/
         PyMOTW.egg-info                    PyMOTW.egg-info/
            README.txt                          README.txt
                   bin                                bin/
                  dist                               dist/
                module                              module
                  motw                                motw
                output                             output/
           pavement.py                         pavement.py
      paver-minilib.zip                   paver-minilib.zip
              setup.py                            setup.py
   sitemap_gen_config.xml              sitemap_gen_config.xml
                sphinx                             sphinx/
             structure                          structure/
             trace.txt                           trace.txt
                 utils                               utils/
```

See Also:

dircache (http://docs.python.org/library/dircache.html) The standard library documentation for this module.

6.11   filecmp—Compare Files

Purpose Compare files and directories on the file system.
Python Version 2.1 and later

The `filecmp` module includes functions and a class for comparing files and directories on the file system.

6.11.1   Example Data

The examples in this discussion use a set of test files created by `filecmp_mkexamples.py`.

```python
import os

def mkfile(filename, body=None):
    with open(filename, 'w') as f:
        f.write(body or filename)
    return

def make_example_dir(top):
    if not os.path.exists(top):
        os.mkdir(top)
    curdir = os.getcwd()
    os.chdir(top)

    os.mkdir('dir1')
    os.mkdir('dir2')

    mkfile('dir1/file_only_in_dir1')
    mkfile('dir2/file_only_in_dir2')

    os.mkdir('dir1/dir_only_in_dir1')
    os.mkdir('dir2/dir_only_in_dir2')

    os.mkdir('dir1/common_dir')
    os.mkdir('dir2/common_dir')

    mkfile('dir1/common_file', 'this file is the same')
    mkfile('dir2/common_file', 'this file is the same')

    mkfile('dir1/not_the_same')
    mkfile('dir2/not_the_same')

    mkfile('dir1/file_in_dir1', 'This is a file in dir1')
    os.mkdir('dir2/file_in_dir1')

    os.chdir(curdir)
    return
```

```
if __name__ == '__main__':
    os.chdir(os.path.dirname(__file__) or os.getcwd())
    make_example_dir('example')
    make_example_dir('example/dir1/common_dir')
    make_example_dir('example/dir2/common_dir')
```

Running `filecmp_mkexamples.py` produces a tree of files under the directory `example`:

```
$ find example

example
example/dir1
example/dir1/common_dir
example/dir1/common_dir/dir1
example/dir1/common_dir/dir1/common_dir
example/dir1/common_dir/dir1/common_file
example/dir1/common_dir/dir1/dir_only_in_dir1
example/dir1/common_dir/dir1/file_in_dir1
example/dir1/common_dir/dir1/file_only_in_dir1
example/dir1/common_dir/dir1/not_the_same
example/dir1/common_dir/dir2
example/dir1/common_dir/dir2/common_dir
example/dir1/common_dir/dir2/common_file
example/dir1/common_dir/dir2/dir_only_in_dir2
example/dir1/common_dir/dir2/file_in_dir1
example/dir1/common_dir/dir2/file_only_in_dir2
example/dir1/common_dir/dir2/not_the_same
example/dir1/common_file
example/dir1/dir_only_in_dir1
example/dir1/file_in_dir1
example/dir1/file_only_in_dir1
example/dir1/not_the_same
example/dir2
example/dir2/common_dir
example/dir2/common_dir/dir1
example/dir2/common_dir/dir1/common_dir
example/dir2/common_dir/dir1/common_file
example/dir2/common_dir/dir1/dir_only_in_dir1
example/dir2/common_dir/dir1/file_in_dir1
example/dir2/common_dir/dir1/file_only_in_dir1
example/dir2/common_dir/dir1/not_the_same
```

```
example/dir2/common_dir/dir2
example/dir2/common_dir/dir2/common_dir
example/dir2/common_dir/dir2/common_file
example/dir2/common_dir/dir2/dir_only_in_dir2
example/dir2/common_dir/dir2/file_in_dir1
example/dir2/common_dir/dir2/file_only_in_dir2
example/dir2/common_dir/dir2/not_the_same
example/dir2/common_file
example/dir2/dir_only_in_dir2
example/dir2/file_in_dir1
example/dir2/file_only_in_dir2
example/dir2/not_the_same
```

The same directory structure is repeated one time under the "common_dir" directories to give interesting recursive comparison options.

6.11.2 Comparing Files

cmp() compares two files on the file system.

```
import filecmp

print 'common_file:',
print filecmp.cmp('example/dir1/common_file',
                  'example/dir2/common_file'),
print filecmp.cmp('example/dir1/common_file',
                  'example/dir2/common_file',
                  shallow=False)

print 'not_the_same:',
print filecmp.cmp('example/dir1/not_the_same',
                  'example/dir2/not_the_same'),
print filecmp.cmp('example/dir1/not_the_same',
                  'example/dir2/not_the_same',
                  shallow=False)

print 'identical:',
print filecmp.cmp('example/dir1/file_only_in_dir1',
                  'example/dir1/file_only_in_dir1'),
print filecmp.cmp('example/dir1/file_only_in_dir1',
                  'example/dir1/file_only_in_dir1',
                  shallow=False)
```

The *shallow* argument tells `cmp()` whether to look at the contents of the file, in addition to its metadata. The default is to perform a shallow comparison using the information available from `os.stat()` without looking at content. Files of the same size created at the same time are reported as the same, if their contents are not compared.

```
$ python filecmp_cmp.py

common_file: True True
not_the_same: True False
identical: True True
```

To compare a set of files in two directories without recursing, use `cmpfiles()`. The arguments are the names of the directories and a list of files to be checked in the two locations. The list of common files passed in should contain only filenames (directories always result in a mismatch), and the files must be present in both locations. The next example shows a simple way to build the common list. The comparison also takes the *shallow* flag, just as with `cmp()`.

```
import filecmp
import os

# Determine the items that exist in both directories
d1_contents = set(os.listdir('example/dir1'))
d2_contents = set(os.listdir('example/dir2'))
common = list(d1_contents & d2_contents)
common_files = [ f
                 for f in common
                 if os.path.isfile(os.path.join('example/dir1', f))
                 ]
print 'Common files:', common_files

# Compare the directories
match, mismatch, errors = filecmp.cmpfiles('example/dir1',
                                           'example/dir2',
                                           common_files)
print 'Match    :', match
print 'Mismatch:', mismatch
print 'Errors   :', errors
```

`cmpfiles()` returns three lists of filenames containing files that match, files that do not match, and files that could not be compared (due to permission problems or for any other reason).

```
dc = filecmp.dircmp('example/dir1', 'example/dir2')
print 'Left:'
pprint.pprint(dc.left_list)

print '\nRight:'
pprint.pprint(dc.right_list)
```

The files and subdirectories contained in the directories being compared are listed in `left_list` and `right_list`.

```
$ python filecmp_dircmp_list.py

Left:
['common_dir',
 'common_file',
 'dir_only_in_dir1',
 'file_in_dir1',
 'file_only_in_dir1',
 'not_the_same']

Right:
['common_dir',
 'common_file',
 'dir_only_in_dir2',
 'file_in_dir1',
 'file_only_in_dir2',
 'not_the_same']
```

The inputs can be filtered by passing a list of names to ignore to the constructor. By default, the names RCS, CVS, and `tags` are ignored.

```
import filecmp
import pprint

dc = filecmp.dircmp('example/dir1', 'example/dir2',
                    ignore=['common_file'])

print 'Left:'
pprint.pprint(dc.left_list)

print '\nRight:'
pprint.pprint(dc.right_list)
```

In this case, the "`common_file`" is left out of the list of files to be compared.

```
$ python filecmp_dircmp_list_filter.py

Left:
['common_dir',
 'dir_only_in_dir1',
 'file_in_dir1',
 'file_only_in_dir1',
 'not_the_same']

Right:
['common_dir',
 'dir_only_in_dir2',
 'file_in_dir1',
 'file_only_in_dir2',
 'not_the_same']
```

The names of files common to both input directories are saved in `common`, and the files unique to each directory are listed in `left_only` and `right_only`.

```
import filecmp
import pprint

dc = filecmp.dircmp('example/dir1', 'example/dir2')
print 'Common:'
pprint.pprint(dc.common)

print '\nLeft:'
pprint.pprint(dc.left_only)

print '\nRight:'
pprint.pprint(dc.right_only)
```

The "left" directory is the first argument to `dircmp()`, and the "right" directory is the second.

```
$ python filecmp_dircmp_membership.py

Common:
['not_the_same', 'common_file', 'file_in_dir1', 'common_dir']
```

```
Left:
['dir_only_in_dir1', 'file_only_in_dir1']

Right:
['dir_only_in_dir2', 'file_only_in_dir2']
```

The common members can be further broken down into files, directories, and "funny" items (anything that has a different type in the two directories or where there is an error from `os.stat()`).

```
import filecmp
import pprint

dc = filecmp.dircmp('example/dir1', 'example/dir2')
print 'Common:'
pprint.pprint(dc.common)

print '\nDirectories:'
pprint.pprint(dc.common_dirs)

print '\nFiles:'
pprint.pprint(dc.common_files)

print '\nFunny:'
pprint.pprint(dc.common_funny)
```

In the example data, the item named "`file_in_dir1`" is a file in one directory and a subdirectory in the other, so it shows up in the funny list.

```
$ python filecmp_dircmp_common.py

Common:
['not_the_same', 'common_file', 'file_in_dir1', 'common_dir']

Directories:
['common_dir']

Files:
['not_the_same', 'common_file']

Funny:
['file_in_dir1']
```

The differences between files are broken down similarly.

```
import filecmp

dc = filecmp.dircmp('example/dir1', 'example/dir2')
print 'Same      :', dc.same_files
print 'Different :', dc.diff_files
print 'Funny     :', dc.funny_files
```

The file `not_the_same` is only being compared via `os.stat()`, and the contents are not examined, so it is included in the `same_files` list.

```
$ python filecmp_dircmp_diff.py

Same      : ['not_the_same', 'common_file']
Different : []
Funny     : []
```

Finally, the subdirectories are also saved to allow easy recursive comparison.

```
import filecmp

dc = filecmp.dircmp('example/dir1', 'example/dir2')
print 'Subdirectories:'
print dc.subdirs
```

The attribute `subdirs` is a dictionary mapping the directory name to new `dircmp` objects.

```
$ python filecmp_dircmp_subdirs.py

Subdirectories:
{'common_dir': <filecmp.dircmp instance at 0x85da0>}
```

See Also:

filecmp (http://docs.python.org/library/filecmp.html) The standard library documentation for this module.

***Directories* (page 1118)** Listing the contents of a directory using `os` (page 1108).

`difflib` (page 61) Computing the differences between two sequences.

Chapter 7

DATA PERSISTENCE AND EXCHANGE

There are two aspects to preserving data for long-term use: converting the data back and forth between the object in-memory and the storage format, and working with the storage of the converted data. The standard library includes a variety of modules that handle both aspects in different situations.

Two modules convert objects into a format that can be transmitted or stored (a process known as *serializing*). It is most common to use `pickle` for persistence, since it is integrated with some of the other standard library modules that actually store the serialized data, such as `shelve`. `json` is more frequently used for Web-based applications, however, since it integrates better with existing Web service storage tools.

Once the in-memory object is converted to a format that can be saved, the next step is to decide how to store the data. A simple flat-file with serialized objects written one after the other works for data that does not need to be indexed in any way. Python includes a collection of modules for storing key-value pairs in a simple database using one of the DBM format variants when an indexed lookup is needed.

The most straightforward way to take advantage of the DBM format is `shelve`. Open the shelve file, and access it through a dictionary-like API. Objects saved to the database are automatically pickled and saved without any extra work by the caller.

One drawback of `shelve`, though, is that when using the default interface, there is no way to predict which DBM format will be used, since it selects one based on the libraries available on the system where the database is created. The format does not matter if an application will not need to share the database files between hosts with different libraries; but if portability is a requirement, use one of the classes in the module to ensure a specific format is selected.

For Web applications that work with data in JSON already, using `json` and `anydbm` provides another persistence mechanism. Using `anydbm` directly is a little more work than `shelve` because the DBM database keys and values must be strings, and the objects will not be re-created automatically when the value is accessed in the database.

The `sqlite3` in-process relational database is available with most Python distributions for storing data in more complex arrangements than key-value pairs. It stores its database in memory or in a local file, and all access is from within the same process so there is no network communication lag. The compact nature of `sqlite3` makes it especially well suited for embedding in desktop applications or development versions of Web apps.

There are also modules for parsing more formally defined formats, useful for exchanging data between Python programs and applications written in other languages. `xml.etree.ElementTree` can parse XML documents and provides several operating modes for different applications. Besides the parsing tools, `ElementTree` includes an interface for creating well-formed XML documents from objects in memory. The `csv` module can read and write tabular data in formats produced by spreadsheets or database applications, making it useful for bulk loading data or converting the data from one format to another.

7.1 pickle—Object Serialization

Purpose Object serialization.
Python Version 1.4 and later for pickle, 1.5 and later for cPickle

The `pickle` module implements an algorithm for turning an arbitrary Python object into a series of bytes. This process is also called *serializing* the object. The byte stream representing the object can then be transmitted or stored, and later reconstructed to create a new object with the same characteristics.

The `cPickle` module implements the same algorithm, in C instead of Python. It is many times faster than the Python implementation, so it is generally used instead of the pure-Python implementation.

Warning: The documentation for `pickle` makes clear that it offers no security guarantees. In fact, unpickling data can execute arbitrary code. Be careful using `pickle` for inter-process communication or data storage, and do not trust data that cannot be verified as secure. See *Applications of Message Signatures* in the `hmac` section for an example of a secure way to verify the source of a pickled data source.

7.1.1 Importing

Because `cPickle` is faster than `pickle`, it is common to first try to import `cPickle`, giving it an alias of "pickle," and then fall back on the native Python implementation in `pickle` if the import fails. This means the program will use the faster implementation, if it is available, and the portable implementation otherwise.

```
try:
    import cPickle as pickle
except:
    import pickle
```

The API for the C and Python versions is the same, and data can be exchanged between programs using either version of the library.

7.1.2 Encoding and Decoding Data in Strings

This first example uses `dumps()` to encode a data structure as a string, and then prints the string to the console. It uses a data structure made up of entirely built-in types. Instances of any class can be pickled, as will be illustrated in a later example.

```
try:
    import cPickle as pickle
except:
    import pickle
import pprint

data = [ { 'a':'A', 'b':2, 'c':3.0 } ]
print 'DATA:',
pprint.pprint(data)

data_string = pickle.dumps(data)
print 'PICKLE: %r' % data_string
```

By default, the pickle will contain only ASCII characters. A more efficient binary pickle format is also available, but all the examples here use the ASCII output because it is easier to understand in print.

```
$ python pickle_string.py

DATA:[{'a': 'A', 'b': 2, 'c': 3.0}]
PICKLE: "(lp1\n(dp2\nS'a'\nS'A'\nsS'c'\nF3\nsS'b'\nI2\nsa."
```

After the data is serialized, it can be written to a file, a socket, or a pipe, etc. Later, the file can be read and the data unpickled to construct a new object with the same values.

```python
try:
    import cPickle as pickle
except:
    import pickle
import pprint

data1 = [ { 'a':'A', 'b':2, 'c':3.0 } ]
print 'BEFORE: ',
pprint.pprint(data1)

data1_string = pickle.dumps(data1)

data2 = pickle.loads(data1_string)
print 'AFTER : ',
pprint.pprint(data2)

print 'SAME? :', (data1 is data2)
print 'EQUAL?:', (data1 == data2)
```

The newly constructed object is equal to, but not the same object as, the original.

```
$ python pickle_unpickle.py

BEFORE: [{'a': 'A', 'b': 2, 'c': 3.0}]
AFTER : [{'a': 'A', 'b': 2, 'c': 3.0}]
SAME? : False
EQUAL?: True
```

7.1.3 Working with Streams

In addition to dumps() and loads(), pickle provides convenience functions for working with file-like streams. It is possible to write multiple objects to a stream and then read them from the stream without knowing in advance how many objects are written or how big they are.

```python
try:
    import cPickle as pickle
except:
    import pickle
```

```python
import pprint
from StringIO import StringIO


class SimpleObject(object):

    def __init__(self, name):
        self.name = name
        self.name_backwards = name[::-1]
        return

data = []
data.append(SimpleObject('pickle'))
data.append(SimpleObject('cPickle'))
data.append(SimpleObject('last'))

# Simulate a file with StringIO
out_s = StringIO()

# Write to the stream
for o in data:
    print 'WRITING : %s (%s)' % (o.name, o.name_backwards)
    pickle.dump(o, out_s)
    out_s.flush()

# Set up a read-able stream
in_s = StringIO(out_s.getvalue())

# Read the data
while True:
    try:
        o = pickle.load(in_s)
    except EOFError:
        break
    else:
        print 'READ    : %s (%s)' % (o.name, o.name_backwards)
```

The example simulates streams using two `StringIO` buffers. The first receives
the pickled objects, and its value is fed to a second from which `load()` reads. A simple
database format could use pickles to store objects, too (see `shelve`).

```
$ python pickle_stream.py

WRITING : pickle (elkcip)
WRITING : cPickle (elkciPc)
```

```
WRITING : last (tsal)
READ    : pickle (elkcip)
READ    : cPickle (elkciPc)
READ    : last (tsal)
```

Besides storing data, pickles are handy for inter-process communication. For example, `os.fork()` and `os.pipe()` can be used to establish worker processes that read job instructions from one pipe and write the results to another pipe. The core code for managing the worker pool and sending jobs in and receiving responses can be reused, since the job and response objects do not have to be based on a particular class. When using pipes or sockets, do not forget to flush after dumping each object, to push the data through the connection to the other end. See the `multiprocessing` module for a reusable worker pool manager.

7.1.4 Problems Reconstructing Objects

When working with custom classes, the class being pickled must appear in the name-space of the process reading the pickle. Only the data for the instance is pickled, not the class definition. The class name is used to find the constructor to create the new object when unpickling. This example writes instances of a class to a file.

```
try:
    import cPickle as pickle
except:
    import pickle
import sys

class SimpleObject(object):
    def __init__(self, name):
        self.name = name
        l = list(name)
        l.reverse()
        self.name_backwards = ''.join(l)
        return

if __name__ == '__main__':
    data = []
    data.append(SimpleObject('pickle'))
    data.append(SimpleObject('cPickle'))
    data.append(SimpleObject('last'))

    filename = sys.argv[1]
```

```
with open(filename, 'wb') as out_s:
    # Write to the stream
    for o in data:
        print 'WRITING: %s (%s)' % (o.name, o.name_backwards)
        pickle.dump(o, out_s)
```

When run, the script creates a file based on the name given as argument on the command line.

```
$ python pickle_dump_to_file_1.py test.dat

WRITING: pickle (elkcip)
WRITING: cPickle (elkciPc)
WRITING: last (tsal)
```

A simplistic attempt to load the resulting pickled objects fails.

```
try:
    import cPickle as pickle
except:
    import pickle
import pprint
from StringIO import StringIO
import sys

filename = sys.argv[1]

with open(filename, 'rb') as in_s:
    # Read the data
    while True:
        try:
            o = pickle.load(in_s)
        except EOFError:
            break
        else:
            print 'READ: %s (%s)' % (o.name, o.name_backwards)
```

This version fails because there is no `SimpleObject` class available.

```
$ python pickle_load_from_file_1.py test.dat
```

```
Traceback (most recent call last):
  File "pickle_load_from_file_1.py", line 25, in <module>
    o = pickle.load(in_s)
AttributeError: 'module' object has no attribute 'SimpleObject'
```

The corrected version, which imports `SimpleObject` from the original script, succeeds. Adding this import statement to the end of the import list allows the script to find the class and construct the object.

from pickle_dump_to_file_1 import SimpleObject

Running the modified script now produces the desired results.

```
$ python pickle_load_from_file_2.py test.dat

READ: pickle (elkcip)
READ: cPickle (elkciPc)
READ: last (tsal)
```

7.1.5   Unpicklable Objects

Not all objects can be pickled. Sockets, file handles, database connections, and other objects with run-time state that depends on the operating system or another process may not be able to be saved in a meaningful way. Objects that have nonpicklable attributes can define __getstate__() and __setstate__() to return a subset of the state of the instance to be pickled. New-style classes can also define __getnewargs__(), which should return arguments to be passed to the class memory allocator (C.__new__()). Use of these features is covered in more detail in the standard library documentation.

7.1.6   Circular References

The pickle protocol automatically handles circular references between objects, so complex data structures do not need any special handling. Consider the directed graph in Figure 7.1. It includes several cycles, yet the correct structure can be pickled and then reloaded.

```
import pickle


class Node(object):
    """A simple digraph"""
```

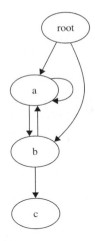

Figure 7.1. Pickling a data structure with cycles

```python
    def __init__(self, name):
        self.name = name
        self.connections = []

    def add_edge(self, node):
        "Create an edge between this node and the other."
        self.connections.append(node)

    def __iter__(self):
        return iter(self.connections)

def preorder_traversal(root, seen=None, parent=None):
    """Generator function to yield the edges in a graph.
    """
    if seen is None:
        seen = set()
    yield (parent, root)
    if root in seen:
        return
    seen.add(root)
    for node in root:
        for parent, subnode in preorder_traversal(node, seen, root):
            yield (parent, subnode)
```

```
def show_edges(root):
    "Print all the edges in the graph."
    for parent, child in preorder_traversal(root):
        if not parent:
            continue
        print '%5s -> %2s (%s)' % \
            (parent.name, child.name, id(child))

# Set up the nodes.
root = Node('root')
a = Node('a')
b = Node('b')
c = Node('c')

# Add edges between them.
root.add_edge(a)
root.add_edge(b)
a.add_edge(b)
b.add_edge(a)
b.add_edge(c)
a.add_edge(a)

print 'ORIGINAL GRAPH:'
show_edges(root)

# Pickle and unpickle the graph to create
# a new set of nodes.
dumped = pickle.dumps(root)
reloaded = pickle.loads(dumped)

print '\nRELOADED GRAPH:'
show_edges(reloaded)
```

The reloaded nodes are not the same object, but the relationship between the nodes is maintained and only one copy of the object with multiple references is reloaded. Both of these statements can be verified by examining the id() values for the nodes before and after being passed through pickle.

```
$ python pickle_cycle.py

ORIGINAL GRAPH:
 root ->   a (4309376848)
    a ->   b (4309376912)
```

```
   b ->   a (4309376848)
   b ->   c (4309376976)
   a ->   a (4309376848)
root ->   b (4309376912)

RELOADED GRAPH:
 root ->   a (4309418128)
   a ->   b (4309418192)
   b ->   a (4309418128)
   b ->   c (4309418256)
   a ->   a (4309418128)
root ->   b (4309418192)
```

See Also:

pickle (http://docs.python.org/lib/module-pickle.html) Standard library documentation for this module.

**Pickle: An interesting stack language
(http://peadrop.com/blog/2007/06/18/pickle-an-interesting-stack-language/)**
A blog post by Alexandre Vassalotti.

Why Python Pickle is Insecure (http://nadiana.com/python-pickle-insecure)
A short example by Nadia Alramli demonstrating a security exploit using pickle.

`shelve` **(page 343)** The `shelve` module uses `pickle` to store data in a DBM database.

7.2   shelve—Persistent Storage of Objects

Purpose The shelve module implements persistent storage for arbitrary Python objects that can be pickled, using a dictionary-like API.

The `shelve` module can be used as a simple persistent storage option for Python objects when a relational database is not required. The shelf is accessed by keys, just as with a dictionary. The values are pickled and written to a database created and managed by `anydbm`.

7.2.1   Creating a New Shelf

The simplest way to use `shelve` is via the `DbfilenameShelf` class. It uses `anydbm` to store the data. The class can be used directly or by calling `shelve.open()`.

```
import shelve
from contextlib import closing
```

```
with closing(shelve.open('test_shelf.db')) as s:
    s['key1'] = { 'int': 10, 'float':9.5, 'string':'Sample data' }
```

To access the data again, open the shelf and use it like a dictionary.

```
import shelve
from contextlib import closing

with closing(shelve.open('test_shelf.db')) as s:
    existing = s['key1']

print existing
```

This is what running both sample scripts produces.

```
$ python shelve_create.py
$ python shelve_existing.py

{'int': 10, 'float': 9.5, 'string': 'Sample data'}
```

The dbm module does not support multiple applications writing to the same database at the same time, but it does support concurrent read-only clients. If a client will not be modifying the shelf, tell shelve to open the database in read-only mode by passing flag='r'.

```
import shelve
from contextlib import closing

with closing(shelve.open('test_shelf.db', flag='r')) as s:
    existing = s['key1']

print existing
```

If the program tries to modify the database while it is opened in read-only mode, an access error exception is generated. The exception type depends on the database module selected by anydbm when the database was created.

7.2.2   Writeback

Shelves do not track modifications to volatile objects, by default. That means if the contents of an item stored in the shelf are changed, the shelf must be updated explicitly by storing the entire item again.

```
import shelve
from contextlib import closing

with closing(shelve.open('test_shelf.db')) as s:
    print s['key1']
    s['key1']['new_value'] = 'this was not here before'

with closing(shelve.open('test_shelf.db', writeback=True)) as s:
    print s['key1']
```

In this example, the dictionary at 'key1' is not stored again, so when the shelf is reopened, the changes will not have been preserved.

```
$ python shelve_create.py
$ python shelve_withoutwriteback.py

{'int': 10, 'float': 9.5, 'string': 'Sample data'}
{'int': 10, 'float': 9.5, 'string': 'Sample data'}
```

To automatically catch changes to volatile objects stored in the shelf, open it with writeback enabled. The *writeback* flag causes the shelf to remember all objects retrieved from the database using an in-memory cache. Each cache object is also written back to the database when the shelf is closed.

```
import shelve
import pprint
from contextlib import closing

with closing(shelve.open('test_shelf.db', writeback=True)) as s:
    print 'Initial data:'
    pprint.pprint(s['key1'])

    s['key1']['new_value'] = 'this was not here before'
    print '\nModified:'
    pprint.pprint(s['key1'])

with closing(shelve.open('test_shelf.db', writeback=True)) as s:
    print '\nPreserved:'
    pprint.pprint(s['key1'])
```

Although it reduces the chance of programmer error and can make object persistence more transparent, using writeback mode may not be desirable in every situation. The cache consumes extra memory while the shelf is open, and pausing to write every cached object back to the database when it is closed slows down the application. All cached objects are written back to the database because there is no way to tell if they have been modified. If the application reads data more than it writes, writeback will impact performance unnecessarily.

```
$ python shelve_create.py
$ python shelve_writeback.py

Initial data:
{'float': 9.5, 'int': 10, 'string': 'Sample data'}

Modified:
{'float': 9.5,
 'int': 10,
 'new_value': 'this was not here before',
 'string': 'Sample data'}

Preserved:
{'float': 9.5,
 'int': 10,
 'new_value': 'this was not here before',
 'string': 'Sample data'}
```

7.2.3   Specific Shelf Types

The earlier examples all used the default shelf implementation. Using `shelve.open()` instead of one of the shelf implementations directly is a common usage pattern, especially if it does not matter what type of database is used to store the data. There are times, however, when the database format is important. In those situations, use `DbfilenameShelf` or `BsdDbShelf` directly, or even subclass `Shelf` for a custom solution.

See Also:

shelve (http://docs.python.org/lib/module-shelve.html) Standard library documentation for this module.

feedcache (www.doughellmann.com/projects/feedcache/) The `feedcache` module uses `shelve` as a default storage option.

shove (http://pypi.python.org/pypi/shove/) Shove implements a similar API with more back-end formats.

anydbm (page 347) The `anydbm` module finds an available DBM library to create a new database.

7.3 anydbm—DBM-Style Databases

Purpose anydbm provides a generic dictionary-like interface to DBM-
   style, string-keyed databases.
Python Version 1.4 and later

anydbm is a front-end for DBM-style databases that use simple string values as keys
to access records containing strings. It uses whichdb to identify databases, and then
opens them with the appropriate module. It is used as a back-end for shelve, which
stores objects in a DBM database using pickle.

7.3.1 Database Types

Python comes with several modules for accessing DBM-style databases. The implementation selected depends on the libraries available on the current system and the
options used when Python was compiled.

dbhash

The dbhash module is the primary back-end for anydbm. It uses the bsddb library to
manage database files. The semantics for using dbhash databases are the same as those
defined by the anydbm API.

gdbm

gdbm is an updated version of the dbm library from the GNU project. It works the same
as the other DBM implementations described here, with a few changes to the flags
supported by open().

Besides the standard 'r', 'w', 'c', and 'n' flags, gdbm.open() supports:

- 'f' to open the database in *fast* mode. In fast mode, writes to the database are
  not synchronized.
- 's' to open the database in *synchronized* mode. Changes to the database are
  written to the file as they are made, rather than being delayed until the database
  is closed or synced explicitly.
- 'u' to open the database unlocked.

dbm

The dbm module provides an interface to one of several C implementations of the dbm
format, depending on how the module was configured during compilation. The module

attribute `library` identifies the name of the library `configure` was able to find when the extension module was compiled.

dumbdbm

The `dumbdbm` module is a portable fallback implementation of the DBM API when no other implementations are available. No external dependencies are required to use `dumbdbm`, but it is slower than most other implementations.

7.3.2   Creating a New Database

The storage format for new databases is selected by looking for each of these modules in order:

- `dbhash`
- `gdbm`
- `dbm`
- `dumbdbm`

The `open()` function takes flags to control how the database file is managed. To create a new database when necessary, use `'c'`. Using `'n'` always creates a new database, overwriting an existing file.

```
import anydbm

db = anydbm.open('/tmp/example.db', 'n')
db['key'] = 'value'
db['today'] = 'Sunday'
db['author'] = 'Doug'
db.close()
```

In this example, the file is always reinitialized.

```
$ python anydbm_new.py
```

`whichdb` reports the type of database that was created.

```
import whichdb

print whichdb.whichdb('/tmp/example.db')
```

Output from the example program will vary, depending on which modules are installed on the system.

```
$ python anydbm_whichdb.py

dbhash
```

7.3.3   Opening an Existing Database

To open an existing database, use flags of either ′r′ (for read-only) or ′w′ (for read-write). Existing databases are automatically given to whichdb to identify, so as long as a file can be identified, the appropriate module is used to open it.

```
import anydbm

db = anydbm.open('/tmp/example.db', 'r')
try:
    print 'keys():', db.keys()
    for k, v in db.iteritems():
        print 'iterating:', k, v
    print 'db["author"] =', db['author']
finally:
    db.close()
```

Once open, db is a dictionary-like object, with support for the usual methods.

```
$ python anydbm_existing.py

keys(): ['author', 'key', 'today']
iterating: author Doug
iterating: key value
iterating: today Sunday
db["author"] = Doug
```

7.3.4   Error Cases

The keys of the database need to be strings.

```
import anydbm

db = anydbm.open('/tmp/example.db', 'w')
```

```
try:
    db[1] = 'one'
except TypeError, err:
    print '%s: %s' % (err.__class__.__name__, err)
finally:
    db.close()
```

Passing another type results in a `TypeError`.

```
$ python anydbm_intkeys.py

TypeError: Integer keys only allowed for Recno and Queue DB's
```

Values must be strings or `None`.

```
import anydbm

db = anydbm.open('/tmp/example.db', 'w')
try:
    db['one'] = 1
except TypeError, err:
    print '%s: %s' % (err.__class__.__name__, err)
finally:
    db.close()
```

A similar `TypeError` is raised if a value is not a string.

```
$ python anydbm_intvalue.py

TypeError: Data values must be of type string or None.
```

See Also:
anydbm (http://docs.python.org/library/anydbm.html) The standard library documentation for this module.

shelve (page 343) Examples for the `shelve` module, which uses `anydbm` to store data.

7.4 whichdb—Identify DBM-Style Database Formats

Purpose Examine existing DBM-style database file to determine what library should be used to open it.

Python Version 1.4 and later

The `whichdb` module contains one function, `whichdb()`, that can be used to examine an existing database file to determine which of the DBM libraries should be used to open it. It returns the string name of the module to use to open the file, or `None` if there is a problem opening the file. If it can open the file but cannot determine the library to use, it returns an empty string.

```
import anydbm
import whichdb

db = anydbm.open('/tmp/example.db', 'n')
db['key'] = 'value'
db.close()


print whichdb.whichdb('/tmp/example.db')
```

The results from running the sample program will vary, depending on the modules available on the system.

```
$ python whichdb_whichdb.py

dbhash
```

See Also:

whichdb (http://docs.python.org/lib/module-whichdb.html) Standard library documentation for this module.

anydbm (page 347) The `anydbm` module uses the best available DBM implementation when creating new databases.

shelve (page 343) The `shelve` module provides a mapping-style API for DBM databases.

7.5 sqlite3—Embedded Relational Database

Purpose Implements an embedded relational database with SQL support.
Python Version 2.5 and later

The `sqlite3` module provides a DB-API 2.0 compliant interface to SQLite, an in-process relational database. SQLite is designed to be embedded in applications, instead of using a separate database server program, such as MySQL, PostgreSQL, or Oracle. It is fast, rigorously tested, and flexible, making it suitable for prototyping and production deployment for some applications.

7.5.1   Creating a Database

An SQLite database is stored as a single file on the file system. The library manages access to the file, including locking it to prevent corruption when multiple writers use it. The database is created the first time the file is accessed, but the application is responsible for managing the table definitions, or *schema*, within the database.

This example looks for the database file before opening it with `connect()` so it knows when to create the schema for new databases.

```python
import os
import sqlite3

db_filename = 'todo.db'

db_is_new = not os.path.exists(db_filename)

conn = sqlite3.connect(db_filename)

if db_is_new:
    print 'Need to create schema'
else:
    print 'Database exists, assume schema does, too.'

conn.close()
```

Running the script twice shows that it creates the empty file if it does not exist.

```
$ ls *.db

ls: *.db: No such file or directory

$ python sqlite3_createdb.py

Need to create schema

$ ls *.db

todo.db

$ python sqlite3_createdb.py

Database exists, assume schema does, too.
```

Table 7.1. The "project" Table

Column	Type	Description
name	text	Project name
description	text	Long project description
deadline	date	Due date for the entire project

Table 7.2. The "task" Table

Column	Type	Description
id	number	Unique task identifier
priority	integer	Numerical priority; lower is more important
details	text	Full task details
status	text	Task status (one of new, pending, done, or canceled).
deadline	date	Due date for this task
completed_on	date	When the task was completed
project	text	The name of the project for this task

After creating the new database file, the next step is to create the schema to define the tables within the database. The remaining examples in this section all use the same database schema with tables for managing tasks. The details of the database schema are presented in Table 7.1 and Table 7.2.

These are the *data definition language* (DDL) statements to create the tables.

```
-- Schema for to-do application examples.

-- Projects are high-level activities made up of tasks
create table project (
    name        text primary key,
    description text,
    deadline    date
);

-- Tasks are steps that can be taken to complete a project
create table task (
    id          integer primary key autoincrement not null,
    priority    integer default 1,
    details     text,
    status      text,
```

```
    deadline    date,
    completed_on date,
    project     text not null references project(name)
);
```

The `executescript()` method of the `Connection` can be used to run the DDL instructions to create the schema.

```python
import os
import sqlite3

db_filename = 'todo.db'
schema_filename = 'todo_schema.sql'

db_is_new = not os.path.exists(db_filename)

with sqlite3.connect(db_filename) as conn:
    if db_is_new:
        print 'Creating schema'
        with open(schema_filename, 'rt') as f:
            schema = f.read()
        conn.executescript(schema)

        print 'Inserting initial data'

        conn.executescript("""
        insert into project (name, description, deadline)
        values ('pymotw', 'Python Module of the Week', '2010-11-01');

        insert into task (details, status, deadline, project)
        values ('write about select', 'done', '2010-10-03',
                'pymotw');

        insert into task (details, status, deadline, project)
        values ('write about random', 'waiting', '2010-10-10',
                'pymotw');

        insert into task (details, status, deadline, project)
        values ('write about sqlite3', 'active', '2010-10-17',
                'pymotw');
        """)
    else:
        print 'Database exists, assume schema does, too.'
```

After the tables are created, a few **insert** statements create a sample project and related tasks. The **sqlite3** command line program can be used to examine the contents of the database.

```
$ python sqlite3_create_schema.py

Creating schema
Inserting initial data

$ sqlite3 todo.db 'select * from task'

1|1|write about select|done|2010-10-03||pymotw
2|1|write about random|waiting|2010-10-10||pymotw
3|1|write about sqlite3|active|2010-10-17||pymotw
```

7.5.2   Retrieving Data

To retrieve the values saved in the `task` table from within a Python program, create a `cursor` from a database connection. A cursor produces a consistent view of the data and is the primary means of interacting with a transactional database system like SQLite.

```
import sqlite3

db_filename = 'todo.db'

with sqlite3.connect(db_filename) as conn:
    cursor = conn.cursor()

    cursor.execute("""
    select id, priority, details, status, deadline from task
    where project = 'pymotw'
    """)

    for row in cursor.fetchall():
        task_id, priority, details, status, deadline = row
        print '%2d {%d} %-20s [%-8s] (%s)' % \
            (task_id, priority, details, status, deadline)
```

Querying is a two-step process. First, run the query with the cursor's `execute()` method to tell the database engine what data to collect. Then, use `fetchall()` to retrieve the results. The return value is a sequence of tuples containing the values for the columns included in the **select** clause of the query.

```
$ python sqlite3_select_tasks.py

 1 {1} write about select   [done    ] (2010-10-03)
 2 {1} write about random   [waiting ] (2010-10-10)
 3 {1} write about sqlite3  [active  ] (2010-10-17)
```

The results can be retrieved one at a time with fetchone() or in fixed-size batches with fetchmany().

```
import sqlite3

db_filename = 'todo.db'

with sqlite3.connect(db_filename) as conn:
    cursor = conn.cursor()

    cursor.execute("""
    select name, description, deadline from project
    where name = 'pymotw'
    """)
    name, description, deadline = cursor.fetchone()

    print 'Project details for %s (%s) due %s' % \
        (description, name, deadline)

    cursor.execute("""
    select id, priority, details, status, deadline from task
    where project = 'pymotw' order by deadline
    """)

    print '\nNext 5 tasks:'
    for row in cursor.fetchmany(5):
        task_id, priority, details, status, deadline = row
        print '%2d {%d} %-25s [%-8s] (%s)' % \
            (task_id, priority, details, status, deadline)
```

The value passed to fetchmany() is the maximum number of items to return. If fewer items are available, the sequence returned will be smaller than the maximum value.

```
$ python sqlite3_select_variations.py

Project details for Python Module of the Week (pymotw) due 2010-11-01

Next 5 tasks:
 1 {1} write about select       [done    ] (2010-10-03)
 2 {1} write about random       [waiting ] (2010-10-10)
 3 {1} write about sqlite3      [active  ] (2010-10-17)
```

7.5.3   Query Metadata

The DB-API 2.0 specification says that after `execute()` has been called, the `cursor` should set its `description` attribute to hold information about the data that will be returned by the fetch methods. The API specifications say that the description value is a sequence of tuples containing the column name, type, display size, internal size, precision, scale, and a flag that says whether null values are accepted.

```
import sqlite3

db_filename = 'todo.db'

with sqlite3.connect(db_filename) as conn:
    cursor = conn.cursor()

    cursor.execute("""
    select * from task where project = 'pymotw'
    """)

    print 'Task table has these columns:'
    for colinfo in cursor.description:
        print colinfo
```

Because `sqlite3` does not enforce type or size constraints on data inserted into a database, only the column name value is filled in.

```
$ python sqlite3_cursor_description.py

Task table has these columns:
('id', None, None, None, None, None, None)
('priority', None, None, None, None, None, None)
('details', None, None, None, None, None, None)
('status', None, None, None, None, None, None)
```

```
('deadline', None, None, None, None, None, None)
('completed_on', None, None, None, None, None, None)
('project', None, None, None, None, None, None)
```

7.5.4   Row Objects

By default, the values returned by the fetch methods as "rows" from the database are tuples. The caller is responsible for knowing the order of the columns in the query and extracting individual values from the tuple. When the number of values in a query grows, or the code working with the data is spread out in a library, it is usually easier to work with an object and access values using their column names. That way, the number and order of the tuple contents can change over time as the query is edited, and code depending on the query results is less likely to break.

Connection objects have a row_factory property that allows the calling code to control the type of object created to represent each row in the query result set. sqlite3 also includes a Row class intended to be used as a row factory. Column values can be accessed through Row instances by using the column index or name.

```
import sqlite3

db_filename = 'todo.db'

with sqlite3.connect(db_filename) as conn:
    # Change the row factory to use Row
    conn.row_factory = sqlite3.Row

    cursor = conn.cursor()

    cursor.execute("""
    select name, description, deadline from project
    where name = 'pymotw'
    """)
    name, description, deadline = cursor.fetchone()

    print 'Project details for %s (%s) due %s' % (
        description, name, deadline)

    cursor.execute("""
    select id, priority, status, deadline, details from task
    where project = 'pymotw' order by deadline
    """)
```

```
print '\nNext 5 tasks:'
for row in cursor.fetchmany(5):
    print '%2d {%d} %-25s [%-8s] (%s)' % (
        row['id'], row['priority'], row['details'],
        row['status'], row['deadline'],
        )
```

This version of the `sqlite3_select_variations.py` example has been rewritten using `Row` instances instead of tuples. The row from the project table is still printed by accessing the column values through position, but the **print** statement for tasks uses keyword lookup instead, so it does not matter that the order of the columns in the query has been changed.

```
$ python sqlite3_row_factory.py

Project details for Python Module of the Week (pymotw) due 2010-11-01

Next 5 tasks:
 1 {1} write about select        [done     ] (2010-10-03)
 2 {1} write about random        [waiting  ] (2010-10-10)
 3 {1} write about sqlite3       [active   ] (2010-10-17)
```

7.5.5 Using Variables with Queries

Using queries defined as literal strings embedded in a program is inflexible. For example, when another project is added to the database, the query to show the top five tasks should be updated to work with either project. One way to add more flexibility is to build an SQL statement with the desired query by combining values in Python. However, building a query string in this way is dangerous and should be avoided. Failing to correctly escape special characters in the variable parts of the query can result in SQL parsing errors, or worse, a class of security vulnerabilities known as *SQL-injection attacks*, which allow intruders to execute arbitrary SQL statements in the database.

The proper way to use dynamic values with queries is through *host variables* passed to `execute()` along with the SQL instruction. A placeholder value in the SQL statement is replaced with the value of the host variable when the statement is executed. Using host variables instead of inserting arbitrary values into the SQL statement before it is parsed avoids injection attacks because there is no chance that the untrusted values will affect how the SQL statement is parsed. SQLite supports two forms for queries with placeholders, positional and named.

Positional Parameters

A question mark (?) denotes a positional argument, passed to `execute()` as a member of a tuple.

```
import sqlite3
import sys

db_filename = 'todo.db'
project_name = sys.argv[1]

with sqlite3.connect(db_filename) as conn:
    cursor = conn.cursor()

    query = """select id, priority, details, status, deadline from task
        where project = ?
        """

    cursor.execute(query, (project_name,))

    for row in cursor.fetchall():
        task_id, priority, details, status, deadline = row
        print '%2d {%d} %-20s [%-8s] (%s)' % (
            task_id, priority, details, status, deadline)
```

The command line argument is passed safely to the query as a positional argument, and there is no chance for bad data to corrupt the database.

```
$ python sqlite3_argument_positional.py pymotw

 1 {1} write about select    [done    ] (2010-10-03)
 2 {1} write about random    [waiting ] (2010-10-10)
 3 {1} write about sqlite3   [active  ] (2010-10-17)
```

Named Parameters

Use named parameters for more complex queries with a lot of parameters, or where some parameters are repeated multiple times within the query. Named parameters are prefixed with a colon (e.g., :param_name).

```
import sqlite3
import sys
```

```
db_filename = 'todo.db'
project_name = sys.argv[1]

with sqlite3.connect(db_filename) as conn:
    cursor = conn.cursor()

    query = """select id, priority, details, status, deadline from task
            where project = :project_name
            order by deadline, priority
            """

    cursor.execute(query, {'project_name':project_name})

    for row in cursor.fetchall():
        task_id, priority, details, status, deadline = row
        print '%2d {%d} %-25s [%-8s] (%s)' % (\
            task_id, priority, details, status, deadline)
```

Neither positional nor named parameters need to be quoted or escaped, since they are given special treatment by the query parser.

```
$ python sqlite3_argument_named.py pymotw

 1 {1} write about select        [done    ] (2010-10-03)
 2 {1} write about random        [waiting ] (2010-10-10)
 3 {1} write about sqlite3       [active  ] (2010-10-17)
```

Query parameters can be used with **select**, **insert**, and **update** statements. They can appear in any part of the query where a literal value is legal.

```
import sqlite3
import sys

db_filename = 'todo.db'
id = int(sys.argv[1])
status = sys.argv[2]

with sqlite3.connect(db_filename) as conn:
    cursor = conn.cursor()
    query = "update task set status = :status where id = :id"
    cursor.execute(query, {'status':status, 'id':id})
```

This **update** statement uses two named parameters. The `id` value is used to find the right row to modify, and the `status` value is written to the table.

```
$ python sqlite3_argument_update.py 2 done
$ python sqlite3_argument_named.py pymotw

1 {1} write about select      [done   ] (2010-10-03)
2 {1} write about random      [done   ] (2010-10-10)
3 {1} write about sqlite3     [active ] (2010-10-17)
```

7.5.6   Bulk Loading

To apply the same SQL instruction to a large set of data, use `executemany()`. This is useful for loading data, since it avoids looping over the inputs in Python and lets the underlying library apply loop optimizations. This example program reads a list of tasks from a comma-separated value file using the `csv` module and loads them into the database.

```python
import csv
import sqlite3
import sys

db_filename = 'todo.db'
data_filename = sys.argv[1]

SQL = """
    insert into task (details, priority, status, deadline, project)
    values (:details, :priority, 'active', :deadline, :project)
    """

with open(data_filename, 'rt') as csv_file:
    csv_reader = csv.DictReader(csv_file)

    with sqlite3.connect(db_filename) as conn:
        cursor = conn.cursor()
        cursor.executemany(SQL, csv_reader)
```

The sample data file `tasks.csv` contains:

```
deadline,project,priority,details
2010-10-02,pymotw,2,"finish reviewing markup"
```

```
2010-10-03,pymotw,2,"revise chapter intros"
2010-10-03,pymotw,1,"subtitle"
```

Running the program produces:

```
$ python sqlite3_load_csv.py tasks.csv
$ python sqlite3_argument_named.py pymotw

4 {2} finish reviewing markup    [active ] (2010-10-02)
1 {1} write about select         [done   ] (2010-10-03)
6 {1} subtitle                   [active ] (2010-10-03)
5 {2} revise chapter intros      [active ] (2010-10-03)
2 {1} write about random         [done   ] (2010-10-10)
3 {1} write about sqlite3        [active ] (2010-10-17)
```

7.5.7 Defining New Column Types

SQLite has native support for integer, floating point, and text columns. Data of these types is converted automatically by `sqlite3` from Python's representation to a value that can be stored in the database, and back again, as needed. Integer values are loaded from the database into `int` or `long` variables, depending on the size of the value. Text is saved and retrieved as `unicode`, unless the `text_factory` for the `Connection` has been changed.

Although SQLite only supports a few data types internally, `sqlite3` includes facilities for defining custom types to allow a Python application to store any type of data in a column. Conversion for types beyond those supported by default is enabled in the database connection using the `detect_types` flag. Use `PARSE_DECLTYPES` if the column was declared using the desired type when the table was defined.

```python
import sqlite3
import sys

db_filename = 'todo.db'

sql = "select id, details, deadline from task"

def show_deadline(conn):
    conn.row_factory = sqlite3.Row
    cursor = conn.cursor()
    cursor.execute(sql)
    row = cursor.fetchone()
```

```
    for col in ['id', 'details', 'deadline']:
        print '   %-8s   %-30r %s' % (col, row[col], type(row[col]))
    return

print 'Without type detection:'
with sqlite3.connect(db_filename) as conn:
    show_deadline(conn)

print '\nWith type detection:'
with sqlite3.connect(db_filename,
                     detect_types=sqlite3.PARSE_DECLTYPES,
                     ) as conn:
    show_deadline(conn)
```

sqlite3 provides converters for date and timestamp columns, using the classes date and datetime from the datetime module to represent the values in Python. Both date-related converters are enabled automatically when type detection is turned on.

```
$ python sqlite3_date_types.py

Without type detection:
  id        1                               <type 'int'>
  details   u'write about select'           <type 'unicode'>
  deadline  u'2010-10-03'                    <type 'unicode'>

With type detection:
  id        1                               <type 'int'>
  details   u'write about select'           <type 'unicode'>
  deadline  datetime.date(2010, 10, 3)      <type 'datetime.date'>
```

Two functions need to be registered to define a new type. The *adapter* takes the Python object as input and returns a byte string that can be stored in the database. The *converter* receives the string from the database and returns a Python object. Use register_adapter() to define an adapter function, and register_converter() for a converter function.

```
import sqlite3
try:
    import cPickle as pickle
except:
    import pickle
```

```python
db_filename = 'todo.db'


def adapter_func(obj):
    """Convert from in-memory to storage representation.
    """
    print 'adapter_func(%s)\n' % obj
    return pickle.dumps(obj)


def converter_func(data):
    """Convert from storage to in-memory representation.
    """
    print 'converter_func(%r)\n' % data
    return pickle.loads(data)


class MyObj(object):
    def __init__(self, arg):
        self.arg = arg
    def __str__(self):
        return 'MyObj(%r)' % self.arg


# Register the functions for manipulating the type.
sqlite3.register_adapter(MyObj, adapter_func)
sqlite3.register_converter("MyObj", converter_func)

# Create some objects to save.  Use a list of tuples so
# the sequence can be passed directly to executemany().
to_save = [ (MyObj('this is a value to save'),),
            (MyObj(42),),
            ]

with sqlite3.connect(db_filename,
                     detect_types=sqlite3.PARSE_DECLTYPES) as conn:
    # Create a table with column of type "MyObj"
    conn.execute("""
    create table if not exists obj (
        id      integer primary key autoincrement not null,
        data    MyObj
    )
    """)
    cursor = conn.cursor()

    # Insert the objects into the database
    cursor.executemany("insert into obj (data) values (?)", to_save)
```

```
# Query the database for the objects just saved
cursor.execute("select id, data from obj")
for obj_id, obj in cursor.fetchall():
    print 'Retrieved', obj_id, obj, type(obj)
    print
```

This example uses `pickle` to save an object to a string that can be stored in the database, a useful technique for storing arbitrary objects, but one that does not allow querying based on object attributes. A real *object-relational mapper*, such as SQLAlchemy, that stores attribute values in separate columns will be more useful for large amounts of data.

```
$ python sqlite3_custom_type.py

adapter_func(MyObj('this is a value to save'))

adapter_func(MyObj(42))

converter_func("ccopy_reg\n_reconstructor\np1\n(c__main__\nMyObj\np2
\nc__builtin__\nobject\np3\nNtRp4\n(dp5\nS'arg'\np6\nS'this is a val
ue to save'\np7\nsb.")

converter_func("ccopy_reg\n_reconstructor\np1\n(c__main__\nMyObj\np2
\nc__builtin__\nobject\np3\nNtRp4\n(dp5\nS'arg'\np6\nI42\nsb.")

Retrieved 1 MyObj('this is a value to save') <class '__main__.MyObj'
>

Retrieved 2 MyObj(42) <class '__main__.MyObj'>
```

7.5.8 Determining Types for Columns

There are two sources for type information about the values returned by a query. The original table declaration can be used to identify the type of a real column, as shown earlier. A type specifier can also be included in the **select** clause of the query itself using the form `as "name [type]"`.

```
import sqlite3
try:
    import cPickle as pickle
except:
    import pickle
```

```
db_filename = 'todo.db'

def adapter_func(obj):
    """Convert from in-memory to storage representation.
    """
    print 'adapter_func(%s)\n' % obj
    return pickle.dumps(obj)

def converter_func(data):
    """Convert from storage to in-memory representation.
    """
    print 'converter_func(%r)\n' % data
    return pickle.loads(data)


class MyObj(object):
    def __init__(self, arg):
        self.arg = arg
    def __str__(self):
        return 'MyObj(%r)' % self.arg

# Register the functions for manipulating the type.
sqlite3.register_adapter(MyObj, adapter_func)
sqlite3.register_converter("MyObj", converter_func)

# Create some objects to save.  Use a list of tuples so we can pass
# this sequence directly to executemany().
to_save = [ (MyObj('this is a value to save'),),
            (MyObj(42),),
            ]

with sqlite3.connect(db_filename,
                     detect_types=sqlite3.PARSE_COLNAMES) as conn:
    # Create a table with column of type "text"
    conn.execute("""
    create table if not exists obj2 (
        id     integer primary key autoincrement not null,
        data   text
    )
    """)
    cursor = conn.cursor()

    # Insert the objects into the database
    cursor.executemany("insert into obj2 (data) values (?)", to_save)
```

```
    # Query the database for the objects just saved,
    # using a type specifier to convert the text
    # to objects.
    cursor.execute('select id, data as "pickle [MyObj]" from obj2')
    for obj_id, obj in cursor.fetchall():
        print 'Retrieved', obj_id, obj, type(obj)
        print
```

Use the `detect_types` flag `PARSE_COLNAMES` when the type is part of the query instead of the original table definition.

```
$ python sqlite3_custom_type_column.py

adapter_func(MyObj('this is a value to save'))

adapter_func(MyObj(42))

converter_func("ccopy_reg\n_reconstructor\np1\n(c__main__\nMyObj\np2
\nc__builtin__\nobject\np3\nNtRp4\n(dp5\nS'arg'\np6\nS'this is a val
ue to save'\np7\nsb.")

converter_func("ccopy_reg\n_reconstructor\np1\n(c__main__\nMyObj\np2
\nc__builtin__\nobject\np3\nNtRp4\n(dp5\nS'arg'\np6\nI42\nsb.")

Retrieved 1 MyObj('this is a value to save') <class '__main__.MyObj'
>

Retrieved 2 MyObj(42) <class '__main__.MyObj'>
```

7.5.9 Transactions

One of the key features of relational databases is the use of *transactions* to maintain a consistent internal state. With transactions enabled, several changes can be made through one connection without effecting any other users until the results are *committed* and flushed to the actual database.

Preserving Changes

Changes to the database, either through **insert** or **update** statements, need to be saved by explicitly calling `commit()`. This requirement gives an application an opportunity to make several related changes together, so they are stored *atomically* instead of incrementally, and avoids a situation where partial updates are seen by different clients connecting to the database simultaneously.

The effect of calling `commit()` can be seen with a program that uses several connections to the database. A new row is inserted with the first connection, and then two attempts are made to read it back using separate connections.

```python
import sqlite3

db_filename = 'todo.db'

def show_projects(conn):
    cursor = conn.cursor()
    cursor.execute('select name, description from project')
    for name, desc in cursor.fetchall():
        print '  ', name
    return

with sqlite3.connect(db_filename) as conn1:

    print 'Before changes:'
    show_projects(conn1)

    # Insert in one cursor
    cursor1 = conn1.cursor()
    cursor1.execute("""
    insert into project (name, description, deadline)
    values ('virtualenvwrapper', 'Virtualenv Extensions',
            '2011-01-01')
    """)

    print '\nAfter changes in conn1:'
    show_projects(conn1)

    # Select from another connection, without committing first
    print '\nBefore commit:'
    with sqlite3.connect(db_filename) as conn2:
        show_projects(conn2)

    # Commit then select from another connection
    conn1.commit()
    print '\nAfter commit:'
    with sqlite3.connect(db_filename) as conn3:
        show_projects(conn3)
```

When `show_projects()` is called before `conn1` has been committed, the results depend on which connection is used. Since the change was made through `conn1`, it sees the altered data. However, `conn2` does not. After committing, the new connection `conn3` sees the inserted row.

```
$ python sqlite3_transaction_commit.py

Before changes:
   pymotw

After changes in conn1:
   pymotw
   virtualenvwrapper

Before commit:
   pymotw

After commit:
   pymotw
   virtualenvwrapper
```

Discarding Changes

Uncommitted changes can also be discarded entirely using `rollback()`. The `commit()` and `rollback()` methods are usually called from different parts of the same `try:except` block, with errors triggering a rollback.

```python
import sqlite3

db_filename = 'todo.db'

def show_projects(conn):
    cursor = conn.cursor()
    cursor.execute('select name, description from project')
    for name, desc in cursor.fetchall():
        print '  ', name
    return

with sqlite3.connect(db_filename) as conn:

    print 'Before changes:'
    show_projects(conn)
```

```
try:

    # Insert
    cursor = conn.cursor()
    cursor.execute("""delete from project
                where name = 'virtualenvwrapper'
                """)

    # Show the settings
    print '\nAfter delete:'
    show_projects(conn)

    # Pretend the processing caused an error
    raise RuntimeError('simulated error')

except Exception, err:
    # Discard the changes
    print 'ERROR:', err
    conn.rollback()

else:
    # Save the changes
    conn.commit()

# Show the results
print '\nAfter rollback:'
show_projects(conn)
```

After calling `rollback()`, the changes to the database are no longer present.

```
$ python sqlite3_transaction_rollback.py

Before changes:
   pymotw
   virtualenvwrapper

After delete:
   pymotw
ERROR: simulated error

After rollback:
   pymotw
   virtualenvwrapper
```

7.5.10 Isolation Levels

`sqlite3` supports three locking modes, called *isolation levels*, that control the technique used to prevent incompatible changes between connections. The isolation level is set by passing a string as the *isolation_level* argument when a connection is opened, so different connections can use different values.

This program demonstrates the effect of different isolation levels on the order of events in threads using separate connections to the same database. Four threads are created. Two threads write changes to the database by updating existing rows. The other two threads attempt to read all the rows from the `task` table.

```python
import logging
import sqlite3
import sys
import threading
import time

logging.basicConfig(
    level=logging.DEBUG,
    format='%(asctime)s (%(threadName)-10s) %(message)s',
    )

db_filename = 'todo.db'
isolation_level = sys.argv[1]


def writer():
    my_name = threading.currentThread().name
    with sqlite3.connect(db_filename,
                         isolation_level=isolation_level) as conn:
        cursor = conn.cursor()
        cursor.execute('update task set priority = priority + 1')
        logging.debug('waiting to synchronize')
        ready.wait()  # synchronize threads
        logging.debug('PAUSING')
        time.sleep(1)
        conn.commit()
        logging.debug('CHANGES COMMITTED')
    return


def reader():
    my_name = threading.currentThread().name
    with sqlite3.connect(db_filename,
                         isolation_level=isolation_level) as conn:
```

```
    cursor = conn.cursor()
    logging.debug('waiting to synchronize')
    ready.wait() # synchronize threads
    logging.debug('wait over')
    cursor.execute('select * from task')
    logging.debug('SELECT EXECUTED')
    results = cursor.fetchall()
    logging.debug('results fetched')
return


if __name__ == '__main__':
    ready = threading.Event()

    threads = [
        threading.Thread(name='Reader 1', target=reader),
        threading.Thread(name='Reader 2', target=reader),
        threading.Thread(name='Writer 1', target=writer),
        threading.Thread(name='Writer 2', target=writer),
        ]

    [ t.start() for t in threads ]

    time.sleep(1)
    logging.debug('setting ready')
    ready.set()

    [ t.join() for t in threads ]
```

The threads are synchronized using an `Event` from the `threading` module. The `writer()` function connects and makes changes to the database, but does not commit before the event fires. The `reader()` function connects, and then waits to query the database until after the synchronization event occurs.

Deferred

The default isolation level is `DEFERRED`. Using deferred mode locks the database, but only once a change is begun. All the previous examples use deferred mode.

```
$ python sqlite3_isolation_levels.py DEFERRED

2010-12-04 09:06:51,793 (Reader 1  ) waiting to synchronize
2010-12-04 09:06:51,794 (Reader 2  ) waiting to synchronize
2010-12-04 09:06:51,795 (Writer 1  ) waiting to synchronize
```

```
2010-12-04 09:06:52,796 (MainThread) setting ready
2010-12-04 09:06:52,797 (Writer 1  ) PAUSING
2010-12-04 09:06:52,797 (Reader 1  ) wait over
2010-12-04 09:06:52,798 (Reader 1  ) SELECT EXECUTED
2010-12-04 09:06:52,798 (Reader 1  ) results fetched
2010-12-04 09:06:52,799 (Reader 2  ) wait over
2010-12-04 09:06:52,800 (Reader 2  ) SELECT EXECUTED
2010-12-04 09:06:52,800 (Reader 2  ) results fetched
2010-12-04 09:06:53,799 (Writer 1  ) CHANGES COMMITTED
2010-12-04 09:06:53,829 (Writer 2  ) waiting to synchronize
2010-12-04 09:06:53,829 (Writer 2  ) PAUSING
2010-12-04 09:06:54,832 (Writer 2  ) CHANGES COMMITTED
```

Immediate

Immediate mode locks the database as soon as a change starts and prevents other cursors from making changes until the transaction is committed. It is suitable for a database with complicated writes, but more readers than writers, since the readers are not blocked while the transaction is ongoing.

```
$ python sqlite3_isolation_levels.py IMMEDIATE
```

```
2010-12-04 09:06:54,914 (Reader 1  ) waiting to synchronize
2010-12-04 09:06:54,915 (Reader 2  ) waiting to synchronize
2010-12-04 09:06:54,916 (Writer 1  ) waiting to synchronize
2010-12-04 09:06:55,917 (MainThread) setting ready
2010-12-04 09:06:55,918 (Reader 1  ) wait over
2010-12-04 09:06:55,919 (Reader 2  ) wait over
2010-12-04 09:06:55,919 (Writer 1  ) PAUSING
2010-12-04 09:06:55,919 (Reader 1  ) SELECT EXECUTED
2010-12-04 09:06:55,919 (Reader 1  ) results fetched
2010-12-04 09:06:55,920 (Reader 2  ) SELECT EXECUTED
2010-12-04 09:06:55,920 (Reader 2  ) results fetched
2010-12-04 09:06:56,922 (Writer 1  ) CHANGES COMMITTED
2010-12-04 09:06:56,951 (Writer 2  ) waiting to synchronize
2010-12-04 09:06:56,951 (Writer 2  ) PAUSING
2010-12-04 09:06:57,953 (Writer 2  ) CHANGES COMMITTED
```

Exclusive

Exclusive mode locks the database to all readers and writers. Its use should be limited in situations where database performance is important, since each exclusive connection blocks all other users.

```
$ python sqlite3_isolation_levels.py EXCLUSIVE

2010-12-04 09:06:58,042 (Reader 1  ) waiting to synchronize
2010-12-04 09:06:58,043 (Reader 2  ) waiting to synchronize
2010-12-04 09:06:58,044 (Writer 1  ) waiting to synchronize
2010-12-04 09:06:59,045 (MainThread) setting ready
2010-12-04 09:06:59,045 (Writer 1  ) PAUSING
2010-12-04 09:06:59,046 (Reader 2  ) wait over
2010-12-04 09:06:59,045 (Reader 1  ) wait over
2010-12-04 09:07:00,048 (Writer 1  ) CHANGES COMMITTED
2010-12-04 09:07:00,076 (Reader 1  ) SELECT EXECUTED
2010-12-04 09:07:00,076 (Reader 1  ) results fetched
2010-12-04 09:07:00,079 (Reader 2  ) SELECT EXECUTED
2010-12-04 09:07:00,079 (Reader 2  ) results fetched
2010-12-04 09:07:00,090 (Writer 2  ) waiting to synchronize
2010-12-04 09:07:00,090 (Writer 2  ) PAUSING
2010-12-04 09:07:01,093 (Writer 2  ) CHANGES COMMITTED
```

Because the first writer has started making changes, the readers and second writer block until it commits. The `sleep()` call introduces an artificial delay in the writer thread to highlight the fact that the other connections are blocking.

Autocommit

The *isolation_level* parameter for the connection can also be set to `None` to enable autocommit mode. With autocommit enabled, each `execute()` call is committed immediately when the statement finishes. Autocommit mode is suited for short transactions, such as those that insert a small amount of data into a single table. The database is locked for as little time as possible, so there is less chance of contention between threads.

In `sqlite3_autocommit.py`, the explicit call to `commit()` has been removed and the isolation level is set to `None`, but otherwise, it is the same as `sqlite3_isolation_levels.py`. The output is different, however, since both writer threads finish their work before either reader starts querying.

```
$ python sqlite3_autocommit.py

2010-12-04 09:07:01,176 (Reader 1  ) waiting to synchronize
2010-12-04 09:07:01,177 (Reader 2  ) waiting to synchronize
2010-12-04 09:07:01,181 (Writer 1  ) waiting to synchronize
2010-12-04 09:07:01,184 (Writer 2  ) waiting to synchronize
2010-12-04 09:07:02,180 (MainThread) setting ready
```

```
2010-12-04 09:07:02,181 (Writer 1  ) PAUSING
2010-12-04 09:07:02,181 (Reader 1  ) wait over
2010-12-04 09:07:02,182 (Reader 1  ) SELECT EXECUTED
2010-12-04 09:07:02,182 (Reader 1  ) results fetched
2010-12-04 09:07:02,183 (Reader 2  ) wait over
2010-12-04 09:07:02,183 (Reader 2  ) SELECT EXECUTED
2010-12-04 09:07:02,184 (Reader 2  ) results fetched
2010-12-04 09:07:02,184 (Writer 2  ) PAUSING
```

7.5.11   In-Memory Databases

SQLite supports managing an entire database in RAM, instead of relying on a disk file. In-memory databases are useful for automated testing, when the database does not need to be preserved between test runs, or when experimenting with a schema or other database features. To open an in-memory database, use the string `':memory:'` instead of a filename when creating the `Connection`. Each `':memory:'` connection creates a separate database instance, so changes made by a cursor in one do not effect other connections.

7.5.12   Exporting the Contents of a Database

The contents of an in-memory database can be saved using the `iterdump()` method of the `Connection`. The iterator returned by `iterdump()` produces a series of strings that together build SQL instructions to recreate the state of the database.

```python
import sqlite3

schema_filename = 'todo_schema.sql'

with sqlite3.connect(':memory:') as conn:
    conn.row_factory = sqlite3.Row

    print 'Creating schema'
    with open(schema_filename, 'rt') as f:
        schema = f.read()
    conn.executescript(schema)

    print 'Inserting initial data'
    conn.execute("""
        insert into project (name, description, deadline)
        values ('pymotw', 'Python Module of the Week', '2010-11-01')
        """)
```

```
data = [
    ('write about select', 'done', '2010-10-03', 'pymotw'),
    ('write about random', 'waiting', '2010-10-10', 'pymotw'),
    ('write about sqlite3', 'active', '2010-10-17', 'pymotw'),
    ]
conn.executemany("""
    insert into task (details, status, deadline, project)
    values (?, ?, ?, ?)
    """, data)

print 'Dumping:'
for text in conn.iterdump():
    print text
```

`iterdump()` can also be used with databases saved to files, but it is most useful for preserving a database that would not otherwise be saved. This output has been edited to fit on the page while remaining syntactically correct.

```
$ python sqlite3_iterdump.py

Creating schema
Inserting initial data
Dumping:
BEGIN TRANSACTION;
CREATE TABLE project (
    name        text primary key,
    description text,
    deadline    date
);
INSERT INTO "project" VALUES('pymotw','Python Module of the
Week','2010-11-01');
CREATE TABLE task (
    id           integer primary key autoincrement not null,
    priority     integer default 1,
    details      text,
    status       text,
    deadline     date,
    completed_on date,
    project      text not null references project(name)
);
INSERT INTO "task" VALUES(1,1,'write about
select','done','2010-10-03',NULL,'pymotw');
INSERT INTO "task" VALUES(2,1,'write about
```

```
random','waiting','2010-10-10',NULL,'pymotw');
INSERT INTO "task" VALUES(3,1,'write about
sqlite3','active','2010-10-17',NULL,'pymotw');
DELETE FROM sqlite_sequence;
INSERT INTO "sqlite_sequence" VALUES('task',3);
COMMIT;
```

7.5.13   Using Python Functions in SQL

SQL syntax supports calling functions during queries, either in the column list or **where** clause of the **select** statement. This feature makes it possible to process data before returning it from the query and can be used to convert between different formats, perform calculations that would be clumsy in pure SQL, and reuse application code.

```python
import sqlite3

db_filename = 'todo.db'

def encrypt(s):
    print 'Encrypting %r' % s
    return s.encode('rot-13')

def decrypt(s):
    print 'Decrypting %r' % s
    return s.encode('rot-13')


with sqlite3.connect(db_filename) as conn:

    conn.create_function('encrypt', 1, encrypt)
    conn.create_function('decrypt', 1, decrypt)
    cursor = conn.cursor()

    # Raw values
    print 'Original values:'
    query = "select id, details from task"
    cursor.execute(query)
    for row in cursor.fetchall():
        print row

    print '\nEncrypting...'
    query = "update task set details = encrypt(details)"
    cursor.execute(query)
```

```
print '\nRaw encrypted values:'
query = "select id, details from task"
cursor.execute(query)
for row in cursor.fetchall():
    print row

print '\nDecrypting in query...'
query = "select id, decrypt(details) from task"
cursor.execute(query)
for row in cursor.fetchall():
    print row
```

Functions are exposed using the `create_function()` method of the `Connection`. The parameters are the name of the function (as it should be used from within SQL), the number of arguments the function takes, and the Python function to expose.

```
$ python sqlite3_create_function.py

Original values:
(1, u'write about select')
(2, u'write about random')
(3, u'write about sqlite3')
(4, u'finish reviewing markup')
(5, u'revise chapter intros')
(6, u'subtitle')

Encrypting...
Encrypting u'write about select'
Encrypting u'write about random'
Encrypting u'write about sqlite3'
Encrypting u'finish reviewing markup'
Encrypting u'revise chapter intros'
Encrypting u'subtitle'

Raw encrypted values:
(1, u'jevgr nobhg fryrpg')
(2, u'jevgr nobhg enaqbz')
(3, u'jevgr nobhg fdyvgr3')
(4, u'svavfu erivrjvat znexhc')
(5, u'erivfr puncgre vagebf')
(6, u'fhogvgyr')
Decrypting in query...
```

```
Decrypting u'jevgr nobhg fryrpg'
Decrypting u'jevgr nobhg enaqbz'
Decrypting u'jevgr nobhg fdyvgr3'
Decrypting u'svavfu erivrjvat znexhc'
Decrypting u'erivfr puncgre vagebf'
Decrypting u'fhogvgyr'
(1, u'write about select')
(2, u'write about random')
(3, u'write about sqlite3')
(4, u'finish reviewing markup')
(5, u'revise chapter intros')
(6, u'subtitle')
```

7.5.14 Custom Aggregation

An aggregation function collects many pieces of individual data and summarizes it in some way. Examples of built-in aggregation functions are avg() (average), min(), max(), and count().

The API for aggregators used by sqlite3 is defined in terms of a class with two methods. The step() method is called once for each data value as the query is processed. The finalize() method is called one time at the end of the query and should return the aggregate value. This example implements an aggregator for the arithmetic *mode*. It returns the value that appears most frequently in the input.

```python
import sqlite3
import collections

db_filename = 'todo.db'

class Mode(object):
    def __init__(self):
        self.counter = collections.Counter()
    def step(self, value):
        print 'step(%r)' % value
        self.counter[value] += 1
    def finalize(self):
        result, count = self.counter.most_common(1)[0]
        print 'finalize() -> %r (%d times)' % (result, count)
        return result

with sqlite3.connect(db_filename) as conn:
```

```
conn.create_aggregate('mode', 1, Mode)

cursor = conn.cursor()
cursor.execute("""
select mode(deadline) from task where project = 'pymotw'
""")
row = cursor.fetchone()
print 'mode(deadline) is:', row[0]
```

The aggregator class is registered with the `create_aggregate()` method of the `Connection`. The parameters are the name of the function (as it should be used from within SQL), the number of arguments the `step()` method takes, and the class to use.

```
$ python sqlite3_create_aggregate.py

step(u'2010-10-03')
step(u'2010-10-10')
step(u'2010-10-17')
step(u'2010-10-02')
step(u'2010-10-03')
step(u'2010-10-03')
finalize() -> u'2010-10-03' (3 times)
mode(deadline) is: 2010-10-03
```

7.5.15   Custom Sorting

A *collation* is a comparison function used in the **order by** section of an SQL query. Custom collations can be used to compare data types that could not otherwise be sorted by SQLite internally. For example, a custom collation would be needed to sort the pickled objects saved in `sqlite3_custom_type.py`.

```
import sqlite3
try:
    import cPickle as pickle
except:
    import pickle

db_filename = 'todo.db'

def adapter_func(obj):
    return pickle.dumps(obj)
```

```python
def converter_func(data):
    return pickle.loads(data)

class MyObj(object):
    def __init__(self, arg):
        self.arg = arg
    def __str__(self):
        return 'MyObj(%r)' % self.arg
    def __cmp__(self, other):
        return cmp(self.arg, other.arg)

# Register the functions for manipulating the type.
sqlite3.register_adapter(MyObj, adapter_func)
sqlite3.register_converter("MyObj", converter_func)

def collation_func(a, b):
    a_obj = converter_func(a)
    b_obj = converter_func(b)
    print 'collation_func(%s, %s)' % (a_obj, b_obj)
    return cmp(a_obj, b_obj)

with sqlite3.connect(db_filename,
                     detect_types=sqlite3.PARSE_DECLTYPES,
                     ) as conn:
    # Define the collation
    conn.create_collation('unpickle', collation_func)

    # Clear the table and insert new values
    conn.execute('delete from obj')
    conn.executemany('insert into obj (data) values (?)',
                     [(MyObj(x),) for x in xrange(5, 0, -1)],
                     )

    # Query the database for the objects just saved
    print 'Querying:'
    cursor = conn.cursor()
    cursor.execute("""
    select id, data from obj order by data collate unpickle
    """)
    for obj_id, obj in cursor.fetchall():
        print obj_id, obj
```

The arguments to the collation function are byte strings, so they must be unpickled and converted to `MyObj` instances before the comparison can be performed.

```
$ python sqlite3_create_collation.py

Querying:
collation_func(MyObj(5), MyObj(4))
collation_func(MyObj(4), MyObj(3))
collation_func(MyObj(4), MyObj(2))
collation_func(MyObj(3), MyObj(2))
collation_func(MyObj(3), MyObj(1))
collation_func(MyObj(2), MyObj(1))
7 MyObj(1)
6 MyObj(2)
5 MyObj(3)
4 MyObj(4)
3 MyObj(5)
```

7.5.16 Threading and Connection Sharing

For historical reasons having to do with old versions of SQLite, `Connection` objects cannot be shared between threads. Each thread must create its own connection to the database.

```python
import sqlite3
import sys
import threading
import time

db_filename = 'todo.db'
isolation_level = None # autocommit mode

def reader(conn):
    my_name = threading.currentThread().name
    print 'Starting thread'
    try:
        cursor = conn.cursor()
        cursor.execute('select * from task')
        results = cursor.fetchall()
        print 'results fetched'
```

```
    except Exception, err:
        print 'ERROR:', err
    return


if __name__ == '__main__':

    with sqlite3.connect(db_filename,
                         isolation_level=isolation_level,
                         ) as conn:
        t = threading.Thread(name='Reader 1',
                             target=reader,
                             args=(conn,),
                             )
        t.start()
        t.join()
```

Attempts to share a connection between threads result in an exception.

```
$ python sqlite3_threading.py

Starting thread
ERROR: SQLite objects created in a thread can only be used in that
same thread.The object was created in thread id 4299299872 and
this is thread id 4311166976
```

7.5.17 Restricting Access to Data

Although SQLite does not have user access controls found in other, larger, relational databases, it does have a mechanism for limiting access to columns. Each connection can install an *authorizer function* to grant or deny access to columns at runtime based on any desired criteria. The authorizer function is invoked during the parsing of SQL statements and is passed five arguments. The first is an action code indicating the type of operation being performed (reading, writing, deleting, etc.). The rest of the arguments depend on the action code. For SQLITE_READ operations, the arguments are the name of the table, the name of the column, the location in the SQL statement where the access is occurring (main query, trigger, etc.), and None.

```
import sqlite3

db_filename = 'todo.db'
```

```
def authorizer_func(action, table, column, sql_location, ignore):
    print '\nauthorizer_func(%s, %s, %s, %s, %s)' % \
        (action, table, column, sql_location, ignore)

    response = sqlite3.SQLITE_OK # be permissive by default

    if action == sqlite3.SQLITE_SELECT:
        print 'requesting permission to run a select statement'
        response = sqlite3.SQLITE_OK

    elif action == sqlite3.SQLITE_READ:
        print 'requesting access to column %s.%s from %s' % \
            (table, column, sql_location)
        if column == 'details':
            print '  ignoring details column'
            response = sqlite3.SQLITE_IGNORE
        elif column == 'priority':
            print '  preventing access to priority column'
            response = sqlite3.SQLITE_DENY

    return response

with sqlite3.connect(db_filename) as conn:
    conn.row_factory = sqlite3.Row
    conn.set_authorizer(authorizer_func)

    print 'Using SQLITE_IGNORE to mask a column value:'
    cursor = conn.cursor()
    cursor.execute("""
    select id, details from task where project = 'pymotw'
    """)
    for row in cursor.fetchall():
        print row['id'], row['details']

    print '\nUsing SQLITE_DENY to deny access to a column:'
    cursor.execute("""
    select id, priority from task where project = 'pymotw'
    """)
    for row in cursor.fetchall():
        print row['id'], row['details']
```

This example uses SQLITE_IGNORE to cause the strings from the task.details column to be replaced with null values in the query results. It also prevents all access to the `task.priority` column by returning `SQLITE_DENY`, which in turn causes SQLite to raise an exception.

```
$ python sqlite3_set_authorizer.py

Using SQLITE_IGNORE to mask a column value:

authorizer_func(21, None, None, None, None)
requesting permission to run a select statement

authorizer_func(20, task, id, main, None)
requesting access to column task.id from main

authorizer_func(20, task, details, main, None)
requesting access to column task.details from main
  ignoring details column

authorizer_func(20, task, project, main, None)
requesting access to column task.project from main
1 None
2 None
3 None
4 None
5 None
6 None

Using SQLITE_DENY to deny access to a column:

authorizer_func(21, None, None, None, None)
requesting permission to run a select statement

authorizer_func(20, task, id, main, None)
requesting access to column task.id from main

authorizer_func(20, task, priority, main, None)
requesting access to column task.priority from main
  preventing access to priority column
Traceback (most recent call last):
  File "sqlite3_set_authorizer.py", line 51, in <module>
    """)
sqlite3.DatabaseError: access to task.priority is prohibited
```

The possible action codes are available as constants in `sqlite3`, with names prefixed `SQLITE_`. Each type of SQL statement can be flagged, and access to individual columns can be controlled as well.

See Also:

sqlite3 (http://docs.python.org/library/sqlite3.html) The standard library documentation for this module.

PEP 249 (www.python.org/dev/peps/pep-0249)—DB API 2.0 Specification A standard interface for modules that provide access to relational databases.

SQLite (www.sqlite.org/) The official site of the SQLite library.

`shelve` **(page 343)** Key-value store for saving arbitrary Python objects.

SQLAlchemy (http://sqlalchemy.org/) A popular object-relational mapper that supports SQLite among many other relational databases.

7.6   xml.etree.ElementTree—XML Manipulation API

> **Purpose** Generate and parse XML documents.
> **Python Version** 2.5 and later

The ElementTree library includes tools for parsing XML using event-based and document-based APIs, searching parsed documents with XPath expressions, and creating new or modifying existing documents.

Note: All examples in this section use the Python implementation of ElementTree for simplicity, but there is also a C implementation in `xml.etree.cElementTree`.

7.6.1   Parsing an XML Document

Parsed XML documents are represented in memory by `ElementTree` and `Element` objects connected in a tree structure based on the way the nodes in the XML document are nested.

Parsing an entire document with `parse()` returns an `ElementTree` instance. The tree knows about all data in the input document, and the nodes of the tree can be searched or manipulated in place. While this flexibility can make working with the parsed document more convenient, it typically takes more memory than an event-based parsing approach since the entire document must be loaded at one time.

The memory footprint of small, simple documents (such as this list of podcasts represented as an OPML outline) is not significant:

```
<?xml version="1.0" encoding="UTF-8"?>
<opml version="1.0">
<head>
    <title>My Podcasts</title>
    <dateCreated>Sun, 07 Mar 2010 15:53:26 GMT</dateCreated>
```

```
    <dateModified>Sun, 07 Mar 2010 15:53:26 GMT</dateModified>
  </head>
  <body>
    <outline text="Fiction">
      <outline
          text="tor.com / category / tordotstories" type="rss"
          xmlUrl="http://www.tor.com/rss/category/TorDotStories"
          htmlUrl="http://www.tor.com/" />
    </outline>
    <outline text="Python">
      <outline
          text="PyCon Podcast" type="rss"
          xmlUrl="http://advocacy.python.org/podcasts/pycon.rss"
          htmlUrl="http://advocacy.python.org/podcasts/" />
      <outline
          text="A Little Bit of Python" type="rss"
          xmlUrl="http://advocacy.python.org/podcasts/littlebit.rss"
          htmlUrl="http://advocacy.python.org/podcasts/" />
    </outline>
  </body>
</opml>
```

To parse the file, pass an open file handle to `parse()`.

```
from xml.etree import ElementTree

with open('podcasts.opml', 'rt') as f:
    tree = ElementTree.parse(f)

print tree
```

It will read the data, parse the XML, and return an `ElementTree` object.

```
$ python ElementTree_parse_opml.py

<xml.etree.ElementTree.ElementTree object at 0x100dca350>
```

7.6.2   Traversing the Parsed Tree

To visit all children in order, use `iter()` to create a generator that iterates over the `ElementTree` instance.

```
from xml.etree import ElementTree
import pprint

with open('podcasts.opml', 'rt') as f:
    tree = ElementTree.parse(f)

for node in tree.iter():
    print node.tag
```

This example prints the entire tree, one tag at a time.

```
$ python ElementTree_dump_opml.py

opml
head
title
dateCreated
dateModified
body
outline
outline
outline
outline
outline
```

To print only the groups of names and feed URLs for the podcasts, leave out all data in the header section by iterating over only the outline nodes and print the *text* and *xmlUrl* attributes by looking up the values in the attrib dictionary.

```
from xml.etree import ElementTree

with open('podcasts.opml', 'rt') as f:
    tree = ElementTree.parse(f)

for node in tree.iter('outline'):
    name = node.attrib.get('text')
    url = node.attrib.get('xmlUrl')
    if name and url:
        print '  %s' % name
        print '    %s' % url
    else:
        print name
```

The `'outline'` argument to `iter()` means processing is limited to only nodes with the tag `'outline'`.

```
$ python ElementTree_show_feed_urls.py

Fiction
  tor.com / category / tordotstories
    http://www.tor.com/rss/category/TorDotStories
Python
  PyCon Podcast
    http://advocacy.python.org/podcasts/pycon.rss
  A Little Bit of Python
    http://advocacy.python.org/podcasts/littlebit.rss
```

7.6.3 Finding Nodes in a Document

Walking the entire tree like this, searching for relevant nodes, can be error prone. The previous example had to look at each outline node to determine if it was a group (nodes with only a `text` attribute) or a podcast (with both `text` and `xmlUrl`). To produce a simple list of the podcast feed URLs, without names or groups, the logic could be simplified using `findall()` to look for nodes with more descriptive search characteristics.

As a first pass at converting the first version, an XPath argument can be used to look for all outline nodes.

```
from xml.etree import ElementTree

with open('podcasts.opml', 'rt') as f:
    tree = ElementTree.parse(f)

for node in tree.findall('.//outline'):
    url = node.attrib.get('xmlUrl')
    if url:
        print url
```

The logic in this version is not substantially different than the version using `getiterator()`. It still has to check for the presence of the URL, except that it does not print the group name when the URL is not found.

```
$ python ElementTree_find_feeds_by_tag.py
```

```
http://www.tor.com/rss/category/TorDotStories
http://advocacy.python.org/podcasts/pycon.rss
http://advocacy.python.org/podcasts/littlebit.rss
```

It is possible to take advantage of the fact that the outline nodes are only nested two levels deep. Changing the search path to `.//outline/outline` means the loop will process only the second level of outline nodes.

```
from xml.etree import ElementTree

with open('podcasts.opml', 'rt') as f:
    tree = ElementTree.parse(f)

for node in tree.findall('.//outline/outline'):
    url = node.attrib.get('xmlUrl')
    print url
```

All outline nodes nested two levels deep in the input are expected to have the *xmlURL* attribute referring to the podcast feed, so the loop can skip checking for the attribute before using it.

```
$ python ElementTree_find_feeds_by_structure.py

http://www.tor.com/rss/category/TorDotStories
http://advocacy.python.org/podcasts/pycon.rss
http://advocacy.python.org/podcasts/littlebit.rss
```

This version is limited to the existing structure, though, so if the outline nodes are ever rearranged into a deeper tree, it will stop working.

7.6.4 Parsed Node Attributes

The items returned by `findall()` and `iter()` are `Element` objects, each representing a node in the XML parse tree. Each `Element` has attributes for accessing data pulled out of the XML. This can be illustrated with a somewhat more contrived example input file, `data.xml`.

```
1  <?xml version="1.0" encoding="UTF-8"?>
2  <top>
3    <child>Regular text.</child>
4    <child_with_tail>Regular text.</child_with_tail>"Tail" text.
```

```
5    <with_attributes name="value" foo="bar" />
6    <entity_expansion attribute="This &#38; That ">
7      That &#38; This
8    </entity_expansion>
9  </top>
```

The *attributes* of a node are available in the `attrib` property, which acts like a dictionary.

```python
from xml.etree import ElementTree

with open('data.xml', 'rt') as f:
    tree = ElementTree.parse(f)

node = tree.find('./with_attributes')
print node.tag
for name, value in sorted(node.attrib.items()):
    print '  %-4s = "%s"' % (name, value)
```

The node on line five of the input file has two attributes, `name` and `foo`.

```
$ python ElementTree_node_attributes.py

with_attributes
  foo  = "bar"
  name = "value"
```

The text content of the nodes is available, along with the *tail* text that comes after the end of a close tag.

```python
from xml.etree import ElementTree

with open('data.xml', 'rt') as f:
    tree = ElementTree.parse(f)

for path in [ './child', './child_with_tail' ]:
    node = tree.find(path)
    print node.tag
    print '  child node text:', node.text
    print '  and tail text   :', node.tail
```

The `child` node on line three contains embedded text, and the node on line four has text with a tail (including whitespace).

```
$ python ElementTree_node_text.py

child
  child node text: Regular text.
  and tail text  :

child_with_tail
  child node text: Regular text.
  and tail text  : "Tail" text.
```

XML entity references embedded in the document are converted to the appropriate characters before values are returned.

```
from xml.etree import ElementTree

with open('data.xml', 'rt') as f:
    tree = ElementTree.parse(f)

node = tree.find('entity_expansion')
print node.tag
print '  in attribute:', node.attrib['attribute']
print '  in text     :', node.text.strip()
```

The automatic conversion means the implementation detail of representing certain characters in an XML document can be ignored.

```
$ python ElementTree_entity_references.py

entity_expansion
  in attribute: This & That
  in text     : That & This
```

7.6.5 Watching Events While Parsing

The other API for processing XML documents is event based. The parser generates `start` events for opening tags and `end` events for closing tags. Data can be extracted from the document during the parsing phase by iterating over the event stream, which is convenient if it is not necessary to manipulate the entire document afterward or hold the entire parsed document in memory.

These are the types of events.

start A new tag has been encountered. The closing angle bracket of the tag was processed, but not the contents.

end The closing angle bracket of a closing tag has been processed. All the children were already processed.

start-ns Start a namespace declaration.

end-ns End a namespace declaration.

iterparse() returns an iterable that produces tuples containing the name of the event and the node triggering the event.

```python
from xml.etree.ElementTree import iterparse

depth = 0
prefix_width = 8
prefix_dots = '.' * prefix_width
line_template = ''.join([ '{prefix:<0.{prefix_len}}',
                          '{event:<8}',
                          '{suffix:<{suffix_len}} ',
                          '{node.tag:<12} ',
                          '{node_id}',
                          ])

EVENT_NAMES = ['start', 'end', 'start-ns', 'end-ns']

for (event, node) in iterparse('podcasts.opml', EVENT_NAMES):
    if event == 'end':
        depth -= 1

    prefix_len = depth * 2

    print line_template.format(
        prefix=prefix_dots,
        prefix_len=prefix_len,
        suffix='',
        suffix_len=(prefix_width - prefix_len),
        node=node,
        node_id=id(node),
        event=event,
        )

    if event == 'start':
        depth += 1
```

By default, only `end` events are generated. To see other events, pass the list of desired event names to `iterparse()`, as in this example.

```
$ python ElementTree_show_all_events.py

start           opml        4309429072
..start         head        4309429136
....start       title       4309429200
....end         title       4309429200
....start       dateCreated 4309429392
....end         dateCreated 4309429392
....start       dateModified 4309429584
....end         dateModified 4309429584
..end           head        4309429136
..start         body        4309429968
....start       outline     4309430032
......start     outline     4309430096
......end       outline     4309430096
....end         outline     4309430032
....start       outline     4309430160
......start     outline     4309430224
......end       outline     4309430224
......start     outline     4309459024
......end       outline     4309459024
....end         outline     4309430160
..end           body        4309429968
end             opml        4309429072
```

The event style of processing is more natural for some operations, such as converting XML input to some other format. This technique can be used to convert lists of podcasts (from the earlier examples) from an XML file to a CSV file, so they can be loaded into a spreadsheet or database application.

```python
import csv
from xml.etree.ElementTree import iterparse
import sys

writer = csv.writer(sys.stdout, quoting=csv.QUOTE_NONNUMERIC)

group_name = ''

for (event, node) in iterparse('podcasts.opml', events=['start']):
```

```
if node.tag != 'outline':
    # Ignore anything not part of the outline
    continue
if not node.attrib.get('xmlUrl'):
    # Remember the current group
    group_name = node.attrib['text']
else:
    # Output a podcast entry
    writer.writerow( (group_name, node.attrib['text'],
                     node.attrib['xmlUrl'],
                     node.attrib.get('htmlUrl', ''),
                     )
                   )
```

This conversion program does not need to hold the entire parsed input file in memory, and processing each node as it is encountered in the input is more efficient.

```
$ python ElementTree_write_podcast_csv.py

"Fiction","tor.com / category / tordotstories","http://www.tor.com/r\
ss/category/TorDotStories","http://www.tor.com/"
"Python","PyCon Podcast","http://advocacy.python.org/podcasts/pycon.\
rss","http://advocacy.python.org/podcasts/"
"Python","A Little Bit of Python","http://advocacy.python.org/podcas\
ts/littlebit.rss","http://advocacy.python.org/podcasts/"
```

> **Note:** The output from `ElementTree_write_podcast_csv.py` has been reformatted to fit on this page. The output lines ending with \ indicate an artificial line break.

7.6.6 Creating a Custom Tree Builder

A potentially more efficient means of handling parse events is to replace the standard tree builder behavior with a custom version. The `ElementTree` parser uses an `XMLTreeBuilder` to process the XML and call methods on a target class to save the results. The usual output is an `ElementTree` instance created by the default `TreeBuilder` class. Replacing `TreeBuilder` with another class allows it to receive the events before the `Element` nodes are instantiated, saving that portion of the overhead.

The XML-to-CSV converter from the previous section can be reimplemented as a tree builder.

```python
import csv
from xml.etree.ElementTree import XMLTreeBuilder
import sys

class PodcastListToCSV(object):

    def __init__(self, outputFile):
        self.writer = csv.writer(outputFile,
                                 quoting=csv.QUOTE_NONNUMERIC)
        self.group_name = ''
        return

    def start(self, tag, attrib):
        if tag != 'outline':
            # Ignore anything not part of the outline
            return
        if not attrib.get('xmlUrl'):
            # Remember the current group
            self.group_name = attrib['text']
        else:
            # Output a podcast entry
            self.writer.writerow( (self.group_name, attrib['text'],
                                   attrib['xmlUrl'],
                                   attrib.get('htmlUrl', ''),
                                   )
                                )

    def end(self, tag):
        # Ignore closing tags
        pass
    def data(self, data):
        # Ignore data inside nodes
        pass
    def close(self):
        # Nothing special to do here
        return


target = PodcastListToCSV(sys.stdout)
parser = XMLTreeBuilder(target=target)
with open('podcasts.opml', 'rt') as f:
    for line in f:
        parser.feed(line)
parser.close()
```

PodcastListToCSV implements the TreeBuilder protocol. Each time a new XML tag is encountered, start() is called with the tag name and attributes. When a closing tag is seen, end() is called with the name. In between, data() is called when a node has content (the tree builder is expected to keep up with the "current" node). When all the input is processed, close() is called. It can return a value, which will be returned to the user of the XMLTreeBuilder.

```
$ python ElementTree_podcast_csv_treebuilder.py

"Fiction","tor.com / category / tordotstories","http://www.tor.com/r\
ss/category/TorDotStories","http://www.tor.com/"
"Python","PyCon Podcast","http://advocacy.python.org/podcasts/pycon.\
rss","http://advocacy.python.org/podcasts/"
"Python","A Little Bit of Python","http://advocacy.python.org/podcas\
ts/littlebit.rss","http://advocacy.python.org/podcasts/"
```

> **Note:** The output from ElementTree_podcast_csv_treebuidler.py has been reformatted to fit on this page. The output lines ending with \ indicate an artificial line break.

7.6.7 Parsing Strings

To work with smaller bits of XML text, especially string literals that might be embedded in the source of a program, use XML() and the string containing the XML to be parsed as the only argument.

```
from xml.etree.ElementTree import XML

parsed = XML('''
<root>
  <group>
    <child id="a">This is child "a".</child>
    <child id="b">This is child "b".</child>
  </group>
  <group>
    <child id="c">This is child "c".</child>
  </group>
</root>
''')

print 'parsed =', parsed
```

```python
def show_node(node):
    print node.tag
    if node.text is not None and node.text.strip():
        print '   text: "%s"' % node.text
    if node.tail is not None and node.tail.strip():
        print '   tail: "%s"' % node.tail
    for name, value in sorted(node.attrib.items()):
        print '   %-4s = "%s"' % (name, value)
    for child in node:
        show_node(child)
    return

for elem in parsed:
    show_node(elem)
```

Unlike with `parse()`, the return value is an `Element` instance instead of an `ElementTree`. An `Element` supports the iterator protocol directly, so there is no need to call `getiterator()`.

```
$ python ElementTree_XML.py

parsed = <Element 'root' at 0x100dcba50>
group
child
  text: "This is child "a"."
  id   = "a"
child
  text: "This is child "b"."
  id   = "b"
group
child
  text: "This is child "c"."
  id   = "c"
```

For structured XML that uses the `id` attribute to identify unique nodes of interest, `XMLID()` is a convenient way to access the parse results.

```python
from xml.etree.ElementTree import XMLID

tree, id_map = XMLID('''
<root>
```

```
  <group>
    <child id="a">This is child "a".</child>
    <child id="b">This is child "b".</child>
  </group>
  <group>
    <child id="c">This is child "c".</child>
  </group>
</root>
''')


for key, value in sorted(id_map.items()):
    print '%s = %s' % (key, value)
```

XMLID() returns the parsed tree as an Element object, along with a dictionary mapping the id attribute strings to the individual nodes in the tree.

```
$ python ElementTree_XMLID.py

a = <Element 'child' at 0x100dcab90>
b = <Element 'child' at 0x100dcac50>
c = <Element 'child' at 0x100dcae90>
```

See Also:

Outline Processor Markup Language, OPML (http://www.opml.org/) Dave Winer's OPML specification and documentation.

XML Path Language, XPath (http://www.w3.org/TR/xpath/) A syntax for identifying parts of an XML document.

XPath Support in ElementTree (http://effbot.org/zone/element-xpath.htm) Part of Fredrick Lundh's original documentation for ElementTree.

csv (page 411) Read and write comma-separated-value files.

7.6.8   Building Documents with Element Nodes

In addition to its parsing capabilities, xml.etree.ElementTree also supports creating well-formed XML documents from Element objects constructed in an application. The Element class used when a document is parsed also knows how to generate a serialized form of its contents, which can then be written to a file or other data stream.

There are three helper functions useful for creating a hierarchy of Element nodes. Element() creates a standard node, SubElement() attaches a new node to a parent, and Comment() creates a node that serializes using XML's comment syntax.

```
from xml.etree.ElementTree import ( Element,
                                     SubElement,
                                     Comment,
                                     tostring,
                                     )

top = Element('top')

comment = Comment('Generated for PyMOTW')
top.append(comment)

child = SubElement(top, 'child')
child.text = 'This child contains text.'

child_with_tail = SubElement(top, 'child_with_tail')
child_with_tail.text = 'This child has regular text.'
child_with_tail.tail = 'And "tail" text.'

child_with_entity_ref = SubElement(top, 'child_with_entity_ref')
child_with_entity_ref.text = 'This & that'

print tostring(top)
```

The output contains only the XML nodes in the tree, not the XML declaration with version and encoding.

```
$ python ElementTree_create.py

<top><!--Generated for PyMOTW--><child>This child contains text.</ch
ild><child_with_tail>This child has regular text.</child_with_tail>A
nd "tail" text.<child_with_entity_ref>This &amp; that</child_with_en
tity_ref></top>
```

The & character in the text of `child_with_entity_ref` is converted to the entity reference `&amp;` automatically.

7.6.9 Pretty-Printing XML

`ElementTree` makes no effort to format the output of `tostring()` so it is easy to read, because adding extra whitespace changes the contents of the document. To make the output easier to follow, the rest of the examples will use `xml.dom.minidom` to reparse the XML and then use its `toprettyxml()` method.

```
from xml.etree import ElementTree
from xml.dom import minidom

def prettify(elem):
    """Return a pretty-printed XML string for the Element.
    """
    rough_string = ElementTree.tostring(elem, 'utf-8')
    reparsed = minidom.parseString(rough_string)
    return reparsed.toprettyxml(indent="  ")
```

The updated example now looks like the following:

```
from xml.etree.ElementTree import Element, SubElement, Comment
from ElementTree_pretty import prettify

top = Element('top')

comment = Comment('Generated for PyMOTW')
top.append(comment)

child = SubElement(top, 'child')
child.text = 'This child contains text.'

child_with_tail = SubElement(top, 'child_with_tail')
child_with_tail.text = 'This child has regular text.'
child_with_tail.tail = 'And "tail" text.'

child_with_entity_ref = SubElement(top, 'child_with_entity_ref')
child_with_entity_ref.text = 'This & that'

print prettify(top)
```

The output is easier to read.

```
$ python ElementTree_create_pretty.py

<?xml version="1.0" ?>
<top>
  <!--Generated for PyMOTW-->
  <child>
    This child contains text.
  </child>
```

```
<child_with_tail>
  This child has regular text.
</child_with_tail>
And &quot;tail&quot; text.
<child_with_entity_ref>
  This &amp; that
</child_with_entity_ref>
</top>
```

In addition to the extra whitespace for formatting, the `xml.dom.minidom` pretty-printer also adds an XML declaration to the output.

7.6.10   Setting Element Properties

The previous example created nodes with tags and text content, but did not set any attributes of the nodes. Many of the examples from *Parsing an XML Document* worked with an OPML file listing podcasts and their feeds. The `outline` nodes in the tree used attributes for the group names and podcast properties. `ElementTree` can be used to construct a similar XML file from a CSV input file, setting all the element attributes as the tree is constructed.

```
import csv
from xml.etree.ElementTree import ( Element,
                                    SubElement,
                                    Comment,
                                    tostring,
                                    )
import datetime
from ElementTree_pretty import prettify

generated_on = str(datetime.datetime.now())

# Configure one attribute with set()
root = Element('opml')
root.set('version', '1.0')

root.append(
    Comment('Generated by ElementTree_csv_to_xml.py for PyMOTW')
    )

head = SubElement(root, 'head')
title = SubElement(head, 'title')
```

```
title.text = 'My Podcasts'
dc = SubElement(head, 'dateCreated')
dc.text = generated_on
dm = SubElement(head, 'dateModified')
dm.text = generated_on

body = SubElement(root, 'body')

with open('podcasts.csv', 'rt') as f:
    current_group = None
    reader = csv.reader(f)
    for row in reader:
        group_name, podcast_name, xml_url, html_url = row
        if current_group is None or group_name != current_group.text:
            # Start a new group
            current_group = SubElement(body, 'outline',
                                       {'text':group_name})
        # Add this podcast to the group,
        # setting all its attributes at
        # once.
        podcast = SubElement(current_group, 'outline',
                             {'text':podcast_name,
                              'xmlUrl':xml_url,
                              'htmlUrl':html_url,
                              })

print prettify(root)
```

This example uses two techniques to set the attribute values of new nodes. The root node is configured using `set()` to change one attribute at a time. The podcast nodes are given all their attributes at once by passing a dictionary to the node factory.

```
$ python ElementTree_csv_to_xml.py

<?xml version="1.0" ?>
<opml version="1.0">
  <!--Generated by ElementTree_csv_to_xml.py for PyMOTW-->
  <head>
    <title>
      My Podcasts
    </title>
    <dateCreated>
```

```
        2010-12-03 08:48:58.065172
    </dateCreated>
    <dateModified>
        2010-12-03 08:48:58.065172
    </dateModified>
  </head>
  <body>
    <outline text="Books and Fiction">
        <outline htmlUrl="http://www.tor.com/" text="tor.com / categor
y / tordotstories" xmlUrl="http://www.tor.com/rss/category/TorDotSto
ries"/>
    </outline>
    <outline text="Python">
        <outline htmlUrl="http://advocacy.python.org/podcasts/" text="
PyCon Podcast" xmlUrl="http://advocacy.python.org/podcasts/pycon.rss
"/>
    </outline>
    <outline text="Python">
        <outline htmlUrl="http://advocacy.python.org/podcasts/" text="
A Little Bit of Python" xmlUrl="http://advocacy.python.org/podcasts/
littlebit.rss"/>
    </outline>
    <outline text="Python">
        <outline htmlUrl="" text="Django Dose Everything Feed" xmlUrl=
"http://djangodose.com/everything/feed/"/>
    </outline>
  </body>
</opml>
```

7.6.11 Building Trees from Lists of Nodes

Multiple children can be added to an `Element` instance together with the `extend()` method. The argument to `extend()` is any iterable, including a `list` or another `Element` instance.

```
from xml.etree.ElementTree import Element, tostring
from ElementTree_pretty import prettify

top = Element('top')

children = [
    Element('child', num=str(i))
```

```
    for i in xrange(3)
    ]

top.extend(children)

print prettify(top)
```

When a `list` is given, the nodes in the list are added directly to the new parent.

```
$ python ElementTree_extend.py

<?xml version="1.0" ?>
<top>
  <child num="0"/>
  <child num="1"/>
  <child num="2"/>
</top>
```

When another `Element` instance is given, the children of that node are added to the new parent.

```
from xml.etree.ElementTree import Element, SubElement, tostring, XML
from ElementTree_pretty import prettify

top = Element('top')

parent = SubElement(top, 'parent')

children = XML(
    '<root><child num="0" /><child num="1" /><child num="2" /></root>'
    )
parent.extend(children)

print prettify(top)
```

In this case, the node with tag `root` created by parsing the XML string has three children, which are added to the `parent` node. The `root` node is not part of the output tree.

```
$ python ElementTree_extend_node.py

<?xml version="1.0" ?>
<top>
```

```
  <parent>
    <child num="0"/>
    <child num="1"/>
    <child num="2"/>
  </parent>
</top>
```

It is important to understand that `extend()` does not modify any existing parent-child relationships with the nodes. If the values passed to `extend()` exist somewhere in the tree already, they will still be there and will be repeated in the output.

```
from xml.etree.ElementTree import Element, SubElement, tostring, XML
from ElementTree_pretty import prettify

top = Element('top')

parent_a = SubElement(top, 'parent', id='A')
parent_b = SubElement(top, 'parent', id='B')

# Create children
children = XML(
    '<root><child num="0" /><child num="1" /><child num="2" /></root>'
    )

# Set the id to the Python object id of the node
# to make duplicates easier to spot.
for c in children:
    c.set('id', str(id(c)))

# Add to first parent
parent_a.extend(children)

print 'A:'
print prettify(top)
print

# Copy nodes to second parent
parent_b.extend(children)

print 'B:'
print prettify(top)
print
```

Setting the `id` attribute of these children to the Python unique object identifier highlights the fact that the same node objects appear in the output tree more than once.

```
$ python ElementTree_extend_node_copy.py

A:
<?xml version="1.0" ?>
<top>
  <parent id="A">
    <child id="4309786256" num="0"/>
    <child id="4309786320" num="1"/>
    <child id="4309786512" num="2"/>
  </parent>
  <parent id="B"/>
</top>


B:
<?xml version="1.0" ?>
<top>
  <parent id="A">
    <child id="4309786256" num="0"/>
    <child id="4309786320" num="1"/>
    <child id="4309786512" num="2"/>
  </parent>
  <parent id="B">
    <child id="4309786256" num="0"/>
    <child id="4309786320" num="1"/>
    <child id="4309786512" num="2"/>
  </parent>
</top>
```

7.6.12 Serializing XML to a Stream

`tostring()` is implemented by writing to an in-memory file-like object and then returning a string representing the entire element tree. When working with large amounts of data, it will take less memory and make more efficient use of the I/O libraries to write directly to a file handle using the `write()` method of `ElementTree`.

```
import sys
from xml.etree.ElementTree import ( Element,
                                    SubElement,
```

```
                                    Comment,
                                    ElementTree,
                                    )

top = Element('top')

comment = Comment('Generated for PyMOTW')
top.append(comment)

child = SubElement(top, 'child')
child.text = 'This child contains text.'

child_with_tail = SubElement(top, 'child_with_tail')
child_with_tail.text = 'This child has regular text.'
child_with_tail.tail = 'And "tail" text.'

child_with_entity_ref = SubElement(top, 'child_with_entity_ref')
child_with_entity_ref.text = 'This & that'

empty_child = SubElement(top, 'empty_child')

ElementTree(top).write(sys.stdout)
```

The example uses `sys.stdout` to write to the console, but it could also write to an open file or socket.

```
$ python ElementTree_write.py

<top><!--Generated for PyMOTW--><child>This child contains text.</ch
ild><child_with_tail>This child has regular text.</child_with_tail>A
nd "tail" text.<child_with_entity_ref>This &amp; that</child_with_en
tity_ref><empty_child /></top>
```

The last node in the tree contains no text or subnodes, so it is written as an empty tag, `<empty_child />`. `write()` takes a *method* argument to control the handling for empty nodes.

```
import sys
from xml.etree.ElementTree import Element, SubElement, ElementTree

top = Element('top')
```

```
child = SubElement(top, 'child')
child.text = 'Contains text.'

empty_child = SubElement(top, 'empty_child')

for method in [ 'xml', 'html', 'text' ]:
    print method
    ElementTree(top).write(sys.stdout, method=method)
    print '\n'
```

Three methods are supported.

xml The default method, produces `<empty_child />`.

html Produces the tag pair, as is required in HTML documents (`<empty_child>`
`</empty_child>`).

text Prints only the text of nodes, and skips empty tags entirely.

```
$ python ElementTree_write_method.py

xml
<top><child>Contains text.</child><empty_child /></top>

html
<top><child>Contains text.</child><empty_child></empty_child></top>

text
Contains text.
```

See Also:

Outline Processor Markup Language, OPML (www.opml.org/) Dave Winer's
OPML specification and documentation.

**Pretty-Print XML with Python—Indenting XML
(http://renesd.blogspot.com/2007/05/pretty-print-xml-with-python.html)**
A tip from Rene Dudfield for pretty-printing XML in Python.

xml.etree.ElementTree (http://docs.python.org/library/xml.etree.elementtree.html)
The standard library documentation for this module.

ElementTree Overview (http://effbot.org/zone/element-index.htm) Fredrick
Lundh's original documentation and links to the development versions of the
ElementTree library.

**Process XML in Python with ElementTree
(http://www.ibm.com/developerworks/library/x-matters28/)** IBM Developer-
Works article by David Mertz.

lxml.etree (http://codespeak.net/lxml/) A separate implementation of the Element-Tree API based on `libxml2` with more complete XPath support.

7.7   csv—Comma-Separated Value Files

Purpose Read and write comma-separated value files.
Python Version 2.3 and later.

The `csv` module can be used to work with data exported from spreadsheets and databases into text files formatted with fields and records, commonly referred to as *comma-separated value* (CSV) format because commas are often used to separate the fields in a record.

> **Note:** The Python 2.5 version of `csv` does not support Unicode data. There are also issues with ASCII NUL characters. Using UTF-8 or printable ASCII is recommended.

7.7.1   Reading

Use `reader()` to create an object for reading data from a CSV file. The reader can be used as an iterator to process the rows of the file in order. For example

```
import csv
import sys

with open(sys.argv[1], 'rt') as f:
    reader = csv.reader(f)
    for row in reader:
        print row
```

The first argument to `reader()` is the source of text lines. In this case, it is a file, but any iterable is accepted (a `StringIO` instance, `list`, etc.). Other optional arguments can be given to control how the input data is parsed.

```
"Title 1","Title 2","Title 3"
1,"a",08/18/07
2,"b",08/19/07
3,"c",08/20/07
```

As it is read, each row of the input data is parsed and converted to a `list` of strings.

```
$ python csv_reader.py testdata.csv

['Title 1', 'Title 2', 'Title 3']
['1', 'a', '08/18/07']
['2', 'b', '08/19/07']
['3', 'c', '08/20/07']
```

The parser handles line breaks embedded within strings in a row, which is why a "row" is not always the same as a "line" of input from the file.

```
"Title 1","Title 2","Title 3"
1,"first line
second line",08/18/07
```

Fields with line breaks in the input retain the internal line breaks when they are returned by the parser.

```
$ python csv_reader.py testlinebreak.csv

['Title 1', 'Title 2', 'Title 3']
['1', 'first line\nsecond line', '08/18/07']
```

7.7.2   Writing

Writing CSV files is just as easy as reading them. Use `writer()` to create an object for writing, and then iterate over the rows using `writerow()` to print them.

```
import csv
import sys

with open(sys.argv[1], 'wt') as f:
    writer = csv.writer(f)
    writer.writerow( ('Title 1', 'Title 2', 'Title 3') )
    for i in range(3):
        writer.writerow( (i+1,
                          chr(ord('a') + i),
                          '08/%02d/07' % (i+1),
                          )
                        )

print open(sys.argv[1], 'rt').read()
```

The output does not look exactly like the exported data used in the reader example.

```
$ python csv_writer.py testout.csv

Title 1,Title 2,Title 3
1,a,08/01/07
2,b,08/02/07
3,c,08/03/07
```

Quoting

The default quoting behavior is different for the writer, so the second and third columns in the previous example are not quoted. To add quoting, set the *quoting* arguments to one of the other quoting modes.

```
writer = csv.writer(f, quoting=csv.QUOTE_NONNUMERIC)
```

In this case, QUOTE_NONNUMERIC adds quotes around all columns containing values that are not numbers.

```
$ python csv_writer_quoted.py testout_quoted.csv

"Title 1","Title 2","Title 3"
1,"a","08/01/07"
2,"b","08/02/07"
3,"c","08/03/07"
```

There are four different quoting options defined as constants in the csv module.

QUOTE_ALL Quote everything, regardless of type.

QUOTE_MINIMAL Quote fields with special characters (anything that would confuse a parser configured with the same dialect and options). This is the default.

QUOTE_NONNUMERIC Quote all fields that are not integers or floats. When used with the reader, input fields that are not quoted are converted to floats.

QUOTE_NONE Do not quote anything on output. When used with the reader, quote characters are included in the field values (normally, they are treated as delimiters and stripped).

7.7.3   Dialects

There is no well-defined standard for comma-separated value files, so the parser needs to be flexible. This flexibility means there are many parameters to control how csv parses or writes data. Rather than passing each of these parameters to the reader and writer separately, they are grouped together into a *dialect* object.

Dialect classes can be registered by name so that callers of the `csv` module do not need to know the parameter settings in advance. The complete list of registered dialects can be retrieved with `list_dialects()`.

```
import csv

print csv.list_dialects()
```

The standard library includes two dialects: `excel` and `excel-tabs`. The `excel` dialect is for working with data in the default export format for Microsoft Excel, and it also works with OpenOffice or NeoOffice.

```
$ python csv_list_dialects.py

['excel-tab', 'excel']
```

Creating a Dialect

If, instead of using commas to delimit fields, the input file uses pipes (|), like this

```
"Title 1"|"Title 2"|"Title 3"
1|"first line
second line"|08/18/07
```

a new dialect can be registered using the appropriate delimiter.

```
import csv

csv.register_dialect('pipes', delimiter='|')

with open('testdata.pipes', 'r') as f:
    reader = csv.reader(f, dialect='pipes')
    for row in reader:
        print row
```

Using the "pipes" dialect, the file can be read just as with the comma-delimited file.

```
$ python csv_dialect.py

['Title 1', 'Title 2', 'Title 3']
['1', 'first line\nsecond line', '08/18/07']
```

Table 7.3. CSV Dialect Parameters

Attribute	Default	Meaning
delimiter	,	Field separator (one character)
doublequote	True	Flag controlling whether `quotechar` instances are doubled
escapechar	None	Character used to indicate an escape sequence
lineterminator	\r\n	String used by writer to terminate a line
quotechar	"	String to surround fields containing special values (one character)
quoting	QUOTE_MINIMAL	Controls quoting behavior described earlier
skipinitialspace	False	Ignore whitespace after the field delimiter

Dialect Parameters

A dialect specifies all the tokens used when parsing or writing a data file. Table 7.3 lists the aspects of the file format that can be specified, from the way columns are delimited to the character used to escape a token.

```
import csv
import sys

csv.register_dialect('escaped',
                     escapechar='\\',
                     doublequote=False,
                     quoting=csv.QUOTE_NONE,
                     )
csv.register_dialect('singlequote',
                     quotechar="'",
                     quoting=csv.QUOTE_ALL,
                     )

quoting_modes = dict( (getattr(csv,n), n)
                     for n in dir(csv)
                     if n.startswith('QUOTE_')
                     )

for name in sorted(csv.list_dialects()):
    print 'Dialect: "%s"\n' % name
```

```
dialect = csv.get_dialect(name)

print ' delimiter    = %-6r    skipinitialspace = %r' % (
    dialect.delimiter, dialect.skipinitialspace)
print ' doublequote = %-6r    quoting          = %s' % (
    dialect.doublequote, quoting_modes[dialect.quoting])
print ' quotechar   = %-6r    lineterminator   = %r' % (
    dialect.quotechar, dialect.lineterminator)
print ' escapechar  = %-6r' % dialect.escapechar
print

writer = csv.writer(sys.stdout, dialect=dialect)
writer.writerow(
    ('col1', 1, '10/01/2010',
     'Special chars: " \' %s to parse' % dialect.delimiter)
    )
print
```

This program shows how the same data appears in several different dialects.

```
$ python csv_dialect_variations.py

Dialect: "escaped"

  delimiter   = ','       skipinitialspace = 0
  doublequote = 0         quoting          = QUOTE_NONE
  quotechar   = '"'       lineterminator   = '\r\n'
  escapechar  = '\\'

col1,1,10/01/2010,Special chars: \" ' \, to parse

Dialect: "excel"

  delimiter   = ','       skipinitialspace = 0
  doublequote = 1         quoting          = QUOTE_MINIMAL
  quotechar   = '"'       lineterminator   = '\r\n'
  escapechar  = None

col1,1,10/01/2010,"Special chars: "" ' , to parse"

Dialect: "excel-tab"

  delimiter   = '\t'      skipinitialspace = 0
  doublequote = 1         quoting          = QUOTE_MINIMAL
```

```
quotechar    = '"'            lineterminator    = '\r\n'
escapechar   = None


col1     1         10/01/2010       "Special chars: "" '       to parse"


Dialect: "singlequote"

  delimiter   = ','           skipinitialspace = 0
  doublequote = 1             quoting          = QUOTE_ALL
  quotechar   = "'"           lineterminator   = '\r\n'
  escapechar  = None

'col1','1','10/01/2010','Special chars: " '' , to parse'
```

Automatically Detecting Dialects

The best way to configure a dialect for parsing an input file is to know the correct settings in advance. For data where the dialect parameters are unknown, the `Sniffer` class can be used to make an educated guess. The `sniff()` method takes a sample of the input data and an optional argument giving the possible delimiter characters.

```
import csv
from StringIO import StringIO
import textwrap

csv.register_dialect('escaped',
                     escapechar='\\',
                     doublequote=False,
                     quoting=csv.QUOTE_NONE)
csv.register_dialect('singlequote',
                     quotechar="'",
                     quoting=csv.QUOTE_ALL)


# Generate sample data for all known dialects
samples = []
for name in sorted(csv.list_dialects()):
    buffer = StringIO()
    dialect = csv.get_dialect(name)
    writer = csv.writer(buffer, dialect=dialect)
    writer.writerow(
        ('col1', 1, '10/01/2010',
         'Special chars " \' %s to parse' % dialect.delimiter)
        )
    samples.append( (name, dialect, buffer.getvalue()) )
```

```
# Guess the dialect for a given sample, and then use the results to
# parse the data.
sniffer = csv.Sniffer()
for name, expected, sample in samples:
    print 'Dialect: "%s"\n' % name
    dialect = sniffer.sniff(sample, delimiters=',\t')
    reader = csv.reader(StringIO(sample), dialect=dialect)
    print reader.next()
    print
```

`sniff()` returns a `Dialect` instance with the settings to be used for parsing the data. The results are not always perfect, as demonstrated by the "escaped" dialect in the example.

```
$ python csv_dialect_sniffer.py

Dialect: "escaped"

['col1', '1', '10/01/2010', 'Special chars \\" \' \\', ' to parse']

Dialect: "excel"

['col1', '1', '10/01/2010', 'Special chars " \' , to parse']

Dialect: "excel-tab"

['col1', '1', '10/01/2010', 'Special chars " \' \t to parse']

Dialect: "singlequote"

['col1', '1', '10/01/2010', 'Special chars " \' , to parse']
```

7.7.4   Using Field Names

In addition to working with sequences of data, the `csv` module includes classes for working with rows as dictionaries so that the fields can be named. The `DictReader` and `DictWriter` classes translate rows to dictionaries instead of lists. Keys for the dictionary can be passed in or inferred from the first row in the input (when the row contains headers).

```
import csv
import sys

with open(sys.argv[1], 'rt') as f:
    reader = csv.DictReader(f)
    for row in reader:
        print row
```

The dictionary-based reader and writer are implemented as wrappers around the sequence-based classes, and they use the same methods and arguments. The only difference in the reader API is that rows are returned as dictionaries instead of lists or tuples.

```
$ python csv_dictreader.py testdata.csv

{'Title 1': '1', 'Title 3': '08/18/07', 'Title 2': 'a'}
{'Title 1': '2', 'Title 3': '08/19/07', 'Title 2': 'b'}
{'Title 1': '3', 'Title 3': '08/20/07', 'Title 2': 'c'}
```

The DictWriter must be given a list of field names so it knows how to order the columns in the output.

```
import csv
import sys

with open(sys.argv[1], 'wt') as f:

    fieldnames = ('Title 1', 'Title 2', 'Title 3')
    headers = dict( (n,n) for n in fieldnames )

    writer = csv.DictWriter(f, fieldnames=fieldnames)
    writer.writerow(headers)

    for i in range(3):
        writer.writerow({ 'Title 1':i+1,
                          'Title 2':chr(ord('a') + i),
                          'Title 3':'08/%02d/07' % (i+1),
                          })

print open(sys.argv[1], 'rt').read()
```

The field names are not written to the file automatically, so they need to be written explicitly before any other data.

```
$ python csv_dictwriter.py testout.csv

Title 1,Title 2,Title 3
1,a,08/01/07
2,b,08/02/07
3,c,08/03/07
```

See Also:

csv (http://docs.python.org/library/csv.html) The standard library documentation for this module.

PEP 305 (www.python.org/dev/peps/pep-0305) CSV File API.

Chapter 8

DATA COMPRESSION AND ARCHIVING

Although modern computer systems have an ever-increasing storage capacity, the growth of data being produced is unrelenting. *Lossless* compression algorithms make up for some of the shortfall in capacity by trading time spent compressing or decompressing data for the space needed to store it. Python includes interfaces to the most popular compression libraries so it can read and write files interchangeably.

zlib and gzip expose the GNU zip library, and bz2 provides access to the more recent bzip2 format. Both formats work on streams of data, without regard to input format, and provide interfaces for reading and writing compressed files transparently. Use these modules for compressing a single file or data source.

The standard library also includes modules to manage *archive* formats for combining several files into a single file that can be managed as a unit. tarfile reads and writes the UNIX tape archive format, an old standard still widely used today because of its flexibility. zipfile works with archives based on the format popularized by the PC program PKZIP, originally used under MS-DOS and Windows, but now also used on other platforms because of the simplicity of its API and portability of the format.

8.1 zlib—GNU zlib Compression

Purpose Low-level access to GNU zlib compression library.
Python Version 2.5 and later

The zlib module provides a lower-level interface to many of the functions in the zlib compression library from the GNU project.

8.1.1 Working with Data in Memory

The simplest way to work with `zlib` requires holding all the data to be compressed or decompressed in memory:

```
import zlib
import binascii

original_data = 'This is the original text.'
print 'Original      :', len(original_data), original_data

compressed = zlib.compress(original_data)
print 'Compressed    :', len(compressed), binascii.hexlify(compressed)

decompressed = zlib.decompress(compressed)
print 'Decompressed :', len(decompressed), decompressed
```

The `compress()` and `decompress()` functions both take a string argument and return a string.

```
$ python zlib_memory.py

Original      : 26 This is the original text.
Compressed    : 32 789c0bc9c82c5600a2928c5485fca2ccf4ccbcc41c8592d
48a123d007f2f097e
Decompressed : 26 This is the original text.
```

The previous example demonstrates that, for short text, the compressed version of a string can be bigger than the uncompressed version. While the actual results depend on the input data, for short bits of text, it is interesting to observe the compression overhead.

```
import zlib

original_data = 'This is the original text.'

fmt = '%15s  %15s'
print fmt % ('len(data)', 'len(compressed)')
print fmt % ('-' * 15, '-' * 15)

for i in xrange(5):
    data = original_data * i
```

```
compressed = zlib.compress(data)
highlight = '*' if len(data) < len(compressed) else ''
print fmt % (len(data), len(compressed)), highlight
```

The * in the output highlight the lines where the compressed data takes up more memory than the uncompressed version.

```
$ python zlib_lengths.py

     len(data)   len(compressed)
--------------   ---------------
            0                 8 *
           26                32 *
           52                35
           78                35
          104                36
```

8.1.2   Incremental Compression and Decompression

The in-memory approach has drawbacks that make it impractical for real-world use cases, primarily that the system needs enough memory to hold both the uncompressed and compressed versions resident in memory at the same time. The alternative is to use Compress and Decompress objects to manipulate data incrementally, so that the entire data set does not have to fit into memory.

```
import zlib
import binascii

compressor = zlib.compressobj(1)

with open('lorem.txt', 'r') as input:
    while True:
        block = input.read(64)
        if not block:
            break
        compressed = compressor.compress(block)
        if compressed:
            print 'Compressed: %s' % binascii.hexlify(compressed)
        else:
            print 'buffering...'
    remaining = compressor.flush()
    print 'Flushed: %s' % binascii.hexlify(remaining)
```

This example reads small blocks of data from a plain-text file and passes it to `compress()`. The compressor maintains an internal buffer of compressed data. Since the compression algorithm depends on checksums and minimum block sizes, the compressor may not be ready to return data each time it receives more input. If it does not have an entire compressed block ready, it returns an empty string. When all the data is fed in, the `flush()` method forces the compressor to close the final block and return the rest of the compressed data.

```
$ python zlib_incremental.py

Compressed: 7801
buffering...
buffering...
buffering...
buffering...
buffering...
Flushed: 55904b6ac4400c44f73e451da0f129b20c2110c85e696b8c40ddedd167ce1
f7915025a087daa9ef4be8c07e4f21c38962e834b800647435fd3b90747b2810eb9c4b
bcc13ac123bded6e4bef1c91ee40d3c6580e3ff52aad2e8cb2eb6062dad74a89ca904c
bb0f2545e0db4b1f2e01955b8c511cb2ac08967d228af1447c8ec72e40c4c714116e60
cdef171bb6c0feaa255dff1c507c2c4439ec9605b7e0ba9fc54bae39355cb89fd6ebe5
841d673c7b7bc68a46f575a312eebd220d4b32441bdc1b36ebf0aedef3d57ea4b26dd9
86dd39af57dfb05d32279de
```

8.1.3 Mixed Content Streams

The `Decompress` class returned by `decompressobj()` can also be used in situations where compressed and uncompressed data are mixed together.

```python
import zlib

lorem = open('lorem.txt', 'rt').read()
compressed = zlib.compress(lorem)
combined = compressed + lorem

decompressor = zlib.decompressobj()
decompressed = decompressor.decompress(combined)

decompressed_matches = decompressed == lorem
print 'Decompressed matches lorem:', decompressed_matches
```

```
unused_matches = decompressor.unused_data == lorem
print 'Unused data matches lorem :', unused_matches
```

After decompressing all the data, the *unused_data* attribute contains any data not used.

```
$ python zlib_mixed.py

Decompressed matches lorem: True
Unused data matches lorem : True
```

8.1.4   Checksums

In addition to compression and decompression functions, `zlib` includes two functions for computing checksums of data, `adler32()` and `crc32()`. Neither checksum is billed as cryptographically secure, and they are only intended for use for data-integrity verification.

```
import zlib

data = open('lorem.txt', 'r').read()

cksum = zlib.adler32(data)
print 'Adler32: %12d' % cksum
print '       : %12d' % zlib.adler32(data, cksum)

cksum = zlib.crc32(data)
print 'CRC-32 : %12d' % cksum
print '       : %12d' % zlib.crc32(data, cksum)
```

Both functions take the same arguments, a string of data and an optional value to be used as a starting point for the checksum. They return a 32-bit signed integer value that can also be passed back on subsequent calls as a new starting point argument to produce a *running* checksum.

```
$ python zlib_checksums.py

Adler32:    -752715298
       :     669447099
CRC-32 :   -1256596780
       :   -1424888665
```

8.1.5 Compressing Network Data

The server in the next listing uses the stream compressor to respond to requests consisting of filenames by writing a compressed version of the file to the socket used to communicate with the client. It has some artificial chunking in place to illustrate the buffering that occurs when the data passed to `compress()` or `decompress()` does not result in a complete block of compressed or uncompressed output.

```python
import zlib
import logging
import SocketServer
import binascii

BLOCK_SIZE = 64

class ZlibRequestHandler(SocketServer.BaseRequestHandler):

    logger = logging.getLogger('Server')

    def handle(self):
        compressor = zlib.compressobj(1)

        # Find out what file the client wants
        filename = self.request.recv(1024)
        self.logger.debug('client asked for: "%s"', filename)

        # Send chunks of the file as they are compressed
        with open(filename, 'rb') as input:
            while True:
                block = input.read(BLOCK_SIZE)
                if not block:
                    break
                self.logger.debug('RAW "%s"', block)
                compressed = compressor.compress(block)
                if compressed:
                    self.logger.debug('SENDING "%s"',
                                      binascii.hexlify(compressed))
                    self.request.send(compressed)
                else:
                    self.logger.debug('BUFFERING')
```

```
    # Send any data being buffered by the compressor
    remaining = compressor.flush()
    while remaining:
        to_send = remaining[:BLOCK_SIZE]
        remaining = remaining[BLOCK_SIZE:]
        self.logger.debug('FLUSHING "%s"',
                          binascii.hexlify(to_send))
        self.request.send(to_send)
    return


if __name__ == '__main__':
    import socket
    import threading
    from cStringIO import StringIO

    logging.basicConfig(level=logging.DEBUG,
                        format='%(name)s: %(message)s',
                        )
    logger = logging.getLogger('Client')

    # Set up a server, running in a separate thread
    address = ('localhost', 0) # let the kernel assign a port
    server = SocketServer.TCPServer(address, ZlibRequestHandler)
    ip, port = server.server_address # what port was assigned?

    t = threading.Thread(target=server.serve_forever)
    t.setDaemon(True)
    t.start()
```

The client connects to the socket and requests a file. Then it loops, receiving blocks of compressed data. Since a block may not contain enough information to decompress it entirely, the remainder of any data received earlier is combined with the new data and passed to the decompressor. As the data is decompressed, it is appended to a buffer, which is compared against the file contents at the end of the processing loop.

```
    # Connect to the server as a client
    logger.info('Contacting server on %s:%s', ip, port)
    s = socket.socket(socket.AF_INET, socket.SOCK_STREAM)
    s.connect((ip, port))
```

```python
# Ask for a file
requested_file = 'lorem.txt'
logger.debug('sending filename: "%s"', requested_file)
len_sent = s.send(requested_file)
# Receive a response
buffer = StringIO()
decompressor = zlib.decompressobj()
while True:
    response = s.recv(BLOCK_SIZE)
    if not response:
        break
    logger.debug('READ "%s"', binascii.hexlify(response))


    # Include any unconsumed data when feeding the decompressor.
    to_decompress = decompressor.unconsumed_tail + response
    while to_decompress:
        decompressed = decompressor.decompress(to_decompress)
        if decompressed:
            logger.debug('DECOMPRESSED "%s"', decompressed)
            buffer.write(decompressed)
            # Look for unconsumed data due to buffer overflow
            to_decompress = decompressor.unconsumed_tail
        else:
            logger.debug('BUFFERING')
            to_decompress = None


# deal with data reamining inside the decompressor buffer
remainder = decompressor.flush()
if remainder:
    logger.debug('FLUSHED "%s"', remainder)
    buffer.write(reaminder)


full_response = buffer.getvalue()
lorem = open('lorem.txt', 'rt').read()
logger.debug('response matches file contents: %s',
             full_response == lorem)

# Clean up
s.close()
server.socket.close()
```

> **Warning:** This server has obvious security implications. Do not run it on a system on the open Internet or in any environment where security might be an issue.

```
$ python zlib_server.py

Client: Contacting server on 127.0.0.1:55085
Client: sending filename: "lorem.txt"
Server: client asked for: "lorem.txt"
Server: RAW "Lorem ipsum dolor sit amet, consectetuer adipiscing elit
. Donec
"
Server: SENDING "7801"
Server: RAW "egestas, enim et consectetuer ullamcorper, lectus ligula
 rutrum "
Server: BUFFERING
Server: RAW "leo, a
elementum elit tortor eu quam. Duis tincidunt nisi ut ant"
Server: BUFFERING
Server: RAW "e. Nulla
facilisi. Sed tristique eros eu libero. Pellentesque ve"
Server: BUFFERING
Server: RAW "l arcu. Vivamus
purus orci, iaculis ac, suscipit sit amet, pulvi"
Server: BUFFERING
Server: RAW "nar eu,
lacus.
"
Server: BUFFERING
Server: FLUSHING "55904b6ac4400c44f73e451da0f129b20c2110c85e696b8c40d
dedd167ce1f7915025a087daa9ef4be8c07e4f21c38962e834b800647435fd3b90747
b2810eb9"
Server: FLUSHING "c4bbcc13ac123bded6e4bef1c91ee40d3c6580e3ff52aad2e8c
b2eb6062dad74a89ca904cbb0f2545e0db4b1f2e01955b8c511cb2ac08967d228af14
47c8ec72"
Server: FLUSHING "e40c4c714116e60cdef171bb6c0feaa255dff1c507c2c4439ec
9605b7e0ba9fc54bae39355cb89fd6ebe5841d673c7b7bc68a46f575a312eebd220d4
b32441bd"
Server: FLUSHING "c1b36ebf0aedef3d57ea4b26dd986dd39af57dfb05d32279de"
Client: READ "780155904b6ac4400c44f73e451da0f129b20c2110c85e696b8c40d
dedd167ce1f7915025a087daa9ef4be8c07e4f21c38962e834b800647435fd3b90747
b281"
```

```
Client: DECOMPRESSED "Lorem ipsum dolor sit amet, consectetuer "
Client: READ "0eb9c4bbcc13ac123bded6e4bef1c91ee40d3c6580e3ff52aad2e8c
b2eb6062dad74a89ca904cbb0f2545e0db4b1f2e01955b8c511cb2ac08967d228af14
47c8"
Client: DECOMPRESSED "adipiscing elit. Donec
egestas, enim et consectetuer ullamcorper, lectus ligula rutrum leo,
a
elementum elit tortor eu quam. Duis ti"
Client: READ "ec72e40c4c714116e60cdef171bb6c0feaa255dff1c507c2c4439ec
9605b7e0ba9fc54bae39355cb89fd6ebe5841d673c7b7bc68a46f575a312eebd220d4
b324"
Client: DECOMPRESSED "ncidunt nisi ut ante. Nulla
facilisi. Sed tristique eros eu libero. Pellentesque vel arcu. Vivamu
s
purus orci, iacu"
Client: READ "41bdc1b36ebf0aedef3d57ea4b26dd986dd39af57dfb05d32279de"
Client: DECOMPRESSED "lis ac, suscipit sit amet, pulvinar eu,
lacus.
"
Client: response matches file contents: True
```

See Also:

zlib (http://docs.python.org/library/zlib.html) The standard library documentation for this module.

www.zlib.net/ Home page for zlib library.

www.zlib.net/manual.html Complete zlib documentation.

bz2 (page 436) The `bz2` module provides a similar interface to the bzip2 compression library.

gzip (page 430) The `gzip` module includes a higher-level (file-based) interface to the zlib library.

8.2   gzip—Read and Write GNU Zip Files

Purpose Read and write gzip files.
Python Version 1.5.2 and later

The `gzip` module provides a file-like interface to GNU zip files, using `zlib` to compress and uncompress the data.

8.2.1   Writing Compressed Files

The module-level function `open()` creates an instance of the file-like class `GzipFile`. The usual methods for writing and reading data are provided.

```
import gzip
import os

outfilename = 'example.txt.gz'
with gzip.open(outfilename, 'wb') as output:
    output.write('Contents of the example file go here.\n')

print outfilename, 'contains', os.stat(outfilename).st_size, 'bytes'
os.system('file -b --mime %s' % outfilename)
```

To write data into a compressed file, open the file with mode `'w'`.

```
$ python gzip_write.py

application/x-gzip; charset=binary
example.txt.gz contains 68 bytes
```

Different amounts of compression can be used by passing a *compresslevel* argument. Valid values range from 1 to 9, inclusive. Lower values are faster and result in less compression. Higher values are slower and compress more, up to a point.

```
import gzip
import os
import hashlib

def get_hash(data):
    return hashlib.md5(data).hexdigest()

data = open('lorem.txt', 'r').read() * 1024
cksum = get_hash(data)

print 'Level  Size        Checksum'
print '-----  ----------  --------------------------------'
print 'data   %10d  %s' % (len(data), cksum)

for i in xrange(1, 10):
    filename = 'compress-level-%s.gz' % i
```

```
with gzip.open(filename, 'wb', compresslevel=i) as output:
    output.write(data)
size = os.stat(filename).st_size
cksum = get_hash(open(filename, 'rb').read())
print '%5d  %10d  %s' % (i, size, cksum)
```

The center column of numbers in the output shows the size in bytes of the files produced by compressing the input. For this input data, the higher compression values do not necessarily pay off in decreased storage space. Results will vary, depending on the input data.

```
$ python gzip_compresslevel.py

Level  Size        Checksum
-----  ----------  --------------------------------
data      754688   e4c0f9433723971563f08a458715119c
    1       9839   3fbd996cd4d63acc70047fb62646f2ba
    2       8260   427bf6183d4518bcd05611d4f114a07c
    3       8221   078331b777a11572583e3fdaa120b845
    4       4160   f73c478ffcba30bfe0b1d08d0f597394
    5       4160   022d920880e24c1895219a31105a89c8
    6       4160   45ba520d6af45e279a56bb9c67294b82
    7       4160   9a834b8a2c649d4b8d509cb12cc580e2
    8       4160   c1aafc7d7d58cba4ef21dfce6fd1f443
    9       4160   78039211f5777f9f34cf770c2eaafc6d
```

A `GzipFile` instance also includes a `writelines()` method that can be used to write a sequence of strings.

```
import gzip
import itertools
import os

with gzip.open('example_lines.txt.gz', 'wb') as output:
    output.writelines(
        itertools.repeat('The same line, over and over.\n', 10)
    )

os.system('gzcat example_lines.txt.gz')
```

As with a regular file, the input lines need to include a newline character.

```
$ python gzip_writelines.py

The same line, over and over.
The same line, over and over.
The same line, over and over.
The same line, over and over.
The same line, over and over.
The same line, over and over.
The same line, over and over.
The same line, over and over.
The same line, over and over.
The same line, over and over.
```

8.2.2 Reading Compressed Data

To read data back from previously compressed files, open the file with binary read mode
('rb') so no text-based translation of line endings is performed.

```
import gzip

with gzip.open('example.txt.gz', 'rb') as input_file:
    print input_file.read()
```

This example reads the file written by gzip_write.py from the previous section.

```
$ python gzip_read.py

Contents of the example file go here.
```

While reading a file, it is also possible to seek and read only part of the data.

```
import gzip

with gzip.open('example.txt.gz', 'rb') as input_file:
    print 'Entire file:'
    all_data = input_file.read()
    print all_data

    expected = all_data[5:15]

    # rewind to beginning
    input_file.seek(0)
```

```
    # move ahead 5 bytes
    input_file.seek(5)
    print 'Starting at position 5 for 10 bytes:'
    partial = input_file.read(10)
    print partial

    print
    print expected == partial
```

The `seek()` position is relative to the *uncompressed* data, so the caller does not need to know that the data file is compressed.

```
$ python gzip_seek.py

Entire file:
Contents of the example file go here.

Starting at position 5 for 10 bytes:
nts of the

True
```

8.2.3 Working with Streams

The `GzipFile` class can be used to wrap other types of data streams so they can use compression as well. This is useful when the data is being transmitted over a socket or an existing (already open) file handle. A `StringIO` buffer can also be used.

```
import gzip
from cStringIO import StringIO
import binascii

uncompressed_data = 'The same line, over and over.\n' * 10
print 'UNCOMPRESSED:', len(uncompressed_data)
print uncompressed_data

buf = StringIO()
with gzip.GzipFile(mode='wb', fileobj=buf) as f:
    f.write(uncompressed_data)
```

```
compressed_data = buf.getvalue()
print 'COMPRESSED:', len(compressed_data)
print binascii.hexlify(compressed_data)

inbuffer = StringIO(compressed_data)
with gzip.GzipFile(mode='rb', fileobj=inbuffer) as f:
    reread_data = f.read(len(uncompressed_data))

print
print 'REREAD:', len(reread_data)
print reread_data
```

One benefit of using `GzipFile` over `zlib` is that it supports the file API. However, when rereading the previously compressed data, an explicit length is passed to `read()`. Leaving off the length resulted in a CRC error, possibly because `StringIO` returned an empty string before reporting EOF. When working with streams of compressed data, either prefix the data with an integer representing the actual amount of data to be read or use the incremental decompression API in `zlib`.

```
$ python gzip_StringIO.py

UNCOMPRESSED: 300
The same line, over and over.
The same line, over and over.
The same line, over and over.
The same line, over and over.
The same line, over and over.
The same line, over and over.
The same line, over and over.
The same line, over and over.
The same line, over and over.
The same line, over and over.

COMPRESSED: 51
1f8b08001f96f24c02ff0bc94855284ecc4d55c8c9cc4bd551c82f4b2d5248cc4
b0133f4b8424665916401d3e717802c010000

REREAD: 300
The same line, over and over.
The same line, over and over.
The same line, over and over.
```

```
The same line, over and over.
The same line, over and over.
The same line, over and over.
The same line, over and over.
The same line, over and over.
The same line, over and over.
The same line, over and over.
```

See Also:

gzip (http://docs.python.org/library/gzip.html) The standard library documentation for this module.

bz2 (page 436) The `bz2` module uses the bzip2 compression format.

tarfile (page 448) The `tarfile` module includes built-in support for reading compressed tar archives.

zlib (page 421) The `zlib` module is a lower-level interface to gzip compression.

zipfile (page 457) The `zipfile` module gives access to ZIP archives.

8.3 bz2—bzip2 Compression

Purpose Perform bzip2 compression.
Python Version 2.3 and later

The `bz2` module is an interface for the bzip2 library, used to compress data for storage or transmission. There are three APIs provided:

- "one shot" compression/decompression functions for operating on a blob of data
- iterative compression/decompression objects for working with streams of data
- a file-like class that supports reading and writing as with an uncompressed file

8.3.1 One-Shot Operations in Memory

The simplest way to work with `bz2` is to load all the data to be compressed or decompressed in memory and then use `compress()` and `decompress()` to transform it.

```python
import bz2
import binascii

original_data = 'This is the original text.'
print 'Original     : %d bytes' % len(original_data)
print original_data
```

```
print
compressed = bz2.compress(original_data)
print 'Compressed   : %d bytes' % len(compressed)
hex_version = binascii.hexlify(compressed)
for i in xrange(len(hex_version)/40 + 1):
    print hex_version[i*40:(i+1)*40]

print
decompressed = bz2.decompress(compressed)
print 'Decompressed : %d bytes' % len(decompressed)
print decompressed
```

The compressed data contains non-ASCII characters, so it needs to be converted to its hexadecimal representation before it can be printed. In the output from these examples, the hexadecimal version is reformatted to have, at most, 40 characters on each line.

```
$ python bz2_memory.py

Original    : 26 bytes
This is the original text.

Compressed  : 62 bytes
425a683931415926535916be35a6000002938040
01040022e59c402000314c000111e93d434da223
028cf9e73148cae0a0d6ed7f17724538509016be
35a6

Decompressed : 26 bytes
This is the original text.
```

For short text, the compressed version can be significantly longer than the original. While the actual results depend on the input data, it is interesting to observe the compression overhead.

```
import bz2

original_data = 'This is the original text.'

fmt = '%15s  %15s'
print fmt % ('len(data)', 'len(compressed)')
print fmt % ('-' * 15, '-' * 15)
```

```
for i in xrange(5):
    data = original_data * i
    compressed = bz2.compress(data)
    print fmt % (len(data), len(compressed)),
    print '*' if len(data) < len(compressed) else ''
```

The output lines ending with * show the points where the compressed data is longer than the raw input.

```
$ python bz2_lengths.py

      len(data)    len(compressed)
-----------------  ----------------
              0                14 *
             26                62 *
             52                68 *
             78                70
            104                72
```

8.3.2   Incremental Compression and Decompression

The in-memory approach has obvious drawbacks that make it impractical for real-world use cases. The alternative is to use BZ2Compressor and BZ2Decompressor objects to manipulate data incrementally so that the entire data set does not have to fit into memory.

```
import bz2
import binascii

compressor = bz2.BZ2Compressor()

with open('lorem.txt', 'r') as input:
    while True:
        block = input.read(64)
        if not block:
            break
        compressed = compressor.compress(block)
        if compressed:
            print 'Compressed: %s' % binascii.hexlify(compressed)
        else:
            print 'buffering...'
```

```
remaining = compressor.flush()
print 'Flushed: %s' % binascii.hexlify(remaining)
```

This example reads small blocks of data from a plain-text file and passes it to `compress()`. The compressor maintains an internal buffer of compressed data. Since the compression algorithm depends on checksums and minimum block sizes, the compressor may not be ready to return data each time it receives more input. If it does not have an entire compressed block ready, it returns an empty string. When all the data is fed in, the `flush()` method forces the compressor to close the final block and return the rest of the compressed data.

```
$ python bz2_incremental.py

buffering...
buffering...
buffering...
buffering...
Flushed: 425a6839314159265359ba83a48c000014d5800010400504052fa7fe00300
0ba9112793d4ca789068698a0d1a341901a0d53f4d1119a8d4c9e812d755a67c107983
87682c7ca7b5a3bb75da77755eb81c1cb1ca94c4b6faf209c52a90aaa4d16a4a1b9c16
7a01c8d9ef32589d831e77df7a5753a398b11660e392126fc18a72a1088716cc8dedda
5d489da410748531278043d70a8a131c2b8adcd6a221bdb8c7ff76b88c1d5342ee48a7
0a12175074918
```

8.3.3 Mixed Content Streams

`BZ2Decompressor` can also be used in situations where compressed and uncompressed data are mixed together.

```
import bz2

lorem = open('lorem.txt', 'rt').read()
compressed = bz2.compress(lorem)
combined = compressed + lorem

decompressor = bz2.BZ2Decompressor()
decompressed = decompressor.decompress(combined)

decompressed_matches = decompressed == lorem
print 'Decompressed matches lorem:', decompressed_matches
```

```
unused_matches = decompressor.unused_data == lorem
print 'Unused data matches lorem :', unused_matches
```

After decompressing all the data, the *unused_data* attribute contains any data not used.

```
$ python bz2_mixed.py

Decompressed matches lorem: True
Unused data matches lorem : True
```

8.3.4   Writing Compressed Files

BZ2File can be used to write to and read from bzip2-compressed files using the usual methods for writing and reading data.

```
import bz2
import contextlib
import os

with contextlib.closing(bz2.BZ2File('example.bz2', 'wb')) as output:
    output.write('Contents of the example file go here.\n')

os.system('file example.bz2')
```

To write data into a compressed file, open the file with mode 'w'.

```
$ python bz2_file_write.py

example.bz2: bzip2 compressed data, block size = 900k
```

Different compression levels can be used by passing a *compresslevel* argument. Valid values range from 1 to 9, inclusive. Lower values are faster and result in less compression. Higher values are slower and compress more, up to a point.

```
import bz2
import os

data = open('lorem.txt', 'r').read() * 1024
print 'Input contains %d bytes' % len(data)

for i in xrange(1, 10):
    filename = 'compress-level-%s.bz2' % i
```

```
with bz2.BZ2File(filename, 'wb', compresslevel=i) as output:
    output.write(data)
os.system('cksum %s' % filename)
```

The center column of numbers in the script output is the size in bytes of the files produced. For this input data, the higher compression values do not always pay off in decreased storage space for the same input data. Results will vary for other inputs.

```
$ python bz2_file_compresslevel.py

3018243926 8771 compress-level-1.bz2
1942389165 4949 compress-level-2.bz2
2596054176 3708 compress-level-3.bz2
1491394456 2705 compress-level-4.bz2
1425874420 2705 compress-level-5.bz2
2232840816 2574 compress-level-6.bz2
447681641 2394 compress-level-7.bz2
3699654768 1137 compress-level-8.bz2
3103658384 1137 compress-level-9.bz2
Input contains 754688 bytes
```

A BZ2File instance also includes a writelines() method that can be used to write a sequence of strings.

```
import bz2
import contextlib
import itertools
import os

with contextlib.closing(bz2.BZ2File('lines.bz2', 'wb')) as output:
    output.writelines(
        itertools.repeat('The same line, over and over.\n', 10),
    )

os.system('bzcat lines.bz2')
```

The lines should end in a newline character, as when writing to a regular file.

```
$ python bz2_file_writelines.py

The same line, over and over.
The same line, over and over.
```

```
The same line, over and over.
The same line, over and over.
The same line, over and over.
The same line, over and over.
The same line, over and over.
The same line, over and over.
The same line, over and over.
The same line, over and over.
```

8.3.5   Reading Compressed Files

To read data back from previously compressed files, open the file with binary read mode
('rb') so no text-based translation of line endings is performed.

```
import bz2
import contextlib

with contextlib.closing(bz2.BZ2File('example.bz2', 'rb')) as input:
    print input.read()
```

This example reads the file written by bz2_file_write.py from the previous
section.

```
$ python bz2_file_read.py

Contents of the example file go here.
```

While reading a file, it is also possible to seek and to read only part of the data.

```
import bz2
import contextlib

with contextlib.closing(bz2.BZ2File('example.bz2', 'rb')) as input:
    print 'Entire file:'
    all_data = input.read()
    print all_data

    expected = all_data[5:15]
```

```
# rewind to beginning
input.seek(0)

# move ahead 5 bytes
input.seek(5)
print 'Starting at position 5 for 10 bytes:'
partial = input.read(10)
print partial

print
print expected == partial
```

The `seek()` position is relative to the *uncompressed* data, so the caller does not even need to be aware that the data file is compressed. This allows a `BZ2File` instance to be passed to a function expecting a regular uncompressed file.

```
$ python bz2_file_seek.py

Entire file:
Contents of the example file go here.

Starting at position 5 for 10 bytes:
nts of the

True
```

8.3.6   Compressing Network Data

The code in the next example responds to requests consisting of filenames by writing a compressed version of the file to the socket used to communicate with the client. It has some artificial chunking in place to illustrate the buffering that occurs when the data passed to `compress()` or `decompress()` does not result in a complete block of compressed or uncompressed output.

```
import bz2
import logging
import SocketServer
import binascii

BLOCK_SIZE = 32


class Bz2RequestHandler(SocketServer.BaseRequestHandler):
```

```
    logger = logging.getLogger('Server')

def handle(self):
    compressor = bz2.BZ2Compressor()

    # Find out what file the client wants
    filename = self.request.recv(1024)
    self.logger.debug('client asked for: "%s"', filename)

    # Send chunks of the file as they are compressed
    with open(filename, 'rb') as input:
        while True:
            block = input.read(BLOCK_SIZE)
            if not block:
                break
            self.logger.debug('RAW "%s"', block)
            compressed = compressor.compress(block)
            if compressed:
                self.logger.debug('SENDING "%s"',
                                  binascii.hexlify(compressed))
                self.request.send(compressed)
            else:
                self.logger.debug('BUFFERING')

    # Send any data being buffered by the compressor
    remaining = compressor.flush()
    while remaining:
        to_send = remaining[:BLOCK_SIZE]
        remaining = remaining[BLOCK_SIZE:]
        self.logger.debug('FLUSHING "%s"',
                          binascii.hexlify(to_send))
        self.request.send(to_send)
    return
```

The main program starts a server in a thread, combining SocketServer and Bz2RequestHandler.

```
if __name__ == '__main__':
    import socket
    import sys
    from cStringIO import StringIO
    import threading
```

```python
logging.basicConfig(level=logging.DEBUG,
                    format='%(name)s: %(message)s',
                    )

# Set up a server, running in a separate thread
address = ('localhost', 0) # let the kernel assign a port
server = SocketServer.TCPServer(address, Bz2RequestHandler)
ip, port = server.server_address # what port was assigned?

t = threading.Thread(target=server.serve_forever)
t.setDaemon(True)
t.start()

logger = logging.getLogger('Client')

# Connect to the server
logger.info('Contacting server on %s:%s', ip, port)
s = socket.socket(socket.AF_INET, socket.SOCK_STREAM)
s.connect((ip, port))

# Ask for a file
requested_file = (sys.argv[0]
                  if len(sys.argv) > 1
                  else 'lorem.txt')
logger.debug('sending filename: "%s"', requested_file)
len_sent = s.send(requested_file)

# Receive a response
buffer = StringIO()
decompressor = bz2.BZ2Decompressor()
while True:
    response = s.recv(BLOCK_SIZE)
    if not response:
        break
    logger.debug('READ "%s"', binascii.hexlify(response))

    # Include any unconsumed data when feeding the decompressor.
    decompressed = decompressor.decompress(response)
    if decompressed:
        logger.debug('DECOMPRESSED "%s"', decompressed)
        buffer.write(decompressed)
    else:
        logger.debug('BUFFERING')
```

```
full_response = buffer.getvalue()
lorem = open(requested_file, 'rt').read()
logger.debug('response matches file contents: %s',
             full_response == lorem)

# Clean up
server.shutdown()
server.socket.close()
s.close()
```

It then opens a socket to communicate with the server as a client and requests the file. The default file, `lorem.txt`, contains this text.

```
Lorem ipsum dolor sit amet, consectetuer adipiscing elit. Donec
egestas, enim et consectetuer ullamcorper, lectus ligula rutrum leo,
a elementum elit tortor eu quam. Duis tincidunt nisi ut ante. Nulla
facilisi.
```

Warning: This implementation has obvious security implications. Do not run it on a server on the open Internet or in any environment where security might be an issue.

Running `bz2_server.py` produces:

```
$ python bz2_server.py

Client: Contacting server on 127.0.0.1:55091
Client: sending filename: "lorem.txt"
Server: client asked for: "lorem.txt"
Server: RAW "Lorem ipsum dolor sit amet, cons"
Server: BUFFERING
Server: RAW "ectetuer adipiscing elit. Donec
"
Server: BUFFERING
Server: RAW "egestas, enim et consectetuer ul"
Server: BUFFERING
Server: RAW "lamcorper, lectus ligula rutrum "
Server: BUFFERING
Server: RAW "leo,
```

```
a elementum elit tortor eu "
Server: BUFFERING
Server: RAW "quam. Duis tincidunt nisi ut ant"
Server: BUFFERING
Server: RAW "e. Nulla
facilisi.
"
Server: BUFFERING
Server: FLUSHING "425a6839314159265359ba83a48c000014d580001040050405
2fa7fe003000ba"
Server: FLUSHING "9112793d4ca789068698a0d1a341901a0d53f4d1119a8d4c9e
812d755a67c107"
Server: FLUSHING "98387682c7ca7b5a3bb75da77755eb81c1cb1ca94c4b6faf20
9c52a90aaa4d16"
Server: FLUSHING "a4a1b9c167a01c8d9ef32589d831e77df7a5753a398b11660e
392126fc18a72a"
Server: FLUSHING "1088716cc8dedda5d489da410748531278043d70a8a131c2b8
adcd6a221bdb8c"
Server: FLUSHING "7ff76b88c1d5342ee48a70a12175074918"
Client: READ "425a6839314159265359ba83a48c000014d5800010400504052fa7
fe003000ba"
Client: BUFFERING
Client: READ "9112793d4ca789068698a0d1a341901a0d53f4d1119a8d4c9e812d
755a67c107"
Client: BUFFERING
Client: READ "98387682c7ca7b5a3bb75da77755eb81c1cb1ca94c4b6faf209c52
a90aaa4d16"
Client: BUFFERING
Client: READ "a4a1b9c167a01c8d9ef32589d831e77df7a5753a398b11660e3921
26fc18a72a"
Client: BUFFERING
Client: READ "1088716cc8dedda5d489da410748531278043d70a8a131c2b8adcd
6a221bdb8c"
Client: BUFFERING
Client: READ "7ff76b88c1d5342ee48a70a12175074918"
Client: DECOMPRESSED "Lorem ipsum dolor sit amet, consectetuer adipi
scing elit. Donec
egestas, enim et consectetuer ullamcorper, lectus ligula rutrum leo,
a elementum elit tortor eu quam. Duis tincidunt nisi ut ante. Nulla
facilisi.
"
Client: response matches file contents: True
```

See Also:

bz2 (http://docs.python.org/library/bz2.html) The standard library documentation for this module.

bzip2.org (www.bzip.org/) The home page for **bzip2**.

`gzip` **(page 430)** A file-like interface to GNU zip compressed files.

`zlib` **(page 421)** The `zlib` module for GNU zip compression.

8.4 tarfile—Tar Archive Access

Purpose Read and write tar archives.
Python Version 2.3 and later

The `tarfile` module provides read and write access to UNIX tar archives, including compressed files. In addition to the POSIX standards, several GNU tar extensions are supported. UNIX special file types, such as hard and soft links, and device nodes are also handled.

> **Note:** Although `tarfile` implements a UNIX format, it can be used to create and read tar archives under Microsoft Windows, too.

8.4.1 Testing Tar Files

The `is_tarfile()` function returns a Boolean indicating whether or not the filename passed as an argument refers to a valid tar archive.

```
import tarfile

for filename in [ 'README.txt', 'example.tar',
                  'bad_example.tar', 'notthere.tar' ]:
    try:
        print '%15s  %s' % (filename, tarfile.is_tarfile(filename))
    except IOError, err:
        print '%15s  %s' % (filename, err)
```

If the file does not exist, `is_tarfile()` raises an `IOError`.

```
$ python tarfile_is_tarfile.py

    README.txt  False
   example.tar  True
```

```
bad_example.tar   False
   notthere.tar    [Errno 2] No such file or directory: 'notthere.tar'
```

8.4.2 Reading Metadata from an Archive

Use the `TarFile` class to work directly with a tar archive. It supports methods for reading data about existing archives, as well as modifying the archives by adding additional files.

To read the names of the files in an existing archive, use `getnames()`.

```
import tarfile
from contextlib import closing

with closing(tarfile.open('example.tar', 'r')) as t:
    print t.getnames()
```

The return value is a list of strings with the names of the archive contents.

```
$ python tarfile_getnames.py

['README.txt', '__init__.py']
```

In addition to names, metadata about the archive members is available as instances of `TarInfo` objects.

```
import tarfile
import time
from contextlib import closing

with closing(tarfile.open('example.tar', 'r')) as t:
    for member_info in t.getmembers():
        print member_info.name
        print '\tModified:\t', time.ctime(member_info.mtime)
        print '\tMode    :\t', oct(member_info.mode)
        print '\tType    :\t', member_info.type
        print '\tSize    :\t', member_info.size, 'bytes'
        print
```

Load the metadata via `getmembers()` and `getmember()`.

```
$ python tarfile_getmembers.py
```

```
README.txt
        Modified:         Sun Nov 28 13:30:14 2010
        Mode    :         0644
        Type    :         0
        Size    :         75 bytes

__init__.py
        Modified:         Sun Nov 14 09:39:38 2010
        Mode    :         0644
        Type    :         0
        Size    :         22 bytes
```

If the name of the archive member is known in advance, its `TarInfo` object can be retrieved with `getmember()`.

```
import tarfile
import time
from contextlib import closing

with closing(tarfile.open('example.tar', 'r')) as t:
    for filename in [ 'README.txt', 'notthere.txt' ]:
        try:
            info = t.getmember(filename)
        except KeyError:
            print 'ERROR: Did not find %s in tar archive' % filename
        else:
            print '%s is %d bytes' % (info.name, info.size)
```

If the archive member is not present, `getmember()` raises a `KeyError`.

```
$ python tarfile_getmember.py

README.txt is 75 bytes
ERROR: Did not find notthere.txt in tar archive
```

8.4.3   Extracting Files from an Archive

To access the data from an archive member within a program, use the `extractfile()` method, passing the member's name.

```
import tarfile
from contextlib import closing
```

```
with closing(tarfile.open('example.tar', 'r')) as t:
    for filename in [ 'README.txt', 'notthere.txt' ]:
        try:
            f = t.extractfile(filename)
        except KeyError:
            print 'ERROR: Did not find %s in tar archive' % filename
        else:
            print filename, ':'
            print f.read()
```

The return value is a file-like object from which the contents of the archive member can be read.

```
$ python tarfile_extractfile.py

README.txt :
The examples for the tarfile module use this file and example.tar as
data.

ERROR: Did not find notthere.txt in tar archive
```

To unpack the archive and write the files to the file system, use `extract()` or `extractall()` instead.

```
import tarfile
import os
from contextlib import closing

os.mkdir('outdir')
with closing(tarfile.open('example.tar', 'r')) as t:
    t.extract('README.txt', 'outdir')
print os.listdir('outdir')
```

The member or members are read from the archive and written to the file system, starting in the directory named in the arguments.

```
$ python tarfile_extract.py

['README.txt']
```

The standard library documentation includes a note stating that extractall() is safer than extract(), especially for working with streaming data where rewinding to read an earlier part of the input is not possible. It should be used in most cases.

```
import tarfile
import os
from contextlib import closing

os.mkdir('outdir')
with closing(tarfile.open('example.tar', 'r')) as t:
    t.extractall('outdir')
print os.listdir('outdir')
```

With extractall(), the first argument is the name of the directory where the files should be written.

```
$ python tarfile_extractall.py

['__init__.py', 'README.txt']
```

To extract specific files from the archive, pass their names or TarInfo metadata containers to extractall().

```
import tarfile
import os
from contextlib import closing

os.mkdir('outdir')
with closing(tarfile.open('example.tar', 'r')) as t:
    t.extractall('outdir',
                 members=[t.getmember('README.txt')],
                 )
print os.listdir('outdir')
```

When a *members* list is provided, only the named files are extracted.

```
$ python tarfile_extractall_members.py

['README.txt']
```

8.4.4 Creating New Archives

To create a new archive, open the `TarFile` with a mode of `'w'`.

```
import tarfile
from contextlib import closing

print 'creating archive'
with closing(tarfile.open('tarfile_add.tar', mode='w')) as out:
    print 'adding README.txt'
    out.add('README.txt')

print
print 'Contents:'
with closing(tarfile.open('tarfile_add.tar', mode='r')) as t:
    for member_info in t.getmembers():
        print member_info.name
```

Any existing file is truncated and a new archive is started. To add files, use the `add()` method.

```
$ python tarfile_add.py

creating archive
adding README.txt

Contents:
README.txt
```

8.4.5 Using Alternate Archive Member Names

It is possible to add a file to an archive using a name other than the original filename by constructing a `TarInfo` object with an alternate *arcname* and passing it to `addfile()`.

```
import tarfile
from contextlib import closing

print 'creating archive'
with closing(tarfile.open('tarfile_addfile.tar', mode='w')) as out:
    print 'adding README.txt as RENAMED.txt'
```

```
    info = out.gettarinfo('README.txt', arcname='RENAMED.txt')
    out.addfile(info)

print
print 'Contents:'
with closing(tarfile.open('tarfile_addfile.tar', mode='r')) as t:
    for member_info in t.getmembers():
        print member_info.name
```

The archive includes only the changed filename

```
$ python tarfile_addfile.py

creating archive
adding README.txt as RENAMED.txt

Contents:
RENAMED.txt
```

8.4.6   Writing Data from Sources Other than Files

Sometimes, it is necessary to write data into an archive directly from memory. Rather than writing the data to a file, and then adding that file to the archive, you can use `addfile()` to add data from an open file-like handle.

```
import tarfile
from cStringIO import StringIO
from contextlib import closing

data = 'This is the data to write to the archive.'

with closing(tarfile.open('addfile_string.tar', mode='w')) as out:
    info = tarfile.TarInfo('made_up_file.txt')
    info.size = len(data)
    out.addfile(info, StringIO(data))

print 'Contents:'
with closing(tarfile.open('addfile_string.tar', mode='r')) as t:
    for member_info in t.getmembers():
        print member_info.name
        f = t.extractfile(member_info)
        print f.read()
```

By first constructing a `TarInfo` object, the archive member can be given any name desired. After setting the size, the data is written to the archive using `addfile()` and a `StringIO` buffer as a source of the data.

```
$ python tarfile_addfile_string.py

Contents:
made_up_file.txt
This is the data to write to the archive.
```

8.4.7 Appending to Archives

In addition to creating new archives, it is possible to append to an existing file by using mode `'a'`.

```python
import tarfile
from contextlib import closing

print 'creating archive'
with closing(tarfile.open('tarfile_append.tar', mode='w')) as out:
    out.add('README.txt')

print 'contents:',
with closing(tarfile.open('tarfile_append.tar', mode='r')) as t:
    print [m.name for m in t.getmembers()]

print 'adding index.rst'
with closing(tarfile.open('tarfile_append.tar', mode='a')) as out:
    out.add('index.rst')

print 'contents:',
with closing(tarfile.open('tarfile_append.tar', mode='r')) as t:
    print [m.name for m in t.getmembers()]
```

The resulting archive ends up with two members.

```
$ python tarfile_append.py

creating archive
contents: ['README.txt']
adding index.rst
contents: ['README.txt', 'index.rst']
```

8.4.8 Working with Compressed Archives

Besides regular tar archive files, the `tarfile` module can work with archives compressed via the gzip or bzip2 protocols. To open a compressed archive, modify the mode string passed to `open()` to include `":gz"` or `":bz2"`, depending on the desired compression method.

```python
import tarfile
import os

fmt = '%-30s %-10s'
print fmt % ('FILENAME', 'SIZE')
print fmt % ('README.txt', os.stat('README.txt').st_size)

for filename, write_mode in [
    ('tarfile_compression.tar', 'w'),
    ('tarfile_compression.tar.gz', 'w:gz'),
    ('tarfile_compression.tar.bz2', 'w:bz2'),
    ]:
    out = tarfile.open(filename, mode=write_mode)
    try:
        out.add('README.txt')
    finally:
        out.close()

    print fmt % (filename, os.stat(filename).st_size),
    print [m.name
           for m in tarfile.open(filename, 'r:*').getmembers()
           ]
```

When opening an existing archive for reading, specify `"r:*"` to have `tarfile` determine the compression method to use automatically.

```
$ python tarfile_compression.py

FILENAME                        SIZE
README.txt                      75
tarfile_compression.tar         10240      ['README.txt']
tarfile_compression.tar.gz      212        ['README.txt']
tarfile_compression.tar.bz2     187        ['README.txt']
```

See Also:

tarfile (http://docs.python.org/library/tarfile.html) The standard library documentation for this module.

GNU tar manual (www.gnu.org/software/tar/manual/html_node/Standard.html)
  Documentation of the tar format, including extensions.
bz2 (page 436) bzip2 compression.
contextlib (page 163) The `contextlib` module includes `closing()`, for managing file handles in **with** statements.
gzip (page 430) GNU zip compression.
zipfile (page 457) Similar access for ZIP archives.

8.5 zipfile—ZIP Archive Access

Purpose Read and write ZIP archive files.
Python Version 1.6 and later

The `zipfile` module can be used to manipulate ZIP archive files, the format popularized by the PC program PKZIP.

8.5.1 Testing ZIP Files

The `is_zipfile()` function returns a Boolean indicating whether or not the filename passed as an argument refers to a valid ZIP archive.

```
import zipfile

for filename in [ 'README.txt', 'example.zip',
                  'bad_example.zip', 'notthere.zip' ]:
    print '%15s  %s' % (filename, zipfile.is_zipfile(filename))
```

If the file does not exist at all, `is_zipfile()` returns `False`.

```
$ python zipfile_is_zipfile.py

      README.txt  False
     example.zip  True
 bad_example.zip  False
    notthere.zip  False
```

8.5.2 Reading Metadata from an Archive

Use the `ZipFile` class to work directly with a ZIP archive. It supports methods for reading data about existing archives, as well as modifying the archives by adding additional files.

```
import zipfile

with zipfile.ZipFile('example.zip', 'r') as zf:
    print zf.namelist()
```

The `namelist()` method returns the names of the files in an existing archive.

```
$ python zipfile_namelist.py

['README.txt']
```

The list of names is only part of the information available from the archive, though. To access all the metadata about the ZIP contents, use the `infolist()` or `getinfo()` methods.

```
import datetime
import zipfile

def print_info(archive_name):
    with zipfile.ZipFile(archive_name) as zf:
        for info in zf.infolist():
            print info.filename
            print '\tComment     :', info.comment
            mod_date = datetime.datetime(*info.date_time)
            print '\tModified    :', mod_date
            if info.create_system == 0:
                system = 'Windows'
            elif info.create_system == 3:
                system = 'Unix'
            else:
                system = 'UNKNOWN'
            print '\tSystem      :', system
            print '\tZIP version :', info.create_version
            print '\tCompressed  :', info.compress_size, 'bytes'
            print '\tUncompressed:', info.file_size, 'bytes'
            print

if __name__ == '__main__':
    print_info('example.zip')
```

There are additional fields other than those printed here, but deciphering the values into anything useful requires careful reading of the *PKZIP Application Note* with the ZIP file specification.

```
$ python zipfile_infolist.py

README.txt
        Comment      :
        Modified     : 2010-11-15 06:48:02
        System       : Unix
        ZIP version  : 30
        Compressed   : 65 bytes
        Uncompressed : 76 bytes
```

If the name of the archive member is known in advance, its `ZipInfo` object can be retrieved directly with `getinfo()`.

```
import zipfile

with zipfile.ZipFile('example.zip') as zf:
    for filename in [ 'README.txt', 'notthere.txt' ]:
        try:
            info = zf.getinfo(filename)
        except KeyError:
            print 'ERROR: Did not find %s in zip file' % filename
        else:
            print '%s is %d bytes' % (info.filename, info.file_size)
```

If the archive member is not present, `getinfo()` raises a `KeyError`.

```
$ python zipfile_getinfo.py

README.txt is 76 bytes
ERROR: Did not find notthere.txt in zip file
```

8.5.3 Extracting Archived Files from an Archive

To access the data from an archive member, use the `read()` method, passing the member's name.

```
import zipfile

with zipfile.ZipFile('example.zip') as zf:
    for filename in [ 'README.txt', 'notthere.txt' ]:
        try:
            data = zf.read(filename)
        except KeyError:
            print 'ERROR: Did not find %s in zip file' % filename
        else:
            print filename, ':'
            print data
        print
```

The data is automatically decompressed, if necessary.

```
$ python zipfile_read.py

README.txt :
The examples for the zipfile module use
this file and example.zip as data.


ERROR: Did not find notthere.txt in zip file
```

8.5.4 Creating New Archives

To create a new archive, instantiate the ZipFile with a mode of 'w'. Any existing file is truncated and a new archive is started. To add files, use the write() method.

```
from zipfile_infolist import print_info
import zipfile

print 'creating archive'
with zipfile.ZipFile('write.zip', mode='w') as zf:
    print 'adding README.txt'
    zf.write('README.txt')

print
print_info('write.zip')
```

By default, the contents of the archive are not compressed.

```
$ python zipfile_write.py

creating archive
adding README.txt

README.txt
        Comment     :
        Modified    : 2010-11-15 06:48:00
        System      : Unix
        ZIP version : 20
        Compressed  : 76 bytes
        Uncompressed: 76 bytes
```

To add compression, the zlib module is required. If zlib is available, the compression mode for individual files or for the archive as a whole can be set using zipfile.ZIP_DEFLATED. The default compression mode is zipfile.ZIP_STORED, which adds the input data to the archive without compressing it.

```python
from zipfile_infolist import print_info
import zipfile
try:
    import zlib
    compression = zipfile.ZIP_DEFLATED
except:
    compression = zipfile.ZIP_STORED

modes = { zipfile.ZIP_DEFLATED: 'deflated',
          zipfile.ZIP_STORED:   'stored',
          }

print 'creating archive'
with zipfile.ZipFile('write_compression.zip', mode='w') as zf:
    mode_name = modes[compression]
    print 'adding README.txt with compression mode', mode_name
    zf.write('README.txt', compress_type=compression)

print
print_info('write_compression.zip')
```

This time, the archive member is compressed.

```
$ python zipfile_write_compression.py

creating archive
adding README.txt with compression mode deflated

README.txt
        Comment      :
        Modified     : 2010-11-15 06:48:00
        System       : Unix
        ZIP version  : 20
        Compressed   : 65 bytes
        Uncompressed : 76 bytes
```

8.5.5 Using Alternate Archive Member Names

Pass an *arcname* value to `write()` to add a file to an archive using a name other than the original filename.

```
from zipfile_infolist import print_info
import zipfile

with zipfile.ZipFile('write_arcname.zip', mode='w') as zf:
    zf.write('README.txt', arcname='NOT_README.txt')

print_info('write_arcname.zip')
```

There is no sign of the original filename in the archive.

```
$ python zipfile_write_arcname.py

NOT_README.txt
        Comment      :
        Modified     : 2010-11-15 06:48:00
        System       : Unix
        ZIP version  : 20
        Compressed   : 76 bytes
        Uncompressed : 76 bytes
```

8.5.6 Writing Data from Sources Other than Files

Sometimes it is necessary to write to a ZIP archive using data that did not come from an existing file. Rather than writing the data to a file, and then adding that file to the ZIP archive, use the `writestr()` method to add a string of bytes to the archive directly.

```
from zipfile_infolist import print_info
import zipfile

msg = 'This data did not exist in a file.'
with zipfile.ZipFile('writestr.zip',
                     mode='w',
                     compression=zipfile.ZIP_DEFLATED,
                     ) as zf:
    zf.writestr('from_string.txt', msg)

print_info('writestr.zip')

with zipfile.ZipFile('writestr.zip', 'r') as zf:
    print zf.read('from_string.txt')
```

In this case, the *compress_type* argument to `ZipFile` is used to compress the data, since `writestr()` does not take an argument to specify the compression.

```
$ python zipfile_writestr.py

from_string.txt
        Comment    :
        Modified   : 2010-11-28 13:48:46
        System     : Unix
        ZIP version : 20
        Compressed  : 36 bytes
        Uncompressed: 34 bytes

This data did not exist in a file.
```

8.5.7   Writing with a ZipInfo Instance

Normally, the modification date is computed when a file or string is added to the archive. A `ZipInfo` instance can be passed to `writestr()` to define the modification date and other metadata.

```
import time
import zipfile
from zipfile_infolist import print_info
```

```
msg = 'This data did not exist in a file.'

with zipfile.ZipFile('writestr_zipinfo.zip',
                     mode='w',
                     ) as zf:
    info = zipfile.ZipInfo('from_string.txt',
                           date_time=time.localtime(time.time()),
                           )
    info.compress_type=zipfile.ZIP_DEFLATED
    info.comment='Remarks go here'
    info.create_system=0
    zf.writestr(info, msg)

print_info('writestr_zipinfo.zip')
```

In this example, the modified time is set to the current time, the data is compressed, and a false value for *create_system* is used. A simple comment is also associated with the new file.

```
$ python zipfile_writestr_zipinfo.py

from_string.txt
        Comment      : Remarks go here
        Modified     : 2010-11-28 13:48:46
        System       : Windows
        ZIP version  : 20
        Compressed   : 36 bytes
        Uncompressed : 34 bytes
```

8.5.8   Appending to Files

In addition to creating new archives, it is possible to append to an existing archive or add an archive at the end of an existing file (such as an .exe file for a self-extracting archive). To open a file to append to it, use mode 'a'.

```
from zipfile_infolist import print_info
import zipfile

print 'creating archive'
with zipfile.ZipFile('append.zip', mode='w') as zf:
    zf.write('README.txt')
```

```
print
print_info('append.zip')

print 'appending to the archive'
with zipfile.ZipFile('append.zip', mode='a') as zf:
    zf.write('README.txt', arcname='README2.txt')

print
print_info('append.zip')
```

The resulting archive contains two members:

```
$ python zipfile_append.py

creating archive

README.txt
        Comment      :
        Modified     : 2010-11-15 06:48:00
        System       : Unix
        ZIP version  : 20
        Compressed   : 76 bytes
        Uncompressed : 76 bytes

appending to the archive

README.txt
        Comment      :
        Modified     : 2010-11-15 06:48:00
        System       : Unix
        ZIP version  : 20
        Compressed   : 76 bytes
        Uncompressed : 76 bytes

README2.txt
        Comment      :
        Modified     : 2010-11-15 06:48:00
        System       : Unix
        ZIP version  : 20
        Compressed   : 76 bytes
        Uncompressed : 76 bytes
```

8.5.9 Python ZIP Archives

Python can import modules from inside ZIP archives using `zipimport`, if those archives appear in `sys.path`. The `PyZipFile` class can be used to construct a module suitable for use in this way. The extra method `writepy()` tells `PyZipFile` to scan a directory for `.py` files and add the corresponding `.pyo` or `.pyc` file to the archive. If neither compiled form exists, a `.pyc` file is created and added.

```
import sys
import zipfile

if __name__ == '__main__':
    with zipfile.PyZipFile('pyzipfile.zip', mode='w') as zf:
        zf.debug = 3
        print 'Adding python files'
        zf.writepy('.')
    for name in zf.namelist():
        print name

    print
    sys.path.insert(0, 'pyzipfile.zip')
    import zipfile_pyzipfile
    print 'Imported from:', zipfile_pyzipfile.__file__
```

With the debug attribute of the `PyZipFile` set to 3, verbose debugging is enabled and output is produced as it compiles each `.py` file it finds.

```
$ python zipfile_pyzipfile.py

Adding python files
Adding package in . as .
Adding ./__init__.pyc
Adding ./zipfile_append.pyc
Adding ./zipfile_getinfo.pyc
Adding ./zipfile_infolist.pyc
Compiling ./zipfile_is_zipfile.py
Adding ./zipfile_is_zipfile.pyc
Adding ./zipfile_namelist.pyc
Adding ./zipfile_printdir.pyc
Adding ./zipfile_pyzipfile.pyc
Adding ./zipfile_read.pyc
Adding ./zipfile_write.pyc
```

```
Adding ./zipfile_write_arcname.pyc
Adding ./zipfile_write_compression.pyc
Adding ./zipfile_writestr.pyc
Adding ./zipfile_writestr_zipinfo.pyc
__init__.pyc
zipfile_append.pyc
zipfile_getinfo.pyc
zipfile_infolist.pyc
zipfile_is_zipfile.pyc
zipfile_namelist.pyc
zipfile_printdir.pyc
zipfile_pyzipfile.pyc
zipfile_read.pyc
zipfile_write.pyc
zipfile_write_arcname.pyc
zipfile_write_compression.pyc
zipfile_writestr.pyc
zipfile_writestr_zipinfo.pyc

Imported from: pyzipfile.zip/zipfile_pyzipfile.pyc
```

8.5.10   Limitations

The `zipfile` module does not support ZIP files with appended comments or multidisk archives. It does support ZIP files larger than 4 GB that use the ZIP64 extensions.

See Also:

`tarfile` **(page 448)** Read and write tar archives.

zipfile (http://docs.python.org/library/zipfile.html) The standard library documentation for this module.

`zipimport` **(page 1240)** Import Python modules from ZIP archives.

`zlib` **(page 421)** ZIP compression library.

PKZIP Application Note (www.pkware.com/documents/casestudies/APPNOTE. TXT) Official specification for the ZIP archive format.

Chapter 9

CRYPTOGRAPHY

Encryption secures messages so that they can be verified as accurate and protected from interception. Python's cryptography support includes `hashlib` for generating signatures of message content using standard algorithms, such as MD5 and SHA, and `hmac` for verifying that a message has not been altered in transmission.

9.1 hashlib—Cryptographic Hashing

Purpose Generate cryptographic hashes and message digests.
Python Version 2.5 and later

The `hashlib` module deprecates the separate `md5` and `sha` modules and makes their API consistent. To work with a specific hash algorithm, use the appropriate constructor function to create a hash object. From there, the objects use the same API, no matter what algorithm is being used.

Since `hashlib` is "backed" by OpenSSL, all algorithms provided by that library are available, including

- md5
- sha1
- sha224
- sha256
- sha384
- sha512

9.1.1 Sample Data

All the examples in this section use the same sample data:

```
import hashlib
```

```
lorem = '''Lorem ipsum dolor sit amet, consectetur adipisicing elit,
sed do eiusmod tempor incididunt ut labore et dolore magna aliqua. Ut
enim ad minim veniam, quis nostrud exercitation ullamco laboris nisi
ut aliquip ex ea commodo consequat. Duis aute irure dolor in
reprehenderit in voluptate velit esse cillum dolore eu fugiat nulla
pariatur. Excepteur sint occaecat cupidatat non proident, sunt in
culpa qui officia deserunt mollit anim id est laborum.'''
```

9.1.2 MD5 Example

To calculate the MD5 hash, or *digest*, for a block of data (here an ASCII string), first
create the hash object, and then add the data and call `digest()` or `hexdigest()`.

```
import hashlib

from hashlib_data import lorem

h = hashlib.md5()
h.update(lorem)
print h.hexdigest()
```

This example uses the `hexdigest()` method instead of `digest()` because the
output is formatted so it can be printed clearly. If a binary digest value is acceptable,
use `digest()`.

```
$ python hashlib_md5.py

1426f365574592350315090e295ac273
```

9.1.3 SHA1 Example

A SHA1 digest is calculated in the same way.

```
import hashlib

from hashlib_data import lorem
```

```
h = hashlib.sha1()
h.update(lorem)
print h.hexdigest()
```

The digest value is different in this example because the algorithm changed from MD5 to SHA1.

```
$ python hashlib_sha1.py

8173396ba8a560b89a3f3e2fcc024b044bc83d0a
```

9.1.4 Creating a Hash by Name

Sometimes, it is more convenient to refer to the algorithm by name in a string rather than by using the constructor function directly. It is useful, for example, to be able to store the hash type in a configuration file. In those cases, use `new()` to create a hash calculator.

```
import hashlib
import sys


try:
    hash_name = sys.argv[1]
except IndexError:
    print 'Specify the hash name as the first argument.'
else:
    try:
        data = sys.argv[2]
    except IndexError:
        from hashlib_data import lorem as data

    h = hashlib.new(hash_name)
    h.update(data)
    print h.hexdigest()
```

When run with a variety of arguments:

```
$ python hashlib_new.py sha1

8173396ba8a560b89a3f3e2fcc024b044bc83d0a
```

```
$ python hashlib_new.py sha256

dca37495608c68ec23bbb54ab9675bf0152db63e5a51ab1061dc9982b843e767

$ python hashlib_new.py sha512

0e3d4bc1cbc117382fa077b147a7ff6363f6cbc7508877460f978a566a0adb6dbb4c8
b89f56514da98eb94d7135e1b7ad7fc4a2d747c02af67fcd4e571bd54de

$ python hashlib_new.py md5

1426f365574592350315090e295ac273
```

9.1.5 Incremental Updates

The update() method of the hash calculators can be called repeatedly. Each time, the digest is updated based on the additional text fed in. Updating incrementally is more efficient than reading an entire file into memory, and it produces the same results.

```python
import hashlib

from hashlib_data import lorem

h = hashlib.md5()
h.update(lorem)
all_at_once = h.hexdigest()


def chunkize(size, text):
    "Return parts of the text in size-based increments."
    start = 0
    while start < len(text):
        chunk = text[start:start+size]
        yield chunk
        start += size
    return


h = hashlib.md5()
for chunk in chunkize(64, lorem):
    h.update(chunk)
line_by_line = h.hexdigest()
```

```
print 'All at once :', all_at_once
print 'Line by line:', line_by_line
print 'Same        :', (all_at_once == line_by_line)
```

This example demonstrates how to update a digest incrementally as data is read or otherwise produced.

```
$ python hashlib_update.py

All at once : 1426f365574592350315090e295ac273
Line by line: 1426f365574592350315090e295ac273
Same        : True
```

See Also:
hashlib (http://docs.python.org/library/hashlib.html) The standard library documentation for this module.

Voidspace: IronPython and hashlib (www.voidspace.org.uk/python/weblog/arch_d7_2006_10_07.shtml#e497) A wrapper for `hashlib` that works with IronPython.

hmac (page 473) The `hmac` module.

OpenSSL (http://www.openssl.org/) An open source encryption toolkit.

9.2   hmac—Cryptographic Message Signing and Verification

Purpose The `hmac` module implements keyed-hashing for message authentication, as described in RFC 2104.

Python Version 2.2 and later

The HMAC algorithm can be used to verify the integrity of information passed between applications or stored in a potentially vulnerable location. The basic idea is to generate a cryptographic hash of the actual data combined with a shared secret key. The resulting hash can then be used to check the transmitted or stored message to determine a level of trust, without transmitting the secret key.

Warning: Disclaimer: This book does not offer expert security advice. For the full details on HMAC, check out **RFC 2104** (http://tools.ietf.org/html/rfc2104.html).

9.2.1   Signing Messages

The `new()` function creates a new object for calculating a message signature. This example uses the default MD5 hash algorithm.

```
import hmac

digest_maker = hmac.new('secret-shared-key-goes-here')

with open('lorem.txt', 'rb') as f:
    while True:
        block = f.read(1024)
        if not block:
            break
        digest_maker.update(block)

digest = digest_maker.hexdigest()
print digest
```

When run, the code reads a data file and computes an HMAC signature for it.

```
$ python hmac_simple.py

4bcb287e284f8c21e87e14ba2dc40b16
```

9.2.2   SHA vs. MD5

Although the default cryptographic algorithm for `hmac` is MD5, that is not the most secure method to use. MD5 hashes have some weaknesses, such as collisions (where two different messages produce the same hash). The SHA-1 algorithm is considered to be stronger and should be used instead.

```
import hmac
import hashlib

digest_maker = hmac.new('secret-shared-key-goes-here',
                        '',
                        hashlib.sha1)

with open('hmac_sha.py', 'rb') as f:
    while True:
        block = f.read(1024)
```

```
    if not block:
        break
    digest_maker.update(block)

digest = digest_maker.hexdigest()
print digest
```

The `new()` function takes three arguments. The first is the secret key, which should be shared between the two endpoints that are communicating so both ends can use the same value. The second value is an initial message. If the message content that needs to be authenticated is small, such as a timestamp or an HTTP POST, the entire body of the message can be passed to `new()` instead of using the `update()` method. The last argument is the digest module to be used. The default is `hashlib.md5`. This example substitutes `hashlib.sha1`.

```
$ python hmac_sha.py

b9e8c6737883a9d3a258a0b5090559b7e8e2efcb
```

9.2.3 Binary Digests

The previous examples used the `hexdigest()` method to produce printable digests. The hexdigest is a different representation of the value calculated by the `digest()` method, which is a binary value that may include unprintable or non-ASCII characters, including NUL. Some Web services (Google checkout, Amazon S3) use the base64 encoded version of the binary digest instead of the hexdigest.

```
import base64
import hmac
import hashlib

with open('lorem.txt', 'rb') as f:
    body = f.read()

hash = hmac.new('secret-shared-key-goes-here', body, hashlib.sha1)
digest = hash.digest()
print base64.encodestring(digest)
```

The base64 encoded string ends in a newline, which frequently needs to be stripped off when embedding the string in http headers or other formatting-sensitive contexts.

```
$ python hmac_base64.py
```

olW2DoXHGJEKGU0aE9fOwSVE/o4=

9.2.4 Applications of Message Signatures

HMAC authentication should be used for any public network service and any time data is stored where security is important. For example, when sending data through a pipe or socket, that data should be signed and then the signature should be tested before the data is used. The extended example given here is available in the file `hmac_pickle.py`.

The first step is to establish a function to calculate a digest for a string and a simple class to be instantiated and passed through a communication channel.

```python
import hashlib
import hmac
try:
    import cPickle as pickle
except:
    import pickle
import pprint
from StringIO import StringIO


def make_digest(message):
    "Return a digest for the message."
    hash = hmac.new('secret-shared-key-goes-here',
                    message,
                    hashlib.sha1)
    return hash.hexdigest()


class SimpleObject(object):
    """A very simple class to demonstrate checking digests before
    unpickling.
    """
    def __init__(self, name):
        self.name = name
    def __str__(self):
        return self.name
```

Next, create a `StringIO` buffer to represent the socket or pipe. The example uses a naive, but easy to parse, format for the data stream. The digest and length of the data are written, followed by a new line. The serialized representation of the object, generated by `pickle`, follows. A real system would not want to depend on a length value, since if the digest is wrong, the length is probably wrong as well. Some sort of terminator sequence not likely to appear in the real data would be more appropriate.

The example program then writes two objects to the stream. The first is written using the correct digest value.

```
# Simulate a writable socket or pipe with StringIO
out_s = StringIO()

# Write a valid object to the stream:
#   digest\nlength\npickle
o = SimpleObject('digest matches')
pickled_data = pickle.dumps(o)
digest = make_digest(pickled_data)
header = '%s %s' % (digest, len(pickled_data))
print 'WRITING:', header
out_s.write(header + '\n')
out_s.write(pickled_data)
```

The second object is written to the stream with an invalid digest, produced by calculating the digest for some other data instead of the pickle.

```
# Write an invalid object to the stream
o = SimpleObject('digest does not match')
pickled_data = pickle.dumps(o)
digest = make_digest('not the pickled data at all')
header = '%s %s' % (digest, len(pickled_data))
print '\nWRITING:', header
out_s.write(header + '\n')
out_s.write(pickled_data)

out_s.flush()
```

Now that the data is in the `StringIO` buffer, it can be read back out again. Start by reading the line of data with the digest and data length. Then read the remaining data, using the length value. `pickle.load()` could read directly from the stream, but that assumes a trusted data stream, and this data is not yet trusted enough to unpickle it. Reading the pickle as a string from the stream, without actually unpickling the object, is safer.

```
# Simulate a readable socket or pipe with StringIO
in_s = StringIO(out_s.getvalue())

# Read the data
while True:
    first_line = in_s.readline()
    if not first_line:
        break
    incoming_digest, incoming_length = first_line.split(' ')
    incoming_length = int(incoming_length)
    print '\nREAD:', incoming_digest, incoming_length

    incoming_pickled_data = in_s.read(incoming_length)
```

Once the pickled data is in memory, the digest value can be recalculated and compared against the data read. If the digests match, it is safe to trust the data and unpickle it.

```
    actual_digest = make_digest(incoming_pickled_data)
    print 'ACTUAL:', actual_digest

    if incoming_digest != actual_digest:
        print 'WARNING: Data corruption'
    else:
        obj = pickle.loads(incoming_pickled_data)
        print 'OK:', obj
```

The output shows that the first object is verified and the second is deemed "corrupted," as expected.

```
$ python hmac_pickle.py

WRITING: 387632cfa3d18cd19bdfe72b61ac395dfcdc87c9 124

WRITING: b01b209e28d7e053408ebe23b90fe5c33bc6a0ec 131

READ: 387632cfa3d18cd19bdfe72b61ac395dfcdc87c9 124
ACTUAL: 387632cfa3d18cd19bdfe72b61ac395dfcdc87c9
OK: digest matches

READ: b01b209e28d7e053408ebe23b90fe5c33bc6a0ec 131
```

```
ACTUAL: dec53ca1ad3f4b657dd81d514f17f735628b6828
WARNING: Data corruption
```

See Also:

hmac (http://docs.python.org/library/hmac.html) The standard library documentation for this module.

RFC 2104 (http://tools.ietf.org/html/rfc2104.html) HMAC: Keyed-Hashing for Message Authentication.

hashlib (page 469) The `hashlib` module provides MD5 and SHA1 hash generators.

pickle (page 334) Serialization library.

WikiPedia: MD5 (http://en.wikipedia.org/wiki/MD5) Description of the MD5 hashing algorithm.

Authenticating to Amazon S3 Web Service (http://docs.amazonwebservices.com/AmazonS3/2006-03-01/index.html? S3_Authentication.html) Instructions for authenticating to S3 using HMAC-SHA1 signed credentials.

Chapter 10

PROCESSES AND THREADS

Python includes sophisticated tools for managing concurrent operations using processes and threads. Even many relatively simple programs can be made to run faster by applying techniques for running parts of the job concurrently using these modules.

`subprocess` provides an API for creating and communicating with secondary processes. It is especially good for running programs that produce or consume text, since the API supports passing data back and forth through the standard input and output channels of the new process.

The `signal` module exposes the UNIX signal mechanism for sending events to other processes. The signals are processed asynchronously, usually by interrupting what the program is doing when the signal arrives. Signalling is useful as a coarse messaging system, but other inter-process communication techniques are more reliable and can deliver more complicated messages.

`threading` includes a high-level, object-oriented API for working with concurrency from Python. `Thread` objects run concurrently within the same process and share memory. Using threads is an easy way to scale for tasks that are more I/O bound than CPU bound. The `multiprocessing` module mirrors `threading`, except that instead of a `Thread` class it provides a `Process`. Each `Process` is a true system process without shared memory, but `multiprocessing` provides features for sharing data and passing messages between them. In many cases, converting from threads to processes is as simple as changing a few **import** statements.

10.1 subprocess—Spawning Additional Processes

Purpose Start and communicate with additional processes.
Python Version 2.4 and later

The `subprocess` module provides a consistent way to create and work with additional processes. It offers a higher-level interface than some of the other modules available in the standard libary, and it is intended to replace functions such as `os.system()`, `os.spawnv()`, the variations of `popen()` in the `os` and `popen2` modules, as well as the `commands()` module. To make it easier to compare `subprocess` with those other modules, many of the examples in this section re-create the ones used for `os` and `popen2`.

The `subprocess` module defines one class, `Popen`, and a few wrapper functions that use that class. The constructor for `Popen` takes arguments to set up the new process so the parent can communicate with it via pipes. It provides all the functionality of the other modules and functions it replaces, and more. The API is consistent for all uses, and many of the extra steps of overhead needed (such as closing extra file descriptors and ensuring the pipes are closed) are "built in" instead of being handled by the application code separately.

Note: The API for working on UNIX and Windows is roughly the same, but the underlying implementation is slightly different. All examples shown here were tested on Mac OS X. Behavior on a non-UNIX OS will vary.

10.1.1   Running External Commands

To run an external command without interacting with it in the same way as `os.system()`, use the `call()` function.

```
import subprocess

# Simple command
subprocess.call(['ls', '-1'])
```

The command line arguments are passed as a list of strings, which avoids the need for escaping quotes or other special characters that might be interpreted by the shell.

```
$ python subprocess_os_system.py

__init__.py
index.rst
interaction.py
repeater.py
signal_child.py
signal_parent.py
```

```
subprocess_check_call.py
subprocess_check_output.py
subprocess_check_output_error.py
subprocess_check_output_error_trap_output.py
subprocess_os_system.py
subprocess_pipes.py
subprocess_popen2.py
subprocess_popen3.py
subprocess_popen4.py
subprocess_popen_read.py
subprocess_popen_write.py
subprocess_shell_variables.py
subprocess_signal_parent_shell.py
subprocess_signal_setsid.py
```

Setting the *shell* argument to a true value causes `subprocess` to spawn an intermediate shell process, which then runs the command. The default is to run the command directly.

import subprocess

```
# Command with shell expansion
subprocess.call('echo $HOME', shell=True)
```

Using an intermediate shell means that variables, glob patterns, and other special shell features in the command string are processed before the command is run.

```
$ python subprocess_shell_variables.py

/Users/dhellmann
```

Error Handling

The return value from `call()` is the exit code of the program. The caller is responsible for interpreting it to detect errors. The `check_call()` function works like `call()`, except that the exit code is checked, and if it indicates an error happened, then a `CalledProcessError` exception is raised.

import subprocess

```
try:
    subprocess.check_call(['false'])
```

```
except subprocess.CalledProcessError as err:
    print 'ERROR:', err
```

The **false** command always exits with a nonzero status code, which
check_call() interprets as an error.

```
$ python subprocess_check_call.py

ERROR: Command '['false']' returned nonzero exit status 1
```

Capturing Output

The standard input and output channels for the process started by call() are bound to
the parent's input and output. That means the calling program cannot capture the output
of the command. Use check_output() to capture the output for later processing.

```
import subprocess

output = subprocess.check_output(['ls', '-1'])
print 'Have %d bytes in output' % len(output)
print output
```

The ls -1 command runs successfully, so the text it prints to standard output is
captured and returned.

```
$ python subprocess_check_output.py

Have 462 bytes in output
__init__.py
index.rst
interaction.py
repeater.py
signal_child.py
signal_parent.py
subprocess_check_call.py
subprocess_check_output.py
subprocess_check_output_error.py
subprocess_check_output_error_trap_output.py
subprocess_os_system.py
subprocess_pipes.py
subprocess_popen2.py
subprocess_popen3.py
```

```
subprocess_popen4.py
subprocess_popen_read.py
subprocess_popen_write.py
subprocess_shell_variables.py
subprocess_signal_parent_shell.py
subprocess_signal_setsid.py
```

The next example runs a series of commands in a subshell. Messages are sent to standard output and standard error before the commands exit with an error code.

```
import subprocess

try:
    output = subprocess.check_output(
        'echo to stdout; echo to stderr 1>&2; exit 1',
        shell=True,
        )
except subprocess.CalledProcessError as err:
    print 'ERROR:', err
else:
    print 'Have %d bytes in output' % len(output)
    print output
```

The message to standard error is printed to the console, but the message to standard output is hidden.

```
$ python subprocess_check_output_error.py

to stderr
ERROR: Command 'echo to stdout; echo to stderr 1>&2; exit 1' returned
nonzero exit status 1
```

To prevent error messages from commands run through `check_output()` from being written to the console, set the *stderr* parameter to the constant STDOUT.

```
import subprocess

try:
    output = subprocess.check_output(
        'echo to stdout; echo to stderr 1>&2; exit 1',
        shell=True,
```

```
        stderr=subprocess.STDOUT,
        )
except subprocess.CalledProcessError as err:
    print 'ERROR:', err
else:
    print 'Have %d bytes in output' % len(output)
    print output
```

Now the error and standard output channels are merged together, so if the command prints error messages, they are captured and not sent to the console.

```
$ python subprocess_check_output_error_trap_output.py

ERROR: Command 'echo to stdout; echo to stderr 1>&2; exit 1' returned
nonzero exit status 1
```

10.1.2   Working with Pipes Directly

The functions `call()`, `check_call()`, and `check_output()` are wrappers around the `Popen` class. Using `Popen` directly gives more control over how the command is run and how its input and output streams are processed. For example, by passing different arguments for *stdin*, *stdout*, and *stderr*, it is possible to mimic the variations of `os.popen()`.

One-Way Communication with a Process

To run a process and read all its output, set the *stdout* value to `PIPE` and call `communicate()`.

```
import subprocess

print 'read:'
proc = subprocess.Popen(['echo', '"to stdout"'],
                        stdout=subprocess.PIPE,
                        )
stdout_value = proc.communicate()[0]
print '\tstdout:', repr(stdout_value)
```

This is similar to the way `popen()` works, except that the reading is managed internally by the `Popen` instance.

```
$ python subprocess_popen_read.py
```

```
read:
        stdout: '"to stdout"\n'
```

To set up a pipe to allow the calling program to write data to it, set *stdin* to `PIPE`.

```
import subprocess

print 'write:'
proc = subprocess.Popen(['cat', '-'],
                             stdin=subprocess.PIPE,
                             )
proc.communicate('\tstdin: to stdin\n')
```

To send data to the standard input channel of the process one time, pass the data to `communicate()`. This is similar to using `popen()` with mode `'w'`.

```
$ python -u subprocess_popen_write.py
```

```
write:
        stdin: to stdin
```

Bidirectional Communication with a Process

To set up the `Popen` instance for reading and writing at the same time, use a combination of the previous techniques.

```
import subprocess

print 'popen2:'

proc = subprocess.Popen(['cat', '-'],
                             stdin=subprocess.PIPE,
                             stdout=subprocess.PIPE,
                             )
msg = 'through stdin to stdout'
stdout_value = proc.communicate(msg)[0]
print '\tpass through:', repr(stdout_value)
```

This sets up the pipe to mimic `popen2()`.

```
$ python -u subprocess_popen2.py

popen2:
        pass through: 'through stdin to stdout'
```

Capturing Error Output

It is also possible watch both of the streams for *stdout* and *stderr*, as with `popen3()`.

```
import subprocess

print 'popen3:'
proc = subprocess.Popen('cat -; echo "to stderr" 1>&2',
                        shell=True,
                        stdin=subprocess.PIPE,
                        stdout=subprocess.PIPE,
                        stderr=subprocess.PIPE,
                        )
msg = 'through stdin to stdout'
stdout_value, stderr_value = proc.communicate(msg)
print '\tpass through:', repr(stdout_value)
print '\tstderr       :', repr(stderr_value)
```

Reading from *stderr* works the same as with *stdout*. Passing `PIPE` tells `Popen` to attach to the channel, and `communicate()` reads all the data from it before returning.

```
$ python -u subprocess_popen3.py

popen3:
        pass through: 'through stdin to stdout'
        stderr       : 'to stderr\n'
```

Combining Regular and Error Output

To direct the error output from the process to its standard output channel, use `STDOUT` for *stderr* instead of `PIPE`.

```
import subprocess

print 'popen4:'
proc = subprocess.Popen('cat -; echo "to stderr" 1>&2',
                        shell=True,
```

```
                              stdin=subprocess.PIPE,
                              stdout=subprocess.PIPE,
                              stderr=subprocess.STDOUT,
                              )
msg = 'through stdin to stdout\n'
stdout_value, stderr_value = proc.communicate(msg)
print '\tcombined output:', repr(stdout_value)
print '\tstderr value   :', repr(stderr_value)
```

Combining the output in this way is similar to how `popen4()` works.

```
$ python -u subprocess_popen4.py

popen4:
        combined output: 'through stdin to stdout\nto stderr\n'
        stderr value    : None
```

10.1.3 Connecting Segments of a Pipe

Multiple commands can be connected into a *pipeline*, similar to the way the UNIX shell works, by creating separate `Popen` instances and chaining their inputs and outputs together. The `stdout` attribute of one `Popen` instance is used as the *stdin* argument for the next in the pipeline, instead of the constant `PIPE`. The output is read from the `stdout` handle for the final command in the pipeline.

```
import subprocess

cat = subprocess.Popen(['cat', 'index.rst'],
                       stdout=subprocess.PIPE,
                       )

grep = subprocess.Popen(['grep', '.. include::'],
                        stdin=cat.stdout,
                        stdout=subprocess.PIPE,
                        )

cut = subprocess.Popen(['cut', '-f', '3', '-d:'],
                       stdin=grep.stdout,
                       stdout=subprocess.PIPE,
                       )

end_of_pipe = cut.stdout
```

```
print 'Included files:'
for line in end_of_pipe:
    print '\t', line.strip()
```

The example reproduces the following command line.

```
cat index.rst | grep ".. include" | cut -f 3 -d:
```

The pipeline reads the reStructuredText source file for this section and finds all the lines that include other files. Then it prints the names of the files being included.

```
$ python -u subprocess_pipes.py

Included files:
        subprocess_os_system.py
        subprocess_shell_variables.py
        subprocess_check_call.py
        subprocess_check_output.py
        subprocess_check_output_error.py
        subprocess_check_output_error_trap_output.py
        subprocess_popen_read.py
        subprocess_popen_write.py
        subprocess_popen2.py
        subprocess_popen3.py
        subprocess_popen4.py
        subprocess_pipes.py
        repeater.py
        interaction.py
        signal_child.py
        signal_parent.py
        subprocess_signal_parent_shell.py
        subprocess_signal_setsid.py
```

10.1.4   Interacting with Another Command

All the previous examples assume a limited amount of interaction. The `communicate()` method reads all the output and waits for the child process to exit before returning. It is also possible to write to and read from the individual pipe handles used by the Popen instance incrementally, as the program runs. A simple echo program that reads from standard input and writes to standard output illustrates this technique.

The script `repeater.py` is used as the child process in the next example. It reads from *stdin* and writes the values to *stdout*, one line at a time until there is no more input. It also writes a message to `stderr` when it starts and stops, showing the lifetime of the child process.

```python
import sys

sys.stderr.write('repeater.py: starting\n')
sys.stderr.flush()

while True:
    next_line = sys.stdin.readline()
    if not next_line:
        break
    sys.stdout.write(next_line)
    sys.stdout.flush()

sys.stderr.write('repeater.py: exiting\n')
sys.stderr.flush()
```

The next interaction example uses the `stdin` and `stdout` file handles owned by the `Popen` instance in different ways. In the first example, a sequence of five numbers is written to `stdin` of the process, and after each write, the next line of output is read back. In the second example, the same five numbers are written, but the output is read all at once using `communicate()`.

```python
import subprocess

print 'One line at a time:'
proc = subprocess.Popen('python repeater.py',
                        shell=True,
                        stdin=subprocess.PIPE,
                        stdout=subprocess.PIPE,
                        )
for i in range(5):
    proc.stdin.write('%d\n' % i)
    output = proc.stdout.readline()
    print output.rstrip()
remainder = proc.communicate()[0]
print remainder
```

```
print
print 'All output at once:'
proc = subprocess.Popen('python repeater.py',
                          shell=True,
                          stdin=subprocess.PIPE,
                          stdout=subprocess.PIPE,
                          )
for i in range(5):
    proc.stdin.write('%d\n' % i)

output = proc.communicate()[0]
print output
```

The `repeater.py: exiting` lines come at different points in the output for each loop style.

```
$ python -u interaction.py

One line at a time:
repeater.py: starting
0
1
2
3
4
repeater.py: exiting


All output at once:
repeater.py: starting
repeater.py: exiting
0
1
2
3
4
```

10.1.5 Signaling between Processes

The process management examples for the `os` module include a demonstration of signaling between processes using `os.fork()` and `os.kill()`. Since each `Popen` instance provides a *pid* attribute with the process id of the child process, it is possible to do something similar with `subprocess`. The next example combines two scripts. This child process sets up a signal handler for the USR signal.

```python
import os
import signal
import time
import sys

pid = os.getpid()
received = False

def signal_usr1(signum, frame):
    "Callback invoked when a signal is received"
    global received
    received = True
    print 'CHILD %6s: Received USR1' % pid
    sys.stdout.flush()

print 'CHILD %6s: Setting up signal handler' % pid
sys.stdout.flush()
signal.signal(signal.SIGUSR1, signal_usr1)
print 'CHILD %6s: Pausing to wait for signal' % pid
sys.stdout.flush()
time.sleep(3)

if not received:
    print 'CHILD %6s: Never received signal' % pid
```

This script runs as the parent process. It starts `signal_child.py`, then sends the USR1 signal.

```python
import os
import signal
import subprocess
import time
import sys

proc = subprocess.Popen(['python', 'signal_child.py'])
print 'PARENT      : Pausing before sending signal...'
sys.stdout.flush()
time.sleep(1)
print 'PARENT      : Signaling child'
```

```
sys.stdout.flush()
os.kill(proc.pid, signal.SIGUSR1)
```

This is the output.

```
$ python signal_parent.py

PARENT        : Pausing before sending signal...
CHILD   11298: Setting up signal handler
CHILD   11298: Pausing to wait for signal
PARENT        : Signaling child
CHILD   11298: Received USR1
```

Process Groups / Sessions

If the process created by `Popen` spawns subprocesses, those children will not receive any signals sent to the parent. That means when using the *shell* argument to `Popen`, it will be difficult to cause the command started in the shell to terminate by sending `SIGINT` or `SIGTERM`.

```
import os
import signal
import subprocess
import tempfile
import time
import sys

script = '''#!/bin/sh
echo "Shell script in process $$"
set -x
python signal_child.py
'''
script_file = tempfile.NamedTemporaryFile('wt')
script_file.write(script)
script_file.flush()

proc = subprocess.Popen(['sh', script_file.name], close_fds=True)
print 'PARENT        : Pausing before signaling %s...' % proc.pid
sys.stdout.flush()
time.sleep(1)
print 'PARENT        : Signaling child %s' % proc.pid
sys.stdout.flush()
```

```
os.kill(proc.pid, signal.SIGUSR1)
time.sleep(3)
```

The pid used to send the signal does not match the pid of the child of the shell script waiting for the signal, because in this example, there are three separate processes interacting.

1. The program `subprocess_signal_parent_shell.py`
2. The shell process running the script created by the main Python program
3. The program `signal_child.py`

```
$ python subprocess_signal_parent_shell.py

PARENT       : Pausing before signaling 11301...
Shell script in process 11301
+ python signal_child.py
CHILD  11302: Setting up signal handler
CHILD  11302: Pausing to wait for signal
PARENT       : Signaling child 11301
CHILD  11302: Never received signal
```

To send signals to descendants without knowing their process id, use a *process group* to associate the children so they can be signaled together. The process group is created with `os.setsid()`, setting the "session id" to the process id of the current process. All child processes inherit their session id from their parent, and since it should only be set in the shell created by `Popen` and its descendants, `os.setsid()` should not be called in the same process where the `Popen` is created. Instead, the function is passed to `Popen` as the *preexec_fn* argument so it is run after the `fork()` inside the new process, before it uses `exec()` to run the shell. To signal the entire process group, use `os.killpg()` with the `pid` value from the `Popen` instance.

```
import os
import signal
import subprocess
import tempfile
import time
import sys

script = '''#!/bin/sh
echo "Shell script in process $$"
```

```
set -x
python signal_child.py
'''

script_file = tempfile.NamedTemporaryFile('wt')
script_file.write(script)
script_file.flush()

def show_setting_sid():
    print 'Calling os.setsid() from %s' % os.getpid()
    sys.stdout.flush()
    os.setsid()

proc = subprocess.Popen(['sh', script_file.name],
                        close_fds=True,
                        preexec_fn=show_setting_sid,
                        )
print 'PARENT      : Pausing before signaling %s...' % proc.pid
sys.stdout.flush()
time.sleep(1)
print 'PARENT      : Signaling process group %s' % proc.pid
sys.stdout.flush()
os.killpg(proc.pid, signal.SIGUSR1)
time.sleep(3)
```

The sequence of events is:

1. The parent program instantiates `Popen`.
2. The `Popen` instance forks a new process.
3. The new process runs `os.setsid()`.
4. The new process runs `exec()` to start the shell.
5. The shell runs the shell script.
6. The shell script forks again, and that process execs Python.
7. Python runs `signal_child.py`.
8. The parent program signals the process group using the pid of the shell.
9. The shell and Python processes receive the signal.
10. The shell ignores the signal.
11. The Python process running `signal_child.py` invokes the signal handler.

```
$ python subprocess_signal_setsid.py

Calling os.setsid() from 11305
PARENT      : Pausing before signaling 11305...
Shell script in process 11305
+ python signal_child.py
CHILD   11306: Setting up signal handler
CHILD   11306: Pausing to wait for signal
PARENT      : Signaling process group 11305
CHILD   11306: Received USR1
```

See Also:

subprocess (http://docs.python.org/lib/module-subprocess.html) Standard   library
 documentation for this module.

UNIX Signals and Process Groups
 (www.frostbytes.com/~jimf/papers/signals/signals.html) A good description
 of UNIX signaling and how process groups work.

os (page 1108) Although `subprocess` replaces many of them, the functions for
 working with processes found in the `os` module are still widely used in existing
 code.

signal (page 497) More details about using the `signal` module.

Advanced Programming in the UNIX(R) Environment
 (www.amazon.com/Programming-Environment-Addison-Wesley-
 Professional-Computing/dp/0201433079/ref=pd_bbs_3/002-2842372-
 4768037?ie=UTF8&s=books&qid=1182098757&sr=8-3)   Covers
 working with multiple processes, such as handling signals, closing duplicated
 file descriptors, etc.

pipes UNIX shell command pipeline templates in the standard library.

10.2   signal—Asynchronous System Events

> **Purpose** Send and receive asynchronous system events.
> **Python Version** 1.4 and later

Signals are an operating system feature that provide a means of notifying a program
of an event and having it handled asynchronously. They can be generated by the
system itself or sent from one process to another. Since signals interrupt the regular

flow of the program, it is possible that some operations (especially I/O) may produce errors if a signal is received in the middle.

Signals are identified by integers and are defined in the operating system C headers. Python exposes the signals appropriate for the platform as symbols in the `signal` module. The examples in this section use `SIGINT` and `SIGUSR1`. Both are typically defined for all UNIX and UNIX-like systems.

Note: Programming with UNIX signal handlers is a nontrivial endeavor. This is an introduction and does not include all the details needed to use signals successfully on every platform. There is some degree of standardization across versions of UNIX, but there is also some variation. Consult the operating system documentation if you run into trouble.

10.2.1 Receiving Signals

As with other forms of event-based programming, signals are received by establishing a callback function, called a *signal handler*, that is invoked when the signal occurs. The arguments to the signal handler are the signal number and the stack frame from the point in the program that was interrupted by the signal.

```python
import signal
import os
import time

def receive_signal(signum, stack):
    print 'Received:', signum

# Register signal handlers
signal.signal(signal.SIGUSR1, receive_signal)
signal.signal(signal.SIGUSR2, receive_signal)

# Print the process ID so it can be used with 'kill'
# to send this program signals.
print 'My PID is:', os.getpid()

while True:
    print 'Waiting...'
    time.sleep(3)
```

This example script loops indefinitely, pausing for a few seconds each time. When a signal comes in, the `sleep()` call is interrupted and the signal handler `receive_signal()` prints the signal number. After the signal handler returns, the loop continues.

Send signals to the running program using `os.kill()` or the UNIX command line program **kill**.

```
$ python signal_signal.py

My PID is: 71387
Waiting...
Waiting...
Waiting...
Received: 30
Waiting...
Waiting...
Received: 31
Waiting...
Waiting...
Traceback (most recent call last):
  File "signal_signal.py", line 25, in <module>
    time.sleep(3)
KeyboardInterrupt
```

The previous output was produced by running `signal_signal.py` in one window, and then in another window running

```
$ kill -USR1 $pid
$ kill -USR2 $pid
$ kill -INT $pid
```

10.2.2 Retrieving Registered Handlers

To see what signal handlers are registered for a signal, use `getsignal()`. Pass the signal number as argument. The return value is the registered handler or one of the special values `SIG_IGN` (if the signal is being ignored), `SIG_DFL` (if the default behavior is being used), or `None` (if the existing signal handler was registered from C, rather than from Python).

```python
import signal

def alarm_received(n, stack):
    return

signal.signal(signal.SIGALRM, alarm_received)

signals_to_names = dict(
    (getattr(signal, n), n)
    for n in dir(signal)
    if n.startswith('SIG') and '_' not in n
    )

for s, name in sorted(signals_to_names.items()):
    handler = signal.getsignal(s)
    if handler is signal.SIG_DFL:
        handler = 'SIG_DFL'
    elif handler is signal.SIG_IGN:
        handler = 'SIG_IGN'
    print '%-10s (%2d):' % (name, s), handler
```

Again, since each OS may have different signals defined, the output on other systems may vary. This is from OS X:

```
$ python signal_getsignal.py

SIGHUP     ( 1): SIG_DFL
SIGINT     ( 2): <built-in function default_int_handler>
SIGQUIT    ( 3): SIG_DFL
SIGILL     ( 4): SIG_DFL
SIGTRAP    ( 5): SIG_DFL
SIGIOT     ( 6): SIG_DFL
SIGEMT     ( 7): SIG_DFL
SIGFPE     ( 8): SIG_DFL
SIGKILL    ( 9): None
SIGBUS     (10): SIG_DFL
SIGSEGV    (11): SIG_DFL
SIGSYS     (12): SIG_DFL
SIGPIPE    (13): SIG_IGN
SIGALRM    (14): <function alarm_received at 0x10045b398>
SIGTERM    (15): SIG_DFL
SIGURG     (16): SIG_DFL
SIGSTOP    (17): None
SIGTSTP    (18): SIG_DFL
SIGCONT    (19): SIG_DFL
```

```
SIGCHLD      (20):  SIG_DFL
SIGTTIN      (21):  SIG_DFL
SIGTTOU      (22):  SIG_DFL
SIGIO        (23):  SIG_DFL
SIGXCPU      (24):  SIG_DFL
SIGXFSZ      (25):  SIG_IGN
SIGVTALRM    (26):  SIG_DFL
SIGPROF      (27):  SIG_DFL
SIGWINCH     (28):  SIG_DFL
SIGINFO      (29):  SIG_DFL
SIGUSR1      (30):  SIG_DFL
SIGUSR2      (31):  SIG_DFL
```

10.2.3 Sending Signals

The function for sending signals from within Python is os.kill(). Its use is covered in the section on the os module, *Creating Processes with os.fork()*.

10.2.4 Alarms

Alarms are a special sort of signal, where the program asks the OS to notify it after some period of time has elapsed. As the standard module documentation for os points out, this is useful for avoiding blocking indefinitely on an I/O operation or other system call.

```
import signal
import time

def receive_alarm(signum, stack):
    print 'Alarm :', time.ctime()

# Call receive_alarm in 2 seconds
signal.signal(signal.SIGALRM, receive_alarm)
signal.alarm(2)

print 'Before:', time.ctime()
time.sleep(4)
print 'After :', time.ctime()
```

In this example, the call to sleep() does not last the full four seconds.

```
$ python signal_alarm.py

Before: Sun Aug 17 10:51:09 2008
```

```
Alarm : Sun Aug 17 10:51:11 2008
After : Sun Aug 17 10:51:11 2008
```

10.2.5   Ignoring Signals

To ignore a signal, register SIG_IGN as the handler. This script replaces the default handler for SIGINT with SIG_IGN and registers a handler for SIGUSR1. Then it uses signal.pause() to wait for a signal to be received.

```
import signal
import os
import time

def do_exit(sig, stack):
    raise SystemExit('Exiting')

signal.signal(signal.SIGINT, signal.SIG_IGN)
signal.signal(signal.SIGUSR1, do_exit)

print 'My PID:', os.getpid()

signal.pause()
```

Normally, SIGINT (the signal sent by the shell to a program when the user presses Ctrl-C) raises a KeyboardInterrupt. This example ignores SIGINT and raises SystemExit when it sees SIGUSR1. Each ^C in the output represents an attempt to use Ctrl-C to kill the script from the terminal. Using kill -USR1 72598 from another terminal eventually causes the script to exit.

```
$ python signal_ignore.py

My PID: 72598
^C^C^C^CExiting
```

10.2.6   Signals and Threads

Signals and threads do not generally mix well because only the main thread of a process will receive signals. The following example sets up a signal handler, waits for the signal in one thread, and sends the signal from another thread.

```python
import signal
import threading
import os
import time

def signal_handler(num, stack):
    print 'Received signal %d in %s' % \
        (num, threading.currentThread().name)

signal.signal(signal.SIGUSR1, signal_handler)

def wait_for_signal():
    print 'Waiting for signal in', threading.currentThread().name
    signal.pause()
    print 'Done waiting'

# Start a thread that will not receive the signal
receiver = threading.Thread(target=wait_for_signal, name='receiver')
receiver.start()
time.sleep(0.1)

def send_signal():
    print 'Sending signal in', threading.currentThread().name
    os.kill(os.getpid(), signal.SIGUSR1)

sender = threading.Thread(target=send_signal, name='sender')
sender.start()
sender.join()

# Wait for the thread to see the signal (not going to happen!)
print 'Waiting for', receiver.name
signal.alarm(2)
receiver.join()
```

The signal handlers were all registered in the main thread because this is a requirement of the `signal` module implementation for Python, regardless of underlying platform support for mixing threads and signals. Although the receiver thread calls `signal.pause()`, it does not receive the signal. The `signal.alarm(2)` call near the end of the example prevents an infinite block, since the receiver thread will never exit.

```
$ python signal_threads.py

Waiting for signal in receiver
Sending signal in sender
Received signal 30 in MainThread
Waiting for receiver
Alarm clock
```

Although alarms can be set in any thread, they are always received by the main thread.

```python
import signal
import time
import threading

def signal_handler(num, stack):
    print time.ctime(), 'Alarm in', threading.currentThread().name

signal.signal(signal.SIGALRM, signal_handler)

def use_alarm():
    t_name = threading.currentThread().name
    print time.ctime(), 'Setting alarm in', t_name
    signal.alarm(1)
    print time.ctime(), 'Sleeping in', t_name
    time.sleep(3)
    print time.ctime(), 'Done with sleep in', t_name

# Start a thread that will not receive the signal
alarm_thread = threading.Thread(target=use_alarm,
                                name='alarm_thread')
alarm_thread.start()
time.sleep(0.1)

# Wait for the thread to see the signal (not going to happen!)
print time.ctime(), 'Waiting for', alarm_thread.name
alarm_thread.join()

print time.ctime(), 'Exiting normally'
```

The alarm does not abort the `sleep()` call in `use_alarm()`.

```
$ python signal_threads_alarm.py

Sun Nov 28 14:26:51 2010 Setting alarm in alarm_thread
Sun Nov 28 14:26:51 2010 Sleeping in alarm_thread
Sun Nov 28 14:26:52 2010 Waiting for alarm_thread
Sun Nov 28 14:26:54 2010 Done with sleep in alarm_thread
Sun Nov 28 14:26:54 2010 Alarm in MainThread
Sun Nov 28 14:26:54 2010 Exiting normally
```

See Also:

signal (http://docs.python.org/lib/module-signal.html) Standard library documentation for this module.

Creating Processes with os.fork() (page 1122) The `kill()` function can be used to send signals between processes.

10.3 threading—Manage Concurrent Operations

> **Purpose** Builds on the `thread` module to more easily manage several threads of execution.
>
> **Python Version** 1.5.2 and later

Using threads allows a program to run multiple operations concurrently in the same process space. The `threading` module builds on the low-level features of `thread` to make working with threads easier.

10.3.1 Thread Objects

The simplest way to use a `Thread` is to instantiate it with a target function and call `start()` to let it begin working.

```python
import threading

def worker():
    """thread worker function"""
    print 'Worker'
    return

threads = []
for i in range(5):
    t = threading.Thread(target=worker)
```

```
    threads.append(t)
    t.start()
```

The output is five lines with `"Worker"` on each:

```
$ python threading_simple.py

Worker
Worker
Worker
Worker
Worker
```

It is useful to be able to spawn a thread and pass it arguments to tell it what work to do. Any type of object can be passed as an argument to the thread. This example passes a number, which the thread then prints.

```
import threading

def worker(num):
    """thread worker function"""
    print 'Worker: %s' % num
    return

threads = []
for i in range(5):
    t = threading.Thread(target=worker, args=(i,))
    threads.append(t)
    t.start()
```

The integer argument is now included in the message printed by each thread:

```
$ python -u threading_simpleargs.py

Worker: 0
Worker: 1
Worker: 2
Worker: 3
Worker: 4
```

10.3.2   Determining the Current Thread

Using arguments to identify or name the thread is cumbersome and unnecessary. Each Thread instance has a name with a default value that can be changed as the thread is created. Naming threads is useful in server processes made up of multiple service threads handling different operations.

```
import threading
import time

def worker():
    print threading.currentThread().getName(), 'Starting'
    time.sleep(2)
    print threading.currentThread().getName(), 'Exiting'

def my_service():
    print threading.currentThread().getName(), 'Starting'
    time.sleep(3)
    print threading.currentThread().getName(), 'Exiting'

t = threading.Thread(name='my_service', target=my_service)
w = threading.Thread(name='worker', target=worker)
w2 = threading.Thread(target=worker) # use default name

w.start()
w2.start()
t.start()
```

The debug output includes the name of the current thread on each line. The lines with "Thread-1" in the thread name column correspond to the unnamed thread w2.

```
$ python -u threading_names.py

worker Starting
Thread-1 Starting
my_service Starting
worker Exiting
Thread-1 Exiting
my_service Exiting
```

Most programs do not use **print** to debug. The `logging` module supports embedding the thread name in every log message using the formatter code `%(threadName)s`. Including thread names in log messages makes it possible to trace those messages back to their source.

```python
import logging
import threading
import time

logging.basicConfig(
    level=logging.DEBUG,
    format='[%(levelname)s] (%(threadName)-10s) %(message)s',
    )

def worker():
    logging.debug('Starting')
    time.sleep(2)
    logging.debug('Exiting')

def my_service():
    logging.debug('Starting')
    time.sleep(3)
    logging.debug('Exiting')

t = threading.Thread(name='my_service', target=my_service)
w = threading.Thread(name='worker', target=worker)
w2 = threading.Thread(target=worker) # use default name

w.start()
w2.start()
t.start()
```

`logging` is also thread-safe, so messages from different threads are kept distinct in the output.

```
$ python threading_names_log.py

[DEBUG] (worker    ) Starting
[DEBUG] (Thread-1  ) Starting
[DEBUG] (my_service) Starting
[DEBUG] (worker    ) Exiting
[DEBUG] (Thread-1  ) Exiting
[DEBUG] (my_service) Exiting
```

10.3.3 Daemon vs. Non-Daemon Threads

Up to this point, the example programs have implicitly waited to exit until all threads have completed their work. Programs sometimes spawn a thread as a *daemon* that runs without blocking the main program from exiting. Using daemon threads is useful for services where there may not be an easy way to interrupt the thread, or where letting the thread die in the middle of its work does not lose or corrupt data (for example, a thread that generates "heartbeats" for a service monitoring tool). To mark a thread as a daemon, call its `setDaemon()` method with `True`. The default is for threads to not be daemons.

```python
import threading
import time
import logging

logging.basicConfig(level=logging.DEBUG,
                    format='(%(threadName)-10s) %(message)s',
                    )

def daemon():
    logging.debug('Starting')
    time.sleep(2)
    logging.debug('Exiting')

d = threading.Thread(name='daemon', target=daemon)
d.setDaemon(True)

def non_daemon():
    logging.debug('Starting')
    logging.debug('Exiting')

t = threading.Thread(name='non-daemon', target=non_daemon)

d.start()
t.start()
```

The output does not include the "Exiting" message from the daemon thread, since all of the non-daemon threads (including the main thread) exit before the daemon thread wakes up from its two-second sleep.

```
$ python threading_daemon.py

(daemon    ) Starting
```

```
(non-daemon) Starting
(non-daemon) Exiting
```

To wait until a daemon thread has completed its work, use the `join()` method.

```python
import threading
import time
import logging

logging.basicConfig(level=logging.DEBUG,
                    format='(%(threadName)-10s) %(message)s',
                    )

def daemon():
    logging.debug('Starting')
    time.sleep(2)
    logging.debug('Exiting')

d = threading.Thread(name='daemon', target=daemon)
d.setDaemon(True)

def non_daemon():
    logging.debug('Starting')
    logging.debug('Exiting')

t = threading.Thread(name='non-daemon', target=non_daemon)

d.start()
t.start()

d.join()
t.join()
```

Waiting for the daemon thread to exit using `join()` means it has a chance to produce its "Exiting" message.

```
$ python threading_daemon_join.py

(daemon    ) Starting
(non-daemon) Starting
(non-daemon) Exiting
(daemon    ) Exiting
```

By default, `join()` blocks indefinitely. It is also possible to pass a float value representing the number of seconds to wait for the thread to become inactive. If the thread does not complete within the timeout period, `join()` returns anyway.

```python
import threading
import time
import logging

logging.basicConfig(level=logging.DEBUG,
                    format='(%(threadName)-10s) %(message)s',
                    )

def daemon():
    logging.debug('Starting')
    time.sleep(2)
    logging.debug('Exiting')

d = threading.Thread(name='daemon', target=daemon)
d.setDaemon(True)

def non_daemon():
    logging.debug('Starting')
    logging.debug('Exiting')

t = threading.Thread(name='non-daemon', target=non_daemon)

d.start()
t.start()

d.join(1)
print 'd.isAlive()', d.isAlive()
t.join()
```

Since the timeout passed is less than the amount of time the daemon thread sleeps, the thread is still "alive" after `join()` returns.

```
$ python threading_daemon_join_timeout.py

(daemon    ) Starting
(non-daemon) Starting
(non-daemon) Exiting
d.isAlive() True
```

10.3.4 Enumerating All Threads

It is not necessary to retain an explicit handle to all the daemon threads to ensure they have completed before exiting the main process. `enumerate()` returns a list of active `Thread` instances. The list includes the current thread, and since joining the current thread introduces a deadlock situation, it must be skipped.

```python
import random
import threading
import time
import logging

logging.basicConfig(level=logging.DEBUG,
                    format='(%(threadName)-10s) %(message)s',
                    )


def worker():
    """thread worker function"""
    t = threading.currentThread()
    pause = random.randint(1,5)
    logging.debug('sleeping %s', pause)
    time.sleep(pause)
    logging.debug('ending')
    return

for i in range(3):
    t = threading.Thread(target=worker)
    t.setDaemon(True)
    t.start()

main_thread = threading.currentThread()
for t in threading.enumerate():
    if t is main_thread:
        continue
    logging.debug('joining %s', t.getName())
    t.join()
```

Because the worker is sleeping for a random amount of time, the output from this program may vary.

```
$ python threading_enumerate.py

(Thread-1  ) sleeping 5
```

```
(Thread-2  ) sleeping 4
(Thread-3  ) sleeping 2
(MainThread) joining Thread-1
(Thread-3  ) ending
(Thread-2  ) ending
(Thread-1  ) ending
(MainThread) joining Thread-2
(MainThread) joining Thread-3
```

10.3.5   Subclassing Thread

At start-up, a `Thread` does some basic initialization and then calls its `run()` method, which calls the target function passed to the constructor. To create a subclass of `Thread`, override `run()` to do whatever is necessary.

```python
import threading
import logging

logging.basicConfig(level=logging.DEBUG,
                    format='(%(threadName)-10s) %(message)s',
                    )


class MyThread(threading.Thread):

    def run(self):
        logging.debug('running')
        return


for i in range(5):
    t = MyThread()
    t.start()
```

The return value of `run()` is ignored.

```
$ python threading_subclass.py

(Thread-1  ) running
(Thread-2  ) running
(Thread-3  ) running
(Thread-4  ) running
(Thread-5  ) running
```

Because the *args* and *kwargs* values passed to the `Thread` constructor are saved in private variables using names prefixed with '`__`', they are not easily accessed from a subclass. To pass arguments to a custom thread type, redefine the constructor to save the values in an instance attribute visible from the subclass.

```python
import threading
import logging

logging.basicConfig(level=logging.DEBUG,
                    format='(%(threadName)-10s) %(message)s',
                    )


class MyThreadWithArgs(threading.Thread):

    def __init__(self, group=None, target=None, name=None,
                 args=(), kwargs=None, verbose=None):
        threading.Thread.__init__(self, group=group,
                                  target=target,
                                  name=name,
                                  verbose=verbose)
        self.args = args
        self.kwargs = kwargs
        return

    def run(self):
        logging.debug('running with %s and %s',
                      self.args, self.kwargs)
        return


for i in range(5):
    t = MyThreadWithArgs(args=(i,),
                         kwargs={'a':'A', 'b':'B'})
    t.start()
```

MyThreadWithArgs uses the same API as `Thread`, but another class could easily change the constructor method to take more or different arguments more directly related to the purpose of the thread, as with any other class.

```
$ python threading_subclass_args.py

(Thread-1  ) running with (0,) and {'a': 'A', 'b': 'B'}
(Thread-2  ) running with (1,) and {'a': 'A', 'b': 'B'}
(Thread-3  ) running with (2,) and {'a': 'A', 'b': 'B'}
```

```
(Thread-4 ) running with (3,) and {'a': 'A', 'b': 'B'}
(Thread-5 ) running with (4,) and {'a': 'A', 'b': 'B'}
```

10.3.6 Timer Threads

One example of a reason to subclass Thread is provided by Timer, also included in threading. A Timer starts its work after a delay and can be canceled at any point within that delay time period.

```
import threading
import time
import logging

logging.basicConfig(level=logging.DEBUG,
                    format='(%(threadName)-10s) %(message)s',
                    )

def delayed():
    logging.debug('worker running')
    return

t1 = threading.Timer(3, delayed)
t1.setName('t1')
t2 = threading.Timer(3, delayed)
t2.setName('t2')

logging.debug('starting timers')
t1.start()
t2.start()

logging.debug('waiting before canceling %s', t2.getName())
time.sleep(2)
logging.debug('canceling %s', t2.getName())
t2.cancel()
logging.debug('done')
```

The second timer is never run, and the first timer appears to run after the rest of the main program is done. Since it is not a daemon thread, it is joined implicitly when the main thread is done.

```
$ python threading_timer.py

(MainThread) starting timers
```

```
(MainThread) waiting before canceling t2
(MainThread) canceling t2
(MainThread) done
(t1        ) worker running
```

10.3.7   Signaling between Threads

Although the point of using multiple threads is to run separate operations concurrently, there are times when it is important to be able to synchronize the operations in two or more threads. Event objects are a simple way to communicate between threads safely. An Event manages an internal flag that callers can control with the set() and clear() methods. Other threads can use wait() to pause until the flag is set, effectively blocking progress until allowed to continue.

```python
import logging
import threading
import time

logging.basicConfig(level=logging.DEBUG,
                    format='(%(threadName)-10s) %(message)s',
                    )

def wait_for_event(e):
    """Wait for the event to be set before doing anything"""
    logging.debug('wait_for_event starting')
    event_is_set = e.wait()
    logging.debug('event set: %s', event_is_set)

def wait_for_event_timeout(e, t):
    """Wait t seconds and then timeout"""
    while not e.isSet():
        logging.debug('wait_for_event_timeout starting')
        event_is_set = e.wait(t)
        logging.debug('event set: %s', event_is_set)
        if event_is_set:
            logging.debug('processing event')
        else:
            logging.debug('doing other work')

e = threading.Event()
t1 = threading.Thread(name='block',
```

```
                    target=wait_for_event,
                    args=(e,))
t1.start()

t2 = threading.Thread(name='nonblock',
                    target=wait_for_event_timeout,
                    args=(e, 2))
t2.start()

logging.debug('Waiting before calling Event.set()')
time.sleep(3)
e.set()
logging.debug('Event is set')
```

The `wait()` method takes an argument representing the number of seconds to wait for the event before timing out. It returns a Boolean indicating whether or not the event is set, so the caller knows why `wait()` returned. The `isSet()` method can be used separately on the event without fear of blocking.

In this example, `wait_for_event_timeout()` checks the event status without blocking indefinitely. The `wait_for_event()` blocks on the call to `wait()`, which does not return until the event status changes.

```
$ python threading_event.py

(block     ) wait_for_event starting
(nonblock  ) wait_for_event_timeout starting
(MainThread) Waiting before calling Event.set()
(nonblock  ) event set: False
(nonblock  ) doing other work
(nonblock  ) wait_for_event_timeout starting
(MainThread) Event is set
(block     ) event set: True
(nonblock  ) event set: True
(nonblock  ) processing event
```

10.3.8 Controlling Access to Resources

In addition to synchronizing the operations of threads, it is also important to be able to control access to shared resources to prevent corruption or missed data. Python's built-in data structures (lists, dictionaries, etc.) are thread-safe as a side effect of having atomic byte-codes for manipulating them (the GIL is not released in the middle of an update). Other data structures implemented in Python, or simpler types like integers and floats, do not have that protection. To guard against simultaneous access to an object, use a `Lock` object.

```python
import logging
import random
import threading
import time


logging.basicConfig(level=logging.DEBUG,
                    format='(%(threadName)-10s) %(message)s',
                    )

class Counter(object):
    def __init__(self, start=0):
        self.lock = threading.Lock()
        self.value = start
    def increment(self):
        logging.debug('Waiting for lock')
        self.lock.acquire()
        try:
            logging.debug('Acquired lock')
            self.value = self.value + 1
        finally:
            self.lock.release()

def worker(c):
    for i in range(2):
        pause = random.random()
        logging.debug('Sleeping %0.02f', pause)
        time.sleep(pause)
        c.increment()
    logging.debug('Done')

counter = Counter()
for i in range(2):
    t = threading.Thread(target=worker, args=(counter,))
    t.start()

logging.debug('Waiting for worker threads')
main_thread = threading.currentThread()
```

```
for t in threading.enumerate():
    if t is not main_thread:
        t.join()
logging.debug('Counter: %d', counter.value)
```

In this example, the `worker()` function increments a `Counter` instance, which manages a `Lock` to prevent two threads from changing its internal state at the same time. If the `Lock` was not used, there is a possibility of missing a change to the value attribute.

```
$ python threading_lock.py

(Thread-1  ) Sleeping 0.94
(Thread-2  ) Sleeping 0.32
(MainThread) Waiting for worker threads
(Thread-2  ) Waiting for lock
(Thread-2  ) Acquired lock
(Thread-2  ) Sleeping 0.54
(Thread-1  ) Waiting for lock
(Thread-1  ) Acquired lock
(Thread-1  ) Sleeping 0.84
(Thread-2  ) Waiting for lock
(Thread-2  ) Acquired lock
(Thread-2  ) Done
(Thread-1  ) Waiting for lock
(Thread-1  ) Acquired lock
(Thread-1  ) Done
(MainThread) Counter: 4
```

To find out whether another thread has acquired the lock without holding up the current thread, pass False for the *blocking* argument to `acquire()`. In the next example, `worker()` tries to acquire the lock three separate times and counts how many attempts it has to make to do so. In the meantime, `lock_holder()` cycles between holding and releasing the lock, with short pauses in each state used to simulate load.

```
import logging
import threading
import time

logging.basicConfig(level=logging.DEBUG,
                    format='(%(threadName)-10s) %(message)s',
                    )
```

```python
def lock_holder(lock):
    logging.debug('Starting')
    while True:
        lock.acquire()
        try:
            logging.debug('Holding')
            time.sleep(0.5)
        finally:
            logging.debug('Not holding')
            lock.release()
        time.sleep(0.5)
    return


def worker(lock):
    logging.debug('Starting')
    num_tries = 0
    num_acquires = 0
    while num_acquires < 3:
        time.sleep(0.5)
        logging.debug('Trying to acquire')
        have_it = lock.acquire(0)
        try:
            num_tries += 1
            if have_it:
                logging.debug('Iteration %d: Acquired',
                              num_tries)
                num_acquires += 1
            else:
                logging.debug('Iteration %d: Not acquired',
                              num_tries)
        finally:
            if have_it:
                lock.release()
    logging.debug('Done after %d iterations', num_tries)


lock = threading.Lock()

holder = threading.Thread(target=lock_holder,
                          args=(lock,),
                          name='LockHolder')
holder.setDaemon(True)
holder.start()
```

```
worker = threading.Thread(target=worker,
                          args=(lock,),
                          name='Worker')
worker.start()
```

It takes `worker()` more than three iterations to acquire the lock three separate times.

```
$ python threading_lock_noblock.py

(LockHolder) Starting
(LockHolder) Holding
(Worker    ) Starting
(LockHolder) Not holding
(Worker    ) Trying to acquire
(Worker    ) Iteration 1: Acquired
(LockHolder) Holding
(Worker    ) Trying to acquire
(Worker    ) Iteration 2: Not acquired
(LockHolder) Not holding
(Worker    ) Trying to acquire
(Worker    ) Iteration 3: Acquired
(LockHolder) Holding
(Worker    ) Trying to acquire
(Worker    ) Iteration 4: Not acquired
(LockHolder) Not holding
(Worker    ) Trying to acquire
(Worker    ) Iteration 5: Acquired
(Worker    ) Done after 5 iterations
```

Re-entrant Locks

Normal `Lock` objects cannot be acquired more than once, even by the same thread. This limitation can introduce undesirable side effects if a lock is accessed by more than one function in the same call chain.

```
import threading

lock = threading.Lock()

print 'First try :', lock.acquire()
print 'Second try:', lock.acquire(0)
```

In this case, the second call to `acquire()` is given a zero timeout to prevent it from blocking because the lock has been obtained by the first call.

```
$ python threading_lock_reacquire.py

First try : True
Second try: False
```

In a situation where separate code from the same thread needs to "reacquire" the lock, use an RLock instead.

```
import threading

lock = threading.RLock()

print 'First try :', lock.acquire()
print 'Second try:', lock.acquire(0)
```

The only change to the code from the previous example is substituting RLock for Lock.

```
$ python threading_rlock.py

First try : True
Second try: 1
```

Locks as Context Managers

Locks implement the context manager API and are compatible with the **with** statement. Using **with** removes the need to explicitly acquire and release the lock.

```
import threading
import logging

logging.basicConfig(level=logging.DEBUG,
                    format='(%(threadName)-10s) %(message)s',
                    )

def worker_with(lock):
    with lock:
        logging.debug('Lock acquired via with')
```

```
def worker_no_with(lock):
    lock.acquire()
    try:
        logging.debug('Lock acquired directly')
    finally:
        lock.release()

lock = threading.Lock()
w = threading.Thread(target=worker_with, args=(lock,))
nw = threading.Thread(target=worker_no_with, args=(lock,))

w.start()
nw.start()
```

The two functions `worker_with()` and `worker_no_with()` manage the lock in equivalent ways.

```
$ python threading_lock_with.py

(Thread-1  ) Lock acquired via with
(Thread-2  ) Lock acquired directly
```

10.3.9 Synchronizing Threads

In addition to using `Event`s, another way of synchronizing threads is through using a `Condition` object. Because the `Condition` uses a `Lock`, it can be tied to a shared resource, allowing multiple threads to wait for the resource to be updated. In this example, the `consumer()` threads wait for the `Condition` to be set before continuing. The `producer()` thread is responsible for setting the condition and notifying the other threads that they can continue.

```
import logging
import threading
import time

logging.basicConfig(
    level=logging.DEBUG,
    format='%(asctime)s (%(threadName)-2s) %(message)s',
    )

def consumer(cond):
    """wait for the condition and use the resource"""
```

```
        logging.debug('Starting consumer thread')
        t = threading.currentThread()
        with cond:
            cond.wait()
            logging.debug('Resource is available to consumer')

def producer(cond):
    """set up the resource to be used by the consumer"""
    logging.debug('Starting producer thread')
    with cond:
        logging.debug('Making resource available')
        cond.notifyAll()


condition = threading.Condition()
c1 = threading.Thread(name='c1', target=consumer,
                      args=(condition,))
c2 = threading.Thread(name='c2', target=consumer,
                      args=(condition,))
p = threading.Thread(name='p', target=producer,
                     args=(condition,))


c1.start()
time.sleep(2)
c2.start()
time.sleep(2)
p.start()
```

The threads use **with** to acquire the lock associated with the `Condition`. Using the `acquire()` and `release()` methods explicitly also works.

```
$ python threading_condition.py

2010-11-15 09:24:53,544 (c1) Starting consumer thread
2010-11-15 09:24:55,545 (c2) Starting consumer thread
2010-11-15 09:24:57,546 (p ) Starting producer thread
2010-11-15 09:24:57,546 (p ) Making resource available
2010-11-15 09:24:57,547 (c2) Resource is available to consumer
2010-11-15 09:24:57,547 (c1) Resource is available to consumer
```

10.3.10 Limiting Concurrent Access to Resources

It is sometimes useful to allow more than one worker access to a resource at a time, while still limiting the overall number. For example, a connection pool might support a fixed number of simultaneous connections, or a network application might support a fixed number of concurrent downloads. A Semaphore is one way to manage those connections.

```python
import logging
import random
import threading
import time

logging.basicConfig(
    level=logging.DEBUG,
    format='%(asctime)s (%(threadName)-2s) %(message)s',
    )


class ActivePool(object):
    def __init__(self):
        super(ActivePool, self).__init__()
        self.active = []
        self.lock = threading.Lock()
    def makeActive(self, name):
        with self.lock:
            self.active.append(name)
            logging.debug('Running: %s', self.active)
    def makeInactive(self, name):
        with self.lock:
            self.active.remove(name)
            logging.debug('Running: %s', self.active)


def worker(s, pool):
    logging.debug('Waiting to join the pool')
    with s:
        name = threading.currentThread().getName()
        pool.makeActive(name)
        time.sleep(0.1)
        pool.makeInactive(name)

pool = ActivePool()
s = threading.Semaphore(2)
for i in range(4):
    t = threading.Thread(target=worker,
                         name=str(i),
                         args=(s, pool))
    t.start()
```

In this example, the `ActivePool` class simply serves as a convenient way to track which threads are able to run at a given moment. A real resource pool would allocate a connection or some other value to the newly active thread and reclaim the value when the thread is done. Here, it is just used to hold the names of the active threads to show that, at most, two are running concurrently.

```
$ python threading_semaphore.py

2010-11-15 09:24:57,618 (0 ) Waiting to join the pool
2010-11-15 09:24:57,619 (0 ) Running: ['0']
2010-11-15 09:24:57,619 (1 ) Waiting to join the pool
2010-11-15 09:24:57,619 (1 ) Running: ['0', '1']
2010-11-15 09:24:57,620 (2 ) Waiting to join the pool
2010-11-15 09:24:57,620 (3 ) Waiting to join the pool
2010-11-15 09:24:57,719 (0 ) Running: ['1']
2010-11-15 09:24:57,720 (1 ) Running: []
2010-11-15 09:24:57,721 (2 ) Running: ['2']
2010-11-15 09:24:57,721 (3 ) Running: ['2', '3']
2010-11-15 09:24:57,821 (2 ) Running: ['3']
2010-11-15 09:24:57,822 (3 ) Running: []
```

10.3.11 Thread-Specific Data

While some resources need to be locked so multiple threads can use them, others need to be protected so that they are hidden from threads that do not "own" them. The `local()` function creates an object capable of hiding values from view in separate threads.

```
import random
import threading
import logging

logging.basicConfig(level=logging.DEBUG,
                    format='(%(threadName)-10s) %(message)s',
                    )


def show_value(data):
    try:
        val = data.value
    except AttributeError:
        logging.debug('No value yet')
    else:
        logging.debug('value=%s', val)
```

```python
def worker(data):
    show_value(data)
    data.value = random.randint(1, 100)
    show_value(data)


local_data = threading.local()
show_value(local_data)
local_data.value = 1000
show_value(local_data)


for i in range(2):
    t = threading.Thread(target=worker, args=(local_data,))
    t.start()
```

The attribute `local_data.value` is not present for any thread until it is set in that thread.

```
$ python threading_local.py

(MainThread) No value yet
(MainThread) value=1000
(Thread-1  ) No value yet
(Thread-1  ) value=71
(Thread-2  ) No value yet
(Thread-2  ) value=38
```

To initialize the settings so all threads start with the same value, use a subclass and set the attributes in `__init__()`.

```python
import random
import threading
import logging

logging.basicConfig(level=logging.DEBUG,
                    format='(%(threadName)-10s) %(message)s',
                    )


def show_value(data):
    try:
        val = data.value
```

```
    except AttributeError:
        logging.debug('No value yet')
    else:
        logging.debug('value=%s', val)

def worker(data):
    show_value(data)
    data.value = random.randint(1, 100)
    show_value(data)

class MyLocal(threading.local):
    def __init__(self, value):
        logging.debug('Initializing %r', self)
        self.value = value

local_data = MyLocal(1000)
show_value(local_data)

for i in range(2):
    t = threading.Thread(target=worker, args=(local_data,))
    t.start()
```

__init__() is invoked on the same object (note the id() value), once in each thread to set the default values.

```
$ python threading_local_defaults.py

(MainThread) Initializing <__main__.MyLocal object at 0x100e16050>
(MainThread) value=1000
(Thread-1  ) Initializing <__main__.MyLocal object at 0x100e16050>
(Thread-1  ) value=1000
(Thread-1  ) value=19
(Thread-2  ) Initializing <__main__.MyLocal object at 0x100e16050>
(Thread-2  ) value=1000
(Thread-2  ) value=55
```

See Also:

threading (http://docs.python.org/lib/module-threading.html) Standard library documentation for this module.

thread Lower-level thread API.

multiprocessing (page 529) An API for working with processes; it mirrors the threading API.

Queue (page 96) Thread-safe queue, useful for passing messages between threads.

10.4   multiprocessing—Manage Processes like Threads

Purpose Provides an API for managing processes.
Python Version 2.6 and later

The `multiprocessing` module includes an API for dividing up work between multiple processes based on the API for `threading`. In some cases, `multiprocessing` is a drop-in replacement and can be used instead of `threading` to take advantage of multiple CPU cores to avoid computational bottlenecks associated with Python's global interpreter lock.

Due to the similarity, the first few examples here are modified from the `threading` examples. Features provided by `multiprocessing` but not available in `threading` are covered later.

10.4.1   Multiprocessing Basics

The simplest way to spawn a second process is to instantiate a `Process` object with a target function and call `start()` to let it begin working.

```
import multiprocessing

def worker():
    """worker function"""
    print 'Worker'
    return

if __name__ == '__main__':
    jobs = []
    for i in range(5):
        p = multiprocessing.Process(target=worker)
        jobs.append(p)
        p.start()
```

The output includes the word "Worker" printed five times, although it may not come out entirely clean, depending on the order of execution, because each process is competing for access to the output stream.

```
$ python multiprocessing_simple.py

Worker
Worker
```

```
Worker
Worker
Worker
```

It is usually more useful to be able to spawn a process with arguments to tell it what work to do. Unlike with `threading`, in order to pass arguments to a `multiprocessing Process`, the arguments must be able to be serialized using `pickle`. This example passes each worker a number to be printed.

```python
import multiprocessing

def worker(num):
    """thread worker function"""
    print 'Worker:', num
    return

if __name__ == '__main__':
    jobs = []
    for i in range(5):
        p = multiprocessing.Process(target=worker, args=(i,))
        jobs.append(p)
        p.start()
```

The integer argument is now included in the message printed by each worker:

```
$ python multiprocessing_simpleargs.py

Worker: 0
Worker: 1
Worker: 4
Worker: 2
Worker: 3
```

10.4.2   Importable Target Functions

One difference between the `threading` and `multiprocessing` examples is the extra protection for __main__ used in the `multiprocessing` examples. Due to the way the new processes are started, the child process needs to be able to import the script containing the target function. Wrapping the main part of the application in a check for __main__ ensures that it is not run recursively in each child as the module is imported. Another approach is to import the target function from a separate script. For example, `multiprocessing_import_main.py` uses a worker function defined in a second module.

```
import multiprocessing
import multiprocessing_import_worker

if __name__ == '__main__':
    jobs = []
    for i in range(5):
        p = multiprocessing.Process(
            target=multiprocessing_import_worker.worker,
            )
        jobs.append(p)
        p.start()
```

The worker function is defined in `multiprocessing_import_worker.py`.

```
def worker():
    """worker function"""
    print 'Worker'
    return
```

Calling the main program produces output similar to the first example.

```
$ python multiprocessing_import_main.py

Worker
Worker
Worker
Worker
Worker
```

10.4.3 Determining the Current Process

Passing arguments to identify or name the process is cumbersome and unnecessary. Each `Process` instance has a name with a default value that can be changed as the process is created. Naming processes is useful for keeping track of them, especially in applications with multiple types of processes running simultaneously.

```
import multiprocessing
import time
```

```python
def worker():
    name = multiprocessing.current_process().name
    print name, 'Starting'
    time.sleep(2)
    print name, 'Exiting'

def my_service():
    name = multiprocessing.current_process().name
    print name, 'Starting'
    time.sleep(3)
    print name, 'Exiting'

if __name__ == '__main__':
    service = multiprocessing.Process(name='my_service',
                                        target=my_service)
    worker_1 = multiprocessing.Process(name='worker 1',
                                        target=worker)
    worker_2 = multiprocessing.Process(target=worker) # default name

    worker_1.start()
    worker_2.start()
    service.start()
```

The debug output includes the name of the current process on each line. The lines with `Process-3` in the name column correspond to the unnamed process `worker_1`.

```
$ python multiprocessing_names.py

worker 1 Starting
worker 1 Exiting
Process-3 Starting
Process-3 Exiting
my_service Starting
my_service Exiting
```

10.4.4 Daemon Processes

By default, the main program will not exit until all the children have exited. There are times when starting a background process that runs without blocking the main program from exiting is useful, such as in services where there may not be an easy way to interrupt the worker or where letting it die in the middle of its work does not lose or corrupt data (for example, a task that generates "heartbeats" for a service monitoring tool).

To mark a process as a daemon, set its `daemon` attribute to `True`. The default is for processes to not be daemons.

```python
import multiprocessing
import time
import sys

def daemon():
    p = multiprocessing.current_process()
    print 'Starting:', p.name, p.pid
    sys.stdout.flush()
    time.sleep(2)
    print 'Exiting :', p.name, p.pid
    sys.stdout.flush()


def non_daemon():
    p = multiprocessing.current_process()
    print 'Starting:', p.name, p.pid
    sys.stdout.flush()
    print 'Exiting :', p.name, p.pid
    sys.stdout.flush()


if __name__ == '__main__':
    d = multiprocessing.Process(name='daemon', target=daemon)
    d.daemon = True

    n = multiprocessing.Process(name='non-daemon', target=non_daemon)
    n.daemon = False

    d.start()
    time.sleep(1)
    n.start()
```

The output does not include the "Exiting" message from the daemon process, since all non-daemon processes (including the main program) exit before the daemon process wakes up from its two-second sleep.

```
$ python multiprocessing_daemon.py

Starting: daemon 9842
```

```
Starting: non-daemon 9843
Exiting : non-daemon 9843
```

The daemon process is terminated automatically before the main program exits, which avoids leaving orphaned processes running. This can be verified by looking for the process id value printed when the program runs and then checking for that process with a command like **ps**.

10.4.5 Waiting for Processes

To wait until a process has completed its work and exited, use the `join()` method.

```python
import multiprocessing
import time
import sys

def daemon():
    name = multiprocessing.current_process().name
    print 'Starting:', name
    time.sleep(2)
    print 'Exiting :', name

def non_daemon():
    name = multiprocessing.current_process().name
    print 'Starting:', name
    print 'Exiting :', name

if __name__ == '__main__':
    d = multiprocessing.Process(name='daemon',
                                target=daemon)
    d.daemon = True

    n = multiprocessing.Process(name='non-daemon',
                                target=non_daemon)
    n.daemon = False

    d.start()
    time.sleep(1)
    n.start()

    d.join()
    n.join()
```

Since the main process waits for the daemon to exit using `join()`, the "Exiting" message is printed this time.

```
$ python multiprocessing_daemon_join.py

Starting: non-daemon
Exiting : non-daemon
Starting: daemon
Exiting : daemon
```

By default, `join()` blocks indefinitely. It is also possible to pass a timeout argument (a float representing the number of seconds to wait for the process to become inactive). If the process does not complete within the timeout period, `join()` returns anyway.

```python
import multiprocessing
import time
import sys

def daemon():
    name = multiprocessing.current_process().name
    print 'Starting:', name
    time.sleep(2)
    print 'Exiting :', name

def non_daemon():
    name = multiprocessing.current_process().name
    print 'Starting:', name
    print 'Exiting :', name

if __name__ == '__main__':
    d = multiprocessing.Process(name='daemon',
                                target=daemon)
    d.daemon = True

    n = multiprocessing.Process(name='non-daemon',
                                target=non_daemon)
    n.daemon = False

    d.start()
    n.start()
```

```
    d.join(1)
    print 'd.is_alive()', d.is_alive()
    n.join()
```

Since the timeout passed is less than the amount of time the daemon sleeps, the process is still "alive" after `join()` returns.

```
$ python multiprocessing_daemon_join_timeout.py

Starting: non-daemon
Exiting : non-daemon
d.is_alive() True
```

10.4.6 Terminating Processes

Although it is better to use the *poison pill* method of signaling to a process that it should exit (see *Passing Messages to Processes*, later in this chapter), if a process appears hung or deadlocked, it can be useful to be able to kill it forcibly. Calling `terminate()` on a process object kills the child process.

```
import multiprocessing
import time

def slow_worker():
    print 'Starting worker'
    time.sleep(0.1)
    print 'Finished worker'

if __name__ == '__main__':
    p = multiprocessing.Process(target=slow_worker)
    print 'BEFORE:', p, p.is_alive()

    p.start()
    print 'DURING:', p, p.is_alive()

    p.terminate()
    print 'TERMINATED:', p, p.is_alive()

    p.join()
    print 'JOINED:', p, p.is_alive()
```

> **Note:** It is important to `join()` the process after terminating it in order to give the process management code time to update the status of the object to reflect the termination.

```
$ python multiprocessing_terminate.py

BEFORE: <Process(Process-1, initial)> False
DURING: <Process(Process-1, started)> True
TERMINATED: <Process(Process-1, started)> True
JOINED: <Process(Process-1, stopped[SIGTERM])> False
```

10.4.7 Process Exit Status

The status code produced when the process exits can be accessed via the `exitcode` attribute. The ranges allowed are listed in Table 10.1.

Table 10.1. Multiprocessing Exit Codes

Exit Code	Meaning
== 0	No error was produced.
> 0	The process had an error, and exited with that code.
< 0	The process was killed with a signal of $-1 * $ `exitcode`.

```python
import multiprocessing
import sys
import time

def exit_error():
    sys.exit(1)

def exit_ok():
    return

def return_value():
    return 1

def raises():
    raise RuntimeError('There was an error!')
```

```
def terminated():
    time.sleep(3)

if __name__ == '__main__':
    jobs = []
    for f in [exit_error, exit_ok, return_value, raises, terminated]:
        print 'Starting process for', f.func_name
        j = multiprocessing.Process(target=f, name=f.func_name)
        jobs.append(j)
        j.start()

    jobs[-1].terminate()

    for j in jobs:
        j.join()
        print '%15s.exitcode = %s' % (j.name, j.exitcode)
```

Processes that raise an exception automatically get an exitcode of 1.

```
$ python multiprocessing_exitcode.py

Starting process for exit_error
Starting process for exit_ok
Starting process for return_value
Starting process for raises
Starting process for terminated
Process raises:
Traceback (most recent call last):
  File "/Library/Frameworks/Python.framework/Versions/2.7/lib/python
2.7/multiprocessing/process.py", line 232, in _bootstrap
    self.run()
  File "/Library/Frameworks/Python.framework/Versions/2.7/lib/python
2.7/multiprocessing/process.py", line 88, in run
    self._target(*self._args, **self._kwargs)
  File "multiprocessing_exitcode.py", line 24, in raises
    raise RuntimeError('There was an error!')
RuntimeError: There was an error!
    exit_error.exitcode = 1
       exit_ok.exitcode = 0
  return_value.exitcode = 0
        raises.exitcode = 1
    terminated.exitcode = -15
```

10.4.8   Logging

When debugging concurrency issues, it can be useful to have access to the internals of the objects provided by `multiprocessing`. There is a convenient module-level function to enable logging called `log_to_stderr()`. It sets up a logger object using `logging` and adds a handler so that log messages are sent to the standard error channel.

```
import multiprocessing
import logging
import sys


def worker():
    print 'Doing some work'
    sys.stdout.flush()


if __name__ == '__main__':
    multiprocessing.log_to_stderr(logging.DEBUG)
    p = multiprocessing.Process(target=worker)
    p.start()
    p.join()
```

By default, the logging level is set to `NOTSET` so no messages are produced. Pass a different level to initialize the logger to the level of detail desired.

```
$ python multiprocessing_log_to_stderr.py

[INFO/Process-1] child process calling self.run()
Doing some work
[INFO/Process-1] process shutting down
[DEBUG/Process-1] running all "atexit" finalizers with priority >= 0
[DEBUG/Process-1] running the remaining "atexit" finalizers
[INFO/Process-1] process exiting with exitcode 0
[INFO/MainProcess] process shutting down
[DEBUG/MainProcess] running all "atexit" finalizers with priority >= 0
[DEBUG/MainProcess] running the remaining "atexit" finalizers
```

To manipulate the logger directly (change its level setting or add handlers), use `get_logger()`.

```
import multiprocessing
import logging
```

```
import sys

def worker():
    print 'Doing some work'
    sys.stdout.flush()

if __name__ == '__main__':
    multiprocessing.log_to_stderr()
    logger = multiprocessing.get_logger()
    logger.setLevel(logging.INFO)
    p = multiprocessing.Process(target=worker)
    p.start()
    p.join()
```

The logger can also be configured through the `logging` configuration file API, using the name `multiprocessing`.

```
$ python multiprocessing_get_logger.py

[INFO/Process-1] child process calling self.run()
Doing some work
[INFO/Process-1] process shutting down
[INFO/Process-1] process exiting with exitcode 0
[INFO/MainProcess] process shutting down
```

10.4.9 Subclassing Process

Although the simplest way to start a job in a separate process is to use `Process` and pass a target function, it is also possible to use a custom subclass.

```
import multiprocessing

class Worker(multiprocessing.Process):

    def run(self):
        print 'In %s' % self.name
        return

if __name__ == '__main__':
    jobs = []
    for i in range(5):
        p = Worker()
        jobs.append(p)
```

```
        p.start()
    for j in jobs:
        j.join()
```

The derived class should override `run()` to do its work.

```
$ python multiprocessing_subclass.py

In Worker-1
In Worker-2
In Worker-3
In Worker-4
In Worker-5
```

10.4.10 Passing Messages to Processes

As with threads, a commonly used pattern for multiple processes is to divide a job up among several workers to run in parallel. Effective use of multiple processes usually requires some communication between them, so that work can be divided and results can be aggregated. A simple way to communicate between processes with multiprocessing is to use a `Queue` to pass messages back and forth. Any object that can be serialized with `pickle` can pass through a `Queue`.

```
import multiprocessing

class MyFancyClass(object):

    def __init__(self, name):
        self.name = name

    def do_something(self):
        proc_name = multiprocessing.current_process().name
        print 'Doing something fancy in %s for %s!' % \
            (proc_name, self.name)

def worker(q):
    obj = q.get()
    obj.do_something()

if __name__ == '__main__':
    queue = multiprocessing.Queue()
```

```
p = multiprocessing.Process(target=worker, args=(queue,))
p.start()

queue.put(MyFancyClass('Fancy Dan'))

# Wait for the worker to finish
queue.close()
queue.join_thread()
p.join()
```

This short example passes only a single message to a single worker, and then the main process waits for the worker to finish.

```
$ python multiprocessing_queue.py

Doing something fancy in Process-1 for Fancy Dan!
```

A more complex example shows how to manage several workers consuming data from a `JoinableQueue` and passing results back to the parent process. The *poison pill* technique is used to stop the workers. After setting up the real tasks, the main program adds one "stop" value per worker to the job queue. When a worker encounters the special value, it breaks out of its processing loop. The main process uses the task queue's `join()` method to wait for all the tasks to finish before processing the results.

```
import multiprocessing
import time

class Consumer(multiprocessing.Process):

    def __init__(self, task_queue, result_queue):
        multiprocessing.Process.__init__(self)
        self.task_queue = task_queue
        self.result_queue = result_queue

    def run(self):
        proc_name = self.name
        while True:
            next_task = self.task_queue.get()
            if next_task is None:
                # Poison pill means shutdown
```

```python
            print '%s: Exiting' % proc_name
            self.task_queue.task_done()
            break
        print '%s: %s' % (proc_name, next_task)
        answer = next_task()
        self.task_queue.task_done()
        self.result_queue.put(answer)
    return


class Task(object):
    def __init__(self, a, b):
        self.a = a
        self.b = b
    def __call__(self):
        time.sleep(0.1) # pretend to take some time to do the work
        return '%s * %s = %s' % (self.a, self.b, self.a * self.b)
    def __str__(self):
        return '%s * %s' % (self.a, self.b)


if __name__ == '__main__':
    # Establish communication queues
    tasks = multiprocessing.JoinableQueue()
    results = multiprocessing.Queue()

    # Start consumers
    num_consumers = multiprocessing.cpu_count() * 2
    print 'Creating %d consumers' % num_consumers
    consumers = [ Consumer(tasks, results)
                  for i in xrange(num_consumers) ]
    for w in consumers:
        w.start()

    # Enqueue jobs
    num_jobs = 10
    for i in xrange(num_jobs):
        tasks.put(Task(i, i))

    # Add a poison pill for each consumer
    for i in xrange(num_consumers):
        tasks.put(None)
```

```
# Wait for all the tasks to finish
tasks.join()

# Start printing results
while num_jobs:
    result = results.get()
    print 'Result:', result
    num_jobs -= 1
```

Although the jobs enter the queue in order, their execution is parallelized so there is no guarantee about the order in which they will be completed.

```
$ python -u multiprocessing_producer_consumer.py

Creating 4 consumers
Consumer-1: 0 * 0
Consumer-2: 1 * 1
Consumer-3: 2 * 2
Consumer-4: 3 * 3
Consumer-4: 4 * 4
Consumer-1: 5 * 5
Consumer-3: 6 * 6
Consumer-2: 7 * 7
Consumer-1: 8 * 8
Consumer-4: 9 * 9
Consumer-3: Exiting
Consumer-2: Exiting
Consumer-1: Exiting
Consumer-4: Exiting
Result: 0 * 0 = 0
Result: 3 * 3 = 9
Result: 2 * 2 = 4
Result: 1 * 1 = 1
Result: 5 * 5 = 25
Result: 4 * 4 = 16
Result: 6 * 6 = 36
Result: 7 * 7 = 49
Result: 9 * 9 = 81
Result: 8 * 8 = 64
```

10.4.11   Signaling between Processes

The `Event` class provides a simple way to communicate state information between processes. An event can be toggled between set and unset states. Users of the event object can wait for it to change from unset to set, using an optional timeout value.

```python
import multiprocessing
import time

def wait_for_event(e):
    """Wait for the event to be set before doing anything"""
    print 'wait_for_event: starting'
    e.wait()
    print 'wait_for_event: e.is_set()->', e.is_set()

def wait_for_event_timeout(e, t):
    """Wait t seconds and then timeout"""
    print 'wait_for_event_timeout: starting'
    e.wait(t)
    print 'wait_for_event_timeout: e.is_set()->', e.is_set()


if __name__ == '__main__':
    e = multiprocessing.Event()
    w1 = multiprocessing.Process(name='block',
                                 target=wait_for_event,
                                 args=(e,))
    w1.start()

    w2 = multiprocessing.Process(name='nonblock',
                                 target=wait_for_event_timeout,
                                 args=(e, 2))
    w2.start()

    print 'main: waiting before calling Event.set()'
    time.sleep(3)
    e.set()
    print 'main: event is set'
```

When `wait()` times out it returns without an error. The caller is responsible for checking the state of the event using `is_set()`.

```
$ python -u multiprocessing_event.py

main: waiting before calling Event.set()
wait_for_event: starting
wait_for_event_timeout: starting
wait_for_event_timeout: e.is_set()-> False
main: event is setwait_for_event: e.is_set()->
 True
```

10.4.12 Controlling Access to Resources

In situations when a single resource needs to be shared between multiple processes, a
Lock can be used to avoid conflicting accesses.

```
import multiprocessing
import sys

def worker_with(lock, stream):
    with lock:
        stream.write('Lock acquired via with\n')

def worker_no_with(lock, stream):
    lock.acquire()
    try:
        stream.write('Lock acquired directly\n')
    finally:
        lock.release()

lock = multiprocessing.Lock()
w = multiprocessing.Process(target=worker_with,
                            args=(lock, sys.stdout))
nw = multiprocessing.Process(target=worker_no_with,
                            args=(lock, sys.stdout))

w.start()
nw.start()

w.join()
nw.join()
```

In this example, the messages printed to the console may be jumbled together if
the two processes do not synchronize their access of the output stream with the lock.

```
$ python multiprocessing_lock.py

Lock acquired via with
Lock acquired directly
```

10.4.13 Synchronizing Operations

Condition objects can be used to synchronize parts of a workflow so that some run in parallel but others run sequentially, even if they are in separate processes.

```python
import multiprocessing
import time


def stage_1(cond):
    """perform first stage of work,
    then notify stage_2 to continue
    """
    name = multiprocessing.current_process().name
    print 'Starting', name
    with cond:
        print '%s done and ready for stage 2' % name
        cond.notify_all()


def stage_2(cond):
    """wait for the condition telling us stage_1 is done"""
    name = multiprocessing.current_process().name
    print 'Starting', name
    with cond:
        cond.wait()
        print '%s running' % name


if __name__ == '__main__':
    condition = multiprocessing.Condition()
    s1 = multiprocessing.Process(name='s1',
                                 target=stage_1,
                                 args=(condition,))
    s2_clients = [
        multiprocessing.Process(name='stage_2[%d]' % i,
                                target=stage_2,
                                args=(condition,))
        for i in range(1, 3)
        ]
```

```
    for c in s2_clients:
        c.start()
        time.sleep(1)
    s1.start()

    s1.join()
    for c in s2_clients:
        c.join()
```

In this example, two processes run the second stage of a job in parallel, but only after the first stage is done.

```
$ python multiprocessing_condition.py

Starting s1
s1 done and ready for stage 2
Starting stage_2[1]
stage_2[1] running
Starting stage_2[2]
stage_2[2] running
```

10.4.14 Controlling Concurrent Access to Resources

It may be useful to allow more than one worker access to a resource at a time, while still limiting the overall number. For example, a connection pool might support a fixed number of simultaneous connections, or a network application might support a fixed number of concurrent downloads. A `Semaphore` is one way to manage those connections.

```
import random
import multiprocessing
import time


class ActivePool(object):
    def __init__(self):
        super(ActivePool, self).__init__()
        self.mgr = multiprocessing.Manager()
        self.active = self.mgr.list()
        self.lock = multiprocessing.Lock()
    def makeActive(self, name):
        with self.lock:
            self.active.append(name)
    def makeInactive(self, name):
```

```
            with self.lock:
                self.active.remove(name)
        def __str__(self):
            with self.lock:
                return str(self.active)


def worker(s, pool):
    name = multiprocessing.current_process().name
    with s:
        pool.makeActive(name)
        print 'Now running: %s' % str(pool)
        time.sleep(random.random())
        pool.makeInactive(name)


if __name__ == '__main__':
    pool = ActivePool()
    s = multiprocessing.Semaphore(3)
    jobs = [
        multiprocessing.Process(target=worker,
                                name=str(i),
                                args=(s, pool),
                                )
        for i in range(10)
        ]

    for j in jobs:
        j.start()

    for j in jobs:
        j.join()
        print 'Now running: %s' % str(pool)
```

In this example, the `ActivePool` class simply serves as a convenient way to track which processes are running at a given moment. A real resource pool would probably allocate a connection or some other value to the newly active process and reclaim the value when the task is done. Here, the pool is just used to hold the names of the active processes to show that only three are running concurrently.

```
$ python multiprocessing_semaphore.py

Now running: ['0', '1', '3']
Now running: ['0', '1', '3']
Now running: ['3', '2', '5']
```

```
Now running: ['0', '1', '3']
Now running: ['1', '3', '2']
Now running: ['2', '6', '7']
Now running: ['3', '2', '6']
Now running: ['6', '4', '8']
Now running: ['4', '8', '9']
Now running: ['6', '7', '4']
Now running: ['1', '3', '2']
Now running: ['3', '2', '5']
Now running: ['6', '7', '4']
Now running: ['6', '7', '4']
Now running: []
Now running: []
Now running: []
Now running: []
Now running: []
Now running: []
```

10.4.15 Managing Shared State

In the previous example, the list of active processes is maintained centrally in the `ActivePool` instance via a special type of list object created by a `Manager`. The `Manager` is responsible for coordinating shared information state between all of its users.

```python
import multiprocessing
import pprint

def worker(d, key, value):
    d[key] = value

if __name__ == '__main__':
    mgr = multiprocessing.Manager()
    d = mgr.dict()
    jobs = [ multiprocessing.Process(target=worker, args=(d, i, i*2))
            for i in range(10)
            ]
    for j in jobs:
        j.start()
    for j in jobs:
```

```
        j.join()
    print 'Results:', d
```

By creating the list through the manager, it is shared and updates are seen in all processes. Dictionaries are also supported.

```
$ python multiprocessing_manager_dict.py

Results: {0: 0, 1: 2, 2: 4, 3: 6, 4: 8, 5: 10, 6: 12, 7: 14,
8: 16, 9: 18}
```

10.4.16   Shared Namespaces

In addition to dictionaries and lists, a `Manager` can create a shared `Namespace`.

```
import multiprocessing

def producer(ns, event):
    ns.value = 'This is the value'
    event.set()

def consumer(ns, event):
    try:
        value = ns.value
    except Exception, err:
        print 'Before event, error:', str(err)
    event.wait()
    print 'After event:', ns.value

if __name__ == '__main__':
    mgr = multiprocessing.Manager()
    namespace = mgr.Namespace()
    event = multiprocessing.Event()
    p = multiprocessing.Process(target=producer,
                                args=(namespace, event))
    c = multiprocessing.Process(target=consumer,
                                args=(namespace, event))

    c.start()
    p.start()
```

```
    c.join()
    p.join()
```

Any named value added to the `Namespace` is visible to all clients that receive the `Namespace` instance.

```
$ python multiprocessing_namespaces.py

Before event, error: 'Namespace' object has no attribute 'value'
After event: This is the value
```

It is important to know that updates to the contents of mutable values in the namespace are not propagated automatically.

```
import multiprocessing

def producer(ns, event):
    # DOES NOT UPDATE GLOBAL VALUE!
    ns.my_list.append('This is the value')
    event.set()

def consumer(ns, event):
    print 'Before event:', ns.my_list
    event.wait()
    print 'After event :', ns.my_list

if __name__ == '__main__':
    mgr = multiprocessing.Manager()
    namespace = mgr.Namespace()
    namespace.my_list = []

    event = multiprocessing.Event()
    p = multiprocessing.Process(target=producer,
                                args=(namespace, event))
    c = multiprocessing.Process(target=consumer,
                                args=(namespace, event))

    c.start()
    p.start()

    c.join()
    p.join()
```

To update the list, attach it to the namespace object again.

```
$ python multiprocessing_namespaces_mutable.py

Before event: []
After event : []
```

10.4.17   Process Pools

The `Pool` class can be used to manage a fixed number of workers for simple cases where the work to be done can be broken up and distributed between workers independently. The return values from the jobs are collected and returned as a list. The pool arguments include the number of processes and a function to run when starting the task process (invoked once per child).

```python
import multiprocessing

def do_calculation(data):
    return data * 2

def start_process():
    print 'Starting', multiprocessing.current_process().name

if __name__ == '__main__':
    inputs = list(range(10))
    print 'Input   :', inputs

    builtin_outputs = map(do_calculation, inputs)
    print 'Built-in:', builtin_outputs

    pool_size = multiprocessing.cpu_count() * 2
    pool = multiprocessing.Pool(processes=pool_size,
                                initializer=start_process,
                                )
    pool_outputs = pool.map(do_calculation, inputs)
    pool.close() # no more tasks
    pool.join()  # wrap up current tasks

    print 'Pool    :', pool_outputs
```

The result of the `map()` method is functionally equivalent to the built-in `map()`, except that individual tasks run in parallel. Since the pool is processing its inputs in parallel, `close()` and `join()` can be used to synchronize the main process with the task processes to ensure proper cleanup.

```
$ python multiprocessing_pool.py

Input    : [0, 1, 2, 3, 4, 5, 6, 7, 8, 9]
Built-in: [0, 2, 4, 6, 8, 10, 12, 14, 16, 18]
Starting PoolWorker-3
Starting PoolWorker-1
Starting PoolWorker-4
Starting PoolWorker-2
Pool     : [0, 2, 4, 6, 8, 10, 12, 14, 16, 18]
```

By default, `Pool` creates a fixed number of worker processes and passes jobs to them until there are no more jobs. Setting the *maxtasksperchild* parameter tells the pool to restart a worker process after it has finished a few tasks, preventing long-running workers from consuming ever-more system resources.

```python
import multiprocessing

def do_calculation(data):
    return data * 2

def start_process():
    print 'Starting', multiprocessing.current_process().name

if __name__ == '__main__':
    inputs = list(range(10))
    print 'Input    :', inputs

    builtin_outputs = map(do_calculation, inputs)
    print 'Built-in:', builtin_outputs

    pool_size = multiprocessing.cpu_count() * 2
    pool = multiprocessing.Pool(processes=pool_size,
                                initializer=start_process,
                                maxtasksperchild=2,
                                )
    pool_outputs = pool.map(do_calculation, inputs)
    pool.close() # no more tasks
    pool.join()  # wrap up current tasks

    print 'Pool     :', pool_outputs
```

The pool restarts the workers when they have completed their allotted tasks, even if there is no more work. In this output, eight workers are created, even though there are only ten tasks and each worker can complete two of them at a time.

```
$ python multiprocessing_pool_maxtasksperchild.py

Input    : [0, 1, 2, 3, 4, 5, 6, 7, 8, 9]
Built-in: [0, 2, 4, 6, 8, 10, 12, 14, 16, 18]
Starting PoolWorker-1
Starting PoolWorker-2
Starting PoolWorker-3
Starting PoolWorker-4
Starting PoolWorker-5
Starting PoolWorker-6
Starting PoolWorker-7
Starting PoolWorker-8
Pool     : [0, 2, 4, 6, 8, 10, 12, 14, 16, 18]
```

10.4.18 Implementing MapReduce

The `Pool` class can be used to create a simple single-server MapReduce implementation. Although it does not give the full benefits of distributed processing, it does illustrate how easy it is to break down some problems into distributable units of work.

In a MapReduce-based system, input data is broken down into chunks for processing by different worker instances. Each chunk of input data is *mapped* to an intermediate state using a simple transformation. The intermediate data is then collected together and partitioned based on a key value so that all related values are together. Finally, the partitioned data is *reduced* to a result set.

```
import collections
import itertools
import multiprocessing

class SimpleMapReduce(object):

    def __init__(self, map_func, reduce_func, num_workers=None):
        """
        map_func
```

> *Function to map inputs to intermediate data. Takes as*
> *argument one input value and returns a tuple with the key*
> *and a value to be reduced.*
>
> *reduce_func*
>
>   *Function to reduce partitioned version of intermediate data*
>   *to final output. Takes as argument a key as produced by*
>   *map_func and a sequence of the values associated with that*
>   *key.*
>
> *num_workers*
>
>   *The number of workers to create in the pool. Defaults to*
>   *the number of CPUs available on the current host.*

```python
        """
        self.map_func = map_func
        self.reduce_func = reduce_func
        self.pool = multiprocessing.Pool(num_workers)

    def partition(self, mapped_values):
        """Organize the mapped values by their key.
        Returns an unsorted sequence of tuples with a key
        and a sequence of values.
        """
        partitioned_data = collections.defaultdict(list)
        for key, value in mapped_values:
            partitioned_data[key].append(value)
        return partitioned_data.items()

    def __call__(self, inputs, chunksize=1):
        """Process the inputs through the map and reduce functions
        given.

        inputs
          An iterable containing the input data to be processed.

        chunksize=1
          The portion of the input data to hand to each worker.  This
          can be used to tune performance during the mapping phase.
        """
        map_responses = self.pool.map(self.map_func,
                                        inputs,
```

```
                                     chunksize=chunksize)
        partitioned_data = self.partition(
            itertools.chain(*map_responses)
            )
        reduced_values = self.pool.map(self.reduce_func,
                                       partitioned_data)
        return reduced_values
```

The following example script uses `SimpleMapReduce` to count the "words" in the reStructuredText source for this article, ignoring some of the markup.

```python
import multiprocessing
import string

from multiprocessing_mapreduce import SimpleMapReduce

def file_to_words(filename):
    """Read a file and return a sequence of
    (word, occurrences) values.
    """
    STOP_WORDS = set([
            'a', 'an', 'and', 'are', 'as', 'be', 'by', 'for', 'if',
            'in', 'is', 'it', 'of', 'or', 'py', 'rst', 'that', 'the',
            'to', 'with',
            ])
    TR = string.maketrans(string.punctuation,
                          ' ' * len(string.punctuation))

    print multiprocessing.current_process().name, 'reading', filename
    output = []

    with open(filename, 'rt') as f:
        for line in f:
            if line.lstrip().startswith('..'): # Skip comment lines
                continue
            line = line.translate(TR) # Strip punctuation
            for word in line.split():
                word = word.lower()
                if word.isalpha() and word not in STOP_WORDS:
                    output.append( (word, 1) )
    return output

def count_words(item):
```

```
"""Convert the partitioned data for a word to a
tuple containing the word and the number of occurrences.
"""
word, occurrences = item
return (word, sum(occurrences))


if __name__ == '__main__':
    import operator
    import glob

    input_files = glob.glob('*.rst')

    mapper = SimpleMapReduce(file_to_words, count_words)
    word_counts = mapper(input_files)
    word_counts.sort(key=operator.itemgetter(1))
    word_counts.reverse()

    print '\nTOP 20 WORDS BY FREQUENCY\n'
    top20 = word_counts[:20]
    longest = max(len(word) for word, count in top20)
    for word, count in top20:
        print '%-*s: %5s' % (longest+1, word, count)
```

The `file_to_words()` function converts each input file to a sequence of tuples containing the word and the number 1 (representing a single occurrence). The data is divided up by `partition()` using the word as the key, so the resulting structure consists of a key and a sequence of 1 values representing each occurrence of the word. The partitioned data is converted to a set of tuples containing a word and the count for that word by `count_words()` during the reduction phase.

```
$ python multiprocessing_wordcount.py

PoolWorker-1 reading basics.rst
PoolWorker-1 reading index.rst
PoolWorker-2 reading communication.rst
PoolWorker-2 reading mapreduce.rst

TOP 20 WORDS BY FREQUENCY

process         :    81
multiprocessing :    43
```

```
worker      :    38
after       :    34
starting    :    33
running     :    32
processes   :    32
python      :    31
start       :    29
class       :    28
literal     :    27
header      :    27
pymotw      :    27
end         :    27
daemon      :    23
now         :    22
func        :    21
can         :    21
consumer    :    20
mod         :    19
```

See Also:

multiprocessing (http://docs.python.org/library/multiprocessing.html) The standard library documentation for this module.

MapReduce (http://en.wikipedia.org/wiki/MapReduce) Overview of MapReduce on Wikipedia.

MapReduce: Simplified Data Processing on Large Clusters (http://labs.google.com/papers/mapreduce.html) Google Labs presentation and paper on MapReduce.

operator (page 153) Operator tools such as `itemgetter()`.

threading (page 505) High-level API for working with threads.

Chapter 11

NETWORKING

Network communication is used to retrieve data needed for an algorithm running locally, share information for distributed processing, and manage cloud services. Python's standard library comes complete with modules for creating network services, as well as for accessing existing services remotely.

The low-level `socket` library provides direct access to the native C socket library and can be used to communicate with any network service. `select` watches multiple sockets simultaneously and is useful for allowing network servers to communicate with multiple clients simultaneously.

The frameworks in `SocketServer` abstract out a lot of the repetitive work necessary to create a new network server. The classes can be combined to create servers that fork or use threads and support TCP or UDP. Only the actual message handling needs to be provided by the application.

`asyncore` implements an asynchronous networking stack with a callback-based API. It encapsulates the polling loop and buffering, and invokes appropriate handlers when data is received. The framework in `asynchat` simplifies the work needed to create bidirectional message-based protocols on top of `asyncore`.

11.1 socket—Network Communication

Purpose Provides access to network communication.
Python Version 1.4 and later

The `socket` module exposes the low-level C API for communicating over a network using the BSD socket interface. It includes the `socket` class, for handling the actual data channel, and also includes functions for network-related tasks, such as converting a server's name to an address and formatting data to be sent across the network.

11.1.1   Addressing, Protocol Families, and Socket Types

A *socket* is one endpoint of a communication channel used by programs to pass data back and forth locally or across the Internet. Sockets have two primary properties controlling the way they send data: the *address family* controls the OSI network layer protocol used, and the *socket type* controls the transport layer protocol.

Python supports three address families. The most common, AF_INET, is used for IPv4 Internet addressing. IPv4 addresses are four bytes long and are usually represented as a sequence of four numbers, one per byte, separated by dots (e.g., 10.1.1.5 and 127.0.0.1). These values are more commonly referred to as "IP addresses." Almost all Internet networking currently is done using IP version 4.

AF_INET6 is used for IPv6 Internet addressing. IPv6 is the "next generation" version of the Internet protocol. It supports 128-bit addresses, traffic shaping, and routing features not available under IPv4. Adoption of IPv6 is still limited, but continues to grow.

AF_UNIX is the address family for UNIX Domain Sockets (UDS), an inter-process communication protocol available on POSIX-compliant systems. The implementation of UDS typically allows the operating system to pass data directly from process to process, without going through the network stack. This is more efficient than using AF_INET, but because the file system is used as the namespace for addressing, UDS is restricted to processes on the same system. The appeal of using UDS over other IPC mechanisms, such as named pipes or shared memory, is that the programming interface is the same as for IP networking. This means the application can take advantage of efficient communication when running on a single host, but use the same code when sending data across the network.

Note: The AF_UNIX constant is only defined on systems where UDS is supported.

The socket type is usually either SOCK_DGRAM for *user datagram protocol* (UDP) or SOCK_STREAM for *transmission control protocol* (TCP). UDP does not require transmission handshaking or other setup, but offers lower reliability of delivery. UDP messages may be delivered out of order, more than once, or not at all. TCP, by contrast, ensures that each message is delivered exactly once and in the correct order. That extra reliability may impose additional latency, however, since packets may need to be retransmitted. Most application protocols that deliver a large amount of data, such as HTTP, are built on top of TCP. UDP is commonly used for protocols where order is less important (since the message fits in a single packet, e.g., DNS), or for *multicasting* (sending the same data to several hosts).

> **Note:** Python's `socket` module supports other socket types, but they are less commonly used and so are not covered here. Refer to the standard library documentation for more details.

Looking Up Hosts on the Network

`socket` includes functions to interface with the domain name services on the network so a program can convert the host name of a server into its numerical network address. Applications do not need to convert addresses explicitly before using them to connect to a server, but it can be useful when reporting errors to include the numerical address as well as the name value being used.

To find the official name of the current host, use `gethostname()`.

```
import socket

print socket.gethostname()
```

The name returned will depend on the network settings for the current system, and it may change if it is on a different network (such as a laptop attached to a wireless LAN).

```
$ python socket_gethostname.py

farnsworth.hellfly.net
```

Use `gethostbyname()` to consult the operating system hostname resolution API and convert the name of a server to its numerical address.

```
import socket

for host in [ 'homer', 'www', 'www.python.org', 'nosuchname' ]:
    try:
        print '%s : %s' % (host, socket.gethostbyname(host))
    except socket.error, msg:
        print '%s : %s' % (host, msg)
```

If the DNS configuration of the current system includes one or more domains in the search, the name argument does not need to be a fully qualified name (i.e., it does not need to include the domain name as well as the base hostname). If the name cannot be found, an exception of type `socket.error` is raised.

```
$ python socket_gethostbyname.py

homer : 192.168.1.8
www : 192.168.1.8
www.python.org : 82.94.164.162
nosuchname : [Errno 8] nodename nor servname provided, or not known
```

For access to more naming information about a server, use the function `gethostbyname_ex()`. It returns the canonical hostname of the server, any aliases, and all the available IP addresses that can be used to reach it.

```python
import socket

for host in [ 'homer', 'www', 'www.python.org', 'nosuchname' ]:
    print host
    try:
        hostname, aliases, addresses = socket.gethostbyname_ex(host)
        print '   Hostname:', hostname
        print '   Aliases :', aliases
        print '  Addresses:', addresses
    except socket.error as msg:
        print 'ERROR:', msg
    print
```

Having all known IP addresses for a server lets a client implement its own load-balancing or fail-over algorithms.

```
$ python socket_gethostbyname_ex.py

homer
  Hostname: homer.hellfly.net
  Aliases : []
 Addresses: ['192.168.1.8']

www
  Hostname: homer.hellfly.net
  Aliases : ['www.hellfly.net']
 Addresses: ['192.168.1.8']

www.python.org
  Hostname: www.python.org
```

```
   Aliases : []
   Addresses: ['82.94.164.162']

nosuchname
ERROR: [Errno 8] nodename nor servname provided, or not known
```

Use getfqdn() to convert a partial name to a fully qualified domain name.

import socket

for host **in** ['homer', 'www']:
    print '*%6s* : *%s*' % (host, socket.getfqdn(host))

The name returned will not necessarily match the input argument in any way if the input is an alias, such as www is here.

```
$ python socket_getfqdn.py

 homer : homer.hellfly.net
   www : homer.hellfly.net
```

When the address of a server is available, use gethostbyaddr() to do a "reverse" lookup for the name.

import socket

hostname, aliases, addresses = socket.gethostbyaddr('*192.168.1.8*')

print '*Hostname :*', hostname
print '*Aliases   :*', aliases
print '*Addresses:*', addresses

The return value is a tuple containing the full hostname, any aliases, and all IP addresses associated with the name.

```
$ python socket_gethostbyaddr.py

Hostname : homer.hellfly.net
Aliases   : ['8.1.168.192.in-addr.arpa']
Addresses: ['192.168.1.8']
```

Finding Service Information

In addition to an IP address, each socket address includes an integer *port number*. Many applications can run on the same host, listening on a single IP address, but only one socket at a time can use a port at that address. The combination of IP address, protocol, and port number uniquely identify a communication channel and ensure that messages sent through a socket arrive at the correct destination.

Some of the port numbers are preallocated for a specific protocol. For example, email servers using SMTP communicate with each other over port number 25 using TCP, and Web clients and servers use port 80 for HTTP. The port numbers for network services with standardized names can be looked up using `getservbyname()`.

```python
import socket
from urlparse import urlparse

for url in [ 'http://www.python.org',
             'https://www.mybank.com',
             'ftp://prep.ai.mit.edu',
             'gopher://gopher.micro.umn.edu',
             'smtp://mail.example.com',
             'imap://mail.example.com',
             'imaps://mail.example.com',
             'pop3://pop.example.com',
             'pop3s://pop.example.com',
             ]:
    parsed_url = urlparse(url)
    port = socket.getservbyname(parsed_url.scheme)
    print '%6s : %s' % (parsed_url.scheme, port)
```

Although a standardized service is unlikely to change ports, looking up the value with a system call instead of hard coding it is more flexible when new services are added in the future.

```
$ python socket_getservbyname.py

   http : 80
  https : 443
    ftp : 21
 gopher : 70
   smtp : 25
   imap : 143
  imaps : 993
```

```
pop3 : 110
pop3s : 995
```

To reverse the service port lookup, use `getservbyport()`.

```python
import socket
import urlparse

for port in [ 80, 443, 21, 70, 25, 143, 993, 110, 995 ]:
    print urlparse.urlunparse(
        (socket.getservbyport(port), 'example.com', '/', '', '', '')
        )
```

The reverse lookup is useful for constructing URLs to services from arbitrary addresses.

```
$ python socket_getservbyport.py

http://example.com/
https://example.com/
ftp://example.com/
gopher://example.com/
smtp://example.com/
imap://example.com/
imaps://example.com/
pop3://example.com/
pop3s://example.com/
```

The number assigned to a transport protocol can be retrieved with `getprotobyname()`.

```python
import socket

def get_constants(prefix):
    """Create a dictionary mapping socket module
    constants to their names.
    """
    return dict( (getattr(socket, n), n)
                 for n in dir(socket)
                 if n.startswith(prefix)
                 )

protocols = get_constants('IPPROTO_')
```

```
for name in [ 'icmp', 'udp', 'tcp' ]:
    proto_num = socket.getprotobyname(name)
    const_name = protocols[proto_num]
    print '%4s -> %2d (socket.%-12s = %2d)' % \
        (name, proto_num, const_name, getattr(socket, const_name))
```

The values for protocol numbers are standardized and defined as constants in socket with the prefix IPPROTO_.

```
$ python socket_getprotobyname.py

icmp ->  1 (socket.IPPROTO_ICMP =  1)
 udp -> 17 (socket.IPPROTO_UDP  = 17)
 tcp ->  6 (socket.IPPROTO_TCP  =  6)
```

Looking Up Server Addresses

getaddrinfo() converts the basic address of a service into a list of tuples with all the information necessary to make a connection. The contents of each tuple will vary, containing different network families or protocols.

```
import socket

def get_constants(prefix):
    """Create a dictionary mapping socket module
    constants to their names.
    """
    return dict( (getattr(socket, n), n)
                 for n in dir(socket)
                 if n.startswith(prefix)
                 )

families = get_constants('AF_')
types = get_constants('SOCK_')
protocols = get_constants('IPPROTO_')

for response in socket.getaddrinfo('www.python.org', 'http'):

    # Unpack the response tuple
    family, socktype, proto, canonname, sockaddr = response

    print 'Family        :', families[family]
    print 'Type          :', types[socktype]
    print 'Protocol      :', protocols[proto]
```

```
print 'Canonical name:', canonname
print 'Socket address:', sockaddr
print
```

This program demonstrates how to look up the connection information for `www.python.org`.

```
$ python socket_getaddrinfo.py

Family         : AF_INET
Type           : SOCK_DGRAM
Protocol       : IPPROTO_UDP
Canonical name:
Socket address: ('82.94.164.162', 80)

Family         : AF_INET
Type           : SOCK_STREAM
Protocol       : IPPROTO_TCP
Canonical name:
Socket address: ('82.94.164.162', 80)
```

`getaddrinfo()` takes several arguments for filtering the result list. The *host* and *port* values given in the example are required arguments. The optional arguments are *family*, *socktype*, *proto*, and *flags*. The optional values should be either 0 or one of the constants defined by `socket`.

```
import socket

def get_constants(prefix):
    """Create a dictionary mapping socket module
    constants to their names.
    """
    return dict( (getattr(socket, n), n)
                  for n in dir(socket)
                  if n.startswith(prefix)
                )

families = get_constants('AF_')
types = get_constants('SOCK_')
protocols = get_constants('IPPROTO_')

for response in socket.getaddrinfo('www.doughellmann.com', 'http',
                                    socket.AF_INET,      # family
```

```
                             socket.SOCK_STREAM,   # socktype
                             socket.IPPROTO_TCP,   # protocol
                             socket.AI_CANONNAME,  # flags
                             ):

    # Unpack the response tuple
    family, socktype, proto, canonname, sockaddr = response

    print 'Family        :', families[family]
    print 'Type          :', types[socktype]
    print 'Protocol      :', protocols[proto]
    print 'Canonical name:', canonname
    print 'Socket address:', sockaddr
    print
```

Since *flags* includes AI_CANONNAME, the canonical name of the server, which may be different from the value used for the lookup if the host has any aliases, is included in the results this time. Without the flag, the canonical name value is left empty.

```
$ python socket_getaddrinfo_extra_args.py

Family         : AF_INET
Type           : SOCK_STREAM
Protocol       : IPPROTO_TCP
Canonical name: homer.doughellmann.com
Socket address: ('192.168.1.8', 80)
```

IP Address Representations

Network programs written in C use the data type struct sockaddr to represent IP addresses as binary values (instead of the string addresses usually found in Python programs). To convert IPv4 addresses between the Python representation and the C representation, use inet_aton() and inet_ntoa().

```
import binascii
import socket
import struct
import sys

for string_address in [ '192.168.1.1', '127.0.0.1' ]:
    packed = socket.inet_aton(string_address)
    print 'Original:', string_address
```

```
print 'Packed   :', binascii.hexlify(packed)
print 'Unpacked:', socket.inet_ntoa(packed)
print
```

The four bytes in the packed format can be passed to C libraries, transmitted safely over the network, or saved to a database compactly.

```
$ python socket_address_packing.py

Original: 192.168.1.1
Packed   : c0a80101
Unpacked: 192.168.1.1

Original: 127.0.0.1
Packed   : 7f000001
Unpacked: 127.0.0.1
```

The related functions `inet_pton()` and `inet_ntop()` work with both IPv4 and IPv6 addresses, producing the appropriate format based on the address family parameter passed in.

```
import binascii
import socket
import struct
import sys

string_address = '2002:ac10:10a:1234:21e:52ff:fe74:40e'
packed = socket.inet_pton(socket.AF_INET6, string_address)

print 'Original:', string_address
print 'Packed   :', binascii.hexlify(packed)
print 'Unpacked:', socket.inet_ntop(socket.AF_INET6, packed)
```

An IPv6 address is already a hexadecimal value, so converting the packed version to a series of hex digits produces a string similar to the original value.

```
$ python socket_ipv6_address_packing.py

Original: 2002:ac10:10a:1234:21e:52ff:fe74:40e
Packed   : 2002ac10010a1234021e52fffe74040e
Unpacked: 2002:ac10:10a:1234:21e:52ff:fe74:40e
```

See Also:

IPv6 (http://en.wikipedia.org/wiki/IPv6) Wikipedia article discussing Internet Protocol Version 6 (IPv6).

OSI Networking Model (http://en.wikipedia.org/wiki/OSI_model) Wikipedia article describing the seven layer model of networking implementation.

Assigned Internet Protocol Numbers
(www.iana.org/assignments/protocol-numbers/protocol-numbers.xml) List of standard protocol names and numbers.

11.1.2 TCP/IP Client and Server

Sockets can be configured to act as a *server* and listen for incoming messages, or connect to other applications as a *client*. After both ends of a TCP/IP socket are connected, communication is bidirectional.

Echo Server

This sample program, based on the one in the standard library documentation, receives incoming messages and echos them back to the sender. It starts by creating a TCP/IP socket.

```
import socket
import sys

# Create a TCP/IP socket
sock = socket.socket(socket.AF_INET, socket.SOCK_STREAM)
```

Then `bind()` is used to associate the socket with the server address. In this case, the address is `localhost`, referring to the current server, and the port number is 10000.

```
# Bind the socket to the port
server_address = ('localhost', 10000)
print >>sys.stderr, 'starting up on %s port %s' % server_address
sock.bind(server_address)
```

Calling `listen()` puts the socket into server mode, and `accept()` waits for an incoming connection. The integer argument is the number of connections the system should queue up in the background before rejecting new clients. This example only expects to work with one connection at a time.

```
# Listen for incoming connections
sock.listen(1)

while True:
    # Wait for a connection
    print >>sys.stderr, 'waiting for a connection'
    connection, client_address = sock.accept()
```

accept() returns an open connection between the server and client, along with the client address. The connection is actually a different socket on another port (assigned by the kernel). Data is read from the connection with recv() and transmitted with sendall().

```
    try:
        print >>sys.stderr, 'connection from', client_address

        # Receive the data in small chunks and retransmit it
        while True:
            data = connection.recv(16)
            print >>sys.stderr, 'received "%s"' % data
            if data:
                print >>sys.stderr, 'sending data back to the client'
                connection.sendall(data)
            else:
                print >>sys.stderr, 'no data from', client_address
                break

    finally:
        # Clean up the connection
        connection.close()
```

When communication with a client is finished, the connection needs to be cleaned up using close(). This example uses a try:finally block to ensure that close() is always called, even in the event of an error.

Echo Client

The client program sets up its socket differently from the way a server does. Instead of binding to a port and listening, it uses connect() to attach the socket directly to the remote address.

```
import socket
import sys

# Create a TCP/IP socket
sock = socket.socket(socket.AF_INET, socket.SOCK_STREAM)

# Connect the socket to the port where the server is listening
server_address = ('localhost', 10000)
print >>sys.stderr, 'connecting to %s port %s' % server_address
sock.connect(server_address)
```

After the connection is established, data can be sent through the `socket` with `sendall()` and received with `recv()`, just as in the server.

```
try:

    # Send data
    message = 'This is the message.  It will be repeated.'
    print >>sys.stderr, 'sending "%s"' % message
    sock.sendall(message)

    # Look for the response
    amount_received = 0
    amount_expected = len(message)

    while amount_received < amount_expected:
        data = sock.recv(16)
        amount_received += len(data)
        print >>sys.stderr, 'received "%s"' % data

finally:
    print >>sys.stderr, 'closing socket'
    sock.close()
```

When the entire message is sent and a copy received, the socket is closed to free up the port.

Client and Server Together

The client and server should be run in separate terminal windows, so they can communicate with each other. The server output shows the incoming connection and data, as well as the response sent back to the client.

```
$ python ./socket_echo_server.py

starting up on localhost port 10000
waiting for a connection
connection from ('127.0.0.1', 52186)
received "This is the mess"
sending data back to the client
received "age.  It will be"
sending data back to the client
received " repeated."
sending data back to the client
received ""
no data from ('127.0.0.1', 52186)
waiting for a connection
```

The client output shows the outgoing message and the response from the server.

```
$ python socket_echo_client.py

connecting to localhost port 10000
sending "This is the message.  It will be repeated."
received "This is the mess"
received "age.  It will be"
received " repeated."
closing socket

$
```

Easy Client Connections

TCP/IP clients can save a few steps by using the convenience function `create_connection()` to connect to a server. The function takes one argument, a two-value tuple containing the server address, and derives the best address to use for the connection.

```
import socket
import sys


def get_constants(prefix):
    """Create a dictionary mapping socket module
    constants to their names.
    """
```

```python
    return dict( (getattr(socket, n), n)
                for n in dir(socket)
                if n.startswith(prefix)
                )

families = get_constants('AF_')
types = get_constants('SOCK_')
protocols = get_constants('IPPROTO_')

# Create a TCP/IP socket
sock = socket.create_connection(('localhost', 10000))

print >>sys.stderr, 'Family  :', families[sock.family]
print >>sys.stderr, 'Type    :', types[sock.type]
print >>sys.stderr, 'Protocol:', protocols[sock.proto]
print >>sys.stderr

try:

    # Send data
    message = 'This is the message.  It will be repeated.'
    print >>sys.stderr, 'sending "%s"' % message
    sock.sendall(message)

    amount_received = 0
    amount_expected = len(message)

    while amount_received < amount_expected:
        data = sock.recv(16)
        amount_received += len(data)
        print >>sys.stderr, 'received "%s"' % data

finally:
    print >>sys.stderr, 'closing socket'
    sock.close()
```

create_connection() uses getaddrinfo() to find candidate connection parameters and returns a socket opened with the first configuration that creates a successful connection. The family, type, and proto attributes can be examined to determine the type of socket being returned.

```
$ python socket_echo_client_easy.py
```

```
Family  : AF_INET
Type    : SOCK_STREAM
Protocol: IPPROTO_TCP

sending "This is the message.  It will be repeated."
received "This is the mess"
received "age.  It will be"
received " repeated."
closing socket
```

Choosing an Address for Listening

It is important to bind a server to the correct address so that clients can communicate with it. The previous examples all used `'localhost'` as the IP address, which limits connections to clients running on the same server. Use a public address of the server, such as the value returned by `gethostname()`, to allow other hosts to connect. This example modifies the echo server to listen on an address specified via a command line argument.

```python
import socket
import sys

# Create a TCP/IP socket
sock = socket.socket(socket.AF_INET, socket.SOCK_STREAM)

# Bind the socket to the address given on the command line
server_name = sys.argv[1]
server_address = (server_name, 10000)
print >>sys.stderr, 'starting up on %s port %s' % server_address
sock.bind(server_address)
sock.listen(1)

while True:
    print >>sys.stderr, 'waiting for a connection'
    connection, client_address = sock.accept()
    try:
        print >>sys.stderr, 'client connected:', client_address
        while True:
            data = connection.recv(16)
            print >>sys.stderr, 'received "%s"' % data
            if data:
                connection.sendall(data)
```

```
        else:
            break
    finally:
        connection.close()
```

A similar modification to the client program is needed before the server can be tested.

```python
import socket
import sys

# Create a TCP/IP socket
sock = socket.socket(socket.AF_INET, socket.SOCK_STREAM)

# Connect the socket to the port on the server given by the caller
server_address = (sys.argv[1], 10000)
print >>sys.stderr, 'connecting to %s port %s' % server_address
sock.connect(server_address)

try:

    message = 'This is the message.  It will be repeated.'
    print >>sys.stderr, 'sending "%s"' % message
    sock.sendall(message)

    amount_received = 0
    amount_expected = len(message)
    while amount_received < amount_expected:
        data = sock.recv(16)
        amount_received += len(data)
        print >>sys.stderr, 'received "%s"' % data

finally:
    sock.close()
```

After starting the server with the argument `farnsworth.hellfly.net`, the **netstat** command shows it listening on the address for the named host.

```
$ host farnsworth.hellfly.net

farnsworth.hellfly.net has address 192.168.1.17
```

```
$ netstat -an

Active Internet connections (including servers)
Proto Recv-Q Send-Q  Local Address        Foreign Address   (state)
...
tcp4       0      0  192.168.1.17.10000   *.*               LISTEN
...
```

Running the client on another host, passing `farnsworth.hellfly.net` as the host where the server is running, produces the following.

```
$ hostname

homer

$ python socket_echo_client_explicit.py farnsworth.hellfly.net

connecting to farnsworth.hellfly.net port 10000
sending "This is the message.  It will be repeated."
received "This is the mess"
received "age.  It will be"
received " repeated."
```

And the server produces the following output.

```
$ python ./socket_echo_server_explicit.py farnsworth.hellfly.net

starting up on farnsworth.hellfly.net port 10000
waiting for a connection
client connected: ('192.168.1.8', 57471)
received "This is the mess"
received "age.  It will be"
received " repeated."
received ""
waiting for a connection
```

Many servers have more than one network interface, and therefore, more than one IP address. Rather than running separate copies of a service bound to each IP address, use the special address `INADDR_ANY` to listen on all addresses at the same time. Although `socket` defines a constant for `INADDR_ANY`, it is an integer value and must be converted to a dotted-notation string address before it can be passed to `bind()`. As a shortcut, use "`0.0.0.0`" or an empty string (`''`) instead of doing the conversion.

```python
import socket
import sys

# Create a TCP/IP socket
sock = socket.socket(socket.AF_INET, socket.SOCK_STREAM)

# Bind the socket to the address given on the command line
server_address = ('', 10000)
sock.bind(server_address)
print >>sys.stderr, 'starting up on %s port %s' % sock.getsockname()
sock.listen(1)

while True:
    print >>sys.stderr, 'waiting for a connection'
    connection, client_address = sock.accept()
    try:
        print >>sys.stderr, 'client connected:', client_address
        while True:
            data = connection.recv(16)
            print >>sys.stderr, 'received "%s"' % data
            if data:
                connection.sendall(data)
            else:
                break
    finally:
        connection.close()
```

To see the actual address being used by a socket, call its `getsockname()` method. After starting the service, running **netstat** again shows it listening for incoming connections on any address.

```
$ netstat -an

Active Internet connections (including servers)
Proto Recv-Q Send-Q  Local Address    Foreign Address   (state)
...
tcp4       0      0  *.10000          *.*               LISTEN
...
```

11.1.3 User Datagram Client and Server

The user datagram protocol (UDP) works differently from TCP/IP. Where TCP is a *stream-oriented* protocol, ensuring that all the data is transmitted in the right order, UDP is a *message-oriented* protocol. UDP does not require a long-lived connection, so setting up a UDP socket is a little simpler. On the other hand, UDP messages must fit within a single packet (for IPv4, that means they can only hold 65,507 bytes because the 65,535-byte packet also includes header information) and delivery is not guaranteed as it is with TCP.

Echo Server

Since there is no connection, per se, the server does not need to listen for and accept connections. It only needs to use `bind()` to associate its socket with a port and then wait for individual messages.

```python
import socket
import sys

# Create a UDP socket
sock = socket.socket(socket.AF_INET, socket.SOCK_DGRAM)

# Bind the socket to the port
server_address = ('localhost', 10000)
print >>sys.stderr, 'starting up on %s port %s' % server_address
sock.bind(server_address)
```

Messages are read from the socket using `recvfrom()`, which returns the data as well as the address of the client from which it was sent.

```python
while True:
    print >>sys.stderr, '\nwaiting to receive message'
    data, address = sock.recvfrom(4096)

    print >>sys.stderr, 'received %s bytes from %s' % \
        (len(data), address)
    print >>sys.stderr, data

    if data:
        sent = sock.sendto(data, address)
        print >>sys.stderr, 'sent %s bytes back to %s' % \
            (sent, address)
```

Echo Client

The UDP echo client is similar the server, but does not use `bind()` to attach its socket to an address. It uses `sendto()` to deliver its message directly to the server and `recvfrom()` to receive the response.

```
import socket
import sys

# Create a UDP socket
sock = socket.socket(socket.AF_INET, socket.SOCK_DGRAM)

server_address = ('localhost', 10000)
message = 'This is the message.  It will be repeated.'

try:

    # Send data
    print >>sys.stderr, 'sending "%s"' % message
    sent = sock.sendto(message, server_address)

    # Receive response
    print >>sys.stderr, 'waiting to receive'
    data, server = sock.recvfrom(4096)
    print >>sys.stderr, 'received "%s"' % data

finally:
    print >>sys.stderr, 'closing socket'
    sock.close()
```

Client and Server Together

Running the server produces the following.

```
$ python ./socket_echo_server_dgram.py

starting up on localhost port 10000

waiting to receive message
received 42 bytes from ('127.0.0.1', 50139)
This is the message.  It will be repeated.
sent 42 bytes back to ('127.0.0.1', 50139)

waiting to receive message
```

This is the client output

```
$ python ./socket_echo_client_dgram.py
```

```
sending "This is the message.  It will be repeated."
waiting to receive
received "This is the message.  It will be repeated."
closing socket
```

11.1.4   UNIX Domain Sockets

From the programmer's perspective, there are two essential differences between using a UNIX domain socket and an TCP/IP socket. First, the address of the socket is a path on the file system, rather than a tuple containing the server name and port. Second, the node created in the file system to represent the socket persists after the socket is closed and needs to be removed each time the server starts up. The echo server example from earlier can be updated to use UDS by making a few changes in the setup section.

```
import socket
import sys
import os

server_address = './uds_socket'

# Make sure the socket does not already exist
try:
    os.unlink(server_address)
except OSError:
    if os.path.exists(server_address):
        raise
```

The `socket` needs to be created with address family `AF_UNIX`.

```
# Create a UDS socket
sock = socket.socket(socket.AF_UNIX, socket.SOCK_STREAM)
```

Binding the socket and managing the incoming connections works the same as with TCP/IP sockets.

```
# Bind the socket to the address
print >>sys.stderr, 'starting up on %s' % server_address
sock.bind(server_address)
```

```
# Listen for incoming connections
sock.listen(1)

while True:
    # Wait for a connection
    print >>sys.stderr, 'waiting for a connection'
    connection, client_address = sock.accept()
    try:
        print >>sys.stderr, 'connection from', client_address

        # Receive the data in small chunks and retransmit it
        while True:
            data = connection.recv(16)
            print >>sys.stderr, 'received "%s"' % data
            if data:
                print >>sys.stderr, 'sending data back to the client'
                connection.sendall(data)
            else:
                print >>sys.stderr, 'no data from', client_address
                break

    finally:
        # Clean up the connection
        connection.close()
```

The client setup also needs to be modified to work with UDS. It should assume the file system node for the socket exists, since the server creates it by binding to the address.

```
import socket
import sys

# Create a UDS socket
sock = socket.socket(socket.AF_UNIX, socket.SOCK_STREAM)

# Connect the socket to the port where the server is listening
server_address = './uds_socket'
print >>sys.stderr, 'connecting to %s' % server_address
try:
    sock.connect(server_address)
except socket.error, msg:
```

```
print >>sys.stderr, msg
sys.exit(1)
```

Sending and receiving data works the same way in the UDS client as the TCP/IP client from before.

```
try:

    # Send data
    message = 'This is the message.  It will be repeated.'
    print >>sys.stderr, 'sending "%s"' % message
    sock.sendall(message)

    amount_received = 0
    amount_expected = len(message)

    while amount_received < amount_expected:
        data = sock.recv(16)
        amount_received += len(data)
        print >>sys.stderr, 'received "%s"' % data

finally:
    print >>sys.stderr, 'closing socket'
    sock.close()
```

The program output is mostly the same, with appropriate updates for the address information. The server shows the messages received and sent back to the client.

```
$ python ./socket_echo_server_uds.py

starting up on ./uds_socket
waiting for a connection
connection from
received "This is the mess"
sending data back to the client
received "age.  It will be"
sending data back to the client
received " repeated."
sending data back to the client
received ""
```

```
no data from
waiting for a connection
```

The client sends the message all at once and receives parts of it back incrementally.

```
$ python socket_echo_client_uds.py

connecting to ./uds_socket
sending "This is the message.  It will be repeated."
received "This is the mess"
received "age.  It will be"
received " repeated."
closing socket
```

Permissions

Since the UDS socket is represented by a node on the file system, standard file system permissions can be used to control access to the server.

```
$ ls -l ./uds_socket

srwxr-xr-x  1 dhellmann  dhellmann  0 Sep 20 08:24 ./uds_socket

$ sudo chown root ./uds_socket

$ ls -l ./uds_socket

srwxr-xr-x  1 root  dhellmann  0 Sep 20 08:24 ./uds_socket
```

Running the client as a user other than `root` now results in an error because the process does not have permission to open the socket.

```
$ python socket_echo_client_uds.py

connecting to ./uds_socket
[Errno 13] Permission denied
```

Communication between Parent and Child Processes

The `socketpair()` function is useful for setting up UDS sockets for inter-process communication under UNIX. It creates a pair of connected sockets that can be used to communicate between a parent process and a child process after the child is forked.

```
import socket
import os

parent, child = socket.socketpair()

pid = os.fork()

if pid:
    print 'in parent, sending message'
    child.close()
    parent.sendall('ping')
    response = parent.recv(1024)
    print 'response from child:', response
    parent.close()

else:
    print 'in child, waiting for message'
    parent.close()
    message = child.recv(1024)
    print 'message from parent:', message
    child.sendall('pong')
    child.close()
```

By default, a UDS socket is created, but the caller can also pass address family, socket type, and even protocol options to control how the sockets are created.

```
$ python socket_socketpair.py

in child, waiting for message
message from parent: ping
in parent, sending message
response from child: pong
```

11.1.5 Multicast

Point-to-point connections handle a lot of communication needs, but passing the same information between many peers becomes challenging as the number of direct connections grows. Sending messages separately to each recipient consumes additional processing time and bandwidth, which can be a problem for applications such as streaming video or audio. Using *multicast* to deliver messages to more than one endpoint at a time achieves better efficiency because the network infrastructure ensures that the packets are delivered to all recipients.

Multicast messages are always sent using UDP, since TCP requires an end-to-end communication channel. The addresses for multicast, called *multicast groups*, are a subset of the regular IPv4 address range (224.0.0.0 through 230.255.255.255) reserved for multicast traffic. These addresses are treated specially by network routers and switches, so messages sent to the group can be distributed over the Internet to all recipients that have joined the group.

> **Note:** Some managed switches and routers have multicast traffic disabled by default. If you have trouble with the example programs, check your network hardware settings.

Sending Multicast Messages

This modified echo client will send a message to a multicast group and then report all the responses it receives. Since it has no way of knowing how many responses to expect, it uses a timeout value on the socket to avoid blocking indefinitely while waiting for an answer.

```
import socket
import struct
import sys

message = 'very important data'
multicast_group = ('224.3.29.71', 10000)

# Create the datagram socket
sock = socket.socket(socket.AF_INET, socket.SOCK_DGRAM)

# Set a timeout so the socket does not block indefinitely when trying
# to receive data.
sock.settimeout(0.2)
```

The socket also needs to be configured with a *time-to-live* value (TTL) for the messages. The TTL controls how many networks will receive the packet. Set the TTL with the IP_MULTICAST_TTL option and setsockopt(). The default, 1, means that the packets are not forwarded by the router beyond the current network segment. The value can range up to 255 and should be packed into a single byte.

```
# Set the time-to-live for messages to 1 so they do not go past the
# local network segment.
```

```
ttl = struct.pack('b', 1)
sock.setsockopt(socket.IPPROTO_IP, socket.IP_MULTICAST_TTL, ttl)
```

The rest of the sender looks like the UDP echo client, except that it expects multiple responses so uses a loop to call `recvfrom()` until it times out.

```
try:

    # Send data to the multicast group
    print >>sys.stderr, 'sending "%s"' % message
    sent = sock.sendto(message, multicast_group)

    # Look for responses from all recipients
    while True:
        print >>sys.stderr, 'waiting to receive'
        try:
            data, server = sock.recvfrom(16)
        except socket.timeout:
            print >>sys.stderr, 'timed out, no more responses'
            break
        else:
            print >>sys.stderr, 'received "%s" from %s' % \
                (data, server)

finally:
    print >>sys.stderr, 'closing socket'
    sock.close()
```

Receiving Multicast Messages

The first step to establishing a multicast receiver is to create the UDP socket.

```
import socket
import struct
import sys

multicast_group = '224.3.29.71'
server_address = ('', 10000)

# Create the socket
sock = socket.socket(socket.AF_INET, socket.SOCK_DGRAM)

# Bind to the server address
sock.bind(server_address)
```

After the regular socket is created and bound to a port, it can be added to the multicast group by using `setsockopt()` to change the `IP_ADD_MEMBERSHIP` option. The option value is the 8-byte packed representation of the multicast group address followed by the network interface on which the server should listen for the traffic, identified by its IP address. In this case, the receiver listens on all interfaces using `INADDR_ANY`.

```python
# Tell the operating system to add the socket to the multicast group
# on all interfaces.
group = socket.inet_aton(multicast_group)
mreq = struct.pack('4sL', group, socket.INADDR_ANY)
sock.setsockopt(socket.IPPROTO_IP, socket.IP_ADD_MEMBERSHIP, mreq)
```

The main loop for the receiver is just like the regular UDP echo server.

```python
# Receive/respond loop
while True:
    print >>sys.stderr, '\nwaiting to receive message'
    data, address = sock.recvfrom(1024)

    print >>sys.stderr, 'received %s bytes from %s' % \
        (len(data), address)
    print >>sys.stderr, data

    print >>sys.stderr, 'sending acknowledgement to', address
    sock.sendto('ack', address)
```

Example Output

This example shows the multicast receiver running on two different hosts. A has address `192.168.1.17` and B has address `192.168.1.8`.

```
[A]$ python ./socket_multicast_receiver.py

waiting to receive message
received 19 bytes from ('192.168.1.17', 51382)
very important data
sending acknowledgement to ('192.168.1.17', 51382)


[B]$ python ./socket_multicast_receiver.py

waiting to receive message
received 19 bytes from ('192.168.1.17', 51382)
```

```
very important data
sending acknowledgement to ('192.168.1.17', 51382)
```

The sender is running on host A.

```
$ python ./socket_multicast_sender.py

sending "very important data"
waiting to receive
received "ack" from ('192.168.1.17', 10000)
waiting to receive
received "ack" from ('192.168.1.8', 10000)
waiting to receive
timed out, no more responses
closing socket
```

The message is sent one time, and two acknowledgements of the outgoing message are received, one from each of host A and host B.

See Also:

Multicast (http://en.wikipedia.org/wiki/Multicast) Wikipedia article describing technical details of multicasting.

IP Multicast (http://en.wikipedia.org/wiki/IP_multicast) Wikipedia article about IP multicasting, with information about addressing.

11.1.6   Sending Binary Data

Sockets transmit streams of bytes. Those bytes can contain text messages, as in the previous examples, or they can be made up of binary data that has been encoded for transmission. To prepare binary data values for transmission, pack them into a buffer with `struct`.

This client program encodes an integer, a string of two characters, and a floating-point value into a sequence of bytes that can be passed to the socket for transmission.

```
import binascii
import socket
import struct
import sys

# Create a TCP/IP socket
sock = socket.socket(socket.AF_INET, socket.SOCK_STREAM)
```

```
server_address = ('localhost', 10000)
sock.connect(server_address)

values = (1, 'ab', 2.7)
packer = struct.Struct('I 2s f')
packed_data = packer.pack(*values)

print 'values =', values

try:

    # Send data
    print >>sys.stderr, 'sending %r' % binascii.hexlify(packed_data)
    sock.sendall(packed_data)

finally:
    print >>sys.stderr, 'closing socket'
    sock.close()
```

When sending multibyte binary data between two systems, it is important to ensure that both sides of the connection know what order the bytes are in and how to assemble them back into the correct order for the local architecture. The server program uses the same `Struct` specifier to unpack the bytes it receives so they are interpreted in the correct order.

```
import binascii
import socket
import struct
import sys

# Create a TCP/IP socket
sock = socket.socket(socket.AF_INET, socket.SOCK_STREAM)
server_address = ('localhost', 10000)
sock.bind(server_address)
sock.listen(1)

unpacker = struct.Struct('I 2s f')

while True:
    print >>sys.stderr, '\nwaiting for a connection'
    connection, client_address = sock.accept()
```

```
try:
    data = connection.recv(unpacker.size)
    print >>sys.stderr, 'received %r' % binascii.hexlify(data)
    unpacked_data = unpacker.unpack(data)
    print >>sys.stderr, 'unpacked:', unpacked_data

finally:
    connection.close()
```

Running the client produces the following:

```
$ python ./socket_binary_client.py

values = (1, 'ab', 2.7)
sending '0100000061620000cdcc2c40'
closing socket
```

And the server shows the values it receives.

```
$ python ./socket_binary_server.py

waiting for a connection
received '0100000061620000cdcc2c40'
unpacked: (1, 'ab', 2.700000047683716)

waiting for a connection
```

The floating-point value loses some precision as it is packed and unpacked, but otherwise, the data is transmitted as expected. One thing to keep in mind is that, depending on the value of the integer, it may be more efficient to convert it to text and then transmit, instead of using `struct`. The integer 1 uses one byte when represented as a string, but four when packed into the structure.

See Also:
struct (page 102) Converting between strings and other data types.

11.1.7   Nonblocking Communication and Timeouts

By default, a `socket` is configured so that sending or receiving data *blocks*, stopping program execution until the socket is ready. Calls to `send()` wait for buffer space to be available for the outgoing data, and calls to `recv()` wait for the other program to send data that can be read. This form of I/O operation is easy to understand, but can lead to inefficient operation and even deadlocks if both programs end up waiting for the other to send or receive data.

There are a few ways to work around this situation. One is to use a separate thread for communicating with each socket. This can introduce other complexities, though, with communication between the threads. Another option is to change the socket to not block at all and return immediately if it is not ready to handle the operation. Use the `setblocking()` method to change the blocking flag for a socket. The default value is 1, which means to block. Passing a value of 0 turns off blocking. If the socket has blocking turned off and it is not ready for the operation, then `socket.error` is raised.

A compromise solution is to set a timeout value for socket operations. Use `settimeout()` to change the timeout of a `socket` to a floating-point value representing the number of seconds to block before deciding the socket is not ready for the operation. When the timeout expires, a `timeout` exception is raised.

See Also:

socket (http://docs.python.org/library/socket.html) The standard library documentation for this module.

Socket Programming HOWTO (http://docs.python.org/howto/sockets.html) An instructional guide by Gordon McMillan, included in the standard library documentation.

select (page 594) Testing a socket to see if it is ready for reading or writing for nonblocking I/O.

SocketServer (page 609) Framework for creating network servers.

urllib (page 651) and urllib2 (page 667) Most network clients should use the more convenient libraries for accessing remote resources through a URL.

asyncore (page 619) and asynchat (page 629) Frameworks for asynchronous communication.

Unix Network Programming, Volume 1: The Sockets Networking API, 3/E By W. Richard Stevens, Bill Fenner, and Andrew M. Rudoff. Published by Addison-Wesley Professional, 2004. ISBN-10: 0131411551

11.2 select—Wait for I/O Efficiently

Purpose Wait for notification that an input or output channel is ready.
Python Version 1.4 and later

The `select` module provides access to platform-specific I/O monitoring functions. The most portable interface is the POSIX function `select()`, which is available on UNIX and Windows. The module also includes `poll()`, a UNIX-only API, and several options that only work with specific variants of UNIX.

11.2.1 Using select()

Python's `select()` function is a direct interface to the underlying operating system implementation. It monitors sockets, open files, and pipes (anything with a `fileno()` method that returns a valid file descriptor) until they become readable or writable or a communication error occurs. `select()` makes it easier to monitor multiple connections at the same time, and it is more efficient than writing a polling loop in Python using socket timeouts, because the monitoring happens in the operating system network layer, instead of the interpreter.

> **Note:** Using Python's file objects with `select()` works for UNIX, but is not supported under Windows.

The echo server example from the `socket` section can be extended to watch for more than one connection at a time by using `select()`. The new version starts out by creating a nonblocking TCP/IP socket and configuring it to listen on an address.

```
import select
import socket
import sys
import Queue

# Create a TCP/IP socket
server = socket.socket(socket.AF_INET, socket.SOCK_STREAM)
server.setblocking(0)

# Bind the socket to the port
server_address = ('localhost', 10000)
print >>sys.stderr, 'starting up on %s port %s' % server_address
server.bind(server_address)

# Listen for incoming connections
server.listen(5)
```

The arguments to `select()` are three lists containing communication channels to monitor. The first is a list of the objects to be checked for incoming data to be read, the second contains objects that will receive outgoing data when there is room in their buffer, and the third includes those that may have an error (usually a combination of the input and output channel objects). The next step in the server is to set up the lists containing input sources and output destinations to be passed to `select()`.

```
# Sockets from which we expect to read
inputs = [ server ]

# Sockets to which we expect to write
outputs = [ ]
```

Connections are added to and removed from these lists by the server main loop. Since this version of the server is going to wait for a socket to become writable before sending any data (instead of immediately sending the reply), each output connection needs a queue to act as a buffer for the data to be sent through it.

```
# Outgoing message queues (socket:Queue)
message_queues = {}
```

The main portion of the server program loops, calling `select()` to block and wait for network activity.

```
while inputs:

    # Wait for at least one of the sockets to be ready for processing
    print >>sys.stderr, 'waiting for the next event'
    readable, writable, exceptional = select.select(inputs,
                                                     outputs,
                                                     inputs)
```

`select()` returns three new lists, containing subsets of the contents of the lists passed in. All the sockets in the `readable` list have incoming data buffered and available to be read. All the sockets in the `writable` list have free space in their buffer and can be written to. The sockets returned in `exceptional` have had an error (the actual definition of "exceptional condition" depends on the platform).

The "readable" sockets represent three possible cases. If the socket is the main "server" socket, the one being used to listen for connections, then the "readable" condition means it is ready to accept another incoming connection. In addition to adding the new connection to the list of inputs to monitor, this section sets the client socket to not block.

```
# Handle inputs
for s in readable:
    if s is server:
        # A "readable" socket is ready to accept a connection
        connection, client_address = s.accept()
        print >>sys.stderr, '  connection from', client_address
        connection.setblocking(0)
        inputs.append(connection)

        # Give the connection a queue for data we want to send
        message_queues[connection] = Queue.Queue()
```

The next case is an established connection with a client that has sent data. The data is read with `recv()`, and then it is placed on the queue so it can be sent through the socket and back to the client.

```
    else:
        data = s.recv(1024)
        if data:
            # A readable client socket has data
            print >>sys.stderr, '  received "%s" from %s' % \
                (data, s.getpeername())
            message_queues[s].put(data)
            # Add output channel for response
            if s not in outputs:
                outputs.append(s)
```

A readable socket *without* data available is from a client that has disconnected, and the stream is ready to be closed.

```
        else:
            # Interpret empty result as closed connection
            print >>sys.stderr, '  closing', client_address
            # Stop listening for input on the connection
            if s in outputs:
                outputs.remove(s)
            inputs.remove(s)
            s.close()

            # Remove message queue
            del message_queues[s]
```

There are fewer cases for the writable connections. If there is data in the queue for a connection, the next message is sent. Otherwise, the connection is removed from the list of output connections so that the next time through the loop, `select()` does not indicate that the socket is ready to send data.

```python
# Handle outputs
for s in writable:
    try:
        next_msg = message_queues[s].get_nowait()
    except Queue.Empty:
        # No messages waiting so stop checking for writability.
        print >>sys.stderr, '  ', s.getpeername(), 'queue empty'
        outputs.remove(s)
    else:
        print >>sys.stderr, '  sending "%s" to %s' % \
            (next_msg, s.getpeername())
        s.send(next_msg)
```

Finally, if there is an error with a socket, it is closed.

```python
# Handle "exceptional conditions"
for s in exceptional:
    print >>sys.stderr, 'exception condition on', s.getpeername()
    # Stop listening for input on the connection
    inputs.remove(s)
    if s in outputs:
        outputs.remove(s)
    s.close()

    # Remove message queue
    del message_queues[s]
```

The example client program uses two sockets to demonstrate how the server with `select()` manages multiple connections at the same time. The client starts by connecting each TCP/IP socket to the server.

```python
import socket
import sys

messages = [ 'This is the message. ',
             'It will be sent ',
             'in parts.',
             ]
server_address = ('localhost', 10000)
```

```
# Create a TCP/IP socket
socks = [ socket.socket(socket.AF_INET, socket.SOCK_STREAM),
          socket.socket(socket.AF_INET, socket.SOCK_STREAM),
          ]

# Connect the socket to the port where the server is listening
print >>sys.stderr, 'connecting to %s port %s' % server_address
for s in socks:
    s.connect(server_address)
```

Then it sends one piece of the message at a time via each socket and reads all responses available after writing new data.

```
for message in messages:

    # Send messages on both sockets
    for s in socks:
        print >>sys.stderr, '%s: sending "%s"' % \
            (s.getsockname(), message)
        s.send(message)

    # Read responses on both sockets
    for s in socks:
        data = s.recv(1024)
        print >>sys.stderr, '%s: received "%s"' % \
            (s.getsockname(), data)
        if not data:
            print >>sys.stderr, 'closing socket', s.getsockname()
            s.close()
```

Run the server in one window and the client in another. The output will look like this, with different port numbers.

```
$ python ./select_echo_server.py

starting up on localhost port 10000
waiting for the next event
  connection from ('127.0.0.1', 55472)
waiting for the next event
  connection from ('127.0.0.1', 55473)
  received "This is the message. " from ('127.0.0.1', 55472)
```

```
waiting for the next event
  received "This is the message. " from ('127.0.0.1', 55473)
  sending "This is the message. " to ('127.0.0.1', 55472)
waiting for the next event
  ('127.0.0.1', 55472) queue empty
  sending "This is the message. " to ('127.0.0.1', 55473)
waiting for the next event
  ('127.0.0.1', 55473) queue empty
waiting for the next event
  received "It will be sent " from ('127.0.0.1', 55472)
  received "It will be sent " from ('127.0.0.1', 55473)
waiting for the next event
  sending "It will be sent " to ('127.0.0.1', 55472)
  sending "It will be sent " to ('127.0.0.1', 55473)
waiting for the next event
  ('127.0.0.1', 55472) queue empty
  ('127.0.0.1', 55473) queue empty
waiting for the next event
  received "in parts." from ('127.0.0.1', 55472)
  received "in parts." from ('127.0.0.1', 55473)
waiting for the next event
  sending "in parts." to ('127.0.0.1', 55472)
  sending "in parts." to ('127.0.0.1', 55473)
waiting for the next event
  ('127.0.0.1', 55472) queue empty
  ('127.0.0.1', 55473) queue empty
waiting for the next event
  closing ('127.0.0.1', 55473)
  closing ('127.0.0.1', 55473)
waiting for the next event
```

The client output shows the data being sent and received using both sockets.

```
$ python ./select_echo_multiclient.py

connecting to localhost port 10000
('127.0.0.1', 55821): sending "This is the message. "
('127.0.0.1', 55822): sending "This is the message. "
('127.0.0.1', 55821): received "This is the message. "
('127.0.0.1', 55822): received "This is the message. "
('127.0.0.1', 55821): sending "It will be sent "
('127.0.0.1', 55822): sending "It will be sent "
('127.0.0.1', 55821): received "It will be sent "
```

```
('127.0.0.1', 55822): received "It will be sent "
('127.0.0.1', 55821): sending "in parts."
('127.0.0.1', 55822): sending "in parts."
('127.0.0.1', 55821): received "in parts."
('127.0.0.1', 55822): received "in parts."
```

11.2.2 Nonblocking I/O with Timeouts

`select()` also takes an optional fourth parameter, which is the number of seconds to wait before breaking off monitoring if no channels have become active. Using a timeout value lets a main program call `select()` as part of a larger processing loop, taking other actions between checking for network input.

When the timeout expires, `select()` returns three empty lists. Updating the server example to use a timeout requires adding the extra argument to the `select()` call and handling the empty lists after `select()` returns.

```
# Wait for at least one of the sockets to be ready for processing
print >>sys.stderr, '\nwaiting for the next event'
timeout = 1
readable, writable, exceptional = select.select(inputs,
                                                outputs,
                                                inputs,
                                                timeout)

if not (readable or writable or exceptional):
    print >>sys.stderr, '  timed out, do some other work here'
    continue
```

This "slow" version of the client program pauses after sending each message to simulate latency or other delay in transmission.

```
import socket
import sys
import time

# Create a TCP/IP socket
sock = socket.socket(socket.AF_INET, socket.SOCK_STREAM)

# Connect the socket to the port where the server is listening
server_address = ('localhost', 10000)
print >>sys.stderr, 'connecting to %s port %s' % server_address
sock.connect(server_address)
```

```
time.sleep(1)

messages = [ 'Part one of the message.',
             'Part two of the message.',
             ]
amount_expected = len(''.join(messages))

try:

    # Send data
    for message in messages:
        print >>sys.stderr, 'sending "%s"' % message
        sock.sendall(message)
        time.sleep(1.5)

    # Look for the response
    amount_received = 0

    while amount_received < amount_expected:
        data = sock.recv(16)
        amount_received += len(data)
        print >>sys.stderr, 'received "%s"' % data

finally:
    print >>sys.stderr, 'closing socket'
    sock.close()
```

Running the new server with the slow client produces the following:

```
$ python ./select_echo_server_timeout.py

starting up on localhost port 10000
waiting for the next event
  connection from ('127.0.0.1', 55480)
waiting for the next event
  received "Part one of the message." from ('127.0.0.1', 55480)
waiting for the next event
  sending "Part one of the message." to ('127.0.0.1', 55480)
waiting for the next event
  ('127.0.0.1', 55480) queue empty
waiting for the next event
  received "Part two of the message." from ('127.0.0.1', 55480)
waiting for the next event
  sending "Part two of the message." to ('127.0.0.1', 55480)
```

```
waiting for the next event
  ('127.0.0.1', 55480) queue empty
waiting for the next event
  closing ('127.0.0.1', 55480)
waiting for the next event
```

And this is the client output:

```
$ python ./select_echo_slow_client.py

connecting to localhost port 10000
sending "Part one of the message."
sending "Part two of the message."
received "Part one of the "
received "message.Part two"
received " of the message."
closing socket
```

11.2.3   Using poll()

The poll() function provides similar features to select(), but the underlying implementation is more efficient. The trade-off is that poll() is not supported under Windows, so programs using poll() are less portable.

An echo server built on poll() starts with the same socket configuration code used in the other examples.

```
import select
import socket
import sys
import Queue

# Create a TCP/IP socket
server = socket.socket(socket.AF_INET, socket.SOCK_STREAM)
server.setblocking(0)

# Bind the socket to the port
server_address = ('localhost', 10000)
print >>sys.stderr, 'starting up on %s port %s' % server_address
server.bind(server_address)

# Listen for incoming connections
server.listen(5)
```

```
# Keep up with the queues of outgoing messages
message_queues = {}
```

The timeout value passed to `poll()` is represented in milliseconds, instead of seconds, so in order to pause for a full second, the timeout must be set to `1000`.

```
# Do not block forever (milliseconds)
TIMEOUT = 1000
```

Python implements `poll()` with a class that manages the registered data channels being monitored. Channels are added by calling `register()`, with flags indicating which events are interesting for that channel. The full set of flags is listed in Table 11.1.

Table 11.1. Event Flags for poll()

Event	Description
POLLIN	Input ready
POLLPRI	Priority input ready
POLLOUT	Able to receive output
POLLERR	Error
POLLHUP	Channel closed
POLLNVAL	Channel not open

The echo server will be setting up some sockets just for reading and others to be read from or written to. The appropriate combinations of flags are saved to the local variables READ_ONLY and READ_WRITE.

```
# Commonly used flag sets
READ_ONLY = ( select.POLLIN |
              select.POLLPRI |
              select.POLLHUP |
              select.POLLERR )
READ_WRITE = READ_ONLY | select.POLLOUT
```

The `server` socket is registered so that any incoming connections or data triggers an event.

```
# Set up the poller
poller = select.poll()
poller.register(server, READ_ONLY)
```

Since `poll()` returns a list of tuples containing the file descriptor for the socket and the event flag, a mapping from file descriptor numbers to objects is needed to retrieve the `socket` to read or write from it.

```
# Map file descriptors to socket objects
fd_to_socket = { server.fileno(): server,
                }
```

The server's loop calls `poll()` and then processes the "events" returned by looking up the socket and taking action based on the flag in the event.

```
while True:

    # Wait for at least one of the sockets to be ready for processing
    print >>sys.stderr, 'waiting for the next event'
    events = poller.poll(TIMEOUT)

    for fd, flag in events:

        # Retrieve the actual socket from its file descriptor
        s = fd_to_socket[fd]
```

As with `select()`, when the main server socket is "readable," that really means there is a pending connection from a client. The new connection is registered with the READ_ONLY flags to watch for new data to come through it.

```
        # Handle inputs
        if flag & (select.POLLIN | select.POLLPRI):

            if s is server:
                # A readable socket is ready to accept a connection
                connection, client_address = s.accept()
                print >>sys.stderr, '  connection', client_address
                connection.setblocking(0)
                fd_to_socket[ connection.fileno() ] = connection
                poller.register(connection, READ_ONLY)

                # Give the connection a queue for data to send
                message_queues[connection] = Queue.Queue()
```

Sockets other than the server are existing clients with data buffered and waiting to be read. Use `recv()` to retrieve the data from the buffer.

```
    else:
        data = s.recv(1024)
```

If `recv()` returns any data, it is placed into the outgoing queue for the socket, and the flags for that socket are changed using `modify()` so `poll()` will watch for the socket to be ready to receive data.

```
if data:
    # A readable client socket has data
    print >>sys.stderr, '  received "%s" from %s' % \
        (data, s.getpeername())
    message_queues[s].put(data)
    # Add output channel for response
    poller.modify(s, READ_WRITE)
```

An empty string returned by `recv()` means the client disconnected, so `unregister()` is used to tell the `poll` object to ignore the socket.

```
else:
    # Interpret empty result as closed connection
    print >>sys.stderr, '  closing', client_address
    # Stop listening for input on the connection
    poller.unregister(s)
    s.close()

    # Remove message queue
    del message_queues[s]
```

The `POLLHUP` flag indicates a client that "hung up" the connection without closing it cleanly. The server stops polling clients that disappear.

```
elif flag & select.POLLHUP:
    # Client hung up
    print >>sys.stderr, '  closing', client_address, '(HUP)'
    # Stop listening for input on the connection
    poller.unregister(s)
    s.close()
```

The handling for writable sockets looks like the version used in the example for `select()`, except that `modify()` is used to change the flags for the socket in the poller, instead of removing it from the output list.

```
elif flag & select.POLLOUT:
    # Socket is ready to send data, if there is any to send.
```

```
        try:
            next_msg = message_queues[s].get_nowait()
        except Queue.Empty:
            # No messages waiting so stop checking
            print >>sys.stderr, s.getpeername(), 'queue empty'
            poller.modify(s, READ_ONLY)
        else:
            print >>sys.stderr, '  sending "%s" to %s' % \
                (next_msg, s.getpeername())
            s.send(next_msg)
```

And, finally, any events with POLLERR cause the server to close the socket.

```
    elif flag & select.POLLERR:
        print >>sys.stderr, '  exception on', s.getpeername()
        # Stop listening for input on the connection
        poller.unregister(s)
        s.close()

        # Remove message queue
        del message_queues[s]
```

When the poll-based server is run together with select_echo_multiclient
.py (the client program that uses multiple sockets), this is the output.

```
$ python ./select_poll_echo_server.py

waiting for the next event
waiting for the next event
  connection ('127.0.0.1', 62835)
waiting for the next event
  connection ('127.0.0.1', 62836)
waiting for the next event
  received "This is the message. " from ('127.0.0.1', 62835)
waiting for the next event
  sending "This is the message. " to ('127.0.0.1', 62835)
waiting for the next event
('127.0.0.1', 62835) queue empty
waiting for the next event
  received "This is the message. " from ('127.0.0.1', 62836)
waiting for the next event
  sending "This is the message. " to ('127.0.0.1', 62836)
waiting for the next event
('127.0.0.1', 62836) queue empty
```

```
waiting for the next event
  received "It will be sent " from ('127.0.0.1', 62835)
waiting for the next event
  sending "It will be sent " to ('127.0.0.1', 62835)
waiting for the next event
('127.0.0.1', 62835) queue empty
waiting for the next event
  received "It will be sent " from ('127.0.0.1', 62836)
waiting for the next event
  sending "It will be sent " to ('127.0.0.1', 62836)
waiting for the next event
('127.0.0.1', 62836) queue empty
waiting for the next event
  received "in parts." from ('127.0.0.1', 62835)
  received "in parts." from ('127.0.0.1', 62836)
waiting for the next event
  sending "in parts." to ('127.0.0.1', 62835)
  sending "in parts." to ('127.0.0.1', 62836)
waiting for the next event
('127.0.0.1', 62835) queue empty
('127.0.0.1', 62836) queue empty
waiting for the next event
  closing ('127.0.0.1', 62836)
  closing ('127.0.0.1', 62836)
waiting for the next event
```

11.2.4 Platform-Specific Options

Less portable options provided by `select` are `epoll`, the *edge polling* API supported by Linux; `kqueue`, which uses BSD's *kernel queue*; and `kevent`, BSD's *kernel event* interface. Refer to the operating system library documentation for more detail about how they work.

See Also:

select (http://docs.python.org/library/select.html) The standard library documentation for this module.

Socket Programming HOWTO (http://docs.python.org/howto/sockets.html) An instructional guide by Gordon McMillan, included in the standard library documentation.

socket (page 561) Low-level network communication.

SocketServer (page 609) Framework for creating network server applications.

asyncore (page 619) and asynchat (page 629) Asynchronous I/O framework.

UNIX Network Programming, Volume 1: The Sockets Networking API, 3/E By W. Richard Stevens, Bill Fenner, and Andrew M. Rudoff. Published by Addison-Wesley Professional, 2004. ISBN-10: 0131411551.

11.3 SocketServer—Creating Network Servers

Purpose Creating network servers.
Python Version 1.4 and later

The `SocketServer` module is a framework for creating network servers. It defines classes for handling synchronous network requests (the server request-handler blocks until the request is completed) over TCP, UDP, UNIX streams, and UNIX datagrams. It also provides mix-in classes for easily converting servers to use a separate thread or process for each request.

Responsibility for processing a request is split between a server class and a request-handler class. The server deals with the communication issues, such as listening on a socket and accepting connections, and the request handler deals with the "protocol" issues like interpreting incoming data, processing it, and sending data back to the client. This division of responsibility means that many applications can use one of the existing server classes without any modifications and provide a request to communicate with each other handler class for it to work with the custom protocol.

11.3.1 Server Types

There are five different server classes defined in `SocketServer`. `BaseServer` defines the API and is not intended to be instantiated and used directly. `TCPServer` uses TCP/IP sockets to communicate. `UDPServer` uses datagram sockets. `UnixStreamServer` and `UnixDatagramServer` use UNIX-domain sockets and are only available on UNIX platforms.

11.3.2 Server Objects

To construct a server, pass it an address on which to listen for requests and a request-handler *class* (not instance). The address format depends on the server type and the socket family used. Refer to the `socket` module documentation for details.

Once the server object is instantiated, use either `handle_request()` or `serve_forever()` to process requests. The `serve_forever()` method calls `handle_request()` in an infinite loop, but if an application needs to integrate the server with another event loop or use `select()` to monitor several sockets for different servers, it can call `handle_request()` directly.

11.3.3 Implementing a Server

When creating a server, it is usually sufficient to reuse one of the existing classes and provide a custom request handler class. For other cases, `BaseServer` includes several methods that can be overridden in a subclass.

- `verify_request(request, client_address)`: Return True to process the request or False to ignore it. For example, a server could refuse requests from an IP range or if it is overloaded.
- `process_request(request, client_address)`: Calls `finish_request()` to actually do the work of handling the request. It can also create a separate thread or process, as the mix-in classes do.
- `finish_request(request, client_address)`: Creates a request handler instance using the class given to the server's constructor. Calls `handle()` on the request handler to process the request.

11.3.4 Request Handlers

Request handlers do most of the work of receiving incoming requests and deciding what action to take. The handler is responsible for implementing the protocol on top of the socket layer (i.e., HTTP, XML-RPC, or AMQP). The request handler reads the request from the incoming data channel, processes it, and writes a response back out. Three methods are available to be overridden.

- `setup()`: Prepares the request handler for the request. In the `StreamRequestHandler` the `setup()` method creates file-like objects for reading from and writing to the socket.
- `handle()`: Does the real work for the request. Parses the incoming request, processes the data, and sends a response.
- `finish()`: Cleans up anything created during `setup()`.

Many handlers can be implemented with only a `handle()` method.

11.3.5 Echo Example

This example implements a simple server/request handler pair that accepts TCP connections and echos back any data sent by the client. It starts with the request handler.

```
import logging
import sys
import SocketServer
```

```
logging.basicConfig(level=logging.DEBUG,
                    format='%(name)s: %(message)s',
                    )


class EchoRequestHandler(SocketServer.BaseRequestHandler):

    def __init__(self, request, client_address, server):
        self.logger = logging.getLogger('EchoRequestHandler')
        self.logger.debug('__init__')
        SocketServer.BaseRequestHandler.__init__(self, request,
                                                 client_address,
                                                 server)
        return

    def setup(self):
        self.logger.debug('setup')
        return SocketServer.BaseRequestHandler.setup(self)

    def handle(self):
        self.logger.debug('handle')

        # Echo the back to the client'
        data = self.request.recv(1024)
        self.logger.debug('recv()->"%s"', data)
        self.request.send(data)
        return

    def finish(self):
        self.logger.debug('finish')
        return SocketServer.BaseRequestHandler.finish(self)
```

The only method that actually needs to be implemented is `EchoRequest-Handler.handle()`, but versions of all the methods described earlier are included to illustrate the sequence of calls made. The `EchoServer` class does nothing different from `TCPServer`, except log when each method is called.

```
class EchoServer(SocketServer.TCPServer):

    def __init__(self, server_address,
                 handler_class=EchoRequestHandler,
                 ):
        self.logger = logging.getLogger('EchoServer')
        self.logger.debug('__init__')
```

```
        SocketServer.TCPServer.__init__(self, server_address,
                                        handler_class)
        return

    def server_activate(self):
        self.logger.debug('server_activate')
        SocketServer.TCPServer.server_activate(self)
        return

    def serve_forever(self, poll_interval=0.5):
        self.logger.debug('waiting for request')
        self.logger.info('Handling requests, press <Ctrl-C> to quit')
        SocketServer.TCPServer.serve_forever(self, poll_interval)
        return

    def handle_request(self):
        self.logger.debug('handle_request')
        return SocketServer.TCPServer.handle_request(self)

    def verify_request(self, request, client_address):
        self.logger.debug('verify_request(%s, %s)',
                          request, client_address)
        return SocketServer.TCPServer.verify_request(self, request,
                                                     client_address)

    def process_request(self, request, client_address):
        self.logger.debug('process_request(%s, %s)',
                          request, client_address)
        return SocketServer.TCPServer.process_request(self, request,
                                                      client_address)

    def server_close(self):
        self.logger.debug('server_close')
        return SocketServer.TCPServer.server_close(self)

    def finish_request(self, request, client_address):
        self.logger.debug('finish_request(%s, %s)',
                          request, client_address)
        return SocketServer.TCPServer.finish_request(self, request,
                                                     client_address)

    def close_request(self, request_address):
        self.logger.debug('close_request(%s)', request_address)
        return SocketServer.TCPServer.close_request(self,
                                                    request_address)
```

```
    def shutdown(self):
        self.logger.debug('shutdown()')
        return SocketServer.TCPServer.shutdown(self)
```

The last step is to add a main program that sets up the server to run in a thread and sends it data to illustrate which methods are called as the data is echoed back.

```
if __name__ == '__main__':
    import socket
    import threading

    address = ('localhost', 0) # let the kernel assign a port
    server = EchoServer(address, EchoRequestHandler)
    ip, port = server.server_address # what port was assigned?

    # Start the server in a thread
    t = threading.Thread(target=server.serve_forever)
    t.setDaemon(True) # don't hang on exit
    t.start()

    logger = logging.getLogger('client')
    logger.info('Server on %s:%s', ip, port)

    # Connect to the server
    logger.debug('creating socket')
    s = socket.socket(socket.AF_INET, socket.SOCK_STREAM)
    logger.debug('connecting to server')
    s.connect((ip, port))

    # Send the data
    message = 'Hello, world'
    logger.debug('sending data: "%s"', message)
    len_sent = s.send(message)

    # Receive a response
    logger.debug('waiting for response')
    response = s.recv(len_sent)
    logger.debug('response from server: "%s"', response)

    # Clean up
    server.shutdown()
    logger.debug('closing socket')
    s.close()
    logger.debug('done')
    server.socket.close()
```

Running the program produces the following.

```
$ python SocketServer_echo.py

EchoServer: __init__
EchoServer: server_activate
EchoServer: waiting for request
EchoServer: Handling requests, press <Ctrl-C> to quit
client: Server on 127.0.0.1:62859
client: creating socket
client: connecting to server
EchoServer: verify_request(<socket._socketobject object at 0x100e1b8
a0>, ('127.0.0.1', 62860))
EchoServer: process_request(<socket._socketobject object at 0x100e1b
8a0>, ('127.0.0.1', 62860))
EchoServer: finish_request(<socket._socketobject object at 0x100e1b8
a0>, ('127.0.0.1', 62860))
EchoRequestHandler: __init__
EchoRequestHandler: setup
EchoRequestHandler: handle
client: sending data: "Hello, world"
EchoRequestHandler: recv()->"Hello, world"
EchoRequestHandler: finish
EchoServer: close_request(<socket._socketobject object at 0x100e1b8a
0>)
client: waiting for response
client: response from server: "Hello, world"
EchoServer: shutdown()
client: closing socket
client: done
```

Note: The port number used will change each time the program runs because the
kernel allocates an available port automatically. To make the server listen on a specific port each time, provide that number in the address tuple instead of the 0.

Here is a condensed version of the same server, without the logging calls. Only the
`handle()` method in the request-handler class needs to be provided.

```
import SocketServer

class EchoRequestHandler(SocketServer.BaseRequestHandler):
```

```python
    def handle(self):
        # Echo the back to the client
        data = self.request.recv(1024)
        self.request.send(data)
        return

if __name__ == '__main__':
    import socket
    import threading

    address = ('localhost', 0) # let the kernel assign a port
    server = SocketServer.TCPServer(address, EchoRequestHandler)
    ip, port = server.server_address # what port was assigned?

    t = threading.Thread(target=server.serve_forever)
    t.setDaemon(True) # don't hang on exit
    t.start()

    # Connect to the server
    s = socket.socket(socket.AF_INET, socket.SOCK_STREAM)
    s.connect((ip, port))

    # Send the data
    message = 'Hello, world'
    print 'Sending : "%s"' % message
    len_sent = s.send(message)

    # Receive a response
    response = s.recv(len_sent)
    print 'Received: "%s"' % response

    # Clean up
    server.shutdown()
    s.close()
    server.socket.close()
```

In this case, no special server class is required since the TCPServer handles all the server requirements.

```
$ python SocketServer_echo_simple.py

Sending : "Hello, world"
Received: "Hello, world"
```

11.3.6　Threading and Forking

To add threading or forking support to a server, include the appropriate mix-in in the class hierarchy for the server. The mix-in classes override `process_request()` to start a new thread or process when a request is ready to be handled, and the work is done in the new child.

For threads, use `ThreadingMixIn`.

```python
import threading
import SocketServer

class ThreadedEchoRequestHandler(SocketServer.BaseRequestHandler):

    def handle(self):
        # Echo the back to the client
        data = self.request.recv(1024)
        cur_thread = threading.currentThread()
        response = '%s: %s' % (cur_thread.getName(), data)
        self.request.send(response)
        return

class ThreadedEchoServer(SocketServer.ThreadingMixIn,
                         SocketServer.TCPServer,
                         ):
    pass

if __name__ == '__main__':
    import socket
    import threading

    address = ('localhost', 0) # let the kernel assign a port
    server = ThreadedEchoServer(address, ThreadedEchoRequestHandler)
    ip, port = server.server_address # what port was assigned?

    t = threading.Thread(target=server.serve_forever)
    t.setDaemon(True) # don't hang on exit
    t.start()
    print 'Server loop running in thread:', t.getName()

    # Connect to the server
    s = socket.socket(socket.AF_INET, socket.SOCK_STREAM)
    s.connect((ip, port))
```

```python
# Send the data
message = 'Hello, world'
print 'Sending : "%s"' % message
len_sent = s.send(message)

# Receive a response
response = s.recv(1024)
print 'Received: "%s"' % response

# Clean up
server.shutdown()
s.close()
server.socket.close()
```

The response from this threaded server includes the identifier of the thread where the request is handled.

```
$ python SocketServer_threaded.py

Server loop running in thread: Thread-1
Sending : "Hello, world"
Received: "Thread-2: Hello, world"
```

For separate processes, use `ForkingMixIn`.

```python
import os
import SocketServer

class ForkingEchoRequestHandler(SocketServer.BaseRequestHandler):

    def handle(self):
        # Echo the back to the client
        data = self.request.recv(1024)
        cur_pid = os.getpid()
        response = '%s: %s' % (cur_pid, data)
        self.request.send(response)
        return

class ForkingEchoServer(SocketServer.ForkingMixIn,
                        SocketServer.TCPServer,
                        ):
    pass
```

```
if __name__ == '__main__':
    import socket
    import threading

    address = ('localhost', 0) # let the kernel assign a port
    server = ForkingEchoServer(address, ForkingEchoRequestHandler)
    ip, port = server.server_address # what port was assigned?

    t = threading.Thread(target=server.serve_forever)
    t.setDaemon(True) # don't hang on exit
    t.start()
    print 'Server loop running in process:', os.getpid()

    # Connect to the server
    s = socket.socket(socket.AF_INET, socket.SOCK_STREAM)
    s.connect((ip, port))

    # Send the data
    message = 'Hello, world'
    print 'Sending : "%s"' % message
    len_sent = s.send(message)

    # Receive a response
    response = s.recv(1024)
    print 'Received: "%s"' % response

    # Clean up
    server.shutdown()
    s.close()
    server.socket.close()
```

In this case, the process id of the child is included in the response from the server.

```
$ python SocketServer_forking.py

Server loop running in process: 12797
Sending : "Hello, world"
Received: "12798: Hello, world"
```

See Also:

SocketServer (http://docs.python.org/lib/module-SocketServer.html) Standard library documentation for this module.

asyncore (page 619) Use `asyncore` to create asynchronous servers that do not block while processing a request.

SimpleXMLRPCServer (page 714) XML-RPC server built using `SocketServer`.

11.4 asyncore—Asynchronous I/O

Purpose Asynchronous I/O handler.
Python Version 1.5.2 and later

The `asyncore` module includes tools for working with I/O objects such as sockets so they can be managed asynchronously (instead of using multiple threads or processes). The main class provided is `dispatcher`, a wrapper around a socket that provides hooks for handling events like connecting, reading, and writing when invoked from the main loop function, `loop()`.

11.4.1 Servers

This example illustrates using `asyncore` in a server and client by reimplementing the `EchoServer` from the `SocketServer` examples. Three classes are used in the new implementation. The first, `EchoServer`, receives incoming connections from clients. This demonstration implementation closes down as soon as the first connection is accepted, so it is easier to start and stop the server while experimenting with the code.

```python
import asyncore
import logging

class EchoServer(asyncore.dispatcher):
    """Receives connections and establishes handlers for each client.
    """

    def __init__(self, address):
        self.logger = logging.getLogger('EchoServer')
        asyncore.dispatcher.__init__(self)
        self.create_socket(socket.AF_INET, socket.SOCK_STREAM)
        self.bind(address)
        self.address = self.socket.getsockname()
        self.logger.debug('binding to %s', self.address)
        self.listen(1)
        return
```

```
def handle_accept(self):
    # Called when a client connects to the socket
    client_info = self.accept()
    self.logger.debug('handle_accept() -> %s', client_info[1])
    EchoHandler(sock=client_info[0])
    # Only deal with one client at a time,
    # so close as soon as the handler is set up.
    # Under normal conditions, the server
    # would run forever or until it received
    # instructions to stop.
    self.handle_close()
    return

def handle_close(self):
    self.logger.debug('handle_close()')
    self.close()
    return
```

Each time a new connection is accepted in `handle_accept()`, EchoServer creates a new EchoHandler instance to manage it. The EchoServer and EchoHandler are defined in separate classes because they do different things. When EchoServer accepts a connection, a new socket is established. Rather than try to dispatch to individual clients within EchoServer, an EchoHandler is created to take advantage of the socket map maintained by asyncore.

```
class EchoHandler(asyncore.dispatcher):
    """Handles echoing messages from a single client.
    """

    def __init__(self, sock, chunk_size=256):
        self.chunk_size = chunk_size
        logger_name = 'EchoHandler'
        self.logger = logging.getLogger(logger_name)
        asyncore.dispatcher.__init__(self, sock=sock)
        self.data_to_write = []
        return

    def writable(self):
        """Write if data has been received."""
        response = bool(self.data_to_write)
        self.logger.debug('writable() -> %s', response)
        return response
```

```python
def handle_write(self):
    """Write as much as possible of the
    most recent message received.
    """
    data = self.data_to_write.pop()
    sent = self.send(data[:self.chunk_size])
    if sent < len(data):
        remaining = data[sent:]
        self.data.to_write.append(remaining)
    self.logger.debug('handle_write() -> (%d) %r',
                      sent, data[:sent])
    if not self.writable():
        self.handle_close()

def handle_read(self):
    """Read an incoming message from the client
    and put it into the outgoing queue.
    """
    data = self.recv(self.chunk_size)
    self.logger.debug('handle_read() -> (%d) %r',
                      len(data), data)
    self.data_to_write.insert(0, data)

def handle_close(self):
    self.logger.debug('handle_close()')
    self.close()
```

11.4.2 Clients

To create a client based on `asyncore`, subclass `dispatcher`, and provide implementations for creating the socket, reading, and writing. For `EchoClient`, the socket is created in `__init__()` using the base-class method `create_socket()`. Alternative implementations of the method may be provided, but in this case, a TCP/IP socket is needed so the base-class version is sufficient.

```python
class EchoClient(asyncore.dispatcher):
    """Sends messages to the server and receives responses.
    """

    def __init__(self, host, port, message, chunk_size=128):
        self.message = message
        self.to_send = message
        self.received_data = []
```

```
    self.chunk_size = chunk_size
    self.logger = logging.getLogger('EchoClient')
    asyncore.dispatcher.__init__(self)
    self.create_socket(socket.AF_INET, socket.SOCK_STREAM)
    self.logger.debug('connecting to %s', (host, port))
    self.connect((host, port))
    return
```

The `handle_connect()` hook is present simply to show when it is called. Other types of clients that need to implement connection hand-shaking or protocol negotiation should do that work in `handle_connect()`.

```
def handle_connect(self):
    self.logger.debug('handle_connect()')
```

The `handle_close()` method is also presented to show when it is called during processing. The base-class version closes the socket correctly, so if an application does not need to do extra cleanup on close, the method does not need to be overridden.

```
def handle_close(self):
    self.logger.debug('handle_close()')
    self.close()
    received_message = ''.join(self.received_data)
    if received_message == self.message:
        self.logger.debug('RECEIVED COPY OF MESSAGE')
    else:
        self.logger.debug('ERROR IN TRANSMISSION')
        self.logger.debug('EXPECTED "%s"', self.message)
        self.logger.debug('RECEIVED "%s"', received_message)
    return
```

The `asyncore` loop uses `writable()` and its sibling method `readable()` to decide what actions to take with each dispatcher. Actual use of `poll()` or `select()` on the sockets or file descriptors managed by each dispatcher is handled inside the `asyncore` code and does not need to be implemented in a program using `asyncore`. The program only needs to indicate whether the dispatcher wants to read or write data. In this client, `writable()` returns `True` as long as there is data to send to the server. `readable()` always returns `True` because the client needs to read all the data.

```
def writable(self):
    self.logger.debug('writable() -> %s', bool(self.to_send))
    return bool(self.to_send)
```

```
def readable(self):
    self.logger.debug('readable() -> True')
    return True
```

Each time through the processing loop when `writable()` responds positively, `handle_write()` is invoked. The `EchoClient` splits the message up into parts based on the size restriction given to demonstrate how a much larger multipart message could be transmitted using several iterations through the loop. Each time `handle_write()` is called, another part of the message is written, until it is completely consumed.

```
def handle_write(self):
    sent = self.send(self.to_send[:self.chunk_size])
    self.logger.debug('handle_write() -> (%d) %r',
                      sent, self.to_send[:sent])
    self.to_send = self.to_send[sent:]
```

Similarly, when `readable()` responds positively and there is data to read, `handle_read()` is invoked.

```
def handle_read(self):
    data = self.recv(self.chunk_size)
    self.logger.debug('handle_read() -> (%d) %r',
                      len(data), data)
    self.received_data.append(data)
```

11.4.3 The Event Loop

A short test script is included in the module. It sets up a server and client, and then runs `asyncore.loop()` to process the communications. Creating the clients registers them in a "map" kept internally by `asyncore`. The communication occurs as the loop iterates over the clients. When the client reads zero bytes from a socket that seems readable, the condition is interpreted as a closed connection and `handle_close()` is called.

```
if __name__ == '__main__':
    import socket

    logging.basicConfig(level=logging.DEBUG,
                        format='%(name)-11s: %(message)s',
                        )

    address = ('localhost', 0) # let the kernel assign a port
    server = EchoServer(address)
    ip, port = server.address # find out which port was assigned
```

```
message = open('lorem.txt', 'r').read()
logging.info('Total message length: %d bytes', len(message))

client = EchoClient(ip, port, message=message)

asyncore.loop()
```

This is the output of running the program.

```
$ python asyncore_echo_server.py

EchoServer : binding to ('127.0.0.1', 63985)
root       : Total message length: 133 bytes
EchoClient : connecting to ('127.0.0.1', 63985)
EchoClient : readable() -> True
EchoClient : writable() -> True
EchoServer : handle_accept() -> ('127.0.0.1', 63986)
EchoServer : handle_close()
EchoClient : handle_connect()
EchoClient : handle_write() -> (128) 'Lorem ipsum dolor sit amet, cons
ectetuer adipiscing elit. Donec\negestas, enim et consectetuer ullamco
rper, lectus ligula rutrum '
EchoClient : readable() -> True
EchoClient : writable() -> True
EchoHandler: writable() -> False
EchoHandler: handle_read() -> (128) 'Lorem ipsum dolor sit amet, conse
ctetuer adipiscing elit. Donec\negestas, enim et consectetuer ullamcor
per, lectus ligula rutrum '
EchoClient : handle_write() -> (5) 'leo.\n'
EchoClient : readable() -> True
EchoClient : writable() -> False
EchoHandler: writable() -> True
EchoHandler: handle_read() -> (5) 'leo.\n'
EchoHandler: handle_write() -> (128) 'Lorem ipsum dolor sit amet, cons
ectetuer adipiscing elit. Donec\negestas, enim et consectetuer ullamco
rper, lectus ligula rutrum '
EchoHandler: writable() -> True
EchoClient : readable() -> True
EchoClient : writable() -> False
EchoHandler: writable() -> True
EchoClient : handle_read() -> (128) 'Lorem ipsum dolor sit amet, conse
ctetuer adipiscing elit. Donec\negestas, enim et consectetuer ullamcor
```

```
per, lectus ligula rutrum '
EchoHandler: handle_write() -> (5) 'leo.\n'
EchoHandler: writable() -> False
EchoHandler: handle_close()
EchoClient : readable() -> True
EchoClient : writable() -> False
EchoClient : handle_read() -> (5) 'leo.\n'
EchoClient : readable() -> True
EchoClient : writable() -> False
EchoClient : handle_close()
EchoClient : RECEIVED COPY OF MESSAGE
EchoClient : handle_read() -> (0) ''
```

In this example, the server, handler, and client objects are all being maintained in the same socket map by `asyncore` in a single process. To separate the server from the client, instantiate them from separate scripts and run `asyncore.loop()` in both. When a dispatcher is closed, it is removed from the map maintained by `asyncore`, and the loop exits when the map is empty.

11.4.4 Working with Other Event Loops

It is sometimes necessary to integrate the `asyncore` event loop with an event loop from the parent application. For example, a GUI application would not want the UI to block until all asynchronous transfers are handled—that would defeat the purpose of making them asynchronous. To make this sort of integration easy, `asyncore.loop()` accepts arguments to set a timeout and to limit the number of times the loop is run. The effect of these options on the client can be demonstrated with an HTTP client based on the version in the standard library documentation for `asyncore`.

```python
import asyncore
import logging
import socket
from cStringIO import StringIO
import urlparse


class HttpClient(asyncore.dispatcher):

    def __init__(self, url):
        self.url = url
        self.logger = logging.getLogger(self.url)
        self.parsed_url = urlparse.urlparse(url)
```

```
        asyncore.dispatcher.__init__(self)
        self.write_buffer = 'GET %s HTTP/1.0\r\n\r\n' % self.url
        self.read_buffer = StringIO()
        self.create_socket(socket.AF_INET, socket.SOCK_STREAM)
        address = (self.parsed_url.netloc, 80)
        self.logger.debug('connecting to %s', address)
        self.connect(address)

    def handle_connect(self):
        self.logger.debug('handle_connect()')

    def handle_close(self):
        self.logger.debug('handle_close()')
        self.close()

    def writable(self):
        is_writable = (len(self.write_buffer) > 0)
        if is_writable:
            self.logger.debug('writable() -> %s', is_writable)
        return is_writable

    def readable(self):
        self.logger.debug('readable() -> True')
        return True

    def handle_write(self):
        sent = self.send(self.write_buffer)
        self.logger.debug('handle_write() -> "%s"',
                          self.write_buffer[:sent])
        self.write_buffer = self.write_buffer[sent:]

    def handle_read(self):
        data = self.recv(8192)
        self.logger.debug('handle_read() -> %d bytes', len(data))
        self.read_buffer.write(data)
```

This main program uses the client class in a **while** loop, reading or writing data once per iteration.

```
import asyncore
import logging

from asyncore_http_client import HttpClient
```

```
logging.basicConfig(level=logging.DEBUG,
                    format='%(name)s: %(message)s',
                    )

clients = [
    HttpClient('http://www.doughellmann.com/'),
    ]

loop_counter = 0
while asyncore.socket_map:
    loop_counter += 1
    logging.debug('loop_counter=%s', loop_counter)
    asyncore.loop(timeout=1, count=1)
```

Instead of a custom local **while** loop, `asyncore.loop()` could be called in the same manner from a GUI toolkit idle handler or other mechanism for doing a small amount of work when the UI is not busy with other event handlers.

```
$ python asyncore_loop.py

http://www.doughellmann.com/: connecting to ('www.doughellmann.com',
 80)
root: loop_counter=1
http://www.doughellmann.com/: readable() -> True
http://www.doughellmann.com/: writable() -> True
http://www.doughellmann.com/: handle_connect()
http://www.doughellmann.com/: handle_write() -> "GET http://www.doug
hellmann.com/ HTTP/1.0

"
root: loop_counter=2
http://www.doughellmann.com/: readable() -> True
http://www.doughellmann.com/: handle_read() -> 1448 bytes
root: loop_counter=3
http://www.doughellmann.com/: readable() -> True
http://www.doughellmann.com/: handle_read() -> 2896 bytes
root: loop_counter=4
http://www.doughellmann.com/: readable() -> True
http://www.doughellmann.com/: handle_read() -> 1318 bytes
root: loop_counter=5
http://www.doughellmann.com/: readable() -> True
http://www.doughellmann.com/: handle_close()
http://www.doughellmann.com/: handle_read() -> 0 bytes
```

11.4.5 Working with Files

Normally, `asyncore` is used with sockets, but sometimes it is useful to read files asynchronously, too (to use files when testing network servers without requiring the network setup, or to read or write large data files in parts, for example). For these situations, `asyncore` provides the `file_dispatcher` and `file_wrapper` classes.

This example implements an asynchronous reader for files by responding with another portion of the data each time `handle_read()` is called.

```python
class FileReader(asyncore.file_dispatcher):

    def writable(self):
        return False

    def handle_read(self):
        data = self.recv(64)
        print 'READ: (%d)\n%r' % (len(data), data)

    def handle_expt(self):
        # Ignore events that look like out of band data
        pass

    def handle_close(self):
        self.close()
```

To use `FileReader()`, give it an open file handle as the only argument to the constructor.

```python
reader = FileReader(open('lorem.txt', 'r'))
asyncore.loop()
```

> **Note:** This example was tested under Python 2.7. For Python 2.5 and earlier, `file_dispatcher` does not automatically convert an open file to a file descriptor. Use `os.popen()` to open the file instead, and pass the descriptor to `FileReader`.

Running the program produces this output.

```
$ python asyncore_file_dispatcher.py

READ: (64)
'Lorem ipsum dolor sit amet, consectetuer adipiscing elit. Donec\n'
```

```
READ: (64)
'egestas, enim et consectetuer ullamcorper, lectus ligula rutrum '
READ: (5)
'leo.\n'
READ: (0)
''
```

See Also:

asyncore (http://docs.python.org/library/asyncore.html) The standard library documentation for this module.

asynchat (page 629) The `asynchat` module builds on `asyncore` to provide a framework for implementing protocols based on passing messages back and forth using a set protocol.

SocketServer (page 609) The `SocketServer` module section includes another example of the `EchoServer` with threading and forking variants.

11.5   asynchat—Asynchronous Protocol Handler

Purpose Asynchronous network communication protocol handler.
Python Version 1.5.2 and later

The `asynchat` module builds on `asyncore` to provide a framework for implementing protocols based on passing messages back and forth between server and client. The `async_chat` class is an `asyncore.dispatcher` subclass that receives data and looks for a message terminator. The subclass only needs to specify what to do when data comes in and how to respond once the terminator is found. Outgoing data is queued for transmission via FIFO objects managed by `async_chat`.

11.5.1   Message Terminators

Incoming messages are broken up based on *terminators*, which are managed for each `async_chat` instance via `set_terminator()`. There are three possible configurations.

1. If a string argument is passed to `set_terminator()`, the message is considered complete when that string appears in the input data.
2. If a numeric argument is passed, the message is considered complete when that many bytes have been read.
3. If `None` is passed, message termination is not managed by `async_chat`.

The next `EchoServer` example uses both a simple string terminator and a message length terminator, depending on the context of the incoming data. The HTTP request handler example in the standard library documentation offers another example of how to change the terminator based on the context. It uses a literal terminator while reading HTTP headers and a length value to terminate the HTTP POST request body.

11.5.2 Server and Handler

To make it easier to understand how `asynchat` is different from `asyncore`, the examples here duplicate the functionality of the `EchoServer` example from the `asyncore` discussion. The same pieces are needed: a server object to accept connections, handler objects to deal with communication with each client, and client objects to initiate the conversation.

The `EchoServer` implementation with `asynchat` is essentially the same as the one created for the `asyncore` example, but it has fewer logging calls:

```
import asyncore
import logging
import socket

from asynchat_echo_handler import EchoHandler

class EchoServer(asyncore.dispatcher):
    """Receives connections and establishes handlers for each client.
    """

    def __init__(self, address):
        asyncore.dispatcher.__init__(self)
        self.create_socket(socket.AF_INET, socket.SOCK_STREAM)
        self.bind(address)
        self.address = self.socket.getsockname()
        self.listen(1)
        return

    def handle_accept(self):
        # Called when a client connects to our socket
        client_info = self.accept()
        EchoHandler(sock=client_info[0])
        # Only deal with one client at a time,
        # so close as soon as the handler is set up.
        # Under normal conditions, the server
        # would run forever or until it received
        # instructions to stop.
```

```
        self.handle_close()
        return

    def handle_close(self):
        self.close()
```

This version of `EchoHandler` is based on `asynchat.async_chat` instead of the `asyncore.dispatcher`. It operates at a slightly higher level of abstraction, so reading and writing are handled automatically. The buffer needs to know four things:

- what to do with incoming data (by overriding `handle_incoming_data()`)
- how to recognize the end of an incoming message (via `set_terminator()`)
- what to do when a complete message is received (in `found_terminator()`)
- what data to send (using `push()`)

The example application has two operating modes. It is either waiting for a command of the form `ECHO length\n` or waiting for the data to be echoed. The mode is toggled back and forth by setting an instance variable *process_data* to the method to be invoked when the terminator is found and then changing the terminator, as appropriate.

```
import asynchat
import logging

class EchoHandler(asynchat.async_chat):
    """Handles echoing messages from a single client.
    """

    # Artificially reduce buffer sizes to illustrate
    # sending and receiving partial messages.
    ac_in_buffer_size = 128
    ac_out_buffer_size = 128

    def __init__(self, sock):
        self.received_data = []
        self.logger = logging.getLogger('EchoHandler')
        asynchat.async_chat.__init__(self, sock)
        # Start looking for the ECHO command
        self.process_data = self._process_command
        self.set_terminator('\n')
        return
```

```python
    def collect_incoming_data(self, data):
        """Read an incoming message from the client
        and put it into the outgoing queue.
        """
        self.logger.debug(
            'collect_incoming_data() -> (%d bytes) %r',
            len(data), data)
        self.received_data.append(data)

    def found_terminator(self):
        """The end of a command or message has been seen."""
        self.logger.debug('found_terminator()')
        self.process_data()

    def _process_command(self):
        """Have the full ECHO command"""
        command = ''.join(self.received_data)
        self.logger.debug('_process_command() %r', command)
        command_verb, command_arg = command.strip().split(' ')
        expected_data_len = int(command_arg)
        self.set_terminator(expected_data_len)
        self.process_data = self._process_message
        self.received_data = []

    def _process_message(self):
        """Have read the entire message."""
        to_echo = ''.join(self.received_data)
        self.logger.debug('_process_message() echoing %r',
                          to_echo)
        self.push(to_echo)
        # Disconnect after sending the entire response
        # since we only want to do one thing at a time
        self.close_when_done()
```

As soon as the complete command is found, the handler switches to message-processing mode and waits for the complete set of text to be received. When all the data is available, it is pushed onto the outgoing channel. The handler is set up to be closed once the data is sent.

11.5.3 Client

The client works in much the same way as the handler. As with the `asyncore` implementation, the message to be sent is an argument to the client's constructor. When the socket connection is established, `handle_connect()` is called so the client can send the command and message data.

The command is pushed directly, but a special "producer" class is used for the message text. The producer is polled for chunks of data to send out over the network. When the producer returns an empty string, it is assumed to be empty and writing stops.

The client expects just the message data in response, so it sets an integer terminator and collects data in a list until the entire message has been received.

```python
import asynchat
import logging
import socket


class EchoClient(asynchat.async_chat):
    """Sends messages to the server and receives responses.
    """

    # Artificially reduce buffer sizes to show
    # sending and receiving partial messages.
    ac_in_buffer_size = 128
    ac_out_buffer_size = 128

    def __init__(self, host, port, message):
        self.message = message
        self.received_data = []
        self.logger = logging.getLogger('EchoClient')
        asynchat.async_chat.__init__(self)
        self.create_socket(socket.AF_INET, socket.SOCK_STREAM)
        self.logger.debug('connecting to %s', (host, port))
        self.connect((host, port))
        return

    def handle_connect(self):
        self.logger.debug('handle_connect()')
        # Send the command
        self.push('ECHO %d\n' % len(self.message))
        # Send the data
        self.push_with_producer(
            EchoProducer(self.message,
                         buffer_size=self.ac_out_buffer_size)
            )
        # We expect the data to come back as-is,
        # so set a length-based terminator
        self.set_terminator(len(self.message))
```

```
    def collect_incoming_data(self, data):
        """Read an incoming message from the client
        and add it to the outgoing queue.
        """
        self.logger.debug(
            'collect_incoming_data() -> (%d) %r',
            len(data), data)
        self.received_data.append(data)

    def found_terminator(self):
        self.logger.debug('found_terminator()')
        received_message = ''.join(self.received_data)
        if received_message == self.message:
            self.logger.debug('RECEIVED COPY OF MESSAGE')
        else:
            self.logger.debug('ERROR IN TRANSMISSION')
            self.logger.debug('EXPECTED %r', self.message)
            self.logger.debug('RECEIVED %r', received_message)
        return


class EchoProducer(asynchat.simple_producer):

    logger = logging.getLogger('EchoProducer')

    def more(self):
        response = asynchat.simple_producer.more(self)
        self.logger.debug('more() -> (%s bytes) %r',
                          len(response), response)
        return response
```

11.5.4 Putting It All Together

The main program for this example sets up the client and server in the same `asyncore` main loop.

```
import asyncore
import logging
import socket

from asynchat_echo_server import EchoServer
from asynchat_echo_client import EchoClient
```

```
logging.basicConfig(level=logging.DEBUG,
                     format='%(name)-11s: %(message)s',
                     )

address = ('localhost', 0) # let the kernel give us a port
server = EchoServer(address)
ip, port = server.address # find out what port we were given

message_data = open('lorem.txt', 'r').read()
client = EchoClient(ip, port, message=message_data)

asyncore.loop()
```

Normally, they would run in separate processes, but this makes it easier to show the combined output.

```
$ python asynchat_echo_main.py

EchoClient : connecting to ('127.0.0.1', 52590)
EchoClient : handle_connect()
EchoProducer: more() -> (128 bytes) 'Lorem ipsum dolor sit amet,
consectetuer adipiscing elit. Donec\negestas, enim et consectetue
r ullamcorper, lectus ligula rutrum\n'
EchoProducer: more() -> (38 bytes) 'leo, a elementum elit tortor
eu quam.\n'
EchoProducer: more() -> (0 bytes) ''
EchoHandler: collect_incoming_data() -> (8 bytes) 'ECHO 166'
EchoHandler: found_terminator()
EchoHandler: _process_command() 'ECHO 166'
EchoHandler: collect_incoming_data() -> (119 bytes) 'Lorem ipsum
dolor sit amet, consectetuer adipiscing elit. Donec\negestas, eni
m et consectetuer ullamcorper, lectus ligul'
EchoHandler: collect_incoming_data() -> (47 bytes) 'a rutrum\nleo
, a elementum elit tortor eu quam.\n'
EchoHandler: found_terminator()
EchoHandler: _process_message() echoing 'Lorem ipsum dolor sit am
et, consectetuer adipiscing elit. Donec\negestas, enim et consect
etuer ullamcorper, lectus ligula rutrum\nleo, a elementum elit to
rtor eu quam.\n'
EchoClient : collect_incoming_data() -> (128) 'Lorem ipsum dolor
sit amet, consectetuer adipiscing elit. Donec\negestas, enim et c
```

```
onsectetuer ullamcorper, lectus ligula rutrum\n'
EchoClient : collect_incoming_data() -> (38) 'leo, a elementum el
it tortor eu quam.\n'
EchoClient : found_terminator()
EchoClient : RECEIVED COPY OF MESSAGE
```

See Also:
asynchat (http://docs.python.org/library/asynchat.html) The standard library documentation for this module.

asyncore (page 619) The `asyncore` module implements an lower-level asynchronous I/O event loop.

Chapter 12

THE INTERNET

The Internet is a pervasive aspect of modern computing. Even small, single-use scripts frequently interact with remote services to send or receive data. Python's rich set of tools for working with web protocols makes it well suited for programming web-based applications, either as a client or a server.

The `urlparse` module manipulates URL strings, splitting and combining their components, and is useful in clients and servers.

There are two client-side APIs for accessing web resources. The original `urllib` and updated `urllib2` offer similar APIs for retrieving content remotely, but `urllib2` is easier to extend with new protocols and the `urllib2.Request` provides a way to add custom headers to outgoing requests.

HTTP POST requests are usually "form encoded" with `urllib`. Binary data sent through a POST should be encoded with `base64` first, to comply with the message format standard.

Well-behaved clients that access many sites as spiders or crawlers should use `robotparser` to ensure they have permission before placing a heavy load on the remote server.

To create a custom web server with Python, without requiring any external frameworks, use `BaseHTTPServer` as a starting point. It handles the HTTP protocol, so the only customization needed is the application code for responding to the incoming requests.

Session state in the server can be managed through cookies created and parsed by the `Cookie` module. Full support for expiration, path, domain, and other cookie settings makes it easy to configure the session.

The `uuid` module is used for generating identifiers for resources that need unique values. UUIDs are good for automatically generating Uniform Resource Name (URN) values, where the name of the resource needs to be unique but does not need to convey any meaning.

Python's standard library includes support for two web-based remote procedure-call mechanisms. The JavaScript Object Notation (JSON) encoding scheme used in AJAX communication is implemented in `json`. It works equally well in the client or the server. Complete XML-RPC client and server libraries are also included in `xmlrpclib` and `SimpleXMLRPCServer`, respectively.

12.1   urlparse—Split URLs into Components

Purpose Split URL into components.
Python Version 1.4 and later

The `urlparse` module provides functions for breaking URLs down into their component parts, as defined by the relevant RFCs.

12.1.1   Parsing

The return value from the `urlparse()` function is an object that acts like a `tuple` with six elements.

```
from urlparse import urlparse

url = 'http://netloc/path;param?query=arg#frag'
parsed = urlparse(url)
print parsed
```

The parts of the URL available through the tuple interface are the scheme, network location, path, path-segment parameters (separated from the path by a semicolon), query, and fragment.

```
$ python urlparse_urlparse.py

ParseResult(scheme='http', netloc='netloc', path='/path',
params='param', query='query=arg', fragment='frag')
```

Although the return value acts like a tuple, it is really based on a `namedtuple`, a subclass of `tuple` that supports accessing the parts of the URL via named attributes as well as indexes. In addition to being easier to use for the programmer, the attribute API also offers access to several values not available in the `tuple` API.

```
from urlparse import urlparse

url = 'http://user:pwd@NetLoc:80/path;param?query=arg#frag'
parsed = urlparse(url)
print 'scheme   :', parsed.scheme
print 'netloc   :', parsed.netloc
print 'path     :', parsed.path
print 'params   :', parsed.params
print 'query    :', parsed.query
print 'fragment:', parsed.fragment
print 'username:', parsed.username
print 'password:', parsed.password
print 'hostname:', parsed.hostname, '(netloc in lowercase)'
print 'port     :', parsed.port
```

The *username* and *password* are available when present in the input URL and set to `None` when not. The *hostname* is the same value as *netloc*, in all lowercase. And the *port* is converted to an integer when present and `None` when not.

```
$ python urlparse_urlparseattrs.py

scheme   : http
netloc   : user:pwd@NetLoc:80
path     : /path
params   : param
query    : query=arg
fragment: frag
username: user
password: pwd
hostname: netloc (netloc in lowercase)
port     : 80
```

The `urlsplit()` function is an alternative to `urlparse()`. It behaves a little differently because it does not split the parameters from the URL. This is useful for URLs following RFC 2396, which supports parameters for each segment of the path.

```
from urlparse import urlsplit

url = 'http://user:pwd@NetLoc:80/p1;param/p2;param?query=arg#frag'
parsed = urlsplit(url)
print parsed
print 'scheme   :', parsed.scheme
```

```
print 'netloc  :', parsed.netloc
print 'path    :', parsed.path
print 'query   :', parsed.query
print 'fragment:', parsed.fragment
print 'username:', parsed.username
print 'password:', parsed.password
print 'hostname:', parsed.hostname, '(netloc in lowercase)'
print 'port    :', parsed.port
```

Since the parameters are not split out, the tuple API will show five elements instead of six, and there is no *params* attribute.

```
$ python urlparse_urlsplit.py

SplitResult(scheme='http', netloc='user:pwd@NetLoc:80',
path='/p1;param/p2;param', query='query=arg', fragment='frag')
scheme  : http
netloc  : user:pwd@NetLoc:80
path    : /p1;param/p2;param
query   : query=arg
fragment: frag
username: user
password: pwd
hostname: netloc (netloc in lowercase)
port    : 80
```

To simply strip the fragment identifier from a URL, such as when finding a base page name from a URL, use urldefrag().

```
from urlparse import urldefrag

original = 'http://netloc/path;param?query=arg#frag'
print 'original:', original
url, fragment = urldefrag(original)
print 'url     :', url
print 'fragment:', fragment
```

The return value is a tuple containing the base URL and the fragment.

```
$ python urlparse_urldefrag.py

original: http://netloc/path;param?query=arg#frag
url     : http://netloc/path;param?query=arg
fragment: frag
```

12.1.2   Unparsing

There are several ways to assemble the parts of a split URL back together into a single string. The parsed URL object has a `geturl()` method.

```
from urlparse import urlparse

original = 'http://netloc/path;param?query=arg#frag'
print 'ORIG   :', original
parsed = urlparse(original)
print 'PARSED:', parsed.geturl()
```

`geturl()` only works on the object returned by `urlparse()` or `urlsplit()`.

```
$ python urlparse_geturl.py

ORIG   : http://netloc/path;param?query=arg#frag
PARSED: http://netloc/path;param?query=arg#frag
```

A regular tuple containing strings can be combined into a URL with `urlunparse()`.

```
from urlparse import urlparse, urlunparse

original = 'http://netloc/path;param?query=arg#frag'
print 'ORIG   :', original
parsed = urlparse(original)
print 'PARSED:', type(parsed), parsed
t = parsed[:]
print 'TUPLE :', type(t), t
print 'NEW   :', urlunparse(t)
```

While the `ParseResult` returned by `urlparse()` can be used as a tuple, this example explicitly creates a new tuple to show that `urlunparse()` works with normal tuples, too.

```
$ python urlparse_urlunparse.py

ORIG   : http://netloc/path;param?query=arg#frag
PARSED: <class 'urlparse.ParseResult'> ParseResult(scheme='http',
netloc='netloc', path='/path', params='param', query='query=arg',
fragment='frag')
```

```
TUPLE : <type 'tuple'> ('http', 'netloc', '/path', 'param',
'query=arg', 'frag')
NEW    : http://netloc/path;param?query=arg#frag
```

If the input URL included superfluous parts, those may be dropped from the reconstructed URL.

```
from urlparse import urlparse, urlunparse

original = 'http://netloc/path;?#'
print 'ORIG   :', original
parsed = urlparse(original)
print 'PARSED:', type(parsed), parsed
t = parsed[:]
print 'TUPLE :', type(t), t
print 'NEW    :', urlunparse(t)
```

In this case, *parameters*, *query*, and *fragment* are all missing in the original URL. The new URL does not look the same as the original, but it is equivalent according to the standard.

```
$ python urlparse_urlunparseextra.py

ORIG   : http://netloc/path;?#
PARSED: <class 'urlparse.ParseResult'> ParseResult(scheme='http',
netloc='netloc', path='/path', params='', query='', fragment='')
TUPLE : <type 'tuple'> ('http', 'netloc', '/path', '', '', '')
NEW    : http://netloc/path
```

12.1.3   Joining

In addition to parsing URLs, urlparse includes urljoin() for constructing absolute URLs from relative fragments.

```
from urlparse import urljoin

print urljoin('http://www.example.com/path/file.html',
              'anotherfile.html')
print urljoin('http://www.example.com/path/file.html',
              '../anotherfile.html')
```

In the example, the relative portion of the path (". . /") is taken into account when the second URL is computed.

```
$ python urlparse_urljoin.py

http://www.example.com/path/anotherfile.html
http://www.example.com/anotherfile.html
```

Nonrelative paths are handled in the same way as `os.path.join()` handles them.

```
from urlparse import urljoin

print urljoin('http://www.example.com/path/',
              '/subpath/file.html')
print urljoin('http://www.example.com/path/',
              'subpath/file.html')
```

If the path being joined to the URL starts with a slash (/), it resets the URL's path to the top level. If it does not start with a slash, it is appended to the end of the URL's path.

```
$ python urlparse_urljoin_with_path.py

http://www.example.com/subpath/file.html
http://www.example.com/path/subpath/file.html
```

See Also:
urlparse (http://docs.python.org/lib/module-urlparse.html) Standard library documentation for this module.
urllib (page 651) Retrieve the contents of a resource identified by a URL.
urllib2 (page 657) Alternative API for accessing remote URLs.
RFC 1738 (http://tools.ietf.org/html/rfc1738.html) Uniform Resource Locator (URL) syntax.
RFC 1808 (http://tools.ietf.org/html/rfc1808.html) Relative URLs.
RFC 2396 (http://tools.ietf.org/html/rfc2396.html) Uniform Resource Identifier (URI) generic syntax.
RFC 3986 (http://tools.ietf.org/html/rfc3986.html) Uniform Resource Identifier (URI) syntax.

12.2 BaseHTTPServer—Base Classes for Implementing Web Servers

Purpose BaseHTTPServer includes classes that can form the basis of a web server.
Python Version 1.4 and later

BaseHTTPServer uses classes from SocketServer to create base classes for making HTTP servers. HTTPServer can be used directly, but the BaseHTTPRequestHandler is intended to be extended to handle each protocol method (GET, POST, etc.).

12.2.1 HTTP GET

To add support for an HTTP method in a request-handler class, implement the method do_METHOD(), replacing *METHOD* with the name of the HTTP method (e.g., do_GET(), do_POST(), etc.). For consistency, the request-handler methods take no arguments. All the parameters for the request are parsed by BaseHTTPRequestHandler and stored as instance attributes of the request instance.

This example request handler illustrates how to return a response to the client and includes some local attributes that can be useful in building the response.

```
from BaseHTTPServer import BaseHTTPRequestHandler
import urlparse

class GetHandler(BaseHTTPRequestHandler):

    def do_GET(self):
        parsed_path = urlparse.urlparse(self.path)
        message_parts = [
                'CLIENT VALUES:',
                'client_address=%s (%s)' % (self.client_address,
                                            self.address_string()),
                'command=%s' % self.command,
                'path=%s' % self.path,
                'real path=%s' % parsed_path.path,
                'query=%s' % parsed_path.query,
                'request_version=%s' % self.request_version,
                '',
                'SERVER VALUES:',
                'server_version=%s' % self.server_version,
                'sys_version=%s' % self.sys_version,
```

```
                'protocol_version=%s' % self.protocol_version,
                '',
                'HEADERS RECEIVED:',
                ]
        for name, value in sorted(self.headers.items()):
            message_parts.append('%s=%s' % (name, value.rstrip()))
        message_parts.append('')
        message = '\r\n'.join(message_parts)
        self.send_response(200)
        self.end_headers()
        self.wfile.write(message)
        return


if __name__ == '__main__':
    from BaseHTTPServer import HTTPServer
    server = HTTPServer(('localhost', 8080), GetHandler)
    print 'Starting server, use <Ctrl-C> to stop'
    server.serve_forever()
```

The message text is assembled and then written to `wfile`, the file handle wrapping the response socket. Each response needs a response code, set via `send_response()`. If an error code is used (404, 501, etc.), an appropriate default error message is included in the header, or a message can be passed with the error code.

To run the request handler in a server, pass it to the constructor of `HTTPServer`, as in the __main__ processing portion of the sample script.

Then start the server.

```
$ python BaseHTTPServer_GET.py

Starting server, use <Ctrl-C> to stop
```

In a separate terminal, use **curl** to access it.

```
$ curl -i http://localhost:8080/?foo=bar

HTTP/1.0 200 OK

Server: BaseHTTP/0.3 Python/2.5.1
Date: Sun, 09 Dec 2007 16:00:34 GMT

CLIENT VALUES:
client_address=('127.0.0.1', 51275) (localhost)
```

```
command=GET
path=/?foo=bar
real path=/
query=foo=bar
request_version=HTTP/1.1

SERVER VALUES:
server_version=BaseHTTP/0.3
sys_version=Python/2.5.1
protocol_version=HTTP/1.0
```

12.2.2   HTTP POST

Supporting POST requests is a little more work because the base class does not parse
the form data automatically. The cgi module provides the FieldStorage class, which
knows how to parse the form if it is given the correct inputs.

```python
from BaseHTTPServer import BaseHTTPRequestHandler
import cgi

class PostHandler(BaseHTTPRequestHandler):

    def do_POST(self):
        # Parse the form data posted
        form = cgi.FieldStorage(
            fp=self.rfile,
            headers=self.headers,
            environ={'REQUEST_METHOD':'POST',
                     'CONTENT_TYPE':self.headers['Content-Type'],
                     })

        # Begin the response
        self.send_response(200)
        self.end_headers()
        self.wfile.write('Client: %s\n' % str(self.client_address))
        self.wfile.write('User-agent: %s\n' %
                        str(self.headers['user-agent']))
        self.wfile.write('Path: %s\n' % self.path)
        self.wfile.write('Form data:\n')

        # Echo back information about what was posted in the form
        for field in form.keys():
            field_item = form[field]
```

```
        if field_item.filename:
            # The field contains an uploaded file
            file_data = field_item.file.read()
            file_len = len(file_data)
            del file_data
            self.wfile.write(
                '\tUploaded %s as "%s" (%d bytes)\n' % \
                    (field, field_item.filename, file_len))
        else:
            # Regular form value
            self.wfile.write('\t%s=%s\n' %
                                (field, form[field].value))
    return

if __name__ == '__main__':
    from BaseHTTPServer import HTTPServer
    server = HTTPServer(('localhost', 8080), PostHandler)
    print 'Starting server, use <Ctrl-C> to stop'
    server.serve_forever()
```

Run the server in one window.

```
$ python BaseHTTPServer_POST.py

Starting server, use <Ctrl-C> to stop
```

The arguments to **curl** can include form data to be posted to the server by using the -F option. The last argument, -F datafile=@BaseHTTPServer_GET.py, posts the contents of the file BaseHTTPServer_GET.py to illustrate reading file data from the form.

```
$ curl http://localhost:8080/ -F name=dhellmann -F foo=bar \
-F datafile=@BaseHTTPServer_GET.py

Client: ('127.0.0.1', 65029)
User-agent: curl/7.19.7 (universal-apple-darwin10.0) libcurl/7.19.7
OpenSSL/0.9.8l zlib/1.2.3
Path: /
Form data:
    Uploaded datafile as "BaseHTTPServer_GET.py" (2580 bytes)
    foo=bar
    name=dhellmann
```

12.2.3 Threading and Forking

HTTPServer is a simple subclass of SocketServer.TCPServer and does not use multiple threads or processes to handle requests. To add threading or forking, create a new class using the appropriate mix-in from SocketServer.

```python
from BaseHTTPServer import HTTPServer, BaseHTTPRequestHandler
from SocketServer import ThreadingMixIn
import threading

class Handler(BaseHTTPRequestHandler):

    def do_GET(self):
        self.send_response(200)
        self.end_headers()
        message = threading.currentThread().getName()
        self.wfile.write(message)
        self.wfile.write('\n')
        return

class ThreadedHTTPServer(ThreadingMixIn, HTTPServer):
    """Handle requests in a separate thread."""

if __name__ == '__main__':
    server = ThreadedHTTPServer(('localhost', 8080), Handler)
    print 'Starting server, use <Ctrl-C> to stop'
    server.serve_forever()
```

Run the server in the same way as the other examples.

```
$ python BaseHTTPServer_threads.py

Starting server, use <Ctrl-C> to stop
```

Each time the server receives a request, it starts a new thread or process to handle it.

```
$ curl http://localhost:8080/

Thread-1

$ curl http://localhost:8080/
```

```
Thread-2

$ curl http://localhost:8080/

Thread-3
```

Swapping `ForkingMixIn` for `ThreadingMixIn` would achieve similar results, using separate processes instead of threads.

12.2.4   Handling Errors

Handle errors by calling `send_error()`, passing the appropriate error code and an optional error message. The entire response (with headers, status code, and body) is generated automatically.

```
from BaseHTTPServer import BaseHTTPRequestHandler

class ErrorHandler(BaseHTTPRequestHandler):

    def do_GET(self):
        self.send_error(404)
        return

if __name__ == '__main__':
    from BaseHTTPServer import HTTPServer
    server = HTTPServer(('localhost', 8080), ErrorHandler)
    print 'Starting server, use <Ctrl-C> to stop'
    server.serve_forever()
```

In this case, a 404 error is always returned.

```
$ python BaseHTTPServer_errors.py

Starting server, use <Ctrl-C> to stop
```

The error message is reported to the client using an HTML document, as well as the header to indicate an error code.

```
$ curl -i http://localhost:8080/

HTTP/1.0 404 Not Found
Server: BaseHTTP/0.3 Python/2.5.1
```

```
Date: Sun, 09 Dec 2007 15:49:44 GMT
Content-Type: text/html
Connection: close

<head>
<title>Error response</title>
</head>
<body>
<h1>Error response</h1>
<p>Error code 404.
<p>Message: Not Found.
<p>Error code explanation: 404 = Nothing matches the given URI.
</body>
```

12.2.5 Setting Headers

The `send_header` method adds header data to the HTTP response. It takes two arguments: the name of the header and the value.

```python
from BaseHTTPServer import BaseHTTPRequestHandler
import urlparse
import time

class GetHandler(BaseHTTPRequestHandler):

    def do_GET(self):
        self.send_response(200)
        self.send_header('Last-Modified',
                         self.date_time_string(time.time()))
        self.end_headers()
        self.wfile.write('Response body\n')
        return

if __name__ == '__main__':
    from BaseHTTPServer import HTTPServer
    server = HTTPServer(('localhost', 8080), GetHandler)
    print 'Starting server, use <Ctrl-C> to stop'
    server.serve_forever()
```

This example sets the `Last-Modified` header to the current timestamp, formatted according to RFC 2822.

```
$ curl -i http://localhost:8080/

HTTP/1.0 200 OK
Server: BaseHTTP/0.3 Python/2.7
Date: Sun, 10 Oct 2010 13:58:32 GMT
Last-Modified: Sun, 10 Oct 2010 13:58:32 -0000

Response body
```

The server logs the request to the terminal, as in the other examples.

```
$ python BaseHTTPServer_send_header.py

Starting server, use <Ctrl-C> to stop
```

See Also:
BaseHTTPServer (http://docs.python.org/library/basehttpserver.html) The standard library documentation for this module.
SocketServer (page 609) The SocketServer module provides the base class that handles the raw socket connection.
RFC 2822 (http://tools.ietf.org/html/rfc2822.html) The "Internet Message Format" specifies a format for text-based messages, such as email and HTTP responses.

12.3   urllib—Network Resource Access

Purpose Accessing remote resources that do not need authentication, cookies, etc.
Python Version 1.4 and later

The urllib module provides a simple interface for network resource access. It also includes functions for encoding and quoting arguments to be passed over HTTP to a server.

12.3.1   Simple Retrieval with Cache

Downloading data is a common operation, and urllib includes the urlretrieve() function to meet this need. urlretrieve() takes arguments for the URL, a temporary file to hold the data, a function to report on download progress, and data to pass if the URL refers to a form where data should be posted. If no filename is given, urlretrieve() creates a temporary file. The calling program can delete the file directly or treat the file as a cache and use urlcleanup() to remove it.

This example uses an HTTP GET request to retrieve some data from a web server.

```python
import urllib
import os

def reporthook(blocks_read, block_size, total_size):
    """total_size is reported in bytes.
    block_size is the amount read each time.
    blocks_read is the number of blocks successfully read.
    """
    if not blocks_read:
        print 'Connection opened'
        return
    if total_size < 0:
        # Unknown size
        print 'Read %d blocks (%d bytes)' % (blocks_read,
                                             blocks_read * block_size)
    else:
        amount_read = blocks_read * block_size
        print 'Read %d blocks, or %d/%d' % \
            (blocks_read, amount_read, total_size)
    return

try:
    filename, msg = urllib.urlretrieve(
        'http://blog.doughellmann.com/',
        reporthook=reporthook)
    print
    print 'File:', filename
    print 'Headers:'
    print msg
    print 'File exists before cleanup:', os.path.exists(filename)

finally:
    urllib.urlcleanup()

    print 'File still exists:', os.path.exists(filename)
```

Each time data is read from the server, reporthook() is called to report the download progress. The three arguments are the number of blocks read so far, the size (in bytes) of the blocks, and the size (in bytes) of the resource being downloaded. When the server does not return a `Content-length` header, `urlretrieve()` does not know how big the data should be and passes −1 as the *total_size* argument.

```
$ python urllib_urlretrieve.py

Connection opened
Read 1 blocks (8192 bytes)
Read 2 blocks (16384 bytes)
Read 3 blocks (24576 bytes)
Read 4 blocks (32768 bytes)
Read 5 blocks (40960 bytes)
Read 6 blocks (49152 bytes)
Read 7 blocks (57344 bytes)
Read 8 blocks (65536 bytes)
Read 9 blocks (73728 bytes)
Read 10 blocks (81920 bytes)
Read 11 blocks (90112 bytes)
Read 12 blocks (98304 bytes)

File: /var/folders/9R/9R1t+tR02Raxzk+F71Q50U+++Uw/-Tmp-/tmpYI9AuC
Headers:
Content-Type: text/html; charset=UTF-8
Expires: Fri, 07 Jan 2011 14:23:06 GMT
Date: Fri, 07 Jan 2011 14:23:06 GMT
Last-Modified: Tue, 04 Jan 2011 12:32:04 GMT
ETag: "f2108552-7c52-4c50-8838-8300645c40be"
X-Content-Type-Options: nosniff
X-XSS-Protection: 1; mode=block
Server: GSE
Cache-Control: public, max-age=0, proxy-revalidate, must-revalidate
Age: 0

File exists before cleanup: True
File still exists: False
```

12.3.2 Encoding Arguments

Arguments can be passed to the server by encoding them and appending them to the URL.

```
import urllib

query_args = { 'q':'query string', 'foo':'bar' }
encoded_args = urllib.urlencode(query_args)
```

```
print 'Encoded:', encoded_args

url = 'http://localhost:8080/?' + encoded_args
print urllib.urlopen(url).read()
```

The query, in the list of client values, contains the encoded query arguments.

```
$ python urllib_urlencode.py

Encoded: q=query+string&foo=bar
CLIENT VALUES:
client_address=('127.0.0.1', 54415) (localhost)
command=GET
path=/?q=query+string&foo=bar
real path=/
query=q=query+string&foo=bar
request_version=HTTP/1.0

SERVER VALUES:
server_version=BaseHTTP/0.3
sys_version=Python/2.5.1
protocol_version=HTTP/1.0
```

To pass a sequence of values using separate occurrences of the variable in the query string, set *doseq* to True when calling `urlencode()`.

```
import urllib

query_args = { 'foo':['foo1', 'foo2'] }
print 'Single  :', urllib.urlencode(query_args)
print 'Sequence:', urllib.urlencode(query_args, doseq=True  )
```

The result is a query string with several values associated with the same name.

```
$ python urllib_urlencode_doseq.py

Single  : foo=%5B%27foo1%27%2C+%27foo2%27%5D
Sequence: foo=foo1&foo=foo2
```

To decode the query string, see the `FieldStorage` class from the `cgi` module.

Special characters within the query arguments that might cause parse problems with the URL on the server side are "quoted" when passed to `urlencode()`. To quote them locally to make safe versions of the strings, use the `quote()` or `quote_plus()` functions directly.

```
import urllib

url = 'http://localhost:8080/~dhellmann/'
print 'urlencode() :', urllib.urlencode({'url':url})
print 'quote()     :', urllib.quote(url)
print 'quote_plus():', urllib.quote_plus(url)
```

The quoting implementation in `quote_plus()` is more aggressive about the characters it replaces.

```
$ python urllib_quote.py

urlencode() : url=http%3A%2F%2Flocalhost%3A8080%2F%7Edhellmann%2F
quote()     : http%3A//localhost%3A8080/%7Edhellmann/
quote_plus(): http%3A%2F%2Flocalhost%3A8080%2F%7Edhellmann%2F
```

To reverse the quote operations, use `unquote()` or `unquote_plus()`, as appropriate.

```
import urllib

print urllib.unquote('http%3A//localhost%3A8080/%7Edhellmann/')
print urllib.unquote_plus(
    'http%3A%2F%2Flocalhost%3A8080%2F%7Edhellmann%2F'
    )
```

The encoded value is converted back to a normal string URL.

```
$ python urllib_unquote.py

http://localhost:8080/~dhellmann/
http://localhost:8080/~dhellmann/
```

12.3.3 Paths vs. URLs

Some operating systems use different values for separating the components of paths in local files than URLs. To make code portable, use the functions `pathname2url()` and `url2pathname()` to convert back and forth.

> **Note:** Since these examples were prepared under Mac OS X, they have to explicitly import the Windows versions of the functions. Using the versions of the functions exported by `urllib` provides the correct defaults for the current platform, so most programs do not need to do this.

```python
import os

from urllib import pathname2url, url2pathname

print '== Default =='
path = '/a/b/c'
print 'Original:', path
print 'URL     :', pathname2url(path)
print 'Path    :', url2pathname('/d/e/f')
print

from nturl2path import pathname2url, url2pathname

print '== Windows, without drive letter =='
path = r'\a\b\c'
print 'Original:', path
print 'URL     :', pathname2url(path)
print 'Path    :', url2pathname('/d/e/f')
print

print '== Windows, with drive letter =='
path = r'C:\a\b\c'
print 'Original:', path
print 'URL     :', pathname2url(path)
print 'Path    :', url2pathname('/d/e/f')
```

There are two Windows examples, with and without the drive letter at the prefix of the path.

```
$ python urllib_pathnames.py

== Default ==
Original: /a/b/c
URL     : /a/b/c
Path    : /d/e/f
```

```
== Windows, without drive letter ==
Original: \a\b\c
URL      : /a/b/c
Path     : \d\e\f

== Windows, with drive letter ==
Original: C:\a\b\c
URL      : ///C:/a/b/c
Path     : \d\e\f
```

See Also:
urllib (http://docs.python.org/lib/module-urllib.html) Standard library documentation for this module.
urllib2 (page 657) Updated API for working with URL-based services.
urlparse (page 638) Parse URL values to access their components.

12.4 urllib2—Network Resource Access

> **Purpose** A library for opening URLs that can be extended by defining custom protocol handlers.
> **Python Version** 2.1 and later

The urllib2 module provides an updated API for using Internet resources identified by URLs. It is designed to be extended by individual applications to support new protocols or add variations to existing protocols (such as handling HTTP basic authentication).

12.4.1 HTTP GET

> **Note:** The test server for these examples is in BaseHTTPServer_GET.py, from the examples for the BaseHTTPServer module. Start the server in one terminal window, and then run these examples in another.

As with urllib, an HTTP GET operation is the simplest use of urllib2. Pass the URL to urlopen() to get a "file-like" handle to the remote data.

```
import urllib2

response = urllib2.urlopen('http://localhost:8080/')
print 'RESPONSE:', response
print 'URL     :', response.geturl()

headers = response.info()
print 'DATE     :', headers['date']
print 'HEADERS :'
print '---------'
print headers

data = response.read()
print 'LENGTH  :', len(data)
print 'DATA     :'
print '---------'
print data
```

The example server accepts the incoming values and formats a plain-text response to send back. The return value from `urlopen()` gives access to the headers from the HTTP server through the `info()` method and the data for the remote resource via methods like `read()` and `readlines()`.

```
$ python urllib2_urlopen.py

RESPONSE: <addinfourl at 11940488 whose fp = <socket._fileobject
object at 0xb573f0>>
URL     : http://localhost:8080/
DATE    : Sun, 19 Jul 2009 14:01:31 GMT
HEADERS :
---------
Server: BaseHTTP/0.3 Python/2.6.2
Date: Sun, 19 Jul 2009 14:01:31 GMT

LENGTH  : 349
DATA    :
---------
CLIENT VALUES:
client_address=('127.0.0.1', 55836) (localhost)
command=GET
path=/
real path=/
```

```
query=
request_version=HTTP/1.1

SERVER VALUES:
server_version=BaseHTTP/0.3
sys_version=Python/2.6.2
protocol_version=HTTP/1.0

HEADERS RECEIVED:
accept-encoding=identity
connection=close
host=localhost:8080
user-agent=Python-urllib/2.6
```

The file-like object returned by `urlopen()` is iterable.

```
import urllib2

response = urllib2.urlopen('http://localhost:8080/')
for line in response:
    print line.rstrip()
```

This example strips the trailing newlines and carriage returns before printing the output.

```
$ python urllib2_urlopen_iterator.py

CLIENT VALUES:
client_address=('127.0.0.1', 55840) (localhost)
command=GET
path=/
real path=/
query=
request_version=HTTP/1.1

SERVER VALUES:
server_version=BaseHTTP/0.3
sys_version=Python/2.6.2
protocol_version=HTTP/1.0

HEADERS RECEIVED:
accept-encoding=identity
```

```
connection=close
host=localhost:8080
user-agent=Python-urllib/2.6
```

12.4.2   Encoding Arguments

Arguments can be passed to the server by encoding them with `urllib.urlencode()` and appending them to the URL.

```python
import urllib
import urllib2

query_args = { 'q':'query string', 'foo':'bar' }
encoded_args = urllib.urlencode(query_args)
print 'Encoded:', encoded_args

url = 'http://localhost:8080/?' + encoded_args
print urllib2.urlopen(url).read()
```

The list of client values returned in the example output contains the encoded query arguments.

```
$ python urllib2_http_get_args.py

Encoded: q=query+string&foo=bar
CLIENT VALUES:
client_address=('127.0.0.1', 55849) (localhost)
command=GET
path=/?q=query+string&foo=bar
real path=/
query=q=query+string&foo=bar
request_version=HTTP/1.1

SERVER VALUES:
server_version=BaseHTTP/0.3
sys_version=Python/2.6.2
protocol_version=HTTP/1.0

HEADERS RECEIVED:
accept-encoding=identity
connection=close
```

```
host=localhost:8080
user-agent=Python-urllib/2.6
```

12.4.3 HTTP POST

> **Note:** The test server for these examples is in `BaseHTTPServer_POST.py`, from the examples for the `BaseHTTPServer` module. Start the server in one terminal window, and then run these examples in another.

To send form-encoded data to the remote server using POST instead GET, pass the encoded query arguments as data to `urlopen()`.

```python
import urllib
import urllib2

query_args = { 'q':'query string', 'foo':'bar' }
encoded_args = urllib.urlencode(query_args)
url = 'http://localhost:8080/'
print urllib2.urlopen(url, encoded_args).read()
```

The server can decode the form data and access the individual values by name.

```
$ python urllib2_urlopen_post.py

Client: ('127.0.0.1', 55943)
User-agent: Python-urllib/2.6
Path: /
Form data:
    q=query string
    foo=bar
```

12.4.4 Adding Outgoing Headers

`urlopen()` is a convenience function that hides some of the details of how the request is made and handled. More precise control is possible by using a `Request` instance directly. For example, custom headers can be added to the outgoing request to control the format of data returned, specify the version of a document cached locally, and tell the remote server the name of the software client communicating with it.

As the output from the earlier examples shows, the default *User-agent* header value is made up of the constant `Python-urllib`, followed by the Python interpreter version. When creating an application that will access web resources owned by someone else, it is courteous to include real user-agent information in the requests, so they can identify the source of the hits more easily. Using a custom agent also allows them to control crawlers using a `robots.txt` file (see the `robotparser` module).

```python
import urllib2

request = urllib2.Request('http://localhost:8080/')
request.add_header(
    'User-agent',
    'PyMOTW (http://www.doughellmann.com/PyMOTW/)',
    )

response = urllib2.urlopen(request)
data = response.read()
print data
```

After creating a `Request` object, use `add_header()` to set the user-agent value before opening the request. The last line of the output shows the custom value.

```
$ python urllib2_request_header.py

CLIENT VALUES:
client_address=('127.0.0.1', 55876) (localhost)
command=GET
path=/
real path=/
query=
request_version=HTTP/1.1

SERVER VALUES:
server_version=BaseHTTP/0.3
sys_version=Python/2.6.2
protocol_version=HTTP/1.0

HEADERS RECEIVED:
accept-encoding=identity
connection=close
host=localhost:8080
user-agent=PyMOTW (http://www.doughellmann.com/PyMOTW/)
```

12.4.5   Posting Form Data from a Request

The outgoing data can be added to the `Request` to have it posted to the server.

```
import urllib
import urllib2

query_args = { 'q':'query string', 'foo':'bar' }

request = urllib2.Request('http://localhost:8080/')
print 'Request method before data:', request.get_method()

request.add_data(urllib.urlencode(query_args))
print 'Request method after data :', request.get_method()
request.add_header(
    'User-agent',
    'PyMOTW (http://www.doughellmann.com/PyMOTW/)',
    )

print
print 'OUTGOING DATA:'
print request.get_data()

print
print 'SERVER RESPONSE:'
print urllib2.urlopen(request).read()
```

The HTTP method used by the `Request` automatically changes from GET to POST after the data is added.

```
$ python urllib2_request_post.py

Request method before data: GET
Request method after data : POST

OUTGOING DATA:
q=query+string&foo=bar

SERVER RESPONSE:
Client: ('127.0.0.1', 56044)
User-agent: PyMOTW (http://www.doughellmann.com/PyMOTW/)
Path: /
Form data:
```

```
q=query string
foo=bar
```

> **Note:**   Although the method is named `add_data()`, its effect is *not* cumulative. Each call replaces the previous data.

12.4.6   Uploading Files

Encoding files for upload requires a little more work than simple forms. A complete MIME message needs to be constructed in the body of the request so that the server can distinguish incoming form fields from uploaded files.

```python
import itertools
import mimetools
import mimetypes
from cStringIO import StringIO
import urllib
import urllib2


class MultiPartForm(object):
    """Accumulate the data to be used when posting a form."""

    def __init__(self):
        self.form_fields = []
        self.files = []
        self.boundary = mimetools.choose_boundary()
        return

    def get_content_type(self):
        return 'multipart/form-data; boundary=%s' % self.boundary

    def add_field(self, name, value):
        """Add a simple field to the form data."""
        self.form_fields.append((name, value))
        return

    def add_file(self, fieldname, filename, fileHandle,
                 mimetype=None):
        """Add a file to be uploaded."""
        body = fileHandle.read()
        if mimetype is None:
```

```
            mimetype = ( mimetypes.guess_type(filename)[0]
                         or
                         'application/octet-stream'
                         )
        self.files.append((fieldname, filename, mimetype, body))
        return

    def __str__(self):
        """Return a string representing the form data,
        including attached files.
        """
        # Build a list of lists, each containing "lines" of the
        # request.  Each part is separated by a boundary string.
        # Once the list is built, return a string where each
        # line is separated by '\r\n'.
        parts = []
        part_boundary = '--' + self.boundary

        # Add the form fields
        parts.extend(
            [ part_boundary,
              'Content-Disposition: form-data; name="%s"' % name,
              '',
              value,
            ]
            for name, value in self.form_fields
            )

        # Add the files to upload
        parts.extend([
            part_boundary,
            'Content-Disposition: file; name="%s"; filename="%s"' % \
               (field_name, filename),
            'Content-Type: %s' % content_type,
            '',
            body,
          ]
          for field_name, filename, content_type, body in self.files
          )

        # Flatten the list and add closing boundary marker, and
        # then return CR+LF separated data
        flattened = list(itertools.chain(*parts))
```

```
            flattened.append('--' + self.boundary + '--')
            flattened.append('')
            return '\r\n'.join(flattened)

if __name__ == '__main__':
    # Create the form with simple fields
    form = MultiPartForm()
    form.add_field('firstname', 'Doug')
    form.add_field('lastname', 'Hellmann')

    # Add a fake file
    form.add_file(
        'biography', 'bio.txt',
        fileHandle=StringIO('Python developer and blogger.'))

    # Build the request
    request = urllib2.Request('http://localhost:8080/')
    request.add_header(
        'User-agent',
        'PyMOTW (http://www.doughellmann.com/PyMOTW/)')
    body = str(form)
    request.add_header('Content-type', form.get_content_type())
    request.add_header('Content-length', len(body))
    request.add_data(body)

    print
    print 'OUTGOING DATA:'
    print request.get_data()

    print
    print 'SERVER RESPONSE:'
    print urllib2.urlopen(request).read()
```

The `MultiPartForm` class can represent an arbitrary form as a multipart MIME message with attached files.

```
$ python urllib2_upload_files.py

OUTGOING DATA:
--192.168.1.17.527.30074.1248020372.206.1
Content-Disposition: form-data; name="firstname"
```

```
Doug
--192.168.1.17.527.30074.1248020372.206.1
Content-Disposition: form-data; name="lastname"

Hellmann
--192.168.1.17.527.30074.1248020372.206.1
Content-Disposition: file; name="biography"; filename="bio.txt"
Content-Type: text/plain

Python developer and blogger.
--192.168.1.17.527.30074.1248020372.206.1--


SERVER RESPONSE:
Client: ('127.0.0.1', 57126)
User-agent: PyMOTW (http://www.doughellmann.com/PyMOTW/)
Path: /
Form data:
    lastname=Hellmann
    Uploaded biography as "bio.txt" (29 bytes)
    firstname=Doug
```

12.4.7 Creating Custom Protocol Handlers

urllib2 has built-in support for HTTP(S), FTP, and local file access. To add support for other URL types, register another protocol handler. For example, to support URLs pointing to arbitrary files on remote NFS servers, without requiring users to mount the path before accessing the file, create a class derived from BaseHandler and with a method nfs_open().

The protocol-specific open() method is given a single argument, the Request instance, and it should return an object with a read() method that can be used to read the data, an info() method to return the response headers, and geturl() to return the actual URL of the file being read. A simple way to achieve that result is to create an instance of urllib.addurlinfo, passing the headers, URL, and open file handle in to the constructor.

```
import mimetypes
import os
import tempfile
import urllib
```

```python
import urllib2

class NFSFile(file):
    def __init__(self, tempdir, filename):
        self.tempdir = tempdir
        file.__init__(self, filename, 'rb')
    def close(self):
        print 'NFSFile:'
        print '   unmounting %s' % os.path.basename(self.tempdir)
        print '   when %s is closed' % os.path.basename(self.name)
        return file.close(self)

class FauxNFSHandler(urllib2.BaseHandler):

    def __init__(self, tempdir):
        self.tempdir = tempdir

    def nfs_open(self, req):
        url = req.get_selector()
        directory_name, file_name = os.path.split(url)
        server_name = req.get_host()
        print 'FauxNFSHandler simulating mount:'
        print '   Remote path: %s' % directory_name
        print '   Server      : %s' % server_name
        print '   Local path : %s' % os.path.basename(tempdir)
        print '   Filename    : %s' % file_name
        local_file = os.path.join(tempdir, file_name)
        fp = NFSFile(tempdir, local_file)
        content_type = ( mimetypes.guess_type(file_name)[0]
                    or
                    'application/octet-stream'
                    )
        stats = os.stat(local_file)
        size = stats.st_size
        headers = { 'Content-type': content_type,
                'Content-length': size,
                }
        return urllib.addinfourl(fp, headers, req.get_full_url())

if __name__ == '__main__':
    tempdir = tempfile.mkdtemp()
    try:
        # Populate the temporary file for the simulation
```

```
    with open(os.path.join(tempdir, 'file.txt'), 'wt') as f:
        f.write('Contents of file.txt')

    # Construct an opener with our NFS handler
    # and register it as the default opener.
    opener = urllib2.build_opener(FauxNFSHandler(tempdir))
    urllib2.install_opener(opener)

    # Open the file through a URL.
    response = urllib2.urlopen(
        'nfs://remote_server/path/to/the/file.txt'
        )
    print
    print 'READ CONTENTS:', response.read()
    print 'URL          :', response.geturl()
    print 'HEADERS:'
    for name, value in sorted(response.info().items()):
        print '  %-15s = %s' % (name, value)
    response.close()
finally:
    os.remove(os.path.join(tempdir, 'file.txt'))
    os.removedirs(tempdir)
```

The `FauxNFSHandler` and `NFSFile` classes print messages to illustrate where a
real implementation would add mount and unmount calls. Since this is just a simulation,
`FauxNFSHandler` is primed with the name of a temporary directory where it should
look for all its files.

```
$ python urllib2_nfs_handler.py

FauxNFSHandler simulating mount:
  Remote path: /path/to/the
  Server     : remote_server
  Local path : tmpoqqoAV
  Filename   : file.txt

READ CONTENTS: Contents of file.txt
URL          : nfs://remote_server/path/to/the/file.txt
HEADERS:
  Content-length  = 20
  Content-type    = text/plain
```

```
NFSFile:
  unmounting tmpoqqoAV
  when file.txt is closed
```

See Also:

urllib2 (http://docs.python.org/library/urllib2.html) The standard library documentation for this module.

urllib (page 651) Original URL handling library.

urlparse (page 638) Work with the URL string itself.

urllib2 – The Missing Manual (www.voidspace.org.uk/python/articles/urllib2. shtml) Michael Foord's write-up on using `urllib2`.

Upload Scripts (www.voidspace.org.uk/python/cgi.shtml#upload) Example scripts from Michael Foord that illustrate how to upload a file using HTTP and then receive the data on the server.

HTTP client to POST using multipart/form-data (http://code.activestate.com/ recipes/146306) Python cookbook recipe showing how to encode and post data, including files, over HTTP.

Form content types (www.w3.org/TR/REC-html40/interact/forms.html# h-17.13.4) W3C specification for posting files or large amounts of data via HTTP forms.

mimetypes Map filenames to mimetype.

mimetools Tools for parsing MIME messages.

12.5 base64—Encode Binary Data with ASCII

Purpose The `base64` module contains functions for translating binary data into a subset of ASCII suitable for transmission using plain-text protocols.

Python Version 1.4 and later

The Base64, Base32, and Base16 encodings convert 8-bit bytes to values with 6, 5, or 4 bits of useful data per byte, allowing non-ASCII bytes to be encoded as ASCII characters for transmission over protocols that require plain ASCII, such as SMTP. The *base* values correspond to the length of the alphabet used in each encoding. There are also URL-safe variations of the original encodings that use slightly different alphabets.

12.5.1 Base64 Encoding

This is a basic example of encoding some text.

```
import base64
import textwrap

# Load this source file and strip the header.
with open(__file__, 'rt') as input:
    raw = input.read()
    initial_data = raw.split('#end_pymotw_header')[1]

encoded_data = base64.b64encode(initial_data)

num_initial = len(initial_data)

# There will never be more than 2 padding bytes.
padding = 3 - (num_initial % 3)

print '%d bytes before encoding' % num_initial
print 'Expect %d padding bytes' % padding
print '%d bytes after encoding' % len(encoded_data)
print
print encoded_data
```

The output shows that the 168 bytes of the original source expand to 224 bytes after being encoded.

Note: There are no carriage returns in the encoded data produced by the library, but the output has been wrapped artificially to make it fit better on the page.

```
$ python base64_b64encode.py

168 bytes before encoding
Expect 3 padding bytes
224 bytes after encoding

CgppbXBvcnQgYmFzZTY0CmltcG9ydCB0ZXh0d3JhcAoKIyBMb2FkIHRoaXMgc291c
mNlIGZpbGUgYW5kIHN0cmlwIHRoZSBoZWFkZXIuCndpdGggb3BlbihfX2ZpbGVfXy
wgJ3J0JykgYXMgaW5wdXQ6CiAgICByYXcgPSBpbnB1dC5yZWFkKCkKICAgIGluaXR
pYWxfZGF0YSA9IHJhdy5zcGxpdCgn
```

12.5.2   Base64 Decoding

b64decode() converts the encoded string back to the original form by taking four bytes and converting them to the original three, using a lookup table.

```
import base64

original_string = 'This is the data, in the clear.'
print 'Original:', original_string

encoded_string = base64.b64encode(original_string)
print 'Encoded :', encoded_string

decoded_string = base64.b64decode(encoded_string)
print 'Decoded :', decoded_string
```

The encoding process looks at each sequence of 24 bits in the input (three bytes) and encodes those same 24 bits spread over four bytes in the output. The equal signs at the end of the output are padding inserted because the number of bits in the original string was not evenly divisible by 24, in this example.

```
$ python base64_b64decode.py

Original: This is the data, in the clear.
Encoded : VGhpcyBpcyB0aGUgZGF0YSwgaW4gdGhlIGNsZWFyLg==
Decoded : This is the data, in the clear.
```

12.5.3   URL-Safe Variations

Because the default Base64 alphabet may use + and /, and those two characters are used in URLs, it is often necessary to use an alternate encoding with substitutes for those characters.

```
import base64

encodes_with_pluses = chr(251) + chr(239)
encodes_with_slashes = chr(255) * 2

for original in [ encodes_with_pluses, encodes_with_slashes ]:
    print 'Original         :', repr(original)
    print 'Standard encoding:', base64.standard_b64encode(original)
    print 'URL-safe encoding:', base64.urlsafe_b64encode(original)
    print
```

The + is replaced with a – and / is replaced with underscore (_). Otherwise, the alphabet is the same.

```
$ python base64_urlsafe.py

Original           : '\xfb\xef'
Standard encoding: ++8=
URL-safe encoding: --8=

Original           : '\xff\xff'
Standard encoding: //8=
URL-safe encoding: __8=
```

12.5.4   Other Encodings

Besides Base64, the module provides functions for working with Base32 and Base16 (hex) encoded data.

```
import base64

original_string = 'This is the data, in the clear.'
print 'Original:', original_string

encoded_string = base64.b32encode(original_string)
print 'Encoded :', encoded_string

decoded_string = base64.b32decode(encoded_string)
print 'Decoded :', decoded_string
```

The Base32 alphabet includes the 26 uppercase letters from the ASCII set and the digits 2 through 7.

```
$ python base64_base32.py

Original: This is the data, in the clear.
Encoded : KRUGS4ZANFZSA5DIMUQGIYLUMEWCA2LOEB2GQZJAMNWGKYLSFY======
Decoded : This is the data, in the clear.
```

The Base16 functions work with the hexadecimal alphabet.

```
import base64

original_string = 'This is the data, in the clear.'
print 'Original:', original_string

encoded_string = base64.b16encode(original_string)
print 'Encoded :', encoded_string
```

```
decoded_string = base64.b16decode(encoded_string)
print 'Decoded :', decoded_string
```

Each time the number of encoding bits goes down, the output in the encoded format takes up more space.

```
$ python base64_base16.py

Original: This is the data, in the clear.
Encoded : 54686973206973207468652064617461612C20696E2074686520636C6561
722E
Decoded : This is the data, in the clear.
```

See Also:

base64 (http://docs.python.org/library/base64.html) The standard library documentation for this module.

RFC 3548 (http://tools.ietf.org/html/rfc3548.html) The Base16, Base32, and Base64 data encodings.

12.6   robotparser—Internet Spider Access Control

Purpose Parse `robots.txt` file used to control Internet spiders.
Python Version 2.1.3 and later

`robotparser` implements a parser for the `robots.txt` file format, including a function that checks if a given user-agent can access a resource. It is intended for use in well-behaved spiders or other crawler applications that need to either be throttled or otherwise restricted.

12.6.1   robots.txt

The `robots.txt` file format is a simple text-based access control system for computer programs that automatically access web resources ("spiders," "crawlers," etc.). The file is made up of records that specify the user-agent identifier for the program followed by a list of URLs (or URL prefixes) the agent may not access.

This is the `robots.txt` file for `http://www.doughellmann.com/`.

```
User-agent: *
Disallow: /admin/
Disallow: /downloads/
```

```
Disallow: /media/
Disallow: /static/
Disallow: /codehosting/
```

It prevents access to some parts of the site that are expensive to compute and would overload the server if a search engine tried to index them. For a more complete set of examples of `robots.txt`, refer to *The Web Robots Page* (see the references list later in this section).

12.6.2 Testing Access Permissions

Using the data presented earlier, a simple crawler can test whether it is allowed to download a page using `RobotFileParser.can_fetch()`.

```
import robotparser
import urlparse

AGENT_NAME = 'PyMOTW'
URL_BASE = 'http://www.doughellmann.com/'
parser = robotparser.RobotFileParser()
parser.set_url(urlparse.urljoin(URL_BASE, 'robots.txt'))
parser.read()

PATHS = [
    '/',
    '/PyMOTW/',
    '/admin/',
    '/downloads/PyMOTW-1.92.tar.gz',
    ]

for path in PATHS:
    print '%6s : %s' % (parser.can_fetch(AGENT_NAME, path), path)
    url = urlparse.urljoin(URL_BASE, path)
    print '%6s : %s' % (parser.can_fetch(AGENT_NAME, url), url)
    print
```

The URL argument to `can_fetch()` can be a path relative to the root of the site or a full URL.

```
$ python robotparser_simple.py

  True : /
  True : http://www.doughellmann.com/
```

```
True  :  /PyMOTW/
True  :  http://www.doughellmann.com/PyMOTW/

False :  /admin/
False :  http://www.doughellmann.com/admin/

False :  /downloads/PyMOTW-1.92.tar.gz
False :  http://www.doughellmann.com/downloads/PyMOTW-1.92.tar.gz
```

12.6.3 Long-Lived Spiders

An application that takes a long time to process the resources it downloads or that is throttled to pause between downloads should check for new robots.txt files periodically, based on the age of the content it has downloaded already. The age is not managed automatically, but there are convenience methods to make tracking it easier.

```python
import robotparser
import time
import urlparse

AGENT_NAME = 'PyMOTW'
parser = robotparser.RobotFileParser()
# Using the local copy
parser.set_url('robots.txt')
parser.read()
parser.modified()

PATHS = [
    '/',
    '/PyMOTW/',
    '/admin/',
    '/downloads/PyMOTW-1.92.tar.gz',
    ]

for path in PATHS:
    age = int(time.time() - parser.mtime())
    print 'age:', age,
    if age > 1:
        print 'rereading robots.txt'
        parser.read()
        parser.modified()
```

```
else:
    print
print '%6s : %s' % (parser.can_fetch(AGENT_NAME, path), path)
# Simulate a delay in processing
time.sleep(1)
print
```

This extreme example downloads a new `robots.txt` file if the one it has is more than one second old.

```
$ python robotparser_longlived.py

age: 0
  True : /

age: 1
  True : /PyMOTW/

age: 2 rereading robots.txt
 False : /admin/

age: 1
 False : /downloads/PyMOTW-1.92.tar.gz
```

A nicer version of the long-lived application might request the modification time for the file before downloading the entire thing. On the other hand, `robots.txt` files are usually fairly small, so it is not that much more expensive to just retrieve the entire document again.

See Also:

robotparser (http://docs.python.org/library/robotparser.html) The standard library documentation for this module.

The Web Robots Page (www.robotstxt.org/orig.html) Description of `robots.txt` format.

12.7   Cookie—HTTP Cookies

> **Purpose** The Cookie module defines classes for parsing and creating HTTP cookie headers.
>
> **Python Version** 2.1 and later

The `Cookie` module implements a parser for cookies that is mostly RFC 2109 compliant. The implementation is a little less strict than the standard because MSIE 3.0x does not support the entire standard.

12.7.1 Creating and Setting a Cookie

Cookies are used as state management for browser-based applications, and as such, are usually set by the server to be stored and returned by the client. Here is the simplest example of creating a cookie.

```
import Cookie

c = Cookie.SimpleCookie()
c['mycookie'] = 'cookie_value'
print c
```

The output is a valid `Set-Cookie` header ready to be passed to the client as part of the HTTP response.

```
$ python Cookie_setheaders.py

Set-Cookie: mycookie=cookie_value
```

12.7.2 Morsels

It is also possible to control the other aspects of a cookie, such as the expiration, path, and domain. In fact, all the RFC attributes for cookies can be managed through the `Morsel` object representing the cookie value.

```
import Cookie
import datetime

def show_cookie(c):
    print c
    for key, morsel in c.iteritems():
        print
        print 'key =', morsel.key
        print '  value =', morsel.value
        print '  coded_value =', morsel.coded_value
        for name in morsel.keys():
```

```
        if morsel[name]:
            print '    %s = %s' % (name, morsel[name])

c = Cookie.SimpleCookie()

# A cookie with a value that has to be encoded to fit into the header
c['encoded_value_cookie'] = '"cookie_value"'
c['encoded_value_cookie']['comment'] = 'Value has escaped quotes'

# A cookie that only applies to part of a site
c['restricted_cookie'] = 'cookie_value'
c['restricted_cookie']['path'] = '/sub/path'
c['restricted_cookie']['domain'] = 'PyMOTW'
c['restricted_cookie']['secure'] = True

# A cookie that expires in 5 minutes
c['with_max_age'] = 'expires in 5 minutes'
c['with_max_age']['max-age'] = 300 # seconds

# A cookie that expires at a specific time
c['expires_at_time'] = 'cookie_value'
time_to_live = datetime.timedelta(hours=1)
expires = datetime.datetime(2009, 2, 14, 18, 30, 14) + time_to_live

# Date format: Wdy, DD-Mon-YY HH:MM:SS GMT
expires_at_time = expires.strftime('%a, %d %b %Y %H:%M:%S')
c['expires_at_time']['expires'] = expires_at_time

show_cookie(c)
```

This example includes two different methods for setting stored cookies that expire. One sets the `max-age` to a number of seconds, and the other sets `expires` to a date and time when the cookie should be discarded.

```
$ python Cookie_Morsel.py

Set-Cookie: encoded_value_cookie="\"cookie_value\""; Comment=Value h
as escaped quotes
Set-Cookie: expires_at_time=cookie_value; expires=Sat, 14 Feb 2009 1
9:30:14
Set-Cookie: restricted_cookie=cookie_value; Domain=PyMOTW; Path=/sub
/path; secure
```

```
Set-Cookie: with_max_age="expires in 5 minutes"; Max-Age=300
key = restricted_cookie
  value = cookie_value
  coded_value = cookie_value
  domain = PyMOTW
  secure = True
  path = /sub/path

key = with_max_age
  value = expires in 5 minutes
  coded_value = "expires in 5 minutes"
  max-age = 300

key = encoded_value_cookie
  value = "cookie_value"
  coded_value = "\"cookie_value\""
  comment = Value has escaped quotes

key = expires_at_time
  value = cookie_value
  coded_value = cookie_value
  expires = Sat, 14 Feb 2009 19:30:14
```

Both the `Cookie` and `Morsel` objects act like dictionaries. A `Morsel` responds to a fixed set of keys:

- expires
- path
- comment
- domain
- max-age
- secure
- version

The keys for a `Cookie` instance are the names of the individual cookies being stored. That information is also available from the key attribute of the `Morsel`.

12.7.3 Encoded Values

The cookie header needs values to be encoded so they can be parsed properly.

```
import Cookie

c = Cookie.SimpleCookie()
c['integer'] = 5
c['string_with_quotes'] = 'He said, "Hello, World!"'

for name in ['integer', 'string_with_quotes']:
    print c[name].key
    print '  %s' % c[name]
    print '    value=%r' % c[name].value
    print '    coded_value=%r' % c[name].coded_value
    print
```

Morsel.value is always the decoded value of the cookie, while Morsel .coded_value is always the representation to be used for transmitting the value to the client. Both values are always strings. Values saved to a cookie that are not strings are converted automatically.

```
$ python Cookie_coded_value.py

integer
  Set-Cookie: integer=5
  value='5'
  coded_value='5'

string_with_quotes
  Set-Cookie: string_with_quotes="He said, \"Hello, World!\""
  value='He said, "Hello, World!"'
  coded_value='"He said, \\"Hello, World!\\""'
```

12.7.4 Receiving and Parsing Cookie Headers

Once the client receives the Set-Cookie headers, it will return those cookies to the server on subsequent requests using a Cookie header. An incoming Cookie header string may contain several cookie values, separated by semicolons (;).

```
Cookie: integer=5; string_with_quotes="He said, \"Hello, World!\""
```

Depending on the web server and framework, cookies are available directly from either the headers or the HTTP_COOKIE environment variable.

```
import Cookie

HTTP_COOKIE = '; '.join([
        r'integer=5',
        r'string_with_quotes="He said, \"Hello, World!\""',
        ])

print 'From constructor:'
c = Cookie.SimpleCookie(HTTP_COOKIE)
print c

print
print 'From load():'
c = Cookie.SimpleCookie()
c.load(HTTP_COOKIE)
print c
```

To decode them, pass the string without the header prefix to `SimpleCookie` when instantiating it, or use the `load()` method.

```
$ python Cookie_parse.py

From constructor:
Set-Cookie: integer=5
Set-Cookie: string_with_quotes="He said, \"Hello, World!\""

From load():
Set-Cookie: integer=5
Set-Cookie: string_with_quotes="He said, \"Hello, World!\""
```

12.7.5 Alternative Output Formats

Besides using the `Set-Cookie` header, servers may deliver JavaScript that adds cookies to a client. `SimpleCookie` and `Morsel` provide JavaScript output via the `js_output()` method.

```
import Cookie

c = Cookie.SimpleCookie()
c['mycookie'] = 'cookie_value'
```

```
c['another_cookie'] = 'second value'
print c.js_output()
```

The result is a complete `script` tag with statements to set the cookies.

```
$ python Cookie_js_output.py

<script type="text/javascript">
<!-- begin hiding
document.cookie = "another_cookie=\"second value\"";
// end hiding -->
</script>

<script type="text/javascript">
<!-- begin hiding
document.cookie = "mycookie=cookie_value";
// end hiding -->
</script>
```

12.7.6 Deprecated Classes

All these examples have used `SimpleCookie`. The `Cookie` module also provides two other classes, `SerialCookie` and `SmartCookie`. `SerialCookie` can handle any values that can be pickled. `SmartCookie` figures out whether a value needs to be unpickled or if it is a simple value.

> **Warning:** Since both these classes use `pickle`, they are potential security holes and should not be used. It is safer to store state on the server and give the client a session key instead.

See Also:

Cookie (http://docs.python.org/library/cookie.html) The standard library documentation for this module.

cookielib The `cookielib` module for working with cookies on the client side.

RFC 2109 (http://tools.ietf.org/html/rfc2109.html) HTTP State Management Mechanism.

12.8   uuid—Universally Unique Identifiers

Purpose   The `uuid` module implements Universally Unique Identifiers, as
described in RFC 4122.
Python Version   2.5 and later

RFC 4122 defines a system for creating universally unique identifiers for resources in
a way that does not require a central registrar. UUID values are 128 bits long and, as
the reference guide says, "can guarantee uniqueness across space and time." They are
useful for generating identifiers for documents, hosts, application clients, and other situations where a unique value is necessary. The RFC is specifically focused on creating
a Uniform Resource Name namespace and covers three main algorithms.

- Using IEEE 802 MAC addresses as a source of uniqueness
- Using pseudorandom numbers
- Using well-known strings combined with cryptographic hashing

In all cases, the seed value is combined with the system clock and a clock sequence
value used to maintain uniqueness in case the clock is set backwards.

12.8.1   UUID 1—IEEE 802 MAC Address

UUID version 1 values are computed using the MAC address of the host. The `uuid`
module uses `getnode()` to retrieve the MAC value of the current system.

```
import uuid

print hex(uuid.getnode())
```

If a system has more than one network card, and so more than one MAC, any one
of the values may be returned.

```
$ python uuid_getnode.py

0x1e5274040e
```

To generate a UUID for a host, identified by its MAC address, use the `uuid1()`
function. The node identifier argument is optional; leave the field blank to use the value
returned by `getnode()`.

```
import uuid

u = uuid.uuid1()

print u
print type(u)
print 'bytes    :', repr(u.bytes)
print 'hex      :', u.hex
print 'int      :', u.int
print 'urn      :', u.urn
print 'variant  :', u.variant
print 'version  :', u.version
print 'fields   :', u.fields
print '\ttime_low              : ', u.time_low
print '\ttime_mid              : ', u.time_mid
print '\ttime_hi_version       : ', u.time_hi_version
print '\tclock_seq_hi_variant: ', u.clock_seq_hi_variant
print '\tclock_seq_low         : ', u.clock_seq_low
print '\tnode                  : ', u.node
print '\ttime                  : ', u.time
print '\tclock_seq             : ', u.clock_seq
```

The components of the UUID object returned can be accessed through read-only instance attributes. Some attributes, such as *hex*, *int*, and *urn*, are different representations of the UUID value.

```
$ python uuid_uuid1.py

c7887eee-ea6a-11df-a6cf-001e5274040e
<class 'uuid.UUID'>
bytes   : '\xc7\x88~\xee\xea j\x11\xdf\xa6\xcf\x00\x1eRt\x04\x0e'
hex     : c7887eeeea6a11dfa6cf001e5274040e
int     : 265225098046419456611671377169708483598
urn     : urn:uuid:c7887eee-ea6a-11df-a6cf-001e5274040e
variant : specified in RFC 4122
version : 1
fields  : (3347611374L, 60010L, 4575L, 166L, 207L, 130232353806L)
          time_low             : 3347611374
          time_mid             : 60010
          time_hi_version      : 4575
          clock_seq_hi_variant: 166
          clock_seq_low        : 207
```

```
node          :   130232353806
time          :   135084258179448558
clock_seq     :   9935
```

Because of the time component, each call to `uuid1()` returns a new value.

```
import uuid

for i in xrange(3):
    print uuid.uuid1()
```

In this output, only the time component (at the beginning of the string) changes.

```
$ python uuid_uuid1_repeat.py

c794da9c-ea6a-11df-9382-001e5274040e
c797121c-ea6a-11df-9e67-001e5274040e
c79713a1-ea6a-11df-ac7d-001e5274040e
```

Because each computer has a different MAC address, running the sample program on different systems will produce entirely different values. This example passes explicit node ids to simulate running on different hosts.

```
import uuid

for node in [ 0x1ec200d9e0, 0x1e5274040e ]:
    print uuid.uuid1(node), hex(node)
```

In addition to a different time value, the node identifier at the end of the UUID also changes.

```
$ python uuid_uuid1_othermac.py

c7a313a8-ea6a-11df-a228-001ec200d9e0 0x1ec200d9e0
c7a3f751-ea6a-11df-988b-001e5274040e 0x1e5274040e
```

12.8.2   UUID 3 and 5—Name-Based Values

It is also useful in some contexts to create UUID values from names instead of random or time-based values. Versions 3 and 5 of the UUID specification use cryptographic hash values (MD5 or SHA-1, respectively) to combine namespace-specific seed values with names. There are several well-known namespaces, identified by predefined UUID values, for working with DNS, URLs, ISO OIDs, and X.500 Distinguished Names. New application-specific namespaces can be defined by generating and saving UUID values.

```python
import uuid

hostnames = ['www.doughellmann.com', 'blog.doughellmann.com']

for name in hostnames:
    print name
    print '  MD5   :', uuid.uuid3(uuid.NAMESPACE_DNS, name)
    print '  SHA-1 :', uuid.uuid5(uuid.NAMESPACE_DNS, name)
    print
```

To create a UUID from a DNS name, pass `uuid.NAMESPACE_DNS` as the namespace argument to `uuid3()` or `uuid5()`.

```
$ python uuid_uuid3_uuid5.py

www.doughellmann.com
  MD5   : bcd02e22-68f0-3046-a512-327cca9def8f
  SHA-1 : e3329b12-30b7-57c4-8117-c2cd34a87ce9

blog.doughellmann.com
  MD5   : 9bdabfce-dfd6-37ab-8a3f-7f7293bcf111
  SHA-1 : fa829736-7ef8-5239-9906-b4775a5abacb
```

The UUID value for a given name in a namespace is always the same, no matter when or where it is calculated.

```python
import uuid

namespace_types = sorted(n
                         for n in dir(uuid)
                         if n.startswith('NAMESPACE_')
                         )
name = 'www.doughellmann.com'

for namespace_type in namespace_types:
    print namespace_type
    namespace_uuid = getattr(uuid, namespace_type)
```

```
    print ' ', uuid.uuid3(namespace_uuid, name)
    print ' ', uuid.uuid3(namespace_uuid, name)
    print
```

Values for the same name in the namespaces are different.

```
$ python uuid_uuid3_repeat.py

NAMESPACE_DNS
  bcd02e22-68f0-3046-a512-327cca9def8f
  bcd02e22-68f0-3046-a512-327cca9def8f

NAMESPACE_OID
  e7043ac1-4382-3c45-8271-d5c083e41723
  e7043ac1-4382-3c45-8271-d5c083e41723

NAMESPACE_URL
  5d0fdaa9-eafd-365e-b4d7-652500dd1208
  5d0fdaa9-eafd-365e-b4d7-652500dd1208

NAMESPACE_X500
  4a54d6e7-ce68-37fb-b0ba-09acc87cabb7
  4a54d6e7-ce68-37fb-b0ba-09acc87cabb7
```

12.8.3   UUID 4—Random Values

Sometimes, host-based and namespace-based UUID values are not "different enough." For example, in cases where UUID is intended to be used as a hash key, a more random sequence of values with more differentiation is desirable to avoid collisions in the hash table. Having values with fewer common digits also makes it easier to find them in log files. To add greater differentiation in UUIDs, use `uuid4()` to generate them using random input values.

```
import uuid

for i in xrange(3):
    print uuid.uuid4()
```

The source of randomness depends on which C libraries are available when `uuid` is imported. If `libuuid` (or `uuid.dll`) can be loaded and it contains a function for generating random values, it is used. Otherwise, `os.urandom()` or the `random` module are used.

```
$ python uuid_uuid4.py

b2637198-4629-44c2-8b9b-07a6ff601a89
d1b850c6-f842-4a25-a993-6d6160dda761
50fb5234-abce-40b8-b034-ba3637dad6fc
```

12.8.4 Working with UUID Objects

In addition to generating new UUID values, it is possible to parse strings in standard formats to create UUID objects, making it easier to handle comparisons and sorting operations.

```
import uuid

def show(msg, l):
    print msg
    for v in l:
        print ' ', v
    print

input_values = [
    'urn:uuid:f2f84497-b3bf-493a-bba9-7c68e6def80b',
    '{417a5ebb-01f7-4ed5-aeac-3d56cd5037b0}',
    '2115773a-5bf1-11dd-ab48-001ec200d9e0',
    ]

show('input_values', input_values)

uuids = [ uuid.UUID(s) for s in input_values ]
show('converted to uuids', uuids)

uuids.sort()
show('sorted', uuids)
```

Surrounding curly braces are removed from the input, as are dashes (–). If the string has a prefix containing `urn:` and/or `uuid:`, it is also removed. The remaining text must be a string of 16 hexadecimal digits, which are then interpreted as a UUID value.

```
$ python uuid_uuid_objects.py

input_values
  urn:uuid:f2f84497-b3bf-493a-bba9-7c68e6def80b
  {417a5ebb-01f7-4ed5-aeac-3d56cd5037b0}
  2115773a-5bf1-11dd-ab48-001ec200d9e0

converted to uuids
  f2f84497-b3bf-493a-bba9-7c68e6def80b
  417a5ebb-01f7-4ed5-aeac-3d56cd5037b0
  2115773a-5bf1-11dd-ab48-001ec200d9e0

sorted
  2115773a-5bf1-11dd-ab48-001ec200d9e0
  417a5ebb-01f7-4ed5-aeac-3d56cd5037b0
  f2f84497-b3bf-493a-bba9-7c68e6def80b
```

See Also:

uuid (http://docs.python.org/lib/module-uuid.html) The Standard library documentation for this module.

RFC 4122 (http://tools.ietf.org/html/rfc4122.html) A Universally Unique Identifier (UUID) URN Namespace.

12.9 json—JavaScript Object Notation

Purpose Encode Python objects as JSON strings, and decode JSON strings into Python objects.
Python Version 2.6 and later

The `json` module provides an API similar to `pickle` for converting in-memory Python objects to a serialized representation known as JavaScript Object Notation (JSON). Unlike pickle, JSON has the benefit of having implementations in many languages (especially JavaScript). It is most widely used for communicating between the web server and the client in an AJAX application, but it is also useful for other inter-application communication needs.

12.9.1 Encoding and Decoding Simple Data Types

The encoder understands Python's native types by default (`string`, `unicode`, `int`, `float`, `list`, `tuple`, and `dict`).

```
import json

data = [ { 'a':'A', 'b':(2, 4), 'c':3.0 } ]
print 'DATA:', repr(data)

data_string = json.dumps(data)
print 'JSON:', data_string
```

Values are encoded in a manner superficially similar to Python's `repr()` output.

```
$ python json_simple_types.py

DATA: [{'a': 'A', 'c': 3.0, 'b': (2, 4)}]
JSON: [{"a": "A", "c": 3.0, "b": [2, 4]}]
```

Encoding, and then redecoding, may not give exactly the same type of object.

```
import json

data = [ { 'a':'A', 'b':(2, 4), 'c':3.0 } ]
print 'DATA    :', data

data_string = json.dumps(data)
print 'ENCODED:', data_string

decoded = json.loads(data_string)
print 'DECODED:', decoded

print 'ORIGINAL:', type(data[0]['b'])
print 'DECODED :', type(decoded[0]['b'])
```

In particular, strings are converted to unicode objects and tuples become lists.

```
$ python json_simple_types_decode.py

DATA    : [{'a': 'A', 'c': 3.0, 'b': (2, 4)}]
ENCODED: [{"a": "A", "c": 3.0, "b": [2, 4]}]
DECODED: [{'a': 'A', 'c': 3.0, 'b': [2, 4]}]
ORIGINAL: <type 'tuple'>
DECODED : <type 'list'>
```

12.9.2 Human-Consumable vs. Compact Output

Another benefit of JSON over `pickle` is that the results are human-readable. The `dumps()` function accepts several arguments to make the output even nicer. For example, the *sort_keys* flag tells the encoder to output the keys of a dictionary in sorted, instead of random, order.

```python
import json

data = [ { 'a':'A', 'b':(2, 4), 'c':3.0 } ]
print 'DATA:', repr(data)

unsorted = json.dumps(data)
print 'JSON:', json.dumps(data)
print 'SORT:', json.dumps(data, sort_keys=True)

first = json.dumps(data, sort_keys=True)
second = json.dumps(data, sort_keys=True)

print 'UNSORTED MATCH:', unsorted == first
print 'SORTED MATCH  :', first == second
```

Sorting makes it easier to scan the results by eye and also makes it possible to compare JSON output in tests.

```
$ python json_sort_keys.py

DATA: [{'a': 'A', 'c': 3.0, 'b': (2, 4)}]
JSON: [{"a": "A", "c": 3.0, "b": [2, 4]}]
SORT: [{"a": "A", "b": [2, 4], "c": 3.0}]
UNSORTED MATCH: False
SORTED MATCH  : True
```

For highly nested data structures, specify a value for *indent* so the output is formatted nicely as well.

```python
import json

data = [ { 'a':'A', 'b':(2, 4), 'c':3.0 } ]
print 'DATA:', repr(data)

print 'NORMAL:', json.dumps(data, sort_keys=True)
print 'INDENT:', json.dumps(data, sort_keys=True, indent=2)
```

When indent is a non-negative integer, the output more closely resembles that of pprint, with leading spaces for each level of the data structure matching the indent level.

```
$ python json_indent.py

DATA: [{'a': 'A', 'c': 3.0, 'b': (2, 4)}]
NORMAL: [{"a": "A", "b": [2, 4], "c": 3.0}]
INDENT: [
  {
    "a": "A",
    "b": [
      2,
      4
    ],
    "c": 3.0
  }
]
```

Verbose output like this increases the number of bytes needed to transmit the same amount of data, however, so it is not intended for use in a production environment. In fact, it is possible to adjust the settings for separating data in the encoded output to make it even more compact than the default.

```
import json

data = [ { 'a':'A', 'b':(2, 4), 'c':3.0 } ]
print 'DATA:', repr(data)

print 'repr(data)             :', len(repr(data))

plain_dump = json.dumps(data)
print 'dumps(data)            :', len(plain_dump)

small_indent = json.dumps(data, indent=2)
print 'dumps(data, indent=2)  :', len(small_indent)

with_separators = json.dumps(data, separators=(',',':'))
print 'dumps(data, separators):', len(with_separators)
```

The *separators* argument to dumps() should be a tuple containing the strings to separate items in a list and keys from values in a dictionary. The default is (', ', ': '). By removing the whitespace, a more compact output is produced.

```
$ python json_compact_encoding.py

DATA: [{'a': 'A', 'c': 3.0, 'b': (2, 4)}]
repr(data)              : 35
dumps(data)             : 35
dumps(data, indent=2)   : 76
dumps(data, separators) : 29
```

12.9.3 Encoding Dictionaries

The JSON format expects the keys to a dictionary to be strings. Trying to encode a dictionary with nonstring types as keys produces an exception. (The exception type depends on whether the pure-Python version of the module is loaded or the C speed-ups are available, but it will be either `TypeError` or `ValueError`.) One way to work around that limitation is to tell the encoder to skip over nonstring keys using the *skipkeys* argument.

```python
import json

data = [ { 'a':'A', 'b':(2, 4), 'c':3.0, ('d',):'D tuple' } ]

print 'First attempt'
try:
    print json.dumps(data)
except (TypeError, ValueError), err:
    print 'ERROR:', err

print
print 'Second attempt'
print json.dumps(data, skipkeys=True)
```

Rather than raising an exception, the nonstring key is ignored.

```
$ python json_skipkeys.py

First attempt
ERROR: keys must be a string

Second attempt
[{"a": "A", "c": 3.0, "b": [2, 4]}]
```

12.9.4 Working with Custom Types

All the examples so far have used Python's built-in types because those are supported by `json` natively. It is common to need to encode custom classes, as well, and there are two ways to do that.

Given this class to encode

```
class MyObj(object):
    def __init__(self, s):
        self.s = s
    def __repr__(self):
        return '<MyObj(%s)>' % self.s
```

The simple way of encoding a `MyObj` instance is to define a function to convert an unknown type to a known type. It does not need to do the encoding, so it should just convert one object to another.

```
import json
import json_myobj

obj = json_myobj.MyObj('instance value goes here')

print 'First attempt'
try:
    print json.dumps(obj)
except TypeError, err:
    print 'ERROR:', err

def convert_to_builtin_type(obj):
    print 'default(', repr(obj), ')'
    # Convert objects to a dictionary of their representation
    d = { '__class__':obj.__class__.__name__,
          '__module__':obj.__module__,
          }
    d.update(obj.__dict__)
    return d

print
print 'With default'
print json.dumps(obj, default=convert_to_builtin_type)
```

In `convert_to_builtin_type()`, instances of classes not recognized by `json` are converted to dictionaries with enough information to re-create the object if a program has access to the Python modules necessary.

```
$ python json_dump_default.py

First attempt
ERROR: <MyObj(instance value goes here)> is not JSON serializable

With default
default( <MyObj(instance value goes here)> )
{"s": "instance value goes here", "__module__": "json_myobj",
"__class__": "MyObj"}
```

To decode the results and create a `MyObj()` instance, use the *object_hook* argument to `loads()` to tie in to the decoder so the class can be imported from the module and used to create the instance.

The *object_hook* is called for each dictionary decoded from the incoming data stream, providing a chance to convert the dictionary to another type of object. The hook function should return the object the calling application should receive instead of the dictionary.

```python
import json


def dict_to_object(d):
    if '__class__' in d:
        class_name = d.pop('__class__')
        module_name = d.pop('__module__')
        module = __import__(module_name)
        print 'MODULE:', module.__name__
        class_ = getattr(module, class_name)
        print 'CLASS:', class_
        args = dict( (key.encode('ascii'), value)
                     for key, value in d.items())
        print 'INSTANCE ARGS:', args
        inst = class_(**args)
    else:
        inst = d
    return inst

encoded_object = '''
    [{"s": "instance value goes here",
      "__module__": "json_myobj", "__class__": "MyObj"}]
    '''
```

```
myobj_instance = json.loads(encoded_object,
                            object_hook=dict_to_object)
print myobj_instance
```

Since `json` converts string values to unicode objects, they need to be reencoded as ASCII strings before they can be used as keyword arguments to the class constructor.

```
$ python json_load_object_hook.py

MODULE: json_myobj
CLASS: <class 'json_myobj.MyObj'>
INSTANCE ARGS: {'s': 'instance value goes here'}
[<MyObj(instance value goes here)>]
```

Similar hooks are available for the built-in types integers (*parse_int*), floating-point numbers (*parse_float*), and constants (*parse_constant*).

12.9.5   Encoder and Decoder Classes

Besides the convenience functions already covered, the `json` module provides classes for encoding and decoding. Using the classes directly gives access to extra APIs for customizing their behavior.

The `JSONEncoder` uses an iterable interface for producing "chunks" of encoded data, making it easier to write to files or network sockets without having to represent an entire data structure in memory.

```
import json

encoder = json.JSONEncoder()
data = [ { 'a':'A', 'b':(2, 4), 'c':3.0 } ]

for part in encoder.iterencode(data):
    print 'PART:', part
```

The output is generated in logical units, rather than being based on any size value.

```
$ python json_encoder_iterable.py

PART: [
PART: {
PART: "a"
```

```
PART: :
PART: "A"
PART: ,
PART: "c"
PART: :
PART: 3.0
PART: ,
PART: "b"
PART: :
PART: [2
PART: , 4
PART: ]
PART: }
PART: ]
```

The `encode()` method is basically equivalent to the value produced by the expression `' '.join(encoder.iterencode())`, with some extra error checking up front.

To encode arbitrary objects, override the `default()` method with an implementation similar to the one used in `convert_to_builtin_type()`.

```python
import json
import json_myobj

class MyEncoder(json.JSONEncoder):

    def default(self, obj):
        print 'default(', repr(obj), ')'
        # Convert objects to a dictionary of their representation
        d = { '__class__':obj.__class__.__name__,
              '__module__':obj.__module__,
            }
        d.update(obj.__dict__)
        return d

obj = json_myobj.MyObj('internal data')
print obj
print MyEncoder().encode(obj)
```

The output is the same as the previous implementation.

```
$ python json_encoder_default.py
```

```
<MyObj(internal data)>
default( <MyObj(internal data)> )
{"s": "internal data", "__module__": "json_myobj", "__class__":
"MyObj"}
```

Decoding text, and then converting the dictionary into an object, takes a little more work to set up than the previous implementation, but not much.

```
import json

class MyDecoder(json.JSONDecoder):

    def __init__(self):
        json.JSONDecoder.__init__(self,
                                  object_hook=self.dict_to_object)

    def dict_to_object(self, d):
        if '__class__' in d:
            class_name = d.pop('__class__')
            module_name = d.pop('__module__')
            module = __import__(module_name)
            print 'MODULE:', module.__name__
            class_ = getattr(module, class_name)
            print 'CLASS:', class_
            args = dict( (key.encode('ascii'), value)
                        for key, value in d.items())
            print 'INSTANCE ARGS:', args
            inst = class_(**args)
        else:
            inst = d
        return inst

encoded_object = '''
[{"s": "instance value goes here",
  "__module__": "json_myobj", "__class__": "MyObj"}]
'''

myobj_instance = MyDecoder().decode(encoded_object)
print myobj_instance
```

And the output is the same as the earlier example.

```
$ python json_decoder_object_hook.py

MODULE: json_myobj
CLASS: <class 'json_myobj.MyObj'>
INSTANCE ARGS: {'s': 'instance value goes here'}
[<MyObj(instance value goes here)>]
```

12.9.6 Working with Streams and Files

All the examples so far have assumed that the encoded version of the entire data structure could be held in memory at one time. With large data structures, it may be preferable to write the encoding directly to a file-like object. The convenience functions load() and dump() accept references to a file-like object to use for reading or writing.

```
import json
from StringIO import StringIO

data = [ { 'a':'A', 'b':(2, 4), 'c':3.0 } ]

f = StringIO()
json.dump(data, f)

print f.getvalue()
```

A socket or normal file handle would work the same way as the StringIO buffer used in this example.

```
$ python json_dump_file.py

[{"a": "A", "c": 3.0, "b": [2, 4]}]
```

Although it is not optimized to read only part of the data at a time, the load() function still offers the benefit of encapsulating the logic of generating objects from stream input.

```
import json
from StringIO import StringIO

f = StringIO('[{"a": "A", "c": 3.0, "b": [2, 4]}]')
print json.load(f)
```

Just as for `dump()`, any file-like object can be passed to `load()`.

```
$ python json_load_file.py

[{'a': 'A', 'c': 3.0, 'b': [2, 4]}]
```

12.9.7 Mixed Data Streams

`JSONDecoder` includes `raw_decode()`, a method for decoding a data structure followed by more data, such as JSON data with trailing text. The return value is the object created by decoding the input data and an index into that data indicating where decoding left off.

```python
import json

decoder = json.JSONDecoder()
def get_decoded_and_remainder(input_data):
    obj, end = decoder.raw_decode(input_data)
    remaining = input_data[end:]
    return (obj, end, remaining)

encoded_object = '[{"a": "A", "c": 3.0, "b": [2, 4]}]'
extra_text = 'This text is not JSON.'

print 'JSON first:'
data = ' '.join([encoded_object, extra_text])
obj, end, remaining = get_decoded_and_remainder(data)

print 'Object              :', obj
print 'End of parsed input :', end
print 'Remaining text      :', repr(remaining)

print
print 'JSON embedded:'
try:
    data = ' '.join([extra_text, encoded_object, extra_text])
    obj, end, remaining = get_decoded_and_remainder(data)
except ValueError, err:
    print 'ERROR:', err
```

Unfortunately, this only works if the object appears at the beginning of the input.

```
$ python json_mixed_data.py

JSON first:
Object              : [{'a': 'A', 'c': 3.0, 'b': [2, 4]}]
End of parsed input : 35
Remaining text      : ' This text is not JSON.'

JSON embedded:
ERROR: No JSON object could be decoded
```

See Also:

json (http://docs.python.org/library/json.html) The standard library documentation
   for this module.

JavaScript Object Notation (http://json.org/) JSON home, with documentation and
   implementations in other languages.

simplejson (http://code.google.com/p/simplejson/) `simplejson`, from Bob Ippolito
   et al. is the externally maintained development version of the `json` library included with Python 2.6 and later. It maintains backwards compatibility with
   Python 2.4 and Python 2.5.

jsonpickle (http://code.google.com/p/jsonpickle/) `jsonpickle` allows for any
   Python object to be serialized into JSON.

12.10   xmlrpclib—Client Library for XML-RPC

Purpose Client-side library for XML-RPC communication.
Python Version 2.2 and later

XML-RPC is a lightweight remote procedure call protocol built on top of HTTP and
XML. The `xmlrpclib` module lets a Python program communicate with an XML-RPC
server written in any language.

   All the examples in this section use the server defined in `xmlrpclib_`
`server.py`, available in the source distribution and included here for reference.

```
from SimpleXMLRPCServer import SimpleXMLRPCServer
from xmlrpclib import Binary
import datetime

server = SimpleXMLRPCServer(('localhost', 9000),
                            logRequests=True,
                            allow_none=True)
```

```
server.register_introspection_functions()
server.register_multicall_functions()

class ExampleService:

    def ping(self):
        """Simple function to respond when called
        to demonstrate connectivity.
        """
        return True

    def now(self):
        """Returns the server current date and time."""
        return datetime.datetime.now()

    def show_type(self, arg):
        """Illustrates how types are passed in and out of
        server methods.

        Accepts one argument of any type.
        Returns a tuple with string representation of the value,
        the name of the type, and the value itself.
        """
        return (str(arg), str(type(arg)), arg)

    def raises_exception(self, msg):
        "Always raises a RuntimeError with the message passed in"
        raise RuntimeError(msg)

    def send_back_binary(self, bin):
        """Accepts single Binary argument, and unpacks and
        repacks it to return it."""
        data = bin.data
        response = Binary(data)
        return response

server.register_instance(ExampleService())

try:
    print 'Use Control-C to exit'
    server.serve_forever()
except KeyboardInterrupt:
    print 'Exiting'
```

12.10.1 Connecting to a Server

The simplest way to connect a client to a server is to instantiate a `ServerProxy` object, giving it the URI of the server. For example, the demo server runs on port 9000 of localhost.

```
import xmlrpclib

server = xmlrpclib.ServerProxy('http://localhost:9000')
print 'Ping:', server.ping()
```

In this case, the `ping()` method of the service takes no arguments and returns a single Boolean value.

```
$ python xmlrpclib_ServerProxy.py

Ping: True
```

Other options are available to support alternate transport. Both HTTP and HTTPS are supported out of the box, both with basic authentication. To implement a new communication channel, only a new transport class is needed. It could be an interesting exercise, for example, to implement XML-RPC over SMTP.

```
import xmlrpclib

server = xmlrpclib.ServerProxy('http://localhost:9000', verbose=True)
print 'Ping:', server.ping()
```

The *verbose* option gives debugging information useful for resolving communication errors.

```
$ python xmlrpclib_ServerProxy_verbose.py

Ping: connect: (localhost, 9000)
connect fail: ('localhost', 9000)
connect: (localhost, 9000)
connect fail: ('localhost', 9000)
connect: (localhost, 9000)
send: 'POST /RPC2 HTTP/1.0\r\nHost: localhost:9000\r\nUser-Agent:
 xmlrpclib.py/1.0.1 (by www.pythonware.com)\r\nContent-Type: text
/xml\r\nContent-Length: 98\r\n\r\n'
```

```
send: "<?xml version='1.0'?>\n<methodCall>\n<methodName>ping</met
hodName>\n<params>\n</params>\n</methodCall>\n"
reply: 'HTTP/1.0 200 OK\r\n'
header: Server: BaseHTTP/0.3 Python/2.5.1
header: Date: Sun, 06 Jul 2008 19:56:13 GMT
header: Content-type: text/xml
header: Content-length: 129
body: "<?xml version='1.0'?>\n<methodResponse>\n<params>\n<param
>\n<value><boolean>1</boolean></value>\n</param>\n</params>\n</m
ethodResponse>\n"
True
```

The default encoding can be changed from UTF-8 if an alternate system is needed.

```
import xmlrpclib

server = xmlrpclib.ServerProxy('http://localhost:9000',
                               encoding='ISO-8859-1')
print 'Ping:', server.ping()
```

The server automatically detects the correct encoding.

```
$ python xmlrpclib_ServerProxy_encoding.py

Ping: True
```

The *allow_none* option controls whether Python's None value is automatically translated to a nil value or whether it causes an error.

```
import xmlrpclib

server = xmlrpclib.ServerProxy('http://localhost:9000',
                               allow_none=True)
print 'Allowed:', server.show_type(None)

server = xmlrpclib.ServerProxy('http://localhost:9000',
                               allow_none=False)
try:
    server.show_type(None)
except TypeError as err:
    print 'ERROR:', err
```

The error is raised locally if the client does not allow None, but it can also be raised from within the server if it is not configured to allow None.

```
$ python xmlrpclib_ServerProxy_allow_none.py

Allowed: ['None', "<type 'NoneType'>", None]
ERROR: cannot marshal None unless allow_none is enabled
```

12.10.2 Data Types

The XML-RPC protocol recognizes a limited set of common data types. The types can be passed as arguments or return values and combined to create more complex data structures.

```python
import xmlrpclib
import datetime

server = xmlrpclib.ServerProxy('http://localhost:9000')

for t, v in [ ('boolean', True),
              ('integer', 1),
              ('float', 2.5),
              ('string', 'some text'),
              ('datetime', datetime.datetime.now()),
              ('array', ['a', 'list']),
              ('array', ('a', 'tuple')),
              ('structure', {'a':'dictionary'}),
            ]:
    as_string, type_name, value = server.show_type(v)
    print '%-12s:' % t, as_string
    print '%12s ' % '', type_name
    print '%12s ' % '', value
```

The simple types are

```
$ python xmlrpclib_types.py

boolean    : True
             <type 'bool'>
             True
integer    : 1
             <type 'int'>
             1
```

```
float         : 2.5
                <type 'float'>
                2.5
string        : some text
                <type 'str'>
                some text
datetime      : 20101128T20:15:21
                <type 'instance'>
                20101128T20:15:21
array         : ['a', 'list']
                <type 'list'>
                ['a', 'list']
array         : ['a', 'tuple']
                <type 'list'>
                ['a', 'tuple']
structure     : {'a': 'dictionary'}
                <type 'dict'>
                {'a': 'dictionary'}
```

The supported types can be nested to create values of arbitrary complexity.

```
import xmlrpclib
import datetime
import pprint

server = xmlrpclib.ServerProxy('http://localhost:9000')

data = { 'boolean':True,
         'integer': 1,
         'floating-point number': 2.5,
         'string': 'some text',
         'datetime': datetime.datetime.now(),
         'array': ['a', 'list'],
         'array': ('a', 'tuple'),
         'structure': {'a':'dictionary'},
         }
arg = []
for i in range(3):
    d = {}
    d.update(data)
    d['integer'] = i
    arg.append(d)
```

```
print 'Before:'
pprint.pprint(arg)

print
print 'After:'
pprint.pprint(server.show_type(arg)[-1])
```

This program passes a list of dictionaries containing all the supported types to the sample server, which returns the data. Tuples are converted to lists, and datetime instances are converted to DateTime objects. Otherwise, the data is unchanged.

```
$ python xmlrpclib_types_nested.py

Before:
[{'array': ('a', 'tuple'),
  'boolean': True,
  'datetime': datetime.datetime(2008, 7, 6, 16, 24, 52, 348849),
  'floating-point number': 2.5,
  'integer': 0,
  'string': 'some text',
  'structure': {'a': 'dictionary'}},
 {'array': ('a', 'tuple'),
  'boolean': True,
  'datetime': datetime.datetime(2008, 7, 6, 16, 24, 52, 348849),
  'floating-point number': 2.5,
  'integer': 1,
  'string': 'some text',
  'structure': {'a': 'dictionary'}},
 {'array': ('a', 'tuple'),
  'boolean': True,
  'datetime': datetime.datetime(2008, 7, 6, 16, 24, 52, 348849),
  'floating-point number': 2.5,
  'integer': 2,
  'string': 'some text',
  'structure': {'a': 'dictionary'}}]

After:
[{'array': ['a', 'tuple'],
  'boolean': True,
  'datetime': <DateTime '20080706T16:24:52' at a5be18>,
  'floating-point number': 2.5,
  'integer': 0,
```

```
            'string': 'some text',
            'structure': {'a': 'dictionary'}},
 {'array': ['a', 'tuple'],
            'boolean': True,
            'datetime': <DateTime '20080706T16:24:52' at a5bf30>,
            'floating-point number': 2.5,
            'integer': 1,
            'string': 'some text',
            'structure': {'a': 'dictionary'}},
 {'array': ['a', 'tuple'],
            'boolean': True,
            'datetime': <DateTime '20080706T16:24:52' at a5bf80>,
            'floating-point number': 2.5,
            'integer': 2,
            'string': 'some text',
            'structure': {'a': 'dictionary'}}]
```

XML-RPC supports dates as a native type, and `xmlrpclib` can use one of two classes to represent the date values in the outgoing proxy or when they are received from the server. By default an internal version of `DateTime` is used, but the *use_datetime* option turns on support for using the classes in the `datetime` module.

12.10.3 Passing Objects

Instances of Python classes are treated as structures and passed as a dictionary, with the attributes of the object as values in the dictionary.

```
import xmlrpclib
import pprint

class MyObj:
    def __init__(self, a, b):
        self.a = a
        self.b = b
    def __repr__(self):
        return 'MyObj(%s, %s)' % (repr(self.a), repr(self.b))

server = xmlrpclib.ServerProxy('http://localhost:9000')

o = MyObj(1, 'b goes here')
print 'o  :', o
pprint.pprint(server.show_type(o))
```

```
o2 = MyObj(2, o)
print 'o2 :', o2
pprint.pprint(server.show_type(o2))
```

When the value is sent back to the client from the server, the result is a dictionary on the client, since there is nothing encoded in the values to tell the server (or the client) that it should be instantiated as part of a class.

```
$ python xmlrpclib_types_object.py

o  : MyObj(1, 'b goes here')
    ["{'a': 1, 'b': 'b goes here'}", "<type 'dict'>",
 {'a': 1, 'b': 'b goes here'}]
o2 : MyObj(2, MyObj(1, 'b goes here'))
["{'a': 2, 'b': {'a': 1, 'b': 'b goes here'}}",
 "<type 'dict'>",
 {'a': 2, 'b': {'a': 1, 'b': 'b goes here'}}]
```

12.10.4   Binary Data

All values passed to the server are encoded and escaped automatically. However, some data types may contain characters that are not valid XML. For example, binary image data may include byte values in the ASCII control range 0 to 31. To pass binary data, it is best to use the `Binary` class to encode it for transport.

```
import xmlrpclib

server = xmlrpclib.ServerProxy('http://localhost:9000')

s = 'This is a string with control characters' + '\0'
print 'Local string:', s

data = xmlrpclib.Binary(s)
print 'As binary:', server.send_back_binary(data)

try:
    print 'As string:', server.show_type(s)
except xmlrpclib.Fault as err:
    print '\nERROR:', err
```

If the string containing a NULL byte is passed to `show_type()`, an exception is raised in the XML parser.

```
$ python xmlrpclib_Binary.py

Local string: This is a string with control characters
As binary: This is a string with control characters
As string:
ERROR: <Fault 1: "<class 'xml.parsers.expat.ExpatError'>:not
well-formed (invalid token): line 6, column 55">
```

Binary objects can also be used to send objects using `pickle`. The normal security issues related to sending what amounts to executable code over the wire apply here (i.e., do not do this unless the communication channel is secure).

```
import xmlrpclib
import cPickle as pickle
import pprint

class MyObj:
    def __init__(self, a, b):
        self.a = a
        self.b = b
    def __repr__(self):
        return 'MyObj(%s, %s)' % (repr(self.a), repr(self.b))

server = xmlrpclib.ServerProxy('http://localhost:9000')

o = MyObj(1, 'b goes here')
print 'Local:', id(o)
print o

print '\nAs object:'
pprint.pprint(server.show_type(o))

p = pickle.dumps(o)
b = xmlrpclib.Binary(p)
r = server.send_back_binary(b)

o2 = pickle.loads(r.data)
print '\nFrom pickle:', id(o2)
pprint.pprint(o2)
```

The data attribute of the `Binary` instance contains the pickled version of the object, so it has to be unpickled before it can be used. That results in a different object (with a new id value).

```
$ python xmlrpclib_Binary_pickle.py

Local: 4321077872
MyObj(1, 'b goes here')

As object:
["{'a': 1, 'b': 'b goes here'}", "<type 'dict'>",
 {'a': 1, 'b': 'b goes here'}]

From pickle: 4321252344
MyObj(1, 'b goes here')
```

12.10.5   Exception Handling

Since the XML-RPC server might be written in any language, exception classes cannot be transmitted directly. Instead, exceptions raised in the server are converted to `Fault` objects and raised as exceptions locally in the client.

```
import xmlrpclib

server = xmlrpclib.ServerProxy('http://localhost:9000')
try:
    server.raises_exception('A message')
except Exception, err:
    print 'Fault code:', err.faultCode
    print 'Message   :', err.faultString
```

The original error message is saved in the `faultString` attribute, and `fault-Code` is set to an XML-RPC error number.

```
$ python xmlrpclib_exception.py

Fault code: 1
Message   : <type 'exceptions.RuntimeError'>:A message
```

12.10.6   Combining Calls into One Message

Multicall is an extension to the XML-RPC protocol that allows more than one call to be sent at the same time, with the responses collected and returned to the caller. The `MultiCall` class was added to `xmlrpclib` in Python 2.4.

```
import xmlrpclib

server = xmlrpclib.ServerProxy('http://localhost:9000')

multicall = xmlrpclib.MultiCall(server)
multicall.ping()
multicall.show_type(1)
multicall.show_type('string')

for i, r in enumerate(multicall()):
    print i, r
```

To use a `MultiCall` instance, invoke the methods on it as with a `ServerProxy`, and then call the object with no arguments to actually run the remote functions. The return value is an iterator that yields the results from all the calls.

```
$ python xmlrpclib_MultiCall.py

0 True
1 ['1', "<type 'int'>", 1]
2 ['string', "<type 'str'>", 'string']
```

If one of the calls causes a `Fault`, the exception is raised when the result is produced from the iterator and no more results are available.

```
import xmlrpclib

server = xmlrpclib.ServerProxy('http://localhost:9000')

multicall = xmlrpclib.MultiCall(server)
multicall.ping()
multicall.show_type(1)
multicall.raises_exception('Next to last call stops execution')
multicall.show_type('string')

try:
    for i, r in enumerate(multicall()):
        print i, r
except xmlrpclib.Fault as err:
    print 'ERROR:', err
```

Since the third response, from `raises_exception()`, generates an exception, the response from `show_type()` is not accessible.

```
$ python xmlrpclib_MultiCall_exception.py

0 True
1 ['1', "<type 'int'>", 1]
ERROR: <Fault 1: "<type 'exceptions.RuntimeError'>:Next to last call
stops execution">
```

See Also:
xmlrpclib (http://docs.python.org/lib/module-xmlrpclib.html) The Standard library
    documentation for this module.
`SimpleXMLRPCServer` **(page 714)** An XML-RPC server implementation.

12.11   SimpleXMLRPCServer—An XML-RPC Server

Purpose Implements an XML-RPC server.
Python Version 2.2 and later

The `SimpleXMLRPCServer` module contains classes for creating cross-platform, language-independent servers using the XML-RPC protocol. Client libraries exist for many other languages besides Python, making XML-RPC an easy choice for building RPC-style services.

> **Note:** All the examples provided here include a client module as well to interact with the demonstration server. To run the examples, use two separate shell windows, one for the server and one for the client.

12.11.1   A Simple Server

This simple server example exposes a single function that takes the name of a directory and returns the contents. The first step is to create the `SimpleXMLRPCServer` instance and then tell it where to listen for incoming requests ('localhost' port 9000 in this case). The next step is to define a function to be part of the service and register it so the server knows how to call it. The final step is to put the server into an infinite loop receiving and responding to requests.

> **Warning:** This implementation has obvious security implications. Do not run it on a server on the open Internet or in any environment where security might be an issue.

```python
from SimpleXMLRPCServer import SimpleXMLRPCServer
import logging
import os

# Set up logging
logging.basicConfig(level=logging.DEBUG)

server = SimpleXMLRPCServer(('localhost', 9000), logRequests=True)

# Expose a function
def list_contents(dir_name):
    logging.debug('list_contents(%s)', dir_name)
    return os.listdir(dir_name)
server.register_function(list_contents)

# Start the server
try:
    print 'Use Control-C to exit'
    server.serve_forever()
except KeyboardInterrupt:
    print 'Exiting'
```

The server can be accessed at the URL `http://localhost:9000` using the client class from `xmlrpclib`. This example code illustrates how to call the `list_contents()` service from Python.

```python
import xmlrpclib

proxy = xmlrpclib.ServerProxy('http://localhost:9000')
print proxy.list_contents('/tmp')
```

The `ServerProxy` is connected to the server using its base URL, and then methods are called directly on the proxy. Each method invoked on the proxy is translated into a request to the server. The arguments are formatted using XML and then sent to the server in a POST message. The server unpacks the XML and determines which function to call based on the method name invoked from the client. The arguments are passed to the function, and the return value is translated back to XML to be returned to the client.

Starting the server gives:

```
$ python SimpleXMLRPCServer_function.py

Use Control-C to exit
```

Running the client in a second window shows the contents of the /tmp directory.

```
$ python SimpleXMLRPCServer_function_client.py

['.s.PGSQL.5432', '.s.PGSQL.5432.lock', '.X0-lock', '.X11-unix',
'ccc_exclude.1mkahl', 'ccc_exclude.BKG3gb', 'ccc_exclude.M5jrgo',
'ccc_exclude.SPecwL', 'com.hp.launchport', 'emacs527',
'hsperfdata_dhellmann', 'launch-8hGHUp', 'launch-RQnlcc',
'launch-trsdly', 'launchd-242.T5UzTy', 'var_backups']
```

After the request is finished, log output appears in the server window.

```
$ python SimpleXMLRPCServer_function.py

Use Control-C to exit
DEBUG:root:list_contents(/tmp)
localhost - - [29/Jun/2008 09:32:07] "POST /RPC2 HTTP/1.0" 200 -
```

The first line of output is from the `logging.debug()` call inside `list_contents()`. The second line is from the server logging the request because *logRequests* is `True`.

12.11.2 Alternate API Names

Sometimes, the function names used inside a module or library are not the names that should be used in the external API. Names may change because a platform-specific implementation is loaded, the service API is built dynamically based on a configuration file, or real functions are to be replaced with stubs for testing. To register a function with an alternate name, pass the name as the second argument to `register_function()`, like this:

```
from SimpleXMLRPCServer import SimpleXMLRPCServer
import os

server = SimpleXMLRPCServer(('localhost', 9000))

# Expose a function with an alternate name
def list_contents(dir_name):
    return os.listdir(dir_name)
server.register_function(list_contents, 'dir')

try:
    print 'Use Control-C to exit'
    server.serve_forever()
except KeyboardInterrupt:
    print 'Exiting'
```

The client should now use the name `dir()` instead of `list_contents()`.

```
import xmlrpclib

proxy = xmlrpclib.ServerProxy('http://localhost:9000')
print 'dir():', proxy.dir('/tmp')
try:
    print '\nlist_contents():', proxy.list_contents('/tmp')
except xmlrpclib.Fault as err:
    print '\nERROR:', err
```

Calling `list_contents()` results in an error, since the server no longer has a handler registered by that name.

```
$ python SimpleXMLRPCServer_alternate_name_client.py

dir(): ['ccc_exclude.GIqLcR', 'ccc_exclude.kzR42t',
'ccc_exclude.LV04nf', 'ccc_exclude.Vfzylm', 'emacs527',
'icssuis527', 'launch-9hTTwf', 'launch-kCXjtT',
'launch-Nwc3AB', 'launch-pwCgej', 'launch-Xrku4Q',
'launch-YtDZBJ', 'launchd-167.AfaNuZ', 'var_backups']

list_contents():
ERROR: <Fault 1: '<type \'exceptions.Exception\'>:method
"list_contents" is not supported'>
```

12.11.3   Dotted API Names

Individual functions can be registered with names that are not normally legal for Python identifiers. For example, a period (.) can be included in the names to separate the namespace in the service. The next example extends the "directory" service to add "create" and "remove" calls. All the functions are registered using the prefix "dir." so that the same server can provide other services using a different prefix. One other difference in this example is that some of the functions return None, so the server has to be told to translate the None values to a nil value.

```python
from SimpleXMLRPCServer import SimpleXMLRPCServer
import os

server = SimpleXMLRPCServer(('localhost', 9000), allow_none=True)

server.register_function(os.listdir, 'dir.list')
server.register_function(os.mkdir, 'dir.create')
server.register_function(os.rmdir, 'dir.remove')

try:
    print 'Use Control-C to exit'
    server.serve_forever()
except KeyboardInterrupt:
    print 'Exiting'
```

To call the service functions in the client, simply refer to them with the dotted name.

```python
import xmlrpclib

proxy = xmlrpclib.ServerProxy('http://localhost:9000')
print 'BEFORE       :', 'EXAMPLE' in proxy.dir.list('/tmp')
print 'CREATE       :', proxy.dir.create('/tmp/EXAMPLE')
print 'SHOULD EXIST :', 'EXAMPLE' in proxy.dir.list('/tmp')
print 'REMOVE       :', proxy.dir.remove('/tmp/EXAMPLE')
print 'AFTER        :', 'EXAMPLE' in proxy.dir.list('/tmp')
```

Assuming there is no /tmp/EXAMPLE file on the current system, this is the output for the sample client script.

```
$ python SimpleXMLRPCServer_dotted_name_client.py
```

```
BEFORE        : False
CREATE        : None
SHOULD EXIST  : True
REMOVE        : None
AFTER         : False
```

12.11.4 Arbitrary API Names

Another interesting feature is the ability to register functions with names that are otherwise invalid Python-object attribute names. This example service registers a function with the name "multiply args."

```python
from SimpleXMLRPCServer import SimpleXMLRPCServer

server = SimpleXMLRPCServer(('localhost', 9000))

def my_function(a, b):
    return a * b
server.register_function(my_function, 'multiply args')

try:
    print 'Use Control-C to exit'
    server.serve_forever()
except KeyboardInterrupt:
    print 'Exiting'
```

Since the registered name contains a space, dot notation cannot be used to access it directly from the proxy. Using getattr() does work, however.

```python
import xmlrpclib

proxy = xmlrpclib.ServerProxy('http://localhost:9000')
print getattr(proxy, 'multiply args')(5, 5)
```

Avoid creating services with names like this, though. This example is provided not necessarily because it is a good idea, but because existing services with arbitrary names exist, and new programs may need to be able to call them.

```
$ python SimpleXMLRPCServer_arbitrary_name_client.py
```

25

12.11.5 Exposing Methods of Objects

The earlier sections talked about techniques for establishing APIs using good naming conventions and namespacing. Another way to incorporate namespacing into an API is to use instances of classes and expose their methods. The first example can be re-created using an instance with a single method.

```python
from SimpleXMLRPCServer import SimpleXMLRPCServer
import os
import inspect

server = SimpleXMLRPCServer(('localhost', 9000), logRequests=True)

class DirectoryService:
    def list(self, dir_name):
        return os.listdir(dir_name)

server.register_instance(DirectoryService())

try:
    print 'Use Control-C to exit'
    server.serve_forever()
except KeyboardInterrupt:
    print 'Exiting'
```

A client can call the method directly as follows.

```python
import xmlrpclib

proxy = xmlrpclib.ServerProxy('http://localhost:9000')
print proxy.list('/tmp')
```

The output is:

```
$ python SimpleXMLRPCServer_instance_client.py

['ccc_exclude.1mkahl', 'ccc_exclude.BKG3gb', 'ccc_exclude.M5jrgo',
'ccc_exclude.SPecwL', 'com.hp.launchport', 'emacs527',
'hsperfdata_dhellmann', 'launch-8hGHUp', 'launch-RQnlcc',
'launch-trsdly', 'launchd-242.T5UzTy', 'var_backups']
```

The "dir." prefix for the service has been lost, though. It can be restored by defining a class to set up a service tree that can be invoked from clients.

```
from SimpleXMLRPCServer import SimpleXMLRPCServer
import os
import inspect

server = SimpleXMLRPCServer(('localhost', 9000), logRequests=True)

class ServiceRoot:
    pass

class DirectoryService:
    def list(self, dir_name):
        return os.listdir(dir_name)

root = ServiceRoot()
root.dir = DirectoryService()

server.register_instance(root, allow_dotted_names=True)

try:
    print 'Use Control-C to exit'
    server.serve_forever()
except KeyboardInterrupt:
    print 'Exiting'
```

By registering the instance of `ServiceRoot` with *allow_dotted_names* enabled, the server has permission to walk the tree of objects when a request comes in to find the named method using `getattr()`.

```
import xmlrpclib

proxy = xmlrpclib.ServerProxy('http://localhost:9000')
print proxy.dir.list('/tmp')
```

The output of `dir.list()` is the same as with the previous implementations.

```
$ python SimpleXMLRPCServer_instance_dotted_names_client.py

['ccc_exclude.1mkahl', 'ccc_exclude.BKG3gb', 'ccc_exclude.M5jrgo',
'ccc_exclude.SPecwL', 'com.hp.launchport', 'emacs527',
'hsperfdata_dhellmann', 'launch-8hGHUp', 'launch-RQnlcc',
'launch-trsdly', 'launchd-242.T5UzTy', 'var_backups']
```

12.11.6   Dispatching Calls

By default, `register_instance()` finds all callable attributes of the instance with names not starting with an underscore ("_") and registers them with their name. To be more careful about the exposed methods, custom dispatching logic can be used, as in the following example.

```python
from SimpleXMLRPCServer import SimpleXMLRPCServer
import os
import inspect

server = SimpleXMLRPCServer(('localhost', 9000), logRequests=True)

def expose(f):
    "Decorator to set exposed flag on a function."
    f.exposed = True
    return f

def is_exposed(f):
    "Test whether another function should be publicly exposed."
    return getattr(f, 'exposed', False)

class MyService:
    PREFIX = 'prefix'

    def _dispatch(self, method, params):
        # Remove our prefix from the method name
        if not method.startswith(self.PREFIX + '.'):
            raise Exception('method "%s" is not supported' % method)

        method_name = method.partition('.')[2]
        func = getattr(self, method_name)
        if not is_exposed(func):
            raise Exception('method "%s" is not supported' % method)

        return func(*params)

    @expose
    def public(self):
        return 'This is public'

    def private(self):
        return 'This is private'
server.register_instance(MyService())
```

```
try:
    print 'Use Control-C to exit'
    server.serve_forever()
except KeyboardInterrupt:
    print 'Exiting'
```

The `public()` method of `MyService` is marked as exposed to the XML-RPC service while `private()` is not. The `_dispatch()` method is invoked when the client tries to access a function that is part of `MyService`. It first enforces the use of a prefix ("`prefix.`" in this case, but any string can be used). Then it requires the function to have an attribute called *exposed* with a true value. The exposed flag is set on a function using a decorator for convenience.

Here are a few sample client calls.

```
import xmlrpclib

proxy = xmlrpclib.ServerProxy('http://localhost:9000')
print 'public():', proxy.prefix.public()
try:
    print 'private():', proxy.prefix.private()
except Exception, err:
    print '\nERROR:', err
try:
    print 'public() without prefix:', proxy.public()
except Exception, err:
    print '\nERROR:', err
```

And here is the resulting output, with the expected error messages trapped and reported.

```
$ python SimpleXMLRPCServer_instance_with_prefix_client.py

public(): This is public
private():
ERROR: <Fault 1: '<type \'exceptions.Exception\'>:method
"prefix.private" is not supported'>
public() without prefix:
ERROR: <Fault 1: '<type \'exceptions.Exception\'>:method
"public" is not supported'>
```

There are several other ways to override the dispatching mechanism, including subclassing directly from `SimpleXMLRPCServer`. Refer to the docstrings in the module for more details.

12.11.7 Introspection API

As with many network services, it is possible to query an XML-RPC server to ask it what methods it supports and learn how to use them. `SimpleXMLRPCServer` includes a set of public methods for performing this introspection. By default, they are turned off, but can be enabled with `register_introspection_functions()`. Support for `system.listMethods()` and `system.methodHelp()` can be added to a service by defining `_listMethods()` and `_methodHelp()` on the service class.

```python
from SimpleXMLRPCServer import ( SimpleXMLRPCServer,
                                 list_public_methods,
                                 )
import os
import inspect

server = SimpleXMLRPCServer(('localhost', 9000), logRequests=True)
server.register_introspection_functions()

class DirectoryService:

    def _listMethods(self):
        return list_public_methods(self)

    def _methodHelp(self, method):
        f = getattr(self, method)
        return inspect.getdoc(f)

    def list(self, dir_name):
        """list(dir_name) => [<filenames>]

        Returns a list containing the contents of
        the named directory.
        """
        return os.listdir(dir_name)

server.register_instance(DirectoryService())

try:
    print 'Use Control-C to exit'
    server.serve_forever()
except KeyboardInterrupt:
    print 'Exiting'
```

In this case, the convenience function `list_public_methods()` scans an instance to return the names of callable attributes that do not start with underscore (_). Redefine `_listMethods()` to apply whatever rules are desired. Similarly, for this basic example, `_methodHelp()` returns the docstring of the function, but could be written to build a help string from another source.

This client queries the server and reports on all the publicly callable methods.

```
import xmlrpclib

proxy = xmlrpclib.ServerProxy('http://localhost:9000')
for method_name in proxy.system.listMethods():
    print '=' * 60
    print method_name
    print '-' * 60
    print proxy.system.methodHelp(method_name)
    print
```

The system methods are included in the results.

```
$ python SimpleXMLRPCServer_introspection_client.py

============================================================
list
------------------------------------------------------------
list(dir_name) => [<filenames>]

Returns a list containing the contents of the named directory.

============================================================
system.listMethods
------------------------------------------------------------
system.listMethods() => ['add', 'subtract', 'multiple']

Returns a list of the methods supported by the server.

============================================================
system.methodHelp
------------------------------------------------------------
system.methodHelp('add') => "Adds two integers together"

Returns a string containing documentation for the specified method.
```

```
================================================================
system.methodSignature
----------------------------------------------------------------
system.methodSignature('add') => [double, int, int]
```

```
Returns a list describing the signature of the method. In the
above example, the add method takes two integers as arguments
and returns a double result.
```

```
This server does NOT support system.methodSignature.
```

See Also:

SimpleXMLRPCServer

> **(http://docs.python.org/lib/module-SimpleXMLRPCServer.html)** The standard library documentation for this module.

XML-RPC How To

> **(http://www.tldp.org/HOWTO/XML-RPC-HOWTO/index.html)** Describes how to use XML-RPC to implement clients and servers in a variety of languages.

XML-RPC Extensions (http://ontosys.com/xml-rpc/extensions.php) Specifies an extension to the XML-RPC protocol.

xmlrpclib (page 702) XML-RPC client library.

Chapter 13

EMAIL

Email is one of the oldest forms of digital communication, but it is still one of the most popular. Python's standard library includes modules for sending, receiving, and storing email messages.

smtplib communicates with a mail server to deliver a message. smtpd can be used to create a custom mail server, and it provides classes useful for debugging email transmission in other applications.

imaplib uses the IMAP protocol to manipulate messages stored on a server. It provides a low-level API for IMAP clients and can query, retrieve, move, and delete messages.

Local message archives can be created and modified with mailbox using several standard formats, including the popular mbox and Maildir formats used by many email client programs.

13.1 smtplib—Simple Mail Transfer Protocol Client

Purpose Interact with SMTP servers, including sending email.
Python Version 1.5.2 and later

smtplib includes the class SMTP, which can be used to communicate with mail servers to send mail.

> **Note:** The email addresses, hostnames, and IP addresses in the following examples have been obscured. Otherwise, the transcripts illustrate the sequence of commands and responses accurately.

13.1.1 Sending an Email Message

The most common use of SMTP is to connect to a mail server and send a message. The mail server host name and port can be passed to the constructor, or connect() can be invoked explicitly. Once connected, call sendmail() with the envelope parameters and the body of the message. The message text should be fully formed and comply with RFC 2882, since smtplib does not modify the contents or headers at all. That means the caller needs to add the From and To headers.

```python
import smtplib
import email.utils
from email.mime.text import MIMEText

# Create the message
msg = MIMEText('This is the body of the message.')
msg['To'] = email.utils.formataddr(('Recipient',
                                    'recipient@example.com'))
msg['From'] = email.utils.formataddr(('Author',
                                      'author@example.com'))
msg['Subject'] = 'Simple test message'

server = smtplib.SMTP('mail')
server.set_debuglevel(True)  # show communication with the server
try:
    server.sendmail('author@example.com',
                    ['recipient@example.com'],
                    msg.as_string())
finally:
    server.quit()
```

In this example, debugging is also turned on to show the communication between the client and the server. Otherwise, the example would produce no output at all.

```
$ python smtplib_sendmail.py

send: 'ehlo farnsworth.local\r\n'
reply: '250-mail.example.com Hello [192.168.1.27], pleased to meet y
ou\r\n'
reply: '250-ENHANCEDSTATUSCODES\r\n'
reply: '250-PIPELINING\r\n'
reply: '250-8BITMIME\r\n'
reply: '250-SIZE\r\n'
```

```
reply: '250-DSN\r\n'
reply: '250-ETRN\r\n'
reply: '250-AUTH GSSAPI DIGEST-MD5 CRAM-MD5\r\n'
reply: '250-DELIVERBY\r\n'
reply: '250 HELP\r\n'
reply: retcode (250); Msg: mail.example.com Hello [192.168.1.27], pl
eased to meet you
ENHANCEDSTATUSCODES
PIPELINING
8BITMIME
SIZE
DSN
ETRN
AUTH GSSAPI DIGEST-MD5 CRAM-MD5
DELIVERBY
HELP
send: 'mail FROM:<author@example.com> size=229\r\n'
reply: '250 2.1.0 <author@example.com>... Sender ok\r\n'
reply: retcode (250); Msg: 2.1.0 <author@example.com>... Sender ok
send: 'rcpt TO:<recipient@example.com>\r\n'
reply: '250 2.1.5 <recipient@example.com>... Recipient ok\r\n'
reply: retcode (250); Msg: 2.1.5 <recipient@example.com>... Recipien
t ok
send: 'data\r\n'
reply: '354 Enter mail, end with "." on a line by itself\r\n'
reply: retcode (354); Msg: Enter mail, end with "." on a line by its
elf
data: (354, 'Enter mail, end with "." on a line by itself')
send: 'Content-Type: text/plain; charset="us-ascii"\r\nMIME-Version:
 1.0\r\nContent-Transfer-Encoding: 7bit\r\nTo: Recipient <recipient@
example.com>\r\nFrom: Author <author@example.com>\r\nSubject: Simple
 test message\r\n\r\nThis is the body of the message.\r\n.\r\n'
reply: '250 2.0.0 oAT1TiRA010200 Message accepted for delivery\r\n'
reply: retcode (250); Msg: 2.0.0 oAT1TiRA010200 Message accepted for
 delivery
data: (250, '2.0.0 oAT1TiRA010200 Message accepted for delivery')
send: 'quit\r\n'
reply: '221 2.0.0 mail.example.com closing connection\r\n'
reply: retcode (221); Msg: 2.0.0 mail.example.com closing connection
```

The second argument to `sendmail()`, the recipients, is passed as a list. Any number of addresses can be included in the list to have the message delivered to each of them in turn. Since the envelope information is separate from the message headers, it is possible to blind carbon copy (BCC) someone by including them in the method argument, but not in the message header.

13.1.2 Authentication and Encryption

The SMTP class also handles authentication and TLS (transport layer security) encryption, when the server supports them. To determine if the server supports TLS, call ehlo() directly to identify the client to the server and ask it what extensions are available. Then, call has_extn() to check the results. After TLS is started, ehlo() must be called again before authenticating.

```python
import smtplib
import email.utils
from email.mime.text import MIMEText
import getpass

# Prompt the user for connection info
to_email = raw_input('Recipient: ')
servername = raw_input('Mail server name: ')
username = raw_input('Mail username: ')
password = getpass.getpass("%s's password: " % username)

# Create the message
msg = MIMEText('Test message from PyMOTW.')
msg.set_unixfrom('author')
msg['To'] = email.utils.formataddr(('Recipient', to_email))
msg['From'] = email.utils.formataddr(('Author',
                                      'author@example.com'))
msg['Subject'] = 'Test from PyMOTW'

server = smtplib.SMTP(servername)
try:
    server.set_debuglevel(True)

    # identify ourselves, prompting server for supported features
    server.ehlo()

    # If we can encrypt this session, do it
    if server.has_extn('STARTTLS'):
        server.starttls()
        server.ehlo() # reidentify ourselves over TLS connection

    server.login(username, password)
```

```
    server.sendmail('author@example.com',
                    [to_email],
                    msg.as_string())
finally:
    server.quit()
```

The STARTTLS extension does not appear in the reply to EHLO after TLS is
enabled.

```
$ python smtplib_authenticated.py

Recipient: recipient@example.com
Mail server name: smtpauth.isp.net
Mail username: user@isp.net
user@isp.net's password:
send: 'ehlo localhost.local\r\n'
reply: '250-elasmtp-isp.net Hello localhost.local [<your IP here>]\r
\n'
reply: '250-SIZE 14680064\r\n'
reply: '250-PIPELINING\r\n'
reply: '250-AUTH PLAIN LOGIN CRAM-MD5\r\n'
reply: '250-STARTTLS\r\n'
reply: '250 HELP\r\n'
reply: retcode (250); Msg: elasmtp-isp.net Hello localhost.local [<y
our IP here>]
SIZE 14680064
PIPELINING
AUTH PLAIN LOGIN CRAM-MD5
STARTTLS
HELP
send: 'STARTTLS\r\n'
reply: '220 TLS go ahead\r\n'
reply: retcode (220); Msg: TLS go ahead
send: 'ehlo localhost.local\r\n'
reply: '250-elasmtp-isp.net Hello localhost.local [<your IP here>]\r
\n'
reply: '250-SIZE 14680064\r\n'
reply: '250-PIPELINING\r\n'
reply: '250-AUTH PLAIN LOGIN CRAM-MD5\r\n'
reply: '250 HELP\r\n'
reply: retcode (250); Msg: elasmtp-isp.net Hello farnsworth.local [<
your
IP here>]
```

```
SIZE 14680064
PIPELINING
AUTH PLAIN LOGIN CRAM-MD5
HELP
send: 'AUTH CRAM-MD5\r\n'
reply: '334 PDExNjkyLjEyMjI2MTI1NzlAZWxhc210cC1tZWFseS5hdGwuc2EuZWFy
dGhsa
W5rLm5ldD4=\r\n'
reply: retcode (334); Msg: PDExNjkyLjEyMjI2MTI1NzlAZWxhc210cC1tZWFse
S5hdG
wuc2EuZWFydGhsaW5rLm5ldD4=
send: 'ZGhlbGxtYW5uQGVhcnRobGluay5uZXQgN2Q1YjAyYTRmMGQ1YzZjM2NjOTNjZ
Dc1MD
QxN2ViYjg=\r\n'
reply: '235 Authentication succeeded\r\n'
reply: retcode (235); Msg: Authentication succeeded
send: 'mail FROM:<author@example.com> size=221\r\n'
reply: '250 OK\r\n'
reply: retcode (250); Msg: OK
send: 'rcpt TO:<recipient@example.com>\r\n'
reply: '250 Accepted\r\n'
reply: retcode (250); Msg: Accepted
send: 'data\r\n'
reply: '354 Enter message, ending with "." on a line by itself\r\n'
reply: retcode (354); Msg: Enter message, ending with "." on a line
by itself
data: (354, 'Enter message, ending with "." on a line by itself')
send: 'Content-Type: text/plain; charset="us-ascii"\r\nMIME-Version:
1.0\r\nContent-Transfer-Encoding: 7bit\r\nTo: Recipient
<recipient@example.com>\r\nFrom: Author <author@example.com>\r\nSubj
ect: Test
from PyMOTW\r\n\r\nTest message from PyMOTW.\r\n.\r\n'
reply: '250 OK id=1KjxNj-00032a-Ux\r\n'
reply: retcode (250); Msg: OK id=1KjxNj-00032a-Ux
data: (250, 'OK id=1KjxNj-00032a-Ux')
send: 'quit\r\n'
reply: '221 elasmtp-isp.net closing connection\r\n'
reply: retcode (221); Msg: elasmtp-isp.net closing connection
```

13.1.3   Verifying an Email Address

The SMTP protocol includes a command to ask a server whether an address is valid.
Usually, VRFY is disabled to prevent spammers from finding legitimate email addresses.

But, if it is enabled, a client can ask the server about an address and receive a status code indicating validity, along with the user's full name, if it is available.

```
import smtplib

server = smtplib.SMTP('mail')
server.set_debuglevel(True) # show communication with the server
try:
    dhellmann_result = server.verify('dhellmann')
    notthere_result = server.verify('notthere')
finally:
    server.quit()

print 'dhellmann:', dhellmann_result
print 'notthere :', notthere_result
```

As the last two lines of output here show, the address `dhellmann` is valid but `notthere` is not.

```
$ python smtplib_verify.py

send: 'vrfy <dhellmann>\r\n'
reply: '250 2.1.5 Doug Hellmann <dhellmann@mail.example.com>\r\n'
reply: retcode (250); Msg: 2.1.5 Doug Hellmann <dhellmann@mail.examp
le.com>
send: 'vrfy <notthere>\r\n'
reply: '550 5.1.1 <notthere>... User unknown\r\n'
reply: retcode (550); Msg: 5.1.1 <notthere>... User unknown
send: 'quit\r\n'
reply: '221 2.0.0 mail.example.com closing connection\r\n'
reply: retcode (221); Msg: 2.0.0 mail.example.com closing connection
dhellmann: (250, '2.1.5 Doug Hellmann <dhellmann@mail.example.com>')
notthere : (550, '5.1.1 <notthere>... User unknown')
```

See Also:
smtplib (http://docs.python.org/lib/module-smtplib.html) The Standard library documentation for this module.

RFC 821 (http://tools.ietf.org/html/rfc821.html) The Simple Mail Transfer Protocol (SMTP) specification.

RFC 1869 (http://tools.ietf.org/html/rfc1869.html) SMTP Service Extensions to the base protocol.

RFC 822 (http://tools.ietf.org/html/rfc822.html) "Standard for the Format of ARPA Internet Text Messages," the original email message format specification.

RFC 2822 (http://tools.ietf.org/html/rfc2822.html) "Internet Message Format" updates to the email message format.

email The Standard library module for parsing email messages.

smtpd (page 734) Implements a simple SMTP server.

13.2   smtpd—Sample Mail Servers

> **Purpose** Includes classes for implementing SMTP servers.
> **Python Version** 2.1 and later

The `smtpd` module includes classes for building simple mail transport protocol servers. It is the server side of the protocol used by `smtplib`.

13.2.1   Mail Server Base Class

The base class for all the provided example servers is `SMTPServer`. It handles communicating with the client and receiving incoming data, and provides a convenient hook to override so the message can be processed once it is fully available.

The constructor arguments are the local address to listen for connections and the remote address where proxied messages should be delivered. The method `process_message()` is provided as a hook to be overridden by a derived class. It is called when the message is completely received, and it is given these arguments.

peer

> The client's address, a tuple containing IP and incoming port.

mailfrom

> The "from" information out of the message envelope, given to the server by the client when the message is delivered. This information does not necessarily match the `From` header in all cases.

rcpttos

> The list of recipients from the message envelope. Again, this list does not always match the `To` header, especially if a recipient is being blind carbon copied.

data

> The full RFC 2822 message body.

The default implementation of `process_message()` raises `NotImplemented-Error`. The next example defines a subclass that overrides the method to print information about the messages it receives.

```
import smtpd
import asyncore

class CustomSMTPServer(smtpd.SMTPServer):

    def process_message(self, peer, mailfrom, rcpttos, data):
        print 'Receiving message from:', peer
        print 'Message addressed from:', mailfrom
        print 'Message addressed to  :', rcpttos
        print 'Message length        :', len(data)
        return

server = CustomSMTPServer(('127.0.0.1', 1025), None)

asyncore.loop()
```

`SMTPServer` uses `asyncore`; so to run the server, call `asyncore.loop()`.

A client is needed to demonstrate the server. One of the examples from the section on `smtplib` can be adapted to create a client to send data to the test server running locally on port 1025.

```
import smtplib
import email.utils
from email.mime.text import MIMEText

# Create the message
msg = MIMEText('This is the body of the message.')
msg['To'] = email.utils.formataddr(('Recipient',
                                    'recipient@example.com'))
msg['From'] = email.utils.formataddr(('Author',
                                      'author@example.com'))
msg['Subject'] = 'Simple test message'

server = smtplib.SMTP('127.0.0.1', 1025)
server.set_debuglevel(True) # show communication with the server
try:
    server.sendmail('author@example.com',
                    ['recipient@example.com'],
                    msg.as_string())
```

```
finally:
    server.quit()
```

To test the programs, run `smtpd_custom.py` in one terminal and `smtpd_senddata.py` in another.

```
$ python smtpd_custom.py

Receiving message from: ('127.0.0.1', 58541)
Message addressed from: author@example.com
Message addressed to  : ['recipient@example.com']
Message length        : 229
```

The debug output from `smtpd_senddata.py` shows all the communication with the server.

```
$ python smtpd_senddata.py

send: 'ehlo farnsworth.local\r\n'
reply: '502 Error: command "EHLO" not implemented\r\n'
reply: retcode (502); Msg: Error: command "EHLO" not implemented
send: 'helo farnsworth.local\r\n'
reply: '250 farnsworth.local\r\n'
reply: retcode (250); Msg: farnsworth.local
send: 'mail FROM:<author@example.com>\r\n'
reply: '250 Ok\r\n'
reply: retcode (250); Msg: Ok
send: 'rcpt TO:<recipient@example.com>\r\n'
reply: '250 Ok\r\n'
reply: retcode (250); Msg: Ok
send: 'data\r\n'
reply: '354 End data with <CR><LF>.<CR><LF>\r\n'
reply: retcode (354); Msg: End data with <CR><LF>.<CR><LF>
data: (354, 'End data with <CR><LF>.<CR><LF>')
send: 'Content-Type: text/plain; charset="us-ascii"\r\nMIME-Version:
 1.0\r\n
Content-Transfer-Encoding: 7bit\r\nTo: Recipient <recipient@example.
com>\r\n
From: Author <author@example.com>\r\nSubject: Simple test message\r\
n\r\nThis
 is the body of the message.\r\n.\r\n'
reply: '250 Ok\r\n'
```

```
reply: retcode (250); Msg: Ok
data: (250, 'Ok')
send: 'quit\r\n'
reply: '221 Bye\r\n'
reply: retcode (221); Msg: Bye
```

To stop the server, press `Ctrl-C`.

13.2.2 Debugging Server

The previous example shows the arguments to `process_message()`, but `smtpd` also includes a server specifically designed for more complete debugging, called `DebuggingServer`. It prints the entire incoming message to the console and then stops processing (it does not proxy the message to a real mail server).

```
import smtpd
import asyncore

server = smtpd.DebuggingServer(('127.0.0.1', 1025), None)

asyncore.loop()
```

Using the `smtpd_senddata.py` client program from earlier, here is the output of the `DebuggingServer`.

```
$ python smtpd_debug.py

---------- MESSAGE FOLLOWS ----------
Content-Type: text/plain; charset="us-ascii"
MIME-Version: 1.0
Content-Transfer-Encoding: 7bit
To: Recipient <recipient@example.com>
From: Author <author@example.com>
Subject: Simple test message
X-Peer: 127.0.0.1

This is the body of the message.
------------ END MESSAGE ------------
```

13.2.3 Proxy Server

The `PureProxy` class implements a straightforward proxy server. Incoming messages are forwarded upstream to the server given as argument to the constructor.

> **Warning:** The standard library documentation for `smtpd` says, "running this has a good chance to make you into an open relay, so please be careful."

The steps for setting up the proxy server are similar to the debug server.

```
import smtpd
import asyncore

server = smtpd.PureProxy(('127.0.0.1', 1025), ('mail', 25))

asyncore.loop()
```

It prints no output, though, so to verify that it is working, look at the mail server logs.

```
Oct 19 19:16:34 homer sendmail[6785]: m9JNGXJb006785:
from=<author@example.com>, size=248, class=0, nrcpts=1,
msgid=<200810192316.m9JNGXJb006785@homer.example.com>,
proto=ESMTP, daemon=MTA, relay=[192.168.1.17]
```

See Also:
smtpd (http://docs.python.org/lib/module-smtpd.html) The Standard library documentation for this module.
smtplib (page 727) Provides a client interface.
email Parses email messages.
asyncore (page 619) Base module for writing asynchronous servers.
RFC 2822 (http://tools.ietf.org/html/rfc2822.html) Defines the email message format.

13.3   imaplib—IMAP4 Client Library

Purpose Client library for IMAP4 communication.
Python Version 1.5.2 and later

`imaplib` implements a client for communicating with Internet Message Access Protocol (IMAP) version 4 servers. The IMAP protocol defines a set of commands sent to the server and the responses delivered back to the client. Most of the commands are available as methods of the `IMAP4` object used to communicate with the server.

These examples discuss part of the IMAP protocol, but they are by no means complete. Refer to RFC 3501 for complete details.

13.3.1 Variations

Three client classes are available for communicating with servers using various mechanisms. The first, IMAP4, uses clear text sockets; IMAP4_SSL uses encrypted communication over SSL sockets; and IMAP4_stream uses the standard input and standard output of an external command. All the examples here will use IMAP4_SSL, but the APIs for the other classes are similar.

13.3.2 Connecting to a Server

There are two steps for establishing a connection with an IMAP server. First, set up the socket connection itself. Second, authenticate as a user with an account on the server. The following example code will read server and user information from a configuration file.

```python
import imaplib
import ConfigParser
import os

def open_connection(verbose=False):
    # Read the config file
    config = ConfigParser.ConfigParser()
    config.read([os.path.expanduser('~/.pymotw')])

    # Connect to the server
    hostname = config.get('server', 'hostname')
    if verbose: print 'Connecting to', hostname
    connection = imaplib.IMAP4_SSL(hostname)

    # Login to our account
    username = config.get('account', 'username')
    password = config.get('account', 'password')
    if verbose: print 'Logging in as', username
    connection.login(username, password)
    return connection

if __name__ == '__main__':
    c = open_connection(verbose=True)
```

```
try:
    print c
finally:
    c.logout()
```

When run, `open_connection()` reads the configuration information from a file in the user's home directory, and then opens the `IMAP4_SSL` connection and authenticates.

```
$ python imaplib_connect.py

Connecting to mail.example.com
Logging in as example
<imaplib.IMAP4_SSL instance at 0x928cb0>
```

The other examples in this section reuse this module, to avoid duplicating the code.

Authentication Failure

If the connection is established but authentication fails, an exception is raised.

```
import imaplib
import ConfigParser
import os

# Read the config file
config = ConfigParser.ConfigParser()
config.read([os.path.expanduser('~/.pymotw')])

# Connect to the server
hostname = config.get('server', 'hostname')
print 'Connecting to', hostname
connection = imaplib.IMAP4_SSL(hostname)

# Login to our account
username = config.get('account', 'username')
password = 'this_is_the_wrong_password'
print 'Logging in as', username
try:
    connection.login(username, password)
except Exception as err:
    print 'ERROR:', err
```

This example uses the wrong password on purpose to trigger the exception.

```
$ python imaplib_connect_fail.py

Connecting to mail.example.com
Logging in as example
ERROR: Authentication failed.
```

13.3.3   Example Configuration

The example account has three mailboxes: `INBOX`, `Archive`, and `2008` (a subfolder of `Archive`). This is the mailbox hierarchy:

- INBOX
- Archive
    - 2008

There is one unread message in the `INBOX` folder and one read message in `Archive/2008`.

13.3.4   Listing Mailboxes

To retrieve the mailboxes available for an account, use the `list()` method.

```
import imaplib
from pprint import pprint
from imaplib_connect import open_connection

c = open_connection()
try:
    typ, data = c.list()
    print 'Response code:', typ
    print 'Response:'
    pprint(data)
finally:
    c.logout()
```

The return value is a `tuple` containing a response code and the data returned by the server. The response code is `OK`, unless an error has occurred. The data for `list()` is a sequence of strings containing *flags*, the *hierarchy delimiter*, and the *mailbox name* for each mailbox.

```
$ python imaplib_list.py

Response code: OK
Response:
['(\\HasNoChildren) "." INBOX',
 '(\\HasChildren) "." "Archive"',
 '(\\HasNoChildren) "." "Archive.2008"']
```

Each response string can be split into three parts using `re` or `csv` (see *IMAP Backup Script* in the references at the end of this section for an example using `csv`).

```python
import imaplib
import re

from imaplib_connect import open_connection

list_response_pattern = re.compile(
    r'\((?P<flags>.*?)\) "(?P<delimiter>.*)" (?P<name>.*)'
    )

def parse_list_response(line):
    match = list_response_pattern.match(line)
    flags, delimiter, mailbox_name = match.groups()
    mailbox_name = mailbox_name.strip('"')
    return (flags, delimiter, mailbox_name)

if __name__ == '__main__':
    c = open_connection()
    try:
        typ, data = c.list()
    finally:
        c.logout()
    print 'Response code:', typ

    for line in data:
        print 'Server response:', line
        flags, delimiter, mailbox_name = parse_list_response(line)
        print 'Parsed response:', (flags, delimiter, mailbox_name)
```

The server quotes the mailbox name if it includes spaces, but those quotes need to be stripped out to use the mailbox name in other calls back to the server later.

```
$ python imaplib_list_parse.py

Response code: OK
Server response: (\HasNoChildren) "." INBOX
Parsed response: ('\\HasNoChildren', '.', 'INBOX')
Server response: (\HasChildren) "." "Archive"
Parsed response: ('\\HasChildren', '.', 'Archive')
Server response: (\HasNoChildren) "." "Archive.2008"
Parsed response: ('\\HasNoChildren', '.', 'Archive.2008')
```

list() takes arguments to specify mailboxes in part of the hierarchy. For example, to list subfolders of Archive, pass "Archive" as the *directory* argument.

```
import imaplib

from imaplib_connect import open_connection

if __name__ == '__main__':
    c = open_connection()
    try:
        typ, data = c.list(directory='Archive')
    finally:
        c.logout()
    print 'Response code:', typ

    for line in data:
        print 'Server response:', line
```

Only the single subfolder is returned.

```
$ python imaplib_list_subfolders.py

Response code: OK
Server response: (\HasNoChildren) "." "Archive.2008"
```

Alternately, to list folders matching a pattern, pass the *pattern* argument.

```
import imaplib

from imaplib_connect import open_connection
```

```
if __name__ == '__main__':
    c = open_connection()
    try:
        typ, data = c.list(pattern='*Archive*')
    finally:
        c.logout()
    print 'Response code:', typ

    for line in data:
        print 'Server response:', line
```

In this case, both `Archive` and `Archive.2008` are included in the response.

```
$ python imaplib_list_pattern.py

Response code: OK
Server response: (\HasChildren) "." "Archive"
Server response: (\HasNoChildren) "." "Archive.2008"
```

13.3.5   Mailbox Status

Use `status()` to ask for aggregated information about the contents. Table 13.1 lists the status conditions defined by the standard.

Table 13.1. IMAP 4 Mailbox Status Conditions

Condition	Meaning
MESSAGES	The number of messages in the mailbox
RECENT	The number of messages with the \Recent flag set
UIDNEXT	The next unique identifier value of the mailbox
UIDVALIDITY	The unique identifier validity value of the mailbox
UNSEEN	The number of messages that do not have the \Seen flag set

The status conditions must be formatted as a space-separated string enclosed in parentheses, the encoding for a "list" in the IMAP4 specification.

```
import imaplib
import re

from imaplib_connect import open_connection
from imaplib_list_parse import parse_list_response
```

```
if __name__ == '__main__':
    c = open_connection()
    try:
        typ, data = c.list()
        for line in data:
            flags, delimiter, mailbox = parse_list_response(line)
            print c.status(
                mailbox,
                '(MESSAGES RECENT UIDNEXT UIDVALIDITY UNSEEN)')
    finally:
        c.logout()
```

The return value is the usual `tuple` containing a response code and a list of information from the server. In this case, the list contains a single string formatted with the name of the mailbox in quotes, and then the status conditions and values in parentheses.

```
$ python imaplib_status.py

('OK', ['"INBOX" (MESSAGES 1 RECENT 0 UIDNEXT 3 UIDVALIDITY
1222003700 UNSEEN 1)'])
('OK', ['"Archive" (MESSAGES 0 RECENT 0 UIDNEXT 1 UIDVALIDITY
1222003809 UNSEEN 0)'])
('OK', ['"Archive.2008" (MESSAGES 1 RECENT 0 UIDNEXT 2 UIDVALIDITY
1222003831 UNSEEN 0)'])
```

13.3.6 Selecting a Mailbox

The basic mode of operation, once the client is authenticated, is to select a mailbox and then interrogate the server regarding the messages in the mailbox. The connection is stateful, so after a mailbox is selected, all commands operate on messages in that mailbox until a new mailbox is selected.

```
import imaplib
import imaplib_connect

c = imaplib_connect.open_connection()
try:
    typ, data = c.select('INBOX')
    print typ, data
    num_msgs = int(data[0])
    print 'There are %d messages in INBOX' % num_msgs
```

```
finally:
    c.close()
    c.logout()
```

The response data contains the total number of messages in the mailbox.

```
$ python imaplib_select.py

OK ['1']
There are 1 messages in INBOX
```

If an invalid mailbox is specified, the response code is NO.

```
import imaplib
import imaplib_connect

c = imaplib_connect.open_connection()
try:
    typ, data = c.select('Does Not Exist')
    print typ, data
finally:
    c.logout()
```

The data contains an error message describing the problem.

```
$ python imaplib_select_invalid.py

NO ["Mailbox doesn't exist: Does Not Exist"]
```

13.3.7 Searching for Messages

After selecting the mailbox, use `search()` to retrieve the IDs of messages in the mailbox.

```
import imaplib
import imaplib_connect
from imaplib_list_parse import parse_list_response

c = imaplib_connect.open_connection()
try:
    typ, mailbox_data = c.list()
```

```
    for line in mailbox_data:
        flags, delimiter, mailbox_name = parse_list_response(line)
        c.select(mailbox_name, readonly=True)
        typ, msg_ids = c.search(None, 'ALL')
        print mailbox_name, typ, msg_ids
finally:
    try:
        c.close()
    except:
        pass
    c.logout()
```

Message ids are assigned by the server and are implementation dependent. The IMAP4 protocol makes a distinction between sequential ids for messages at a given point in time during a transaction and UID identifiers for messages, but not all servers implement both.

```
$ python imaplib_search_all.py

INBOX OK ['1']
Archive OK ['']
Archive.2008 OK ['1']
```

In this case, `INBOX` and `Archive.2008` each have a different message with id 1. The other mailboxes are empty.

13.3.8 Search Criteria

A variety of other search criteria can be used, including looking at dates for the message, flags, and other headers. Refer to section 6.4.4 of RFC 3501 for complete details.

To look for messages with `'test message 2'` in the subject, the search criteria should be constructed as follows.

```
(SUBJECT "test message 2")
```

This example finds all messages with the title "test message 2" in all mailboxes.

```
import imaplib
import imaplib_connect
from imaplib_list_parse import parse_list_response

c = imaplib_connect.open_connection()
```

```
try:
    typ, mailbox_data = c.list()
    for line in mailbox_data:
        flags, delimiter, mailbox_name = parse_list_response(line)
        c.select(mailbox_name, readonly=True)
        typ, msg_ids = c.search(None, '(SUBJECT "test message 2")')
        print mailbox_name, typ, msg_ids
finally:
    try:
        c.close()
    except:
        pass
    c.logout()
```

There is only one such message in the account, and it is in the INBOX.

```
$ python imaplib_search_subject.py

INBOX OK ['1']
Archive OK ['']
Archive.2008 OK ['']
```

Search criteria can also be combined.

```
import imaplib
import imaplib_connect
from imaplib_list_parse import parse_list_response

c = imaplib_connect.open_connection()
try:
    typ, mailbox_data = c.list()
    for line in mailbox_data:
        flags, delimiter, mailbox_name = parse_list_response(line)
        c.select(mailbox_name, readonly=True)
        typ, msg_ids = c.search(
            None,
            '(FROM "Doug" SUBJECT "test message 2")')
        print mailbox_name, typ, msg_ids
finally:
    try:
        c.close()
    except:
        pass
    c.logout()
```

The criteria are combined with a logical **and** operation.

```
$ python imaplib_search_from.py

INBOX OK ['1']
Archive OK ['']
Archive.2008 OK ['']
```

13.3.9   Fetching Messages

The identifiers returned by `search()` are used to retrieve the contents, or partial contents, of messages for further processing using the `fetch()` method. It takes two arguments: the message to fetch and the portion(s) of the message to retrieve.

The *message_ids* argument is a comma-separated list of ids (e.g., `"1"`, `"1,2"`) or id ranges (e.g., `1:2`). The *message_parts* argument is an IMAP list of message segment names. As with search criteria for `search()`, the IMAP protocol specifies named message segments so clients can efficiently retrieve only the parts of the message they actually need. For example, to retrieve the headers of the messages in a mailbox, use `fetch()` with the argument `BODY.PEEK[HEADER]`.

> **Note:** Another way to fetch the headers is `BODY[HEADERS]`, but that form has a side effect of implicitly marking the message as read, which is undesirable in many cases.

```
import imaplib
import pprint
import imaplib_connect

imaplib.Debug = 4
c = imaplib_connect.open_connection()
try:
    c.select('INBOX', readonly=True)
    typ, msg_data = c.fetch('1', '(BODY.PEEK[HEADER] FLAGS)')
    pprint.pprint(msg_data)
finally:
    try:
        c.close()
    except:
        pass
    c.logout()
```

The return value of `fetch()` has been partially parsed so it is somewhat harder to work with than the return value of `list()`. Turning on debugging shows the complete interaction between the client and the server to understand why this is so.

```
$ python imaplib_fetch_raw.py

13:12.54 imaplib version 2.58
13:12.54 new IMAP4 connection, tag=CFKH
13:12.54 < * OK dovecot ready.
13:12.54 > CFKH0 CAPABILITY
13:12.54 < * CAPABILITY IMAP4rev1 SORT THREAD=REFERENCES MULTIAPPEND
 UNSELECT IDLE CHILDREN LISTEXT LIST-SUBSCRIBED NAMESPACE AUTH=PLAIN
13:12.54 < CFKH0 OK Capability completed.
13:12.54 CAPABILITIES: ('IMAP4REV1', 'SORT', 'THREAD=REFERENCES', 'M
ULTIAPPEND', 'UNSELECT', 'IDLE', 'CHILDREN', 'LISTEXT', 'LIST-SUBSCR
IBED', 'NAMESPACE', 'AUTH=PLAIN')
13:12.54 > CFKH1 LOGIN example "password"
13:13.18 < CFKH1 OK Logged in.
13:13.18 > CFKH2 EXAMINE INBOX
13:13.20 < * FLAGS (\Answered \Flagged \Deleted \Seen \Draft $NotJun
k $Junk)
13:13.20 < * OK [PERMANENTFLAGS ()] Read-only mailbox.
13:13.20 < * 2 EXISTS
13:13.20 < * 1 RECENT
13:13.20 < * OK [UNSEEN 1] First unseen.
13:13.20 < * OK [UIDVALIDITY 1222003700] UIDs valid
13:13.20 < * OK [UIDNEXT 4] Predicted next UID
13:13.20 < CFKH2 OK [READ-ONLY] Select completed.
13:13.20 > CFKH3 FETCH 1 (BODY.PEEK[HEADER] FLAGS)
13:13.20 < * 1 FETCH (FLAGS ($NotJunk) BODY[HEADER] {595}
13:13.20 read literal size 595
13:13.20 < )
13:13.20 < CFKH3 OK Fetch completed.
13:13.20 > CFKH4 CLOSE
13:13.21 < CFKH4 OK Close completed.
13:13.21 > CFKH5 LOGOUT
13:13.21 < * BYE Logging out
13:13.21 BYE response: Logging out
13:13.21 < CFKH5 OK Logout completed.
'1 (FLAGS ($NotJunk) BODY[HEADER] {595}',
'Return-Path: <dhellmann@example.com>\r\nReceived: from example.com
(localhost [127.0.0.1])\r\n\tby example.com (8.13.4/8.13.4) with ESM
TP id m8LDTGW4018260\r\n\tfor <example@example.com>; Sun, 21 Sep 200
```

```
8 09:29:16 -0400\r\nReceived: (from dhellmann@localhost)\r\n\tby exa
mple.com (8.13.4/8.13.4/Submit) id m8LDTGZ5018259\r\n\tfor example@e
xample.com; Sun, 21 Sep 2008 09:29:16 -0400\r\nDate: Sun, 21 Sep 200
8 09:29:16 -0400\r\nFrom: Doug Hellmann <dhellmann@example.com>\r\nM
essage-Id: <200809211329.m8LDTGZ5018259@example.com>\r\nTo: example@
example.com\r\nSubject: test message 2\r\n\r\n'),
)']
```

The response from the `FETCH` command starts with the flags, and then it indicates that there are 595 bytes of header data. The client constructs a tuple with the response for the message, and then closes the sequence with a single string containing the right parenthesis (")") the server sends at the end of the fetch response. Because of this formatting, it may be easier to fetch different pieces of information separately or to recombine the response and parse it in the client.

```python
import imaplib
import pprint
import imaplib_connect

c = imaplib_connect.open_connection()
try:
    c.select('INBOX', readonly=True)

    print 'HEADER:'
    typ, msg_data = c.fetch('1', '(BODY.PEEK[HEADER])')
    for response_part in msg_data:
        if isinstance(response_part, tuple):
            print response_part[1]

    print 'BODY TEXT:'
    typ, msg_data = c.fetch('1', '(BODY.PEEK[TEXT])')
    for response_part in msg_data:
        if isinstance(response_part, tuple):
            print response_part[1]

    print '\nFLAGS:'
    typ, msg_data = c.fetch('1', '(FLAGS)')
    for response_part in msg_data:
        print response_part
        print imaplib.ParseFlags(response_part)
finally:
    try:
        c.close()
```

```
except:
    pass
c.logout()
```

Fetching values separately has the added benefit of making it easy to use `Parse-Flags()` to parse the flags from the response.

```
$ python imaplib_fetch_separately.py

HEADER:
Return-Path: <dhellmann@example.com>
Received: from example.com (localhost [127.0.0.1])
    by example.com (8.13.4/8.13.4) with ESMTP id m8LDTGW4018260
    for <example@example.com>; Sun, 21 Sep 2008 09:29:16 -0400
Received: (from dhellmann@localhost)
    by example.com (8.13.4/8.13.4/Submit) id m8LDTGZ5018259
    for example@example.com; Sun, 21 Sep 2008 09:29:16 -0400
Date: Sun, 21 Sep 2008 09:29:16 -0400
From: Doug Hellmann <dhellmann@example.com>
Message-Id: <200809211329.m8LDTGZ5018259@example.com>
To: example@example.com
Subject: test message 2


BODY TEXT:
second message



FLAGS:
1 (FLAGS ($NotJunk))
('$NotJunk',)
```

13.3.10   Whole Messages

As illustrated earlier, the client can ask the server for individual parts of the message separately. It is also possible to retrieve the entire message as an RFC 2822 formatted mail message and parse it with classes from the `email` module.

```
import imaplib
import email
import imaplib_connect

c = imaplib_connect.open_connection()
```

```
try:
    c.select('INBOX', readonly=True)

    typ, msg_data = c.fetch('1', '(RFC822)')
    for response_part in msg_data:
        if isinstance(response_part, tuple):
            msg = email.message_from_string(response_part[1])
            for header in [ 'subject', 'to', 'from' ]:
                print '%-8s: %s' % (header.upper(), msg[header])

finally:
    try:
        c.close()
    except:
        pass
    c.logout()
```

The parser in the `email` module makes it very easy to access and manipulate messages. This example prints just a few of the headers for each message.

```
$ python imaplib_fetch_rfc822.py

SUBJECT : test message 2
TO      : example@example.com
FROM    : Doug Hellmann <dhellmann@example.com>
```

13.3.11 Uploading Messages

To add a new message to a mailbox, construct a `Message` instance and pass it to the `append()` method, along with the timestamp for the message.

```
import imaplib
import time
import email.message
import imaplib_connect

new_message = email.message.Message()
new_message.set_unixfrom('pymotw')
new_message['Subject'] = 'subject goes here'
new_message['From'] = 'pymotw@example.com'
new_message['To'] = 'example@example.com'
new_message.set_payload('This is the body of the message.\n')
```

```
print new_message

c = imaplib_connect.open_connection()
try:
    c.append('INBOX', '',
                imaplib.Time2Internaldate(time.time()),
                str(new_message))

    # Show the headers for all messages in the mailbox
    c.select('INBOX')
    typ, [msg_ids] = c.search(None, 'ALL')
    for num in msg_ids.split():
        typ, msg_data = c.fetch(num, '(BODY.PEEK[HEADER])')
        for response_part in msg_data:
            if isinstance(response_part, tuple):
                print '\n%s:' % num
                print response_part[1]

finally:
    try:
        c.close()
    except:
        pass
    c.logout()
```

The *payload* used in this example is a simple plain-text email body. `Message` also supports MIME-encoded, multipart messages.

```
pymotw
Subject: subject goes here
From: pymotw@example.com
To: example@example.com

This is the body of the message.


1:
Return-Path: <dhellmann@example.com>
Received: from example.com (localhost [127.0.0.1])
    by example.com (8.13.4/8.13.4) with ESMTP id m8LDTGW4018260
    for <example@example.com>; Sun, 21 Sep 2008 09:29:16 -0400
Received: (from dhellmann@localhost)
    by example.com (8.13.4/8.13.4/Submit) id m8LDTGZ5018259
    for example@example.com; Sun, 21 Sep 2008 09:29:16 -0400
```

```
Date: Sun, 21 Sep 2008 09:29:16 -0400
From: Doug Hellmann <dhellmann@example.com>
Message-Id: <200809211329.m8LDTGZ5018259@example.com>
To: example@example.com
Subject: test message 2



2:
Return-Path: <doug.hellmann@example.com>
Message-Id: <0D9C3C50-462A-4FD7-9E5A-11EE222D721D@example.com>
From: Doug Hellmann <doug.hellmann@example.com>
To: example@example.com
Content-Type: text/plain; charset=US-ASCII; format=flowed; delsp=yes
Content-Transfer-Encoding: 7bit
Mime-Version: 1.0 (Apple Message framework v929.2)
Subject: lorem ipsum
Date: Sun, 21 Sep 2008 12:53:16 -0400
X-Mailer: Apple Mail (2.929.2)



3:
pymotw
Subject: subject goes here
From: pymotw@example.com
To: example@example.com
```

13.3.12 Moving and Copying Messages

Once a message is on the server, it can be moved or copied without downloading it using `move()` or `copy()`. These methods operate on message id ranges, just as `fetch()` does.

```
import imaplib
import imaplib_connect

c = imaplib_connect.open_connection()
try:
    # Find the "SEEN" messages in INBOX
    c.select('INBOX')
    typ, [response] = c.search(None, 'SEEN')
    if typ != 'OK':
        raise RuntimeError(response)
```

```
# Create a new mailbox, "Archive.Today"
msg_ids = ','.join(response.split(' '))
typ, create_response = c.create('Archive.Today')
print 'CREATED Archive.Today:', create_response

# Copy the messages
print 'COPYING:', msg_ids
c.copy(msg_ids, 'Archive.Today')

# Look at the results
c.select('Archive.Today')
typ, [response] = c.search(None, 'ALL')
print 'COPIED:', response

finally:
    c.close()
    c.logout()
```

This example script creates a new mailbox under `Archive` and copies the read messages from `INBOX` into it.

```
$ python imaplib_archive_read.py

CREATED Archive.Today: ['Create completed.']
COPYING: 1,2
COPIED: 1 2
```

Running the same script again shows the importance to checking return codes. Instead of raising an exception, the call to `create()` to make the new mailbox reports that the mailbox already exists.

```
$ python imaplib_archive_read.py

CREATED Archive.Today: ['Mailbox exists.']
COPYING: 1,2
COPIED: 1 2 3 4
```

13.3.13 Deleting Messages

Although many modern mail clients use a "Trash folder" model for working with deleted messages, the messages are not usually moved into an actual folder. Instead, their flags are updated to add `\Deleted`. The operation for "emptying" the trash is implemented through the EXPUNGE command. This example script finds the archived messages with "Lorem ipsum" in the subject, sets the deleted flag, and then shows that the messages are still present in the folder by querying the server again.

```python
import imaplib
import imaplib_connect
from imaplib_list_parse import parse_list_response

c = imaplib_connect.open_connection()
try:
    c.select('Archive.Today')

    # What ids are in the mailbox?
    typ, [msg_ids] = c.search(None, 'ALL')
    print 'Starting messages:', msg_ids

    # Find the message(s)
    typ, [msg_ids] = c.search(None, '(SUBJECT "Lorem ipsum")')
    msg_ids = ','.join(msg_ids.split(' '))
    print 'Matching messages:', msg_ids

    # What are the current flags?
    typ, response = c.fetch(msg_ids, '(FLAGS)')
    print 'Flags before:', response

    # Change the Deleted flag
    typ, response = c.store(msg_ids, '+FLAGS', r'(\Deleted)')

    # What are the flags now?
    typ, response = c.fetch(msg_ids, '(FLAGS)')
    print 'Flags after:', response

    # Really delete the message.
    typ, response = c.expunge()
    print 'Expunged:', response

    # What ids are left in the mailbox?
    typ, [msg_ids] = c.search(None, 'ALL')
    print 'Remaining messages:', msg_ids

finally:
    try:
        c.close()
```

```
    except:
        pass
    c.logout()
```

Explicitly calling `expunge()` removes the messages, but calling `close()` has the same effect. The difference is the client is not notified about the deletions when `close()` is called.

```
$ python imaplib_delete_messages.py

Starting messages: 1 2 3 4
Matching messages: 1,3
Flags before: ['1 (FLAGS (\\Seen $NotJunk))', '3 (FLAGS (\\Seen
\\Recent $NotJunk))']
Flags after: ['1 (FLAGS (\\Deleted \\Seen $NotJunk))',
'3 (FLAGS (\\Deleted \\Seen \\Recent $NotJunk))']
Expunged: ['1', '2']
Remaining messages: 1 2
```

See Also:

imaplib (http://docs.python.org/library/imaplib.html) The standard library documentation for this module.

What is IMAP? (www.imap.org/about/whatisIMAP.html) imap.org description of the IMAP protocol.

University of Washington IMAP Information Center (http://www.washington.edu/imap/) Good resource for IMAP information, along with source code.

RFC 3501 (http://tools.ietf.org/html/rfc3501.html) Internet Message Access Protocol.

RFC 2822 (http://tools.ietf.org/html/rfc2822.html) Internet Message Format.

IMAP Backup Script (http://snipplr.com/view/7955/imap-backup-script/) A script to backup email from an IMAP server.

rfc822 The `rfc822` module includes an RFC 822 / RFC 2822 parser.

email The `email` module for parsing email messages.

mailbox (page 758) Local mailbox parser.

ConfigParser (page 861) Read and write configuration files.

IMAPClient (http://imapclient.freshfoo.com/) A higher-level client for talking to IMAP servers, written by Menno Smits.

13.4   mailbox—Manipulate Email Archives

Purpose Work with email messages in various local file formats.
Python Version 1.4 and later

The `mailbox` module defines a common API for accessing email messages stored in local disk formats, including:

- Maildir
- mbox
- MH
- Babyl
- MMDF

There are base classes for `Mailbox` and `Message`, and each mailbox format includes a corresponding pair of subclasses to implement the details for that format.

13.4.1   mbox

The mbox format is the simplest to show in documentation, since it is entirely plain text. Each mailbox is stored as a single file, with all the messages concatenated together. Each time a line starting with `"From "` ("From" followed by a single space) is encountered it is treated as the beginning of a new message. Any time those characters appear at the beginning of a line in the message body, they are escaped by prefixing the line with `">"`.

Creating an mbox Mailbox

Instantiate the `mbox` class by passing the filename to the constructor. If the file does not exist, it is created when `add()` is used to append messages.

```
import mailbox
import email.utils

from_addr = email.utils.formataddr(('Author',
                                    'author@example.com'))
to_addr = email.utils.formataddr(('Recipient',
                                  'recipient@example.com'))

mbox = mailbox.mbox('example.mbox')
mbox.lock()
try:
    msg = mailbox.mboxMessage()
    msg.set_unixfrom('author Sat Feb  7 01:05:34 2009')
    msg['From'] = from_addr
    msg['To'] = to_addr
    msg['Subject'] = 'Sample message 1'
    msg.set_payload('\n'.join(['This is the body.',
                               'From (should be escaped).',
```

```
                                    'There are 3 lines.\n',
                                    ]))
        mbox.add(msg)
        mbox.flush()

        msg = mailbox.mboxMessage()
        msg.set_unixfrom('author')
        msg['From'] = from_addr
        msg['To'] = to_addr
        msg['Subject'] = 'Sample message 2'
        msg.set_payload('This is the second body.\n')
        mbox.add(msg)
        mbox.flush()
finally:
        mbox.unlock()


print open('example.mbox', 'r').read()
```

The result of this script is a new mailbox file with two email messages.

```
$ python mailbox_mbox_create.py

From MAILER-DAEMON Mon Nov 29 02:00:11 2010
From: Author <author@example.com>
To: Recipient <recipient@example.com>
Subject: Sample message 1

This is the body.
>From (should be escaped).
There are 3 lines.

From MAILER-DAEMON Mon Nov 29 02:00:11 2010
From: Author <author@example.com>
To: Recipient <recipient@example.com>
Subject: Sample message 2

This is the second body.
```

Reading an mbox Mailbox

To read an existing mailbox, open it and treat the mbox object like a dictionary. The keys are arbitrary values defined by the mailbox instance and are not necessary meaningful other than as internal identifiers for message objects.

```
import mailbox

mbox = mailbox.mbox('example.mbox')
for message in mbox:
    print message['subject']
```

The open mailbox supports the iterator protocol, but unlike true dictionary objects, the default iterator for a mailbox works on the *values* instead of the *keys*.

```
$ python mailbox_mbox_read.py

Sample message 1
Sample message 2
```

Removing Messages from an mbox Mailbox

To remove an existing message from an mbox file, either use its key with `remove()` or use **del**.

```
import mailbox

mbox = mailbox.mbox('example.mbox')
mbox.lock()
try:
    to_remove = []
    for key, msg in mbox.iteritems():
        if '2' in msg['subject']:
            print 'Removing:', key
            to_remove.append(key)
    for key in to_remove:
        mbox.remove(key)
finally:
    mbox.flush()
    mbox.close()

print open('example.mbox', 'r').read()
```

The `lock()` and `unlock()` methods are used to prevent issues from simultaneous access to the file, and `flush()` forces the changes to be written to disk.

```
$ python mailbox_mbox_remove.py
```

```
Removing: 1
From MAILER-DAEMON Mon Nov 29 02:00:11 2010
From: Author <author@example.com>
To: Recipient <recipient@example.com>
Subject: Sample message 1

This is the body.
>From (should be escaped).
There are 3 lines.
```

13.4.2   Maildir

The Maildir format was created to eliminate the problem of concurrent modification to an mbox file. Instead of using a single file, the mailbox is organized as a directory where each message is contained in its own file. This also allows mailboxes to be nested, so the API for a Maildir mailbox is extended with methods to work with subfolders.

Creating a Maildir Mailbox

The only real difference between creating a `Maildir` and `mbox` is that the argument to the constructor is a directory name instead of a filename. As before, if the mailbox does not exist, it is created when messages are added.

```
import mailbox
import email.utils
import os

from_addr = email.utils.formataddr(('Author',
                                    'author@example.com'))
to_addr = email.utils.formataddr(('Recipient',
                                  'recipient@example.com'))

mbox = mailbox.Maildir('Example')
mbox.lock()
try:
    msg = mailbox.mboxMessage()
    msg.set_unixfrom('author Sat Feb  7 01:05:34 2009')
    msg['From'] = from_addr
    msg['To'] = to_addr
    msg['Subject'] = 'Sample message 1'
    msg.set_payload('\n'.join(['This is the body.',
                               'From (will not be escaped).',
```

```
                                    'There are 3 lines.\n',
                                    ]))
    mbox.add(msg)
    mbox.flush()

    msg = mailbox.mboxMessage()
    msg.set_unixfrom('author Sat Feb  7 01:05:34 2009')
    msg['From'] = from_addr
    msg['To'] = to_addr
    msg['Subject'] = 'Sample message 2'
    msg.set_payload('This is the second body.\n')
    mbox.add(msg)
    mbox.flush()
finally:
    mbox.unlock()


for dirname, subdirs, files in os.walk('Example'):
    print dirname
    print '\tDirectories:', subdirs
    for name in files:
        fullname = os.path.join(dirname, name)
        print
        print '***', fullname
        print open(fullname).read()
        print '*' * 20
```

When messages are added to the mailbox, they go to the `new` subdirectory. After they are read, a client could move them to the `cur` subdirectory.

> **Warning:** Although it is safe to write to the same Maildir from multiple processes, `add()` is not thread-safe. Use a semaphore or other locking device to prevent simultaneous modifications to the mailbox from multiple threads of the same process.

```
$ python mailbox_maildir_create.py

Example
        Directories: ['cur', 'new', 'tmp']
Example/cur
        Directories: []
Example/new
        Directories: []
```

```
*** Example/new/1290996011.M658966P16077Q1.farnsworth.local
From: Author <author@example.com>
To: Recipient <recipient@example.com>
Subject: Sample message 1

This is the body.
From (will not be escaped).
There are 3 lines.

********************

*** Example/new/1290996011.M660614P16077Q2.farnsworth.local
From: Author <author@example.com>
To: Recipient <recipient@example.com>
Subject: Sample message 2

This is the second body.

*******************
Example/tmp
        Directories: []
```

Reading a Maildir Mailbox

Reading from an existing Maildir mailbox works just like an mbox mailbox.

```
import mailbox

mbox = mailbox.Maildir('Example')
for message in mbox:
    print message['subject']
```

The messages are not guaranteed to be read in any particular order.

```
$ python mailbox_maildir_read.py

Sample message 1
Sample message 2
```

Removing Messages from a Maildir Mailbox

To remove an existing message from a Maildir mailbox, either pass its key to `remove()` or use **del**.

```
import mailbox
import os

mbox = mailbox.Maildir('Example')
mbox.lock()
try:
    to_remove = []
    for key, msg in mbox.iteritems():
        if '2' in msg['subject']:
            print 'Removing:', key
            to_remove.append(key)
    for key in to_remove:
        mbox.remove(key)
finally:
    mbox.flush()
    mbox.close()

for dirname, subdirs, files in os.walk('Example'):
    print dirname
    print '\tDirectories:', subdirs
    for name in files:
        fullname = os.path.join(dirname, name)
        print
        print '***', fullname
        print open(fullname).read()
        print '*' * 20
```

There is no way to compute the key for a message, so use `iteritems()` to retrieve the key and message object from the mailbox at the same time.

```
$ python mailbox_maildir_remove.py

Removing: 1290996011.M660614P16077Q2.farnsworth.local
Example
        Directories: ['cur', 'new', 'tmp']
Example/cur
        Directories: []
Example/new
        Directories: []

*** Example/new/1290996011.M658966P16077Q1.farnsworth.local
From: Author <author@example.com>
To: Recipient <recipient@example.com>
```

```
Subject: Sample message 1

This is the body.
From (will not be escaped).
There are 3 lines.


********************
Example/tmp
        Directories: []
```

Maildir Folders

Subdirectories or *folders* of a Maildir mailbox can be managed directly through the methods of the `Maildir` class. Callers can list, retrieve, create, and remove subfolders for a given mailbox.

```python
import mailbox
import os

def show_maildir(name):
    os.system('find %s -print' % name)

mbox = mailbox.Maildir('Example')
print 'Before:', mbox.list_folders()
show_maildir('Example')

print
print '#' * 30
print

mbox.add_folder('subfolder')
print 'subfolder created:', mbox.list_folders()
show_maildir('Example')

subfolder = mbox.get_folder('subfolder')
print 'subfolder contents:', subfolder.list_folders()

print
print '#' * 30
print

subfolder.add_folder('second_level')
print 'second_level created:', subfolder.list_folders()
show_maildir('Example')
```

```
print
print '#' * 30
print

subfolder.remove_folder('second_level')
print 'second_level removed:', subfolder.list_folders()
show_maildir('Example')
```

The directory name for the folder is constructed by prefixing the folder name with a period (.).

```
$ python mailbox_maildir_folders.py

Example
Example/cur
Example/new
Example/new/1290996011.M658966P16077Q1.farnsworth.local
Example/tmp
Example
Example/.subfolder
Example/.subfolder/cur
Example/.subfolder/maildirfolder
Example/.subfolder/new
Example/.subfolder/tmp
Example/cur
Example/new
Example/new/1290996011.M658966P16077Q1.farnsworth.local
Example/tmp
Example
Example/.subfolder
Example/.subfolder/.second_level
Example/.subfolder/.second_level/cur
Example/.subfolder/.second_level/maildirfolder
Example/.subfolder/.second_level/new
Example/.subfolder/.second_level/tmp
Example/.subfolder/cur
Example/.subfolder/maildirfolder
Example/.subfolder/new
Example/.subfolder/tmp
Example/cur
Example/new
Example/new/1290996011.M658966P16077Q1.farnsworth.local
Example/tmp
Example
```

```
Example/.subfolder
Example/.subfolder/cur
Example/.subfolder/maildirfolder
Example/.subfolder/new
Example/.subfolder/tmp
Example/cur
Example/new
Example/new/1290996011.M658966P16077Q1.farnsworth.local
Example/tmp
Before: []


##############################

subfolder created: ['subfolder']
subfolder contents: []


##############################

second_level created: ['second_level']


##############################

second_level removed: []
```

13.4.3   Other Formats

`mailbox` supports a few other formats, but none are as popular as mbox or Maildir. MH is another multifile mailbox format used by some mail handlers. Babyl and MMDF are single-file formats with different message separators than mbox. The single-file formats support the same API as mbox, and MH includes the folder-related methods found in the Maildir class.

See Also:

mailbox (http://docs.python.org/library/mailbox.html) The standard library documentation for this module.

mbox manpage from qmail (http://www.qmail.org/man/man5/mbox.html) Documentation for the mbox format.

Maildir manpage from qmail (http://www.qmail.org/man/man5/maildir.html) Documentation for the Maildir format.

email The `email` module.

mhlib The `mhlib` module.

imaplib (page 738) The `imaplib` module can work with saved email messages on an IMAP server.

Chapter 14

APPLICATION BUILDING BLOCKS

The strength of Python's standard library is its size. It includes implementations of so many aspects of a program's structure that developers can concentrate on what makes their application unique, instead of implementing all the basic pieces over and over again. This chapter covers some of the more frequently reused building blocks that solve problems common to so many applications.

There are three separate modules for parsing command-line arguments using different styles. `getopt` implements the same low-level processing model available to C programs and shell scripts. It has fewer features than other option-parsing libraries, but that simplicity and familiarity make it a popular choice. `optparse` is a more modern, and flexible, replacement for `getopt`. `argparse` is a third interface for parsing and validating command-line arguments, and it deprecates both `getopt` and `optparse`. It supports converting arguments from strings to integers and other types, running callbacks when an option is encountered, setting default values for options not provided by the user, and automatically producing usage instructions for a program.

Interactive programs should use `readline` to give the user a command prompt. It includes tools for managing history, auto-completing parts of commands, and interactive editing with **emacs** and **vi** key-bindings. To securely prompt the user for a password or other secret value, without echoing the value to the screen as it is typed, use `getpass`.

The `cmd` module includes a framework for interactive, command-driven shell-style programs. It provides the main loop and handles the interaction with the user, so the application only needs to implement the processing callbacks for the individual commands.

shlex is a parser for shell-style syntax, with lines made up of tokens separated by whitespace. It is smart about quotes and escape sequences, so text with embedded spaces is treated as a single token. shlex works well as the tokenizer for domain-specific languages, such as configuration files or programming languages.

It is easy to manage application configuration files with ConfigParser. It can save user preferences between program runs and read them the next time an application starts, or even serve as a simple data file format.

Applications being deployed in the real world need to give their users debugging information. Simple error messages and tracebacks are helpful, but when it is difficult to reproduce an issue, a full activity log can point directly to the chain of events that leads to a failure. The logging module includes a full-featured API that manages log files, supports multiple threads, and even interfaces with remote logging daemons for centralized logging.

One of the most common patterns for programs in UNIX environments is a line-by-line filter that reads data, modifies it, and writes it back out. Reading from files is simple enough, but there may not be an easier way to create a filter application than by using the fileinput module. Its API is a line iterator that yields each input line, so the main body of the program is a simple **for** loop. The module handles parsing command-line arguments for filenames to be processed or falling back to reading directly from standard input, so tools built on fileinput can be run directly on a file or as part of a pipeline.

Use atexit to schedule functions to be run as the interpreter is shutting down a program. Registering exit callbacks is useful for releasing resources by logging out of remote services, closing files, etc.

The sched module implements a scheduler for triggering events at set times in the future. The API does not dictate the definition of "time," so anything from true clock time to interpreter steps can be used.

14.1   getopt—Command-Line Option Parsing

Purpose Command-line option parsing.
Python Version 1.4 and later

The getopt module is the original command-line option parser that supports the conventions established by the UNIX function getopt(). It parses an argument sequence, such as sys.argv, and returns a sequence of tuples containing (option, argument) pairs and a sequence of nonoption arguments.

Supported option syntax include short- and long-form options:

```
-a
-bval
-b val
--noarg
--witharg=val
--witharg val
```

14.1.1   Function Arguments

The `getopt()` function takes three arguments.

- The first parameter is the sequence of arguments to be parsed. This usually comes from `sys.argv[1:]` (ignoring the program name in `sys.arg[0]`).
- The second argument is the option definition string for single-character options. If one of the options requires an argument, its letter is followed by a colon.
- The third argument, if used, should be a sequence of the long-style option names. Long-style options can be more than a single character, such as `--noarg` or `--witharg`. The option names in the sequence should not include the "`--`" prefix. If any long option requires an argument, its name should have a suffix of "`=`".

Short- and long-form options can be combined in a single call.

14.1.2   Short-Form Options

This example program accepts three options. The `-a` is a simple flag, while `-b` and `-c` require an argument. The option definition string is `"ab:c:"`.

```
import getopt

opts, args = getopt.getopt(['-a', '-bval', '-c', 'val'], 'ab:c:')

for opt in opts:
    print opt
```

The program passes a list of simulated option values to `getopt()` to show the way they are processed.

```
$ python getopt_short.py

('-a', '')
('-b', 'val')
('-c', 'val')
```

14.1.3   Long-Form Options

For a program that takes two options, --noarg and --witharg, the long-argument sequence should be ['noarg', 'witharg='].

```
import getopt

opts, args = getopt.getopt([ '--noarg',
                             '--witharg', 'val',
                             '--witharg2=another',
                             ],
                           '',
                           [ 'noarg', 'witharg=', 'witharg2=' ])
for opt in opts:
    print opt
```

Since this sample program does not take any short form options, the second argument to getopt() is an empty string.

```
$ python getopt_long.py

('--noarg', '')
('--witharg', 'val')
('--witharg2', 'another')
```

14.1.4   A Complete Example

This example is a more complete program that takes five options: -o, -v, --output, --verbose, and --version. The -o, --output, and --version options each require an argument.

```
import getopt
import sys

version = '1.0'
verbose = False
```

```python
output_filename = 'default.out'

print 'ARGV      :', sys.argv[1:]

try:
    options, remainder = getopt.getopt(
        sys.argv[1:],
        'o:v',
        ['output=',
         'verbose',
         'version=',
         ])
except getopt.GetoptError as err:
    print 'ERROR:', err
    sys.exit(1)

print 'OPTIONS   :', options

for opt, arg in options:
    if opt in ('-o', '--output'):
        output_filename = arg
    elif opt in ('-v', '--verbose'):
        verbose = True
    elif opt == '--version':
        version = arg

print 'VERSION   :', version
print 'VERBOSE   :', verbose
print 'OUTPUT    :', output_filename
print 'REMAINING :', remainder
```

The program can be called in a variety of ways. When it is called without any arguments at all, the default settings are used.

```
$ python getopt_example.py

ARGV      : []
OPTIONS   : []
VERSION   : 1.0
VERBOSE   : False
OUTPUT    : default.out
REMAINING : []
```

A single-letter option can be a separated from its argument by whitespace.

```
$ python getopt_example.py -o foo

ARGV      : ['-o', 'foo']
OPTIONS   : [('-o', 'foo')]
VERSION   : 1.0
VERBOSE   : False
OUTPUT    : foo
REMAINING : []
```

Or the option and value can be combined into a single argument.

```
$ python getopt_example.py -ofoo

ARGV      : ['-ofoo']
OPTIONS   : [('-o', 'foo')]
VERSION   : 1.0
VERBOSE   : False
OUTPUT    : foo
REMAINING : []
```

A long-form option can similarly be separate from the value.

```
$ python getopt_example.py --output foo

ARGV      : ['--output', 'foo']
OPTIONS   : [('--output', 'foo')]
VERSION   : 1.0
VERBOSE   : False
OUTPUT    : foo
REMAINING : []
```

When a long option is combined with its value, the option name and value should be separated by a single =.

```
$ python getopt_example.py --output=foo

ARGV      : ['--output=foo']
OPTIONS   : [('--output', 'foo')]
VERSION   : 1.0
```

```
VERBOSE   : False
OUTPUT    : foo
REMAINING : []
```

14.1.5 Abbreviating Long-Form Options

The long-form option does not have to be spelled out entirely on the command line, as long as a unique prefix is provided.

```
$ python getopt_example.py --o foo

ARGV      : ['--o', 'foo']
OPTIONS   : [('--output', 'foo')]
VERSION   : 1.0
VERBOSE   : False
OUTPUT    : foo
REMAINING : []
```

If a unique prefix is not provided, an exception is raised.

```
$ python getopt_example.py --ver 2.0

ARGV      : ['--ver', '2.0']
ERROR: option --ver not a unique prefix
```

14.1.6 GNU-Style Option Parsing

Normally, option processing stops as soon as the first nonoption argument is encountered.

```
$ python getopt_example.py -v not_an_option --output foo

ARGV      : ['-v', 'not_an_option', '--output', 'foo']
OPTIONS   : [('-v', '')]
VERSION   : 1.0
VERBOSE   : True
OUTPUT    : default.out
REMAINING : ['not_an_option', '--output', 'foo']
```

An additional function `gnu_getopt()` was added to the module in Python 2.3. It allows option and nonoption arguments to be mixed on the command line in any order.

```python
import getopt
import sys

version = '1.0'
verbose = False
output_filename = 'default.out'

print 'ARGV      :', sys.argv[1:]

try:
    options, remainder = getopt.gnu_getopt(
        sys.argv[1:],
        'o:v',
        ['output=',
         'verbose',
         'version=',
         ])
except getopt.GetoptError as err:
    print 'ERROR:', err
    sys.exit(1)

print 'OPTIONS   :', options

for opt, arg in options:
    if opt in ('-o', '--output'):
        output_filename = arg
    elif opt in ('-v', '--verbose'):
        verbose = True
    elif opt == '--version':
        version = arg

print 'VERSION   :', version
print 'VERBOSE   :', verbose
print 'OUTPUT    :', output_filename
print 'REMAINING :', remainder
```

After changing the call in the previous example, the difference becomes clear.

```
$ python getopt_gnu.py -v not_an_option --output foo

ARGV      : ['-v', 'not_an_option', '--output', 'foo']
OPTIONS   : [('-v', ''), ('--output', 'foo')]
VERSION   : 1.0
```

```
VERBOSE   : True
OUTPUT    : foo
REMAINING : ['not_an_option']
```

14.1.7   Ending Argument Processing

If `getopt()` encounters "--" in the input arguments, it stops processing the remaining arguments as options. This feature can be used to pass argument values that look like options, such as filenames that start with a dash ("-").

```
$ python getopt_example.py -v -- --output foo

ARGV      : ['-v', '--', '--output', 'foo']
OPTIONS   : [('-v', '')]
VERSION   : 1.0
VERBOSE   : True
OUTPUT    : default.out
REMAINING : ['--output', 'foo']
```

See Also:
getopt (http://docs.python.org/library/getopt.html) The standard library documentation for this module.
argparse (page 795) The `argparse` module replaces both `getopt` and `optparse`.
optparse (page 777) The `optparse` module.

14.2   optparse—Command-Line Option Parser

> **Purpose** Command-line option parser to replace `getopt`.
> **Python Version** 2.3 and later

The `optparse` module is a modern alternative for command-line option parsing that offers several features not available in `getopt`, including type conversion, option callbacks, and automatic help generation. There are many more features to `optparse` than can be covered here, but this section will introduce some more commonly used capabilities.

14.2.1   Creating an OptionParser

There are two phases to parsing options with `optparse`. First, the `OptionParser` instance is constructed and configured with the expected options. Then, a sequence of options is fed in and processed.

```
import optparse
parser = optparse.OptionParser()
```

Usually, once the parser has been created, each option is added to the parser explicitly, with information about what to do when the option is encountered on the command line. It is also possible to pass a list of options to the `OptionParser` constructor, but that form is not used as frequently.

Defining Options

Options should be added one at a time using the `add_option()` method. Any unnamed string arguments at the beginning of the argument list are treated as option names. To create aliases for an option (i.e., to have a short and long form of the same option), pass multiple names.

Parsing a Command Line

After all the options are defined, the command line is parsed by passing a sequence of argument strings to `parse_args()`. By default, the arguments are taken from `sys.argv[1:]`, but a list can be passed explicitly as well. The options are processed using the GNU/POSIX syntax, so option and argument values can be mixed in the sequence.

The return value from `parse_args()` is a two-part tuple containing a `Values` instance and the list of arguments to the command that were not interpreted as options. The default processing action for options is to store the value using the name given in the *dest* argument to `add_option()`. The `Values` instance returned by `parse_args()` holds the option values as attributes, so if an option's `dest` is set to `"myoption"`, the value is accessed as `options.myoption`.

14.2.2   Short- and Long-Form Options

Here is a simple example with three different options: a Boolean option (-a), a simple string option (-b), and an integer option (-c).

```
import optparse

parser = optparse.OptionParser()
parser.add_option('-a', action="store_true", default=False)
parser.add_option('-b', action="store", dest="b")
parser.add_option('-c', action="store", dest="c", type="int")

print parser.parse_args(['-a', '-bval', '-c', '3'])
```

The options on the command line are parsed with the same rules that `getopt.gnu_getopt()` uses, so there are two ways to pass values to single-character options. The example uses both forms, `-bval` and `-c val`.

```
$ python optparse_short.py

(<Values at 0x100e1b560: {'a': True, 'c': 3, 'b': 'val'}>, [])
```

The type of the value associated with `'c'` in the output is an integer, since the `OptionParser` was told to convert the argument before storing it.

Unlike with `getopt`, "long" option names are not handled any differently by `optparse`.

```
import optparse

parser = optparse.OptionParser()
parser.add_option('--noarg', action="store_true", default=False)
parser.add_option('--witharg', action="store", dest="witharg")
parser.add_option('--witharg2', action="store",
                  dest="witharg2", type="int")

print parser.parse_args([ '--noarg',
                          '--witharg', 'val',
                          '--witharg2=3' ])
```

And the results are similar.

```
$ python optparse_long.py

(<Values at 0x100e1b5a8: {'noarg': True, 'witharg': 'val',
'witharg2': 3}>, [])
```

14.2.3 Comparing with getopt

Since `optparse` is supposed to replace `getopt`, this example reimplements the same example program used in the section about `getopt`.

```
import optparse
import sys

print 'ARGV      :', sys.argv[1:]

parser = optparse.OptionParser()
```

```
parser.add_option('-o', '--output',
                   dest="output_filename",
                   default="default.out",
                   )
parser.add_option('-v', '--verbose',
                   dest="verbose",
                   default=False,
                   action="store_true",
                   )
parser.add_option('--version',
                   dest="version",
                   default=1.0,
                   type="float",
                   )
options, remainder = parser.parse_args()

print 'VERSION    :', options.version
print 'VERBOSE    :', options.verbose
print 'OUTPUT     :', options.output_filename
print 'REMAINING :', remainder
```

The options −o and −−output are aliased by being added at the same time. Either option can be used on the command line.

```
$ python optparse_getoptcomparison.py -o output.txt

ARGV       : ['-o', 'output.txt']
VERSION    : 1.0
VERBOSE    : False
OUTPUT     : output.txt
REMAINING : []

$ python optparse_getoptcomparison.py --output output.txt

ARGV       : ['--output', 'output.txt']
VERSION    : 1.0
VERBOSE    : False
OUTPUT     : output.txt
REMAINING : []
```

Any unique prefix of the long option can also be used.

```
$ python optparse_getoptcomparison.py --out output.txt

ARGV      : ['--out', 'output.txt']
VERSION   : 1.0
VERBOSE   : False
OUTPUT    : output.txt
REMAINING : []
```

14.2.4   Option Values

The default processing action is to store the argument to the option. If a type is provided when the option is defined, the argument value is converted to that type before it is stored.

Setting Defaults

Since options are by definition optional, applications should establish default behavior when an option is not given on the command line. A default value for an individual option can be provided when the option is defined using the argument *default*.

```
import optparse

parser = optparse.OptionParser()
parser.add_option('-o', action="store", default="default value")

options, args = parser.parse_args()

print options.o
```

The default value should match the type expected for the option, since no conversion is performed.

```
$ python optparse_default.py

default value

$ python optparse_default.py -o "different value"

different value
```

Defaults can also be loaded after the options are defined using keyword arguments to set_defaults().

```
import optparse

parser = optparse.OptionParser()
parser.add_option('-o', action="store")

parser.set_defaults(o='default value')

options, args = parser.parse_args()

print options.o
```

This form is useful when loading defaults from a configuration file or other source, instead of hard-coding them.

```
$ python optparse_set_defaults.py

default value

$ python optparse_set_defaults.py -o "different value"

different value
```

All defined options are available as attributes of the Values instance returned by parse_args(), so applications do not need to check for the presence of an option before trying to use its value.

```
import optparse

parser = optparse.OptionParser()
parser.add_option('-o', action="store")

options, args = parser.parse_args()

print options.o
```

If no default value is given for an option, and the option is not specified on the command line, its value is None.

```
$ python optparse_no_default.py

None
```

```
$ python optparse_no_default.py -o "different value"

different value
```

Type Conversion

`optparse` will convert option values from strings to integers, floats, longs, and complex values. To enable the conversion, specify the *type* of the option as an argument to `add_option()`.

import optparse

```
parser = optparse.OptionParser()
parser.add_option('-i', action="store", type="int")
parser.add_option('-f', action="store", type="float")
parser.add_option('-l', action="store", type="long")
parser.add_option('-c', action="store", type="complex")

options, args = parser.parse_args()
```

print *'int   : %-16r %s'* % (type(options.i), options.i)
print *'float   : %-16r %s'* % (type(options.f), options.f)
print *'long   : %-16r %s'* % (type(options.l), options.l)
print *'complex: %-16r %s'* % (type(options.c), options.c)

If an option's value cannot be converted to the specified type, an error is printed and the program exits.

```
$ python optparse_types.py -i 1 -f 3.14 -l 1000000 -c 1+2j

int     : <type 'int'>     1
float   : <type 'float'>   3.14
long    : <type 'long'>    1000000
complex: <type 'complex'>  (1+2j)

$ python optparse_types.py -i a

Usage: optparse_types.py [options]

optparse_types.py: error: option -i: invalid integer value: 'a'
```

Custom conversions can be created by subclassing the `Option` class. Refer to the standard library documentation for more details.

Enumerations

The `choice` type provides validation using a list of candidate strings. Set *type* to choice and provide the list of valid values using the *choices* argument to `add_option()`.

```
import optparse

parser = optparse.OptionParser()

parser.add_option('-c', type='choice', choices=['a', 'b', 'c'])

options, args = parser.parse_args()

print 'Choice:', options.c
```

Invalid inputs result in an error message that shows the allowed list of values.

```
$ python optparse_choice.py -c a

Choice: a

$ python optparse_choice.py -c b

Choice: b

$ python optparse_choice.py -c d

Usage: optparse_choice.py [options]

optparse_choice.py: error: option -c: invalid choice: 'd' (choose
from 'a', 'b', 'c')
```

14.2.5 Option Actions

Unlike `getopt`, which only *parses* the options, `optparse` is an option *processing* library. Options can trigger different actions, specified by the action argument to `add_option()`. Supported actions include storing the argument (singly, or as part of a list), storing a constant value when the option is encountered (including special handling for true/false values for Boolean switches), counting the number of times an option is seen, and calling a callback. The default action is `store`, and it does not need to be specified explicitly.

Constants

When options represent a selection of fixed alternatives, such as operating modes of an application, creating separate explicit options makes it easier to document them. The `store_const` action is intended for this purpose.

```python
import optparse

parser = optparse.OptionParser()
parser.add_option('--earth', action="store_const",
                  const='earth', dest='element',
                  default='earth',
                  )
parser.add_option('--air', action='store_const',
                  const='air', dest='element',
                  )
parser.add_option('--water', action='store_const',
                  const='water', dest='element',
                  )
parser.add_option('--fire', action='store_const',
                  const='fire', dest='element',
                  )

options, args = parser.parse_args()

print options.element
```

The `store_const` action associates a constant value in the application with the option specified by the user. Several options can be configured to store different constant values to the same *dest* name, so the application only has to check a single setting.

```
$ python optparse_store_const.py

earth

$ python optparse_store_const.py --fire

fire
```

Boolean Flags

Boolean options are implemented using special actions for storing true and false constant values.

```
import optparse

parser = optparse.OptionParser()
parser.add_option('-t', action='store_true',
                  default=False, dest='flag')
parser.add_option('-f', action='store_false',
                  default=False, dest='flag')

options, args = parser.parse_args()

print 'Flag:', options.flag
```

True and false versions of the same flag can be created by configuring their *dest* name to the same value.

```
$ python optparse_boolean.py

Flag: False

$ python optparse_boolean.py -t

Flag: True

$ python optparse_boolean.py -f

Flag: False
```

Repeating Options

There are three ways to handle repeated options: overwriting, appending, and counting. The default is to overwrite any existing value so that the last option specified is used. The store action works this way.

Using the append action, it is possible to accumulate values as an option is repeated, creating a list of values. Append mode is useful when multiple responses are allowed, since they can each be listed individually.

```
import optparse

parser = optparse.OptionParser()
parser.add_option('-o', action="append", dest='outputs', default=[])
```

```
options, args = parser.parse_args()
```

print options.outputs

The order of the values given on the command line is preserved, in case it is important for the application.

```
$ python optparse_append.py
```

```
[]
```

```
$ python optparse_append.py -o a.out
```

```
['a.out']
```

```
$ python optparse_append.py -o a.out -o b.out
```

```
['a.out', 'b.out']
```

Sometimes, it is enough to know how many times an option was given, and the associated value is not needed. For example, many applications allow the user to repeat the -v option to increase the level of verbosity of their output. The count action increments a value each time the option appears.

import optparse

```
parser = optparse.OptionParser()
parser.add_option('-v', action="count",
                  dest='verbosity', default=1)
parser.add_option('-q', action='store_const',
                  const=0, dest='verbosity')
```

```
options, args = parser.parse_args()
```

print options.verbosity

Since the -v option does not take an argument, it can be repeated using the syntax -vv as well as through separate individual options.

```
$ python optparse_count.py
```

```
$ python optparse_count.py -v

2

$ python optparse_count.py -v -v

3

$ python optparse_count.py -vv

3

$ python optparse_count.py -q

0
```

Callbacks

Besides saving the arguments for options directly, it is possible to define callback functions to be invoked when the option is encountered on the command line. Callbacks for options take four arguments: the `Option` instance causing the callback, the option string from the command line, any argument value associated with the option, and the `OptionParser` instance doing the parsing work.

```python
import optparse

def flag_callback(option, opt_str, value, parser):
    print 'flag_callback:'
    print '\toption:', repr(option)
    print '\topt_str:', opt_str
    print '\tvalue:', value
    print '\tparser:', parser
    return

def with_callback(option, opt_str, value, parser):
    print 'with_callback:'
    print '\toption:', repr(option)
    print '\topt_str:', opt_str
    print '\tvalue:', value
    print '\tparser:', parser
    return
parser = optparse.OptionParser()
parser.add_option('--flag', action="callback",
                  callback=flag_callback)
```

```
parser.add_option('--with',
                  action="callback",
                  callback=with_callback,
                  type="string",
                  help="Include optional feature")

parser.parse_args(['--with', 'foo', '--flag'])
```

In this example, the `--with` option is configured to take a string argument (other types, such as integers and floats, are supported as well).

```
$ python optparse_callback.py

with_callback:
        option: <Option at 0x100e1b3b0: --with>
        opt_str: --with
        value: foo
        parser: <optparse.OptionParser instance at 0x100da1200>
flag_callback:
        option: <Option at 0x100e1b320: --flag>
        opt_str: --flag
        value: None
        parser: <optparse.OptionParser instance at 0x100da1200>
```

Callbacks can be configured to take multiple arguments using the *nargs* option.

```
import optparse

def with_callback(option, opt_str, value, parser):
    print 'with_callback:'
    print '\toption:', repr(option)
    print '\topt_str:', opt_str
    print '\tvalue:', value
    print '\tparser:', parser
    return

parser = optparse.OptionParser()
parser.add_option('--with',
                  action="callback",
                  callback=with_callback,
                  type="string",
                  nargs=2,
                  help="Include optional feature")

parser.parse_args(['--with', 'foo', 'bar'])
```

In this case, the arguments are passed to the callback function as a `tuple` via the value argument.

```
$ python optparse_callback_nargs.py

with_callback:
        option: <Option at 0x100e1a2d8: --with>
        opt_str: --with
        value: ('foo', 'bar')
        parser: <optparse.OptionParser instance at 0x100da0128>
```

14.2.6   Help Messages

The `OptionParser` automatically adds a help option to all option sets, so the user can pass `--help` on the command line to see instructions for running the program. The help message includes all the options, with an indication of whether or not they take an argument. It is also possible to pass help text to `add_option()` to give a more verbose description of an option.

```
import optparse

parser = optparse.OptionParser()
parser.add_option('--no-foo', action="store_true",
                  default=False,
                  dest="foo",
                  help="Turn off foo",
                  )
parser.add_option('--with', action="store",
                  help="Include optional feature")

parser.parse_args()
```

The options are listed in alphabetical order, with aliases included on the same line. When the option takes an argument, the `dest` name is included as an argument name in the help output. The help text is printed in the right column.

```
$ python optparse_help.py --help

Usage: optparse_help.py [options]

Options:
  -h, --help    show this help message and exit
```

```
--no-foo      Turn off foo
--with=WITH   Include optional feature
```

The name `WITH` printed with the option `--with` comes from the destination variable for the option. For cases where the internal variable name is not descriptive enough to serve in the documentation, the *metavar* argument can be used to set a different name.

```python
import optparse

parser = optparse.OptionParser()
parser.add_option('--no-foo', action="store_true",
                  default=False,
                  dest="foo",
                  help="Turn off foo",
                  )
parser.add_option('--with', action="store",
                  help="Include optional feature",
                  metavar='feature_NAME')

parser.parse_args()
```

The value is printed exactly as it is given, without any changes to capitalization or punctuation.

```
$ python optparse_metavar.py -h

Usage: optparse_metavar.py [options]

Options:
  -h, --help            show this help message and exit
  --no-foo              Turn off foo
  --with=feature_NAME   Include optional feature
```

Organizing Options

Many applications include sets of related options. For example, **rpm** includes separate options for each of its operating modes. `optparse` uses *option groups* to organize options in the help output. The option values are all still saved in a single `Values` instance, so the namespace for option names is still flat.

```python
import optparse

parser = optparse.OptionParser()
```

```
parser.add_option('-q', action='store_const',
                   const='query', dest='mode',
                   help='Query')
parser.add_option('-i', action='store_const',
                   const='install', dest='mode',
                   help='Install')

query_opts = optparse.OptionGroup(
    parser, 'Query Options',
    'These options control the query mode.',
    )
query_opts.add_option('-l', action='store_const',
                      const='list', dest='query_mode',
                      help='List contents')
query_opts.add_option('-f', action='store_const',
                      const='file', dest='query_mode',
                      help='Show owner of file')
query_opts.add_option('-a', action='store_const',
                      const='all', dest='query_mode',
                      help='Show all packages')
parser.add_option_group(query_opts)

install_opts = optparse.OptionGroup(
    parser, 'Installation Options',
    'These options control installation.',
    )
install_opts.add_option(
    '--hash', action='store_true', default=False,
    help='Show hash marks as progress indication')
install_opts.add_option(
    '--force', dest='install_force', action='store_true',
    default=False,
    help='Install, regardless of dependencies or existing version')
parser.add_option_group(install_opts)

print parser.parse_args()
```

Each group has its own section title and description, and the options are displayed together.

```
$ python optparse_groups.py -h
```

```
Usage: optparse_groups.py [options]

Options:
  -h, --help   show this help message and exit
  -q           Query
  -i           Install

  Query Options:
    These options control the query mode.

    -l           List contents
    -f           Show owner of file
    -a           Show all packages

  Installation Options:
    These options control installation.

    --hash       Show hash marks as progress indication
    --force      Install, regardless of dependencies or existing version
```

Application Settings

The automatic help generation facilities use configuration settings to control several aspects of the help output. The program's *usage* string, which shows how the positional arguments are expected, can be set when the `OptionParser` is created.

```python
import optparse

parser = optparse.OptionParser(
    usage='%prog [options] <arg1> <arg2> [<arg3>...]'
    )
parser.add_option('-a', action="store_true", default=False)
parser.add_option('-b', action="store", dest="b")
parser.add_option('-c', action="store", dest="c", type="int")

parser.parse_args()
```

The literal value `%prog` is expanded to the name of the program at runtime, so it can reflect the full path to the script. If the script is run by **python**, instead of running directly, the script name is used.

```
$ python optparse_usage.py -h

Usage: optparse_usage.py [options] <arg1> <arg2> [<arg3>...]

Options:
  -h, --help  show this help message and exit
  -a
  -b B
  -c C
```

The program name can be changed using the *prog* argument.

```
import optparse

parser = optparse.OptionParser(
    usage='%prog [options] <arg1> <arg2> [<arg3>...]',
    prog='my_program_name',
    )
parser.add_option('-a', action="store_true", default=False)
parser.add_option('-b', action="store", dest="b")
parser.add_option('-c', action="store", dest="c", type="int")

parser.parse_args()
```

It is generally a bad idea to hard-code the program name in this way, though, because if the program is renamed, the help will not reflect the change.

```
$ python optparse_prog.py -h

Usage: my_program_name [options] <arg1> <arg2> [<arg3>...]

Options:
  -h, --help  show this help message and exit
  -a
  -b B
  -c C
```

The application version can be set using the *version* argument. When a version value is provided, `optparse` automatically adds a `--version` option to the parser.

```
import optparse

parser = optparse.OptionParser(
    usage='%prog [options] <arg1> <arg2> [<arg3>...]',
    version='1.0',
    )

parser.parse_args()
```

When the user runs the program with the `--version` option, `optparse` prints the version string and then exits.

```
$ python optparse_version.py -h

Usage: optparse_version.py [options] <arg1> <arg2> [<arg3>...]

Options:
  --version   show program's version number and exit
  -h, --help  show this help message and exit

$ python optparse_version.py --version

1.0
```

See Also:
optparse (http://docs.python.org/lib/module-optparse.html) The Standard library documentation for this module.
getopt (page 770) The `getopt` module, replaced by `optparse`.
argparse (page 795) Newer replacement for `optparse`.

14.3   argparse—Command-Line Option and Argument Parsing

Purpose Command-line option and argument parsing.
Python Version 2.7 and later

The `argparse` module was added to Python 2.7 as a replacement for `optparse`. The implementation of `argparse` supports features that would not have been easy to add to `optparse` and that would have required backwards-incompatible API changes. So, a new module was brought into the library instead. `optparse` is still supported, but it is not likely to receive new features.

14.3.1   Comparing with optparse

The API for `argparse` is similar to the one provided by `optparse`, and in many cases, `argparse` can be used as a straightforward replacement by updating the names of the classes and methods used. There are a few places where direct compatibility could not be preserved as new features were added, however.

The decision to upgrade existing programs should be made on a case-by-case basis. If an application includes extra code to work around limitations of `optparse`, upgrading may reduce maintenance work. Use `argparse` for a new program, if it is available on all the platforms where the program will be deployed.

14.3.2   Setting Up a Parser

The first step when using `argparse` is to create a parser object and tell it what arguments to expect. The parser can then be used to process the command-line arguments when the program runs. The constructor for the parser class (`ArgumentParser`) takes several arguments to set up the description used in the help text for the program and other global behaviors or settings.

```
import argparse
parser = argparse.ArgumentParser(
    description='This is a PyMOTW sample program',
    )
```

14.3.3   Defining Arguments

`argparse` is a complete argument-processing library. Arguments can trigger different actions, specified by the *action* argument to `add_argument()`. Supported actions include storing the argument (singly, or as part of a list), storing a constant value when the argument is encountered (including special handling for true/false values for Boolean switches), counting the number of times an argument is seen, and calling a callback to use custom processing instructions.

The default action is to store the argument value. If a type is provided, the value is converted to that type before it is stored. If the *dest* argument is provided, the value is saved using that name when the command-line arguments are parsed.

14.3.4   Parsing a Command Line

After all the arguments are defined, parse the command line by passing a sequence of argument strings to `parse_args()`. By default, the arguments are taken from `sys.argv[1:]`, but any list of strings can be used. The options are processed using the GNU/POSIX syntax, so option and argument values can be mixed in the sequence.

The return value from `parse_args()` is a `Namespace` containing the arguments to the command. The object holds the argument values as attributes, so if the argument's `dest` is set to `"myoption"`, the value is accessible as `args.myoption`.

14.3.5   Simple Examples

Here is a simple example with three different options: a Boolean option (−a), a simple string option (−b), and an integer option (−c).

```
import argparse

parser = argparse.ArgumentParser(description='Short sample app')

parser.add_argument('-a', action="store_true", default=False)
parser.add_argument('-b', action="store", dest="b")
parser.add_argument('-c', action="store", dest="c", type=int)

print parser.parse_args(['-a', '-bval', '-c', '3'])
```

There are a few ways to pass values to single-character options. The previous example uses two different forms, −bval and −c val.

```
$ python argparse_short.py

Namespace(a=True, b='val', c=3)
```

The type of the value associated with `'c'` in the output is an integer, since the `ArgumentParser` was told to convert the argument before storing it.

"Long" option names, with more than a single character in their name, are handled in the same way.

```
import argparse

parser = argparse.ArgumentParser(
    description='Example with long option names',
    )

parser.add_argument('--noarg', action="store_true",
                    default=False)
```

```
parser.add_argument('--witharg', action="store",
                    dest="witharg")
parser.add_argument('--witharg2', action="store",
                    dest="witharg2", type=int)

print parser.parse_args(
    [ '--noarg', '--witharg', 'val', '--witharg2=3' ]
    )
```

The results are similar.

```
$ python argparse_long.py

Namespace(noarg=True, witharg='val', witharg2=3)
```

One area in which `argparse` differs from `optparse` is the treatment of nonoptional argument values. While `optparse` sticks to option parsing, `argparse` is a full command-line argument parser tool and handles nonoptional arguments as well.

```
import argparse

parser = argparse.ArgumentParser(
    description='Example with nonoptional arguments',
    )

parser.add_argument('count', action="store", type=int)
parser.add_argument('units', action="store")

print parser.parse_args()
```

In this example, the "count" argument is an integer and the "units" argument is saved as a string. If either is left off the command line, or the value given cannot be converted to the right type, an error is reported.

```
$ python argparse_arguments.py 3 inches

Namespace(count=3, units='inches')

$ python argparse_arguments.py some inches

usage: argparse_arguments.py [-h] count units
```

```
argparse_arguments.py: error: argument count: invalid int value:
'some'

$ python argparse_arguments.py

usage: argparse_arguments.py [-h] count units
argparse_arguments.py: error: too few arguments
```

Argument Actions

Six built-in actions can be triggered when an argument is encountered.

store Save the value, after optionally converting it to a different type. This is the default action taken if none is specified explicitly.

store_const Save a value defined as part of the argument specification, rather than a value that comes from the arguments being parsed. This is typically used to implement command-line flags that are not Booleans.

store_true / store_false Save the appropriate Boolean value. These actions are used to implement Boolean switches.

append Save the value to a list. Multiple values are saved if the argument is repeated.

append_const Save a value defined in the argument specification to a list.

version Prints version details about the program and then exits.

This example program demonstrates each action type, with the minimum configuration needed for each to work.

```
import argparse

parser = argparse.ArgumentParser()

parser.add_argument('-s', action='store',
                    dest='simple_value',
                    help='Store a simple value')

parser.add_argument('-c', action='store_const',
                    dest='constant_value',
                    const='value-to-store',
                    help='Store a constant value')

parser.add_argument('-t', action='store_true',
                    default=False,
                    dest='boolean_switch',
                    help='Set a switch to true')
```

```
parser.add_argument('-f', action='store_false',
                     default=False,
                     dest='boolean_switch',
                     help='Set a switch to false')

parser.add_argument('-a', action='append',
                     dest='collection',
                     default=[],
                     help='Add repeated values to a list')

parser.add_argument('-A', action='append_const',
                     dest='const_collection',
                     const='value-1-to-append',
                     default=[],
                     help='Add different values to list')
parser.add_argument('-B', action='append_const',
                     dest='const_collection',
                     const='value-2-to-append',
                     help='Add different values to list')

parser.add_argument('--version', action='version',
                     version='%(prog)s 1.0')

results = parser.parse_args()
print 'simple_value     = %r' % results.simple_value
print 'constant_value   = %r' % results.constant_value
print 'boolean_switch   = %r' % results.boolean_switch
print 'collection       = %r' % results.collection
print 'const_collection = %r' % results.const_collection
```

The -t and -f options are configured to modify the same option value, so they act as a Boolean switch. The *dest* values for -A and -B are the same so that their constant values are appended to the same list.

```
$ python argparse_action.py -h

usage: argparse_action.py [-h] [-s SIMPLE_VALUE] [-c] [-t] [-f]
                          [-a COLLECTION] [-A] [-B] [--version]

optional arguments:
  -h, --help       show this help message and exit
  -s SIMPLE_VALUE  Store a simple value
  -c               Store a constant value
```

```
   -t                  Set a switch to true
   -f                  Set a switch to false
   -a COLLECTION       Add repeated values to a list
   -A                  Add different values to list
   -B                  Add different values to list
   --version           show program's version number and exit

$ python argparse_action.py -s value

simple_value     = 'value'
constant_value   = None
boolean_switch   = False
collection       = []
const_collection = []

$ python argparse_action.py -c

simple_value     = None
constant_value   = 'value-to-store'
boolean_switch   = False
collection       = []
const_collection = []

$ python argparse_action.py -t

simple_value     = None
constant_value   = None
boolean_switch   = True
collection       = []
const_collection = []

$ python argparse_action.py -f

simple_value     = None
constant_value   = None
boolean_switch   = False
collection       = []
const_collection = []

$ python argparse_action.py -a one -a two -a three

simple_value     = None
constant_value   = None
boolean_switch   = False
```

```
collection        = ['one', 'two', 'three']
const_collection = []

$ python argparse_action.py -B -A

simple_value      = None
constant_value    = None
boolean_switch    = False
collection        = []
const_collection = ['value-2-to-append', 'value-1-to-append']

$ python argparse_action.py --version

argparse_action.py 1.0
```

Option Prefixes

The default syntax for options is based on the UNIX convention of signifying command-line switches using a dash prefix ("–"). argparse supports other prefixes, so a program can conform to the local platform default (i.e., use "/" on Windows) or follow a different convention.

```
import argparse

parser = argparse.ArgumentParser(
    description='Change the option prefix characters',
    prefix_chars='-+/',
    )

parser.add_argument('-a', action="store_false",
                    default=None,
                    help='Turn A off',
                    )
parser.add_argument('+a', action="store_true",
                    default=None,
                    help='Turn A on',
                    )
parser.add_argument('//noarg', '++noarg',
                    action="store_true",
                    default=False)

print parser.parse_args()
```

Set the *prefix_chars* parameter for the `ArgumentParser` to a string containing all the characters that should be allowed to signify options. It is important to understand that although *prefix_chars* establishes the allowed switch characters, the individual argument definitions specify the syntax for a given switch. This gives explicit control over whether options using different prefixes are aliases (such as might be the case for platform-independent, command-line syntax) or alternatives (e.g., using "+" to indicate turning a switch on and "−" to turn it off). In the previous example, +a and −a are separate arguments, and //noarg can also be given as ++noarg, but not as −−noarg.

```
$ python argparse_prefix_chars.py -h

usage: argparse_prefix_chars.py [-h] [-a] [+a] [//noarg]

Change the option prefix characters

optional arguments:
  -h, --help       show this help message and exit
  -a               Turn A off
  +a               Turn A on
  //noarg, ++noarg

$ python argparse_prefix_chars.py +a

Namespace(a=True, noarg=False)

$ python argparse_prefix_chars.py -a

Namespace(a=False, noarg=False)

$ python argparse_prefix_chars.py //noarg

Namespace(a=None, noarg=True)

$ python argparse_prefix_chars.py ++noarg

Namespace(a=None, noarg=True)

$ python argparse_prefix_chars.py --noarg

usage: argparse_prefix_chars.py [-h] [-a] [+a] [//noarg]
argparse_prefix_chars.py: error: unrecognized arguments: --noarg
```

Sources of Arguments

In the examples so far, the list of arguments given to the parser has come from a list passed in explicitly, or the arguments were taken implicitly from `sys.argv`. Passing the list explicitly is useful when using `argparse` to process command-line-like instructions that do not come from the command line (such as in a configuration file).

```python
import argparse
from ConfigParser import ConfigParser
import shlex

parser = argparse.ArgumentParser(description='Short sample app')

parser.add_argument('-a', action="store_true", default=False)
parser.add_argument('-b', action="store", dest="b")
parser.add_argument('-c', action="store", dest="c", type=int)

config = ConfigParser()
config.read('argparse_with_shlex.ini')
config_value = config.get('cli', 'options')
print 'Config  :', config_value

argument_list = shlex.split(config_value)
print 'Arg List:', argument_list

print 'Results :', parser.parse_args(argument_list)
```

`shlex` makes it easy to split the string stored in the configuration file.

```
$ python argparse_with_shlex.py

Config  : -a -b 2
Arg List: ['-a', '-b', '2']
Results : Namespace(a=True, b='2', c=None)
```

An alternative to processing the configuration file in application code is to tell `argparse` how to recognize an argument that specifies an input file containing a set of arguments to be processed using *fromfile_prefix_chars*.

```python
import argparse
from ConfigParser import ConfigParser
import shlex
```

```
parser = argparse.ArgumentParser(description='Short sample app',
                                 fromfile_prefix_chars='@',
                                 )

parser.add_argument('-a', action="store_true", default=False)
parser.add_argument('-b', action="store", dest="b")
parser.add_argument('-c', action="store", dest="c", type=int)

print parser.parse_args(['@argparse_fromfile_prefix_chars.txt'])
```

This example stops when it finds an argument prefixed with @, and then it reads the named file to find more arguments. For example, an input file `argparse_fromfile_prefix_chars.txt` contains a series of arguments, one per line.

```
-a
-b
2
```

This is the output produced when processing the file.

```
$ python argparse_fromfile_prefix_chars.py

Namespace(a=True, b='2', c=None)
```

14.3.6 Automatically Generated Options

`argparse` will automatically add options to generate help and show the version information for the application, if configured to do so.

The *add_help* argument to `ArgumentParser` controls the help-related options.

```
import argparse

parser = argparse.ArgumentParser(add_help=True)

parser.add_argument('-a', action="store_true", default=False)
parser.add_argument('-b', action="store", dest="b")
parser.add_argument('-c', action="store", dest="c", type=int)

print parser.parse_args()
```

The help options (-h and --help) are added by default, but they can be disabled by setting *add_help* to false.

```
import argparse

parser = argparse.ArgumentParser(add_help=False)

parser.add_argument('-a', action="store_true", default=False)
parser.add_argument('-b', action="store", dest="b")
parser.add_argument('-c', action="store", dest="c", type=int)

print parser.parse_args()
```

Although -h and --help are de facto standard option names for requesting help, some applications or uses of argparse either do not need to provide help or need to use those option names for other purposes.

```
$ python argparse_with_help.py -h

usage: argparse_with_help.py [-h] [-a] [-b B] [-c C]

optional arguments:
  -h, --help  show this help message and exit
  -a
  -b B
  -c C

$ python argparse_without_help.py -h

usage: argparse_without_help.py [-a] [-b B] [-c C]
argparse_without_help.py: error: unrecognized arguments: -h
```

The version options (-v and --version) are added when *version* is set in the ArgumentParser constructor.

```
import argparse

parser = argparse.ArgumentParser(version='1.0')

parser.add_argument('-a', action="store_true", default=False)
parser.add_argument('-b', action="store", dest="b")
parser.add_argument('-c', action="store", dest="c", type=int)

print parser.parse_args()

print 'This is not printed'
```

Both forms of the option print the program's version string and then cause it to exit immediately.

```
$ python argparse_with_version.py -h

usage: argparse_with_version.py [-h] [-v] [-a] [-b B] [-c C]

optional arguments:
  -h, --help     show this help message and exit
  -v, --version  show program's version number and exit
  -a
  -b B
  -c C

$ python argparse_with_version.py -v

1.0

$ python argparse_with_version.py --version

1.0
```

14.3.7   Parser Organization

argparse includes several features for organizing argument parsers, to make implementation easier or to improve the usability of the help output.

Sharing Parser Rules

Programmers commonly to need to implement a suite of command-line tools that all take a set of arguments and then specialize in some way. For example, if the programs all need to authenticate the user before taking any real action, they would all need to support --user and --password options. Rather than add the options explicitly to every ArgumentParser, it is possible to define a parent parser with the shared options and then have the parsers for the individual programs inherit from its options.

The first step is to set up the parser with the shared-argument definitions. Since each subsequent user of the parent parser will try to add the same help options, causing an exception, automatic help generation is turned off in the base parser.

```
import argparse

parser = argparse.ArgumentParser(add_help=False)
```

```
parser.add_argument('--user', action="store")
parser.add_argument('--password', action="store")
```

Next, create another parser with *parents* set.

```
import argparse
import argparse_parent_base

parser = argparse.ArgumentParser(
    parents=[argparse_parent_base.parser],
    )

parser.add_argument('--local-arg',
                    action="store_true",
                    default=False)

print parser.parse_args()
```

And the resulting program takes all three options.

```
$ python argparse_uses_parent.py -h

usage: argparse_uses_parent.py [-h] [--user USER]
                               [--password PASSWORD]
                               [--local-arg]

optional arguments:
  -h, --help            show this help message and exit
  --user USER
  --password PASSWORD
  --local-arg
```

Conflicting Options

The previous example pointed out that adding two argument handlers to a parser using the same argument name causes an exception. The conflict resolution behavior can be changed by passing a *conflict_handler*. The two built-in handlers are `error` (the default) and `resolve`, which picks handlers based on the order in which they are added.

```
import argparse

parser = argparse.ArgumentParser(conflict_handler='resolve')
parser.add_argument('-a', action="store")
parser.add_argument('-b', action="store", help='Short alone')
```

```
parser.add_argument('--long-b', '-b',
                    action="store",
                    help='Long and short together')

print parser.parse_args(['-h'])
```

Since the last handler with a given argument name is used, in this example, the stand-alone option -b is masked by the alias for --long-b.

```
$ python argparse_conflict_handler_resolve.py

usage: argparse_conflict_handler_resolve.py [-h] [-a A]
[--long-b LONG_B]

optional arguments:
  -h, --help              show this help message and exit
  -a A
  --long-b LONG_B, -b LONG_B
                          Long and short together
```

Switching the order of the calls to add_argument() unmasks the stand-alone option.

```
import argparse

parser = argparse.ArgumentParser(conflict_handler='resolve')

parser.add_argument('-a', action="store")
parser.add_argument('--long-b', '-b',
                    action="store",
                    help='Long and short together')
parser.add_argument('-b', action="store", help='Short alone')

print parser.parse_args(['-h'])
```

Now both options can be used together.

```
$ python argparse_conflict_handler_resolve2.py

usage: argparse_conflict_handler_resolve2.py [-h] [-a A]
                                             [--long-b LONG_B]
                                             [-b B]
```

```
optional arguments:
  -h, --help          show this help message and exit
  -a A
  --long-b LONG_B   Long and short together
  -b B                Short alone
```

Argument Groups

`argparse` combines the argument definitions into "groups." By default, it uses two groups, with one for options and another for required position-based arguments.

```
import argparse

parser = argparse.ArgumentParser(description='Short sample app')

parser.add_argument('--optional', action="store_true", default=False)
parser.add_argument('positional', action="store")

print parser.parse_args()
```

The grouping is reflected in the separate "positional arguments" and "optional arguments" section of the help output.

```
$ python argparse_default_grouping.py -h

usage: argparse_default_grouping.py [-h] [--optional] positional

Short sample app

positional arguments:
  positional

optional arguments:
  -h, --help  show this help message and exit
  --optional
```

The grouping can be adjusted to make it more logical in the help, so that related options or values are documented together. The shared-option example from earlier could be written using custom grouping so that the authentication options are shown together in the help.

Create the "authentication" group with `add_argument_group()` and then add each of the authentication-related options to the group, instead of the base parser.

```
import argparse

parser = argparse.ArgumentParser(add_help=False)

group = parser.add_argument_group('authentication')

group.add_argument('--user', action="store")
group.add_argument('--password', action="store")
```

The program using the group-based parent lists it in the *parents* value, just as before.

```
import argparse
import argparse_parent_with_group

parser = argparse.ArgumentParser(
    parents=[argparse_parent_with_group.parser],
    )

parser.add_argument('--local-arg',
                    action="store_true",
                    default=False)

print parser.parse_args()
```

The help output now shows the authentication options together.

```
$ python argparse_uses_parent_with_group.py -h

usage: argparse_uses_parent_with_group.py [-h] [--user USER]
                                          [--password PASSWORD]
                                          [--local-arg]

optional arguments:
  -h, --help            show this help message and exit
  --local-arg
```

```
authentication:
  --user USER
  --password PASSWORD
```

Mutually Exclusive Options

Defining mutually exclusive options is a special case of the option grouping feature. It uses add_mutually_exclusive_group() instead of add_argument_group().

```python
import argparse

parser = argparse.ArgumentParser()

group = parser.add_mutually_exclusive_group()
group.add_argument('-a', action='store_true')
group.add_argument('-b', action='store_true')

print parser.parse_args()
```

argparse enforces the mutual exclusivity, so that only one of the options from the group can be given.

```
$ python argparse_mutually_exclusive.py -h

usage: argparse_mutually_exclusive.py [-h] [-a | -b]

optional arguments:
  -h, --help  show this help message and exit
  -a
  -b

$ python argparse_mutually_exclusive.py -a

Namespace(a=True, b=False)

$ python argparse_mutually_exclusive.py -b

Namespace(a=False, b=True)

$ python argparse_mutually_exclusive.py -a -b

usage: argparse_mutually_exclusive.py [-h] [-a | -b]
```

```
argparse_mutually_exclusive.py: error: argument -b: not allowed with
argument -a
```

Nesting Parsers

The parent parser approach described earlier is one way to share options between related commands. An alternate approach is to combine the commands into a single program and use subparsers to handle each portion of the command-line. The result works in the way svn, hg, and other programs with multiple command-line actions, or subcommands, do.

A program to work with directories on the file system might define commands for creating, deleting, and listing the contents of a directory like this.

```
import argparse

parser = argparse.ArgumentParser()

subparsers = parser.add_subparsers(help='commands')

# A list command
list_parser = subparsers.add_parser(
    'list', help='List contents')
list_parser.add_argument(
    'dirname', action='store',
    help='Directory to list')

# A create command
create_parser = subparsers.add_parser(
    'create', help='Create a directory')
create_parser.add_argument(
    'dirname', action='store',
    help='New directory to create')
create_parser.add_argument(
    '--read-only', default=False, action='store_true',
    help='Set permissions to prevent writing to the directory',
    )

# A delete command
delete_parser = subparsers.add_parser(
    'delete', help='Remove a directory')
delete_parser.add_argument(
    'dirname', action='store', help='The directory to remove')
```

```
delete_parser.add_argument(
    '--recursive', '-r', default=False, action='store_true',
    help='Remove the contents of the directory, too',
    )
```

```
print parser.parse_args()
```

The help output shows the named subparsers as "commands" that can be specified on the command line as positional arguments.

```
$ python argparse_subparsers.py -h

usage: argparse_subparsers.py [-h] {create,list,delete} ...

positional arguments:
  {create,list,delete}   commands
    list                 List contents
    create               Create a directory
    delete               Remove a directory

optional arguments:
  -h, --help             show this help message and exit
```

Each subparser also has its own help, describing the arguments and options for that command.

```
$ python argparse_subparsers.py create -h

usage: argparse_subparsers.py create [-h] [--read-only] dirname

positional arguments:
  dirname      New directory to create

optional arguments:
  -h, --help   show this help message and exit
  --read-only  Set permissions to prevent writing to the directory
```

And when the arguments are parsed, the Namespace object returned by parse_args() includes only the values related to the command specified.

```
$ python argparse_subparsers.py delete -r foo

Namespace(dirname='foo', recursive=True)
```

14.3.8   Advanced Argument Processing

The examples so far have shown simple Boolean flags, options with string or numerical arguments, and positional arguments. argparse also supports sophisticated argument specification for variable-length argument lists, enumerations, and constant values.

Variable Argument Lists

A single argument definition can be configured to consume multiple arguments on the command line being parsed. Set *nargs* to one of the flag values from Table 14.1, based on the number of required or expected arguments.

Table 14.1. Flags for Variable Argument Definitions in argparse

Value	Meaning
N	The absolute number of arguments (e.g., 3)
?	0 or 1 arguments
*	0 or all arguments
+	All, and at least one, arguments

```
import argparse

parser = argparse.ArgumentParser()

parser.add_argument('--three', nargs=3)
parser.add_argument('--optional', nargs='?')
parser.add_argument('--all', nargs='*', dest='all')
parser.add_argument('--one-or-more', nargs='+')

print parser.parse_args()
```

The parser enforces the argument count instructions and generates an accurate syntax diagram as part of the command help text.

```
$ python argparse_nargs.py -h

usage: argparse_nargs.py [-h] [--three THREE THREE THREE]
                         [--optional [OPTIONAL]]
                         [--all [ALL [ALL ...]]]
                         [--one-or-more ONE_OR_MORE [ONE_OR_MORE ...]]

optional arguments:
  -h, --help            show this help message and exit
```

```
    --three THREE THREE THREE
    --optional [OPTIONAL]
    --all [ALL [ALL ...]]
    --one-or-more ONE_OR_MORE [ONE_OR_MORE ...]

$ python argparse_nargs.py

Namespace(all=None, one_or_more=None, optional=None, three=None)

$ python argparse_nargs.py --three

usage: argparse_nargs.py [-h] [--three THREE THREE THREE]
                [--optional [OPTIONAL]]
                [--all [ALL [ALL ...]]]
                [--one-or-more ONE_OR_MORE [ONE_OR_MORE ...]]
argparse_nargs.py: error: argument --three: expected 3
argument(s)

$ python argparse_nargs.py --three a b c

Namespace(all=None, one_or_more=None, optional=None,
three=['a', 'b', 'c'])

$ python argparse_nargs.py --optional

Namespace(all=None, one_or_more=None, optional=None, three=None)

$ python argparse_nargs.py --optional with_value

Namespace(all=None, one_or_more=None, optional='with_value',
three=None)

$ python argparse_nargs.py --all with multiple values

Namespace(all=['with', 'multiple', 'values'], one_or_more=None,
optional=None, three=None)

$ python argparse_nargs.py --one-or-more with_value

Namespace(all=None, one_or_more=['with_value'], optional=None,
three=None)

$ python argparse_nargs.py --one-or-more with multiple values
```

```
Namespace(all=None, one_or_more=['with', 'multiple', 'values'],
optional=None, three=None)

$ python argparse_nargs.py --one-or-more

usage: argparse_nargs.py [-h] [--three THREE THREE THREE]
                [--optional [OPTIONAL]]
                [--all [ALL [ALL ...]]]
                [--one-or-more ONE_OR_MORE [ONE_OR_MORE ...]]
argparse_nargs.py: error: argument --one-or-more: expected
at least one argument
```

Argument Types

argparse treats all argument values as strings, unless it is told to convert the string to another type. The *type* parameter to add_argument() defines a converter function, which is used by the ArgumentParser to transform the argument value from a string to some other type.

```
import argparse

parser = argparse.ArgumentParser()

parser.add_argument('-i', type=int)
parser.add_argument('-f', type=float)
parser.add_argument('--file', type=file)

try:
    print parser.parse_args()
except IOError, msg:
    parser.error(str(msg))
```

Any callable that takes a single string argument can be passed as *type*, including built-in types like int(), float(), and file().

```
$ python argparse_type.py -i 1

Namespace(f=None, file=None, i=1)

$ python argparse_type.py -f 3.14

Namespace(f=3.14, file=None, i=None)
```

```
$ python argparse_type.py --file argparse_type.py

Namespace(f=None, file=<open file 'argparse_type.py', mode 'r' at
0x100d886f0>, i=None)
```

If the type conversion fails, `argparse` raises an exception. `TypeError` and `ValueError` exceptions are trapped automatically and converted to a simple error message for the user. Other exceptions, such as the `IOError` in the next example where the input file does not exist, must be handled by the caller.

```
$ python argparse_type.py -i a

usage: argparse_type.py [-h] [-i I] [-f F] [--file FILE]
argparse_type.py: error: argument -i: invalid int value: 'a'

$ python argparse_type.py -f 3.14.15

usage: argparse_type.py [-h] [-i I] [-f F] [--file FILE]
argparse_type.py: error: argument -f: invalid float value: '3.14.15'

$ python argparse_type.py --file does_not_exist.txt

usage: argparse_type.py [-h] [-i I] [-f F] [--file FILE]
argparse_type.py: error: [Errno 2] No such file or directory:
'does_not_exist.txt'
```

To limit an input argument to a value within a predefined set, use the *choices* parameter.

```
import argparse

parser = argparse.ArgumentParser()

parser.add_argument('--mode', choices=('read-only', 'read-write'))

print parser.parse_args()
```

If the argument to `--mode` is not one of the allowed values, an error is generated and processing stops.

```
$ python argparse_choices.py -h

usage: argparse_choices.py [-h] [--mode {read-only,read-write}]
```

```
optional arguments:
  -h, --help              show this help message and exit
  --mode {read-only,read-write}

$ python argparse_choices.py --mode read-only

Namespace(mode='read-only')

$ python argparse_choices.py --mode invalid

usage: argparse_choices.py [-h] [--mode {read-only,read-write}]
argparse_choices.py: error: argument --mode: invalid choice:
'invalid' (choose from 'read-only', 'read-write')
```

File Arguments

Although `file` objects can be instantiated with a single string argument, that does not include the access mode argument. `FileType` provides a more flexible way of specifying that an argument should be a file, including the mode and buffer size.

```
import argparse

parser = argparse.ArgumentParser()

parser.add_argument('-i', metavar='in-file',
                    type=argparse.FileType('rt'))
parser.add_argument('-o', metavar='out-file',
                    type=argparse.FileType('wt'))

try:
    results = parser.parse_args()
    print 'Input file:', results.i
    print 'Output file:', results.o
except IOError, msg:
    parser.error(str(msg))
```

The value associated with the argument name is the open file handle. The application is responsible for closing the file when it is no longer being used.

```
$ python argparse_FileType.py -h

usage: argparse_FileType.py [-h] [-i in-file] [-o out-file]
```

```
optional arguments:
  -h, --help   show this help message and exit
  -i in-file
  -o out-file
```

```
$ python argparse_FileType.py -i argparse_FileType.py -o tmp_file.txt
```

```
Input file: <open file 'argparse_FileType.py', mode 'rt' at
0x100d886f0>
Output file: <open file 'tmp_file.txt', mode 'wt' at 0x100dfa150>
```

```
$ python argparse_FileType.py -i no_such_file.txt
```

```
usage: argparse_FileType.py [-h] [-i in-file] [-o out-file]
argparse_FileType.py: error: [Errno 2] No such file or directory:
'no_such_file.txt'
```

Custom Actions

In addition to the built-in actions described earlier, custom actions can be defined by providing an object that implements the Action API. The object passed to add_argument() as *action* should take parameters describing the argument being defined (all the same arguments given to add_argument()) and return a callable object that takes as parameters the *parser* processing the arguments, the *namespace* holding the parse results, the *value* of the argument being acted on, and the *option_string* that triggered the action.

A class Action is provided as a convenient starting point for defining new actions. The constructor handles the argument definitions, so only __call__() needs to be overridden in the subclass.

```
import argparse

class CustomAction(argparse.Action):
    def __init__(self,
                 option_strings,
                 dest,
                 nargs=None,
                 const=None,
                 default=None,
                 type=None,
                 choices=None,
                 required=False,
```

```
                help=None,
                metavar=None):
        argparse.Action.__init__(self,
                                 option_strings=option_strings,
                                 dest=dest,
                                 nargs=nargs,
                                 const=const,
                                 default=default,
                                 type=type,
                                 choices=choices,
                                 required=required,
                                 help=help,
                                 metavar=metavar,
                                 )
        print 'Initializing CustomAction'
        for name,value in sorted(locals().items()):
            if name == 'self' or value is None:
                continue
            print '  %s = %r' % (name, value)
        print
        return

    def __call__(self, parser, namespace, values,
                 option_string=None):
        print 'Processing CustomAction for "%s"' % self.dest
        print '  parser = %s' % id(parser)
        print '  values = %r' % values
        print '  option_string = %r' % option_string

        # Do some arbitrary processing of the input values
        if isinstance(values, list):
            values = [ v.upper() for v in values ]
        else:
            values = values.upper()
        # Save the results in the namespace using the destination
        # variable given to our constructor.
        setattr(namespace, self.dest, values)
        print

parser = argparse.ArgumentParser()

parser.add_argument('-a', action=CustomAction)
parser.add_argument('-m', nargs='*', action=CustomAction)
```

```
results = parser.parse_args(['-a', 'value',
                            '-m', 'multivalue',
                            'second'])
print results
```

The type of *values* depends on the value of *nargs*. If the argument allows multiple values, *values* will be a list even if it only contains one item.

The value of *option_string* also depends on the original argument specification. For positional required arguments, *option_string* is always None.

```
$ python argparse_custom_action.py

Initializing CustomAction
dest = 'a'
option_strings = ['-a']
required = False

Initializing CustomAction
dest = 'm'
nargs = '*'
option_strings = ['-m']
required = False

Initializing CustomAction
dest = 'positional'
option_strings = []
required = True

Processing CustomAction for "a"
parser = 4309267472
values = 'value'
option_string = '-a'

Processing CustomAction for "m"
parser = 4309267472
values = ['multivalue', 'second']
option_string = '-m'

Namespace(a='VALUE', m=['MULTIVALUE', 'SECOND'])
```

See Also:

argparse (http://docs.python.org/library/argparse.html) The standard library documentation for this module.

Original argparse (http://pypi.python.org/pypi/argparse) The PyPI page for the version of argparse from outside of the standard libary. This version is compatible with older versions of Python and can be installed separately.

`ConfigParser` **(page 861)** Read and write configuration files.

14.4   readline—The GNU Readline Library

> **Purpose** Provides an interface to the GNU Readline library for interacting with the user at a command prompt.
> **Python Version** 1.4 and later

The `readline` module can be used to enhance interactive command-line programs to make them easier to use. It is primarily used to provide command-line text completion, or "tab completion."

> **Note:** Because `readline` interacts with the console content, printing debug messages makes it difficult to see what is happening in the sample code versus what readline is doing for free. The following examples use the `logging` module to write debug information to a separate file. The log output is shown with each example.

> **Note:** The GNU libraries needed for `readline` are not available on all platforms by default. If your system does not include them, you may need to recompile the Python interpreter to enable the module, after installing the dependencies.

14.4.1   Configuring

There are two ways to configure the underlying readline library, using a configuration file or the `parse_and_bind()` function. Configuration options include the key-binding to invoke completion, editing modes (**vi** or **emacs**), and many other values. Refer to the documentation for the GNU Readline library for details.

The easiest way to enable tab-completion is through a call to `parse_and_bind()`. Other options can be set at the same time. This example changes the editing controls to use "vi" mode instead of the default of "emacs." To edit the current input line, press ESC and then use normal **vi** navigation keys such as j, k, l, and h.

```
import readline

readline.parse_and_bind('tab: complete')
readline.parse_and_bind('set editing-mode vi')
```

```
while True:
    line = raw_input('Prompt ("stop" to quit): ')
    if line == 'stop':
        break
    print 'ENTERED: "%s"' % line
```

The same configuration can be stored as instructions in a file read by the library with a single call. If `myreadline.rc` contains

```
# Turn on tab completion
tab: complete

# Use vi editing mode instead of emacs
set editing-mode vi
```

the file can be read with `read_init_file()`.

```
import readline

readline.read_init_file('myreadline.rc')

while True:
    line = raw_input('Prompt ("stop" to quit): ')
    if line == 'stop':
        break
    print 'ENTERED: "%s"' % line
```

14.4.2   Completing Text

This program has a built-in set of possible commands and uses tab-completion when the user is entering instructions.

```
import readline
import logging

LOG_FILENAME = '/tmp/completer.log'
logging.basicConfig(filename=LOG_FILENAME,
                    level=logging.DEBUG,
                    )

class SimpleCompleter(object):

    def __init__(self, options):
```

```python
        self.options = sorted(options)
        return

    def complete(self, text, state):
        response = None
        if state == 0:
            # This is the first time for this text,
            # so build a match list.
            if text:
                self.matches = [s
                                for s in self.options
                                if s and s.startswith(text)]
                logging.debug('%s matches: %s',
                              repr(text), self.matches)
            else:
                self.matches = self.options[:]
                logging.debug('(empty input) matches: %s',
                              self.matches)

        # Return the state'th item from the match list,
        # if we have that many.
        try:
            response = self.matches[state]
        except IndexError:
            response = None
        logging.debug('complete(%s, %s) => %s',
                      repr(text), state, repr(response))
        return response

def input_loop():
    line = ''
    while line != 'stop':
        line = raw_input('Prompt ("stop" to quit): ')
        print 'Dispatch %s' % line

# Register the completer function
OPTIONS = ['start', 'stop', 'list', 'print']
readline.set_completer(SimpleCompleter(OPTIONS).complete)

# Use the tab key for completion
readline.parse_and_bind('tab: complete')

# Prompt the user for text
input_loop()
```

The `input_loop()` function reads one line after another until the input value is `"stop"`. A more sophisticated program could actually parse the input line and run the command.

The `SimpleCompleter` class keeps a list of "options" that are candidates for auto-completion. The `complete()` method for an instance is designed to be registered with `readline` as the source of completions. The arguments are a *text* string to complete and a *state* value, indicating how many times the function has been called with the same text. The function is called repeatedly, with the state incremented each time. It should return a string if there is a candidate for that state value or `None` if there are no more candidates. The implementation of `complete()` here looks for a set of matches when state is `0`, and then returns all the candidate matches one at a time on subsequent calls.

When run, the initial output is:

```
$ python readline_completer.py

Prompt ("stop" to quit):
```

Pressing TAB twice causes a list of options to be printed.

```
$ python readline_completer.py

Prompt ("stop" to quit):
list    print   start   stop
Prompt ("stop" to quit):
```

The log file shows that `complete()` was called with two separate sequences of state values.

```
$ tail -f /tmp/completer.log

DEBUG:root:(empty input) matches: ['list', 'print', 'start', 'stop']
DEBUG:root:complete('', 0) => 'list'
DEBUG:root:complete('', 1) => 'print'
DEBUG:root:complete('', 2) => 'start'
DEBUG:root:complete('', 3) => 'stop'
DEBUG:root:complete('', 4) => None
DEBUG:root:(empty input) matches: ['list', 'print', 'start', 'stop']
DEBUG:root:complete('', 0) => 'list'
DEBUG:root:complete('', 1) => 'print'
```

```
DEBUG:root:complete('', 2) => 'start'
DEBUG:root:complete('', 3) => 'stop'
DEBUG:root:complete('', 4) => None
```

The first sequence is from the first TAB key-press. The completion algorithm asks for all candidates but does not expand the empty input line. Then, on the second TAB, the list of candidates is recalculated so it can be printed for the user.

If the next input is "l" followed by another TAB, the screen shows the following.

```
Prompt ("stop" to quit): list
```

And the log reflects the different arguments to `complete()`.

```
DEBUG:root:'l' matches: ['list']
DEBUG:root:complete('l', 0) => 'list'
DEBUG:root:complete('l', 1) => None
```

Pressing RETURN now causes `raw_input()` to return the value, and the **while** loop cycles.

```
Dispatch list
Prompt ("stop" to quit):
```

There are two possible completions for a command beginning with "s". Typing "s", and then pressing TAB, finds that "start" and "stop" are candidates, but only partially completes the text on the screen by adding a "t".

This is what the log file shows.

```
DEBUG:root:'s' matches: ['start', 'stop']
DEBUG:root:complete('s', 0) => 'start'
DEBUG:root:complete('s', 1) => 'stop'
DEBUG:root:complete('s', 2) => None
```

And the screen shows the following.

```
Prompt ("stop" to quit): st
```

Warning: If a completer function raises an exception, it is ignored silently and `readline` assumes there are no matching completions.

14.4.3 Accessing the Completion Buffer

The completion algorithm in `SimpleCompleter` is simplistic because it only looks at the text argument passed to the function, but does not use any more of readline's internal state. It is also possible to use `readline` functions to manipulate the text of the input buffer.

```python
import readline
import logging

LOG_FILENAME = '/tmp/completer.log'
logging.basicConfig(filename=LOG_FILENAME,
                    level=logging.DEBUG,
                    )


class BufferAwareCompleter(object):

    def __init__(self, options):
        self.options = options
        self.current_candidates = []
        return

    def complete(self, text, state):
        response = None
        if state == 0:
            # This is the first time for this text,
            # so build a match list.

            origline = readline.get_line_buffer()
            begin = readline.get_begidx()
            end = readline.get_endidx()
            being_completed = origline[begin:end]
            words = origline.split()

            logging.debug('origline=%s', repr(origline))
            logging.debug('begin=%s', begin)
            logging.debug('end=%s', end)
            logging.debug('being_completed=%s', being_completed)
            logging.debug('words=%s', words)

            if not words:
                self.current_candidates = sorted(self.options.keys())
```

```python
        else:
            try:
                if begin == 0:
                    # first word
                    candidates = self.options.keys()
                else:
                    # later word
                    first = words[0]
                    candidates = self.options[first]

                if being_completed:
                    # match options with portion of input
                    # being completed
                    self.current_candidates = [
                        w for w in candidates
                        if w.startswith(being_completed)
                        ]
                else:
                    # matching empty string so use all candidates
                    self.current_candidates = candidates

                logging.debug('candidates=%s',
                              self.current_candidates)

            except (KeyError, IndexError), err:
                logging.error('completion error: %s', err)
                self.current_candidates = []

        try:
            response = self.current_candidates[state]
        except IndexError:
            response = None
        logging.debug('complete(%s, %s) => %s',
                      repr(text), state, response)
        return response


def input_loop():
    line = ''
    while line != 'stop':
        line = raw_input('Prompt ("stop" to quit): ')
        print 'Dispatch %s' % line
```

```
# Register our completer function
readline.set_completer(BufferAwareCompleter(
    {'list':['files', 'directories'],
     'print':['byname', 'bysize'],
     'stop':[],
    }).complete)

# Use the tab key for completion
readline.parse_and_bind('tab: complete')

# Prompt the user for text
input_loop()
```

In this example, commands with suboptions are being completed. The com-plete() method needs to look at the position of the completion within the input buffer to determine whether it is part of the first word or a later word. If the target is the first word, the keys of the options dictionary are used as candidates. If it is not the first word, then the first word is used to find candidates from the options dictionary.

There are three top-level commands, two of which have subcommands.

- list
    - files
    - directories
- print
    - byname
    - bysize
- stop

Following the same sequence of actions as before, pressing TAB twice gives the three top-level commands.

```
$ python readline_buffer.py

Prompt ("stop" to quit):
list    print   stop
Prompt ("stop" to quit):
```

and in the log:

```
DEBUG:root:origline=''
DEBUG:root:begin=0
```

```
DEBUG:root:end=0
DEBUG:root:being_completed=
DEBUG:root:words=[]
DEBUG:root:complete('', 0) => list
DEBUG:root:complete('', 1) => print
DEBUG:root:complete('', 2) => stop
DEBUG:root:complete('', 3) => None
DEBUG:root:origline=''
DEBUG:root:begin=0
DEBUG:root:end=0
DEBUG:root:being_completed=
DEBUG:root:words=[]
DEBUG:root:complete('', 0) => list
DEBUG:root:complete('', 1) => print
DEBUG:root:complete('', 2) => stop
DEBUG:root:complete('', 3) => None
```

If the first word is `"list  "` (with a space after the word), the candidates for completion are different.

```
Prompt ("stop" to quit): list
directories    files
```

The log shows that the text being completed is *not* the full line, but the portion after `list`.

```
DEBUG:root:origline='list '
DEBUG:root:begin=5
DEBUG:root:end=5
DEBUG:root:being_completed=
DEBUG:root:words=['list']
DEBUG:root:candidates=['files', 'directories']
DEBUG:root:complete('', 0) => files
DEBUG:root:complete('', 1) => directories
DEBUG:root:complete('', 2) => None
DEBUG:root:origline='list '
DEBUG:root:begin=5
DEBUG:root:end=5
DEBUG:root:being_completed=
DEBUG:root:words=['list']
DEBUG:root:candidates=['files', 'directories']
DEBUG:root:complete('', 0) => files
DEBUG:root:complete('', 1) => directories
DEBUG:root:complete('', 2) => None
```

14.4.4 Input History

readline tracks the input history automatically. There are two different sets of functions for working with the history. The history for the current session can be accessed
with get_current_history_length() and get_history_item(). That same
history can be saved to a file to be reloaded later using write_history_file() and
read_history_file(). By default, the entire history is saved, but the maximum
length of the file can be set with set_history_length(). A length of −1 means no
limit.

```python
import readline
import logging
import os

LOG_FILENAME = '/tmp/completer.log'
HISTORY_FILENAME = '/tmp/completer.hist'

logging.basicConfig(filename=LOG_FILENAME,
                    level=logging.DEBUG,
                    )

def get_history_items():
    num_items = readline.get_current_history_length() + 1
    return [ readline.get_history_item(i)
             for i in xrange(1, num_items)
             ]

class HistoryCompleter(object):

    def __init__(self):
        self.matches = []
        return

    def complete(self, text, state):
        response = None
        if state == 0:
            history_values = get_history_items()
            logging.debug('history: %s', history_values)
            if text:
                self.matches = sorted(h
                                      for h in history_values
                                      if h and h.startswith(text))
```

```python
        else:
            self.matches = []
        logging.debug('matches: %s', self.matches)
    try:
        response = self.matches[state]
    except IndexError:
        response = None
    logging.debug('complete(%s, %s) => %s',
                  repr(text), state, repr(response))
    return response


def input_loop():
    if os.path.exists(HISTORY_FILENAME):
        readline.read_history_file(HISTORY_FILENAME)
    print 'Max history file length:', readline.get_history_length()
    print 'Start-up history:', get_history_items()
    try:
        while True:
            line = raw_input('Prompt ("stop" to quit): ')
            if line == 'stop':
                break
            if line:
                print 'Adding "%s" to the history' % line
    finally:
        print 'Final history:', get_history_items()
        readline.write_history_file(HISTORY_FILENAME)


# Register our completer function
readline.set_completer(HistoryCompleter().complete)

# Use the tab key for completion
readline.parse_and_bind('tab: complete')

# Prompt the user for text
input_loop()
```

The `HistoryCompleter` remembers everything typed and uses those values when completing subsequent inputs.

```
$ python readline_history.py

Max history file length: -1
```

```
Start-up history: []
Prompt ("stop" to quit): foo
Adding "foo" to the history
Prompt ("stop" to quit): bar
Adding "bar" to the history
Prompt ("stop" to quit): blah
Adding "blah" to the history
Prompt ("stop" to quit): b
bar    blah
Prompt ("stop" to quit): b
Prompt ("stop" to quit): stop
Final history: ['foo', 'bar', 'blah', 'stop']
```

The log shows this output when the "b" is followed by two TABs.

```
DEBUG:root:history: ['foo', 'bar', 'blah']
DEBUG:root:matches: ['bar', 'blah']
DEBUG:root:complete('b', 0) => 'bar'
DEBUG:root:complete('b', 1) => 'blah'
DEBUG:root:complete('b', 2) => None
DEBUG:root:history: ['foo', 'bar', 'blah']
DEBUG:root:matches: ['bar', 'blah']
DEBUG:root:complete('b', 0) => 'bar'
DEBUG:root:complete('b', 1) => 'blah'
DEBUG:root:complete('b', 2) => None
```

When the script is run the second time, all the history is read from the file.

```
$ python readline_history.py

Max history file length: -1
Start-up history: ['foo', 'bar', 'blah', 'stop']
Prompt ("stop" to quit):
```

There are functions for removing individual history items and clearing the entire history, as well.

14.4.5 Hooks

Several hooks are available for triggering actions as part of the interaction sequence. The *start-up* hook is invoked immediately before printing the prompt, and the *preinput* hook is run after the prompt, but before reading text from the user.

```
import readline

def startup_hook():
    readline.insert_text('from start up_hook')

def pre_input_hook():
    readline.insert_text(' from pre_input_hook')
    readline.redisplay()

readline.set_startup_hook(startup_hook)
readline.set_pre_input_hook(pre_input_hook)
readline.parse_and_bind('tab: complete')

while True:
    line = raw_input('Prompt ("stop" to quit): ')
    if line == 'stop':
        break
    print 'ENTERED: "%s"' % line
```

Either hook is a potentially good place to use `insert_text()` to modify the input buffer.

```
$ python readline_hooks.py

Prompt ("stop" to quit): from startup_hook from pre_input_hook
```

If the buffer is modified inside the preinput hook, `redisplay()` must be called to update the screen.

See Also:
readline (http://docs.python.org/library/readline.html) The standard library documentation for this module.

GNU readline (http://tiswww.case.edu/php/chet/readline/readline.html) Documentation for the GNU Readline library.

readline init file format (http://tiswww.case.edu/php/chet/readline/readline.html# SEC10) The initialization and configuration file format.

effbot: The readline module (http://sandbox.effbot.org/librarybook/readline.htm) effbot's guide to the readline module.

pyreadline (https://launchpad.net/pyreadline) pyreadline, developed as a Python-based replacement for readline to be used in iPython (http://ipython.scipy.org/).

cmd (page 839) The `cmd` module uses `readline` extensively to implement tab-completion in the command interface. Some of the examples here were adapted from the code in `cmd`.

rlcompleter `rlcompleter` uses `readline` to add tab-completion to the interactive Python interpreter.

14.5   getpass—Secure Password Prompt

> **Purpose** Prompt the user for a value, usually a password, without echoing what is typed to the console.
> **Python Version** 1.5.2 and later

Many programs that interact with the user via the terminal need to ask the user for password values without showing what the user types on the screen. The `getpass` module provides a portable way to handle such password prompts securely.

14.5.1   Example

The `getpass()` function prints a prompt and then reads input from the user until return is pressed. The input is returned as a string to the caller.

```
import getpass

try:
    p = getpass.getpass()
except Exception, err:
    print 'ERROR:', err
else:
    print 'You entered:', p
```

The default prompt, if none is specified by the caller, is "`Password:`".

```
$ python getpass_defaults.py

Password:
You entered: sekret
```

The prompt can be changed to any value needed.

```
import getpass

p = getpass.getpass(prompt='What is your favorite color? ')
```

```
if p.lower() == 'blue':
    print 'Right.  Off you go.'
else:
    print 'Auuuuugh!'
```

Some programs ask for a "pass phrase," instead of a simple password, to give better security.

```
$ python getpass_prompt.py

What is your favorite color?
Right.  Off you go.

$ python getpass_prompt.py

What is your favorite color?
Auuuuugh!
```

By default, `getpass()` uses `sys.stdout` to print the prompt string. For a program that may produce useful output on `sys.stdout`, it is frequently better to send the prompt to another stream, such as `sys.stderr`.

```
import getpass
import sys

p = getpass.getpass(stream=sys.stderr)
print 'You entered:', p
```

Using `sys.stderr` for the prompt means standard output can be redirected (to a pipe or a file) without seeing the password prompt. The value the user enters is still not echoed back to the screen.

```
$ python getpass_stream.py >/dev/null

Password:
```

14.5.2 Using getpass without a Terminal

Under UNIX `getpass()` always requires a tty it can control via `termios`, so input echoing can be disabled. This means values will not be read from a nonterminal stream redirected to standard input. The results vary when standard input is redirected, based on the Python version. Python 2.5 produces an exception if `sys.stdin` is replaced.

```
$ echo "not sekret" | python2.5 getpass_defaults.py

ERROR: (25, 'Inappropriate ioctl for device')
```

Python 2.6 and 2.7 have been enhanced to try harder to get to the tty for a process, and no error is raised if they can access it.

```
$ echo "not sekret" | python2.7 getpass_defaults.py

Password:
You entered: sekret
```

It is up to the caller to detect when the input stream is not a tty and use an alternate method for reading in that case.

```python
import getpass
import sys

if sys.stdin.isatty():
    p = getpass.getpass('Using getpass: ')
else:
    print 'Using readline'
    p = sys.stdin.readline().rstrip()

print 'Read: ', p
```

With a tty:

```
$ python ./getpass_noterminal.py

Using getpass:
Read:   sekret
```

Without a tty:

```
$ echo "sekret" | python ./getpass_noterminal.py

Using readline
Read:   sekret
```

See Also:

getpass (http://docs.python.org/library/getpass.html) The standard library documentation for this module.

`readline` **(page 823)** Interactive prompt library.

14.6   cmd—Line-Oriented Command Processors

Purpose Create line-oriented command processors.
Python Version 1.4 and later

The `cmd` module contains one public class, `Cmd`, designed to be used as a base class for interactive shells and other command interpreters. By default, it uses `readline` for interactive prompt handling, command-line editing, and command completion.

14.6.1   Processing Commands

A command interpreter created with `Cmd` uses a loop to read all lines from its input, parse them, and then dispatch the command to an appropriate *command handler*. Input lines are parsed into two parts: the command and any other text on the line. If the user enters `foo bar`, and the interpreter class includes a method named `do_foo()`, it is called with `"bar"` as the only argument.

The end-of-file marker is dispatched to `do_EOF()`. If a command handler returns a true value, the program will exit cleanly. So, to give a clean way to exit the interpreter, make sure to implement `do_EOF()` and have it return True.

This simple example program supports the "greet" command.

```
import cmd

class HelloWorld(cmd.Cmd):
    """Simple command processor example."""

    def do_greet(self, line):
        print "hello"

    def do_EOF(self, line):
        return True

if __name__ == '__main__':
    HelloWorld().cmdloop()
```

Running it interactively demonstrates how commands are dispatched and shows some of the features included in `Cmd`.

```
$ python cmd_simple.py

(Cmd)
```

   The first thing to notice is the command prompt, (Cmd). The prompt can be configured through the attribute *prompt*. If the prompt changes as the result of a command processor, the new value is used to query for the next command.

```
(Cmd) help

Undocumented commands:
======================
EOF   greet   help
```

   The **help** command is built into Cmd. With no arguments, **help** shows the list of commands available. If the input includes a command name, the output is more verbose and restricted to details of that command, when available.
   If the command is **greet**, do_greet() is invoked to handle it.

```
(Cmd) greet
hello
```

   If the class does not include a specific command processor for a command, the method default() is called with the entire input line as an argument. The built-in implementation of default() reports an error.

```
(Cmd) foo
*** Unknown syntax: foo
```

   Since do_EOF() returns True, typing Ctrl-D causes the interpreter to exit.

```
(Cmd) ^D$
```

   No newline is printed on exit, so the results are a little messy.

14.6.2   Command Arguments

This example includes a few enhancements to eliminate some of the annoyances and add help for the **greet** command.

```
import cmd

class HelloWorld(cmd.Cmd):
    """Simple command processor example."""
```

```
    def do_greet(self, person):
        """greet [person]
        Greet the named person"""
        if person:
            print "hi,", person
        else:
            print 'hi'

    def do_EOF(self, line):
        return True

    def postloop(self):
        print

if __name__ == '__main__':
    HelloWorld().cmdloop()
```

The docstring added to do_greet() becomes the help text for the command.

```
$ python cmd_arguments.py

(Cmd) help

Documented commands (type help ):
========================================
greet

Undocumented commands:
======================
EOF   help

(Cmd) help greet
greet [person]
        Greet the named person
```

The output shows one optional argument to **greet**, *person*. Although the argument is optional to the command, there is a distinction between the command and the callback method. The method always takes the argument, but sometimes, the value is an empty string. It is left up to the command processor to determine if an empty argument is valid or to do any further parsing and processing of the command. In this example, if a person's name is provided, then the greeting is personalized.

```
(Cmd) greet Alice
hi, Alice
```

```
(Cmd) greet
hi
```

Whether an argument is given by the user or not, the value passed to the command processor does not include the command itself. That simplifies parsing in the command processor, especially if multiple arguments are needed.

14.6.3   Live Help

In the previous example, the formatting of the help text leaves something to be desired. Since it comes from the docstring, it retains the indentation from the source file. The source could be changed to remove the extra whitespace, but that would leave the application code looking poorly formatted. A better solution is to implement a help handler for the **greet** command, named `help_greet()`. The help handler is called to produce help text for the named command.

```python
import cmd

class HelloWorld(cmd.Cmd):
    """Simple command processor example."""

    def do_greet(self, person):
        if person:
            print "hi,", person
        else:
            print 'hi'

    def help_greet(self):
        print '\n'.join([ 'greet [person]',
                          'Greet the named person',
                          ])

    def do_EOF(self, line):
        return True

if __name__ == '__main__':
    HelloWorld().cmdloop()
```

In this example, the text is static but formatted more nicely. It would also be possible to use previous command state to tailor the contents of the help text to the current context.

```
$ python cmd_do_help.py

(Cmd) help greet
greet [person]
Greet the named person
```

It is up to the help handler to actually output the help message and not simply return the help text for handling elsewhere.

14.6.4 Auto-Completion

Cmd includes support for command completion based on the names of the commands with processor methods. The user triggers completion by hitting the tab key at an input prompt. When multiple completions are possible, pressing tab twice prints a list of the options.

```
$ python cmd_do_help.py

(Cmd) <tab><tab>
EOF     greet  help
(Cmd) h<tab>
(Cmd) help
```

Once the command is known, argument completion is handled by methods with the prefix complete_. This allows new completion handlers to assemble a list of possible completions using arbitrary criteria (i.e., querying a database or looking at a file or directory on the file system). In this case, the program has a hard-coded set of "friends" who receive a less formal greeting than named or anonymous strangers. A real program would probably save the list somewhere, read it once and then cache the contents to be scanned, as needed.

```
import cmd

class HelloWorld(cmd.Cmd):
    """Simple command processor example."""

    FRIENDS = [ 'Alice', 'Adam', 'Barbara', 'Bob' ]

    def do_greet(self, person):
        "Greet the person"
```

```
        if person and person in self.FRIENDS:
            greeting = 'hi, %s!' % person
        elif person:
            greeting = "hello, " + person
        else:
            greeting = 'hello'
        print greeting

    def complete_greet(self, text, line, begidx, endidx):
        if not text:
            completions = self.FRIENDS[:]
        else:
            completions = [ f
                            for f in self.FRIENDS
                            if f.startswith(text)
                            ]
        return completions

    def do_EOF(self, line):
        return True


if __name__ == '__main__':
    HelloWorld().cmdloop()
```

When there is input text, `complete_greet()` returns a list of friends that match. Otherwise, the full list of friends is returned.

```
$ python cmd_arg_completion.py

(Cmd) greet <tab><tab>
Adam      Alice     Barbara   Bob
(Cmd) greet A<tab><tab>
Adam    Alice
(Cmd) greet Ad<tab>
(Cmd) greet Adam
hi, Adam!
```

If the name given is not in the list of friends, the formal greeting is given.

```
(Cmd) greet Joe
hello, Joe
```

14.6.5   Overriding Base Class Methods

Cmd includes several methods that can be overridden as hooks for taking actions or altering the base class behavior. This example is not exhaustive, but it contains many of the methods commonly useful.

```
import cmd

class Illustrate(cmd.Cmd):
    "Illustrate the base class method use."

    def cmdloop(self, intro=None):
        print 'cmdloop(%s)' % intro
        return cmd.Cmd.cmdloop(self, intro)

    def preloop(self):
        print 'preloop()'

    def postloop(self):
        print 'postloop()'

    def parseline(self, line):
        print 'parseline(%s) =>' % line,
        ret = cmd.Cmd.parseline(self, line)
        print ret
        return ret

    def onecmd(self, s):
        print 'onecmd(%s)' % s
        return cmd.Cmd.onecmd(self, s)

    def emptyline(self):
        print 'emptyline()'
        return cmd.Cmd.emptyline(self)

    def default(self, line):
        print 'default(%s)' % line
        return cmd.Cmd.default(self, line)

    def precmd(self, line):
        print 'precmd(%s)' % line
        return cmd.Cmd.precmd(self, line)
```

```
    def postcmd(self, stop, line):
        print 'postcmd(%s, %s)' % (stop, line)
        return cmd.Cmd.postcmd(self, stop, line)

    def do_greet(self, line):
        print 'hello,', line

    def do_EOF(self, line):
        "Exit"
        return True

if __name__ == '__main__':
    Illustrate().cmdloop('Illustrating the methods of cmd.Cmd')
```

cmdloop() is the main processing loop of the interpreter. Overriding it is usually not necessary, since the preloop() and postloop() hooks are available.

Each iteration through cmdloop() calls onecmd() to dispatch the command to its processor. The actual input line is parsed with parseline() to create a tuple containing the command and the remaining portion of the line.

If the line is empty, emptyline() is called. The default implementation runs the previous command again. If the line contains a command, first precmd() is called and then the processor is looked up and invoked. If none is found, default() is called instead. Finally, postcmd() is called.

Here is an example session with print statements added.

```
$ python cmd_illustrate_methods.py

cmdloop(Illustrating the methods of cmd.Cmd)
preloop()
Illustrating the methods of cmd.Cmd
(Cmd) greet Bob
precmd(greet Bob)
onecmd(greet Bob)
parseline(greet Bob) => ('greet', 'Bob', 'greet Bob')
hello, Bob
postcmd(None, greet Bob)
(Cmd) ^Dprecmd(EOF)
onecmd(EOF)
parseline(EOF) => ('EOF', '', 'EOF')
postcmd(True, EOF)
postloop()
```

14.6.6   Configuring Cmd through Attributes

In addition to the methods described earlier, there are several attributes for controlling command interpreters. `prompt` can be set to a string to be printed each time the user is asked for a new command. `intro` is the "welcome" message printed at the start of the program. `cmdloop()` takes an argument for this value, or it can be set on the class directly. When printing help, the `doc_header`, `misc_header`, `undoc_header`, and `ruler` attributes are used to format the output.

```python
import cmd

class HelloWorld(cmd.Cmd):
    """Simple command processor example."""

    prompt = 'prompt: '
    intro = "Simple command processor example."

    doc_header = 'doc_header'
    misc_header = 'misc_header'
    undoc_header = 'undoc_header'

    ruler = '-'

    def do_prompt(self, line):
        "Change the interactive prompt"
        self.prompt = line + ': '

    def do_EOF(self, line):
        return True

if __name__ == '__main__':
    HelloWorld().cmdloop()
```

This example class shows a command processor to let the user control the prompt for the interactive session.

```
$ python cmd_attributes.py

Simple command processor example.
prompt: prompt hello
hello: help
```

```
doc_header
----------
prompt

undoc_header
------------
EOF  help

hello:
```

14.6.7   Running Shell Commands

To supplement the standard command processing, Cmd includes two special command prefixes. A question mark (?) is equivalent to the built-in **help** command and can be used in the same way. An exclamation point (!) maps to do_shell() and is intended for "shelling out" to run other commands, as in this example.

```python
import cmd
import subprocess

class ShellEnabled(cmd.Cmd):

    last_output = ''

    def do_shell(self, line):
        "Run a shell command"
        print "running shell command:", line
        sub_cmd = subprocess.Popen(line,
                                   shell=True,
                                   stdout=subprocess.PIPE)
        output = sub_cmd.communicate()[0]
        print output
        self.last_output = output

    def do_echo(self, line):
        """Print the input, replacing '$out' with
        the output of the last shell command.
        """
        # Obviously not robust
        print line.replace('$out', self.last_output)

    def do_EOF(self, line):
        return True
```

```
if __name__ == '__main__':
    ShellEnabled().cmdloop()
```

This **echo** command implementation replaces the string `$out` in its argument with the output from the previous shell command.

```
$ python cmd_do_shell.py

(Cmd) ?

Documented commands (type help ):
========================================
echo   shell

Undocumented commands:
======================
EOF   help

(Cmd) ? shell
Run a shell command
(Cmd) ? echo
Print the input, replacing '$out' with
the output of the last shell command
(Cmd) shell pwd
running shell command: pwd
/Users/dhellmann/Documents/PyMOTW/in_progress/cmd

(Cmd) ! pwd
running shell command: pwd
/Users/dhellmann/Documents/PyMOTW/in_progress/cmd

(Cmd) echo $out
/Users/dhellmann/Documents/PyMOTW/in_progress/cmd

(Cmd)
```

14.6.8 Alternative Inputs

While the default mode for `Cmd()` is to interact with the user through the `readline` library, it is also possible to pass a series of commands to standard input using standard UNIX shell redirection.

```
$ echo help | python cmd_do_help.py
```

```
(Cmd)
Documented commands (type help ):
========================================
greet

Undocumented commands:
=======================
EOF   help

(Cmd)
```

To have the program read a script file directly, a few other changes may be needed. Since `readline` interacts with the terminal/tty device, rather than the standard input stream, it should be disabled when the script will be reading from a file. Also, to avoid printing superfluous prompts, the prompt can be set to an empty string. This example shows how to open a file and pass it as input to a modified version of the `HelloWorld` example.

```python
import cmd

class HelloWorld(cmd.Cmd):
    """Simple command processor example."""

    # Disable rawinput module use
    use_rawinput = False

    # Do not show a prompt after each command read
    prompt = ''

    def do_greet(self, line):
        print "hello,", line

    def do_EOF(self, line):
        return True

if __name__ == '__main__':
    import sys
    with open(sys.argv[1], 'rt') as input:
        HelloWorld(stdin=input).cmdloop()
```

With *use_rawinput* set to False and *prompt* set to an empty string, the script can be called on this input file.

```
greet
greet Alice and Bob
```

It produces this output.

```
$ python cmd_file.py cmd_file.txt

hello,
hello, Alice and Bob
```

14.6.9   Commands from sys.argv

Command-line arguments to the program can also be processed as commands for the interpreter class, instead of reading commands from the console or a file. To use the command-line arguments, call `onecmd()` directly, as in this example.

```python
import cmd


class InteractiveOrCommandLine(cmd.Cmd):
    """Accepts commands via the normal interactive
    prompt or on the command line.
    """

    def do_greet(self, line):
        print 'hello,', line

    def do_EOF(self, line):
        return True


if __name__ == '__main__':
    import sys
    if len(sys.argv) > 1:
        InteractiveOrCommandLine().onecmd(' '.join(sys.argv[1:]))
    else:
        InteractiveOrCommandLine().cmdloop()
```

Since `onecmd()` takes a single string as input, the arguments to the program need to be joined together before being passed in.

```
$ python cmd_argv.py greet Command-Line User

hello, Command-Line User
```

```
$ python cmd_argv.py

(Cmd) greet Interactive User
hello, Interactive User
(Cmd)
```

See Also:

cmd (http://docs.python.org/library/cmd.html) The standard library documentation for this module.

cmd2 (http://pypi.python.org/pypi/cmd2) Drop-in replacement for `cmd` with additional features.

GNU Readline (http://tiswww.case.edu/php/chet/readline/rltop.html)
The GNU Readline library provides functions that allow users to edit input lines as they are typed.

`readline` (page 823) The Python standard library interface to readline.

`subprocess` (page 481) Managing other processes and their output.

14.7 shlex—Parse Shell-Style Syntaxes

Purpose Lexical analysis of shell-style syntaxes.
Python Version 1.5.2 and later

The `shlex` module implements a class for parsing simple shell-like syntaxes. It can be used for writing a domain-specific language or for parsing quoted strings (a task that is more complex than it seems on the surface).

14.7.1 Quoted Strings

A common problem when working with input text is to identify a sequence of quoted words as a single entity. Splitting the text on quotes does not always work as expected, especially if there are nested levels of quotes. Take the following text as an example.

```
This string has embedded "double quotes" and 'single quotes' in it,
and even "a 'nested example'".
```

A naive approach would be to construct a regular expression to find the parts of the text outside the quotes to separate them from the text inside the quotes, or vice versa. That would be unnecessarily complex and prone to errors resulting from edge-cases like apostrophes or even typos. A better solution is to use a true parser, such as the one provided by the `shlex` module. Here is a simple example that prints the tokens identified in the input file using the `shlex` class.

```
import shlex
import sys

if len(sys.argv) != 2:
    print 'Please specify one filename on the command line.'
    sys.exit(1)

filename = sys.argv[1]
body = file(filename, 'rt').read()
print 'ORIGINAL:', repr(body)
print

print 'TOKENS:'
lexer = shlex.shlex(body)
for token in lexer:
    print repr(token)
```

When run on data with embedded quotes, the parser produces the list of expected tokens.

```
$ python shlex_example.py quotes.txt

ORIGINAL: 'This string has embedded "double quotes" and \'single quo
tes\' in it,\nand even "a \'nested example\'".\n'

TOKENS:
'This'
'string'
'has'
'embedded'
'"double quotes"'
'and'
"'single quotes'"
'in'
'it'
','
'and'
'even'
'"a \'nested example\'"'
'.'
```

Isolated quotes such as apostrophes are also handled. Consider this input file.

```
This string has an embedded apostrophe, doesn't it?
```

The token with the embedded apostrophe is no problem.

```
$ python shlex_example.py apostrophe.txt

ORIGINAL: "This string has an embedded apostrophe, doesn't it?"

TOKENS:
'This'
'string'
'has'
'an'
'embedded'
'apostrophe'
','
"doesn't"
'it'
'?'
```

14.7.2 Embedded Comments

Since the parser is intended to be used with command languages, it needs to handle comments. By default, any text following a # is considered part of a comment and ignored. Due to the nature of the parser, only single-character comment prefixes are supported. The set of comment characters used can be configured through the `commenters` property.

```
$ python shlex_example.py comments.txt

ORIGINAL: 'This line is recognized.\n# But this line is ignored.\nAnd
this line is processed.'

TOKENS:
'This'
'line'
'is'
'recognized'
'.'
'And'
'this'
'line'
'is'
'processed'
'.'
```

14.7.3   Split

To split an existing string into component tokens, the convenience function `split()` is a simple wrapper around the parser.

```
import shlex

text = """This text has "quoted parts" inside it."""
print 'ORIGINAL:', repr(text)
print

print 'TOKENS:'
print shlex.split(text)
```

The result is a list.

```
$ python shlex_split.py

ORIGINAL: 'This text has "quoted parts" inside it.'

TOKENS:
['This', 'text', 'has', 'quoted parts', 'inside', 'it.']
```

14.7.4   Including Other Sources of Tokens

The `shlex` class includes several configuration properties that control its behavior. The `source` property enables a feature for code (or configuration) reuse by allowing one token stream to include another. This is similar to the Bourne shell **source** operator, hence the name.

```
import shlex

text = """This text says to source quotes.txt before continuing."""
print 'ORIGINAL:', repr(text)
print

lexer = shlex.shlex(text)
lexer.wordchars += '.'
lexer.source = 'source'

print 'TOKENS:'
for token in lexer:
    print repr(token)
```

The string `source quotes.txt` in the original text receives special handling. Since the `source` property of the lexer is set to `"source"`, when the keyword is encountered, the filename appearing on the next line is automatically included. In order to cause the filename to appear as a single token, the `.` character needs to be added to the list of characters that are included in words (otherwise "`quotes.txt`" becomes three tokens, "`quotes`", "`.`", "`txt`"). This is what the output looks like.

```
$ python shlex_source.py

ORIGINAL: 'This text says to source quotes.txt before continuing.'

TOKENS:
'This'
'text'
'says'
'to'
'This'
'string'
'has'
'embedded'
'"double quotes"'
'and'
"'single quotes'"
'in'
'it'
','
'and'
'even'
'"a \'nested example\'"'
'.'
'before'
'continuing.'
```

The "source" feature uses a method called `sourcehook()` to load the additional input source, so a subclass of `shlex` can provide an alternate implementation that loads data from locations other than files.

14.7.5 Controlling the Parser

An earlier example demonstrated changing the `wordchars` value to control which characters are included in words. It is also possible to set the `quotes` character to use additional or alternative quotes. Each quote must be a single character, so it is not possible to have different open and close quotes (no parsing on parentheses, for example).

```python
import shlex

text = """|Col 1||Col 2||Col 3|"""
print 'ORIGINAL:', repr(text)
print

lexer = shlex.shlex(text)
lexer.quotes = '|'

print 'TOKENS:'
for token in lexer:
    print repr(token)
```

In this example, each table cell is wrapped in vertical bars.

```
$ python shlex_table.py

ORIGINAL: '|Col 1||Col 2||Col 3|'

TOKENS:
'|Col 1|'
'|Col 2|'
'|Col 3|'
```

It is also possible to control the whitespace characters used to split words.

```python
import shlex
import sys

if len(sys.argv) != 2:
    print 'Please specify one filename on the command line.'
    sys.exit(1)

filename = sys.argv[1]
body = file(filename, 'rt').read()
print 'ORIGINAL:', repr(body)
print

print 'TOKENS:'
lexer = shlex.shlex(body)
lexer.whitespace += '.,'
```

```
for token in lexer:
    print repr(token)
```

If the example in `shlex_example.py` is modified to include periods and commas, the results change.

```
$ python shlex_whitespace.py quotes.txt

ORIGINAL: 'This string has embedded "double quotes" and \'single quo
tes\' in it,\nand even "a \'nested example\'".\n'

TOKENS:
'This'
'string'
'has'
'embedded'
'"double quotes"'
'and'
"'single quotes'"
'in'
'it'
'and'
'even'
'"a \'nested example\'"'
```

14.7.6 Error Handling

When the parser encounters the end of its input before all quoted strings are closed, it raises `ValueError`. When that happens, it is useful to examine some of the properties maintained by the parser as it processes the input. For example, `infile` refers to the name of the file being processed (which might be different from the original file, if one file sources another). The `lineno` reports the line when the error is discovered. The `lineno` is typically the end of the file, which may be far away from the first quote. The `token` attribute contains the buffer of text not already included in a valid token. The `error_leader()` method produces a message prefix in a style similar to UNIX compilers, which enables editors such as **emacs** to parse the error and take the user directly to the invalid line.

```
import shlex

text = """This line is ok.
This line has an "unfinished quote.
```

```
This line is ok, too.
"""

print 'ORIGINAL:', repr(text)
print

lexer = shlex.shlex(text)

print 'TOKENS:'
try:
    for token in lexer:
        print repr(token)
except ValueError, err:
    first_line_of_error = lexer.token.splitlines()[0]
    print 'ERROR:', lexer.error_leader(), str(err)
    print 'following "' + first_line_of_error + '"'
```

The example produces this output.

```
$ python shlex_errors.py

ORIGINAL: 'This line is ok.\nThis line has an "unfinished quote.\nTh
is line is ok, too.\n'

TOKENS:
'This'
'line'
'is'
'ok'
'.'
'This'
'line'
'has'
'an'
ERROR: "None", line 4:  No closing quotation
following ""unfinished quote."
```

14.7.7 POSIX vs. Non-POSIX Parsing

The default behavior for the parser is to use a backwards-compatible style, which is not POSIX-compliant. For POSIX behavior, set the *posix* argument when constructing the parser.

```
import shlex

for s in [ 'Do"Not"Separate',
           '"Do"Separate',
           'Escaped \e Character not in quotes',
           'Escaped "\e" Character in double quotes',
           "Escaped '\e' Character in single quotes",
           r"Escaped '\'' \"\'\" single quote",
           r'Escaped "\"" \'\"\' double quote',
           "\"'Strip extra layer of quotes'\"",
           ]:
    print 'ORIGINAL :', repr(s)
    print 'non-POSIX:',

    non_posix_lexer = shlex.shlex(s, posix=False)
    try:
        print repr(list(non_posix_lexer))
    except ValueError, err:
        print 'error(%s)' % err


    print 'POSIX    :',
    posix_lexer = shlex.shlex(s, posix=True)
    try:
        print repr(list(posix_lexer))
    except ValueError, err:
        print 'error(%s)' % err

    print
```

Here are a few examples of the differences in parsing behavior.

```
$ python shlex_posix.py

ORIGINAL : 'Do"Not"Separate'
non-POSIX: ['Do"Not"Separate']
POSIX    : ['DoNotSeparate']

ORIGINAL : '"Do"Separate'
non-POSIX: ['"Do"', 'Separate']
POSIX    : ['DoSeparate']

ORIGINAL : 'Escaped \\e Character not in quotes'
```

```
non-POSIX: ['Escaped', '\\', 'e', 'Character', 'not', 'in',
'quotes']
POSIX    : ['Escaped', 'e', 'Character', 'not', 'in', 'quotes']

ORIGINAL : 'Escaped "\\e" Character in double quotes'
non-POSIX: ['Escaped', '"\\e"', 'Character', 'in', 'double',
'quotes']
POSIX    : ['Escaped', '\\e', 'Character', 'in', 'double', 'quotes']

ORIGINAL : "Escaped '\\e' Character in single quotes"
non-POSIX: ['Escaped', "'\\e'", 'Character', 'in', 'single',
'quotes']
POSIX    : ['Escaped', '\\e', 'Character', 'in', 'single', 'quotes']

ORIGINAL : 'Escaped \'\\\'\' \\"\\\'\\" single quote'
non-POSIX: error(No closing quotation)
POSIX    : ['Escaped', '\\ \\"\\"', 'single', 'quote']

ORIGINAL : 'Escaped "\\"" \\\'\\"\\\' double quote'
non-POSIX: error(No closing quotation)
POSIX    : ['Escaped', '"', '\'"\'', 'double', 'quote']

ORIGINAL : '"\'Strip extra layer of quotes\'"'
non-POSIX: ['"\'Strip extra layer of quotes\'"']
POSIX    : ["'Strip extra layer of quotes'"]
```

See Also:
shlex (http://docs.python.org/lib/module-shlex.html) The Standard library documentation for this module.
cmd (page 839) Tools for building interactive command interpreters.
optparse (page 777) Command-line option parsing.
getopt (page 770) Command-line option parsing.
argparse (page 795) Command-line option parsing.
subprocess (page 481) Run commands after parsing the command line.

14.8 ConfigParser—Work with Configuration Files

Purpose Read and write configuration files similar to Windows INI files.
Python Version 1.5

Use the `ConfigParser` module to manage user-editable configuration files for an application. The contents of the configuration files can be organized into groups, and several option-value types are supported, including integers, floating-point values, and Booleans. Option values can be combined using Python formatting strings, to build longer values such as URLs from shorter values like host names and port numbers.

14.8.1 Configuration File Format

The file format used by `ConfigParser` is similar to the format used by older versions of Microsoft Windows. It consists of one or more named *sections*, each of which can contain individual *options* with names and values.

Config file sections are identified by looking for lines starting with " [" and ending with "] ". The value between the square brackets is the section name and can contain any characters except square brackets.

Options are listed one per line within a section. The line starts with the name of the option, which is separated from the value by a colon (:) or an equal sign (=). Whitespace around the separator is ignored when the file is parsed.

This sample configuration file has a section named "bug_tracker" with three options.

```
[bug_tracker]
url = http://localhost:8080/bugs/
username = dhellmann
password = SECRET
```

14.8.2 Reading Configuration Files

The most common use for a configuration file is to have a user or system administrator edit the file with a regular text editor to set application behavior defaults and then have the application read the file, parse it, and act based on its contents. Use the `read()` method of `SafeConfigParser` to read the configuration file.

```
from ConfigParser import SafeConfigParser

parser = SafeConfigParser()
parser.read('simple.ini')

print parser.get('bug_tracker', 'url')
```

This program reads the `simple.ini` file from the previous section and prints the value of the `url` option from the `bug_tracker` section.

```
$ python ConfigParser_read.py

http://localhost:8080/bugs/
```

The `read()` method also accepts a list of filenames. Each name in turn is scanned, and if the file exists, it is opened and read.

```
from ConfigParser import SafeConfigParser
import glob

parser = SafeConfigParser()

candidates = ['does_not_exist.ini', 'also-does-not-exist.ini',
              'simple.ini', 'multisection.ini',
              ]

found = parser.read(candidates)

missing = set(candidates) - set(found)

print 'Found config files:', sorted(found)
print 'Missing files     :', sorted(missing)
```

`read()` returns a list containing the names of the files successfully loaded, so the program can discover which configuration files are missing and decide whether to ignore them.

```
$ python ConfigParser_read_many.py

Found config files: ['multisection.ini', 'simple.ini']
Missing files     : ['also-does-not-exist.ini', 'does_not_exist.ini']
```

Unicode Configuration Data

Configuration files containing Unicode data should be opened using the `codecs` module to set the proper encoding value. Changing the password value of the original input to contain Unicode characters and saving the results in UTF-8 encoding gives the following.

```
[bug_tracker]
url = http://localhost:8080/bugs/
```

```
username = dhellmann
password = ßéç®ét
```

The `codecs` file handle can be passed to `readfp()`, which uses the `readline()` method of its argument to get lines from the file and parse them.

```
from ConfigParser import SafeConfigParser
import codecs

parser = SafeConfigParser()

# Open the file with the correct encoding
with codecs.open('unicode.ini', 'r', encoding='utf-8') as f:
    parser.readfp(f)

password = parser.get('bug_tracker', 'password')

print 'Password:', password.encode('utf-8')
print 'Type     :', type(password)
print 'repr()   :', repr(password)
```

The value returned by `get()` is a `unicode` object, so in order to print it safely, it must be reencoded as UTF-8.

```
$ python ConfigParser_unicode.py

Password: ßéç®ét
Type    : <type 'unicode'>
repr()  : u'\xdf\xe9\xe7\xae\xe9\u2020'
```

14.8.3   Accessing Configuration Settings

`SafeConfigParser` includes methods for examining the structure of the parsed configuration, including listing the sections and options, and getting their values. This configuration file includes two sections for separate web services.

```
[bug_tracker]
url = http://localhost:8080/bugs/
username = dhellmann
password = SECRET

[wiki]
url = http://localhost:8080/wiki/
```

```
username = dhellmann
password = SECRET
```

And this sample program exercises some of the methods for looking at the configuration data, including `sections()`, `options()`, and `items()`.

```
from ConfigParser import SafeConfigParser

parser = SafeConfigParser()
parser.read('multisection.ini')

for section_name in parser.sections():
    print 'Section:', section_name
    print '  Options:', parser.options(section_name)
    for name, value in parser.items(section_name):
        print '    %s = %s' % (name, value)
    print
```

Both `sections()` and `options()` return lists of strings, while `items()` returns a list of tuples containing the name-value pairs.

```
$ python ConfigParser_structure.py

Section: bug_tracker
  Options: ['url', 'username', 'password']
  url = http://localhost:8080/bugs/
  username = dhellmann
  password = SECRET

Section: wiki
  Options: ['url', 'username', 'password']
  url = http://localhost:8080/wiki/
  username = dhellmann
  password = SECRET
```

Testing Whether Values Are Present

To test if a section exists, use `has_section()`, passing the section name.

```
from ConfigParser import SafeConfigParser

parser = SafeConfigParser()
parser.read('multisection.ini')
```

```
for candidate in [ 'wiki', 'bug_tracker', 'dvcs' ]:
    print '%-12s: %s' % (candidate, parser.has_section(candidate))
```

Testing if a section exists before calling get() avoids exceptions for missing data.

```
$ python ConfigParser_has_section.py

wiki        : True
bug_tracker : True
dvcs        : False
```

Use has_option() to test if an option exists within a section.

```
from ConfigParser import SafeConfigParser

parser = SafeConfigParser()
parser.read('multisection.ini')

SECTIONS = [ 'wiki', 'none' ]
OPTIONS = [ 'username', 'password', 'url', 'description' ]

for section in SECTIONS:
    has_section = parser.has_section(section)
    print '%s section exists: %s' % (section, has_section)
    for candidate in OPTIONS:
        has_option = parser.has_option(section, candidate)
        print '%s.%-12s  : %s' % (section,
                                  candidate,
                                  has_option,
                                  )
    print
```

If the section does not exist, has_option() returns False.

```
$ python ConfigParser_has_option.py

wiki section exists: True
wiki.username    : True
wiki.password    : True
wiki.url         : True
wiki.description : False
```

```
none section exists: False
none.username      : False
none.password      : False
none.url           : False
none.description   : False
```

Value Types

All section and option names are treated as strings, but option values can be strings, integers, floating-point numbers, or Booleans. There is a range of possible Boolean values that are converted true or false. This example file includes one of each.

```
[ints]
positive = 1
negative = -5

[floats]
positive = 0.2
negative = -3.14

[booleans]
number_true = 1
number_false = 0
yn_true = yes
yn_false = no
tf_true = true
tf_false = false
onoff_true = on
onoff_false = false
```

SafeConfigParser does not make any attempt to understand the option type. The application is expected to use the correct method to fetch the value as the desired type. get() always returns a string. Use getint() for integers, getfloat() for floating-point numbers, and getboolean() for Boolean values.

```
from ConfigParser import SafeConfigParser

parser = SafeConfigParser()
parser.read('types.ini')

print 'Integers:'
```

```
for name in parser.options('ints'):
    string_value = parser.get('ints', name)
    value = parser.getint('ints', name)
    print '  %-12s : %-7r -> %d' % (name, string_value, value)
print '\nFloats:'
for name in parser.options('floats'):
    string_value = parser.get('floats', name)
    value = parser.getfloat('floats', name)
    print '  %-12s : %-7r -> %0.2f' % (name, string_value, value)

print '\nBooleans:'
for name in parser.options('booleans'):
    string_value = parser.get('booleans', name)
    value = parser.getboolean('booleans', name)
    print '  %-12s : %-7r -> %s' % (name, string_value, value)
```

Running this program with the example input produces the following.

```
$ python ConfigParser_value_types.py

Integers:
  positive     : '1'      -> 1
  negative     : '-5'     -> -5

Floats:
  positive     : '0.2'    -> 0.20
  negative     : '-3.14' -> -3.14

Booleans:
  number_true  : '1'      -> True
  number_false : '0'      -> False
  yn_true      : 'yes'    -> True
  yn_false     : 'no'     -> False
  tf_true      : 'true'   -> True
  tf_false     : 'false' -> False
  onoff_true   : 'on'     -> True
  onoff_false  : 'false' -> False
```

Options as Flags

Usually, the parser requires an explicit value for each option, but with the `SafeConfigParser` parameter *allow_no_value* set to `True`, an option can appear by itself on a line in the input file and be used as a flag.

```
import ConfigParser

# Require values
try:
    parser = ConfigParser.SafeConfigParser()
    parser.read('allow_no_value.ini')
except ConfigParser.ParsingError, err:
    print 'Could not parse:', err

# Allow stand-alone option names
print '\nTrying again with allow_no_value=True'
parser = ConfigParser.SafeConfigParser(allow_no_value=True)
parser.read('allow_no_value.ini')
for flag in [ 'turn_feature_on', 'turn_other_feature_on' ]:
    print
    print flag
    exists = parser.has_option('flags', flag)
    print '  has_option:', exists
    if exists:
        print '        get:', parser.get('flags', flag)
```

When an option has no explicit value, `has_option()` reports that the option exists and `get()` returns `None`.

```
$ python ConfigParser_allow_no_value.py

Could not parse: File contains parsing errors: allow_no_value.ini
        [line  2]: 'turn_feature_on\n'

Trying again with allow_no_value=True

turn_feature_on
  has_option: True
        get: None

turn_other_feature_on
  has_option: False
```

14.8.4 Modifying Settings

While `SafeConfigParser` is primarily intended to be configured by reading settings from files, settings can also be populated by calling `add_section()` to create a new section and `set()` to add or change an option.

```
import ConfigParser

parser = ConfigParser.SafeConfigParser()

parser.add_section('bug_tracker')
parser.set('bug_tracker', 'url', 'http://localhost:8080/bugs')
parser.set('bug_tracker', 'username', 'dhellmann')
parser.set('bug_tracker', 'password', 'secret')

for section in parser.sections():
    print section
    for name, value in parser.items(section):
        print '  %s = %r' % (name, value)
```

All options must be set as strings, even if they will be retrieved as integer, float, or Boolean values.

```
$ python ConfigParser_populate.py

bug_tracker
  url = 'http://localhost:8080/bugs'
  username = 'dhellmann'
  password = 'secret'
```

Sections and options can be removed from a SafeConfigParser with remove_section() and remove_option().

```
from ConfigParser import SafeConfigParser

parser = SafeConfigParser()
parser.read('multisection.ini')

print 'Read values:\n'
for section in parser.sections():
    print section
    for name, value in parser.items(section):
        print '  %s = %r' % (name, value)

parser.remove_option('bug_tracker', 'password')
parser.remove_section('wiki')

print '\nModified values:\n'
```

```
for section in parser.sections():
    print section
    for name, value in parser.items(section):
        print '  %s = %r' % (name, value)
```

Removing a section deletes any options it contains.

```
$ python ConfigParser_remove.py

Read values:

bug_tracker
  url = 'http://localhost:8080/bugs/'
  username = 'dhellmann'
  password = 'SECRET'
wiki
  url = 'http://localhost:8080/wiki/'
  username = 'dhellmann'
  password = 'SECRET'

Modified values:

bug_tracker
  url = 'http://localhost:8080/bugs/'
  username = 'dhellmann'
```

14.8.5   Saving Configuration Files

Once a `SafeConfigParser` is populated with desired data, it can be saved to a file by calling the `write()` method. This makes it possible to provide a user interface for editing the configuration settings, without having to write any code to manage the file.

```
import ConfigParser
import sys

parser = ConfigParser.SafeConfigParser()

parser.add_section('bug_tracker')
parser.set('bug_tracker', 'url', 'http://localhost:8080/bugs')
parser.set('bug_tracker', 'username', 'dhellmann')
parser.set('bug_tracker', 'password', 'secret')

parser.write(sys.stdout)
```

The `write()` method takes a file-like object as argument. It writes the data out in the INI format so it can be parsed again by `SafeConfigParser`.

```
$ python ConfigParser_write.py

[bug_tracker]
url = http://localhost:8080/bugs
username = dhellmann
password = secret
```

Warning: Comments in the original configuration file are not preserved when reading, modifying, and rewriting a configuration file.

14.8.6   Option Search Path

`SafeConfigParser` uses a multistep search process when looking for an option.

Before starting the option search, the section name is tested. If the section does not exist, and the name is not the special value `DEFAULT`, then `NoSectionError` is raised.

1. If the option name appears in the *vars* dictionary passed to `get()`, the value from *vars* is returned.
2. If the option name appears in the specified section, the value from that section is returned.
3. If the option name appears in the `DEFAULT` section, that value is returned.
4. If the option name appears in the *defaults* dictionary passed to the constructor, that value is returned. If the name is not found in any of those locations, `NoOptionError` is raised.

The search path behavior can be demonstrated using this configuration file.

```
[DEFAULT]
file-only = value from DEFAULT section
init-and-file = value from DEFAULT section
from-section = value from DEFAULT section
from-vars = value from DEFAULT section

[sect]
section-only = value from section in file
```

```
from-section = value from section in file
from-vars = value from section in file
```

This test program includes default settings for options not specified in the configuration file and overrides some values that are defined in the file.

```python
import ConfigParser

# Define the names of the options
option_names = [
    'from-default',
    'from-section', 'section-only',
    'file-only', 'init-only', 'init-and-file',
    'from-vars',
    ]

# Initialize the parser with some defaults
parser = ConfigParser.SafeConfigParser(
    defaults={'from-default':'value from defaults passed to init',
              'init-only':'value from defaults passed to init',
              'init-and-file':'value from defaults passed to init',
              'from-section':'value from defaults passed to init',
              'from-vars':'value from defaults passed to init',
              })

print 'Defaults before loading file:'
defaults = parser.defaults()
for name in option_names:
    if name in defaults:
        print '  %-15s = %r' % (name, defaults[name])

# Load the configuration file
parser.read('with-defaults.ini')

print '\nDefaults after loading file:'
defaults = parser.defaults()
for name in option_names:
    if name in defaults:
        print '  %-15s = %r' % (name, defaults[name])

# Define some local overrides
vars = {'from-vars':'value from vars'}
```

```
# Show the values of all the options
print '\nOption lookup:'
for name in option_names:
    value = parser.get('sect', name, vars=vars)
    print '   %-15s = %r' % (name, value)

# Show error messages for options that do not exist
print '\nError cases:'
try:
    print 'No such option :', parser.get('sect', 'no-option')
except ConfigParser.NoOptionError, err:
    print str(err)


try:
    print 'No such section:', parser.get('no-sect', 'no-option')
except ConfigParser.NoSectionError, err:
    print str(err)
```

The output shows the origin for the value of each option and illustrates the way defaults from different sources override existing values.

```
$ python ConfigParser_defaults.py

Defaults before loading file:
  from-default    = 'value from defaults passed to init'
  from-section    = 'value from defaults passed to init'
  init-only       = 'value from defaults passed to init'
  init-and-file   = 'value from defaults passed to init'
  from-vars       = 'value from defaults passed to init'

Defaults after loading file:
  from-default    = 'value from defaults passed to init'
  from-section    = 'value from DEFAULT section'
  file-only       = 'value from DEFAULT section'
  init-only       = 'value from defaults passed to init'
  init-and-file   = 'value from DEFAULT section'
  from-vars       = 'value from DEFAULT section'

Option lookup:
  from-default    = 'value from defaults passed to init'
  from-section    = 'value from section in file'
  section-only    = 'value from section in file'
  file-only       = 'value from DEFAULT section'
  init-only       = 'value from defaults passed to init'
```

```
  init-and-file   = 'value from DEFAULT section'
  from-vars       = 'value from vars'
Error cases:
No such option : No option 'no-option' in section: 'sect'
No such section: No section: 'no-sect'
```

14.8.7 Combining Values with Interpolation

`SafeConfigParser` provides a feature called *interpolation* that can be used to combine values together. Values containing standard Python format strings trigger the interpolation feature when they are retrieved with `get()`. Options named within the value being fetched are replaced with their values in turn, until no more substitution is necessary.

The URL examples from earlier in this section can be rewritten to use interpolation to make it easier to change only part of the value. For example, this configuration file separates the protocol, hostname, and port from the URL as separate options.

```
[bug_tracker]
protocol = http
server = localhost
port = 8080
url = %(protocol)s://%(server)s:%(port)s/bugs/
username = dhellmann
password = SECRET
```

Interpolation is performed by default each time `get()` is called. Pass a true value in the `raw` argument to retrieve the original value, without interpolation.

```
from ConfigParser import SafeConfigParser

parser = SafeConfigParser()
parser.read('interpolation.ini')

print 'Original value          :', parser.get('bug_tracker', 'url')

parser.set('bug_tracker', 'port', '9090')
print 'Altered port value  :', parser.get('bug_tracker', 'url')

print 'Without interpolation:', parser.get('bug_tracker', 'url',
                                           raw=True)
```

Because the value is computed by `get()`, changing one of the settings being used by the `url` value changes the return value.

```
$ python ConfigParser_interpolation.py

Original value      : http://localhost:8080/bugs/
Altered port value  : http://localhost:9090/bugs/
Without interpolation: %(protocol)s://%(server)s:%(port)s/bugs/
```

Using Defaults

Values for interpolation do not need to appear in the same section as the original option. Defaults can be mixed with override values.

```
[DEFAULT]
url = %(protocol)s://%(server)s:%(port)s/bugs/
protocol = http
server = bugs.example.com
port = 80

[bug_tracker]
server = localhost
port = 8080
username = dhellmann
password = SECRET
```

With this configuration, the value for `url` comes from the DEFAULT section, and the substitution starts by looking in `bug_tracker` and falling back to DEFAULT for pieces not found.

```
from ConfigParser import SafeConfigParser

parser = SafeConfigParser()
parser.read('interpolation_defaults.ini')

print 'URL:', parser.get('bug_tracker', 'url')
```

The `hostname` and `port` values come from the `bug_tracker` section, but the `protocol` comes from DEFAULT.

```
$ python ConfigParser_interpolation_defaults.py

URL: http://localhost:8080/bugs/
```

Substitution Errors

Substitution stops after `MAX_INTERPOLATION_DEPTH` steps to avoid problems due to recursive references.

```
import ConfigParser

parser = ConfigParser.SafeConfigParser()

parser.add_section('sect')
parser.set('sect', 'opt', '%(opt)s')

try:
    print parser.get('sect', 'opt')
except ConfigParser.InterpolationDepthError, err:
    print 'ERROR:', err
```

An `InterpolationDepthError` exception is raised if there are too many substitution steps.

```
$ python ConfigParser_interpolation_recursion.py

ERROR: Value interpolation too deeply recursive:
        section: [sect]
        option : opt
        rawval : %(opt)s
```

Missing values result in an `InterpolationMissingOptionError` exception.

```
import ConfigParser

parser = ConfigParser.SafeConfigParser()

parser.add_section('bug_tracker')
parser.set('bug_tracker', 'url', 'http://%(server)s:%(port)s/bugs')

try:
    print parser.get('bug_tracker', 'url')
except ConfigParser.InterpolationMissingOptionError, err:
    print 'ERROR:', err
```

Since no `server` value is defined, the `url` cannot be constructed.

```
$ python ConfigParser_interpolation_error.py

ERROR: Bad value substitution:
        section: [bug_tracker]
        option : url
        key    : server
        rawval : :%(port)s/bugs
```

See Also:

ConfigParser (http://docs.python.org/library/configparser.html) The standard library documentation for this module.

codecs (page 284) The `codecs` module is for reading and writing Unicode files.

14.9 logging—Report Status, Error, and Informational Messages

Purpose Report status, error, and informational messages.
Python Version 2.3 and later

The `logging` module defines a standard API for reporting errors and status information from applications and libraries. The key benefit of having the logging API provided by a standard library module is that all Python modules can participate in logging, so an application's log can include messages from third-party modules.

14.9.1 Logging in Applications vs. Libraries

Application developers and library authors can both use `logging`, but each audience has different considerations to keep in mind.

Application developers configure the `logging` module, directing the messages to appropriate output channels. It is possible to log messages with different verbosity levels or to different destinations. Handlers for writing log messages to files, HTTP GET/POST locations, email via SMTP, generic sockets, or OS-specific logging mechanisms are all included. It is possible to create custom log destination classes for special requirements not handled by any of the built-in classes.

Developers of libraries can also use `logging` and have even less work to do. Simply create a logger instance for each context, using an appropriate name, and then log messages using the standard levels. As long as a library uses the logging API with consistent naming and level selections, the application can be configured to show or hide messages from the library, as desired.

14.9.2 Logging to a File

Most applications are configured to log to a file. Use the `basicConfig()` function to set up the default handler so that debug messages are written to a file.

```
import logging

LOG_FILENAME = 'logging_example.out'
logging.basicConfig(filename=LOG_FILENAME,
                    level=logging.DEBUG,
                    )

logging.debug('This message should go to the log file')

with open(LOG_FILENAME, 'rt') as f:
    body = f.read()

print 'FILE:'
print body
```

After running the script, the log message is written to `logging_example.out`.

```
$ python logging_file_example.py

FILE:
DEBUG:root:This message should go to the log file
```

14.9.3 Rotating Log Files

Running the script repeatedly causes more messages to be appended to the file. To create a new file each time the program runs, pass a `filemode` argument to `basicConfig()` with a value of `'w'`. Rather than managing the creation of files this way, though, it is better to use a `RotatingFileHandler`, which creates new files automatically and preserves the old log file at the same time.

```
import glob
import logging
import logging.handlers

LOG_FILENAME = 'logging_rotatingfile_example.out'

# Set up a specific logger with our desired output level
my_logger = logging.getLogger('MyLogger')
my_logger.setLevel(logging.DEBUG)
```

```
# Add the log message handler to the logger
handler = logging.handlers.RotatingFileHandler(LOG_FILENAME,
                                               maxBytes=20,
                                               backupCount=5,
                                               )
my_logger.addHandler(handler)

# Log some messages
for i in range(20):
    my_logger.debug('i = %d' % i)

# See what files are created
logfiles = glob.glob('%s*' % LOG_FILENAME)
for filename in logfiles:
    print filename
```

The result is six separate files, each with part of the log history for the application.

```
$ python logging_rotatingfile_example.py

logging_rotatingfile_example.out
logging_rotatingfile_example.out.1
logging_rotatingfile_example.out.2
logging_rotatingfile_example.out.3
logging_rotatingfile_example.out.4
logging_rotatingfile_example.out.5
```

The most current file is always `logging_rotatingfile_example.out`, and each time it reaches the size limit, it is renamed with the suffix `.1`. Each of the existing backup files is renamed to increment the suffix (`.1` becomes `.2`, etc.) and the `.5` file is erased.

> **Note:** Obviously, this example sets the log length much too small as an extreme example. Set *maxBytes* to a more appropriate value in a real program.

14.9.4 Verbosity Levels

Another useful feature of the `logging` API is the ability to produce different messages at different *log levels*. This means code can be instrumented with debug messages, for example, and the log level can be set so that those debug messages are not written on a production system. Table 14.2 lists the logging levels defined by `logging`.

Table 14.2. Logging Levels

Level	Value
CRITICAL	50
ERROR	40
WARNING	30
INFO	20
DEBUG	10
UNSET	0

The log message is only emitted if the handler and logger are configured to emit messages of that level or higher. For example, if a message is CRITICAL and the logger is set to ERROR, the message is emitted (50 > 40). If a message is a WARNING and the logger is set to produce only messages set to ERROR, the message is not emitted (30 < 40).

```
import logging
import sys

LEVELS = { 'debug':logging.DEBUG,
           'info':logging.INFO,
           'warning':logging.WARNING,
           'error':logging.ERROR,
           'critical':logging.CRITICAL,
           }

if len(sys.argv) > 1:
    level_name = sys.argv[1]
    level = LEVELS.get(level_name, logging.NOTSET)
    logging.basicConfig(level=level)

logging.debug('This is a debug message')
logging.info('This is an info message')
logging.warning('This is a warning message')
logging.error('This is an error message')
logging.critical('This is a critical error message')
```

Run the script with an argument like "debug" or "warning" to see which messages show up at different levels.

```
$ python logging_level_example.py debug
```

```
DEBUG:root:This is a debug message
INFO:root:This is an info message
WARNING:root:This is a warning message
ERROR:root:This is an error message
CRITICAL:root:This is a critical error message


$ python logging_level_example.py info


INFO:root:This is an info message
WARNING:root:This is a warning message
ERROR:root:This is an error message
CRITICAL:root:This is a critical error message
```

14.9.5 Naming Logger Instances

All the previous log messages have "root" embedded in them. The `logging` module supports a hierarchy of loggers with different names. An easy way to tell where a specific log message comes from is to use a separate logger object for each module. Every new logger inherits the configuration of its parent, and log messages sent to a logger include the name of that logger. Optionally, each logger can be configured differently, so that messages from different modules are handled in different ways. Here is an example of how to log from different modules so it is easy to trace the source of the message.

```
import logging

logging.basicConfig(level=logging.WARNING)

logger1 = logging.getLogger('package1.module1')
logger2 = logging.getLogger('package2.module2')

logger1.warning('This message comes from one module')
logger2.warning('And this message comes from another module')
```

And here is the output.

```
$ python logging_modules_example.py

WARNING:package1.module1:This message comes from one module
WARNING:package2.module2:And this message comes from another module
```

There are many more options for configuring logging, including different log message formatting options, having messages delivered to multiple destinations, and changing the configuration of a long-running application on the fly using a socket interface. All these options are covered in depth in the library module documentation.

See Also:
logging (http://docs.python.org/library/logging.html) The standard library documentation for this module.

14.10   fileinput—Command-Line Filter Framework

Purpose Create command-line filter programs to process lines from input streams.
Python Version 1.5.2 and later

The `fileinput` module is a framework for creating command-line programs for processing text files as a filter.

14.10.1   Converting M3U Files to RSS

An example of a filter is `m3utorss`, a program to convert a set of MP3 files into an RSS feed that can be shared as a podcast. The inputs to the program are one or more m3u files listing the MP3 files to be distributed. The output is an RSS feed printed to the console. To process the input, the program needs to iterate over the list of filenames and.

- Open each file.
- Read each line of the file.
- Figure out if the line refers to an MP3 file.
- If it does, extract the information from the mp3 file needed for the RSS feed.
- Print the output.

All this file handling could have been coded by hand. It is not that complicated, and with some testing, even the error handling would be right. But `fileinput` handles all the details, so the program is simplified.

```
for line in fileinput.input(sys.argv[1:]):
    mp3filename = line.strip()
    if not mp3filename or mp3filename.startswith('#'):
        continue
    item = SubElement(rss, 'item')
    title = SubElement(item, 'title')
```

```
title.text = mp3filename
encl = SubElement(item, 'enclosure',
                  {'type':'audio/mpeg',
                   'url':mp3filename})
```

The `input()` function takes as argument a list of filenames to examine. If the list is empty, the module reads data from standard input. The function returns an iterator that produces individual lines from the text files being processed. The caller just needs to loop over each line, skipping blanks and comments, to find the references to MP3 files.

Here is the complete program.

```
import fileinput
import sys
import time
from xml.etree.ElementTree import Element, SubElement, tostring
from xml.dom import minidom

# Establish the RSS and channel nodes
rss = Element('rss', {'xmlns:dc':"http://purl.org/dc/elements/1.1/",
                      'version':'2.0',
                      })
channel = SubElement(rss, 'channel')
title = SubElement(channel, 'title')
title.text = 'Sample podcast feed'
desc = SubElement(channel, 'description')
desc.text = 'Generated for PyMOTW'
pubdate = SubElement(channel, 'pubDate')
pubdate.text = time.asctime()
gen = SubElement(channel, 'generator')
gen.text = 'http://www.doughellmann.com/PyMOTW/'

for line in fileinput.input(sys.argv[1:]):
    mp3filename = line.strip()
    if not mp3filename or mp3filename.startswith('#'):
        continue
    item = SubElement(rss, 'item')
    title = SubElement(item, 'title')
    title.text = mp3filename
    encl = SubElement(item, 'enclosure',
                      {'type':'audio/mpeg',
                       'url':mp3filename})
```

```
rough_string = tostring(rss)
reparsed = minidom.parseString(rough_string)
print reparsed.toprettyxml(indent="  ")
```

This sample input file contains the names of several MP3 files.

```
# This is a sample m3u file
episode-one.mp3
episode-two.mp3
```

Running `fileinput_example.py` with the sample input produces XML data using the RSS format.

```
$ python fileinput_example.py sample_data.m3u

<?xml version="1.0" ?>
<rss version="2.0" xmlns:dc="http://purl.org/dc/elements/1.1/">
  <channel>
    <title>
      Sample podcast feed
    </title>
    <description>
      Generated for PyMOTW
    </description>
    <pubDate>
      Sun Nov 28 22:55:09 2010
    </pubDate>
    <generator>
      http://www.doughellmann.com/PyMOTW/
    </generator>
  </channel>
  <item>
    <title>
      episode-one.mp3
    </title>
    <enclosure type="audio/mpeg" url="episode-one.mp3"/>
  </item>
  <item>
    <title>
      episode-two.mp3
    </title>
    <enclosure type="audio/mpeg" url="episode-two.mp3"/>
```

```
    </item>
</rss>
```

14.10.2 Progress Metadata

In the previous example, the filename and line number being processed were not important. Other tools, such as grep-like searching, might need that information. fileinput includes functions for accessing all the metadata about the current line (filename(), filelineno(), and lineno()).

```
import fileinput
import re
import sys

pattern = re.compile(sys.argv[1])

for line in fileinput.input(sys.argv[2:]):
    if pattern.search(line):
        if fileinput.isstdin():
            fmt = '{lineno}:{line}'
        else:
            fmt = '{filename}:{lineno}:{line}'
        print fmt.format(filename=fileinput.filename(),
                         lineno=fileinput.filelineno(),
                         line=line.rstrip())
```

A basic pattern-matching loop can be used to find the occurrences of the string "fileinput" in the source for these examples.

```
$ python fileinput_grep.py fileinput *.py

fileinput_change_subnet.py:10:import fileinput
fileinput_change_subnet.py:17:for line in fileinput.input(files, inp
lace=True):
fileinput_change_subnet_noisy.py:10:import fileinput
fileinput_change_subnet_noisy.py:18:for line in fileinput.input(file
s, inplace=True):
fileinput_change_subnet_noisy.py:19:    if fileinput.isfirstline():
fileinput_change_subnet_noisy.py:21:                        fileinp
ut.filename())
fileinput_example.py:6:"""Example for fileinput module.
fileinput_example.py:10:import fileinput
```

```
fileinput_example.py:30:for line in fileinput.input(sys.argv[1:]):
fileinput_grep.py:10:import fileinput
fileinput_grep.py:16:for line in fileinput.input(sys.argv[2:]):
fileinput_grep.py:18:        if fileinput.isstdin():
fileinput_grep.py:22:            print fmt.format(filename=fileinput.fil
ename(),
fileinput_grep.py:23:                            lineno=fileinput.filel
ineno(),
```

Text can also be read from standard input.

```
$ cat *.py | python fileinput_grep.py fileinput

10:import fileinput
17:for line in fileinput.input(files, inplace=True):
29:import fileinput
37:for line in fileinput.input(files, inplace=True):
38:    if fileinput.isfirstline():
40:                        fileinput.filename())
54:"""Example for fileinput module.
58:import fileinput
78:for line in fileinput.input(sys.argv[1:]):
101:import fileinput
107:for line in fileinput.input(sys.argv[2:]):
109:        if fileinput.isstdin():
113:        print fmt.format(filename=fileinput.filename(),
114:                    lineno=fileinput.filelineno(),
```

14.10.3   In-Place Filtering

Another common file-processing operation is to modify the contents of an in-place file.
For example, a UNIX hosts file might need to be updated if a subnet range changes.

```
##
# Host Database
#
# localhost is used to configure the loopback interface
# when the system is booting.  Do not change this entry.
##
127.0.0.1       localhost
255.255.255.255 broadcasthost
::1             localhost
fe80::1%lo0     localhost
```

```
10.16.177.128   hubert hubert.hellfly.net
10.16.177.132   cubert cubert.hellfly.net
10.16.177.136   zoidberg zoidberg.hellfly.net
```

The safe way to make the change automatically is to create a new file based on the input and then replace the original with the edited copy. `fileinput` supports this method automatically using the *inplace* option.

```python
import fileinput
import sys

from_base = sys.argv[1]
to_base = sys.argv[2]
files = sys.argv[3:]

for line in fileinput.input(files, inplace=True):
    line = line.rstrip().replace(from_base, to_base)
    print line
```

Although the script uses **print**, no output is produced because `fileinput` redirects standard output to the file being overwritten.

```
$ python fileinput_change_subnet.py 10.16. 10.17. etc_hosts.txt
```

The updated file has the changed IP addresses of all the servers on the `10.16.0.0/16` network.

```
##
# Host Database
#
# localhost is used to configure the loopback interface
# when the system is booting.  Do not change this entry.
##
127.0.0.1       localhost
255.255.255.255 broadcasthost
::1             localhost
fe80::1%lo0     localhost
10.17.177.128   hubert hubert.hellfly.net
10.17.177.132   cubert cubert.hellfly.net
10.17.177.136   zoidberg zoidberg.hellfly.net
```

Before processing begins, a backup file is created using the original name plus
.bak.

```
import fileinput
import glob
import sys

from_base = sys.argv[1]
to_base = sys.argv[2]
files = sys.argv[3:]


for line in fileinput.input(files, inplace=True):
    if fileinput.isfirstline():
        sys.stderr.write('Started processing %s\n' %
                         fileinput.filename())
        sys.stderr.write('Directory contains: %s\n' %
                         glob.glob('etc_hosts.txt*'))
    line = line.rstrip().replace(from_base, to_base)
    print line

sys.stderr.write('Finished processing\n')
sys.stderr.write('Directory contains: %s\n' %
                 glob.glob('etc_hosts.txt*'))
```

The backup file is removed when the input is closed.

```
$ python fileinput_change_subnet_noisy.py 10.16. 10.17. etc_hosts.txt

Started processing etc_hosts.txt
Directory contains: ['etc_hosts.txt', 'etc_hosts.txt.bak']
Finished processing
Directory contains: ['etc_hosts.txt']
```

See Also:

fileinput (http://docs.python.org/library/fileinput.html) The standard library documentation for this module.

m3utorss (www.doughellmann.com/projects/m3utorss) Script to convert M3U files
listing MP3s to an RSS file suitable for use as a podcast feed.

***Building Documents with Element Nodes* (page 400)** More details of using Element-
Tree to produce XML.

14.11   atexit—Program Shutdown Callbacks

Purpose Register function(s) to be called when a program is closing down.
Python Version 2.1.3 and later

The `atexit` module provides an interface to register functions to be called when a program closes down normally. The `sys` module also provides a hook, `sys.exitfunc`, but only one function can be registered there. The `atexit` registry can be used by multiple modules and libraries simultaneously.

14.11.1   Examples

This is an example of registering a function via `register()`.

```python
import atexit

def all_done():
    print 'all_done()'

print 'Registering'
atexit.register(all_done)
print 'Registered'
```

Since the program does not do anything else, `all_done()` is called right away.

```
$ python atexit_simple.py

Registering
Registered
all_done()
```

It is also possible to register more than one function and to pass arguments to the registered functions. That can be useful to cleanly disconnect from databases, remove temporary files, etc. Instead of keeping a special list of resources that need to be freed, a separate cleanup function can be registered for each resource.

```python
import atexit

def my_cleanup(name):
    print 'my_cleanup(%s)' % name
```

```
atexit.register(my_cleanup, 'first')
atexit.register(my_cleanup, 'second')
atexit.register(my_cleanup, 'third')
```

The exit functions are called in the reverse of the order in which they are registered. This method allows modules to be cleaned up in the reverse order from which they are imported (and therefore, register their `atexit` functions), which should reduce dependency conflicts.

```
$ python atexit_multiple.py

my_cleanup(third)
my_cleanup(second)
my_cleanup(first)
```

14.11.2 When Are atexit Functions Not Called?

The callbacks registered with `atexit` are not invoked if any of these conditions is met.

- The program dies because of a signal.
- `os._exit()` is invoked directly.
- A fatal error is detected in the interpreter.

An example from the `subprocess` section can be updated to show what happens when a program is killed by a signal. Two files are involved, the parent and the child programs. The parent starts the child, pauses, and then kills it.

```
import os
import signal
import subprocess
import time

proc = subprocess.Popen('atexit_signal_child.py')
print 'PARENT: Pausing before sending signal...'
time.sleep(1)
print 'PARENT: Signaling child'
os.kill(proc.pid, signal.SIGTERM)
```

The child sets up an `atexit` callback, and then sleeps until the signal arrives.

```
import atexit
import time
import sys
```

```
def not_called():
    print 'CHILD: atexit handler should not have been called'

print 'CHILD: Registering atexit handler'
sys.stdout.flush()
atexit.register(not_called)

print 'CHILD: Pausing to wait for signal'
sys.stdout.flush()
time.sleep(5)
```

When run, this is the output.

```
$ python atexit_signal_parent.py

CHILD: Registering atexit handler
CHILD: Pausing to wait for signal
PARENT: Pausing before sending signal...
PARENT: Signaling child
```

The child does not print the message embedded in `not_called()`.

If a program uses `os._exit()`, it can avoid having the `atexit` callbacks invoked.

```
import atexit
import os

def not_called():
    print 'This should not be called'

print 'Registering'
atexit.register(not_called)
print 'Registered'

print 'Exiting...'
os._exit(0)
```

Because this example bypasses the normal exit path, the callback is not run.

```
$ python atexit_os_exit.py
```

To ensure that the callbacks are run, allow the program to terminate by running out of statements to execute or by calling `sys.exit()`.

```
import atexit
import sys

def all_done():
    print 'all_done()'

print 'Registering'
atexit.register(all_done)
print 'Registered'

print 'Exiting...'
sys.exit()
```

This example calls `sys.exit()`, so the registered callbacks are invoked.

```
$ python atexit_sys_exit.py

Registering
Registered
Exiting...
all_done()
```

14.11.3 Handling Exceptions

Tracebacks for exceptions raised in `atexit` callbacks are printed to the console and the last exception raised is reraised to be the final error message of the program.

```
import atexit

def exit_with_exception(message):
    raise RuntimeError(message)

atexit.register(exit_with_exception, 'Registered first')
atexit.register(exit_with_exception, 'Registered second')
```

The registration order controls the execution order. If an error in one callback introduces an error in another (registered earlier, but called later), the final error message might not be the most useful error message to show the user.

```
$ python atexit_exception.py

Error in atexit._run_exitfuncs:
Traceback (most recent call last):
  File "/Library/Frameworks/Python.framework/Versions/2.7/lib/python
```

```
2.7/atexit.py", line 24, in _run_exitfuncs
    func(*targs, **kargs)
  File "atexit_exception.py", line 37, in exit_with_exception
    raise RuntimeError(message)
RuntimeError: Registered second
Error in atexit._run_exitfuncs:
Traceback (most recent call last):
  File "/Library/Frameworks/Python.framework/Versions/2.7/lib/python
2.7/atexit.py", line 24, in _run_exitfuncs
    func(*targs, **kargs)
  File "atexit_exception.py", line 37, in exit_with_exception
    raise RuntimeError(message)
RuntimeError: Registered first
Error in sys.exitfunc:
Traceback (most recent call last):
  File "/Library/Frameworks/Python.framework/Versions/2.7/lib/python
2.7/atexit.py", line 24, in _run_exitfuncs
    func(*targs, **kargs)
  File "atexit_exception.py", line 37, in exit_with_exception
    raise RuntimeError(message)
RuntimeError: Registered first
```

It is usually best to handle and quietly log all exceptions in cleanup functions, since it is messy to have a program dump errors on exit.

See Also:
atexit (http://docs.python.org/library/atexit.html) The standard library documentation for this module.

14.12   sched—Timed Event Scheduler

> **Purpose** Generic event scheduler.
> **Python Version** 1.4 and later

The sched module implements a generic event scheduler for running tasks at specific times. The scheduler class uses a *time* function to learn the current time and a *delay* function to wait for a specific period of time. The actual units of time are not important, which makes the interface flexible enough to be used for many purposes.

The *time* function is called without any arguments and should return a number representing the current time. The *delay* function is called with a single integer argument, using the same scale as the time function, and should wait that many time units before returning. For example, the `time.time()` and `time.sleep()` functions meet these requirements.

To support multithreaded applications, the delay function is called with argument 0 after each event is generated, to ensure that other threads also have a chance to run.

14.12.1 Running Events with a Delay

Events can be scheduled to run after a delay or at a specific time. To schedule them with a delay, use the `enter()` method, which takes four arguments:

- A number representing the delay
- A priority value
- The function to call
- A tuple of arguments for the function

This example schedules two different events to run after two and three seconds, respectively. When the event's time comes up, `print_event()` is called and prints the current time and the name argument passed to the event.

```python
import sched
import time

scheduler = sched.scheduler(time.time, time.sleep)

def print_event(name, start):
    now = time.time()
    elapsed = int(now - start)
    print 'EVENT: %s elapsed=%s name=%s' % (time.ctime(now),
                                            elapsed,
                                            name)

start = time.time()
print 'START:', time.ctime(start)
scheduler.enter(2, 1, print_event, ('first', start))
scheduler.enter(3, 1, print_event, ('second', start))

scheduler.run()
```

This is what running the program produces.

```
$ python sched_basic.py

START: Sun Oct 31 20:48:47 2010
EVENT: Sun Oct 31 20:48:49 2010 elapsed=2 name=first
EVENT: Sun Oct 31 20:48:50 2010 elapsed=3 name=second
```

The time printed for the first event is two seconds after start, and the time for the second event is three seconds after start.

14.12.2   Overlapping Events

The call to `run()` blocks until all the events have been processed. Each event is run in the same thread, so if an event takes longer to run than the delay between events, there will be overlap. The overlap is resolved by postponing the later event. No events are lost, but some events may be called later than they were scheduled. In the next example, `long_event()` sleeps, but it could just as easily delay by performing a long calculation or by blocking on I/O.

```python
import sched
import time

scheduler = sched.scheduler(time.time, time.sleep)

def long_event(name):
    print 'BEGIN EVENT :', time.ctime(time.time()), name
    time.sleep(2)
    print 'FINISH EVENT:', time.ctime(time.time()), name

print 'START:', time.ctime(time.time())
scheduler.enter(2, 1, long_event, ('first',))
scheduler.enter(3, 1, long_event, ('second',))

scheduler.run()
```

The result is that the second event is run immediately after the first event finishes, since the first event took long enough to push the clock past the desired start time of the second event.

```
$ python sched_overlap.py

START: Sun Oct 31 20:48:50 2010
BEGIN EVENT : Sun Oct 31 20:48:52 2010 first
FINISH EVENT: Sun Oct 31 20:48:54 2010 first
```

```
BEGIN EVENT : Sun Oct 31 20:48:54 2010 second
FINISH EVENT: Sun Oct 31 20:48:56 2010 second
```

14.12.3   Event Priorities

If more than one event is scheduled for the same time, the events' priority values are used to determine the order in which they are run.

```
import sched
import time

scheduler = sched.scheduler(time.time, time.sleep)

def print_event(name):
    print 'EVENT:', time.ctime(time.time()), name

now = time.time()
print 'START:', time.ctime(now)
scheduler.enterabs(now+2, 2, print_event, ('first',))
scheduler.enterabs(now+2, 1, print_event, ('second',))

scheduler.run()
```

This example needs to ensure that the events are scheduled for the exact same time, so the `enterabs()` method is used instead of `enter()`. The first argument to `enterabs()` is the time to run the event, instead of the amount of time to delay.

```
$ python sched_priority.py

START: Sun Oct 31 20:48:56 2010
EVENT: Sun Oct 31 20:48:58 2010 second
EVENT: Sun Oct 31 20:48:58 2010 first
```

14.12.4   Canceling Events

Both `enter()` and `enterabs()` return a reference to the event that can be used to cancel it later. Since `run()` blocks, the event has to be canceled in a different thread. For this example, a thread is started to run the scheduler and the main processing thread is used to cancel the event.

```
import sched
import threading
import time
```

```
scheduler = sched.scheduler(time.time, time.sleep)

# Set up a global to be modified by the threads
counter = 0

def increment_counter(name):
    global counter
    print 'EVENT:', time.ctime(time.time()), name
    counter += 1
    print 'NOW:', counter

print 'START:', time.ctime(time.time())
e1 = scheduler.enter(2, 1, increment_counter, ('E1',))
e2 = scheduler.enter(3, 1, increment_counter, ('E2',))

# Start a thread to run the events
t = threading.Thread(target=scheduler.run)
t.start()

# Back in the main thread, cancel the first scheduled event.
scheduler.cancel(e1)

# Wait for the scheduler to finish running in the thread
t.join()

print 'FINAL:', counter
```

Two events were scheduled, but the first was later canceled. Only the second event runs, so the counter variable is only incremented one time.

```
$ python sched_cancel.py

START: Sun Oct 31 20:48:58 2010
EVENT: Sun Oct 31 20:49:01 2010 E2
NOW: 1
FINAL: 1
```

See Also:

sched (http://docs.python.org/lib/module-sched.html) The Standard library documentation for this module.

time (page 173) The time module.

Chapter 15

INTERNATIONALIZATION AND LOCALIZATION

Python comes with two modules for preparing an application to work with multiple natural languages and cultural settings. `gettext` is used to create message catalogs in different languages, so that prompts and error messages can be displayed in a language the user can understand. `locale` changes the way numbers, currency, dates, and times are formatted to consider cultural differences, such as how negative values are indicated and what the local currency symbol is. Both modules interface with other tools and the operating environment to make the Python application fit in with all the other programs on the system.

15.1 gettext—Message Catalogs

Purpose Message catalog API for internationalization.
Python Version 2.1.3 and later

The `gettext` module provides a pure-Python implementation compatible with the GNU **gettext** library for message translation and catalog management. The tools available with the Python source distribution enable you to extract messages from a set of source files, build a message catalog containing translations, and use that message catalog to display an appropriate message for the user at runtime.

Message catalogs can be used to provide internationalized interfaces for a program, showing messages in a language appropriate to the user. They can also be used for other message customizations, including "skinning" an interface for different wrappers or partners.

> **Note:** Although the standard library documentation says all the necessary tools are included with Python, `pygettext.py` failed to extract messages wrapped in the `ungettext` call, even with the appropriate command-line options. These examples use `xgettext` from the GNU **gettext** tool set, instead.

15.1.1   Translation Workflow Overview

The process for setting up and using translations includes five steps.

1. *Identify and mark up literal strings in the source code that contain messages to translate.*
   Start by identifying the messages within the program source that need to be translated and marking the literal strings so the extraction program can find them.
2. *Extract the messages.*
   After the translatable strings in the source are identified, use `xgettext` to extract them and create a `.pot` file, or *translation template*. The template is a text file with copies of all the strings identified and placeholders for their translations.
3. *Translate the messages.*
   Give a copy of the `.pot` file to the translator, changing the extension to `.po`. The `.po` file is an editable source file used as input for the compilation step. The translator should update the header text in the file and provide translations for all the strings.
4. *"Compile" the message catalog from the translation.*
   When the translator sends back the completed `.po` file, compile the text file to the binary catalog format using `msgfmt`. The binary format is used by the runtime catalog lookup code.
5. *Load and activate the appropriate message catalog at runtime.*
   The final step is to add a few lines to the application to configure and load the message catalog and install the translation function. There are a couple of ways to do that, with associated trade-offs.

The rest of this section will examine those steps in a little more detail, starting with the code modifications needed.

15.1.2   Creating Message Catalogs from Source Code

`gettext` works by looking up literal strings in a database of translations and pulling out the appropriate translated string. There are several variations of the functions for accessing the catalog, depending on whether the strings are Unicode or not. The usual pattern is to bind the appropriate lookup function to the name "_" (a single underscore character) so that the code is not cluttered with a lot of calls to functions with longer names.

The message extraction program, xgettext, looks for messages embedded in calls to the catalog lookup functions. It understands different source languages and uses an appropriate parser for each. If the lookup functions are aliased, or extra functions are added, give xgettext the names of additional symbols to consider when extracting messages.

This script has a single message ready to be translated.

```
import gettext

# Set up message catalog access
t = gettext.translation('example', 'locale', fallback=True)
_ = t.ugettext

print _('This message is in the script.')
```

The example uses the Unicode version of the lookup function, ugettext(). The text "This message is in the script." is the message to be substituted from the catalog. Fallback mode is enabled, so if the script is run without a message catalog, the in-lined message is printed.

```
$ python gettext_example.py

This message is in the script.
```

The next step is to extract the message and create the .pot file, using Python's pygettext.py or the GNU tool xgettext.

```
$ xgettext -o example.pot gettext_example.py
```

The output file produced contains the following.

```
# SOME DESCRIPTIVE TITLE.
# Copyright (C) YEAR THE PACKAGE'S COPYRIGHT HOLDER
# This file is distributed under the same license
# as the PACKAGE package.
# FIRST AUTHOR <EMAIL@ADDRESS>, YEAR.
#
```

```
#, fuzzy
msgid ""
msgstr ""
"Project-Id-Version: PACKAGE VERSION\n"
"Report-Msgid-Bugs-To: \n"
"POT-Creation-Date: 2010-11-28 23:16-0500\n"
"PO-Revision-Date: YEAR-MO-DA HO:MI+ZONE\n"
"Last-Translator: FULL NAME <EMAIL@ADDRESS>\n"
"Language-Team: LANGUAGE <LL@li.org>\n"
"Language: \n"
"MIME-Version: 1.0\n"
"Content-Type: text/plain; charset=CHARSET\n"
"Content-Transfer-Encoding: 8bit\n"

#: gettext_example.py:16
msgid "This message is in the script."
msgstr ""
```

Message catalogs are installed into directories organized by *domain* and *language*. The domain is usually a unique value like the application name. In this case, the domain is `gettext_example`. The language value is provided by the user's environment at runtime through one of the environment variables, LANGUAGE, LC_ALL, LC_MESSAGES, or LANG, depending on their configuration and platform. These examples were all run with the language set to en_US.

Now that the template is ready, the next step is to create the required directory structure and copy the template in to the right spot. The `locale` directory inside the PyMOTW source tree will serve as the root of the message catalog directory for these examples, but it is typically better to use a directory accessible system wide so that all users have access to the message catalogs. The full path to the catalog input source is `$localedir/$language/LC_MESSAGES/$domain.po`, and the actual catalog has the filename extension `.mo`.

The catalog is created by copying `example.pot` to `locale/en_US/LC_MESSAGES/example.po` and editing it to change the values in the header and set the alternate messages. The result is shown next.

```
# Messages from gettext_example.py.
# Copyright (C) 2009 Doug Hellmann
# Doug Hellmann <doug.hellmann@gmail.com>, 2009.
#
msgid ""
msgstr ""
```

```
"Project-Id-Version: PyMOTW 1.92\n"
"Report-Msgid-Bugs-To: Doug Hellmann <doug.hellmann@gmail.com>\n"
"POT-Creation-Date: 2009-06-07 10:31+EDT\n"
"PO-Revision-Date: 2009-06-07 10:31+EDT\n"
"Last-Translator: Doug Hellmann <doug.hellmann@gmail.com>\n"
"Language-Team: US English <doug.hellmann@gmail.com>\n"
"MIME-Version: 1.0\n"
"Content-Type: text/plain; charset=UTF-8\n"
"Content-Transfer-Encoding: 8bit\n"


#: gettext_example.py:16
msgid "This message is in the script."
msgstr "This message is in the en_US catalog."
```

The catalog is built from the `.po` file using `msgformat`.

```
$ cd locale/en_US/LC_MESSAGES/; msgfmt -o example.mo example.po
```

Now when the script is run, the message from the catalog is printed instead of the in-line string.

```
$ python gettext_example.py

This message is in the en_US catalog.
```

15.1.3 Finding Message Catalogs at Runtime

As described earlier, the *locale directory* containing the message catalogs is organized based on the language with catalogs named for the *domain* of the program. Different operating systems define their own default value, but `gettext` does not know all these defaults. It uses a default locale directory of `sys.prefix + '/share/locale'`, but most of the time, it is safer to always explicitly give a `localedir` value than to depend on this default being valid. The `find()` function is responsible for locating an appropriate message catalog at runtime.

```
import gettext

catalogs = gettext.find('example', 'locale', all=True)
print 'Catalogs:', catalogs
```

The language portion of the path is taken from one of several environment variables that can be used to configure localization features (LANGUAGE, LC_ALL, LC_MESSAGES, and LANG). The first variable found to be set is used. Multiple languages can be selected by separating the values with a colon (:). To see how that works, use a second message catalog to run a few experiments.

```
$ (cd locale/en_CA/LC_MESSAGES/; msgfmt -o example.mo example.po)
$ python gettext_find.py

Catalogs: ['locale/en_US/LC_MESSAGES/example.mo']

$ LANGUAGE=en_CA python gettext_find.py

Catalogs: ['locale/en_CA/LC_MESSAGES/example.mo']

$ LANGUAGE=en_CA:en_US python gettext_find.py

Catalogs: ['locale/en_CA/LC_MESSAGES/example.mo',
'locale/en_US/LC_MESSAGES/example.mo']

$ LANGUAGE=en_US:en_CA python gettext_find.py

Catalogs: ['locale/en_US/LC_MESSAGES/example.mo',
'locale/en_CA/LC_MESSAGES/example.mo']
```

Although find() shows the complete list of catalogs, only the first one in the sequence is actually loaded for message lookups.

```
$ python gettext_example.py

This message is in the en_US catalog.

$ LANGUAGE=en_CA python gettext_example.py

This message is in the en_CA catalog.

$ LANGUAGE=en_CA:en_US python gettext_example.py

This message is in the en_CA catalog.

$ LANGUAGE=en_US:en_CA python gettext_example.py

This message is in the en_US catalog.
```

15.1.4   Plural Values

While simple message substitution will handle most translation needs, gettext treats pluralization as a special case. Depending on the language, the difference between the singular and plural forms of a message may vary only by the ending of a single word or the entire sentence structure may be different. There may also be different forms depending on the level of plurality. To make managing plurals easier (and, in some cases, possible), a separate set of functions asks for the plural form of a message.

```
from gettext import translation
import sys

t = translation('gettext_plural', 'locale', fallback=True)
num = int(sys.argv[1])
msg = t.ungettext('%(num)d means singular.',
                  '%(num)d means plural.',
                  num)

# Still need to add the values to the message ourself.
print msg % {'num':num}
```

Use ungettext() to access the Unicode version of the plural substitution for a message. The arguments are the messages to be translated and the item count.

```
$ xgettext -L Python -o plural.pot gettext_plural.py
```

Since there are alternate forms to be translated, the replacements are listed in an array. Using an array allows translations for languages with multiple plural forms (e.g., Polish has different forms indicating the relative quantity).

```
# SOME DESCRIPTIVE TITLE.
# Copyright (C) YEAR THE PACKAGE'S COPYRIGHT HOLDER
# This file is distributed under the same license
# as the PACKAGE package.
# FIRST AUTHOR <EMAIL@ADDRESS>, YEAR.
#
#, fuzzy
msgid ""
msgstr ""
"Project-Id-Version: PACKAGE VERSION\n"
"Report-Msgid-Bugs-To: \n"
"POT-Creation-Date: 2010-11-28 23:09-0500\n"
```

```
"PO-Revision-Date: YEAR-MO-DA HO:MI+ZONE\n"
"Last-Translator: FULL NAME <EMAIL@ADDRESS>\n"
"Language-Team: LANGUAGE <LL@li.org>\n"
"Language: \n"
"MIME-Version: 1.0\n"
"Content-Type: text/plain; charset=CHARSET\n"
"Content-Transfer-Encoding: 8bit\n"
"Plural-Forms: nplurals=INTEGER; plural=EXPRESSION;\n"

#: gettext_plural.py:15
#, python-format
msgid "%(num)d means singular."
msgid_plural "%(num)d means plural."
msgstr[0] ""
msgstr[1] ""
```

In addition to filling in the translation strings, the library needs to be told about the way plurals are formed so it knows how to index into the array for any given count value. The line "`Plural-Forms: nplurals=INTEGER; plural= EXPRESSION;\n`" includes two values to replace manually. `nplurals` is an integer indicating the size of the array (the number of translations used), and `plural` is a C language expression for converting the incoming quantity to an index in the array when looking up the translation. The literal string n is replaced with the quantity passed to `ungettext()`.

For example, English includes two plural forms. A quantity of 0 is treated as plural ("0 bananas"). This is the `Plural-Forms` entry.

```
Plural-Forms: nplurals=2; plural=n != 1;
```

The singular translation would then go in position 0 and the plural translation in position 1.

```
# Messages from gettext_plural.py
# Copyright (C) 2009 Doug Hellmann
# This file is distributed under the same license
# as the PyMOTW package.
# Doug Hellmann <doug.hellmann@gmail.com>, 2009.
#
#, fuzzy
msgid ""
msgstr ""
"Project-Id-Version: PyMOTW 1.92\n"
```

```
"Report-Msgid-Bugs-To: Doug Hellmann <doug.hellmann@gmail.com>\n"
"POT-Creation-Date: 2009-06-14 09:29-0400\n"
"PO-Revision-Date: 2009-06-14 09:29-0400\n"
"Last-Translator: Doug Hellmann <doug.hellmann@gmail.com>\n"
"Language-Team: en_US <doug.hellmann@gmail.com>\n"
"MIME-Version: 1.0\n"
"Content-Type: text/plain; charset=UTF-8\n"
"Content-Transfer-Encoding: 8bit\n"
"Plural-Forms: nplurals=2; plural=n != 1;"

#: gettext_plural.py:15
#, python-format
msgid "%(num)d means singular."
msgid_plural "%(num)d means plural."
msgstr[0] "In en_US, %(num)d is singular."
msgstr[1] "In en_US, %(num)d is plural."
```

Running the test script a few times after the catalog is compiled will demonstrate how different values of n are converted to indexes for the translation strings.

```
$ cd locale/en_US/LC_MESSAGES/; msgfmt -o plural.mo plural.po
$ python gettext_plural.py 0

0 means plural.

$ python gettext_plural.py 1

1 means singular.

$ python gettext_plural.py 2

2 means plural.
```

15.1.5 Application vs. Module Localization

The scope of a translation effort defines how `gettext` is installed and used with a body of code.

Application Localization

For application-wide translations, it would be acceptable for the author to install a function like `ungettext()` globally using the `__builtins__` namespace, because they have control over the top level of the application's code.

```
import gettext
gettext.install('gettext_example', 'locale',
                unicode=True, names=['ngettext'])

print _('This message is in the script.')
```

The `install()` function binds `gettext()` to the name `_()` in the __builtins__ namespace. It also adds `ngettext()` and other functions listed in *names*. If *unicode* is true, the Unicode versions of the functions are used instead of the default ASCII versions.

Module Localization

For a library, or individual module, modifying __builtins__ is not a good idea because it may introduce conflicts with an application global value. Instead, import or rebind the names of translation functions by hand at the top of the module.

```
import gettext
t = gettext.translation('gettext_example', 'locale', fallback=True)
_ = t.ugettext
ngettext = t.ungettext

print _('This message is in the script.')
```

15.1.6   Switching Translations

The earlier examples all use a single translation for the duration of the program. Some situations, especially web applications, need to use different message catalogs at different times, without exiting and resetting the environment. For those cases, the class-based API provided in `gettext` will be more convenient. The API calls are essentially the same as the global calls described in this section, but the message catalog object is exposed and can be manipulated directly so that multiple catalogs can be used.

See Also:

gettext (http://docs.python.org/library/gettext.html) The standard library documentation for this module.

locale (page 909) Other localization tools.

GNU gettext (www.gnu.org/software/gettext/) The message catalog formats, API, etc., for this module are all based on the original gettext package from GNU. The catalog file formats are compatible, and the command-line scripts have similar options (if not identical). The GNU gettext manual (www.gnu.org/software/

gettext/manual/gettext.html) has a detailed description of the file formats and describes GNU versions of the tools for working with them.

Plural forms (www.gnu.org/software/gettext/manual/gettext.html#Plural-forms)
Handling of plural forms of words and sentences in different languages.

Internationalizing Python (www.python.org/workshops/1997-10/proceedings/ loewis.html) A paper by Martin von Löwis about techniques for internationalization of Python applications.

Django Internationalization (http://docs.djangoproject.com/en/dev/topics/i18n/)
Another good source of information on using gettext, including real-life examples.

15.2 locale—Cultural Localization API

Purpose Format and parse values that depend on location or language.
Python Version 1.5 and later

The `locale` module is part of Python's internationalization and localization support library. It provides a standard way to handle operations that may depend on the language or location of a user. For example, it handles formatting numbers as currency, comparing strings for sorting, and working with dates. It does not cover translation (see the `gettext` module) or Unicode encoding (see the `codecs` module).

Note: Changing the locale can have application-wide ramifications, so the recommended practice is to avoid changing the value in a library and to let the application set it one time. In the examples in this section, the locale is changed several times within a short program to highlight the differences in the settings of various locales. It is far more likely that an application will set the locale once as it starts up and then will not change it.

This section covers some of the high-level functions in the `locale` module. Others are lower level (`format_string()`) or relate to managing the locale for an application (`resetlocale()`).

15.2.1 Probing the Current Locale

The most common way to let the user change the locale settings for an application is through an environment variable (`LC_ALL`, `LC_CTYPE`, `LANG`, or `LANGUAGE`, depending on the platform). The application then calls `setlocale()` without a hard-coded value, and the environment value is used.

```
import locale
import os
import pprint
import codecs
import sys

sys.stdout = codecs.getwriter('UTF-8')(sys.stdout)

# Default settings based on the user's environment.
locale.setlocale(locale.LC_ALL, '')

print 'Environment settings:'
for env_name in [ 'LC_ALL', 'LC_CTYPE', 'LANG', 'LANGUAGE' ]:
    print '\t%s = %s' % (env_name, os.environ.get(env_name, ''))

# What is the locale?
print
print 'Locale from environment:', locale.getlocale()

template = """
Numeric formatting:

  Decimal point         : "%(decimal_point)s"
  Grouping positions : %(grouping)s
  Thousands separator: "%(thousands_sep)s"

Monetary formatting:

  International currency symbol                 : "%(int_curr_symbol)r"
  Local currency symbol                        : %(currency_symbol)r
    Unicode version                              %(currency_symbol_u)s
  Symbol precedes positive value               : %(p_cs_precedes)s
  Symbol precedes negative value               : %(n_cs_precedes)s
  Decimal point                                : "%(mon_decimal_point)s"
  Digits in fractional values                  : %(frac_digits)s
  Digits in fractional values, international: %(int_frac_digits)s
  Grouping positions                           : %(mon_grouping)s
  Thousands separator                          : "%(mon_thousands_sep)s"
  Positive sign                                : "%(positive_sign)s"
  Positive sign position                       : %(p_sign_posn)s
  Negative sign                                : "%(negative_sign)s"
  Negative sign position                       : %(n_sign_posn)s

"""
```

```
sign_positions = {
    0 : 'Surrounded by parentheses',
    1 : 'Before value and symbol',
    2 : 'After value and symbol',
    3 : 'Before value',
    4 : 'After value',
    locale.CHAR_MAX : 'Unspecified',
    }

info = {}
info.update(locale.localeconv())
info['p_sign_posn'] = sign_positions[info['p_sign_posn']]
info['n_sign_posn'] = sign_positions[info['n_sign_posn']]
# convert the currency symbol to unicode
info['currency_symbol_u'] = info['currency_symbol'].decode('utf-8')

print (template % info)
```

The `localeconv()` method returns a dictionary containing the locale's conventions. The full list of value names and definitions is covered in the standard library documentation.

A Mac running OS X 10.6 with all the variables unset produces this output.

```
$ export LANG=; export LC_CTYPE=; python locale_env_example.py

Environment settings:
        LC_ALL =
        LC_CTYPE =
        LANG =
        LANGUAGE =

Locale from environment: (None, None)

Numeric formatting:

  Decimal point        : "."
  Grouping positions : [3, 3, 0]
  Thousands separator: ","

Monetary formatting:

  International currency symbol                : "'USD '"
  Local currency symbol                       : '$'
    Unicode version                           $
```

```
Symbol precedes positive value              : 1
Symbol precedes negative value              : 1
Decimal point                               : "."
Digits in fractional values                 : 2
Digits in fractional values, international: 2
Grouping positions                          : [3, 3, 0]
Thousands separator                         : ","
Positive sign                               : ""
Positive sign position                      : Before value and symbol
Negative sign                               : "-"
Negative sign position                      : Before value and symbol
```

Running the same script with the LANG variable set shows how the locale and default encoding change.

France (fr_FR):

```
$ LANG=fr_FR LC_CTYPE=fr_FR LC_ALL=fr_FR python locale_env_example.py

Environment settings:
        LC_ALL = fr_FR
        LC_CTYPE = fr_FR
        LANG = fr_FR
        LANGUAGE =

Locale from environment: ('fr_FR', 'ISO8859-1')

Numeric formatting:

  Decimal point      : ","
  Grouping positions : [127]
  Thousands separator: ""

Monetary formatting:

  International currency symbol              : "'EUR '"
  Local currency symbol                     : 'Eu'
    Unicode version                           Eu
  Symbol precedes positive value            : 0
  Symbol precedes negative value            : 0
  Decimal point                             : ","
  Digits in fractional values               : 2
  Digits in fractional values, international: 2
  Grouping positions                        : [3, 3, 0]
```

```
Thousands separator                         : " "
Positive sign                               : ""
Positive sign position                      : Before value and symbol
Negative sign                               : "-"
Negative sign position                      : After value and symbol
```

Spain (es_ES):

```
$ LANG=es_ES LC_CTYPE=es_ES LC_ALL=es_ES python locale_env_example.py
```

```
Environment settings:
        LC_ALL = es_ES
        LC_CTYPE = es_ES
        LANG = es_ES
        LANGUAGE =

Locale from environment: ('es_ES', 'ISO8859-1')

Numeric formatting:

  Decimal point     : ","
  Grouping positions : [127]
  Thousands separator: ""

Monetary formatting:

  International currency symbol        : "'EUR '"
  Local currency symbol               : 'Eu'
    Unicode version                     Eu
  Symbol precedes positive value      : 1
  Symbol precedes negative value      : 1
  Decimal point                       : ","
  Digits in fractional values         : 2
  Digits in fractional values, international: 2
  Grouping positions                  : [3, 3, 0]
  Thousands separator                 : "."
  Positive sign                       : ""
  Positive sign position              : Before value and symbol
  Negative sign                       : "-"
  Negative sign position              : Before value and symbol
```

Portugal (pt_PT):

```
$ LANG=pt_PT LC_CTYPE=pt_PT LC_ALL=pt_PT python locale_env_example.py
```

```
Environment settings:
        LC_ALL = pt_PT
        LC_CTYPE = pt_PT
        LANG = pt_PT
        LANGUAGE =

Locale from environment: ('pt_PT', 'ISO8859-1')

Numeric formatting:

  Decimal point        : ","
  Grouping positions : []
  Thousands separator: " "

Monetary formatting:

  International currency symbol              : "'EUR '"
  Local currency symbol                     : 'Eu'
    Unicode version                         Eu
  Symbol precedes positive value            : 0
  Symbol precedes negative value            : 0
  Decimal point                             : "."
  Digits in fractional values               : 2
  Digits in fractional values, international: 2
  Grouping positions                        : [3, 3, 0]
  Thousands separator                       : "."
  Positive sign                             : ""
  Positive sign position                    : Before value and symbol
  Negative sign                             : "-"
  Negative sign position                    : Before value and symbol
```

Poland (pl_PL):

```
$ LANG=pl_PL LC_CTYPE=pl_PL LC_ALL=pl_PL python locale_env_example.py

Environment settings:
        LC_ALL = pl_PL
        LC_CTYPE = pl_PL
        LANG = pl_PL
        LANGUAGE =

Locale from environment: ('pl_PL', 'ISO8859-2')
```

```
Numeric formatting:

  Decimal point       : ","
  Grouping positions : [3, 3, 0]
  Thousands separator: " "

Monetary formatting:

  International currency symbol               : "'PLN '"
  Local currency symbol                       : 'z\xc5\x82'
    Unicode version                           zł
  Symbol precedes positive value             : 1
  Symbol precedes negative value             : 1
  Decimal point                              : ","
  Digits in fractional values                : 2
  Digits in fractional values, international: 2
  Grouping positions                         : [3, 3, 0]
  Thousands separator                        : " "
  Positive sign                              : ""
  Positive sign position                     : After value
  Negative sign                              : "-"
  Negative sign position                     : After value
```

15.2.2 Currency

The earlier example output shows that changing the locale updates the currency symbol setting and the character to separate whole numbers from decimal fractions. This example loops through several different locales to print a positive and negative currency value formatted for each locale.

```
import locale

sample_locales = [ ('USA',      'en_US'),
                   ('France',   'fr_FR'),
                   ('Spain',    'es_ES'),
                   ('Portugal', 'pt_PT'),
                   ('Poland',   'pl_PL'),
                   ]

for name, loc in sample_locales:
    locale.setlocale(locale.LC_ALL, loc)
    print '%20s: %10s  %10s' % (name,
```

```
                              locale.currency(1234.56),
                              locale.currency(-1234.56))
```

The output is this small table.

```
$ python locale_currency_example.py

        USA:    $1234.56    -$1234.56
     France: 1234,56 Eu   1234,56 Eu-
      Spain: Eu 1234,56   -Eu 1234,56
   Portugal: 1234.56 Eu   -1234.56 Eu
     Poland: zł 1234,56   zł 1234,56-
```

15.2.3 Formatting Numbers

Numbers not related to currency are also formatted differently, depending on the locale. In particular, the *grouping* character used to separate large numbers into readable chunks changes.

```
import locale

sample_locales = [ ('USA',      'en_US'),
                   ('France',   'fr_FR'),
                   ('Spain',    'es_ES'),
                   ('Portugal', 'pt_PT'),
                   ('Poland',   'pl_PL'),
                   ]

print '%20s %15s %20s' % ('Locale', 'Integer', 'Float')
for name, loc in sample_locales:
    locale.setlocale(locale.LC_ALL, loc)

    print '%20s' % name,
    print locale.format('%15d', 123456, grouping=True),
    print locale.format('%20.2f', 123456.78, grouping=True)
```

To format numbers without the currency symbol, use `format()` instead of `currency()`.

```
$ python locale_grouping.py

          Locale          Integer                Float
             USA          123,456           123,456.78
```

France	123456	123456,78
Spain	123456	123456,78
Portugal	123456	123456,78
Poland	123 456	123 456,78

15.2.4   Parsing Numbers

Besides generating output in different formats, the `locale` module helps with parsing input. It includes `atoi()` and `atof()` functions for converting the strings to integer and floating-point values based on the locale's numerical formatting conventions.

```
import locale

sample_data = [ ('USA',      'en_US', '1,234.56'),
                ('France',   'fr_FR', '1234,56'),
                ('Spain',    'es_ES', '1234,56'),
                ('Portugal', 'pt_PT', '1234.56'),
                ('Poland',   'pl_PL', '1 234,56'),
                ]

for name, loc, a in sample_data:
    locale.setlocale(locale.LC_ALL, loc)
    f = locale.atof(a)
    print '%20s: %9s => %f' % (name, a, f)
```

The parser recognizes the grouping and decimal separator values of the locale.

```
$ python locale_atof_example.py

     USA:  1,234.56 => 1234.560000
  France:   1234,56 => 1234.560000
   Spain:   1234,56 => 1234.560000
Portugal:   1234.56 => 1234.560000
  Poland:  1 234,56 => 1234.560000
```

15.2.5   Dates and Times

Another important aspect of localization is date and time formatting.

```
import locale
import time
```

```
sample_locales = [ ('USA',      'en_US'),
                   ('France',   'fr_FR'),
                   ('Spain',    'es_ES'),
                   ('Portugal', 'pt_PT'),
                   ('Poland',   'pl_PL'),
                   ]

for name, loc in sample_locales:
    locale.setlocale(locale.LC_ALL, loc)
    format = locale.nl_langinfo(locale.D_T_FMT)
    print '%20s: %s' % (name, time.strftime(format))
```

This example uses the date formatting string for the locale to print the current date and time.

```
$ python locale_date_example.py

     USA: Sun Nov 28 23:53:58 2010
  France: Dim 28 nov 23:53:58 2010
   Spain: dom 28 nov 23:53:58 2010
Portugal: Dom 28 Nov 23:53:58 2010
  Poland: ndz 28 lis 23:53:58 2010
```

See Also:

locale (http://docs.python.org/library/locale.html) The standard library documentation for this module.

gettext (page 899) Message catalogs for translations.

Chapter 16

DEVELOPER TOOLS

Over the course of its lifetime, Python has evolved an extensive ecosystem of modules intended to make the lives of Python developers easier by eliminating the need to build everything from scratch. That same philosophy has been applied to the tools developers use to do their work, even if they are not used in the final version of a program. This chapter covers the modules included with Python to provide facilities for common development tasks such as testing, debugging, and profiling.

The most basic form of help for developers is the documentation for code they are using. The `pydoc` module generates formatted reference documentation from the docstrings included in the source code for any importable module.

Python includes two testing frameworks for automatically exercising code and verifying that it works correctly. `doctest` extracts test scenarios from examples included in documentation, either inside the source or as stand-alone files. `unittest` is a full-featured automated testing framework with support for fixtures, predefined test suites, and test discovery.

The `trace` module monitors the way Python executes a program, producing a report showing how many times each line was run. That information can be used to find code paths that are not being tested by an automated test suite and to study the function call graph to find dependencies between modules.

Writing and running tests will uncover problems in most programs. Python helps make debugging easier, since in most cases, unhandled errors are printed to the console as tracebacks. When a program is not running in a text console environment, `traceback` can be used to prepare similar output for a log file or message dialog. For situations where a standard traceback does not provide enough information, use `cgitb` to see details like local variable settings at each level of the stack and source context. `cgitb` can also format tracebacks in HTML, for reporting errors in web applications.

Once the location of a problem is identified, stepping through the code using the interactive debugger in the `pdb` module can make it easier to fix by showing what path through the code was followed to get to the error situation and experimenting with changes using live objects and code.

After a program is tested and debugged so that it works correctly, the next step is to work on performance. Using `profile` and `timeit`, a developer can measure the speed of a program and find the slow parts so they can be isolated and improved.

Python programs are run by giving the interpreter a byte-compiled version of the original program source. The byte-compiled versions can be created on the fly or once when the program is packaged. The `compileall` module exposes the interface installation programs and packaging tools used to create files containing the byte code for a module. It can be used in a development environment to make sure a file does not have any syntax errors and to build the byte-compiled files to package when the program is released.

At the source code level, the `pyclbr` module provides a class browser that a text editor or other program can use to scan Python source for interesting symbols, such as functions and classes, without importing the code and potentially triggering side-effects.

16.1 pydoc—Online Help for Modules

Purpose Generates help for Python modules and classes from the code.
Python Version 2.1 and later

The `pydoc` module imports a Python module and uses the contents to generate help text at runtime. The output includes docstrings for any objects that have them, and all the classes, methods, and functions of the module are described.

16.1.1 Plain-Text Help

Running

```
$ pydoc atexit
```

produces plain-text help on the console, using a pager program if one is configured.

16.1.2 HTML Help

`pydoc` will also generate HTML output, either writing a static file to a local directory or starting a web server to browse documentation online.

```
$ pydoc -w atexit
```

Creates `atexit.html` in the current directory.

```
$ pydoc -p 5000
```

Starts a web server listening at `http://localhost:5000/`. The server generates documentation on the fly as you browse.

16.1.3   Interactive Help

`pydoc` also adds a function `help()` to the __builtins__ so the same information can be accessed from the Python interpreter prompt.

```
$ python

Python 2.7 (r27:82508, Jul  3 2010, 21:12:11)
[GCC 4.0.1 (Apple Inc. build 5493)] on darwin
Type "help", "copyright", "credits" or "license" for more
information.
>>> help('atexit')
Help on module atexit:

NAME
    atexit

...
```

See Also:
pydoc (http://docs.python.org/library/pydoc.html) The standard library documentation for this module.
inspect (page 1200) The `inspect` module can be used to retrieve the docstrings for an object programmatically.

16.2   doctest—Testing through Documentation

Purpose Write automated tests as part of the documentation for a module.
Python Version 2.1 and later

`doctest` tests source code by running examples embedded in the documentation and verifying that they produce the expected results. It works by parsing the help text to find examples, running them, and then comparing the output text against the expected value. Many developers find `doctest` easier to use than `unittest` because, in its simplest form, there is no API to learn before using it. However, as the examples become more complex, the lack of fixture management can make writing `doctest` tests more cumbersome than using `unittest`.

16.2.1   Getting Started

The first step to setting up doctests is to use the interactive interpreter to create examples and then copy and paste them into the docstrings in the module. Here, `my_function()` has two examples given.

```
def my_function(a, b):
    """
    >>> my_function(2, 3)
    6
    >>> my_function('a', 3)
    'aaa'
    """
    return a * b
```

To run the tests, use `doctest` as the main program via the `-m` option. Usually, no output is produced while the tests are running, so the next example includes the `-v` option to make the output more verbose.

```
$ python -m doctest -v doctest_simple.py

Trying:
    my_function(2, 3)
Expecting:
    6
ok
Trying:
    my_function('a', 3)
Expecting:
    'aaa'
ok
1 items had no tests:
    doctest_simple
1 items passed all tests:
    2 tests in doctest_simple.my_function
```

```
2 tests in 2 items.
2 passed and 0 failed.
Test passed.
```

Examples cannot usually stand on their own as explanations of a function, so `doctest` also allows for surrounding text. It looks for lines beginning with the interpreter prompt (>>>) to find the beginning of a test case, and the case is ended by a blank line or by the next interpreter prompt. Intervening text is ignored and can have any format as long as it does not look like a test case.

```python
def my_function(a, b):
    """Returns a * b.

    Works with numbers:

    >>> my_function(2, 3)
    6

    and strings:

    >>> my_function('a', 3)
    'aaa'
    """
    return a * b
```

The surrounding text in the updated docstring makes it more useful to a human reader. Because it is ignored by `doctest`, the results are the same.

```
$ python -m doctest -v doctest_simple_with_docs.py

Trying:
    my_function(2, 3)
Expecting:
    6
ok
Trying:
    my_function('a', 3)
Expecting:
    'aaa'
ok
1 items had no tests:
    doctest_simple_with_docs
```

```
1 items passed all tests:
   2 tests in doctest_simple_with_docs.my_function
2 tests in 2 items.
2 passed and 0 failed.
Test passed.
```

16.2.2   Handling Unpredictable Output

There are other cases where the exact output may not be predictable, but should still be testable. For example, local date and time values and object ids change on every test run, the default precision used in the representation of floating-point values depends on compiler options, and object string representations may not be deterministic. Although these conditions cannot be controlled, there are techniques for dealing with them.

For example, in CPython, object identifiers are based on the memory address of the data structure holding the object.

```
class MyClass(object):
    pass


def unpredictable(obj):
    """Returns a new list containing obj.

    >>> unpredictable(MyClass())
    [<doctest_unpredictable.MyClass object at 0x10055a2d0>]
    """
    return [obj]
```

These id values change each time a program runs, because the values are loaded into a different part of memory.

```
$ python -m doctest -v doctest_unpredictable.py

Trying:
unpredictable(MyClass())
Expecting:
[<doctest_unpredictable.MyClass object at 0x10055a2d0>]
**************************************************************
File "doctest_unpredictable.py", line 16, in doctest_unpredicta
ble.unpredictable
Failed example:
unpredictable(MyClass())
```

```
Expected:
[<doctest_unpredictable.MyClass object at 0x10055a2d0>]
Got:
[<doctest_unpredictable.MyClass object at 0x100ea3490>]
2 items had no tests:
doctest_unpredictable
doctest_unpredictable.MyClass
***********************************************************
1 items had failures:
1 of   1 in doctest_unpredictable.unpredictable
1 tests in 3 items.
0 passed and 1 failed.
***Test Failed*** 1 failures.
```

When the tests include values that are likely to change in unpredictable ways, and when the actual value is not important to the test results, use the ELLIPSIS option to tell doctest to ignore portions of the verification value.

```
class MyClass(object):
    pass


def unpredictable(obj):
    """Returns a new list containing obj.

    >>> unpredictable(MyClass()) #doctest: +ELLIPSIS
    [<doctest_ellipsis.MyClass object at 0x...>]
    """
    return [obj]
```

The comment after the call to unpredictable() (#doctest: +ELLIPSIS) tells doctest to turn on the ELLIPSIS option for that test. The . . . replaces the memory address in the object id, so that portion of the expected value is ignored. The actual output matches and the test passes.

```
$ python -m doctest -v doctest_ellipsis.py

Trying:
    unpredictable(MyClass()) #doctest: +ELLIPSIS
Expecting:
    [<doctest_ellipsis.MyClass object at 0x...>]
ok
```

```
2 items had no tests:
    doctest_ellipsis
    doctest_ellipsis.MyClass
1 items passed all tests:
    1 tests in doctest_ellipsis.unpredictable
1 tests in 3 items.
1 passed and 0 failed.
Test passed.
```

There are cases where the unpredictable value cannot be ignored, because that would make the test incomplete or inaccurate. For example, simple tests quickly become more complex when dealing with data types whose string representations are inconsistent. The string form of a dictionary, for example, may change based on the order in which the keys are added.

```python
keys = [ 'a', 'aa', 'aaa' ]

d1 = dict( (k,len(k)) for k in keys )
d2 = dict( (k,len(k)) for k in reversed(keys) )

print 'd1:', d1
print 'd2:', d2
print 'd1 == d2:', d1 == d2

s1 = set(keys)
s2 = set(reversed(keys))

print
print 's1:', s1
print 's2:', s2
print 's1 == s2:', s1 == s2
```

Because of cache collision, the internal key list order is different for the two dictionaries, even though they contain the same values and are considered to be equal. Sets use the same hashing algorithm and exhibit the same behavior.

```
$ python doctest_hashed_values.py

d1: {'a': 1, 'aa': 2, 'aaa': 3}
d2: {'aa': 2, 'a': 1, 'aaa': 3}
d1 == d2: True
```

```
s1: set(['a', 'aa', 'aaa'])
s2: set(['aa', 'a', 'aaa'])
s1 == s2: True
```

The best way to deal with these potential discrepancies is to create tests that produce values that are not likely to change. In the case of dictionaries and sets, that might mean looking for specific keys individually, generating a sorted list of the contents of the data structure, or comparing against a literal value for equality instead of depending on the string representation.

```
def group_by_length(words):
    """Returns a dictionary grouping words into sets by length.

    >>> grouped = group_by_length([ 'python', 'module', 'of',
    ... 'the', 'week' ])
    >>> grouped == { 2:set(['of']),
    ...              3:set(['the']),
    ...              4:set(['week']),
    ...              6:set(['python', 'module']),
    ...              }
    True

    """
    d = {}
    for word in words:
        s = d.setdefault(len(word), set())
        s.add(word)
    return d
```

The single example is actually interpreted as two separate tests, with the first expecting no console output and the second expecting the Boolean result of the comparison operation.

```
$ python -m doctest -v doctest_hashed_values_tests.py

Trying:
    grouped = group_by_length([ 'python', 'module', 'of',
    'the', 'week' ])
Expecting nothing
ok
```

```
Trying:
    grouped == {  2:set(['of']),
                  3:set(['the']),
                  4:set(['week']),
                  6:set(['python', 'module']),
                  }
Expecting:
    True
ok
1 items had no tests:
    doctest_hashed_values_tests
1 items passed all tests:
    2 tests in doctest_hashed_values_tests.group_by_length
2 tests in 2 items.
2 passed and 0 failed.
Test passed.
```

16.2.3 Tracebacks

Tracebacks are a special case of changing data. Since the paths in a traceback depend on the location where a module is installed on the file system on a given system, it would be impossible to write portable tests if they were treated the same as other output.

```
def this_raises():
    """This function always raises an exception.

    >>> this_raises()
    Traceback (most recent call last):
      File "<stdin>", line 1, in <module>
      File "/no/such/path/doctest_tracebacks.py", line 14, in
      this_raises
        raise RuntimeError('here is the error')
    RuntimeError: here is the error
    """
    raise RuntimeError('here is the error')
```

doctest makes a special effort to recognize tracebacks and ignore the parts that might change from system to system.

```
$ python -m doctest -v doctest_tracebacks.py

Trying:
    this_raises()
```

```
Expecting:
    Traceback (most recent call last):
      File "<stdin>", line 1, in <module>
      File "/no/such/path/doctest_tracebacks.py", line 14, in
      this_raises
        raise RuntimeError('here is the error')
    RuntimeError: here is the error
ok
1 items had no tests:
    doctest_tracebacks
1 items passed all tests:
    1 tests in doctest_tracebacks.this_raises
1 tests in 2 items.
1 passed and 0 failed.
Test passed.
```

In fact, the entire body of the traceback is ignored and can be omitted.

```
def this_raises():
    """This function always raises an exception.

    >>> this_raises()
    Traceback (most recent call last):
    RuntimeError: here is the error
    """
    raise RuntimeError('here is the error')
```

When `doctest` sees a traceback header line (either "`Traceback (most recent call last):`" or "`Traceback (innermost last):`", depending on the version of Python being used), it skips ahead to find the exception type and message, ignoring the intervening lines entirely.

```
$ python -m doctest -v doctest_tracebacks_no_body.py

Trying:
    this_raises()
Expecting:
    Traceback (most recent call last):
    RuntimeError: here is the error
ok
1 items had no tests:
    doctest_tracebacks_no_body
```

```
1 items passed all tests:
   1 tests in doctest_tracebacks_no_body.this_raises
1 tests in 2 items.
1 passed and 0 failed.
Test passed.
```

16.2.4   Working around Whitespace

In real-world applications, output usually includes whitespace such as blank lines, tabs, and extra spacing to make it more readable. Blank lines, in particular, cause issues with `doctest` because they are used to delimit tests.

```python
def double_space(lines):
    """Prints a list of lines double-spaced.

    >>> double_space(['Line one.', 'Line two.'])
    Line one.

    Line two.

    """
    for l in lines:
        print l
        print
    return
```

`double_space()` takes a list of input lines and prints them double-spaced with blank lines between them.

```
$ python -m doctest doctest_blankline_fail.py


**************************************************************
File "doctest_blankline_fail.py", line 13, in doctest_blankline
_fail.double_space
Failed example:
double_space(['Line one.', 'Line two.'])
Expected:
Line one.
Got:
Line one.
<BLANKLINE>
```

```
Line two.
<BLANKLINE>
**********************************************************************
1 items had failures:
1 of   1 in doctest_blankline_fail.double_space
***Test Failed*** 1 failures.
```

The test fails, because it interprets the blank line after the line containing `Line one.` in the docstring as the end of the sample output. To match the blank lines, replace them in the sample input with the string `<BLANKLINE>`.

```python
def double_space(lines):
    """Prints a list of lines double-spaced.

    >>> double_space(['Line one.', 'Line two.'])
    Line one.
    <BLANKLINE>
    Line two.
    <BLANKLINE>
    """
    for l in lines:
        print l
        print
    return
```

`doctest` replaces actual blank lines with the same literal before performing the comparison, so now the actual and expected values match and the test passes.

```
$ python -m doctest -v doctest_blankline.py

Trying:
    double_space(['Line one.', 'Line two.'])
Expecting:
    Line one.
    <BLANKLINE>
    Line two.
    <BLANKLINE>
ok
1 items had no tests:
    doctest_blankline
```

```
1 items passed all tests:
   1 tests in doctest_blankline.double_space
1 tests in 2 items.
1 passed and 0 failed.
Test passed.
```

Another pitfall of using text comparisons for tests is that embedded whitespace can also cause tricky problems with tests. This example has a single extra space after the 6.

```
def my_function(a, b):
    """
    >>> my_function(2, 3)
    6
    >>> my_function('a', 3)
    'aaa'
    """
    return a * b
```

Extra spaces can find their way into code via copy-and-paste errors, but since they come at the end of the line, they can go unnoticed in the source file and be invisible in the test failure report as well.

```
$ python -m doctest -v doctest_extra_space.py

Trying:
my_function(2, 3)
Expecting:
6
**********************************************************************
File "doctest_extra_space.py", line 12, in doctest_extra_space.
my_function
Failed example:
my_function(2, 3)
Expected:
6
Got:
6
Trying:
my_function('a', 3)
```

```
Expecting:
    'aaa'
ok
1 items had no tests:
    doctest_extra_space
**********************************************************
1 items had failures:
    1 of   2 in doctest_extra_space.my_function
2 tests in 2 items.
1 passed and 1 failed.
***Test Failed*** 1 failures.
```

Using one of the diff-based reporting options, such as REPORT_NDIFF, shows the difference between the actual and expected values with more detail, and the extra space becomes visible.

```
def my_function(a, b):
    """
    >>> my_function(2, 3) #doctest: +REPORT_NDIFF
    6
    >>> my_function('a', 3)
    'aaa'
    """
    return a * b
```

Unified (REPORT_UDIFF) and context (REPORT_CDIFF) diffs are also available, for output where those formats are more readable.

```
$ python -m doctest -v doctest_ndiff.py

Trying:
    my_function(2, 3) #doctest: +REPORT_NDIFF
Expecting:
    6
**********************************************************
File "doctest_ndiff.py", line 12, in doctest_ndiff.my_function
Failed example:
    my_function(2, 3) #doctest: +REPORT_NDIFF
Differences (ndiff with -expected +actual):
    - 6
    ?  -
    + 6
```

```
Trying:
    my_function('a', 3)
Expecting:
    'aaa'
ok
1 items had no tests:
    doctest_ndiff
****************************************************************
1 items had failures:
    1 of   2 in doctest_ndiff.my_function
2 tests in 2 items.
1 passed and 1 failed.
***Test Failed*** 1 failures.
```

There are cases where it is beneficial to add extra whitespace in the sample output for the test and have `doctest` ignore it. For example, data structures can be easier to read when spread across several lines, even if their representation would fit on a single line.

```
def my_function(a, b):
    """Returns a * b.

    >>> my_function(['A', 'B'], 3) #doctest: +NORMALIZE_WHITESPACE
    ['A', 'B',
     'A', 'B',
     'A', 'B',]

    This does not match because of the extra space after the [ in
    the list.

    >>> my_function(['A', 'B'], 2) #doctest: +NORMALIZE_WHITESPACE
    [ 'A', 'B',
      'A', 'B', ]
    """
    return a * b
```

When `NORMALIZE_WHITESPACE` is turned on, any whitespace in the actual and expected values is considered a match. Whitespace cannot be added to the expected value where none exists in the output, but the length of the whitespace sequence and actual whitespace characters do not need to match. The first test example gets this rule correct and passes, even though there are extra spaces and newlines. The second has extra whitespace after ["and before"], so it fails.

```
$ python -m doctest -v doctest_normalize_whitespace.py

Trying:
my_function(['A', 'B'], 3) #doctest: +NORMALIZE_WHITESPACE
Expecting:
['A', 'B',
'A', 'B',
'A', 'B',]
**********************************************************************
File "doctest_normalize_whitespace.py", line 13, in doctest_nor
malize_whitespace.my_function
Failed example:
my_function(['A', 'B'], 3) #doctest: +NORMALIZE_WHITESPACE
Expected:
['A', 'B',
'A', 'B',
'A', 'B',]
Got:
['A', 'B', 'A', 'B', 'A', 'B']
Trying:
my_function(['A', 'B'], 2) #doctest: +NORMALIZE_WHITESPACE
Expecting:
[ 'A', 'B',
'A', 'B', ]
**********************************************************************
File "doctest_normalize_whitespace.py", line 21, in doctest_nor
malize_whitespace.my_function
Failed example:
my_function(['A', 'B'], 2) #doctest: +NORMALIZE_WHITESPACE
Expected:
[ 'A', 'B',
'A', 'B', ]
Got:
['A', 'B', 'A', 'B']
1 items had no tests:
doctest_normalize_whitespace
**********************************************************************
1 items had failures:
2 of   2 in doctest_normalize_whitespace.my_function
2 tests in 2 items.
0 passed and 2 failed.
***Test Failed*** 2 failures.
```

16.2.5   Test Locations

All the tests in the examples so far have been written in the docstrings of the functions they are testing. That is convenient for users who examine the docstrings for help using the function (especially with `pydoc`), but `doctest` looks for tests in other places, too. The obvious location for additional tests is in the docstrings elsewhere in the module.

```python
#!/usr/bin/env python
# encoding: utf-8

"""Tests can appear in any docstring within the module.

Module-level tests cross class and function boundaries.

>>> A('a') == B('b')
False
"""


class A(object):
    """Simple class.

    >>> A('instance_name').name
    'instance_name'
    """
    def __init__(self, name):
        self.name = name
    def method(self):
        """Returns an unusual value.

        >>> A('name').method()
        'eman'
        """
        return ''.join(reversed(list(self.name)))

class B(A):
    """Another simple class.

    >>> B('different_name').name
    'different_name'
    """
```

Docstrings at the module, class, and function levels can all contain tests.

```
$ python -m doctest -v doctest_docstrings.py

Trying:
    A('a') == B('b')
Expecting:
    False
ok
Trying:
    A('instance_name').name
Expecting:
    'instance_name'
ok
Trying:
    A('name').method()
Expecting:
    'eman'
ok
Trying:
    B('different_name').name
Expecting:
    'different_name'
ok
1 items had no tests:
    doctest_docstrings.A.__init__
4 items passed all tests:
   1 tests in doctest_docstrings
   1 tests in doctest_docstrings.A
   1 tests in doctest_docstrings.A.method
   1 tests in doctest_docstrings.B
4 tests in 5 items.
4 passed and 0 failed.
Test passed.
```

There are cases where tests exist for a module that should be included with the source code but not in the help text for a module, so they need to be placed somewhere other than the docstrings. doctest also looks for a module-level variable called __test__ and uses it to locate other tests. The value of __test__ should be a dictionary that maps test set names (as strings) to strings, modules, classes, or functions.

```
import doctest_private_tests_external

__test__ = {
    'numbers':"""
```

```
>>> my_function(2, 3)
6

>>> my_function(2.0, 3)
6.0
""",

    'strings':"""
>>> my_function('a', 3)
'aaa'

>>> my_function(3, 'a')
'aaa'
""",

    'external':doctest_private_tests_external,

    }

def my_function(a, b):
    """Returns a * b
    """
    return a * b
```

If the value associated with a key is a string, it is treated as a docstring and scanned for tests. If the value is a class or function, `doctest` searches them recursively for docstrings, which are then scanned for tests. In this example, the module `doctest_private_tests_external` has a single test in its docstring.

```
#!/usr/bin/env python
# encoding: utf-8
#
# Copyright (c) 2010 Doug Hellmann.  All rights reserved.
#
"""External tests associated with doctest_private_tests.py.

>>> my_function(['A', 'B', 'C'], 2)
['A', 'B', 'C', 'A', 'B', 'C']
"""
```

After scanning the example file, `doctest` finds a total of five tests to run.

```
$ python -m doctest -v doctest_private_tests.py

Trying:
    my_function(['A', 'B', 'C'], 2)
Expecting:
    ['A', 'B', 'C', 'A', 'B', 'C']
ok
Trying:
    my_function(2, 3)
Expecting:
    6
ok
Trying:
    my_function(2.0, 3)
Expecting:
    6.0
ok
Trying:
    my_function('a', 3)
Expecting:
    'aaa'
ok
Trying:
    my_function(3, 'a')
Expecting:
    'aaa'
ok
2 items had no tests:
    doctest_private_tests
    doctest_private_tests.my_function
3 items passed all tests:
    1 tests in doctest_private_tests.__test__.external
    2 tests in doctest_private_tests.__test__.numbers
    2 tests in doctest_private_tests.__test__.strings
5 tests in 5 items.
5 passed and 0 failed.
Test passed.
```

16.2.6 External Documentation

Mixing tests in with regular code is not the only way to use doctest. Examples embedded in external project documentation files, such as reStructuredText files, can be used as well.

```
def my_function(a, b):
    """Returns a*b
    """
    return a * b
```

The help for this sample module is saved to a separate file, `doctest_in_help.rst`. The examples illustrating how to use the module are included with the help text, and `doctest` can be used to find and run them.

```
=================================
 How to Use doctest_in_help.py
=================================

This library is very simple, since it only has one function called
``my_function()``.

Numbers
=======

``my_function()`` returns the product of its arguments.  For numbers,
that value is equivalent to using the ``*`` operator.

::

    >>> from doctest_in_help import my_function
    >>> my_function(2, 3)
    6

It also works with floating-point values.

::

    >>> my_function(2.0, 3)
    6.0

Non-Numbers
===========

Because ``*`` is also defined on data types other than numbers,
``my_function()`` works just as well if one of the arguments is a
string, a list, or a tuple.
```

```
::

    >>> my_function('a', 3)
    'aaa'

    >>> my_function(['A', 'B', 'C'], 2)
    ['A', 'B', 'C', 'A', 'B', 'C']
```

The tests in the text file can be run from the command line, just as with the Python source modules.

```
$ python -m doctest -v doctest_in_help.rst

Trying:
    from doctest_in_help import my_function
Expecting nothing
ok
Trying:
    my_function(2, 3)
Expecting:
    6
ok
Trying:
    my_function(2.0, 3)
Expecting:
    6.0
ok
Trying:
    my_function('a', 3)
Expecting:
    'aaa'
ok
Trying:
    my_function(['A', 'B', 'C'], 2)
Expecting:
    ['A', 'B', 'C', 'A', 'B', 'C']
ok
1 items passed all tests:
   5 tests in doctest_in_help.rst
5 tests in 1 items.
5 passed and 0 failed.
Test passed.
```

Normally, `doctest` sets up the test execution environment to include the members of the module being tested, so the tests do not need to import the module explicitly. In this case, however, the tests are not defined in a Python module and `doctest` does not know how to set up the global namespace, so the examples need to do the import work themselves. All the tests in a given file share the same execution context, so importing the module once at the top of the file is enough.

16.2.7 Running Tests

The previous examples all use the command-line test-runner built into `doctest`. It is easy and convenient for a single module, but it will quickly become tedious as a package spreads out into multiple files. There are several alternative approaches.

By Module

The instructions to run `doctest` against the source can be included at the bottom of modules.

```python
def my_function(a, b):
    """
    >>> my_function(2, 3)
    6
    >>> my_function('a', 3)
    'aaa'
    """
    return a * b


if __name__ == '__main__':
    import doctest
    doctest.testmod()
```

Calling `testmod()` only if the current module name is __main__ ensures that the tests are only run when the module is invoked as a main program.

```
$ python doctest_testmod.py -v

Trying:
    my_function(2, 3)
Expecting:
    6
ok
Trying:
    my_function('a', 3)
```

```
Expecting:
    'aaa'
ok
1 items had no tests:
    __main__
1 items passed all tests:
   2 tests in __main__.my_function
2 tests in 2 items.
2 passed and 0 failed.
Test passed.
```

The first argument to `testmod()` is a module containing code to be scanned for tests. A separate test script can use this feature to import the real code and run the tests in each module one after another.

```
import doctest_simple

if __name__ == '__main__':
    import doctest
    doctest.testmod(doctest_simple)
```

A test suite can be constructed for the project by importing each module and running its tests.

```
$ python doctest_testmod_other_module.py -v

Trying:
    my_function(2, 3)
Expecting:
    6
ok
Trying:
    my_function('a', 3)
Expecting:
    'aaa'
ok
1 items had no tests:
    doctest_simple
1 items passed all tests:
   2 tests in doctest_simple.my_function
2 tests in 2 items.
2 passed and 0 failed.
Test passed.
```

By File

testfile() works in a way similar to testmod(), allowing the tests to be invoked explicitly in an external file from within the test program.

```
import doctest

if __name__ == '__main__':
    doctest.testfile('doctest_in_help.rst')
```

Both testmod() and testfile() include optional parameters to control the behavior of the tests through the doctest options. Refer to the standard library documentation for more details about those features. Most of the time, they are not needed.

```
$ python doctest_testfile.py -v

Trying:
    from doctest_in_help import my_function
Expecting nothing
ok
Trying:
    my_function(2, 3)
Expecting:
    6
ok
Trying:
    my_function(2.0, 3)
Expecting:
    6.0
ok
Trying:
    my_function('a', 3)
Expecting:
    'aaa'
ok
Trying:
    my_function(['A', 'B', 'C'], 2)
Expecting:
    ['A', 'B', 'C', 'A', 'B', 'C']
ok
1 items passed all tests:
   5 tests in doctest_in_help.rst
5 tests in 1 items.
```

```
5 passed and 0 failed.
Test passed.
```

Unittest Suite

When both `unittest` and `doctest` are used for testing the same code in different situations, the `unittest` integration in `doctest` can be used to run the tests together. Two classes, `DocTestSuite` and `DocFileSuite`, create test suites compatible with the test-runner API of `unittest`.

```
import doctest
import unittest

import doctest_simple

suite = unittest.TestSuite()
suite.addTest(doctest.DocTestSuite(doctest_simple))
suite.addTest(doctest.DocFileSuite('doctest_in_help.rst'))

runner = unittest.TextTestRunner(verbosity=2)
runner.run(suite)
```

The tests from each source are collapsed into a single outcome, instead of being reported individually.

```
$ python doctest_unittest.py

my_function (doctest_simple)
Doctest: doctest_simple.my_function ... ok
doctest_in_help.rst
Doctest: doctest_in_help.rst ... ok

-----------------------------------------------------------
Ran 2 tests in 0.006s

OK
```

16.2.8   Test Context

The execution context created by `doctest` as it runs tests contains a copy of the module-level globals for the test module. Each test source (function, class, module) has its own set of global values to isolate the tests from each other somewhat, so they are less likely to interfere with one another.

```python
class TestGlobals(object):

    def one(self):
        """
        >>> var = 'value'
        >>> 'var' in globals()
        True
        """

    def two(self):
        """
        >>> 'var' in globals()
        False
        """
```

`TestGlobals` has two methods: `one()` and `two()`. The tests in the docstring for `one()` set a global variable, and the test for `two()` looks for it (expecting not to find it).

```
$ python -m doctest -v doctest_test_globals.py

Trying:
    var = 'value'
Expecting nothing
ok
Trying:
    'var' in globals()
Expecting:
    True
ok
Trying:
    'var' in globals()
Expecting:
    False
ok
2 items had no tests:
    doctest_test_globals
    doctest_test_globals.TestGlobals
2 items passed all tests:
   2 tests in doctest_test_globals.TestGlobals.one
```

```
    1 tests in doctest_test_globals.TestGlobals.two
3 tests in 4 items.
3 passed and 0 failed.
Test passed.
```

That does not mean the tests *cannot* interfere with each other, though, if they change the contents of mutable variables defined in the module.

```
_module_data = {}

class TestGlobals(object):

    def one(self):
        """
        >>> TestGlobals().one()
        >>> 'var' in _module_data
        True
        """
        _module_data['var'] = 'value'

    def two(self):
        """
        >>> 'var' in _module_data
        False
        """
```

The module variable `_module_data` is changed by the tests for `one()`, causing the test for `two()` to fail.

```
$ python -m doctest -v doctest_mutable_globals.py

Trying:
TestGlobals().one()
Expecting nothing
ok
Trying:
'var' in _module_data
Expecting:
True
ok
Trying:
'var' in _module_data
```

```
Expecting:
False
********************************************************************
File "doctest_mutable_globals.py", line 24, in doctest_mutable_
globals.TestGlobals.two
Failed example:
'var' in _module_data
Expected:
False
Got:
True
2 items had no tests:
doctest_mutable_globals
doctest_mutable_globals.TestGlobals
1 items passed all tests:
2 tests in doctest_mutable_globals.TestGlobals.one
********************************************************************
1 items had failures:
1 of   1 in doctest_mutable_globals.TestGlobals.two
3 tests in 4 items.
2 passed and 1 failed.
***Test Failed*** 1 failures.
```

If global values are needed for the tests, to parameterize them for an environment for example, values can be passed to `testmod()` and `testfile()` to have the context set up using data controlled by the caller.

See Also:

doctest (http://docs.python.org/library/doctest.html) The standard library documentation for this module.

The Mighty Dictionary (http://blip.tv/file/3332763) Presentation by Brandon Rhodes at PyCon 2010 about the internal operations of the `dict`.

difflib (page 61) Python's sequence difference computation library, used to produce the ndiff output.

Sphinx (http://sphinx.pocoo.org/) As well as being the documentation processing tool for Python's standard library, Sphinx has been adopted by many third-party projects because it is easy to use and produces clean output in several digital and print formats. Sphinx includes an extension for running doctests as it processes documentation source files, so the examples are always accurate.

nose (http://somethingaboutorange.com/mrl/projects/nose/) Third-party test runner with `doctest` support.

py.test (http://codespeak.net/py/dist/test/) Third-party test runner with `doctest` support.

Manuel (http://packages.python.org/manuel/) Third-party documentation-based test runner with more advanced test-case extraction and integration with Sphinx.

16.3   unittest—Automated Testing Framework

Purpose Automated testing framework.
Python Version 2.1 and later

Python's `unittest` module, sometimes called PyUnit, is based on the XUnit framework design by Kent Beck and Erich Gamma. The same pattern is repeated in many other languages, including C, Perl, Java, and Smalltalk. The framework implemented by `unittest` supports fixtures, test suites, and a test runner to enable automated testing.

16.3.1   Basic Test Structure

Tests, as defined by `unittest`, have two parts: code to manage test dependencies (called "fixtures") and the test itself. Individual tests are created by subclassing `Test-Case` and overriding or adding appropriate methods. For example,

```
import unittest

class SimplisticTest(unittest.TestCase):

    def test(self):
        self.failUnless(True)

if __name__ == '__main__':
    unittest.main()
```

In this case, the `SimplisticTest` has a single `test()` method, which would fail if True is ever False.

16.3.2   Running Tests

The easiest way to run unittest tests is to include

```
if __name__ == '__main__':
    unittest.main()
```

at the bottom of each test file, and then simply run the script directly from the command
line.

```
$ python unittest_simple.py

.
----------------------------------------------------------------------
Ran 1 test in 0.000s

OK
```

This abbreviated output includes the amount of time the tests took, along with a
status indicator for each test (the "." on the first line of output means that a test passed).
For more detailed test results, include the –v option:

```
$ python unittest_simple.py -v

test (__main__.SimplisticTest) ... ok

----------------------------------------------------------------------
Ran 1 test in 0.000s

OK
```

16.3.3   Test Outcomes

Tests have three possible outcomes, described in Table 16.1.

There is no explicit way to cause a test to "pass," so a test's status depends on the
presence (or absence) of an exception.

```
import unittest

class OutcomesTest(unittest.TestCase):
```

Table 16.1. Test Case Outcomes

Outcome	Description
ok	The test passes.
FAIL	The test does not pass and raises an AssertionError exception.
ERROR	The test raises any exception other than AssertionError.

```
    def testPass(self):
        return

    def testFail(self):
        self.failIf(True)

    def testError(self):
        raise RuntimeError('Test error!')

if __name__ == '__main__':
    unittest.main()
```

When a test fails or generates an error, the traceback is included in the output.

```
$ python unittest_outcomes.py

EF.
======================================================================
ERROR: testError (__main__.OutcomesTest)
----------------------------------------------------------------------
Traceback (most recent call last):
  File "unittest_outcomes.py", line 42, in testError
    raise RuntimeError('Test error!')
RuntimeError: Test error!


======================================================================
FAIL: testFail (__main__.OutcomesTest)
----------------------------------------------------------------------
Traceback (most recent call last):
  File "unittest_outcomes.py", line 39, in testFail
    self.failIf(True)
AssertionError: True is not False


----------------------------------------------------------------------
Ran 3 tests in 0.001s

FAILED (failures=1, errors=1)
```

In the previous example, testFail() fails and the traceback shows the line with the failure code. It is up to the person reading the test output to look at the code to figure out the meaning of the failed test, though.

```
import unittest

class FailureMessageTest(unittest.TestCase):

    def testFail(self):
        self.failIf(True, 'failure message goes here')

if __name__ == '__main__':
    unittest.main()
```

To make it easier to understand the nature of a test failure, the `fail*()` and `assert*()` methods all accept an argument *msg*, which can be used to produce a more detailed error message.

```
$ python unittest_failwithmessage.py -v

testFail (__main__.FailureMessageTest) ... FAIL

======================================================================
FAIL: testFail (__main__.FailureMessageTest)
----------------------------------------------------------------------
Traceback (most recent call last):
  File "unittest_failwithmessage.py", line 36, in testFail
    self.failIf(True, 'failure message goes here')
AssertionError: failure message goes here


----------------------------------------------------------------------
Ran 1 test in 0.000s

FAILED (failures=1)
```

16.3.4   Asserting Truth

Most tests assert the truth of some condition. There are a few different ways to write truth-checking tests, depending on the perspective of the test author and the desired outcome of the code being tested.

```
import unittest

class TruthTest(unittest.TestCase):

    def testFailUnless(self):
        self.failUnless(True)
```

```
    def testAssertTrue(self):
        self.assertTrue(True)

    def testFailIf(self):
        self.failIf(False)

    def testAssertFalse(self):
        self.assertFalse(False)

if __name__ == '__main__':
    unittest.main()
```

If the code produces a value that can be evaluated as true, the methods failUnless() and assertTrue() should be used. If the code produces a false value, the methods failIf() and assertFalse() make more sense.

```
$ python unittest_truth.py -v

testAssertFalse (__main__.TruthTest) ... ok
testAssertTrue (__main__.TruthTest) ... ok
testFailIf (__main__.TruthTest) ... ok
testFailUnless (__main__.TruthTest) ... ok

----------------------------------------------------------------
Ran 4 tests in 0.000s

OK
```

16.3.5   Testing Equality

As a special case, unittest includes methods for testing the equality of two values.

```
import unittest

class EqualityTest(unittest.TestCase):

    def testExpectEqual(self):
        self.failUnlessEqual(1, 3-2)

    def testExpectEqualFails(self):
        self.failUnlessEqual(2, 3-2)
```

```
    def testExpectNotEqual(self):
        self.failIfEqual(2, 3-2)

    def testExpectNotEqualFails(self):
        self.failIfEqual(1, 3-2)

if __name__ == '__main__':
    unittest.main()
```

When they fail, these special test methods produce error messages including the values being compared.

```
$ python unittest_equality.py -v

testExpectEqual (__main__.EqualityTest) ... ok
testExpectEqualFails (__main__.EqualityTest) ... FAIL
testExpectNotEqual (__main__.EqualityTest) ... ok
testExpectNotEqualFails (__main__.EqualityTest) ... FAIL


======================================================================
FAIL: testExpectEqualFails (__main__.EqualityTest)
----------------------------------------------------------------------
Traceback (most recent call last):
  File "unittest_equality.py", line 39, in testExpectEqualFails
    self.failUnlessEqual(2, 3-2)
AssertionError: 2 != 1


======================================================================
FAIL: testExpectNotEqualFails (__main__.EqualityTest)
----------------------------------------------------------------------
Traceback (most recent call last):
  File "unittest_equality.py", line 45, in testExpectNotEqualFails
    self.failIfEqual(1, 3-2)
AssertionError: 1 == 1


----------------------------------------------------------------------
Ran 4 tests in 0.001s

FAILED (failures=2)
```

16.3.6   Almost Equal?

In addition to strict equality, it is possible to test for near equality of floating-point numbers using `failIfAlmostEqual()` and `failUnlessAlmostEqual()`.

```
import unittest

class AlmostEqualTest(unittest.TestCase):

    def testEqual(self):
        self.failUnlessEqual(1.1, 3.3-2.2)

    def testAlmostEqual(self):
        self.failUnlessAlmostEqual(1.1, 3.3-2.2, places=1)

    def testNotAlmostEqual(self):
        self.failIfAlmostEqual(1.1, 3.3-2.0, places=1)

if __name__ == '__main__':
    unittest.main()
```

The arguments are the values to be compared and the number of decimal places to use for the test.

```
$ python unittest_almostequal.py

.F.
======================================================================
FAIL: testEqual (__main__.AlmostEqualTest)
----------------------------------------------------------------------
Traceback (most recent call last):
  File "unittest_almostequal.py", line 36, in testEqual
    self.failUnlessEqual(1.1, 3.3-2.2)
AssertionError: 1.1 != 1.0999999999999996


----------------------------------------------------------------------
Ran 3 tests in 0.001s

FAILED (failures=1)
```

16.3.7 Testing for Exceptions

As previously mentioned, if a test raises an exception other than `AssertionError`, it is treated as an error. This is very useful for uncovering mistakes while modifying code that has existing test coverage. There are circumstances, however, in which the test should verify that some code does produce an exception. One example is when an invalid value is given to an attribute of an object. In such cases, `failUnlessRaises()` or `assertRaises()` make the code more clear than trapping the exception in the test. Compare these two tests.

```
import unittest

def raises_error(*args, **kwds):
    raise ValueError('Invalid value: ' + str(args) + str(kwds))

class ExceptionTest(unittest.TestCase):

    def testTrapLocally(self):
        try:
            raises_error('a', b='c')
        except ValueError:
            pass
        else:
            self.fail('Did not see ValueError')

    def testFailUnlessRaises(self):
        self.failUnlessRaises(ValueError, raises_error, 'a', b='c')

if __name__ == '__main__':
    unittest.main()
```

The results for both are the same, but the second test using failUnlessRaises() is more succinct.

```
$ python unittest_exception.py -v

testFailUnlessRaises (__main__.ExceptionTest) ... ok
testTrapLocally (__main__.ExceptionTest) ... ok

----------------------------------------------------------------------
Ran 2 tests in 0.000s

OK
```

16.3.8   Test Fixtures

Fixtures are outside resources needed by a test. For example, tests for one class may all need an instance of another class that provides configuration settings or another shared resource. Other test fixtures include database connections and temporary files (many people would argue that using external resources makes such tests not "unit" tests, but they are still tests and still useful). TestCase includes a special hook to configure and clean up any fixtures needed by tests. To configure the fixtures, override setUp(). To clean up, override tearDown().

```
import unittest

class FixturesTest(unittest.TestCase):

    def setUp(self):
        print 'In setUp()'
        self.fixture = range(1, 10)

    def tearDown(self):
        print 'In tearDown()'
        del self.fixture

    def test(self):
        print 'In test()'
        self.failUnlessEqual(self.fixture, range(1, 10))

if __name__ == '__main__':
    unittest.main()
```

When this sample test is run, the order of execution of the fixture and test methods is apparent.

```
$ python -u unittest_fixtures.py

In setUp()
In test()
In tearDown()
.
----------------------------------------------------------------------
Ran 1 test in 0.000s

OK
```

16.3.9 Test Suites

The standard library documentation describes how to organize test suites manually. Automated test discovery is more manageable for large code bases in which related tests are not all in the same place. Tools such as **nose** and **py.test** make it easier to manage tests when they are spread over multiple files and directories.

See Also:

unittest (http://docs.python.org/lib/module-unittest.html) The standard library documentation for this module.

doctest (page 921) An alternate means of running tests embedded in docstrings or external documentation files.

nose (http://somethingaboutorange.com/mrl/projects/nose/) A more sophisticated test manager.

py.test (http://codespeak.net/py/dist/test/) A third-party test runner.

unittest2 (http://pypi.python.org/pypi/unittest2) Ongoing improvements to `unittest`.

16.4   traceback—Exceptions and Stack Traces

Purpose Extract, format, and print exceptions and stack traces.
Python Version 1.4 and later

The `traceback` module works with the call stack to produce error messages. A *traceback* is a stack trace from the point of an exception handler down the call chain to the point where the exception was raised. Tracebacks also can be accessed from the current call stack up from the point of a call (and without the context of an error), which is useful for finding out the paths being followed into a function.

The functions in `traceback` fall into several common categories. There are functions for extracting raw tracebacks from the current runtime environment (either an exception handler for a traceback or the regular stack). The extracted stack trace is a sequence of tuples containing the filename, line number, function name, and text of the source line.

Once extracted, the stack trace can be formatted using functions like `format_exception()`, `format_stack()`, etc. The format functions return a list of strings with messages formatted to be printed. There are shorthand functions for printing the formatted values, as well.

Although the functions in `traceback` mimic the behavior of the interactive interpreter by default, they also are useful for handling exceptions in situations where dumping the full stack trace to the console is not desirable. For example, a web application may need to format the traceback so it looks good in HTML, and an IDE may convert the elements of the stack trace into a clickable list that lets the user browse the source.

16.4.1   Supporting Functions

The examples in this section use the module `traceback_example.py`.

```
import traceback
import sys
```

```
def produce_exception(recursion_level=2):
    sys.stdout.flush()
    if recursion_level:
        produce_exception(recursion_level-1)
    else:
        raise RuntimeError()

def call_function(f, recursion_level=2):
    if recursion_level:
        return call_function(f, recursion_level-1)
    else:
        return f()
```

16.4.2 Working with Exceptions

The simplest way to handle exception reporting is with `print_exc()`. It uses `sys.exc_info()` to obtain the exception information for the current thread, formats the results, and prints the text to a file handle (`sys.stderr`, by default).

```
import traceback
import sys

from traceback_example import produce_exception

print 'print_exc() with no exception:'
traceback.print_exc(file=sys.stdout)
print

try:
    produce_exception()
except Exception, err:
    print 'print_exc():'
    traceback.print_exc(file=sys.stdout)
    print
    print 'print_exc(1):'
    traceback.print_exc(limit=1, file=sys.stdout)
```

In this example, the file handle for `sys.stdout` is substituted so the informational and traceback messages are mingled correctly.

```
$ python traceback_print_exc.py

print_exc() with no exception:
None
```

```
print_exc():
Traceback (most recent call last):
  File "traceback_print_exc.py", line 20, in <module>
    produce_exception()
  File "/Users/dhellmann/Documents/PyMOTW/book/PyMOTW/traceback/trac
eback_example.py", line 16, in produce_exception
    produce_exception(recursion_level-1)
  File "/Users/dhellmann/Documents/PyMOTW/book/PyMOTW/traceback/trac
eback_example.py", line 16, in produce_exception
    produce_exception(recursion_level-1)
  File "/Users/dhellmann/Documents/PyMOTW/book/PyMOTW/traceback/trac
eback_example.py", line 18, in produce_exception
    raise RuntimeError()
RuntimeError

print_exc(1):
Traceback (most recent call last):
  File "traceback_print_exc.py", line 20, in <module>
    produce_exception()
RuntimeError
```

`print_exc()` is just a shortcut for `print_exception()`, which requires explicit arguments.

```
import traceback
import sys

from traceback_example import produce_exception

try:
    produce_exception()
except Exception, err:
    print 'print_exception():'
    exc_type, exc_value, exc_tb = sys.exc_info()
    traceback.print_exception(exc_type, exc_value, exc_tb)
```

The arguments to `print_exception()` are produced by `sys.exc_info()`.

```
$ python traceback_print_exception.py

Traceback (most recent call last):
  File "traceback_print_exception.py", line 16, in <module>
    produce_exception()
```

```
  File "/Users/dhellmann/Documents/PyMOTW/book/PyMOTW/traceback/trac
eback_example.py", line 16, in produce_exception
    produce_exception(recursion_level-1)
  File "/Users/dhellmann/Documents/PyMOTW/book/PyMOTW/traceback/trac
eback_example.py", line 16, in produce_exception
    produce_exception(recursion_level-1)
  File "/Users/dhellmann/Documents/PyMOTW/book/PyMOTW/traceback/trac
eback_example.py", line 18, in produce_exception
    raise RuntimeError()
RuntimeError
print_exception():
```

`print_exception()` uses `format_exception()` to prepare the text.

```
import traceback
import sys
from pprint import pprint

from traceback_example import produce_exception

try:
    produce_exception()
except Exception, err:
    print 'format_exception():'
    exc_type, exc_value, exc_tb = sys.exc_info()
    pprint(traceback.format_exception(exc_type, exc_value, exc_tb))
```

The same three arguments, exception type, exception value, and traceback, are used with `format_exception()`.

```
$ python traceback_format_exception.py

format_exception():
['Traceback (most recent call last):\n',
 '  File "traceback_format_exception.py", line 17, in <module>\n
produce_exception()\n',
 '  File "/Users/dhellmann/Documents/PyMOTW/book/PyMOTW/traceback/tr
aceback_example.py", line 16, in produce_exception\n    produce_exce
ption(recursion_level-1)\n',
 '  File "/Users/dhellmann/Documents/PyMOTW/book/PyMOTW/traceback/tr
aceback_example.py", line 16, in produce_exception\n    produce_exce
ption(recursion_level-1)\n',
```

```
'   File "/Users/dhellmann/Documents/PyMOTW/book/PyMOTW/traceback/tr
aceback_example.py", line 18, in produce_exception\n    raise Runtim
eError()\n',
 'RuntimeError\n']
```

To process the traceback in some other way, such as formatting it differently, use `extract_tb()` to get the data in a usable form.

```python
import traceback
import sys
import os
from traceback_example import produce_exception

try:
    produce_exception()
except Exception, err:
    print 'format_exception():'
    exc_type, exc_value, exc_tb = sys.exc_info()
    for tb_info in traceback.extract_tb(exc_tb):
        filename, linenum, funcname, source = tb_info
        print '%-23s:%s "%s" in %s()' % \
            (os.path.basename(filename),
            linenum,
            source,
            funcname)
```

The return value is a list of entries from each level of the stack represented by the traceback. Each entry is a tuple with four parts: the name of the source file, the line number in that file, the name of the function, and the source text from that line with whitespace stripped (if the source is available).

```
$ python traceback_extract_tb.py

format_exception():
traceback_extract_tb.py:16 "produce_exception()" in <module>()
traceback_example.py    :16 "produce_exception(recursion_level-1)" in
 produce_exception()
traceback_example.py    :16 "produce_exception(recursion_level-1)" in
 produce_exception()
traceback_example.py    :18 "raise RuntimeError()" in produce_excepti
on()
```

16.4.3   Working with the Stack

There is a similar set of functions for performing the same operations with the current call stack instead of a traceback. `print_stack()` prints the current stack, without generating an exception.

```
import traceback
import sys

from traceback_example import call_function

def f():
    traceback.print_stack(file=sys.stdout)

print 'Calling f() directly:'
f()

print
print 'Calling f() from 3 levels deep:'
call_function(f)
```

The output looks like a traceback without an error message.

```
$ python traceback_print_stack.py

Calling f() directly:
  File "traceback_print_stack.py", line 19, in <module>
    f()
  File "traceback_print_stack.py", line 16, in f
    traceback.print_stack(file=sys.stdout)

Calling f() from 3 levels deep:
  File "traceback_print_stack.py", line 23, in <module>
    call_function(f)
  File "/Users/dhellmann/Documents/PyMOTW/book/PyMOTW/traceback/trac
eback_example.py", line 22, in call_function
    return call_function(f, recursion_level-1)
  File "/Users/dhellmann/Documents/PyMOTW/book/PyMOTW/traceback/trac
eback_example.py", line 22, in call_function
    return call_function(f, recursion_level-1)
  File "/Users/dhellmann/Documents/PyMOTW/book/PyMOTW/traceback/trac
eback_example.py", line 24, in call_function
```

```
    return f()
  File "traceback_print_stack.py", line 16, in f
    traceback.print_stack(file=sys.stdout)
```

`format_stack()` prepares the stack trace in the same way that `format_exception()` prepares the traceback.

```
import traceback
import sys
from pprint import pprint

from traceback_example import call_function

def f():
    return traceback.format_stack()

formatted_stack = call_function(f)
pprint(formatted_stack)
```

It returns a list of strings, each of which makes up one line of the output.

```
$ python traceback_format_stack.py

['  File "traceback_format_stack.py", line 19, in <module>\n    form
atted_stack = call_function(f)\n',
 '  File "/Users/dhellmann/Documents/PyMOTW/book/PyMOTW/traceback/tr
aceback_example.py", line 22, in call_function\n    return call_func
tion(f, recursion_level-1)\n',
 '  File "/Users/dhellmann/Documents/PyMOTW/book/PyMOTW/traceback/tr
aceback_example.py", line 22, in call_function\n    return call_func
tion(f, recursion_level-1)\n',
 '  File "/Users/dhellmann/Documents/PyMOTW/book/PyMOTW/traceback/tr
aceback_example.py", line 24, in call_function\n    return f()\n',
 '  File "traceback_format_stack.py", line 17, in f\n    return trac
eback.format_stack()\n']
```

The `extract_stack()` function works like `extract_tb()`.

```
import traceback
import sys
import os
```

```
from traceback_example import call_function

def f():
    return traceback.extract_stack()

stack = call_function(f)
for filename, linenum, funcname, source in stack:
    print '%-26s:%s "%s" in %s()' % \
        (os.path.basename(filename), linenum, source, funcname)
```

It also accepts arguments, not shown here, to start from an alternate place in the stack frame or to limit the depth of traversal.

```
$ python traceback_extract_stack.py

traceback_extract_stack.py:19 "stack = call_function(f)" in <module>
()
traceback_example.py      :22 "return call_function(f, recursion_lev
el-1)" in call_function()
traceback_example.py      :22 "return call_function(f, recursion_lev
el-1)" in call_function()
traceback_example.py      :24 "return f()" in call_function()
traceback_extract_stack.py:17 "return traceback.extract_stack()" in
f()
```

See Also:

traceback (http://docs.python.org/lib/module-traceback.html) The standard library documentation for this module.

sys (page 1055) The `sys` module includes singletons that hold the current exception.

inspect (page 1200) The `inspect` module includes other functions for probing the frames on the stack.

cgitb (page 965) Another module for formatting tracebacks nicely.

16.5 cgitb—Detailed Traceback Reports

> **Purpose** cgitb provides more detailed traceback information than `trace-back`.
>
> **Python Version** 2.2 and later

`cgitb` is a valuable debugging tool in the standard library. It was originally designed for showing errors and debugging information in web applications. It was later updated to include plain-text output as well, but unfortunately was never renamed. This has led to obscurity, and the module is not used as often as it could be.

16.5.1   Standard Traceback Dumps

Python's default exception-handling behavior is to print a traceback to the standard error output stream with the call stack leading up to the error position. This basic output frequently contains enough information to understand the cause of the exception and permit a fix.

```
def func2(a, divisor):
    return a / divisor

def func1(a, b):
    c = b - 5
    return func2(a, c)

func1(1, 5)
```

This sample program has a subtle error in `func2()`.

```
$ python cgitb_basic_traceback.py

Traceback (most recent call last):
  File "cgitb_basic_traceback.py", line 17, in <module>
    func1(1, 5)
  File "cgitb_basic_traceback.py", line 15, in func1
    return func2(a, c)
  File "cgitb_basic_traceback.py", line 11, in func2
    return a / divisor
ZeroDivisionError: integer division or modulo by zero
```

16.5.2   Enabling Detailed Tracebacks

While the basic traceback includes enough information to spot the error, enabling `cgitb` gives more detail. `cgitb` replaces `sys.excepthook` with a function that gives extended tracebacks.

```
import cgitb
cgitb.enable(format='text')
```

The error report from this example is much more extensive than the original. Each frame of the stack is listed, along with the following.

- The full path to the source file, instead of just the base name
- The values of the arguments to each function in the stack
- A few lines of source context from around the line in the error path
- The values of variables in the expression causing the error

Having access to the variables involved in the error stack can help find a logical error that occurs somewhere higher in the stack than the line where the actual exception is generated.

```
$ python cgitb_local_vars.py

<type 'exceptions.ZeroDivisionError'>
Python 2.7: /Users/dhellmann/.virtualenvs/pymotw/bin/python
Sat Dec  4 12:59:15 2010

A problem occurred in a Python script.  Here is the sequence of
function calls leading up to the error, in the order they occurred.

/Users/dhellmann/Documents/PyMOTW/book/PyMOTW/cgitb/cgitb_local_var
s.py in <module>()
   16 def func1(a, b):
   17     c = b - 5
   18     return func2(a, c)
   19
   20 func1(1, 5)
func1 = <function func1>

/Users/dhellmann/Documents/PyMOTW/book/PyMOTW/cgitb/cgitb_local_var
s.py in func1(a=1, b=5)
   16 def func1(a, b):
   17     c = b - 5
   18     return func2(a, c)
   19
   20 func1(1, 5)
global func2 = <function func2>
a = 1
c = 0
```

```
/Users/dhellmann/Documents/PyMOTW/book/PyMOTW/cgitb/cgitb_local_var
s.py in func2(a=1, divisor=0)
   12
   13 def func2(a, divisor):
   14     return a / divisor
   15
   16 def func1(a, b):
a = 1
divisor = 0
<type 'exceptions.ZeroDivisionError'>: integer division or modulo by
zero
    __class__ = <type 'exceptions.ZeroDivisionError'>
    __dict__ = {}
    __doc__ = 'Second argument to a division or modulo operation was
    zero.'
...method references removed...
    args = ('integer division or modulo by zero',)
    message = 'integer division or modulo by zero'

The above is a description of an error in a Python program.  Here is
the original traceback:

Traceback (most recent call last):
  File "cgitb_local_vars.py", line 20, in <module>
    func1(1, 5)
  File "cgitb_local_vars.py", line 18, in func1
    return func2(a, c)
  File "cgitb_local_vars.py", line 14, in func2
    return a / divisor
ZeroDivisionError: integer division or modulo by zero
```

In the case of this code with a `ZeroDivisionError`, it is apparent that the problem is introduced in the computation of the value of `c` in `func1()`, rather than where the value is used in `func2()`.

The end of the output also includes the full details of the exception object (in case it has attributes other than `message` that would be useful for debugging) and the original form of a traceback dump.

16.5.3 Local Variables in Tracebacks

The code in `cgitb` that examines the variables used in the stack frame leading to the error is smart enough to evaluate object attributes to display them, too.

```python
import cgitb
cgitb.enable(format='text', context=12)


class BrokenClass(object):
    """This class has an error.
    """

    def __init__(self, a, b):
        """Be careful passing arguments in here.
        """
        self.a = a
        self.b = b
        self.c = self.a * self.b
        # Really
        # long
        # comment
        # goes
        # here.
        self.d = self.a / self.b
        return

o = BrokenClass(1, 0)
```

If a function or method includes a lot of in-line comments, whitespace, or other code that makes it very long, then having the default of five lines of context may not provide enough direction. When the body of the function is pushed out of the code window displayed, there is not enough context to understand the location of the error. Using a larger context value with cgitb solves this problem. Passing an integer as the *context* argument to enable() controls the amount of code displayed for each line of the traceback.

This output shows that self.a and self.b are involved in the error-prone code.

```
$ python cgitb_with_classes.py | grep -v method

<type 'exceptions.ZeroDivisionError'>
Python 2.7: /Users/dhellmann/.virtualenvs/pymotw/bin/python
Sat Dec  4 12:59:16 2010

A problem occurred in a Python script.  Here is the sequence of
function calls leading up to the error, in the order they occurred.

 /Users/dhellmann/Documents/PyMOTW/book/PyMOTW/cgitb/cgitb_with_clas
```

```
 ses.py in <module>()
   20          self.a = a
   21          self.b = b
   22          self.c = self.a * self.b
   23          # Really
   24          # long
   25          # comment
   26          # goes
   27          # here.
   28          self.d = self.a / self.b
   29          return
   30
   31 o = BrokenClass(1, 0)
o undefined
BrokenClass = <class '__main__.BrokenClass'>

 /Users/dhellmann/Documents/PyMOTW/book/PyMOTW/cgitb/cgitb_with_clas
 ses.py in __init__(self=<__main__.BrokenClass object>, a=1, b=0)
   20          self.a = a
   21          self.b = b
   22          self.c = self.a * self.b
   23          # Really
   24          # long
   25          # comment
   26          # goes
   27          # here.
   28          self.d = self.a / self.b
   29          return
   30
   31 o = BrokenClass(1, 0)
self = <__main__.BrokenClass object>
self.d undefined
self.a = 1
self.b = 0
<type 'exceptions.ZeroDivisionError'>: integer division or modulo by
zero
    __class__ = <type 'exceptions.ZeroDivisionError'>
    __dict__ = {}
    __doc__ = 'Second argument to a division or modulo operation was
    zero.'
...method references removed...
    args = ('integer division or modulo by zero',)
    message = 'integer division or modulo by zero'
```

The above is a description of an error in a Python program. Here is
the original traceback:

```
Traceback (most recent call last):
  File "cgitb_with_classes.py", line 31, in <module>
    o = BrokenClass(1, 0)
  File "cgitb_with_classes.py", line 28, in __init__
    self.d = self.a / self.b
ZeroDivisionError: integer division or modulo by zero
```

16.5.4   Exception Properties

In addition to the local variables from each stack frame, cgitb shows all properties of
the exception object. Extra properties on custom exception types are printed as part of
the error report.

```python
import cgitb
cgitb.enable(format='text')


class MyException(Exception):
    """Add extra properties to a special exception
    """

    def __init__(self, message, bad_value):
        self.bad_value = bad_value
        Exception.__init__(self, message)
        return


raise MyException('Normal message', bad_value=99)
```

In this example, the *bad_value* property is included along with the standard *message* and *args* values.

```
$ python cgitb_exception_properties.py

<class '__main__.MyException'>
Python 2.7: /Users/dhellmann/.virtualenvs/pymotw/bin/python
Sat Dec  4 12:59:16 2010

A problem occurred in a Python script.  Here is the sequence of
function calls leading up to the error, in the order they occurred.
```

```
/Users/dhellmann/Documents/PyMOTW/book/PyMOTW/cgitb/cgitb_exception
_properties.py in <module>()
  18          self.bad_value = bad_value
  19          Exception.__init__(self, message)
  20          return
  21
  22 raise MyException('Normal message', bad_value=99)
MyException = <class '__main__.MyException'>
bad_value undefined
<class '__main__.MyException'>: Normal message
    __class__ = <class '__main__.MyException'>
    __dict__ = {'bad_value': 99}
    __doc__ = 'Add extra properties to a special exception\n    '
    __module__ = '__main__'
...method references removed...
    args = ('Normal message',)
    bad_value = 99
    message = 'Normal message'
```

The above is a description of an error in a Python program. Here is
the original traceback:

```
Traceback (most recent call last):
  File "cgitb_exception_properties.py", line 22, in <module>
    raise MyException('Normal message', bad_value=99)
MyException: Normal message
```

16.5.5 HTML Output

Because cgitb was originally developed for handling exceptions in web applications, no discussion would be complete without mentioning its original HTML output format. The earlier examples all show plain-text output. To produce HTML instead, leave out the *format* argument (or specify "html"). Most modern web applications are constructed using a framework that includes an error-reporting facility, so the HTML form is largely obsolete.

16.5.6 Logging Tracebacks

For many situations, printing the traceback details to standard error is the best resolution. In a production system, however, logging the errors is even better. The enable() function includes an optional argument, *logdir*, to enable error logging. When a directory name is provided, each exception is logged to its own file in the given directory.

```
import cgitb
import os

cgitb.enable(logdir=os.path.join(os.path.dirname(__file__), 'LOGS'),
             display=False,
             format='text',
             )


def func(a, divisor):
    return a / divisor

func(1, 0)
```

Even though the error display is suppressed, a message is printed describing where to go to find the error log.

```
$ python cgitb_log_exception.py

<p>A problem occurred in a Python script.
<p> /Users/dhellmann/Documents/PyMOTW/book/PyMOTW/cgitb/LOGS/tmpy2v8
NM.txt contains the description of this error.

$ ls LOGS

tmpy2v8NM.txt

$ cat LOGS/*.txt

<type 'exceptions.ZeroDivisionError'>
Python 2.7: /Users/dhellmann/.virtualenvs/pymotw/bin/python
Sat Dec  4 12:59:15 2010

A problem occurred in a Python script.  Here is the sequence of
function calls leading up to the error, in the order they occurred.

 /Users/dhellmann/Documents/PyMOTW/book/PyMOTW/cgitb/cgitb_log_excep
 tion.py in <module>()
   17
   18 def func(a, divisor):
   19     return a / divisor
   20
   21 func(1, 0)
func = <function func>
```

```
/Users/dhellmann/Documents/PyMOTW/book/PyMOTW/cgitb/cgitb_log_excep
tion.py in func(a=1, divisor=0)
   17
   18 def func(a, divisor):
   19     return a / divisor
   20
   21 func(1, 0)
a = 1
divisor = 0
<type 'exceptions.ZeroDivisionError'>: integer division or modulo by
zero
    __class__ = <type 'exceptions.ZeroDivisionError'>
    __delattr__ = <method-wrapper '__delattr__' of
    exceptions.ZeroDivisionError object>
    __dict__ = {}
    __doc__ = 'Second argument to a division or modulo operation was
    zero.'
    __format__ = <built-in method __format__ of
    exceptions.ZeroDivisionError object>
    __getattribute__ = <method-wrapper '__getattribute__' of
    exceptions.ZeroDivisionError object>
    __getitem__ = <method-wrapper '__getitem__' of
    exceptions.ZeroDivisionError object>
    __getslice__ = <method-wrapper '__getslice__' of
    exceptions.ZeroDivisionError object>
    __hash__ = <method-wrapper '__hash__' of
    exceptions.ZeroDivisionError object>
    __init__ = <method-wrapper '__init__' of
    exceptions.ZeroDivisionError object>
    __new__ = <built-in method __new__ of type object>
    __reduce__ = <built-in method __reduce__ of
    exceptions.ZeroDivisionError object>
    __reduce_ex__ = <built-in method __reduce_ex__ of
    exceptions.ZeroDivisionError object>
    __repr__ = <method-wrapper '__repr__' of
    exceptions.ZeroDivisionError object>
    __setattr__ = <method-wrapper '__setattr__' of
    exceptions.ZeroDivisionError object>
    __setstate__ = <built-in method __setstate__ of
    exceptions.ZeroDivisionError object>
    __sizeof__ = <built-in method __sizeof__ of
    exceptions.ZeroDivisionError object>
    __str__ = <method-wrapper '__str__' of
```

```
exceptions.ZeroDivisionError object>
__subclasshook__ = <built-in method __subclasshook__ of type
object>
__unicode__ = <built-in method __unicode__ of
exceptions.ZeroDivisionError object>
args = ('integer division or modulo by zero',)
message = 'integer division or modulo by zero'
```

The above is a description of an error in a Python program. Here is
the original traceback:

```
Traceback (most recent call last):
  File "cgitb_log_exception.py", line 21, in <module>
    func(1, 0)
  File "cgitb_log_exception.py", line 19, in func
    return a / divisor
ZeroDivisionError: integer division or modulo by zero
```

See Also:

cgitb (http://docs.python.org/library/cgitb.html) The standard library documentation for this module.

traceback (page 958) The standard library module for working with tracebacks.

inspect (page 1200) The inspect module includes more functions for examining the stack.

sys (page 1055) The sys module provides access to the current exception value and the excepthook handler invoked when an exception occurs.

Improved Traceback Module
(http://thread.gmane.org/gmane.comp.python.devel/110326) Discussion on the Python development mailing list about improvements to the traceback module and related enhancements other developers use locally.

16.6 pdb—Interactive Debugger

Purpose Python's interactive debugger.
Python Version 1.4 and later

pdb implements an interactive debugging environment for Python programs. It includes features to pause a program, look at the values of variables, and watch program execution step by step, so you can understand what the program actually does and find bugs in the logic.

16.6.1   Starting the Debugger

The first step to using `pdb` is causing the interpreter to enter the debugger at the right time. There are a few different ways to do that, depending on the starting conditions and what is being debugged.

From the Command Line

The most straightforward way to use the debugger is to run it from the command line, giving it the program as input so it knows what to run.

```python
1   #!/usr/bin/env python
2   # encoding: utf-8
3   #
4   # Copyright (c) 2010 Doug Hellmann.  All rights reserved.
5   #
6
7   class MyObj(object):
8
9       def __init__(self, num_loops):
10          self.count = num_loops
11
12      def go(self):
13          for i in range(self.count):
14              print i
15          return
16
17  if __name__ == '__main__':
18      MyObj(5).go()
```

Running the debugger from the command line causes it to load the source file and stop execution on the first statement it finds. In this case, it stops before evaluating the definition of the class `MyObj` on line 7.

```
$ python -m pdb pdb_script.py

> .../pdb_script.py(7)<module>()
-> class MyObj(object):
(Pdb)
```

Note: Normally, `pdb` includes the full path to each module in the output when printing a filename. In order to maintain clear examples, the path in the sample output in this section has been replaced with an ellipsis (. . .).

Within the Interpreter

Many Python developers work with the interactive interpreter while developing early versions of modules because it lets them experiment more iteratively without the save/run/repeat cycle needed when creating stand-alone scripts. To run the debugger from within an interactive interpreter, use `run()` or `runeval()`.

```
$ python

Python 2.7 (r27:82508, Jul  3 2010, 21:12:11)
[GCC 4.0.1 (Apple Inc. build 5493)] on darwin
Type "help", "copyright", "credits" or "license" for more information.
>>> import pdb_script
>>> import pdb
>>> pdb.run('pdb_script.MyObj(5).go()')
> <string>(1)<module>()
(Pdb)
```

The argument to `run()` is a string expression that can be evaluated by the Python interpreter. The debugger will parse it, and then pause execution just before the first expression evaluates. The debugger commands described here can be used to navigate and control the execution.

From within a Program

Both of the previous examples start the debugger at the beginning of a program. For a long-running process where the problem appears much later in the program execution, it will be more convenient to start the debugger from inside the program using `set_trace()`.

```
1   #!/usr/bin/env python
2   # encoding: utf-8
3   #
4   # Copyright (c) 2010 Doug Hellmann.  All rights reserved.
5   #
6
7   import pdb
8
9   class MyObj(object):
10
11      def __init__(self, num_loops):
12          self.count = num_loops
13
14      def go(self):
```

```
15          for i in range(self.count):
16              pdb.set_trace()
17              print i
18          return
19
20 if __name__ == '__main__':
21     MyObj(5).go()
```

Line 16 of the sample script triggers the debugger at that point in execution.

```
$ python ./pdb_set_trace.py

> .../pdb_set_trace.py(17)go()
-> print i
(Pdb)
```

set_trace() is just a Python function, so it can be called at any point in a program. This makes it possible to enter the debugger based on conditions inside the program, including from an exception handler or via a specific branch of a control statement.

After a Failure

Debugging a failure after a program terminates is called *post-mortem* debugging. pdb supports post-mortem debugging through the pm() and post_mortem() functions.

```
1  #!/usr/bin/env python
2  # encoding: utf-8
3  #
4  # Copyright (c) 2010 Doug Hellmann.  All rights reserved.
5  #
6
7  class MyObj(object):
8
9      def __init__(self, num_loops):
10         self.count = num_loops
11
12     def go(self):
13         for i in range(self.num_loops):
14             print i
15         return
```

Here the incorrect attribute name on line 13 triggers an `AttributeError` exception, causing execution to stop. `pm()` looks for the active traceback and starts the debugger at the point in the call stack where the exception occurred.

```
$ python

Python 2.7 (r27:82508, Jul  3 2010, 21:12:11)
[GCC 4.0.1 (Apple Inc. build 5493)] on darwin
Type "help", "copyright", "credits" or "license" for more information.
>>> from pdb_post_mortem import MyObj
>>> MyObj(5).go()
Traceback (most recent call last):
  File "<stdin>", line 1, in <module>
  File "pdb_post_mortem.py", line 13, in go
    for i in range(self.num_loops):
AttributeError: 'MyObj' object has no attribute 'num_loops'
>>> import pdb
>>> pdb.pm()
> .../pdb_post_mortem.py(13)go()
-> for i in range(self.num_loops):
(Pdb)
```

16.6.2 Controlling the Debugger

The interface for the debugger is a small command language that lets you move around the call stack, examine and change the values of variables, and control how the debugger executes the program. The interactive debugger uses `readline` to accept commands. Entering a blank line reruns the previous command again, unless it was a **list** operation.

Navigating the Execution Stack

At any point while the debugger is running, use **where** (abbreviated **w**) to find out exactly what line is being executed and where on the call stack the program is. In this case, it is the module `pdb_set_trace.py` at line 17 in the `go()` method.

```
$ python pdb_set_trace.py

> .../pdb_set_trace.py(17)go()
-> print i
```

```
(Pdb) where
  .../pdb_set_trace.py(21)<module>()
-> MyObj(5).go()
> .../pdb_set_trace.py(17)go()
-> print i
```

To add more context around the current location, use **list** (**l**).

```
(Pdb) list
 12                 self.count = num_loops
 13
 14         def go(self):
 15             for i in range(self.count):
 16                 pdb.set_trace()
 17  ->             print i
 18             return
 19
 20     if __name__ == '__main__':
 21         MyObj(5).go()
[EOF]
(Pdb)
```

The default is to list 11 lines around the current line (five before and five after). Using **list** with a single numerical argument lists 11 lines around that line instead of the current line.

```
(Pdb) list 14
  9     class MyObj(object):
 10
 11         def __init__(self, num_loops):
 12             self.count = num_loops
 13
 14         def go(self):
 15             for i in range(self.count):
 16                 pdb.set_trace()
 17  ->             print i
 18             return
 19
```

If **list** receives two arguments, it interprets them as the first and last lines to include in its output.

```
(Pdb) list 5, 19
  5        #
  6
  7        import pdb
  8
  9        class MyObj(object):
 10
 11            def __init__(self, num_loops):
 12                self.count = num_loops
 13
 14            def go(self):
 15                for i in range(self.count):
 16                    pdb.set_trace()
 17    ->              print i
 18                return
 19
```

Move between frames within the current call stack using **up** and **down. up** (abbreviated **u**) moves toward older frames on the stack. **down** (abbreviated **d**) moves toward newer frames.

```
(Pdb) up
> .../pdb_set_trace.py(21)<module>()
-> MyObj(5).go()

(Pdb) down
> .../pdb_set_trace.py(17)go()
-> print i
```

Each time you move up or down the stack, the debugger prints the current location in the same format as produced by **where**.

Examining Variables on the Stack

Each frame on the stack maintains a set of variables, including values local to the function being executed and global state information. pdb provides several ways to examine the contents of those variables.

```
1   #!/usr/bin/env python
2   # encoding: utf-8
3   #
```

```
4   # Copyright (c) 2010 Doug Hellmann.  All rights reserved.
5   #
6
7   import pdb
8
9   def recursive_function(n=5, output='to be printed'):
10      if n > 0:
11          recursive_function(n-1)
12      else:
13          pdb.set_trace()
14          print output
15      return
16
17  if __name__ == '__main__':
18      recursive_function()
```

The **args** command (abbreviated **a**) prints all the arguments to the function active in the current frame. This example also uses a recursive function to show what a deeper stack looks like when printed by **where**.

```
$ python pdb_function_arguments.py

> .../pdb_function_arguments.py(14)recursive_function()
-> return
(Pdb) where
  .../pdb_function_arguments.py(17)<module>()
-> recursive_function()
  .../pdb_function_arguments.py(11)recursive_function()
-> recursive_function(n-1)
  .../pdb_function_arguments.py(11)recursive_function()
-> recursive_function(n-1)
  .../pdb_function_arguments.py(11)recursive_function()
-> recursive_function(n-1)
  .../pdb_function_arguments.py(11)recursive_function()
-> recursive_function(n-1)
  .../pdb_function_arguments.py(11)recursive_function()
-> recursive_function(n-1)
> .../pdb_function_arguments.py(14)recursive_function()
-> return

(Pdb) args
n = 0
```

```
output = to be printed

(Pdb) up
> .../pdb_function_arguments.py(11)recursive_function()
-> recursive_function(n-1)

(Pdb) args
n = 1
output = to be printed

(Pdb)
```

The **p** command evaluates an expression given as argument and prints the result. Python's `print` statement can be used, but it is passed through to the interpreter to be executed rather than run as a command in the debugger.

```
(Pdb) p n
1

(Pdb) print n
1
```

Similarly, prefixing an expression with **!** passes it to the Python interpreter to be evaluated. This feature can be used to execute arbitrary Python statements, including modifying variables. This example changes the value of *output* before letting the debugger continue running the program. The next statement after the call to `set_trace()` prints the value of *output*, showing the modified value.

```
$ python pdb_function_arguments.py

> .../pdb_function_arguments.py(14)recursive_function()
-> print output

(Pdb) !output
'to be printed'

(Pdb) !output='changed value'

(Pdb) continue
changed value
```

For more complicated values such as nested or large data structures, use **pp** to "pretty-print" them. This program reads several lines of text from a file.

```
1   #!/usr/bin/env python
2   # encoding: utf-8
3   #
4   # Copyright (c) 2010 Doug Hellmann.  All rights reserved.
5   #
6
7   import pdb
8
9   with open('lorem.txt', 'rt') as f:
10      lines = f.readlines()
11
12  pdb.set_trace()
```

Printing the variable `lines` with **p** results in output that is difficult to read because it wraps awkwardly. **pp** uses `pprint` to format the value for clean printing.

```
$ python pdb_pp.py

--Return--
> .../pdb_pp.py(12)<module>()->None
-> pdb.set_trace()
(Pdb) p lines
['Lorem ipsum dolor sit amet, consectetuer adipiscing elit. \n',
 'Donec egestas, enim et consecte
tuer ullamcorper, lectus \n', 'ligula rutrum leo, a elementum el
it tortor eu quam.\n']

(Pdb) pp lines
['Lorem ipsum dolor sit amet, consectetuer adipiscing elit. \n',
 'Donec egestas, enim et consectetuer ullamcorper, lectus \n',
 'ligula rutrum leo, a elementum elit tortor eu quam.\n']

(Pdb)
```

Stepping through a Program

In addition to navigating up and down the call stack when the program is paused, it is also possible to step through execution of the program past the point where it enters the debugger.

```
1    #!/usr/bin/env python
2    # encoding: utf-8
3    #
4    # Copyright (c) 2010 Doug Hellmann.  All rights reserved.
5    #
6
7    import pdb
8
9    def f(n):
10       for i in range(n):
11           j = i * n
12           print i, j
13       return
14
15   if __name__ == '__main__':
16       pdb.set_trace()
17       f(5)
```

Use **step** to execute the current line and then stop at the next execution point—either the first statement inside a function being called or the next line of the current function.

```
$ python pdb_step.py

> .../pdb_step.py(17)<module>()
-> f(5)
```

The interpreter pauses at the call to `set_trace()` and gives control to the debugger. The first step causes the execution to enter `f()`.

```
(Pdb) step
--Call--
> .../pdb_step.py(9)f()
-> def f(n):
```

One more step moves execution to the first line of `f()` and starts the loop.

```
(Pdb) step
> .../pdb_step.py(10)f()
-> for i in range(n):
```

Stepping again moves to the first line inside the loop where `j` is defined.

```
(Pdb) step
> .../pdb_step.py(11)f()
-> j = i * n
(Pdb) p i
0
```

The value of i is 0, so after one more step, the value of j should also be 0.

```
(Pdb) step
> .../pdb_step.py(12)f()
-> print i, j

(Pdb) p j
0

(Pdb)
```

Stepping one line at a time like this can become tedious if there is a lot of code to cover before the point where the error occurs, or if the same function is called repeatedly.

```
 1  #!/usr/bin/env python
 2  # encoding: utf-8
 3  #
 4  # Copyright (c) 2010 Doug Hellmann.  All rights reserved.
 5  #
 6
 7  import pdb
 8
 9  def calc(i, n):
10      j = i * n
11      return j
12
13  def f(n):
14      for i in range(n):
15          j = calc(i, n)
16          print i, j
17      return
18
19  if __name__ == '__main__':
20      pdb.set_trace()
21      f(5)
```

In this example, there is nothing wrong with `calc()`, so stepping through it each time it is called in the loop in `f()` obscures the useful output by showing all the lines of `calc()` as they are executed.

```
$ python pdb_next.py

> .../pdb_next.py(21)<module>()
-> f(5)
(Pdb) step
--Call--
> .../pdb_next.py(13)f()
-> def f(n):

(Pdb) step
> .../pdb_next.py(14)f()
-> for i in range(n):

(Pdb) step
> .../pdb_next.py(15)f()
-> j = calc(i, n)

(Pdb) step
--Call--
> .../pdb_next.py(9)calc()
-> def calc(i, n):

(Pdb) step
> .../pdb_next.py(10)calc()
-> j = i * n

(Pdb) step
> .../pdb_next.py(11)calc()
-> return j

(Pdb) step
--Return--
> .../pdb_next.py(11)calc()->0
-> return j

(Pdb) step
> .../pdb_next.py(16)f()
-> print i, j

(Pdb) step
0 0
```

The **next** command is like step, but does not enter functions called from the statement being executed. In effect, it steps all the way through the function call to the next statement in the current function in a single operation.

```
> .../pdb_next.py(14)f()
-> for i in range(n):
(Pdb) step
> .../pdb_next.py(15)f()
-> j = calc(i, n)

(Pdb) next
> .../pdb_next.py(16)f()
-> print i, j

(Pdb)
```

The **until** command is like **next**, except it explicitly continues until execution reaches a line in the same function with a line number higher than the current value. That means, for example, that **until** can be used to step past the end of a loop.

```
$ python pdb_next.py

> .../pdb_next.py(21)<module>()
-> f(5)
(Pdb) step
--Call--
> .../pdb_next.py(13)f()
-> def f(n):

(Pdb) step
> .../pdb_next.py(14)f()
-> for i in range(n):

(Pdb) step
> .../pdb_next.py(15)f()
-> j = calc(i, n)

(Pdb) next
> .../pdb_next.py(16)f()
-> print i, j
```

```
(Pdb) until
0 0
1 5
2 10
3 15
4 20
> .../pdb_next.py(17)f()
-> return

(Pdb)
```

Before the **until** command was run, the current line was 16, the last line of the loop. After **until** ran, execution was on line 17 and the loop had been exhausted.

The **return** command is another shortcut for bypassing parts of a function. It continues executing until the function is about to execute a `return` statement, and then it pauses, providing time to look at the return value before the function returns.

```
$ python pdb_next.py

> .../pdb_next.py(21)<module>()
-> f(5)
(Pdb) step
--Call--
> .../pdb_next.py(13)f()
-> def f(n):

(Pdb) step
> .../pdb_next.py(14)f()
-> for i in range(n):

(Pdb) return
0 0
1 5
2 10
3 15
4 20
--Return--
> .../pdb_next.py(17)f()->None
-> return

(Pdb)
```

16.6.3 Breakpoints

As programs grow longer, even using **next** and **until** will become slow and cumbersome. Instead of stepping through the program by hand, a better solution is to let it run normally until it reaches a point where the debugger should interrupt it. `set_trace()` can start the debugger, but that only works if there is a single point in the program where it should pause. It is more convenient to run the program through the debugger, but tell the debugger where to stop in advance using *breakpoints*. The debugger monitors the program, and when it reaches the location described by a breakpoint, the program is paused before the line is executed.

```
1  #!/usr/bin/env python
2  # encoding: utf-8
3  #
4  # Copyright (c) 2010 Doug Hellmann.  All rights reserved.
5  #
6
7  def calc(i, n):
8      j = i * n
9      print 'j =', j
10     if j > 0:
11         print 'Positive!'
12     return j
13
14 def f(n):
15     for i in range(n):
16         print 'i =', i
17         j = calc(i, n)
18     return
19
20 if __name__ == '__main__':
21     f(5)
```

There are several options to the **break** command used for setting breakpoints, including the line number, file, and function where processing should pause. To set a breakpoint on a specific line of the current file, use `break lineno`.

```
$ python -m pdb pdb_break.py

> .../pdb_break.py(7)<module>()
-> def calc(i, n):
(Pdb) break 11
```

```
Breakpoint 1 at .../pdb_break.py:11

(Pdb) continue
i = 0
j = 0
i = 1
j = 5
> .../pdb_break.py(11)calc()
-> print 'Positive!'

(Pdb)
```

The command **continue** tells the debugger to keep running the program until the next breakpoint. In this case, it runs through the first iteration of the `for` loop in `f()` and stops inside `calc()` during the second iteration.

Breakpoints can also be set to the first line of a function by specifying the function name instead of a line number. This example shows what happens if a breakpoint is added for the `calc()` function.

```
$ python -m pdb pdb_break.py

> .../pdb_break.py(7)<module>()
-> def calc(i, n):
(Pdb) break calc
Breakpoint 1 at .../pdb_break.py:7

(Pdb) continue
i = 0
> .../pdb_break.py(8)calc()
-> j = i * n

(Pdb) where
  .../pdb_break.py(21)<module>()
-> f(5)
  .../pdb_break.py(17)f()
-> j = calc(i, n)
> .../pdb_break.py(8)calc()
-> j = i * n

(Pdb)
```

To specify a breakpoint in another file, prefix the line or function argument with a filename.

```
1  #!/usr/bin/env python
2  # encoding: utf-8
3
4  from pdb_break import f
5
6  f(5)
```

Here a breakpoint is set for line 11 of `pdb_break.py` after starting the main program `pdb_break_remote.py`.

```
$ python -m pdb pdb_break_remote.py

> .../pdb_break_remote.py(4)<module>()
-> from pdb_break import f
(Pdb) break pdb_break.py:11
Breakpoint 1 at .../pdb_break.py:11

(Pdb) continue
i = 0
j = 0
i = 1
j = 5
> .../pdb_break.py(11)calc()
-> print 'Positive!'

(Pdb)
```

The filename can be a full path to the source file or a relative path to a file available on `sys.path`.

To list the breakpoints currently set, use **break** without any arguments. The output includes the file and line number of each breakpoint, as well as information about how many times it has been encountered.

```
$ python -m pdb pdb_break.py

> .../pdb_break.py(7)<module>()
-> def calc(i, n):
(Pdb) break 11
Breakpoint 1 at .../pdb_break.py:11

(Pdb) break
Num Type         Disp Enb   Where
```

```
1    breakpoint    keep yes   at .../pdb_break.py:11

(Pdb) continue
i = 0
j = 0
i = 1
j = 5
> .../pdb/pdb_break.py(11)calc()
-> print 'Positive!'

(Pdb) continue
Positive!
i = 2
j = 10
> .../pdb_break.py(11)calc()
-> print 'Positive!'

(Pdb) break
Num Type          Disp Enb   Where
1    breakpoint    keep yes   at .../pdb_break.py:11
        breakpoint already hit 2 times

(Pdb)
```

Managing Breakpoints

As each new breakpoint is added, it is assigned a numerical identifier. These id numbers are used to enable, disable, and remove the breakpoints interactively. Turning off a breakpoint with **disable** tells the debugger not to stop when that line is reached. The breakpoint is remembered, but ignored.

```
$ python -m pdb pdb_break.py

> .../pdb_break.py(7)<module>()
-> def calc(i, n):
(Pdb) break calc
Breakpoint 1 at .../pdb_break.py:7

(Pdb) break 11
Breakpoint 2 at .../pdb_break.py:11

(Pdb) break
Num Type          Disp Enb   Where
```

```
1      breakpoint     keep yes     at .../pdb_break.py:7
2      breakpoint     keep yes     at .../pdb_break.py:11

(Pdb) disable 1

(Pdb) break
Num Type           Disp Enb     Where
1      breakpoint     keep no      at .../pdb_break.py:7
2      breakpoint     keep yes     at .../pdb_break.py:11

(Pdb) continue
i = 0
j = 0
i = 1
j = 5
> .../pdb_break.py(11)calc()
-> print 'Positive!'

(Pdb)
```

The next debugging session sets two breakpoints in the program and then disables one. The program is run until the remaining breakpoint is encountered, and then the other breakpoint is turned back on with **enable** before execution continues.

```
$ python -m pdb pdb_break.py

> .../pdb_break.py(7)<module>()
-> def calc(i, n):
(Pdb) break calc
Breakpoint 1 at .../pdb_break.py:7

(Pdb) break 16
Breakpoint 2 at .../pdb_break.py:16

(Pdb) disable 1

(Pdb) continue
> .../pdb_break.py(16)f()
-> print 'i =', i

(Pdb) list
 11                print 'Positive!'
 12            return j
 13
```

```
14      def f(n):
15          for i in range(n):
16 B->          print 'i =', i
17              j = calc(i, n)
18          return
19
20      if __name__ == '__main__':
21          f(5)
```

```
(Pdb) continue
i = 0
j = 0
> .../pdb_break.py(16)f()
-> print 'i =', i
```

```
(Pdb) list
 11             print 'Positive!'
 12          return j
 13
 14      def f(n):
 15          for i in range(n):
 16 B->          print 'i =', i
 17              j = calc(i, n)
 18          return
 19
 20      if __name__ == '__main__':
 21          f(5)
```

```
(Pdb) p i
1
```

```
(Pdb) enable 1
```

```
(Pdb) continue
i = 1
> .../pdb_break.py(8)calc()
-> j = i * n
```

```
(Pdb) list
  3      #
  4      # Copyright (c) 2010 Doug Hellmann.  All rights reserved.
  5      #
  6
  7 B  def calc(i, n):
  8  ->      j = i * n
```

```
 9              print 'j =', j
10              if j > 0:
11                  print 'Positive!'
12              return j
13
```

(Pdb)

The lines prefixed with B in the output from **list** show where the breakpoints are set in the program (lines 7 and 16).

Use **clear** to delete a breakpoint entirely.

```
$ python -m pdb pdb_break.py

> .../pdb_break.py(7)<module>()
-> def calc(i, n):
(Pdb) break calc
Breakpoint 1 at .../pdb_break.py:7

(Pdb) break 11
Breakpoint 2 at .../pdb_break.py:11

(Pdb) break 16
Breakpoint 3 at .../pdb_break.py:16

(Pdb) break
Num Type          Disp Enb   Where
1   breakpoint    keep yes   at .../pdb_break.py:7
2   breakpoint    keep yes   at .../pdb_break.py:11
3   breakpoint    keep yes   at .../pdb_break.py:16

(Pdb) clear 2
Deleted breakpoint 2

(Pdb) break
Num Type          Disp Enb   Where
1   breakpoint    keep yes   at .../pdb_break.py:7
3   breakpoint    keep yes   at .../pdb_break.py:16

(Pdb)
```

The other breakpoints retain their original identifiers and are not renumbered.

Temporary Breakpoints

A temporary breakpoint is automatically cleared the first time the program execution hits it. Using a temporary breakpoint makes it easy to reach a particular spot in the program flow quickly, just as with a regular breakpoint since it is cleared immediately. But, it does not interfere with subsequent progress if that part of the program is run repeatedly.

```
$ python -m pdb pdb_break.py

> .../pdb_break.py(7)<module>()
-> def calc(i, n):
(Pdb) tbreak 11
Breakpoint 1 at .../pdb_break.py:11

(Pdb) continue
i = 0
j = 0
i = 1
j = 5
Deleted breakpoint 1
> .../pdb_break.py(11)calc()
-> print 'Positive!'

(Pdb) break

(Pdb) continue
Positive!
i = 2
j = 10
Positive!
i = 3
j = 15
Positive!
i = 4
j = 20
Positive!
The program finished and will be restarted
> .../pdb_break.py(7)<module>()
-> def calc(i, n):

(Pdb)
```

After the program reaches line 11 the first time, the breakpoint is removed and execution does not stop again until the program finishes.

Conditional Breakpoints

Rules can be applied to breakpoints so that execution only stops when the conditions are met. Using conditional breakpoints gives finer control over how the debugger pauses the program than enabling and disabling breakpoints by hand. Conditional breakpoints can be set in two ways. The first is to specify the condition when the breakpoint is set using **break**.

```
$ python -m pdb pdb_break.py

> .../pdb_break.py(7)<module>()
-> def calc(i, n):
(Pdb) break 9, j>0
Breakpoint 1 at .../pdb_break.py:9

(Pdb) break
Num Type         Disp Enb   Where
1   breakpoint   keep yes   at .../pdb_break.py:9
        stop only if j>0

(Pdb) continue
i = 0
j = 0
i = 1
> .../pdb_break.py(9)calc()
-> print 'j =', j

(Pdb)
```

The condition argument must be an expression using values visible in the stack frame where the breakpoint is defined. If the expression evaluates as true, execution stops at the breakpoint.

A condition can also be applied to an existing breakpoint using the **condition** command. The arguments are the breakpoint id and the expression.

```
$ python -m pdb pdb_break.py

> .../pdb_break.py(7)<module>()
-> def calc(i, n):
```

```
(Pdb) break 9
Breakpoint 1 at .../pdb_break.py:9

(Pdb) break
Num Type          Disp Enb   Where
1   breakpoint    keep yes   at .../pdb_break.py:9

(Pdb) condition 1 j>0

(Pdb) break
Num Type          Disp Enb   Where
1   breakpoint    keep yes   at .../pdb_break.py:9
        stop only if j>0

(Pdb)
```

Ignoring Breakpoints

Programs that loop or use a large number of recursive calls to the same function are often easier to debug by "skipping ahead" in the execution, instead of watching every call or breakpoint. The **ignore** command tells the debugger to pass over a breakpoint without stopping. Each time processing encounters the breakpoint, it decrements the ignore counter. When the counter is zero, the breakpoint is reactivated.

```
$ python -m pdb pdb_break.py

> .../pdb_break.py(7)<module>()
-> def calc(i, n):
(Pdb) break 17
Breakpoint 1 at .../pdb_break.py:17

(Pdb) continue
i = 0
> .../pdb_break.py(17)f()
-> j = calc(i, n)

(Pdb) next
j = 0
> .../pdb_break.py(15)f()
-> for i in range(n):

(Pdb) ignore 1 2
Will ignore next 2 crossings of breakpoint 1.
```

```
(Pdb) break
Num Type          Disp Enb   Where
1   breakpoint    keep yes   at .../pdb_break.py:17
        ignore next 2 hits
        breakpoint already hit 1 time

(Pdb) continue
i = 1
j = 5
Positive!
i = 2
j = 10
Positive!
i = 3
> .../pdb_break.py(17)f()
-> j = calc(i, n)

(Pdb) break
Num Type          Disp Enb   Where
1   breakpoint    keep yes   at .../pdb_break.py:17
        breakpoint already hit 4 times
```

Explicitly resetting the ignore count to zero reenables the breakpoint immediately.

```
$ python -m pdb pdb_break.py

> .../pdb_break.py(7)<module>()
-> def calc(i, n):
(Pdb) break 17
Breakpoint 1 at .../pdb_break.py:17

(Pdb) ignore 1 2
Will ignore next 2 crossings of breakpoint 1.

(Pdb) break
Num Type          Disp Enb   Where
1   breakpoint    keep yes   at .../pdb_break.py:17
        ignore next 2 hits

(Pdb) ignore 1 0
Will stop next time breakpoint 1 is reached.

(Pdb) break
```

```
Num Type           Disp Enb   Where
1   breakpoint     keep yes   at .../pdb_break.py:17
```

Triggering Actions on a Breakpoint

In addition to the purely interactive mode, pdb supports basic scripting. Using **commands**, a series of interpreter commands, including Python statements, can be executed when a specific breakpoint is encountered. After running **commands** with the breakpoint number as argument, the debugger prompt changes to (com). Enter commands one at a time, and finish the list with end to save the script and return to the main debugger prompt.

```
$ python -m pdb pdb_break.py

> .../pdb_break.py(7)<module>()
-> def calc(i, n):
(Pdb) break 9
Breakpoint 1 at .../pdb_break.py:9

(Pdb) commands 1
(com) print 'debug i =', i
(com) print 'debug j =', j
(com) print 'debug n =', n
(com) end

(Pdb) continue
i = 0
debug i = 0
debug j = 0
debug n = 5
> .../pdb_break.py(9)calc()
-> print 'j =', j

(Pdb) continue
j = 0
i = 1
debug i = 1
debug j = 5
debug n = 5
> .../pdb_break.py(9)calc()
-> print 'j =', j

(Pdb)
```

This feature is especially useful for debugging code that uses a lot of data structures or variables, since the debugger can be made to print out all the values automatically, instead of doing it manually each time the breakpoint is encountered.

16.6.4 Changing Execution Flow

The **jump** command alters the flow of the program at runtime, without modifying the code. It can skip forward to avoid running some code or backward to run it again. This sample program generates a list of numbers.

```python
#!/usr/bin/env python
# encoding: utf-8
#
# Copyright (c) 2010 Doug Hellmann.  All rights reserved.
#

def f(n):
    result = []
    j = 0
    for i in range(n):
        j = i * n + j
        j += n
        result.append(j)
    return result

if __name__ == '__main__':
    print f(5)
```

When run without interference the output is a sequence of increasing numbers divisible by 5.

```
$ python pdb_jump.py

[5, 15, 30, 50, 75]
```

Jump Ahead

Jumping ahead moves the point of execution past the current location without evaluating any of the statements in between. By skipping over line 13 in the example, the value of j is not incremented and all the subsequent values that depend on it are a little smaller.

```
$ python -m pdb pdb_jump.py

> .../pdb_jump.py(7)<module>()
-> def f(n):
(Pdb) break 12
Breakpoint 1 at .../pdb_jump.py:12

(Pdb) continue
> .../pdb_jump.py(12)f()
-> j += n

(Pdb) p j
0

(Pdb) step
> .../pdb_jump.py(13)f()
-> result.append(j)

(Pdb) p j
5

(Pdb) continue
> .../pdb_jump.py(12)f()
-> j += n

(Pdb) jump 13
> .../pdb_jump.py(13)f()
-> result.append(j)

(Pdb) p j
10

(Pdb) disable 1

(Pdb) continue
[5, 10, 25, 45, 70]

The program finished and will be restarted
> .../pdb_jump.py(7)<module>()
-> def f(n):
(Pdb)
```

Jump Back

Jumps can also move the program execution to a statement that has already been executed, so it can be run again. Here, the value of j is incremented an extra time, so the numbers in the result sequence are all larger than they would otherwise be.

```
$ python -m pdb pdb_jump.py

> .../pdb_jump.py(7)<module>()
-> def f(n):
(Pdb) break 13
Breakpoint 1 at .../pdb_jump.py:13

(Pdb) continue
> .../pdb_jump.py(13)f()
-> result.append(j)

(Pdb) p j
5

(Pdb) jump 12
> .../pdb_jump.py(12)f()
-> j += n

(Pdb) continue
> .../pdb_jump.py(13)f()
-> result.append(j)

(Pdb) p j
10

(Pdb) disable 1

(Pdb) continue
[10, 20, 35, 55, 80]

The program finished and will be restarted
> .../pdb_jump.py(7)<module>()
-> def f(n):
(Pdb)
```

Illegal Jumps

Jumping in and out of certain flow control statements is dangerous or undefined, and therefore, prevented by the debugger.

```python
#!/usr/bin/env python
# encoding: utf-8
#
# Copyright (c) 2010 Doug Hellmann.  All rights reserved.
#

def f(n):
    if n < 0:
        raise ValueError('Invalid n: %s' % n)
    result = []
    j = 0
    for i in range(n):
        j = i * n + j
        j += n
        result.append(j)
    return result


if __name__ == '__main__':
    try:
        print f(5)
    finally:
        print 'Always printed'

    try:
        print f(-5)
    except:
        print 'There was an error'
    else:
        print 'There was no error'

    print 'Last statement'
```

jump can be used to enter a function, but the arguments are not defined and the code is unlikely to work.

```
$ python -m pdb pdb_no_jump.py

> .../pdb_no_jump.py(7)<module>()
-> def f(n):
(Pdb) break 21
Breakpoint 1 at .../pdb_no_jump.py:21

(Pdb) jump 8
> .../pdb_no_jump.py(8)<module>()
-> if n < 0:

(Pdb) p n
*** NameError: NameError("name 'n' is not defined",)

(Pdb) args

(Pdb)
```

jump will not enter the middle of a block such as a **for** loop or **try:except** statement.

```
$ python -m pdb pdb_no_jump.py

> .../pdb_no_jump.py(7)<module>()
-> def f(n):
(Pdb) break 21
Breakpoint 1 at .../pdb_no_jump.py:21

(Pdb) continue
> .../pdb_no_jump.py(21)<module>()
-> print f(5)

(Pdb) jump 26
*** Jump failed: can't jump into the middle of a block

(Pdb)
```

The code in a **finally** block must all be executed, so **jump** will not leave the block.

```
$ python -m pdb pdb_no_jump.py

> .../pdb_no_jump.py(7)<module>()
```

```
-> def f(n):
(Pdb) break 23
Breakpoint 1 at .../pdb_no_jump.py:23

(Pdb) continue
[5, 15, 30, 50, 75]
> .../pdb_no_jump.py(23)<module>()
-> print 'Always printed'

(Pdb) jump 25
*** Jump failed: can't jump into or out of a 'finally' block

(Pdb)
```

And the most basic restriction is that jumping is constrained to the bottom frame on the call stack. After moving up the stack to examine variables, the execution flow cannot be changed at that point.

```
$ python -m pdb pdb_no_jump.py

> .../pdb_no_jump.py(7)<module>()
-> def f(n):
(Pdb) break 11
Breakpoint 1 at .../pdb_no_jump.py:11

(Pdb) continue
> .../pdb_no_jump.py(11)f()
-> j = 0

(Pdb) where
  /Library/Frameworks/Python.framework/Versions/2.7/lib/python2.7/
bdb.py(379)run()
-> exec cmd in globals, locals
  <string>(1)<module>()
  .../pdb_no_jump.py(21)<module>()
-> print f(5)
> .../pdb_no_jump.py(11)f()
-> j = 0

(Pdb) up
> .../pdb_no_jump.py(21)<module>()
```

```
-> print f(5)

(Pdb) jump 25
*** You can only jump within the bottom frame

(Pdb)
```

Restarting a Program

When the debugger reaches the end of the program, it automatically starts it over, but it can also be restarted explicitly without leaving the debugger and losing the current breakpoints or other settings.

```
1   #!/usr/bin/env python
2   # encoding: utf-8
3   #
4   # Copyright (c) 2010 Doug Hellmann.  All rights reserved.
5   #
6
7   import sys
8
9   def f():
10      print 'Command-line args:', sys.argv
11      return
12
13  if __name__ == '__main__':
14      f()
```

Running this program to completion within the debugger prints the name of the script file, since no other arguments were given on the command line.

```
$ python -m pdb pdb_run.py

> .../pdb_run.py(7)<module>()
-> import sys
(Pdb) continue

Command-line args: ['pdb_run.py']
The program finished and will be restarted
> .../pdb_run.py(7)<module>()
-> import sys

(Pdb)
```

The program can be restarted using **run**. Arguments passed to **run** are parsed with `shlex` and passed to the program as though they were command-line arguments, so the program can be restarted with different settings.

```
(Pdb) run a b c "this is a long value"
Restarting pdb_run.py with arguments:
        a b c this is a long value
> .../pdb_run.py(7)<module>()
-> import sys

(Pdb) continue
Command-line args: ['pdb_run.py', 'a', 'b', 'c', 'this is a long value']
The program finished and will be restarted
> .../pdb_run.py(7)<module>()
-> import sys

(Pdb)
```

run can also be used at any other point in processing to restart the program.

```
$ python -m pdb pdb_run.py

> .../pdb_run.py(7)<module>()
-> import sys
(Pdb) break 10
Breakpoint 1 at .../pdb_run.py:10

(Pdb) continue
> .../pdb_run.py(10)f()
-> print 'Command-line args:', sys.argv

(Pdb) run one two three
Restarting pdb_run.py with arguments:
        one two three
> .../pdb_run.py(7)<module>()
-> import sys

(Pdb)
```

16.6.5 Customizing the Debugger with Aliases

Avoid typing complex commands repeatedly by using **alias** to define a shortcut. Alias expansion is applied to the first word of each command. The body of the alias can consist of any command that is legal to type at the debugger prompt, including other debugger commands and pure Python expressions. Recursion is allowed in alias definitions, so one alias can even invoke another.

```
$ python -m pdb pdb_function_arguments.py

> .../pdb_function_arguments.py(7)<module>()
-> import pdb
(Pdb) break 10
Breakpoint 1 at .../pdb_function_arguments.py:10

(Pdb) continue
> .../pdb_function_arguments.py(10)recursive_function()
-> if n > 0:

(Pdb) pp locals().keys()
['output', 'n']

(Pdb) alias pl pp locals().keys()

(Pdb) pl
['output', 'n']
```

Running **alias** without any arguments shows the list of defined aliases. A single argument is assumed to be the name of an alias, and its definition is printed.

```
(Pdb) alias
pl = pp locals().keys()

(Pdb) alias pl
pl = pp locals().keys()
(Pdb)
```

Arguments to the alias are referenced using %n, where *n* is replaced with a number indicating the position of the argument, starting with 1. To consume all the arguments, use %*.

```
$ python -m pdb pdb_function_arguments.py

> .../pdb_function_arguments.py(7)<module>()
-> import pdb
```

```
(Pdb) alias ph !help(%1)

(Pdb) ph locals
Help on built-in function locals in module __builtin__:

locals(...)
    locals() -> dictionary

    Update and return a dictionary containing the current scope's
local variables.
```

Clear the definition of an alias with **unalias**.

```
(Pdb) unalias ph

(Pdb) ph locals
*** SyntaxError: invalid syntax (<stdin>, line 1)

(Pdb)
```

16.6.6   Saving Configuration Settings

Debugging a program involves a lot of repetition: running the code, observing the output, adjusting the code or inputs, and running it again. pdb attempts to cut down on the amount of repetition needed to control the debugging experience, to let you concentrate on the code instead of the debugger. To help reduce the number of times you issue the same commands to the debugger, pdb can read a saved configuration from text files interpreted as it starts.

The file ~/.pdbrc is read first, allowing global personal preferences for all debugging sessions. Then ./.pdbrc is read from the current working directory to set local preferences for a particular project.

```
$ cat ~/.pdbrc

# Show python help
alias ph !help(%1)
# Overridden alias
alias redefined p 'home definition'

$ cat .pdbrc
```

```
# Breakpoints
break 10
# Overridden alias
alias redefined p 'local definition'

$ python -m pdb pdb_function_arguments.py

Breakpoint 1 at .../pdb_function_arguments.py:10
> .../pdb_function_arguments.py(7)<module>()
-> import pdb
(Pdb) alias
ph = !help(%1)
redefined = p 'local definition'

(Pdb) break
Num Type          Disp Enb  Where
1   breakpoint    keep yes  at .../pdb_function_arguments.py:10

(Pdb)
```

Any configuration commands that can be typed at the debugger prompt can be saved in one of the start-up files, but most commands that control the execution (**continue**, **jump**, etc.) cannot. The exception is **run**, which means the command-line arguments for a debugging session can be set in `./.pdbrc` so they are consistent across several runs.

See Also:
pdb (http://docs.python.org/library/pdb.html) The standard library documentation for this module.
`readline` **(page 823)** Interactive prompt-editing library.
`cmd` **(page 839)** Build interactive programs.
`shlex` **(page 852)** Shell command-line parsing.

16.7   trace—Follow Program Flow

> **Purpose** Monitor which statements and functions are executed as a program runs to produce coverage and call-graph information.
> **Python Version** 2.3 and later

The `trace` module is useful for understanding the way a program runs. It watches the statements executed, produces coverage reports, and helps investigate the relationships between functions that call each other.

16.7.1   Example Program

This program will be used in the examples in the rest of the section. It imports another module called `recurse` and then runs a function from it.

```
from recurse import recurse

def main():
    print 'This is the main program.'
    recurse(2)
    return

if __name__ == '__main__':
    main()
```

The `recurse()` function invokes itself until the level argument reaches 0.

```
def recurse(level):
    print 'recurse(%s)' % level
    if level:
        recurse(level-1)
    return

def not_called():
    print 'This function is never called.'
```

16.7.2   Tracing Execution

It is easy to use `trace` directly from the command line. The statements being executed as the program runs are printed when the `--trace` option is given.

```
$ python -m trace --trace trace_example/main.py

 --- modulename: threading, funcname: settrace
threading.py(89):      _trace_hook = func
 --- modulename: trace, funcname: <module>
<string>(1):    --- modulename: trace, funcname: <module>
main.py(7): """
main.py(12): from recurse import recurse
 --- modulename: recurse, funcname: <module>
recurse.py(7): """
recurse.py(12): def recurse(level):
recurse.py(18): def not_called():
```

```
main.py(14): def main():
main.py(19): if __name__ == '__main__':
main.py(20):     main()
 --- modulename: trace, funcname: main
main.py(15):     print 'This is the main program.'
This is the main program.
main.py(16):     recurse(2)
 --- modulename: recurse, funcname: recurse
recurse.py(13):     print 'recurse(%s)' % level
recurse(2)
recurse.py(14):     if level:
recurse.py(15):         recurse(level-1)
 --- modulename: recurse, funcname: recurse
recurse.py(13):     print 'recurse(%s)' % level
recurse(1)
recurse.py(14):     if level:
recurse.py(15):         recurse(level-1)
 --- modulename: recurse, funcname: recurse
recurse.py(13):     print 'recurse(%s)' % level
recurse(0)
recurse.py(14):     if level:
recurse.py(16):     return
recurse.py(16):     return
recurse.py(16):     return
main.py(17):     return
```

The first part of the output shows the setup operations performed by `trace`. The rest of the output shows the entry into each function, including the module where the function is located, and then the lines of the source file as they are executed. The `recurse()` function is entered three times, as expected based on the way it is called in `main()`.

16.7.3 Code Coverage

Running `trace` from the command line with the `--count` option will produce code coverage report information, detailing which lines are run and which are skipped. Since a complex program is usually made up of multiple files, a separate coverage report is produced for each. By default, the coverage report files are written to the same directory as the module, named after the module but with a `.cover` extension instead of `.py`.

```
$ python -m trace --count trace_example/main.py

This is the main program.
recurse(2)
recurse(1)
recurse(0)
```

Two output files are produced. Here is `trace_example/main.cover`.

```
1: from recurse import recurse

1: def main():
1:     print 'This is the main program.'
1:     recurse(2)
1:     return

1: if __name__ == '__main__':
1:     main()
```

And here is `trace_example/recurse.cover`.

```
1: def recurse(level):
3:     print 'recurse(%s)' % level
3:     if level:
2:         recurse(level-1)
3:     return

1: def not_called():
       print 'This function is never called.'
```

> **Note:** Although the line `def recurse(level):` has a count of 1, that does not mean the function was only run once. It means the function *definition* was only executed once.

It is also possible to run the program several times, perhaps with different options, to save the coverage data and produce a combined report.

```
$ python -m trace --coverdir coverdir1 --count --file coverdir1/cove\
rage_report.dat trace_example/main.py
```

```
Skipping counts file 'coverdir1/coverage_report.dat': [Errno 2] No suc
h file or directory: 'coverdir1/coverage_report.dat'
This is the main program.
recurse(2)
recurse(1)
recurse(0)

$ python -m trace --coverdir coverdir1 --count --file coverdir1/cove\
rage_report.dat trace_example/main.py

This is the main program.
recurse(2)
recurse(1)
recurse(0)

$ python -m trace --coverdir coverdir1 --count --file coverdir1/cove\
rage_report.dat trace_example/main.py

This is the main program.
recurse(2)
recurse(1)
recurse(0)
```

To produce reports once the coverage information is recorded to the `.cover` files, use the `--report` option.

```
$ python -m trace --coverdir coverdir1 --report --summary --missing \
--file coverdir1/coverage_report.dat trace_example/main.py

lines   cov%   module    (path)
  599     0%   threading    (/Library/Frameworks/Python.framework/Versi
ons/2.7/lib/python2.7/threading.py)
    8   100%   trace_example.main    (trace_example/main.py)
    8    87%   trace_example.recurse    (trace_example/recurse.py)
```

Since the program ran three times, the coverage report shows values three times higher than the first report. The `--summary` option adds the percent-covered information to the output. The `recurse` module is only 87% covered. Looking at the cover file for `recurse` shows that the body of `not_called()` is indeed never run, indicated by the `>>>>>>` prefix.

```
3: def recurse(level):
9:     print 'recurse(%s)' % level
```

```
   9:       if level:
   6:           recurse(level-1)
   9:       return

   3: def not_called():
>>>>>>       print 'This function is never called.'
```

16.7.4   Calling Relationships

In addition to coverage information, `trace` will collect and report on the relationships between functions that call each other.

For a simple list of the functions called, use `--listfuncs`.

```
$ python -m trace --listfuncs trace_example/main.py

This is the main program.
recurse(2)
recurse(1)
recurse(0)

functions called:
filename: /Library/Frameworks/Python.framework/Versions/2.7/lib/python
2.7/threading.py, modulename: threading, funcname: settrace
filename: <string>, modulename: <string>, funcname: <module>
filename: trace_example/main.py, modulename: main, funcname: <module>
filename: trace_example/main.py, modulename: main, funcname: main
filename: trace_example/recurse.py, modulename: recurse, funcname: <mo
dule>
filename: trace_example/recurse.py, modulename: recurse, funcname: rec
urse
```

For more details about who is doing the calling, use `--trackcalls`.

```
$ python -m trace --listfuncs --trackcalls trace_example/main.py

This is the main program.
recurse(2)
recurse(1)
recurse(0)

calling relationships:

*** /Library/Frameworks/Python.framework/Versions/2.7/lib/python2.7/tr
ace.py ***
```

```
  --> /Library/Frameworks/Python.framework/Versions/2.7/lib/python2.7/
threading.py
     trace.Trace.run -> threading.settrace
  --> <string>
     trace.Trace.run -> <string>.<module>

*** <string> ***
  --> trace_example/main.py
     <string>.<module> -> main.<module>

*** trace_example/main.py ***
     main.<module> -> main.main
  --> trace_example/recurse.py
     main.<module> -> recurse.<module>
     main.main -> recurse.recurse

*** trace_example/recurse.py ***
     recurse.recurse -> recurse.recurse
```

16.7.5 Programming Interface

For more control over the `trace` interface, it can be invoked from within a program using a `Trace` object. `Trace` supports setting up fixtures and other dependencies before running a single function or executing a Python command to be traced.

```
import trace
from trace_example.recurse import recurse

tracer = trace.Trace(count=False, trace=True)
tracer.run('recurse(2)')
```

Since the example only traces into the `recurse()` function, no information from `main.py` is included in the output.

```
$ python trace_run.py

 --- modulename: threading, funcname: settrace
threading.py(89):       _trace_hook = func
 --- modulename: trace_run, funcname: <module>
<string>(1):    --- modulename: recurse, funcname: recurse
recurse.py(13):       print 'recurse(%s)' % level
```

```
recurse(2)
recurse.py(14):     if level:
recurse.py(15):         recurse(level-1)
 --- modulename: recurse, funcname: recurse
recurse.py(13):         print 'recurse(%s)' % level
recurse(1)
recurse.py(14):     if level:
recurse.py(15):         recurse(level-1)
 --- modulename: recurse, funcname: recurse
recurse.py(13):         print 'recurse(%s)' % level
recurse(0)
recurse.py(14):     if level:
recurse.py(16):         return
recurse.py(16):         return
recurse.py(16):         return
```

That same output can be produced with the `runfunc()` method, too.

```
import trace
from trace_example.recurse import recurse

tracer = trace.Trace(count=False, trace=True)
tracer.runfunc(recurse, 2)
```

`runfunc()` accepts arbitrary positional and keyword arguments, which are passed to the function when it is called by the tracer.

```
$ python trace_runfunc.py

 --- modulename: recurse, funcname: recurse
recurse.py(13):         print 'recurse(%s)' % level
recurse(2)
recurse.py(14):     if level:
recurse.py(15):         recurse(level-1)
 --- modulename: recurse, funcname: recurse
recurse.py(13):         print 'recurse(%s)' % level
recurse(1)
recurse.py(14):     if level:
recurse.py(15):         recurse(level-1)
 --- modulename: recurse, funcname: recurse
recurse.py(13):         print 'recurse(%s)' % level
```

```
recurse(0)
recurse.py(14):      if level:
recurse.py(16):      return
recurse.py(16):      return
recurse.py(16):      return
```

16.7.6   Saving Result Data

Counts and coverage information can be recorded as well, just as with the command-line interface. The data must be saved explicitly, using the CoverageResults instance from the Trace object.

```
import trace
from trace_example.recurse import recurse

tracer = trace.Trace(count=True, trace=False)
tracer.runfunc(recurse, 2)

results = tracer.results()
results.write_results(coverdir='coverdir2')
```

This example saves the coverage results to the directory coverdir2.

```
$ python trace_CoverageResults.py

recurse(2)
recurse(1)
recurse(0)

$ find coverdir2

coverdir2
coverdir2/trace_example.recurse.cover
```

The output file contains the following.

```
#!/usr/bin/env python
# encoding: utf-8
#
# Copyright (c) 2008 Doug Hellmann All rights reserved.
#
"""
```

```
        """

        #__version__ = "$Id$"
        #end_pymotw_header

>>>>>> def recurse(level):
    3:      print 'recurse(%s)' % level
    3:      if level:
    2:          recurse(level-1)
    3:      return

>>>>>> def not_called():
>>>>>>      print 'This function is never called.'
```

To save the counts data for generating reports, use the *infile* and *outfile* arguments to Trace.

```
import trace
from trace_example.recurse import recurse

tracer = trace.Trace(count=True,
                     trace=False,
                     outfile='trace_report.dat')
tracer.runfunc(recurse, 2)

report_tracer = trace.Trace(count=False,
                            trace=False,
                            infile='trace_report.dat')
results = tracer.results()
results.write_results(summary=True, coverdir='/tmp')
```

Pass a filename to *infile* to read previously stored data and a filename to *outfile* to write new results after tracing. If *infile* and *outfile* are the same, it has the effect of updating the file with cumulative data.

```
$ python trace_report.py

recurse(2)
recurse(1)
recurse(0)
lines   cov%   module       (path)
    7    57%   trace_example.recurse   (.../recurse.py)
```

16.7.7   Options

The constructor for `Trace` takes several optional parameters to control runtime behavior.

count Boolean. Turns on line-number counting. Defaults to `True`.

countfuncs Boolean. Turns on the list of functions called during the run. Defaults to `False`.

countcallers Boolean. Turns on tracking for callers and callees. Defaults to `False`.

ignoremods Sequence. List of modules or packages to ignore when tracking coverage. Defaults to an empty tuple.

ignoredirs Sequence. List of directories containing modules or packages to be ignored. Defaults to an empty tuple.

infile Name of the file containing cached count values. Defaults to `None`.

outfile Name of the file to use for storing cached count files. Defaults to `None`, and data is not stored.

See Also:

trace (http://docs.python.org/lib/module-trace.html) The standard library documentation for this module.

***Tracing a Program as It Runs* (page 1101)** The `sys` module includes facilities for adding a custom-tracing function to the interpreter at runtime.

coverage.py (http://nedbatchelder.com/code/modules/coverage.html) Ned Batchelder's coverage module.

figleaf (http://darcs.idyll.org/ t/projects/figleaf/doc/) Titus Brown's coverage application.

16.8   profile and pstats—Performance Analysis

> **Purpose** Performance analysis of Python programs.
> **Python Version** 1.4 and later

The `profile` and `cProfile` modules provide APIs for collecting and analyzing statistics about how Python source consumes processor resources.

Note: The output reports in this section have been reformatted to fit on the page. Lines ending with backslash (\) are continued on the next line.

16.8.1 Running the Profiler

The most basic starting point in the `profile` module is `run()`. It takes a string statement as argument and creates a report of the time spent executing different lines of code while running the statement.

```
import profile

def fib(n):
    # from literateprograms.org
    # http://bit.ly/hlOQ5m
    if n == 0:
        return 0
    elif n == 1:
        return 1
    else:
        return fib(n-1) + fib(n-2)

def fib_seq(n):
    seq = [ ]
    if n > 0:
        seq.extend(fib_seq(n-1))
    seq.append(fib(n))
    return seq

profile.run('print fib_seq(20); print')
```

This recursive version of a Fibonacci sequence calculator is especially useful for demonstrating the profile because the performance can be improved significantly. The standard report format shows a summary and then the details for each function executed.

```
$ python profile_fibonacci_raw.py

[0, 1, 1, 2, 3, 5, 8, 13, 21, 34, 55, 89, 144, 233, 377, 610, 987,
1597, 2584, 4181, 6765]

        57356 function calls (66 primitive calls) in 0.746 CPU seconds
```

```
Ordered by: standard name

   ncalls  tottime  percall  cumtime  percall  filename:lineno(function)
       21    0.000    0.000    0.000    0.000  :0(append)
       20    0.000    0.000    0.000    0.000  :0(extend)
        1    0.001    0.001    0.001    0.001  :0(setprofile)
        1    0.000    0.000    0.744    0.744  <string>:1(<module>)
        1    0.000    0.000    0.746    0.746  profile:0(\
                                               print fib_seq(20);print)
        0    0.000             0.000            profile:0(profiler)
 57291/21    0.743    0.000    0.743    0.035  profile_fibonacci_raw.py\
                                               :10(fib)
     21/1    0.001    0.000    0.744    0.744  profile_fibonacci_raw.py\
                                               :20(fib_seq)
```

The raw version takes 57,356 separate function calls and $\frac{3}{4}$ of a second to run. The fact that there are only 66 *primitive* calls says that the vast majority of those 57k calls were recursive. The details about where time was spent are broken out by function in the listing showing the number of calls, total time spent in the function, time per call (`tottime/ncalls`), cumulative time spent in a function, and the ratio of cumulative time to primitive calls.

Not surprisingly, most of the time here is spent calling `fib()` repeatedly. Adding a memoize decorator reduces the number of recursive calls and has a big impact on the performance of this function.

```python
import profile

class memoize:
    # from Avinash Vora's memoize decorator
    # http://bit.ly/fGzfR7
    def __init__(self, function):
        self.function = function
        self.memoized = {}


    def __call__(self, *args):
        try:
            return self.memoized[args]
        except KeyError:
            self.memoized[args] = self.function(*args)
            return self.memoized[args]
```

```
@memoize
def fib(n):
    # from literateprograms.org
    # http://bit.ly/hlOQ5m
    if n == 0:
        return 0
    elif n == 1:
        return 1
    else:
        return fib(n-1) + fib(n-2)


def fib_seq(n):
    seq = [ ]
    if n > 0:
        seq.extend(fib_seq(n-1))
    seq.append(fib(n))
    return seq


if __name__ == '__main__':
    profile.run('print fib_seq(20); print')
```

By remembering the Fibonacci value at each level, most of the recursion is avoided and the run drops down to 145 calls that only take 0.003 seconds. The `ncalls` count for `fib()` shows that it *never* recurses.

```
$ python profile_fibonacci_memoized.py

[0, 1, 1, 2, 3, 5, 8, 13, 21, 34, 55, 89, 144, 233, 377, 610, 987, 1597,
2584, 4181, 6765]

        145 function calls (87 primitive calls) in 0.003 CPU seconds

   Ordered by: standard name

   ncalls  tottime  percall  cumtime  percall filename:lineno(function)
       21    0.000    0.000    0.000    0.000 :0(append)
       20    0.000    0.000    0.000    0.000 :0(extend)
        1    0.001    0.001    0.001    0.001 :0(setprofile)
        1    0.000    0.000    0.002    0.002 <string>:1(<module>)
        1    0.000    0.000    0.003    0.003 profile:0(\
                                              print fib_seq(20); print)
        0    0.000             0.000          profile:0(profiler)
    59/21    0.001    0.000    0.001    0.000 profile_fibonacci_\
                                              memoized.py:17(__call__)
```

```
      21     0.000     0.000     0.001     0.000  profile_fibonacci_\
                                                  memoized.py:24(fib)
    21/1     0.001     0.000     0.002     0.002  profile_fibonacci_\
                                                  memoized.py:35(fib_seq)
```

16.8.2 Running in a Context

Sometimes, instead of constructing a complex expression for `run()`, it is easier to build a simple expression and pass it parameters through a context, using `runctx()`.

```
import profile
from profile_fibonacci_memoized import fib, fib_seq

if __name__ == '__main__':
    profile.runctx('print fib_seq(n); print', globals(), {'n':20})
```

In this example, the value of `n` is passed through the local variable context instead of being embedded directly in the statement passed to `runctx()`.

```
$ python profile_runctx.py

[0, 1, 1, 2, 3, 5, 8, 13, 21, 34, 55, 89, 144, 233, 377, 610, 987,
1597, 2584, 4181, 6765]

         145 function calls (87 primitive calls) in 0.003 CPU seconds

   Ordered by: standard name

   ncalls  tottime  percall  cumtime  percall  filename:lineno(function)
       21    0.000    0.000    0.000    0.000  :0(append)
       20    0.000    0.000    0.000    0.000  :0(extend)
        1    0.001    0.001    0.001    0.001  :0(setprofile)
        1    0.000    0.000    0.002    0.002  <string>:1(<module>)
        1    0.000    0.000    0.003    0.003  profile:0(\
                                               print fib_seq(n); print)
        0    0.000             0.000          profile:0(profiler)
    59/21    0.001    0.000    0.001    0.000  profile_fibonacci_\
                                               memoized.py:17(__call__)
       21    0.000    0.000    0.001    0.000  profile_fibonacci_\
                                               memoized.py:24(fib)
     21/1    0.001    0.000    0.002    0.002  profile_fibonacci_\
                                               memoized.py:35(fib_seq)
```

16.8.3 pstats: Saving and Working with Statistics

The standard report created by the `profile` functions is not very flexible. However, custom reports can be produced by saving the raw profiling data from `run()` and `runctx()` and processing it separately with the `pstats.Stats` class.

This example runs several iterations of the same test and combines the results.

```
import cProfile as profile
import pstats
from profile_fibonacci_memoized import fib, fib_seq

# Create 5 set of stats
filenames = []
for i in range(5):
    filename = 'profile_stats_%d.stats' % i
    profile.run('print %d, fib_seq(20)' % i, filename)

# Read all 5 stats files into a single object
stats = pstats.Stats('profile_stats_0.stats')
for i in range(1, 5):
    stats.add('profile_stats_%d.stats' % i)

# Clean up filenames for the report
stats.strip_dirs()

# Sort the statistics by the cumulative time spent in the function
stats.sort_stats('cumulative')

stats.print_stats()
```

The output report is sorted in descending order of cumulative time spent in the function, and the directory names are removed from the printed filenames to conserve horizontal space on the page.

```
$ python profile_stats.py

0 [0, 1, 1, 2, 3, 5, 8, 13, 21, 34, 55, 89, 144, 233, 377, 610,
 987, 1597, 2584, 4181, 6765]
1 [0, 1, 1, 2, 3, 5, 8, 13, 21, 34, 55, 89, 144, 233, 377, 610,
 987, 1597, 2584, 4181, 6765]
2 [0, 1, 1, 2, 3, 5, 8, 13, 21, 34, 55, 89, 144, 233, 377, 610,
 987, 1597, 2584, 4181, 6765]
```

```
3 [0, 1, 1, 2, 3, 5, 8, 13, 21, 34, 55, 89, 144, 233, 377, 610,
 987, 1597, 2584, 4181, 6765]
4 [0, 1, 1, 2, 3, 5, 8, 13, 21, 34, 55, 89, 144, 233, 377, 610,
 987, 1597, 2584, 4181, 6765]
Sun Aug 31 11:29:36 2008    profile_stats_0.stats
Sun Aug 31 11:29:36 2008    profile_stats_1.stats
Sun Aug 31 11:29:36 2008    profile_stats_2.stats
Sun Aug 31 11:29:36 2008    profile_stats_3.stats
Sun Aug 31 11:29:36 2008    profile_stats_4.stats

         489 function calls (351 primitive calls) in 0.008 CPU seconds

   Ordered by: cumulative time

     ncalls  tottime  percall  cumtime  percall filename:lineno(function)
          5    0.000    0.000    0.007    0.001 <string>:1(<module>)
      105/5    0.004    0.000    0.007    0.001 profile_fibonacci_\
                                                memoized.py:36(fib_seq)
          1    0.000    0.000    0.003    0.003 profile:0(print 0, \
                                                fib_seq(20))
    143/105    0.001    0.000    0.002    0.000 profile_fibonacci_\
                                                memoized.py:19(__call__)
          1    0.000    0.000    0.001    0.001 profile:0(print 4, \
                                                fib_seq(20))
          1    0.000    0.000    0.001    0.001 profile:0(print 1, \
                                                fib_seq(20))
          1    0.000    0.000    0.001    0.001 profile:0(print 2, \
                                                fib_seq(20))
          1    0.000    0.000    0.001    0.001 profile:0(print 3, \
                                                fib_seq(20))
         21    0.000    0.000    0.001    0.000 profile_fibonacci_\
                                                memoized.py:26(fib)
        100    0.001    0.000    0.001    0.000 :0(extend)
        105    0.001    0.000    0.001    0.000 :0(append)
          5    0.001    0.000    0.001    0.000 :0(setprofile)
          0    0.000             0.000          profile:0(profiler)
```

16.8.4   Limiting Report Contents

The output can be restricted by function. This version only shows information about the performance of `fib()` and `fib_seq()` by using a regular expression to match the desired `filename:lineno(function)` values.

```
import profile
import pstats
from profile_fibonacci_memoized import fib, fib_seq

# Read all 5 stats files into a single object
stats = pstats.Stats('profile_stats_0.stats')
for i in range(1, 5):
    stats.add('profile_stats_%d.stats' % i)
stats.strip_dirs()
stats.sort_stats('cumulative')

# limit output to lines with "(fib" in them
stats.print_stats('\(fib')
```

The regular expression includes a literal left parenthesis [(] to match against the function name portion of the location value.

```
$ python profile_stats_restricted.py

Sun Aug 31 11:29:36 2008    profile_stats_0.stats
Sun Aug 31 11:29:36 2008    profile_stats_1.stats
Sun Aug 31 11:29:36 2008    profile_stats_2.stats
Sun Aug 31 11:29:36 2008    profile_stats_3.stats
Sun Aug 31 11:29:36 2008    profile_stats_4.stats

        489 function calls (351 primitive calls) in 0.008 CPU seconds

   Ordered by: cumulative time
   List reduced from 13 to 2 due to restriction <'\\(fib'>

   ncalls  tottime  percall  cumtime  percall filename:lineno(function)
    105/5    0.004    0.000    0.007    0.001 profile_fibonacci_\
                                             memoized.py:36(fib_seq)
       21    0.000    0.000    0.001    0.000 profile_fibonacci_\
                                             memoized.py:26(fib)
```

16.8.5   Caller / Callee Graphs

`Stats` also includes methods for printing the callers and callees of functions.

```
import cProfile as profile
import pstats
from profile_fibonacci_memoized import fib, fib_seq
```

```
# Read all 5 stats files into a single object
stats = pstats.Stats('profile_stats_0.stats')
for i in range(1, 5):
    stats.add('profile_stats_%d.stats' % i)
stats.strip_dirs()
stats.sort_stats('cumulative')

print 'INCOMING CALLERS:'
stats.print_callers('\(fib')

print 'OUTGOING CALLEES:'
stats.print_callees('\(fib')
```

The arguments to `print_callers()` and `print_callees()` work the same as the restriction arguments to `print_stats()`. The output shows the caller, callee, number of calls, and cumulative time.

```
$ python profile_stats_callers.py

INCOMING CALLERS:
   Ordered by: cumulative time
   List reduced from 7 to 2 due to restriction <'\\(fib'>

Function                                     was called by...
                                               ncalls  tottime cumtime
profile_fibonacci_memoized.py:35(fib_seq)  <-       5    0.000   0.001\
   <string>:1(<module>)

                                              100/5    0.000   0.001\
   profile_fibonacci_memoized.py:35(fib_seq)
profile_fibonacci_memoized.py:24(fib)      <-      21    0.000   0.000\
   profile_fibonacci_memoized.py:17(__call__)


OUTGOING CALLEES:
   Ordered by: cumulative time
   List reduced from 7 to 2 due to restriction <'\\(fib'>

Function                                     called...
                                               ncalls  tottime cumtime
profile_fibonacci_memoized.py:35(fib_seq)  ->     105    0.000   0.000\
   profile_fibonacci_memoized.py:17(__call__)
                                              100/5    0.000   0.001\
```

```
profile_fibonacci_memoized.py:35(fib_seq)
                                                105    0.000   0.000\
{method 'append' of 'list' objects}
                                                100    0.000   0.000\
{method 'extend' of 'list' objects}
profile_fibonacci_memoized.py:24(fib)      ->    38    0.000   0.000\
  profile_fibonacci_memoized.py:17(__call__)
```

See Also:

profile and cProfile (http://docs.python.org/lib/module-profile.html) The standard library documentation for this module.

pstats (http://docs.python.org/lib/profile-stats.html) The standard library documentation for `pstats`.

Gprof2Dot   (http://code.google.com/p/jrfonseca/wiki/Gprof2Dot) Visualization tool for profile output data.

Fibonacci numbers (Python)—LiteratePrograms (http://en.literateprograms.org/Fibonacci_numbers_(Python)) An implementation of a Fibonacci sequence generator in Python.

Python Decorators: Syntactic Sugar | avinash.vora (http://avinashv.net/2008/04/python-decorators-syntactic-sugar/) Another memoized Fibonacci sequence generator in Python.

16.9   timeit—Time the Execution of Small Bits of Python Code

Purpose Time the execution of small bits of Python code.
Python Version 2.3 and later

The `timeit` module provides a simple interface for determining the execution time of small bits of Python code. It uses a platform-specific time function to provide the most accurate time calculation possible and reduces the impact of start-up or shutdown costs on the time calculation by executing the code repeatedly.

16.9.1   Module Contents

`timeit` defines a single public class, `Timer`. The constructor for `Timer` takes a statement to be timed and a "setup" statement (used to initialize variables, for example). The Python statements should be strings and can include embedded newlines.

The `timeit()` method runs the setup statement one time and then executes the primary statement repeatedly and returns the amount of time that passes. The argument to `timeit()` controls how many times to run the statement; the default is 1,000,000.

16.9.2 Basic Example

To illustrate how the various arguments to `Timer` are used, here is a simple example that prints an identifying value when each statement is executed.

```
import timeit

# using setitem
t = timeit.Timer("print 'main statement'", "print 'setup'")

print 'TIMEIT:'
print t.timeit(2)

print 'REPEAT:'
print t.repeat(3, 2)
```

When run, the output is:

```
$ python timeit_example.py

TIMEIT:
setup
main statement
main statement
2.86102294922e-06
REPEAT:
setup
main statement
main statement
setup
main statement
main statement
setup
main statement
main statement
[9.5367431640625e-07, 1.9073486328125e-06, 2.1457672119140625e-06]
```

`timeit()` runs the setup statement one time and then calls the main statement *count* times. It returns a single floating-point value representing the cumulative amount of time spent running the main statement.

When `repeat()` is used, it calls `timeit()` several times (three in this case) and all the responses are returned in a list.

16.9.3   Storing Values in a Dictionary

This more complex example compares the amount of time it takes to populate a dictionary with a large number of values using various methods. First, a few constants are needed to configure the `Timer`. The `setup_statement` variable initializes a list of tuples containing strings and integers that the main statements will use to build dictionaries, using the strings as keys and storing the integers as the associated values.

```
import timeit
import sys

# A few constants
range_size=1000
count=1000
setup_statement = "l = [ (str(x), x) for x in range(1000) ]; d = {}"
```

A utility function, `show_results()`, is defined to print the results in a useful format. The `timeit()` method returns the amount of time it takes to execute the statement repeatedly. The output of `show_results()` converts that time into the amount of time it takes per iteration, and then it further reduces the value to the average amount of time it takes to store one item in the dictionary.

```
def show_results(result):
    "Print results in terms of microseconds per pass and per item."
    global count, range_size
    per_pass = 1000000 * (result / count)
    print '%.2f usec/pass' % per_pass,
    per_item = per_pass / range_size
    print '%.2f usec/item' % per_item

print "%d items" % range_size
print "%d iterations" % count
print
```

To establish a baseline, the first configuration tested uses `__setitem__()`. All the other variations avoid overwriting values already in the dictionary, so this simple version should be the fastest.

The first argument to `Timer` is a multiline string, with whitespace preserved to ensure that it parses correctly when run. The second argument is a constant established to initialize the list of values and the dictionary.

```
# Using __setitem__ without checking for existing values first
print '__setitem__:',
t = timeit.Timer("""
for s, i in l:
    d[s] = i
""",
setup_statement)
show_results(t.timeit(number=count))
```

The next variation uses `setdefault()` to ensure that values already in the dictionary are not overwritten.

```
# Using setdefault
print 'setdefault :',
t = timeit.Timer("""
for s, i in l:
    d.setdefault(s, i)
""",
setup_statement)
show_results(t.timeit(number=count))
```

Another way to avoid overwriting existing values is to use `has_key()` to check the contents of the dictionary explicitly.

```
# Using has_key
print 'has_key    :',
t = timeit.Timer("""
for s, i in l:
    if not d.has_key(s):
        d[s] = i
""",
setup_statement)
show_results(t.timeit(number=count))
```

This method adds the value only if a `KeyError` exception is raised when looking for the existing value.

```
# Using exceptions
print 'KeyError   :',
t = timeit.Timer("""
for s, i in l:
    try:
```

```
        existing = d[s]
    except KeyError:
        d[s] = i
""",
setup_statement)
show_results(t.timeit(number=count))
```

And the last method is the relatively new form using "`in`" to determine if a dictionary has a particular key.

```
# Using "in"
print '"not in"    :',
t = timeit.Timer("""
for s, i in l:
    if s not in d:
        d[s] = i
""",
setup_statement)
show_results(t.timeit(number=count))
```

When run, the script produces this output.

```
$ python timeit_dictionary.py

1000 items
1000 iterations

__setitem__: 131.44 usec/pass 0.13 usec/item
setdefault : 282.94 usec/pass 0.28 usec/item
has_key    : 202.40 usec/pass 0.20 usec/item
KeyError   : 142.50 usec/pass 0.14 usec/item
"not in"   : 104.60 usec/pass 0.10 usec/item
```

Those times are for a MacBook Pro running Python 2.7, and they will vary depending on what other programs are running on the system. Experiment with the *range_size* and *count* variables, since different combinations will produce different results.

16.9.4   From the Command Line

In addition to the programmatic interface, `timeit` provides a command-line interface for testing modules without instrumentation.

To run the module, use the −m option to the Python interpreter to find the module and treat it as the main program.

```
$ python -m timeit
```

For example, use this command to get help.

```
$ python -m timeit -h

Tool for measuring execution time of small code snippets.

This module avoids a number of common traps for measuring execution
times.  See also Tim Peters' introduction to the Algorithms chapter in
the Python Cookbook, published by O'Reilly.

...
```

The *statement* argument works a little differently on the command line than the argument to `Timer`. Instead of one long string, pass each line of the instructions as a separate command-line argument. To indent lines (such as inside a loop), embed spaces in the string by enclosing it in quotes.

```
$ python -m timeit -s "d={}" "for i in range(1000):" "  d[str(i)] = i"

1000 loops, best of 3: 559 usec per loop
```

It is also possible to define a function with more complex code and then call the function from the command line.

```
def test_setitem(range_size=1000):
    l = [ (str(x), x) for x in range(range_size) ]
    d = {}
    for s, i in l:
        d[s] = i
```

To run the test, pass in code that imports the modules and runs the test function.

```
$ python -m timeit "import timeit_setitem; timeit_setitem.test_
setitem()"

1000 loops, best of 3: 804 usec per loop
```

See Also:
timeit (http://docs.python.org/lib/module-timeit.html) The standard library documentation for this module.
profile (page 1022) The `profile` module is also useful for performance analysis.

16.10 compileall—Byte-Compile Source Files

Purpose Convert source files to byte-compiled version.
Python Version 1.4 and later

The `compileall` module finds Python source files and compiles them to the byte-code representation, saving the results in `.pyc` or `.pyo` files.

16.10.1 Compiling One Directory

`compile_dir()` is used to recursively scan a directory and byte-compile the files within it.

```
import compileall

compileall.compile_dir('examples')
```

By default, all the subdirectories are scanned to a depth of 10.

```
$ python compileall_compile_dir.py

Listing examples ...
Compiling examples/a.py ...
Listing examples/subdir ...
Compiling examples/subdir/b.py ...
```

To filter directories out, use the `rx` argument to provide a regular expression to match the names to exclude.

```
import compileall
import re

compileall.compile_dir('examples',
    rx=re.compile(r'/subdir'))
```

This version excludes files in the `subdir` subdirectory.

```
$ python compileall_exclude_dirs.py

Listing examples ...
Compiling examples/a.py ...
Listing examples/subdir ...
```

The *maxlevels* argument controls the depth of recursion. For example, to avoid recursion entirely pass 0.

```
import compileall
import re

compileall.compile_dir('examples',
    maxlevels=0,
    rx=re.compile(r'/\.svn'))
```

Only files within the directory passed to compile_dir() are compiled.

```
$ python compileall_recursion_depth.py

Listing examples ...
Compiling examples/a.py ...
```

16.10.2 Compiling sys.path

All the Python source files found in sys.path can be compiled with a single call to compile_path().

```
import compileall
import sys

sys.path[:] = ['examples', 'notthere']
print 'sys.path =', sys.path
compileall.compile_path()
```

This example replaces the default contents of sys.path to avoid permission errors while running the script, but it still illustrates the default behavior. Note that the *maxlevels* value defaults to 0.

```
$ python compileall_path.py

sys.path = ['examples', 'notthere']
Listing examples ...
```

```
Compiling examples/a.py ...
Listing notthere ...
Can't list notthere
```

16.10.3   From the Command Line

It is also possible to invoke `compileall` from the command line so it can be integrated with a build system via a Makefile. Here is an example.

```
$ python -m compileall -h

option -h not recognized
usage: python compileall.py [-l] [-f] [-q] [-d destdir] [-x
regexp] [-i list] [directory|file ...]
-l: don't recurse down
-f: force rebuild even if timestamps are up-to-date
-q: quiet operation
-d destdir: purported directory name for error messages
   if no directory arguments, -l sys.path is assumed
-x regexp: skip files matching the regular expression regexp
   the regexp is searched for in the full path of the file
-i list: expand list with its content (file and directory names)
```

To re-create the earlier example, skipping the `subdir` directory, run this command.

```
$ python -m compileall -x '/subdir' examples

Listing examples ...
Compiling examples/a.py ...
Listing examples/subdir ...
```

See Also:
compileall (http://docs.python.org/library/compileall.html) The standard library documentation for this module.

16.11   pyclbr—Class Browser

Purpose Implements an API suitable for use in a source code editor for making a class browser.
Python Version 1.4 and later

pyclbr can scan Python source to find classes and stand-alone functions. The information about class, method, and function names and line numbers is gathered using tokenize *without* importing the code.

The examples in this section use this source file as input.

```python
"""Example source for pyclbr.
"""


class Base(object):
    """This is the base class.
    """

    def method1(self):
        return


class Sub1(Base):
    """This is the first subclass.
    """


class Sub2(Base):
    """This is the second subclass.
    """


class Mixin:
    """A mixin class.
    """

    def method2(self):
        return


class MixinUser(Sub2, Mixin):
    """Overrides method1 and method2
    """

    def method1(self):
        return

    def method2(self):
        return

    def method3(self):
        return
```

```
def my_function():
    """Stand-alone function.
    """
    return
```

16.11.1   Scanning for Classes

There are two public functions exposed by `pyclbr`. The first, `readmodule()`, takes the name of the module as an argument and returns a dictionary mapping class names to `Class` objects containing the metadata about the class source.

```
import pyclbr
import os
from operator import itemgetter

def show_class(name, class_data):
    print 'Class:', name
    filename = os.path.basename(class_data.file)
    print '\tFile: {0} [{1}]'.format(filename, class_data.lineno)
    show_super_classes(name, class_data)
    show_methods(name, class_data)
    print
    return

def show_methods(class_name, class_data):
    for name, lineno in sorted(class_data.methods.items(),
                               key=itemgetter(1)):
        print '\tMethod: {0} [{1}]'.format(name, lineno)
    return

def show_super_classes(name, class_data):
    super_class_names = []
    for super_class in class_data.super:
        if super_class == 'object':
            continue
        if isinstance(super_class, basestring):
            super_class_names.append(super_class)
        else:
            super_class_names.append(super_class.name)
    if super_class_names:
        print '\tSuper classes:', super_class_names
    return
```

```
example_data = pyclbr.readmodule('pyclbr_example')

for name, class_data in sorted(example_data.items(),
                               key=lambda x:x[1].lineno):
    show_class(name, class_data)
```

The metadata for the class includes the file and the line number where it is defined, as well as the names of super classes. The methods of the class are saved as a mapping between method name and line number. The output shows the classes and the methods listed in order based on their line number in the source file.

```
$ python pyclbr_readmodule.py

Class: Base
        File: pyclbr_example.py [10]
        Method: method1 [14]

Class: Sub1
        File: pyclbr_example.py [17]
        Super classes: ['Base']

Class: Sub2
        File: pyclbr_example.py [21]
        Super classes: ['Base']

Class: Mixin
        File: pyclbr_example.py [25]
        Method: method2 [29]

Class: MixinUser
        File: pyclbr_example.py [32]
        Super classes: ['Sub2', 'Mixin']
        Method: method1 [36]
        Method: method2 [39]
        Method: method3 [42]
```

16.11.2   Scanning for Functions

The other public function in `pyclbr` is `readmodule_ex()`. It does everything that `readmodule()` does and adds functions to the result set.

```
import pyclbr
import os
from operator import itemgetter

example_data = pyclbr.readmodule_ex('pyclbr_example')

for name, data in sorted(example_data.items(), key=lambda x:x[1].
    lineno):
    if isinstance(data, pyclbr.Function):
        print 'Function: {0} [{1}]'.format(name, data.lineno)
```

Each `Function` object has properties much like the `Class` object.

```
$ python pyclbr_readmodule_ex.py

Function: my_function [45]
```

See Also:
pyclbr (http://docs.python.org/library/pyclbr.html) The standard library documentation for this module.
inspect (page 1200) The `inspect` module can discover more metadata about classes and functions, but it requires importing the code.
tokenize The `tokenize` module parses Python source code into tokens.

Chapter 17

RUNTIME FEATURES

This chapter covers the features of the Python standard library that allow a program to interact with the interpreter or the environment in which it runs.

During start-up, the interpreter loads the `site` module to configure settings specific to the current installation. The import path is constructed from a combination of environment settings, interpreter build parameters, and configuration files.

The `sys` module is one of the largest in the standard library. It includes functions for accessing a broad range of interpreter and system settings, including interpreter build settings and limits; command-line arguments and program exit codes; exception handling; thread debugging and control; the import mechanism and imported modules; runtime control flow tracing; and standard input and output streams for the process.

While `sys` is focused on interpreter settings, `os` provides access to operating system information. It can be used for portable interfaces to system calls that return details about the running process, such as its owner and environment variables. It also includes functions for working with the file system and process management.

Python is often used as a cross-platform language for creating portable programs. Even in a program intended to run anywhere, it is occasionally necessary to know the operating system or hardware architecture of the current system. The `platform` module provides functions to retrieve runtime settings

The limits for system resources, such as the maximum process stack size or number of open files, can be probed and changed through the `resource` module. It also reports the current consumption rates so a process can be monitored for resource leaks.

The `gc` module gives access to the internal state of Python's garbage collection system. It includes information useful for detecting and breaking object cycles, turning the collector on and off, and adjusting thresholds that automatically trigger collection sweeps.

The `sysconfig` module holds the compile-time variables from the build scripts. It can be used by build and packaging tools to generate paths and other settings dynamically.

17.1 site—Site-Wide Configuration

The `site` module handles site-specific configuration, especially the import path.

17.1.1 Import Path

`site` is automatically imported each time the interpreter starts up. On import, it extends `sys.path` with site-specific names constructed by combining the prefix values `sys.prefix` and `sys.exec_prefix` with several suffixes. The prefix values used are saved in the module-level variable `PREFIXES` for reference later. Under Windows, the suffixes are an empty string and `lib/site-packages`. For UNIX-like platforms, the values are `lib/python$version/site-packages` (where `$version` is replaced by the major and minor version number of the interpreter, such as `2.7`) and `lib/site-python`.

```
import sys
import os
import platform
import site

if 'Windows' in platform.platform():
    SUFFIXES = [
        '',
        'lib/site-packages',
        ]
else:
    SUFFIXES = [
        'lib/python%s/site-packages' % sys.version[:3],
        'lib/site-python',
        ]

print 'Path prefixes:'
for p in site.PREFIXES:
    print '  ', p

for prefix in sorted(set(site.PREFIXES)):
    print
    print prefix
```

```
for suffix in SUFFIXES:
    print
    print ' ', suffix
    path = os.path.join(prefix, suffix).rstrip(os.sep)
    print '    exists :', os.path.exists(path)
    print '    in path:', path in sys.path
```

Each of the paths resulting from the combinations is tested, and those that exist are added to `sys.path`. This output shows the framework version of Python installed on a Mac OS X system.

```
$ python site_import_path.py

Path prefixes:
   /Library/Frameworks/Python.framework/Versions/2.7
   /Library/Frameworks/Python.framework/Versions/2.7

/Library/Frameworks/Python.framework/Versions/2.7

  lib/python2.7/site-packages
   exists : True
   in path: True

  lib/site-python
   exists : False
   in path: False
```

17.1.2   User Directories

In addition to the global site-packages paths, `site` is responsible for adding the user-specific locations to the import path. The user-specific paths are all based on the `USER_BASE` directory, which is usually located in a part of the file system owned (and writable) by the current user. Inside the `USER_BASE` directory is a `site-packages` directory, with the path accessible as `USER_SITE`.

```
import site

print 'Base:', site.USER_BASE
print 'Site:', site.USER_SITE
```

The `USER_SITE` path name is created using the same platform-specific suffix values described earlier.

```
$ python site_user_base.py

Base: /Users/dhellmann/.local
Site: /Users/dhellmann/.local/lib/python2.7/site-packages
```

The user base directory can be set through the `PYTHONUSERBASE` environment variable and has platform-specific defaults (`~/Python$version/site-packages` for Windows and `~/.local` for non-Windows).

```
$ PYTHONUSERBASE=/tmp/$USER python site_user_base.py

Base: /tmp/dhellmann
Site: /tmp/dhellmann/lib/python2.7/site-packages
```

The user directory is disabled under some circumstances that would pose security issues (for example, if the process is running with a different effective user or group id than the actual user that started it). An application can check the setting by examining `ENABLE_USER_SITE`.

```
import site

status = {
    None:'Disabled for security',
    True:'Enabled',
    False:'Disabled by command-line option',
    }

print 'Flag    :', site.ENABLE_USER_SITE
print 'Meaning:', status[site.ENABLE_USER_SITE]
```

The user directory can also be explicitly disabled on the command line with `-s`.

```
$ python site_enable_user_site.py

Flag    : True
Meaning: Enabled

$ python -s site_enable_user_site.py

Flag    : False
Meaning: Disabled by command-line option
```

17.1.3 Path Configuration Files

As paths are added to the import path, they are also scanned for *path configuration files*. A path configuration file is a plain-text file with the extension `.pth`. Each line in the file can take one of four forms:

- A full or relative path to another location that should be added to the import path.
- A Python statement to be executed. All such lines must begin with an `import` statement.
- Blank lines that are to be ignored.
- A line starting with # that is to be treated as a comment and ignored.

Path configuration files can be used to extend the import path to look in locations that would not have been added automatically. For example, the **Distribute** package adds a path to `easy-install.pth` when it installs a package in development mode using `python setup.py develop`.

The function for extending `sys.path` is public, and it can be used in example programs to show how the path configuration files work. Here is the result given a directory named `with_modules` containing the file `mymodule.py` with this `print` statement. It shows how the module was imported.

```
import os
print 'Loaded', __name__, 'from', __file__[len(os.getcwd())+1:]
```

This script shows how `addsitedir()` extends the import path so the interpreter can find the desired module.

```
import site
import os
import sys

script_directory = os.path.dirname(__file__)
module_directory = os.path.join(script_directory, sys.argv[1])

try:
    import mymodule
except ImportError, err:
    print 'Could not import mymodule:', err

print
before_len = len(sys.path)
```

```
site.addsitedir(module_directory)
print 'New paths:'
for p in sys.path[before_len:]:
    print p.replace(os.getcwd(), '.') # shorten dirname

print
import mymodule
```

After the directory containing the module is added to `sys.path`, the script can import `mymodule` without issue.

```
$ python site_addsitedir.py with_modules

Could not import mymodule: No module named mymodule

New paths:
./with_modules

Loaded mymodule from with_modules/mymodule.py
```

The path changes by `addsitedir()` go beyond simply appending the argument to `sys.path`. If the directory given to `addsitedir()` includes any files matching the pattern `*.pth`, they are loaded as path configuration files. For example, if `with_pth/pymotw.pth` contains

```
# Add a single subdirectory to the path.
./subdir
```

and `mymodule.py` is copied to `with_pth/subdir/mymodule.py`, then it can be imported by adding `with_pth` as a site directory. This is possible even though the module is not in that directory because both `with_pth` and `with_pth/subdir` are added to the import path.

```
$ python site_addsitedir.py with_pth

Could not import mymodule: No module named mymodule

New paths:
./with_pth
./with_pth/subdir

Loaded mymodule from with_pth/subdir/mymodule.py
```

If a site directory contains multiple `.pth` files, they are processed in alphabetical order.

```
$ ls -F multiple_pth

a.pth
b.pth
from_a/
from_b/

$ cat multiple_pth/a.pth

./from_a

$ cat multiple_pth/b.pth

./from_b
```

In this case, the module is found in `multiple_pth/from_a` because `a.pth` is read before `b.pth`.

```
$ python site_addsitedir.py multiple_pth

Could not import mymodule: No module named mymodule

New paths:
./multiple_pth
./multiple_pth/from_a
./multiple_pth/from_b

Loaded mymodule from multiple_pth/from_a/mymodule.py
```

17.1.4 Customizing Site Configuration

The `site` module is also responsible for loading site-wide customization defined by the local site owner in a `sitecustomize` module. Uses for `sitecustomize` include extending the import path and enabling coverage, profiling, or other development tools.

For example, this `sitecustomize.py` script extends the import path with a directory based on the current platform. The platform-specific path in `/opt/python` is added to the import path, so any packages installed there can be imported. A system like this is useful for sharing packages containing compiled extension modules between hosts on a network via a shared file system. Only the `sitecustomize.py` script needs to be installed on each host. The other packages can be accessed from the file server.

```
print 'Loading sitecustomize.py'

import site
import platform
import os
import sys

path = os.path.join('/opt',
                    'python',
                    sys.version[:3],
                    platform.platform(),
                    )
print 'Adding new path', path

site.addsitedir(path)
```

A simple script can be used to show that `sitecustomize.py` is imported before Python starts running your own code.

```
import sys

print 'Running main program'

print 'End of path:', sys.path[-1]
```

Since `sitecustomize` is meant for system-wide configuration, it should be installed somewhere in the default path (usually in the `site-packages` directory). This example sets PYTHONPATH explicitly to ensure the module is picked up.

```
$ PYTHONPATH=with_sitecustomize python with_sitecustomize/site_\
sitecustomize.py

Loading sitecustomize.py
Adding new path /opt/python/2.7/Darwin-10.5.0-i386-64bit
Running main program
End of path: /opt/python/2.7/Darwin-10.5.0-i386-64bit
```

17.1.5 Customizing User Configuration

Similar to `sitecustomize`, the `usercustomize` module can be used to set up user-specific settings each time the interpreter starts up. `usercustomize` is loaded after `sitecustomize` so site-wide customizations can be overridden.

In environments where a user's home directory is shared on several servers running different operating systems or versions, the standard user directory mechanism may not work for user-specific installations of packages. In these cases, a platform-specific directory tree can be used instead.

```
print 'Loading usercustomize.py'

import site
import platform
import os
import sys

path = os.path.expanduser(os.path.join('~',
                                       'python',
                                       sys.version[:3],
                                       platform.platform(),
                                       ))
print 'Adding new path', path

site.addsitedir(path)
```

Another simple script, similar to the one used for `sitecustomize`, can be used to show that `usercustomize.py` is imported before Python starts running other code.

```
import sys

print 'Running main program'

print 'End of path:', sys.path[-1]
```

Since `usercustomize` is meant for user-specific configuration for a user, it should be installed somewhere in the user's default path, but not on the site-wide path. The default `USER_BASE` directory is a good location. This example sets `PYTHONPATH` explicitly to ensure the module is picked up.

```
$ PYTHONPATH=with_usercustomize python with_usercustomize/site_\
usercustomize.py

Loading usercustomize.py
Adding new path /Users/dhellmann/python/2.7/Darwin-10.5.0-i386-64bit
Running main program
End of path: /Users/dhellmann/python/2.7/Darwin-10.5.0-i386-64bit
```

When the user site directory feature is disabled, `usercustomize` is not imported, whether it is located in the user site directory or elsewhere.

```
$ PYTHONPATH=with_usercustomize python -s with_usercustomize/site_\
usercustomize.py

Running main program
End of path: /Library/Frameworks/Python.framework/Versions/2.7/lib/
python2.7/site-packages
```

17.1.6 Disabling the site Module

To maintain backwards-compatibility with versions of Python from before the automatic import was added, the interpreter accepts an `-S` option.

```
$ python -S site_import_path.py

Path prefixes:
   sys.prefix     : /Library/Frameworks/Python.framework/Versions/2.7
   sys.exec_prefix: /Library/Frameworks/Python.framework/Versions/2.7

/Library/Frameworks/Python.framework/Versions/2.7/lib/python2.7/
site-packages
   exists: True
  in path: False
/Library/Frameworks/Python.framework/Versions/2.7/lib/site-python
   exists: False
  in path: False
```

See Also:

site (http://docs.python.org/library/site.html) The standard library documentation for this module.

***Modules and Imports* (page 1080)** Description of how the import path defined in `sys` (page 1055) works.

Running code at Python startup (http://nedbatchelder.com/blog/201001/running_code_at_python_startup. html) Post from Ned Batchelder discussing ways to cause the Python interpreter to run custom initialization code before starting the main program execution.

Distribute (http://packages.python.org/distribute) Distribute is a Python packaging library based on `setuptools` and `distutils`.

17.2 sys—System-Specific Configuration

Purpose Provides system-specific configuration and operations.
Python Version 1.4 and later

The `sys` module includes a collection of services for probing or changing the configuration of the interpreter at runtime and resources for interacting with the operating environment outside of the current program.

See Also:
sys (http://docs.python.org/library/sys.html) The standard library documentation for this module.

17.2.1 Interpreter Settings

`sys` contains attributes and functions for accessing compile-time or runtime configuration settings for the interpreter.

Build-Time Version Information

The version used to build the C interpreter is available in a few forms. `sys.version` is a human-readable string that usually includes the full version number, as well as information about the build date, compiler, and platform. `sys.hexversion` is easier to use for checking the interpreter version since it is a simple integer. When formatted using `hex()`, it is clear that parts of `sys.hexversion` come from the version information also visible in the more readable `sys.version_info` (a five-part tuple representing just the version number).

More specific information about the source that went into the build can be found in the `sys.subversion` tuple, which includes the actual branch and subversion revision that was checked out and built. The separate C API version used by the current interpreter is saved in `sys.api_version`.

```
import sys

print 'Version info:'
print
print 'sys.version       =', repr(sys.version)
print 'sys.version_info =', sys.version_info
print 'sys.hexversion    =', hex(sys.hexversion)
print 'sys.subversion    =', sys.subversion
print 'sys.api_version   =', sys.api_version
```

All the values depend on the actual interpreter used to run the sample program.

```
$ python2.6 sys_version_values.py

Version info:

sys.version       = '2.6.5 (r265:79359, Mar 24 2010, 01:32:55) \n[GCC 4
.0.1 (Apple Inc. build 5493)]'
sys.version_info = (2, 6, 5, 'final', 0)
sys.hexversion    = 0x20605f0
sys.subversion    = ('CPython', 'tags/r265', '79359')
sys.api_version   = 1013

$ python2.7 sys_version_values.py

Version info:

sys.version       = '2.7 (r27:82508, Jul  3 2010, 21:12:11) \n[GCC 4.0.
1 (Apple Inc. build 5493)]'
sys.version_info = sys.version_info(major=2, minor=7, micro=0, release
level='final', serial=0)
sys.hexversion    = 0x20700f0
sys.subversion    = ('CPython', 'tags/r27', '82508')
sys.api_version   = 1013
```

The operating system platform used to build the interpreter is saved as `sys.platform`.

```
import sys

print 'This interpreter was built for:', sys.platform
```

For most UNIX systems, the value comes from combining the output of the command `uname -s` with the first part of the version in `uname -r`. For other operating systems, there is a hard-coded table of values.

```
$ python sys_platform.py

This interpreter was built for: darwin
```

Command-Line Options

The CPython interpreter accepts several command-line options to control its behavior; these options are listed in Table 17.1.

Table 17.1. CPython Command-Line Option Flags

Option	Meaning
-B	Do not write .py[co] files on import
-d	Debug output from parser
-E	Ignore PYTHON* environment variables (such as PYTHONPATH)
-i	Inspect interactively after running script
-O	Optimize generated bytecode slightly
-OO	Remove docstrings in addition to the -O optimizations
-s	Do not add user site directory to sys.path
-S	Do not run "import site" on initialization
-t	Issue warnings about inconsistent tab usage
-tt	Issue errors for inconsistent tab usage
-v	Verbose
-3	Warn about Python 3.x incompatibilities

Some of these are available for programs to check through `sys.flags`.

```
import sys

if sys.flags.debug:
    print 'Debuging'
if sys.flags.py3k_warning:
    print 'Warning about Python 3.x incompatibilities'
if sys.flags.division_warning:
    print 'Warning about division change'
```

```
if sys.flags.division_new:
    print 'New division behavior enabled'
if sys.flags.inspect:
    print 'Will enter interactive mode after running'
if sys.flags.optimize:
    print 'Optimizing byte-code'
if sys.flags.dont_write_bytecode:
    print 'Not writing byte-code files'
if sys.flags.no_site:
    print 'Not importing "site"'
if sys.flags.ignore_environment:
    print 'Ignoring environment'
if sys.flags.tabcheck:
    print 'Checking for mixed tabs and spaces'
if sys.flags.verbose:
    print 'Verbose mode'
if sys.flags.unicode:
    print 'Unicode'
```

Experiment with `sys_flags.py` to learn how the command-line options map to the flag settings.

```
$ python -3 -S -E sys_flags.py

Warning about Python 3.x incompatibilities
Warning about division change
Not importing "site"
Ignoring environment
Checking for mixed tabs and spaces
```

Unicode Defaults

To get the name of the default Unicode encoding the interpreter is using, use `getdefaultencoding()`. The value is set during start-up by `site`, which calls `sys.setdefaultencoding()` and then removes it from the namespace in `sys` to avoid having it called again.

The internal encoding default and the file system encoding may be different for some operating systems, so there is a separate way to retrieve the file system setting. `getfile systemencoding()` returns an OS-specific (*not* file system-specific) value.

```
import sys

print 'Default encoding     :', sys.getdefaultencoding()
print 'File system encoding :', sys.getfilesystemencoding()
```

Rather than changing the global default encoding, most Unicode experts recommend making an application explicitly Unicode-aware. This method provides two benefits: different Unicode encodings for different data sources can be handled more cleanly, and the number of assumptions about encodings in the application code is reduced.

```
$ python sys_unicode.py

Default encoding     : ascii
File system encoding : utf-8
```

Interactive Prompts

The interactive interpreter uses two separate prompts for indicating the default input level (ps1) and the "continuation" of a multiline statement (ps2). The values are only used by the interactive interpreter.

```
>>> import sys
>>> sys.ps1
'>>> '
>>> sys.ps2
'... '
>>>
```

Either prompt or both prompts can be changed to a different string.

```
>>> sys.ps1 = '::: '
::: sys.ps2 = '~~~ '
::: for i in range(3):
~~~    print i
~~~
0
1
2
:::
```

Alternately, any object that can be converted to a string (via __str__) can be used for the prompt.

```
import sys

class LineCounter(object):
    def __init__(self):
        self.count = 0
    def __str__(self):
        self.count += 1
        return '(%3d)> ' % self.count
```

The LineCounter keeps track of how many times it has been used, so the number in the prompt increases each time.

```
$ python

Python 2.6.2 (r262:71600, Apr 16 2009, 09:17:39)
[GCC 4.0.1 (Apple Computer, Inc. build 5250)] on darwin
Type "help", "copyright", "credits" or "license" for more information.
>>> from PyMOTW.sys.sys_ps1 import LineCounter
>>> import sys
>>> sys.ps1 = LineCounter()
(   1)>
(   2)>
(   3)>
```

Display Hook

sys.displayhook is invoked by the interactive interpreter each time the user enters an expression. The *result* of the expression is passed as the only argument to the function.

```
import sys

class ExpressionCounter(object):

    def __init__(self):
        self.count = 0
        self.previous_value = self
```

```
    def __call__(self, value):
        print
        print ' Previous:', self.previous_value
        print ' New     :', value
        print
        if value != self.previous_value:
            self.count += 1
            sys.ps1 = '(%3d)> ' % self.count
        self.previous_value = value
        sys.__displayhook__(value)

print 'installing'
sys.displayhook = ExpressionCounter()
```

The default value (saved in `sys.__displayhook__`) prints the result to stdout and saves it in `.__builtin__._` for easy reference later.

```
$ python

Python 2.6.2 (r262:71600, Apr 16 2009, 09:17:39)
[GCC 4.0.1 (Apple Computer, Inc. build 5250)] on darwin
Type "help", "copyright", "credits" or "license" for more information.
>>> import PyMOTW.sys.sys_displayhook
installing
>>> 1+2

 Previous: <PyMOTW.sys.sys_displayhook.ExpressionCounter object at
 0x9c5f 90>
 New     : 3

3
(  1)> 'abc'

 Previous: 3
 New     : abc

'abc'
(  2)> 'abc'

 Previous: abc
 New     : abc

'abc'
(  2)> 'abc' * 3
```

```
   Previous: abc
   New      : abcabcabc
```

```
'abcabcabc'
(  3)>
```

Install Location

The path to the actual interpreter program is available in `sys.executable` on all systems for which having a path to the interpreter makes sense. This can be useful for ensuring that the correct interpreter is being used, and it also gives clues about paths that might be set based on the interpreter location.

   `sys.prefix` refers to the parent directory of the interpreter installation. It usually includes `bin` and `lib` directories for executables and installed modules, respectively.

import sys

```
print 'Interpreter executable:', sys.executable
print 'Installation prefix   :', sys.prefix
```

This example output was produced on a Mac running a framework build installed from python.org.

```
$ python sys_locations.py

Interpreter executable: /Library/Frameworks/Python.framework/
Versions/2.7/Resources/Python.app/Contents/MacOS/Python
Installation prefix   : /Library/Frameworks/Python.framework/
Versions/2.7
```

17.2.2   Runtime Environment

`sys` provides low-level APIs for interacting with the system outside of an application, by accepting command-line arguments, accessing user input, and passing messages and status values to the user.

Command-Line Arguments

The arguments captured by the interpreter are processed there and are not passed to the program being run. Any remaining options and arguments, including the name of the script itself, are saved to `sys.argv` in case the program does need to use them.

```
import sys

print 'Arguments:', sys.argv
```

In the third example, the -u option is understood by the interpreter and is not passed to the program being run.

```
$ python sys_argv.py

Arguments: ['sys_argv.py']

$ python sys_argv.py -v foo blah

Arguments: ['sys_argv.py', '-v', 'foo', 'blah']

$ python -u sys_argv.py

Arguments: ['sys_argv.py']
```

See Also:
getopt (page 770), optparse (page 777), and argparse (page 795) Modules for parsing command-line arguments.

Input and Output Steams

Following the UNIX paradigm, Python programs can access three file descriptors by default.

```
import sys

print >>sys.stderr, 'STATUS: Reading from stdin'

data = sys.stdin.read()

print >>sys.stderr, 'STATUS: Writing data to stdout'

sys.stdout.write(data)
sys.stdout.flush()

print >>sys.stderr, 'STATUS: Done'
```

stdin is the standard way to read input, usually from a console but also from other programs via a pipeline. stdout is the standard way to write output for a user (to the console) or to be sent to the next program in a pipeline. `stderr` is intended for use with warning or error messages.

```
$ cat sys_stdio.py | python sys_stdio.py

STATUS: Reading from stdin
STATUS: Writing data to stdout
#!/usr/bin/env python
# encoding: utf-8
#
# Copyright (c) 2009 Doug Hellmann All rights reserved.
#
"""
"""
#end_pymotw_header

import sys

print >>sys.stderr, 'STATUS: Reading from stdin'

data = sys.stdin.read()

print >>sys.stderr, 'STATUS: Writing data to stdout'

sys.stdout.write(data)
sys.stdout.flush()

print >>sys.stderr, 'STATUS: Done'
STATUS: Done
```

See Also:

subprocess (page 481) and pipes Both subprocess and pipes have features for pipelining programs together.

Returning Status

To return an exit code from a program, pass an integer value to `sys.exit()`.

```
import sys

exit_code = int(sys.argv[1])
sys.exit(exit_code)
```

A nonzero value means the program exited with an error.

```
$ python sys_exit.py 0 ; echo "Exited $?"

Exited 0

$ python sys_exit.py 1 ; echo "Exited $?"

Exited 1
```

17.2.3 Memory Management and Limits

sys includes several functions for understanding and controlling memory usage.

Reference Counts

Python uses *reference counting* and *garbage collection* for automatic memory management. An object is automatically marked to be collected when its reference count drops to zero. To examine the reference count of an existing object, use getrefcount().

```
import sys

one = []
print 'At start            :', sys.getrefcount(one)

two = one

print 'Second reference :', sys.getrefcount(one)

del two

print 'After del           :', sys.getrefcount(one)
```

The count is actually one higher than expected because a temporary reference to the object is held by getrefcount() itself.

```
$ python sys_getrefcount.py

At start            : 2
Second reference : 3
After del           : 2
```

See Also:
gc (page 1138) Control the garbage collector via the functions exposed in gc.

Object Size

Knowing how many references an object has may help find cycles or a memory leak, but it is not enough to determine what objects are consuming the *most* memory. That requires knowledge about how big objects are.

```
import sys

class OldStyle:
    pass

class NewStyle(object):
    pass

for obj in [ [], (), {}, 'c', 'string', 1, 2.3,
            OldStyle, OldStyle(), NewStyle, NewStyle(),
            ]:
    print '%10s : %s' % (type(obj).__name__, sys.getsizeof(obj))
```

getsizeof() reports the size of an object in bytes.

```
$ python sys_getsizeof.py

      list : 72
     tuple : 56
      dict : 280
       str : 38
       str : 43
       int : 24
     float : 24
  classobj : 104
  instance : 72
      type : 904
  NewStyle : 64
```

The reported size for a custom class does not include the size of the attribute values.

```
import sys

class WithoutAttributes(object):
    pass

class WithAttributes(object):
    def __init__(self):
        self.a = 'a'
        self.b = 'b'
        return

without_attrs = WithoutAttributes()
print 'WithoutAttributes:', sys.getsizeof(without_attrs)

with_attrs = WithAttributes()
print 'WithAttributes:', sys.getsizeof(with_attrs)
```

This can give a false impression of the amount of memory being consumed.

```
$ python sys_getsizeof_object.py

WithoutAttributes: 64
WithAttributes: 64
```

For a more complete estimate of the space used by a class, provide a __sizeof__() method to compute the value by aggregating the sizes of an object's attributes.

```
import sys

class WithAttributes(object):
    def __init__(self):
        self.a = 'a'
        self.b = 'b'
        return
    def __sizeof__(self):
        return object.__sizeof__(self) + \
            sum(sys.getsizeof(v) for v in self.__dict__.values())

my_inst = WithAttributes()
print sys.getsizeof(my_inst)
```

This version adds the base size of the object to the sizes of all the attributes stored in the internal __dict__.

```
$ python sys_getsizeof_custom.py

140
```

Recursion

Allowing infinite recursion in a Python application may introduce a stack overflow in the interpreter itself, leading to a crash. To eliminate this situation, the interpreter provides a way to control the maximum recursion depth using setrecursionlimit() and getrecursionlimit().

```python
import sys

print 'Initial limit:', sys.getrecursionlimit()

sys.setrecursionlimit(10)

print 'Modified limit:', sys.getrecursionlimit()

def generate_recursion_error(i):
    print 'generate_recursion_error(%s)' % i
    generate_recursion_error(i+1)

try:
    generate_recursion_error(1)
except RuntimeError, err:
    print 'Caught exception:', err
```

Once the recursion limit is reached, the interpreter raises a RuntimeError exception so the program has an opportunity to handle the situation.

```
$ python sys_recursionlimit.py

Initial limit: 1000
Modified limit: 10
generate_recursion_error(1)
generate_recursion_error(2)
generate_recursion_error(3)
generate_recursion_error(4)
```

```
generate_recursion_error(5)
generate_recursion_error(6)
generate_recursion_error(7)
generate_recursion_error(8)
Caught exception: maximum recursion depth exceeded while getting
the str of an object
```

Maximum Values

Along with the runtime configurable values, `sys` includes variables defining the maximum values for types that vary from system to system.

```
import sys

print 'maxint     :', sys.maxint
print 'maxsize    :', sys.maxsize
print 'maxunicode:', sys.maxunicode
```

`maxint` is the largest representable regular integer. `maxsize` is the maximum size of a list, dictionary, string, or other data structure dictated by the C interpreter's size type. `maxunicode` is the largest integer Unicode point supported by the interpreter as currently configured.

```
$ python sys_maximums.py

maxint     : 9223372036854775807
maxsize    : 9223372036854775807
maxunicode: 65535
```

Floating-Point Values

The structure `float_info` contains information about the floating-point type representation used by the interpreter, based on the underlying system's float implementation.

```
import sys

print 'Smallest difference (epsilon):', sys.float_info.epsilon
print
print 'Digits (dig)                 :', sys.float_info.dig
print 'Mantissa digits (mant_dig):', sys.float_info.mant_dig
print
print 'Maximum (max):', sys.float_info.max
print 'Minimum (min):', sys.float_info.min
print
```

```
print 'Radix of exponents (radix):', sys.float_info.radix
print
print 'Maximum exponent for radix (max_exp):', sys.float_info.max_exp
print 'Minimum exponent for radix (min_exp):', sys.float_info.min_exp
print
print 'Max. exponent power of 10 (max_10_exp):',\
      sys.float_info.max_10_exp
print 'Min. exponent power of 10 (min_10_exp):',\
      sys.float_info.min_10_exp
print
print 'Rounding for addition (rounds):', sys.float_info.rounds
```

These values depend on the compiler and the underlying system. These examples were produced on OS X 10.6.5.

```
$ python sys_float_info.py

Smallest difference (epsilon): 2.22044604925e-16

Digits (dig)             : 15
Mantissa digits (mant_dig): 53

Maximum (max): 1.79769313486e+308
Minimum (min): 2.22507385851e-308

Radix of exponents (radix): 2

Maximum exponent for radix (max_exp): 1024
Minimum exponent for radix (min_exp): -1021

Max. exponent power of 10 (max_10_exp): 308
Min. exponent power of 10 (min_10_exp): -307

Rounding for addition (rounds): 1
```

See Also:

The `float.h` C header file for the local compiler contains more details about these settings.

Byte Ordering

`byteorder` is set to the native byte order.

```
import sys

print sys.byteorder
```

The value is either `big` for big endian or `little` for little endian.

```
$ python sys_byteorder.py

little
```

See Also:
Endianness (http://en.wikipedia.org/wiki/Byte_order) Description of big and little
    endian memory systems.
array (page 84) and struct (page 102) Other modules that depend on the byte
    order of data.
float.h The C header file for the local compiler contains more details about these
    settings.

17.2.4   Exception Handling

`sys` includes features for trapping and working with exceptions.

Unhandled Exceptions

Many applications are structured with a main loop that wraps execution in a global
exception handler to trap errors not handled at a lower level. Another way to achieve the
same thing is by setting the `sys.excepthook` to a function that takes three arguments
(error type, error value, and traceback) and letting it deal with unhandled errors.

```
import sys

def my_excepthook(type, value, traceback):
    print 'Unhandled error:', type, value

sys.excepthook = my_excepthook

print 'Before exception'

raise RuntimeError('This is the error message')

print 'After exception'
```

Since there is no **try:except** block around the line where the exception is raised,
the following **print** statement is not run, even though the except hook is set.

```
$ python sys_excepthook.py

Before exception
Unhandled error: <type 'exceptions.RuntimeError'> This is the error
message
```

Current Exception

There are times when an explicit exception handler is preferred, either for code clarity or to avoid conflicts with libraries that try to install their own excepthook. In these cases, a common handler function can be created that does not need to have the exception object passed to it explicitly by calling exc_info() to retrieve the current exception for a thread.

The return value of exc_info() is a three-member tuple containing the exception class, an exception instance, and a traceback. Using exc_info() is preferred over the old form (with exc_type, exc_value, and exc_traceback) because it is thread-safe.

```python
import sys
import threading
import time

def do_something_with_exception():
    exc_type, exc_value = sys.exc_info()[:2]
    print 'Handling %s exception with message "%s" in %s' % \
        (exc_type.__name__, exc_value, threading.current_thread().name)

def cause_exception(delay):
    time.sleep(delay)
    raise RuntimeError('This is the error message')

def thread_target(delay):
    try:
        cause_exception(delay)
    except:
        do_something_with_exception()

threads = [ threading.Thread(target=thread_target, args=(0.3,)),
            threading.Thread(target=thread_target, args=(0.1,)),
            ]
for t in threads:
    t.start()
```

```
for t in threads:
    t.join()
```

This example avoids introducing a circular reference between the traceback object and a local variable in the current frame by ignoring that part of the return value from `exc_info()`. If the traceback is needed (e.g., so it can be logged), explicitly delete the local variable (using **del**) to avoid cycles.

```
$ python sys_exc_info.py

Handling RuntimeError exception with message "This is the error
message" in Thread-2
Handling RuntimeError exception with message "This is the error
message" in Thread-1
```

Previous Interactive Exception

In the interactive interpreter, there is only one thread of interaction. Unhandled exceptions in that thread are saved to three variables in `sys` (`last_type`, `last_value`, and `last_traceback`) to make it easy to retrieve them for debugging. Using the post-mortem debugger in `pdb` avoids any need to use the values directly.

```
$ python

Python 2.7 (r27:82508, Jul  3 2010, 21:12:11)
[GCC 4.0.1 (Apple Inc. build 5493)] on darwin
Type "help", "copyright", "credits" or "license" for more information.
>>> def cause_exception():
...     raise RuntimeError('This is the error message')
...
>>> cause_exception()
Traceback (most recent call last):
  File "<stdin>", line 1, in <module>
  File "<stdin>", line 2, in cause_exception
RuntimeError: This is the error message
>>> import pdb
>>> pdb.pm()
> <stdin>(2)cause_exception()
(Pdb) where
  <stdin>(1)<module>()
> <stdin>(2)cause_exception()
(Pdb)
```

See Also:
exceptions (page 1216) Built-in errors.
pdb (page 975) Python debugger.
traceback (page 958) Module for working with tracebacks.

17.2.5   Low-Level Thread Support

`sys` includes low-level functions for controlling and debugging thread behavior.

Check Interval

Python 2 uses a global lock to prevent separate threads from corrupting the interpreter state. At a fixed interval, bytecode execution is paused and the interpreter checks if any signal handlers need to be executed. During the same interval check, the global interpreter lock (GIL) is also released by the current thread and then reacquired, giving other threads an opportunity to take over execution by grabbing the lock first.

The default check interval is 100 bytecodes, and the current value can always be retrieved with `sys.getcheckinterval()`. Changing the interval with `sys.setcheckinterval()` may have an impact on the performance of an application, depending on the nature of the operations being performed.

```
import sys
import threading
from Queue import Queue
import time


def show_thread(q, extraByteCodes):
    for i in range(5):
        for j in range(extraByteCodes):
            pass
        q.put(threading.current_thread().name)
    return


def run_threads(prefix, interval, extraByteCodes):
    print '%s interval = %s with %s extra operations' % \
        (prefix, interval, extraByteCodes)
    sys.setcheckinterval(interval)
    q = Queue()
    threads = [ threading.Thread(target=show_thread,
                                 name='%s T%s' % (prefix, i),
                                 args=(q, extraByteCodes)
                                 )
```

```
            for i in range(3)
            ]
    for t in threads:
        t.start()
    for t in threads:
        t.join()
    while not q.empty():
        print q.get()
    print
    return

run_threads('Default', interval=10, extraByteCodes=1000)
run_threads('Custom', interval=10, extraByteCodes=0)
```

When the check interval is smaller than the number of bytecodes in a thread, the interpreter may give another thread control so that it runs for a while. This is illustrated in the first set of output situation where the check interval is set to 100 (the default) and 1,000 extra loop iterations are performed for each step through the i loop.

On the other hand, when the check interval is *greater* than the number of bytecodes being executed by a thread that does not release control for another reason, the thread will finish its work before the interval comes up. This situation is illustrated by the order of the name values in the queue in the second example.

```
$ python sys_checkinterval.py

Default interval = 10 with 1000 extra operations
Default T0
Default T0
Default T0
Default T1
Default T2
Default T2
Default T0
Default T1
Default T2
Default T0
Default T1
Default T2
Default T1
Default T2
Default T1

Custom interval = 10 with 0 extra operations
```

```
Custom T0
Custom T0
Custom T0
Custom T0
Custom T0
Custom T1
Custom T1
Custom T1
Custom T1
Custom T1
Custom T2
Custom T2
Custom T2
Custom T2
Custom T2
```

Modifying the check interval is not as clearly useful as it might seem. Many other factors may control the context-switching behavior of Python's threads. For example, if a thread performs I/O, it releases the GIL and may therefore allow another thread to take over execution.

```
import sys
import threading
from Queue import Queue
import time

def show_thread(q, extraByteCodes):
    for i in range(5):
        for j in range(extraByteCodes):
            pass
        #q.put(threading.current_thread().name)
        print threading.current_thread().name
    return

def run_threads(prefix, interval, extraByteCodes):
    print '%s interval = %s with %s extra operations' % \
        (prefix, interval, extraByteCodes)
    sys.setcheckinterval(interval)
    q = Queue()
    threads = [ threading.Thread(target=show_thread,
                                 name='%s T%s' % (prefix, i),
                                 args=(q, extraByteCodes)
```

```
                                        )
                        for i in range(3)
                    ]
        for t in threads:
            t.start()
        for t in threads:
            t.join()
        while not q.empty():
            print q.get()
        print
        return


run_threads('Default', interval=100, extraByteCodes=1000)
run_threads('Custom', interval=10, extraByteCodes=0)
```

This example is modified from the first example to show that the thread prints directly to `sys.stdout` instead of appending to a queue. The output is much less predictable.

```
$ python sys_checkinterval_io.py

Default interval = 100 with 1000 extra operations
Default T0
Default T1
Default T1Default T2

Default T0Default T2

Default T2
Default T2
Default T1
Default T2
Default T1
Default T1
Default T0
Default T0
Default T0

Custom interval = 10 with 0 extra operations
Custom T0
Custom T0
Custom T0
```

```
Custom T0
Custom T0
Custom T1
Custom T1
Custom T1
Custom T1
Custom T2
Custom T2
Custom T2
Custom T1Custom T2

Custom T2
```

See Also:

dis (page 1186) Disassembling Python code with the dis module is one way to count
bytecodes.

Debugging

Identifying deadlocks can be one of the most difficult aspects of working with threads.
sys._current_frames() can help by showing exactly where a thread is stopped.

```python
1  #!/usr/bin/env python
2  # encoding: utf-8
3
4  import sys
5  import threading
6  import time
7
8  io_lock = threading.Lock()
9  blocker = threading.Lock()
10
11 def block(i):
12     t = threading.current_thread()
13     with io_lock:
14         print '%s with ident %s going to sleep' % (t.name, t.ident)
15     if i:
16         blocker.acquire()  # acquired but never released
17         time.sleep(0.2)
```

```
18        with io_lock:
19            print t.name, 'finishing'
20        return
21
22    # Create and start several threads that "block"
23    threads = [ threading.Thread(target=block, args=(i,)) for i in range(3) ]
24    for t in threads:
25        t.setDaemon(True)
26        t.start()
27
28    # Map the threads from their identifier to the thread object
29    threads_by_ident = dict((t.ident, t) for t in threads)
30
31    # Show where each thread is "blocked"
32    time.sleep(0.01)
33    with io_lock:
34        for ident, frame in sys._current_frames().items():
35            t = threads_by_ident.get(ident)
36            if not t:
37                # Main thread
38                continue
39            print t.name, 'stopped in', frame.f_code.co_name,
40            print 'at line', frame.f_lineno, 'of', frame.f_code.co_filename
```

The dictionary returned by `sys._current_frames()` is keyed on the thread identifier, rather than its name. A little work is needed to map those identifiers back to the thread object.

Because **Thread-1** does not sleep, it finishes before its status is checked. Since it is no longer active, it does not appear in the output. **Thread-2** acquires the lock *blocker* and then sleeps for a short period. Meanwhile, **Thread-3** tries to acquire *blocker* but cannot because **Thread-2** already has it.

```
$ python sys_current_frames.py

Thread-1 with ident 4300619776 going to sleep
Thread-1 finishing
Thread-2 with ident 4301156352 going to sleep
Thread-3 with ident 4302835712 going to sleep
Thread-3 stopped in block at line 16 of sys_current_frames.py
Thread-2 stopped in block at line 17 of sys_current_frames.py
```

See Also:

threading (page 505) The threading module includes classes for creating Python threads.

Queue (page 96) The Queue module provides a thread-safe implementation of a FIFO data structure.

Python Threads and the Global Interpreter Lock (http://jessenoller.com/2009/02/01/python-threads-and-the-global-interpreter-lock/) Jesse Noller's article from the December 2007 issue of *Python Magazine*.

Inside the Python GIL (www.dabeaz.com/python/GIL.pdf) Presentation by David Beazley describing thread implementation and performance issues, including how the check interval and GIL are related.

17.2.6   Modules and Imports

Most Python programs end up as a combination of several modules with a main application importing them. Whether using the features of the standard library or organizing custom code in separate files to make it easier to maintain, understanding and managing the dependencies for a program is an important aspect of development. sys includes information about the modules available to an application, either as built-ins or after being imported. It also defines hooks for overriding the standard import behavior for special cases.

Imported Modules

sys.modules is a dictionary mapping the names of imported modules to the module object holding the code.

```
import sys
import textwrap

names = sorted(sys.modules.keys())
name_text = ', '.join(names)

print textwrap.fill(name_text, width=65)
```

The contents of sys.modules change as new modules are imported.

```
$ python sys_modules.py

UserDict, __builtin__, __main__, _abcoll, _codecs, _sre,
_warnings, abc, codecs, copy_reg, encodings,
```

```
encodings.__builtin__, encodings.aliases, encodings.codecs,
encodings.encodings, encodings.utf_8, errno, exceptions,
genericpath, linecache, os, os.path, posix, posixpath, re,
signal, site, sre_compile, sre_constants, sre_parse, stat,
string, strop, sys, textwrap, types, warnings, zipimport
```

Built-in Modules

The Python interpreter can be compiled with some C modules built right in, so they do not need to be distributed as separate shared libraries. These modules do not appear in the list of imported modules managed in `sys.modules` because they were not technically imported. The only way to find the available built-in modules is through `sys.builtin_module_names`.

```python
import sys
import textwrap

name_text = ', '.join(sorted(sys.builtin_module_names))

print textwrap.fill(name_text, width=65)
```

The output of this script will vary, especially if run with a custom-built version of the interpreter. This output was created using a copy of the interpreter installed from the standard python.org installer for OS X.

```
$ python sys_builtins.py

__builtin__, __main__, _ast, _codecs, _sre, _symtable, _warnings,
errno, exceptions, gc, imp, marshal, posix, pwd, signal, sys,
thread, xxsubtype, zipimport
```

See Also:
Build Instructions (http://svn.python.org/view/python/trunk/README?view= markup) Instructions for building Python, from the README distributed with the source.

Import Path

The search path for modules is managed as a Python list saved in `sys.path`. The default contents of the path include the directory of the script used to start the application and the current working directory.

```
import sys

for d in sys.path:
    print d
```

The first directory in the search path is the home for the sample script itself. That is followed by a series of platform-specific paths where compiled extension modules (written in C) might be installed. The global `site-packages` directory is listed last.

```
$ python sys_path_show.py

/Users/dhellmann/Documents/PyMOTW/book/PyMOTW/sys
.../lib/python2.7
.../lib/python2.7/plat-darwin
.../lib/python2.7/lib-tk
.../lib/python2.7/plat-mac
.../lib/python2.7/plat-mac/lib-scriptpackages
.../lib/python2.7/site-packages
```

The import search-path list can be modified before starting the interpreter by setting the shell variable `PYTHONPATH` to a colon-separated list of directories.

```
$ PYTHONPATH=/my/private/site-packages:/my/shared/site-packages \
> python sys_path_show.py

/Users/dhellmann/Documents/PyMOTW/book/PyMOTW/sys
/my/private/site-packages
/my/shared/site-packages
.../lib/python2.7
.../lib/python2.7/plat-darwin
.../lib/python2.7/lib-tk
.../lib/python2.7/plat-mac
.../lib/python2.7/plat-mac/lib-scriptpackages
.../lib/python2.7/site-packages
```

A program can also modify its path by adding elements to `sys.path` directly.

```
import sys
import os

base_dir = os.path.dirname(__file__) or '.'
```

```
print 'Base directory:', base_dir

# Insert the package_dir_a directory at the front of the path.
package_dir_a = os.path.join(base_dir, 'package_dir_a')
sys.path.insert(0, package_dir_a)

# Import the example module
import example
print 'Imported example from:', example.__file__
print '\t', example.DATA

# Make package_dir_b the first directory in the search path
package_dir_b = os.path.join(base_dir, 'package_dir_b')
sys.path.insert(0, package_dir_b)

# Reload the module to get the other version
reload(example)
print 'Reloaded example from:', example.__file__
print '\t', example.DATA
```

Reloading an imported module reimports the file and uses the same `module` object to hold the results. Changing the path between the initial import and the call to `reload()` means a different module may be loaded the second time.

```
$ python sys_path_modify.py

Base directory: .
Imported example from: ./package_dir_a/example.pyc
        This is example A
Reloaded example from: ./package_dir_b/example.pyc
        This is example B
```

Custom Importers

Modifying the search path lets a programmer control how standard Python modules are found. But, what if a program needs to import code from somewhere other than the usual `.py` or `.pyc` files on the file system? PEP 302 solves this problem by introducing the idea of *import hooks*, which can trap an attempt to find a module on the search path and take alternative measures to load the code from somewhere else or apply preprocessing to it.

Custom importers are implemented in two separate phases. The *finder* is responsible for locating a module and providing a *loader* to manage the actual import. Custom module finders are added by appending a factory to the `sys.path_hooks` list. On import, each part of the path is given to a finder until one claims support (by not raising `ImportError`). That finder is then responsible for searching data storage represented by its path entry for named modules.

```python
import sys

class NoisyImportFinder(object):

    PATH_TRIGGER = 'NoisyImportFinder_PATH_TRIGGER'

    def __init__(self, path_entry):
        print 'Checking %s:' % path_entry,
        if path_entry != self.PATH_TRIGGER:
            print 'wrong finder'
            raise ImportError()
        else:
            print 'works'
        return

    def find_module(self, fullname, path=None):
        print 'Looking for "%s"' % fullname
        return None

sys.path_hooks.append(NoisyImportFinder)

sys.path.insert(0, NoisyImportFinder.PATH_TRIGGER)

try:
    import target_module
except Exception, e:
    print 'Import failed:', e
```

This example illustrates how the finders are instantiated and queried. The `Noisy-ImportFinder` raises `ImportError` when instantiated with a path entry that does not match its special trigger value, which is obviously not a real path on the file system. This test prevents the `NoisyImportFinder` from breaking imports of real modules.

```
$ python sys_path_hooks_noisy.py

Checking NoisyImportFinder_PATH_TRIGGER: works
Looking for "target_module"
```

```
Checking /Users/dhellmann/Documents/PyMOTW/book/PyMOTW/sys:
wrong finder
Import failed: No module named target_module
```

Importing from a Shelve

When the finder locates a module, it is responsible for returning a *loader* capable of importing that module. This example illustrates a custom importer that saves its module contents in a database created by `shelve`.

First, a script is used to populate the shelf with a package containing a submodule and subpackage.

```python
import sys
import shelve
import os

filename = '/tmp/pymotw_import_example.shelve'
if os.path.exists(filename):
    os.unlink(filename)
db = shelve.open(filename)
try:
    db['data:README'] = """
==============
package README
==============

This is the README for ''package''.
"""
    db['package.__init__'] = """
print 'package imported'
message = 'This message is in package.__init__'
"""
    db['package.module1'] = """
print 'package.module1 imported'
message = 'This message is in package.module1'
"""
    db['package.subpackage.__init__'] = """
print 'package.subpackage imported'
message = 'This message is in package.subpackage.__init__'
"""
    db['package.subpackage.module2'] = """
print 'package.subpackage.module2 imported'
message = 'This message is in package.subpackage.module2'
```

```
    """
        db['package.with_error'] = """
    print 'package.with_error being imported'
    raise ValueError('raising exception to break import')
    """
        print 'Created %s with:' % filename
        for key in sorted(db.keys()):
            print '\t', key
    finally:
        db.close()
```

A real packaging script would read the contents from the file system, but using hard-coded values is sufficient for a simple example like this one.

```
$ python sys_shelve_importer_create.py

Created /tmp/pymotw_import_example.shelve with:
        data:README
        package.__init__
        package.module1
        package.subpackage.__init__
        package.subpackage.module2
        package.with_error
```

The custom importer needs to provide finder and loader classes that know how to look in a shelf for the source of a module or package.

```
import contextlib
import imp
import os
import shelve
import sys


def _mk_init_name(fullname):
    """Return the name of the __init__ module
    for a given package name.
    """
    if fullname.endswith('.__init__'):
        return fullname
    return fullname + '.__init__'


def _get_key_name(fullname, db):
    """Look in an open shelf for fullname or
```

```
    fullname.__init__, return the name found.
    """
    if fullname in db:
        return fullname
    init_name = _mk_init_name(fullname)
    if init_name in db:
        return init_name
    return None


class ShelveFinder(object):
    """Find modules collected in a shelve archive."""

    def __init__(self, path_entry):
        if not os.path.isfile(path_entry):
            raise ImportError
        try:
            # Test the path_entry to see if it is a valid shelf
            with contextlib.closing(shelve.open(path_entry, 'r')):
                pass
        except Exception, e:
            raise ImportError(str(e))
        else:
            print 'shelf added to import path:', path_entry
            self.path_entry = path_entry
        return

    def __str__(self):
        return '<%s for "%s">' % (self.__class__.__name__,
                                  self.path_entry)

    def find_module(self, fullname, path=None):
        path = path or self.path_entry
        print '\nlooking for "%s"\n  in %s' % (fullname, path)
        with contextlib.closing(shelve.open(self.path_entry, 'r')
                                ) as db:
            key_name = _get_key_name(fullname, db)
            if key_name:
                print '  found it as %s' % key_name
                return ShelveLoader(path)
        print '  not found'
        return None


class ShelveLoader(object):
    """Load source for modules from shelve databases."""
```

```python
    def __init__(self, path_entry):
        self.path_entry = path_entry
        return

    def _get_filename(self, fullname):
        # Make up a fake filename that starts with the path entry
        # so pkgutil.get_data() works correctly.
        return os.path.join(self.path_entry, fullname)

    def get_source(self, fullname):
        print 'loading source for "%s" from shelf' % fullname
        try:
            with contextlib.closing(shelve.open(self.path_entry, 'r')
                                    ) as db:
                key_name = _get_key_name(fullname, db)
                if key_name:
                    return db[key_name]
                raise ImportError('could not find source for %s' %
                                  fullname)
        except Exception, e:
            print 'could not load source:', e
            raise ImportError(str(e))

    def get_code(self, fullname):
        source = self.get_source(fullname)
        print 'compiling code for "%s"' % fullname
        return compile(source, self._get_filename(fullname),
                       'exec', dont_inherit=True)

    def get_data(self, path):
        print 'looking for data\n  in %s\n  for "%s"' % \
            (self.path_entry, path)
        if not path.startswith(self.path_entry):
            raise IOError
        path = path[len(self.path_entry)+1:]
        key_name = 'data:' + path
        try:
            with contextlib.closing(shelve.open(self.path_entry, 'r')
                                    ) as db:
                return db[key_name]
        except Exception, e:
            # Convert all errors to IOError
            raise IOError
```

```
def is_package(self, fullname):
    init_name = _mk_init_name(fullname)
    with contextlib.closing(shelve.open(self.path_entry, 'r')
                            ) as db:
        return init_name in db

def load_module(self, fullname):
    source = self.get_source(fullname)

    if fullname in sys.modules:
        print 'reusing existing module from import of "%s"' % \
            fullname
        mod = sys.modules[fullname]
    else:
        print 'creating a new module object for "%s"' % fullname
        mod = sys.modules.setdefault(fullname,
                                     imp.new_module(fullname))

    # Set a few properties required by PEP 302
    mod.__file__ = self._get_filename(fullname)
    mod.__name__ = fullname
    mod.__path__ = self.path_entry
    mod.__loader__ = self
    mod.__package__ = '.'.join(fullname.split('.')[:-1])

    if self.is_package(fullname):
        print 'adding path for package'
        # Set __path__ for packages
        # so we can find the submodules.
        mod.__path__ = [ self.path_entry ]
    else:
        print 'imported as regular module'

    print 'execing source...'
    exec source in mod.__dict__
    print 'done'
    return mod
```

Now `ShelveFinder` and `ShelveLoader` can be used to import code from a shelf. This example shows importing the `package` just created.

```
import sys
import sys_shelve_importer
```

```
def show_module_details(module):
    print '    message     :', module.message
    print '    __name__    :', module.__name__
    print '    __package__:', module.__package__
    print '    __file__    :', module.__file__
    print '    __path__    :', module.__path__
    print '    __loader__  :', module.__loader__

filename = '/tmp/pymotw_import_example.shelve'
sys.path_hooks.append(sys_shelve_importer.ShelveFinder)
sys.path.insert(0, filename)

print 'Import of "package":'
import package

print
print 'Examine package details:'
show_module_details(package)

print
print 'Global settings:'
print 'sys.modules entry:'
print sys.modules['package']
```

The shelf is added to the import path the first time an import occurs after the path is modified. The finder recognizes the shelf and returns a loader, which is used for all imports from that shelf. The initial package-level import creates a new module object and then uses **exec** to run the source loaded from the shelf. It uses the new module as the namespace so that names defined in the source are preserved as module-level attributes.

```
$ python sys_shelve_importer_package.py

Import of "package":
shelf added to import path: /tmp/pymotw_import_example.shelve

looking for "package"
  in /tmp/pymotw_import_example.shelve
  found it as package.__init__
loading source for "package" from shelf
creating a new module object for "package"
adding path for package
```

```
execing source...
package imported
done
```

```
Examine package details:
  message    : This message is in package.__init__
  __name__   : package
  __package__:
  __file__   : /tmp/pymotw_import_example.shelve/package
  __path__   : ['/tmp/pymotw_import_example.shelve']
  __loader__ : <sys_shelve_importer.ShelveLoader object at 0x1006d42d0>
```

```
Global settings:
sys.modules entry:
<module 'package' from '/tmp/pymotw_import_example.shelve/package'>
```

Custom Package Importing

Loading other modules and subpackages proceeds in the same way.

```python
import sys
import sys_shelve_importer


def show_module_details(module):
    print '  message    :', module.message
    print '  __name__   :', module.__name__
    print '  __package__:', module.__package__
    print '  __file__   :', module.__file__
    print '  __path__   :', module.__path__
    print '  __loader__ :', module.__loader__


filename = '/tmp/pymotw_import_example.shelve'
sys.path_hooks.append(sys_shelve_importer.ShelveFinder)
sys.path.insert(0, filename)

print 'Import of "package.module1":'
import package.module1

print
print 'Examine package.module1 details:'
show_module_details(package.module1)

print
```

```
print 'Import of "package.subpackage.module2":'
import package.subpackage.module2

print
print 'Examine package.subpackage.module2 details:'
show_module_details(package.subpackage.module2)
```

The finder receives the entire dotted name of the module to load and returns a `ShelveLoader` configured to load modules from the path entry pointing to the shelf file. The fully qualified module name is passed to the loader's `load_module()` method, which constructs and returns a `module` instance.

```
$ python sys_shelve_importer_module.py

Import of "package.module1":
shelf added to import path: /tmp/pymotw_import_example.shelve

looking for "package"
  in /tmp/pymotw_import_example.shelve
  found it as package.__init__
loading source for "package" from shelf
creating a new module object for "package"
adding path for package
execing source...
package imported
done

looking for "package.module1"
  in /tmp/pymotw_import_example.shelve
  found it as package.module1
loading source for "package.module1" from shelf
creating a new module object for "package.module1"
imported as regular module
execing source...
package.module1 imported
done

Examine package.module1 details:
  message     : This message is in package.module1
  __name__    : package.module1
  __package__ : package
  __file__    : /tmp/pymotw_import_example.shelve/package.module1
```

```
    __path__   : /tmp/pymotw_import_example.shelve
    __loader__ : <sys_shelve_importer.ShelveLoader object at 0x1006d42d0
>


Import of "package.subpackage.module2":

looking for "package.subpackage"
  in /tmp/pymotw_import_example.shelve
  found it as package.subpackage.__init__
loading source for "package.subpackage" from shelf
creating a new module object for "package.subpackage"
adding path for package
execing source...
package.subpackage imported
done

looking for "package.subpackage.module2"
  in /tmp/pymotw_import_example.shelve
  found it as package.subpackage.module2
loading source for "package.subpackage.module2" from shelf
creating a new module object for "package.subpackage.module2"
imported as regular module
execing source...
package.subpackage.module2 imported
done

Examine package.subpackage.module2 details:
  message    : This message is in package.subpackage.module2
  __name__   : package.subpackage.module2
  __package__: package.subpackage
  __file__   : /tmp/pymotw_import_example.shelve/package.subpackage.mo
dule2
  __path__   : /tmp/pymotw_import_example.shelve
  __loader__ : <sys_shelve_importer.ShelveLoader object at 0x1006d4390
>
```

Reloading Modules in a Custom Importer

Reloading a module is handled slightly differently. Instead of creating a new module object, the existing module is reused.

```
import sys
import sys_shelve_importer
```

```
filename = '/tmp/pymotw_import_example.shelve'
sys.path_hooks.append(sys_shelve_importer.ShelveFinder)
sys.path.insert(0, filename)

print 'First import of "package":'
import package

print
print 'Reloading "package":'
reload(package)
```

By reusing the same object, existing references to the module are preserved, even if class or function definitions are modified by the reload.

```
$ python sys_shelve_importer_reload.py

First import of "package":
shelf added to import path: /tmp/pymotw_import_example.shelve

looking for "package"
  in /tmp/pymotw_import_example.shelve
  found it as package.__init__
loading source for "package" from shelf
creating a new module object for "package"
adding path for package
execing source...
package imported
done

Reloading "package":

looking for "package"
  in /tmp/pymotw_import_example.shelve
  found it as package.__init__
loading source for "package" from shelf
reusing existing module from import of "package"
adding path for package
execing source...
package imported
done
```

Handling Import Errors

When a module cannot be located by any finder, ImportError is raised by the main import code.

```
import sys
import sys_shelve_importer

filename = '/tmp/pymotw_import_example.shelve'
sys.path_hooks.append(sys_shelve_importer.ShelveFinder)
sys.path.insert(0, filename)

try:
    import package.module3
except ImportError, e:
    print 'Failed to import:', e
```

Other errors during the import are propagated.

```
$ python sys_shelve_importer_missing.py

shelf added to import path: /tmp/pymotw_import_example.shelve

looking for "package"
  in /tmp/pymotw_import_example.shelve
  found it as package.__init__
loading source for "package" from shelf
creating a new module object for "package"
adding path for package
execing source...
package imported
done

looking for "package.module3"
  in /tmp/pymotw_import_example.shelve
  not found
Failed to import: No module named module3
```

Package Data

In addition to defining the API for loading executable Python code, PEP 302 defines an optional API for retrieving package data intended for distributing data files, documentation, and other noncode resources used by a package. By implementing `get_data()`, a loader can allow calling applications to support retrieval of data associated with the package, without considering how the package is actually installed (especially without assuming that the package is stored as files on a file system).

```
import sys
import sys_shelve_importer
```

```
import os
import pkgutil

filename = '/tmp/pymotw_import_example.shelve'
sys.path_hooks.append(sys_shelve_importer.ShelveFinder)
sys.path.insert(0, filename)

import package

readme_path = os.path.join(package.__path__[0], 'README')

readme = pkgutil.get_data('package', 'README')
# Equivalent to:
#   readme = package.__loader__.get_data(readme_path)
print readme

foo_path = os.path.join(package.__path__[0], 'foo')
try:
    foo = pkgutil.get_data('package', 'foo')
    # Equivalent to:
    #   foo = package.__loader__.get_data(foo_path)
except IOError as err:
    print 'ERROR: Could not load "foo"', err
else:
    print foo
```

get_data() takes a path based on the module or package that owns the data. It returns the contents of the resource "file" as a string or raises IOError if the resource does not exist.

```
$ python sys_shelve_importer_get_data.py

shelf added to import path: /tmp/pymotw_import_example.shelve

looking for "package"
  in /tmp/pymotw_import_example.shelve
  found it as package.__init__
loading source for "package" from shelf
creating a new module object for "package"
adding path for package
execing source...
package imported
done
```

```
looking for data
  in /tmp/pymotw_import_example.shelve
  for "/tmp/pymotw_import_example.shelve/README"


===============
package README
===============

This is the README for ``package``.

looking for data
  in /tmp/pymotw_import_example.shelve
  for "/tmp/pymotw_import_example.shelve/foo"
ERROR: Could not load "foo"
```

See Also:
pkgutil (page 1247) Includes `get_data()` for retrieving data from a package.

Importer Cache

Searching through all the hooks each time a module is imported can become expensive. To save time, `sys.path_importer_cache` is maintained as a mapping between a path entry and the loader that can use the value to find modules.

```python
import sys

print 'PATH:'
for name in sys.path:
    if name.startswith(sys.prefix):
        name = '...' + name[len(sys.prefix):]
    print ' ', name

print
print 'IMPORTERS:'
for name, cache_value in sys.path_importer_cache.items():
    name = name.replace(sys.prefix, '...')
    print '  %s: %r' % (name, cache_value)
```

A cache value of `None` means to use the default file system loader. Directories on the path that do not exist are associated with an `imp.NullImporter` instance, since they cannot be used to import modules. In the example output, several `zipimport.zipimporter` instances are used to manage EGG files found on the path.

```
$ python sys_path_importer_cache.py

PATH:
  /Users/dhellmann/Documents/PyMOTW/book/PyMOTW/sys
  .../lib/python2.7/site-packages/distribute-0.6.10-py2.7.egg
  .../lib/python2.7/site-packages/pip-0.7.2-py2.7.egg
  .../lib/python27.zip
  .../lib/python2.7
  .../lib/python2.7/plat-darwin
  .../lib/python2.7/plat-mac
  .../lib/python2.7/plat-mac/lib-scriptpackages
  .../lib/python2.7/lib-tk
  .../lib/python2.7/lib-old
  .../lib/python2.7/lib-dynload
  .../lib/python2.7/site-packages

IMPORTERS:
  sys_path_importer_cache.py: <imp.NullImporter object at 0x100d02080>
  .../lib/python27.zip: <imp.NullImporter object at 0x100d02030>
  .../lib/python2.7/lib-dynload: None
  .../lib/python2.7/encodings: None
  .../lib/python2.7: None
  .../lib/python2.7/lib-old: None
  .../lib/python2.7/site-packages: None
  .../lib/python2.7/plat-darwin: None
  .../lib/python2.7/: None
  .../lib/python2.7/plat-mac/lib-scriptpackages: None
  .../lib/python2.7/plat-mac: None
  .../lib/python2.7/site-packages/pip-0.7.2-py2.7.egg: None
  .../lib/python2.7/lib-tk: None
  .../lib/python2.7/site-packages/distribute-0.6.10-py2.7.egg: None
```

Meta-Path

The `sys.meta_path` further extends the sources of potential imports by allowing a finder to be searched *before* the regular `sys.path` is scanned. The API for a finder on the meta-path is the same as for a regular path. The difference is that the metafinder is not limited to a single entry in `sys.path`—it can search anywhere at all.

```
import sys
import sys_shelve_importer
import imp
```

```python
class NoisyMetaImportFinder(object):

    def __init__(self, prefix):
        print 'Creating NoisyMetaImportFinder for %s' % prefix
        self.prefix = prefix
        return

    def find_module(self, fullname, path=None):
        print 'looking for "%s" with path "%s"' % (fullname, path)
        name_parts = fullname.split('.')
        if name_parts and name_parts[0] == self.prefix:
            print ' ... found prefix, returning loader'
            return NoisyMetaImportLoader(path)
        else:
            print ' ... not the right prefix, cannot load'
        return None


class NoisyMetaImportLoader(object):

    def __init__(self, path_entry):
        self.path_entry = path_entry
        return

    def load_module(self, fullname):
        print 'loading %s' % fullname
        if fullname in sys.modules:
            mod = sys.modules[fullname]
        else:
            mod = sys.modules.setdefault(fullname,
                                         imp.new_module(fullname))


        # Set a few properties required by PEP 302
        mod.__file__ = fullname
        mod.__name__ = fullname
        # always looks like a package
        mod.__path__ = [ 'path-entry-goes-here' ]
        mod.__loader__ = self
        mod.__package__ = '.'.join(fullname.split('.')[:-1])

        return mod
```

```
# Install the meta-path finder
sys.meta_path.append(NoisyMetaImportFinder('foo'))

# Import some modules that are "found" by the meta-path finder
print
import foo

print
import foo.bar

# Import a module that is not found
print
try:
    import bar
except ImportError, e:
    pass
```

Each finder on the meta-path is interrogated before sys.path is searched, so there is always an opportunity to have a central importer load modules without explicitly modifying sys.path. Once the module is "found," the loader API works in the same way as for regular loaders (although this example is truncated for simplicity).

```
$ python sys_meta_path.py

Creating NoisyMetaImportFinder for foo

looking for "foo" with path "None"
 ... found prefix, returning loader
loading foo

looking for "foo.bar" with path "['path-entry-goes-here']"
 ... found prefix, returning loader
loading foo.bar

looking for "bar" with path "None"
 ... not the right prefix, cannot load
```

See Also:
imp (page 1235) The imp module provides tools used by importers.

`importlib` Base classes and other tools for creating custom importers.

**The Quick Guide to Python Eggs (http://peak.telecommunity.com/DevCenter/
   PythonEggs)** PEAK documentation for working with EGGs.

**Python 3 stdlib module "importlib" (http://docs.python.org/py3k/library/
   importlib.html)** Python 3.x includes abstract base classes that make it easier to
   create custom importers.

PEP 302 (www.python.org/dev/peps/pep-0302) Import hooks.

`zipimport` **(page 1410)** Implements importing Python modules from inside ZIP
   archives.

**Import this, that, and the other thing: custom importers
   (http://us.pycon.org/2010/conference/talks/?filter=core)** Brett Cannon's Py-
   Con 2010 presentation.

17.2.7 Tracing a Program as It Runs

There are two ways to inject code to watch a program run: *tracing* and *profiling*. They
are similar, but they are intended for different purposes and so have different constraints. The easiest, but least efficient, way to monitor a program is through a *trace
hook*, which can be used to write a debugger, monitor code coverage, or achieve many
other purposes.

The trace hook is modified by passing a callback function to `sys.settrace()`.
The callback will receive three arguments: the stack frame from the code being run, a
string naming the type of notification, and an event-specific argument value. Table 17.2
lists the seven event types for different levels of information that occur as a program is
being executed.

Table 17.2. Event Hooks for settrace()

Event	When it occurs	Argument value
call	Before a function is executed	None
line	Before a line is executed	None
return	Before a function returns	The value being returned
exception	After an exception occurs	The (exception, value, traceback) tuple
c_call	Before a C function is called	The C function object
c_return	After a C function returns	None
c_exception	After a C function throws an error	None

Tracing Function Calls

A `call` event is generated before every function call. The frame passed to the callback can be used to find out which function is being called and from where.

```python
#!/usr/bin/env python
# encoding: utf-8

import sys

def trace_calls(frame, event, arg):
    if event != 'call':
        return
    co = frame.f_code
    func_name = co.co_name
    if func_name == 'write':
        # Ignore write() calls from print statements
        return
    func_line_no = frame.f_lineno
    func_filename = co.co_filename
    caller = frame.f_back
    caller_line_no = caller.f_lineno
    caller_filename = caller.f_code.co_filename
    print 'Call to %s\n  on line %s of %s\n  from line %s of %s\n' % \
        (func_name, func_line_no, func_filename,
            caller_line_no, caller_filename)
    return

def b():
    print 'in b()\n'

def a():
    print 'in a()\n'
    b()

sys.settrace(trace_calls)
a()
```

This example ignores calls to `write()`, as used by **print** to write to `sys.stdout`.

```
$ python sys_settrace_call.py

Call to a
```

```
on line 27 of sys_settrace_call.py
from line 32 of sys_settrace_call.py

in a()

Call to b
  on line 24 of sys_settrace_call.py
  from line 29 of sys_settrace_call.py

in b()
```

Tracing Inside Functions

The trace hook can return a new hook to be used inside the new scope (the *local* trace function). It is possible, for instance, to control tracing to only run line-by-line within certain modules or functions.

```python
1   #!/usr/bin/env python
2   # encoding: utf-8
3
4   import sys
5
6   def trace_lines(frame, event, arg):
7       if event != 'line':
8           return
9       co = frame.f_code
10      func_name = co.co_name
11      line_no = frame.f_lineno
12      filename = co.co_filename
13      print '  %s line %s' % (func_name, line_no)
14
15  def trace_calls(frame, event, arg):
16      if event != 'call':
17          return
18      co = frame.f_code
19      func_name = co.co_name
20      if func_name == 'write':
21          # Ignore write() calls from print statements
22          return
23      line_no = frame.f_lineno
24      filename = co.co_filename
```

```
25      print 'Call to %s on line %s of %s' % \
26          (func_name, line_no, filename)
27      if func_name in TRACE_INTO:
28          # Trace into this function
29          return trace_lines
30      return
31
32  def c(input):
33      print 'input =', input
34      print 'Leaving c()'
35
36  def b(arg):
37      val = arg * 5
38      c(val)
39      print 'Leaving b()'
40
41  def a():
42      b(2)
43      print 'Leaving a()'
44
45  TRACE_INTO = ['b']
46
47  sys.settrace(trace_calls)
48  a()
```

In this example, the global list of functions is kept in the variable TRACE_INTO, so when trace_calls() runs, it can return trace_lines() to enable tracing inside of b().

```
$ python sys_settrace_line.py

Call to a on line 41 of sys_settrace_line.py
Call to b on line 36 of sys_settrace_line.py
  b line 37
  b line 38
Call to c on line 32 of sys_settrace_line.py
input = 10
Leaving c()
  b line 39
Leaving b()
Leaving a()
```

Watching the Stack

Another useful way to use the hooks is to keep up with which functions are being called and what their return values are. To monitor return values, watch for the `return` event.

```python
#!/usr/bin/env python
# encoding: utf-8

import sys

def trace_calls_and_returns(frame, event, arg):
    co = frame.f_code
    func_name = co.co_name
    if func_name == 'write':
        # Ignore write() calls from print statements
        return
    line_no = frame.f_lineno
    filename = co.co_filename
    if event == 'call':
        print 'Call to %s on line %s of %s' % (func_name,
                                               line_no,
                                               filename)
        return trace_calls_and_returns
    elif event == 'return':
        print '%s => %s' % (func_name, arg)
    return

def b():
    print 'in b()'
    return 'response_from_b '

def a():
    print 'in a()'
    val = b()
    return val * 2

sys.settrace(trace_calls_and_returns)
a()
```

The local trace function is used for watching return events, which means `trace_calls_and_returns()` needs to return a reference to itself when a function is called, so the return value can be monitored.

```
$ python sys_settrace_return.py

Call to a on line 27 of sys_settrace_return.py
in a()
Call to b on line 23 of sys_settrace_return.py
in b()
b => response_from_b
a => response_from_b response_from_b
```

Exception Propagation

Exceptions can be monitored by looking for the `exception` event in a local trace function. When an exception occurs, the trace hook is called with a tuple containing the type of exception, the exception object, and a traceback object.

```python
1  #!/usr/bin/env python
2  # encoding: utf-8
3
4  import sys
5
6  def trace_exceptions(frame, event, arg):
7      if event != 'exception':
8          return
9      co = frame.f_code
10     func_name = co.co_name
11     line_no = frame.f_lineno
12     filename = co.co_filename
13     exc_type, exc_value, exc_traceback = arg
14     print 'Tracing exception:\n%s "%s"\non line %s of %s\n' % \
15         (exc_type.__name__, exc_value, line_no, func_name)
16
17 def trace_calls(frame, event, arg):
18     if event != 'call':
19         return
20     co = frame.f_code
21     func_name = co.co_name
22     if func_name in TRACE_INTO:
23         return trace_exceptions
24
25 def c():
26     raise RuntimeError('generating exception in c()')
27
28 def b():
```

```
29        c()
30        print 'Leaving b()'
31
32   def a():
33        b()
34        print 'Leaving a()'
35
36   TRACE_INTO = ['a', 'b', 'c']
37
38   sys.settrace(trace_calls)
39   try:
40        a()
41   except Exception, e:
42        print 'Exception handler:', e
```

Take care to limit where the local function is applied because some of the internals of formatting error messages generate, and ignore, their own exceptions. Every exception is seen by the trace hook, whether the caller catches and ignores it or not.

```
$ python sys_settrace_exception.py

Tracing exception:
RuntimeError "generating exception in c()"
on line 26 of c

Tracing exception:
RuntimeError "generating exception in c()"
on line 29 of b

Tracing exception:
RuntimeError "generating exception in c()"
on line 33 of a

Exception handler: generating exception in c()
```

See Also:
profile (page 1022) The `profile` module documentation shows how to use a ready-made profiler.
trace (page 1012) The `trace` module implements several code analysis features.
Types and Members (http://docs.python.org/library/inspect.html#types-and-members) The descriptions of frame and code objects and their attributes.

**Tracing python code (www.dalkescientific.com/writings/diary/archive/
2005/04/20/tracing_python_code.html)** Another `settrace()` tutorial.
**Wicked hack: Python bytecode tracing (http://nedbatchelder.com/blog/200804/
wicked_hack_python_bytecode_tracing.html)** Ned Batchelder's experiments
with tracing with more granularity than source line level.

17.3 os—Portable Access to Operating System Specific Features

Purpose Portable access to operating system specific features.
Python Version 1.4 and later

The `os` module provides a wrapper for platform-specific modules such as `posix`, `nt`,
and `mac`. The API for functions available on all platforms should be the same, so using
the `os` module offers some measure of portability. Not all functions are available on
every platform, however. Many of the process management functions described in this
summary are not available for Windows.

The Python documentation for the `os` module is subtitled "Miscellaneous operating system interfaces." The module consists mostly of functions for creating and managing running processes or file system content (files and directories), with a few other
bits of functionality thrown in besides.

17.3.1 Process Owner

The first set of functions provided by `os` is used for determining and changing the
process owner ids. These are most frequently used by authors of daemons or special
system programs that need to change permission level rather than run as `root`. This
section does not try to explain all the intricate details of UNIX security, process owners,
etc. See the references list at the end of this section for more details.

The following example shows the real and effective user and group information
for a process, and then changes the effective values. This is similar to what a daemon
would need to do when it starts as root during a system boot, to lower the privilege level
and run as a different user.

Note: Before running the example, change the `TEST_GID` and `TEST_UID` values
to match a real user.

```python
import os

TEST_GID=501
TEST_UID=527


def show_user_info():
    print 'User (actual/effective)  : %d / %d' % \
        (os.getuid(), os.geteuid())
    print 'Group (actual/effective) : %d / %d' % \
        (os.getgid(), os.getegid())
    print 'Actual Groups   :', os.getgroups()
    return

print 'BEFORE CHANGE:'
show_user_info()
print

try:
    os.setegid(TEST_GID)
except OSError:
    print 'ERROR: Could not change effective group.  Rerun as root.'
else:
    print 'CHANGED GROUP:'
    show_user_info()
    print

try:
    os.seteuid(TEST_UID)
except OSError:
    print 'ERROR: Could not change effective user.  Rerun as root.'
else:
    print 'CHANGE USER:'
    show_user_info()
    print
```

When run as user with id of 527 and group 501 on OS X, this output is produced.

```
$ python os_process_user_example.py

BEFORE CHANGE:
User (actual/effective)  : 527 / 527
Group (actual/effective) : 501 / 501
```

```
Actual Groups    : [501, 102, 204, 100, 98, 80, 61, 12, 500, 101]

CHANGED GROUP:
User (actual/effective)    : 527 / 527
Group (actual/effective) : 501 / 501
Actual Groups    : [501, 102, 204, 100, 98, 80, 61, 12, 500, 101]

CHANGE USER:
User (actual/effective)    : 527 / 527
Group (actual/effective) : 501 / 501
Actual Groups    : [501, 102, 204, 100, 98, 80, 61, 12, 500, 101]
```

The values do not change because when it is not running as root, a process cannot change its effective owner value. Any attempt to set the effective user id or group id to anything other than that of the current user causes an OSError. Running the same script using **sudo** so that it starts out with root privileges is a different story.

```
$ sudo python os_process_user_example.py

BEFORE CHANGE:
User (actual/effective)    : 0 / 0
Group (actual/effective) : 0 / 0
Actual Groups    : [0, 204, 100, 98, 80, 61, 29, 20, 12, 9, 8,
5, 4, 3, 2, 1]

CHANGED GROUP:
User (actual/effective)    : 0 / 0
Group (actual/effective) : 0 / 501
Actual Groups    : [501, 204, 100, 98, 80, 61, 29, 20, 12, 9,
8, 5, 4, 3, 2, 1]

CHANGE USER:
User (actual/effective)    : 0 / 527
Group (actual/effective) : 0 / 501
Actual Groups    : [501, 204, 100, 98, 80, 61, 29, 20, 12, 9,
8, 5, 4, 3, 2, 1]
```

In this case, since it starts as root, the script can change the effective user and group for the process. Once the effective UID is changed, the process is limited to the permissions of that user. Because nonroot users cannot change their effective group, the program needs to change the group before changing the user.

17.3.2   Process Environment

Another feature of the operating system exposed to a program though the `os` module is the environment. Variables set in the environment are visible as strings that can be read through `os.environ` or `getenv()`. Environment variables are commonly used for configuration values, such as search paths, file locations, and debug flags. This example shows how to retrieve an environment variable and pass a value through to a child process.

```
import os

print 'Initial value:', os.environ.get('TESTVAR', None)
print 'Child process:'
os.system('echo $TESTVAR')

os.environ['TESTVAR'] = 'THIS VALUE WAS CHANGED'

print
print 'Changed value:', os.environ['TESTVAR']
print 'Child process:'
os.system('echo $TESTVAR')

del os.environ['TESTVAR']

print
print 'Removed value:', os.environ.get('TESTVAR', None)
print 'Child process:'
os.system('echo $TESTVAR')
```

The `os.environ` object follows the standard Python mapping API for retrieving and setting values. Changes to `os.environ` are exported for child processes.

```
$ python -u os_environ_example.py

Initial value: None
Child process:


Changed value: THIS VALUE WAS CHANGED
Child process:
THIS VALUE WAS CHANGED
```

```
Removed value: None
Child process:
```

17.3.3   Process Working Directory

Operating systems with hierarchical file systems have a concept of the *current working directory*—the directory on the file system the process uses as the starting location when files are accessed with relative paths. The current working directory can be retrieved with `getcwd()` and changed with `chdir()`.

```
import os

print 'Starting:', os.getcwd()

print 'Moving up one:', os.pardir
os.chdir(os.pardir)

print 'After move:', os.getcwd()
```

`os.curdir` and `os.pardir` are used to refer to the current and parent directories in a portable manner.

```
$ python os_cwd_example.py

Starting: /Users/dhellmann/Documents/PyMOTW/book/PyMOTW/os
Moving up one: ..
After move: /Users/dhellmann/Documents/PyMOTW/book/PyMOTW
```

17.3.4   Pipes

The `os` module provides several functions for managing the I/O of child processes using pipes. The functions all work essentially the same way, but return different file handles depending on the type of input or output desired. For the most part, these functions are made obsolete by the `subprocess` module (added in Python 2.4), but it is likely that legacy code uses them.

The most commonly used pipe function is `popen()`. It creates a new process running the command given and attaches a single stream to the input or output of that process, depending on the *mode* argument.

> **Note:** Although the `popen()` functions work on Windows, some of these examples assume a UNIX-like shell.

```
import os

print 'popen, read:'
stdout = os.popen('echo "to stdout"', 'r')
try:
    stdout_value = stdout.read()
finally:
    stdout.close()
print '\tstdout:', repr(stdout_value)

print '\npopen, write:'
stdin = os.popen('cat -', 'w')
try:
    stdin.write('\tstdin: to stdin\n')
finally:
    stdin.close()
```

The descriptions of the streams also assume UNIX-like terminology.

- stdin—The "standard input" stream for a process (file descriptor 0) is readable by the process. This is usually where terminal input goes.
- stdout—The "standard output" stream for a process (file descriptor 1) is writable by the process and is used for displaying regular output to the user.
- stderr—The "standard error" stream for a process (file descriptor 2) is writable by the process and is used for conveying error messages.

```
$ python -u os_popen.py

popen, read:
    stdout: 'to stdout\n'

popen, write:
    stdin: to stdin
```

The caller can only read from or write to the streams associated with the child process, which limits their usefulness. The other file descriptors for the child process are inherited from the parent, so the output of the cat – command in the second example appears on the console because its standard output file descriptor is the same as the one used by the parent script.

The other popen() variants provide additional streams, so it is possible to work with stdin, stdout, and stderr, as needed. For example, popen2() returns a write-only stream attached to stdin of the child process and a read-only stream attached to its stdout.

```
import os

print 'popen2:'
stdin, stdout = os.popen2('cat -')
try:
    stdin.write('through stdin to stdout')
finally:
    stdin.close()
try:
    stdout_value = stdout.read()
finally:
    stdout.close()
print '\tpass through:', repr(stdout_value)
```

This simplistic example illustrates bidirectional communication. The value written to stdin is read by `cat` (because of the ` - ` argument) and then written back to stdout. A more complicated process could pass other types of messages back and forth through the pipe—even serialized objects.

```
$ python -u os_popen2.py

popen2:
    pass through: 'through stdin to stdout'
```

In most cases, it is desirable to have access to both stdout and stderr. The stdout stream is used for message passing, and the stderr stream is used for errors. Reading them separately reduces the complexity for parsing any error messages. The `popen3()` function returns three open streams tied to stdin, stdout, and stderr of the new process.

```
import os

print 'popen3:'
stdin, stdout, stderr = os.popen3('cat -; echo ";to stderr" 1>&2')
try:
    stdin.write('through stdin to stdout')
finally:
    stdin.close()
try:
    stdout_value = stdout.read()
finally:
    stdout.close()
```

```
print '\tpass through:', repr(stdout_value)
try:
    stderr_value = stderr.read()
finally:
    stderr.close()
print '\tstderr:', repr(stderr_value)
```

The program has to read from and close both stdout and stderr separately. There are some issues related to flow control and sequencing when dealing with I/O for multiple processes. The I/O is buffered, and if the caller expects to be able to read all the data from a stream, then the child process must close that stream to indicate the end of file. For more information on these issues, refer to the *Flow Control Issues* section of the Python library documentation.

```
$ python -u os_popen3.py

popen3:
    pass through: 'through stdin to stdout'
    stderr: ';to stderr\n'
```

And finally, `popen4()` returns two streams: stdin and a merged stdout/stderr. This is useful when the results of the command need to be logged but not parsed directly.

```
import os

print 'popen4:'
stdin, stdout_and_stderr = os.popen4('cat -; echo ";to stderr" 1>&2')
try:
    stdin.write('through stdin to stdout')
finally:
    stdin.close()
try:
    stdout_value = stdout_and_stderr.read()
finally:
    stdout_and_stderr.close()
print '\tcombined output:', repr(stdout_value)
```

All the messages written to both stdout and stderr are read together.

```
$ python -u os_popen4.py

popen4:
    combined output: 'through stdin to stdout;to stderr\n'
```

Besides accepting a single-string command to be given to the shell for parsing, `popen2()`, `popen3()`, and `popen4()` also accept a sequence of strings containing the command followed by its arguments.

```
import os

print 'popen2, cmd as sequence:'
stdin, stdout = os.popen2(['cat', '-'])
try:
    stdin.write('through stdin to stdout')
finally:
    stdin.close()
try:
    stdout_value = stdout.read()
finally:
    stdout.close()
print '\tpass through:', repr(stdout_value)
```

When arguments are passed as a list instead of as a single string, they are not processed by a shell before the command is run.

```
$ python -u os_popen2_seq.py

popen2, cmd as sequence:
    pass through: 'through stdin to stdout'
```

17.3.5 File Descriptors

`os` includes the standard set of functions for working with low-level *file descriptors* (integers representing open files owned by the current process). This is a lower-level API than is provided by `file` objects. These functions are not covered here because it is generally easier to work directly with `file` objects. Refer to the library documentation for details.

17.3.6 File System Permissions

Detailed information about a file can be accessed using `stat()` or `lstat()` (for checking the status of something that might be a symbolic link).

```
import os
import sys
import time
```

```
if len(sys.argv) == 1:
    filename = __file__
else:
    filename = sys.argv[1]

stat_info = os.stat(filename)

print 'os.stat(%s):' % filename
print '\tSize:', stat_info.st_size
print '\tPermissions:', oct(stat_info.st_mode)
print '\tOwner:', stat_info.st_uid
print '\tDevice:', stat_info.st_dev
print '\tLast modified:', time.ctime(stat_info.st_mtime)
```

The output will vary depending on how the example code was installed. Try passing different filenames on the command line to `os_stat.py`.

```
$ python os_stat.py

os.stat(os_stat.py):
    Size: 1516
    Permissions: 0100644
    Owner: 527
    Device: 234881026
    Last modified: Sun Nov 14 09:40:36 2010
```

On UNIX-like systems, file permissions can be changed using `chmod()`, passing the mode as an integer. Mode values can be constructed using constants defined in the `stat` module. This example toggles the user's execute permission bit.

```
import os
import stat

filename = 'os_stat_chmod_example.txt'
if os.path.exists(filename):
    os.unlink(filename)
with open(filename, 'wt') as f:
    f.write('contents')

# Determine what permissions are already set using stat
existing_permissions = stat.S_IMODE(os.stat(filename).st_mode)

if not os.access(filename, os.X_OK):
```

```
    print 'Adding execute permission'
    new_permissions = existing_permissions | stat.S_IXUSR
else:
    print 'Removing execute permission'
    # use xor to remove the user execute permission
    new_permissions = existing_permissions ^ stat.S_IXUSR

os.chmod(filename, new_permissions)
```

The script assumes it has the permissions necessary to modify the mode of the file when run.

```
$ python os_stat_chmod.py

Adding execute permission
```

17.3.7 Directories

There are several functions for working with directories on the file system, including creating contents, listing contents, and removing them.

```
import os

dir_name = 'os_directories_example'

print 'Creating', dir_name
os.makedirs(dir_name)

file_name = os.path.join(dir_name, 'example.txt')
print 'Creating', file_name
with open(file_name, 'wt') as f:
    f.write('example file')

print 'Listing', dir_name
print os.listdir(dir_name)

print 'Cleaning up'
os.unlink(file_name)
os.rmdir(dir_name)
```

There are two sets of functions for creating and deleting directories. When creating a new directory with mkdir(), all the parent directories must already exist. When removing a directory with `rmdir()`, only the leaf directory (the last part of the path) is actually removed. In contrast, `makedirs()` and `removedirs()` operate on all the nodes in the path. `makedirs()` will create any parts of the path that do not exist, and `removedirs()` will remove all the parent directories, as long as they are empty.

```
$ python os_directories.py

Creating os_directories_example
Creating os_directories_example/example.txt
Listing os_directories_example
['example.txt']
Cleaning up
```

17.3.8 Symbolic Links

For platforms and file systems that support them, there are functions for working with symlinks.

```
import os

link_name = '/tmp/' + os.path.basename(__file__)

print 'Creating link %s -> %s' % (link_name, __file__)
os.symlink(__file__, link_name)

stat_info = os.lstat(link_name)
print 'Permissions:', oct(stat_info.st_mode)

print 'Points to:', os.readlink(link_name)

# Cleanup
os.unlink(link_name)
```

Use `symlink()` to create a symbolic link and `readlink()` for reading it to determine the original file pointed to by the link. The `lstat()` function is like `stat()`, but it operates on symbolic links.

```
$ python os_symlinks.py

Creating link /tmp/os_symlinks.py -> os_symlinks.py
Permissions: 0120755
Points to: os_symlinks.py
```

17.3.9 Walking a Directory Tree

The function `walk()` traverses a directory recursively and, for each directory, generates a `tuple` containing the directory path, any immediate subdirectories of that path, and a list of the names of any files in that directory.

```python
import os, sys

# If we are not given a path to list, use /tmp
if len(sys.argv) == 1:
    root = '/tmp'
else:
    root = sys.argv[1]

for dir_name, sub_dirs, files in os.walk(root):
    print dir_name
    # Make the subdirectory names stand out with /
    sub_dirs = [ '%s/' % n for n in sub_dirs ]
    # Mix the directory contents together
    contents = sub_dirs + files
    contents.sort()
    # Show the contents
    for c in contents:
        print '\t%s' % c
    print
```

This example shows a recursive directory listing.

```
$ python os_walk.py ../zipimport

../zipimport
    __init__.py
    __init__.pyc
    example_package/
    index.rst
    zipimport_example.zip
    zipimport_find_module.py
    zipimport_find_module.pyc
    zipimport_get_code.py
    zipimport_get_code.pyc
    zipimport_get_data.py
    zipimport_get_data.pyc
    zipimport_get_data_nozip.py
    zipimport_get_data_nozip.pyc
```

```
zipimport_get_data_zip.py
zipimport_get_data_zip.pyc
zipimport_get_source.py
zipimport_get_source.pyc
zipimport_is_package.py
zipimport_is_package.pyc
zipimport_load_module.py
zipimport_load_module.pyc
zipimport_make_example.py
zipimport_make_example.pyc

../zipimport/example_package
    README.txt
    __init__.py
    __init__.pyc
```

17.3.10 Running External Commands

> **Warning:** Many of these functions for working with processes have limited portability. For a more consistent way to work with processes in a platform-independent manner, see the `subprocess` module instead.

The most basic way to run a separate command, without interacting with it at all, is `system()`. It takes a single-string argument, which is the command line to be executed by a subprocess running a shell.

```
import os

# Simple command
os.system('pwd')
```

The return value of `system()` is the exit value of the shell running the program packed into a 16-bit number, with the high byte the exit status and the low byte the signal number that caused the process to die, or zero.

```
$ python -u os_system_example.py

/Users/dhellmann/Documents/PyMOTW/book/PyMOTW/os
```

Since the command is passed directly to the shell for processing, it can include shell syntax such as globbing or environment variables.

```
import os

# Command with shell expansion
os.system('echo $TMPDIR')
```

The environment variable $TMPDIR in this string is expanded when the shell runs the command line.

```
$ python -u os_system_shell.py

/var/folders/9R/9R1t+tR02Raxzk+F71Q50U+++Uw/-Tmp-/
```

Unless the command is explicitly run in the background, the call to system() blocks until it is complete. Standard input, output, and error channels from the child process are tied to the appropriate streams owned by the caller by default, but can be redirected using shell syntax.

```
import os
import time

print 'Calling...'
os.system('date; (sleep 3; date) &')

print 'Sleeping...'
time.sleep(5)
```

This is getting into shell trickery, though, and there are better ways to accomplish the same thing.

```
$ python -u os_system_background.py

Calling...
Sat Dec  4 14:47:07 EST 2010
Sleeping...
Sat Dec  4 14:47:10 EST 2010
```

17.3.11 Creating Processes with os.fork()

The POSIX functions fork() and exec() (available under Mac OS X, Linux, and other UNIX variants) are exposed via the os module. Entire books have been written about reliably using these functions, so check the library or a bookstore for more details than this introduction presents.

To create a new process as a clone of the current process, use `fork()`.

```
import os

pid = os.fork()

if pid:
    print 'Child process id:', pid
else:
    print 'I am the child'
```

The output will vary based on the state of the system each time the example is run, but it will look something like this.

```
$ python -u os_fork_example.py

I am the child
Child process id: 14133
```

After the fork, two processes are running the same code. For a program to tell which one it is in, it needs to check the return value of `fork()`. If the value is 0, the current process is the child. If it is not 0, the program is running in the parent process and the return value is the process id of the child process.

The parent can send signals to the child process using `kill()` and the `signal` module. First, define a signal handler to be invoked when the signal is received.

```
import os
import signal
import time

def signal_usr1(signum, frame):
    "Callback invoked when a signal is received"
    pid = os.getpid()
    print 'Received USR1 in process %s' % pid
```

Then invoke `fork()`, and in the parent, pause a short amount of time before sending a `USR1` signal using `kill()`. The short pause gives the child process time to set up the signal handler.

```
print 'Forking...'
child_pid = os.fork()
if child_pid:
    print 'PARENT: Pausing before sending signal...'
    time.sleep(1)
    print 'PARENT: Signaling %s' % child_pid
    os.kill(child_pid, signal.SIGUSR1)
```

In the child, set up the signal handler and go to sleep for a while to give the parent time to send the signal.

```
else:
    print 'CHILD: Setting up signal handler'
    signal.signal(signal.SIGUSR1, signal_usr1)
    print 'CHILD: Pausing to wait for signal'
    time.sleep(5)
```

A real application would not need (or want) to call `sleep()`.

```
$ python os_kill_example.py

Forking...
PARENT: Pausing before sending signal...
PARENT: Signaling 14136
Forking...
CHILD: Setting up signal handler
CHILD: Pausing to wait for signal
Received USR1 in process 14136
```

A simple way to handle separate behavior in the child process is to check the return value of `fork()` and branch. More complex behavior may call for more code separation than a simple branch. In other cases, an existing program may need to be wrapped. For both of these situations, the `exec*()` series of functions can be used to run another program.

```
import os

child_pid = os.fork()
if child_pid:
    os.waitpid(child_pid, 0)
else:
    os.execlp('pwd', 'pwd', '-P')
```

When a program is run by `exec()`, the code from that program replaces the code from the existing process.

```
$ python os_exec_example.py

/Users/dhellmann/Documents/PyMOTW/book/PyMOTW/os
```

There are many variations of `exec()`, depending on the form in which the arguments are available, whether the path and environment of the parent process should be copied to the child, etc. For all variations, the first argument is a path or filename, and the remaining arguments control how that program runs. They are either passed as command-line arguments, or they override the process "environment" (see `os.environ` and `os.getenv`). Refer to the library documentation for complete details.

17.3.12   Waiting for a Child

Many computationally intensive programs use multiple processes to work around the threading limitations of Python and the global interpreter lock. When starting several processes to run separate tasks, the master will need to wait for one or more of them to finish before starting new ones, to avoid overloading the server. There are a few different ways to do that using `wait()` and related functions.

When it does not matter which child process might exit first, use `wait()`. It returns as soon as any child process exits.

```python
import os
import sys
import time

for i in range(2):
    print 'PARENT %s: Forking %s' % (os.getpid(), i)
    worker_pid = os.fork()
    if not worker_pid:
        print 'WORKER %s: Starting' % i
        time.sleep(2 + i)
        print 'WORKER %s: Finishing' % i
        sys.exit(i)

for i in range(2):
    print 'PARENT: Waiting for %s' % i
    done = os.wait()
    print 'PARENT: Child done:', done
```

The return value from `wait()` is a tuple containing the process id and exit status combined into a 16-bit value. The low byte is the number of the signal that killed the process, and the high byte is the status code returned by the process when it exited.

```
$ python os_wait_example.py

PARENT 14154: Forking 0
PARENT 14154: Forking 1
WORKER 0: Starting
PARENT: Waiting for 0
WORKER 1: Starting
WORKER 0: Finishing
PARENT: Child done: (14155, 0)
PARENT: Waiting for 1
WORKER 1: Finishing
PARENT: Child done: (14156, 256)
```

To wait for a specific process, use `waitpid()`.

```python
import os
import sys
import time

workers = []
for i in range(2):
    print 'PARENT %d: Forking %s' % (os.getpid(), i)
    worker_pid = os.fork()
    if not worker_pid:
        print 'WORKER %s: Starting' % i
        time.sleep(2 + i)
        print 'WORKER %s: Finishing' % i
        sys.exit(i)
    workers.append(worker_pid)

for pid in workers:
    print 'PARENT: Waiting for %s' % pid
    done = os.waitpid(pid, 0)
    print 'PARENT: Child done:', done
```

Pass the process id of the target process. `waitpid()` blocks until that process exits.

```
$ python os_waitpid_example.py

PARENT 14162: Forking 0
```

```
PARENT 14162: Forking 1
PARENT: Waiting for 14163
WORKER 0: Starting
WORKER 1: Starting
WORKER 0: Finishing
PARENT: Child done: (14163, 0)
PARENT: Waiting for 14164
WORKER 1: Finishing
PARENT: Child done: (14164, 256)
```

`wait3()` and `wait4()` work in a similar manner, but return more detailed information about the child process with the pid, exit status, and resource usage.

17.3.13 Spawn

As a convenience, the `spawn()` family of functions handles the `fork()` and `exec()` in one statement.

```
import os

os.spawnlp(os.P_WAIT, 'pwd', 'pwd', '-P')
```

The first argument is a mode indicating whether or not to wait for the process to finish before returning. This example waits. Use `P_NOWAIT` to let the other process start, but then resume in the current process.

```
$ python os_spawn_example.py

/Users/dhellmann/Documents/PyMOTW/book/PyMOTW/os
```

17.3.14 File System Permissions

The function `access()` can be used to test the access rights a process has for a file.

```
import os

print 'Testing:', __file__
print 'Exists:', os.access(__file__, os.F_OK)
print 'Readable:', os.access(__file__, os.R_OK)
print 'Writable:', os.access(__file__, os.W_OK)
print 'Executable:', os.access(__file__, os.X_OK)
```

The results will vary depending on how the example code is installed, but the output will be similar to the following.

```
$ python os_access.py

Testing: os_access.py
Exists: True
Readable: True
Writable: True
Executable: False
```

The library documentation for `access()` includes two special warnings. First, there is not much sense in calling `access()` to test whether a file can be opened before actually calling `open()` on it. There is a small, but real, window of time between the two calls during which the permissions on the file could change. The other warning applies mostly to networked file systems that extend the POSIX permission semantics. Some file system types may respond to the POSIX call that a process has permission to access a file, and then report a failure when the attempt is made using `open()` for some reason not tested via the POSIX call. All in all, it is better to call `open()` with the required mode and catch the `IOError` raised if a problem occurs.

See Also:

os (http://docs.python.org/lib/module-os.html) The standard library documentation for this module.

Flow Control Issues (http://docs.python.org/library/popen2.html#popen2-flow-control) The standard library documentation of `popen2()` and how to prevent deadlocks.

signal (page 497) The section on the `signal` module goes over signal handling techniques in more detail.

subprocess (page 481) The `subprocess` module supersedes `os.popen()`.

multiprocessing (page 529) The `multiprocessing` module makes working with extra processes easier.

***Working with Directory Trees* (page 276)** The `shutil` (page 271) module also includes functions for working with directory trees.

tempfile (page 265) The `tempfile` module for working with temporary files.

UNIX Manual Page Introduction (www.scit.wlv.ac.uk/cgi-bin/mansec?2+intro) Includes definitions of real and effective ids, etc.

Speaking UNIX, Part 8 (www.ibm.com/developerworks/aix/library/auspeakingunix8/index.html) Learn how UNIX multitasks.

UNIX Concepts (www.linuxhq.com/guides/LUG/node67.html) For more discussion of stdin, stdout, and stderr.

Delve into UNIX Process Creation (www.ibm.com/developerworks/aix/library/auunixprocess.html) Explains the life cycle of a UNIX process.

Advanced Programming in the UNIX(R) Environment By W. Richard Stevens and Stephen A. Rago. Published by Addison-Wesley Professional, 2005. ISBN-10: 0201433079. Covers working with multiple processes, such as handling signals, closing duplicated file descriptors, etc.

17.4 platform—System Version Information

Purpose Probe the underlying platform's hardware, operating system, and interpreter version information.

Python Version 2.3 and later

Although Python is often used as a cross-platform language, it is occasionally necessary to know what sort of system a program is running on. Build tools need that information, but an application might also know that some of the libraries or external commands it uses have different interfaces on different operating systems. For example, a tool to manage the network configuration of an operating system can define a portable representation of network interfaces, aliases, IP addresses, etc. But when the time comes to edit the configuration files, it must know more about the host so it can use the correct operating system configuration commands and files. The `platform` module includes the tools for learning about the interpreter, operating system, and hardware platform where a program is running.

> **Note:** The example output in this section was generated on three systems: a Mac-Book Pro3,1 running OS X 10.6.5; a VMware Fusion VM running CentOS 5.5; and a Dell PC running Microsoft Windows 2008. Python was installed on the OS X and Windows systems using the precompiled installer from python.org. The Linux system is running an interpreter built from source locally.

17.4.1 Interpreter

There are four functions for getting information about the current Python interpreter. `python_version()` and `python_version_tuple()` return different forms of the interpreter version with major, minor, and patch-level components.

`python_compiler()` reports on the compiler used to build the interpreter. And `python_build()` gives a version string for the interpreter build.

```
import platform

print 'Version       :', platform.python_version()
print 'Version tuple:', platform.python_version_tuple()
print 'Compiler      :', platform.python_compiler()
print 'Build         :', platform.python_build()
```

OS X:

```
$ python platform_python.py

Version       : 2.7.0
Version tuple: ('2', '7', '0')
Compiler      : GCC 4.0.1 (Apple Inc. build 5493)
Build         : ('r27:82508', 'Jul  3 2010 21:12:11')
```

Linux:

```
$ python platform_python.py

Version       : 2.7.0
Version tuple: ('2', '7', '0')
Compiler      : GCC 4.1.2 20080704 (Red Hat 4.1.2-46)
Build         : ('r27', 'Aug 20 2010 11:37:51')
```

Windows:

```
C:> python.exe platform_python.py

Version       : 2.7.0
Version tuple: ['2', '7', '0']
Compiler      : MSC v.1500 64 bit (AMD64)
Build         : ('r27:82525', 'Jul  4 2010 07:43:08')
```

17.4.2 Platform

The `platform()` function returns a string containing a general-purpose platform identifier. The function accepts two optional Boolean arguments. If *aliased* is True, the names in the return value are converted from a formal name to their more common form. When *terse* is true, a minimal value with some parts dropped is returned instead of the full string.

```
import platform

print 'Normal :', platform.platform()
print 'Aliased:', platform.platform(aliased=True)
print 'Terse  :', platform.platform(terse=True)
```

OS X:

```
$ python platform_platform.py

Normal : Darwin-10.5.0-i386-64bit
Aliased: Darwin-10.5.0-i386-64bit
Terse  : Darwin-10.5.0
```

Linux:

```
$ python platform_platform.py

Normal : Linux-2.6.18-194.3.1.el5-i686-with-redhat-5.5-Final
Aliased: Linux-2.6.18-194.3.1.el5-i686-with-redhat-5.5-Final
Terse  : Linux-2.6.18-194.3.1.el5-i686-with-glibc2.3
```

Windows:

```
C:> python.exe platform_platform.py

Normal : Windows-2008ServerR2-6.1.7600
Aliased: Windows-2008ServerR2-6.1.7600
Terse  : Windows-2008ServerR2
```

17.4.3 Operating System and Hardware Info

More detailed information about the operating system and the hardware the interpreter is running under can be retrieved as well. uname() returns a tuple containing the system, node, release, version, machine, and processor values. Individual values can be accessed through functions of the same names, listed in Table 17.3.

Table 17.3. Platform Information Functions

Function	Return Value
system()	Operating system name
node()	Host name of the server, not fully qualified
release()	Operating system release number
version()	More detailed system version
machine()	A hardware-type identifier, such as 'i386'
processor()	A real identifier for the processor (the same value as machine() in many cases)

```
import platform

print 'uname:', platform.uname()

print
print 'system   :', platform.system()
print 'node     :', platform.node()
print 'release  :', platform.release()
print 'version  :', platform.version()
print 'machine  :', platform.machine()
print 'processor:', platform.processor()
```

OS X:

```
$ python platform_os_info.py

uname: ('Darwin', 'farnsworth.local', '10.5.0', 'Darwin Kernel
Version 10.5.0: Fri Nov  5 23:20:39 PDT 2010;
root:xnu-1504.9.17~1/RELEASE_I386', 'i386', 'i386')

system   : Darwin
node     : farnsworth.local
release  : 10.5.0
version  : Darwin Kernel Version 10.5.0: Fri Nov  5 23:20:39 PDT
2010; root:xnu-1504.9.17~1/RELEASE_I386
machine  : i386
processor: i386
```

Linux:

```
$ python platform_os_info.py
```

```
uname: ('Linux', 'hermes.hellfly.net', '2.6.18-194.3.1.el5',
'#1 SMP Thu May 13 13:09:10 EDT 2010', 'i686', 'i686')

system   : Linux
node     : hermes.hellfly.net
release  : 2.6.18-194.3.1.el5
version  : #1 SMP Thu May 13 13:09:10 EDT 2010
machine  : i686
processor: i686
```

Windows:

```
C:> python.exe platform_os_info.py

uname: ('Windows', 'dhellmann', '2008ServerR2', '6.1.7600',
'AMD64', 'Intel64 Family 6 Model 15 Stepping 11, GenuineIntel')

system   : Windows
node     : dhellmann
release  : 2008ServerR2
version  : 6.1.7600
machine  : AMD64
processor: Intel64 Family 6 Model 15 Stepping 11, GenuineIntel
```

17.4.4   Executable Architecture

Individual program architecture information can be probed using the `architecture()` function. The first argument is the path to an executable program (defaulting to `sys.executable`, the Python interpreter). The return value is a tuple containing the bit architecture and the linkage format used.

```
import platform

print 'interpreter:', platform.architecture()
print '/bin/ls    :', platform.architecture('/bin/ls')
```

OS X:

```
$ python platform_architecture.py

interpreter: ('64bit', '')
/bin/ls    : ('64bit', '')
```

Linux:

```
$ python platform_architecture.py

interpreter: ('32bit', 'ELF')
/bin/ls    : ('32bit', 'ELF')
```

Windows:

```
C:> python.exe platform_architecture.py

interpreter  : ('64bit', 'WindowsPE')
iexplore.exe : ('64bit', '')
```

See Also:
platform (http://docs.python.org/lib/module-platform.html) The standard library
documentation for this module.

17.5   resource—System Resource Management

> **Purpose** Manage the system resource limits for a UNIX program.
> **Python Version** 1.5.2 and later

The functions in `resource` probe the current system resources consumed by a process
and place limits on them to control how much load a program can impose on a system.

17.5.1   Current Usage

Use `getrusage()` to probe the resources used by the current process and/or its children. The return value is a data structure containing several resource metrics based on
the current state of the system.

Note: Not all the resource values gathered are displayed here. Refer to the standard
library documentation for `resource` for a more complete list.

```
import resource
import time

usage = resource.getrusage(resource.RUSAGE_SELF)
for name, desc in [
```

```
    ('ru_utime', 'User time'),
    ('ru_stime', 'System time'),
    ('ru_maxrss', 'Max. Resident Set Size'),
    ('ru_ixrss', 'Shared Memory Size'),
    ('ru_idrss', 'Unshared Memory Size'),
    ('ru_isrss', 'Stack Size'),
    ('ru_inblock', 'Block inputs'),
    ('ru_oublock', 'Block outputs'),
    ]:
    print '%-25s (%-10s) = %s' % (desc, name, getattr(usage, name))
```

Because the test program is extremely simple, it does not use very many resources.

```
$ python resource_getrusage.py

User time                (ru_utime  ) = 0.013974
System time              (ru_stime  ) = 0.013182
Max. Resident Set Size   (ru_maxrss ) = 5378048
Shared Memory Size       (ru_ixrss  ) = 0
Unshared Memory Size     (ru_idrss  ) = 0
Stack Size               (ru_isrss  ) = 0
Block inputs             (ru_inblock) = 0
Block outputs            (ru_oublock) = 1
```

17.5.2   Resource Limits

Separate from the current actual usage, it is possible to check the *limits* imposed on the application and then change them.

```
import resource

print 'Resource limits (soft/hard):'
for name, desc in [
    ('RLIMIT_CORE', 'core file size'),
    ('RLIMIT_CPU',  'CPU time'),
    ('RLIMIT_FSIZE', 'file size'),
    ('RLIMIT_DATA', 'heap size'),
    ('RLIMIT_STACK', 'stack size'),
    ('RLIMIT_RSS', 'resident set size'),
    ('RLIMIT_NPROC', 'number of processes'),
    ('RLIMIT_NOFILE', 'number of open files'),
    ('RLIMIT_MEMLOCK', 'lockable memory address'),
    ]:
```

```
limit_num = getattr(resource, name)
soft, hard = resource.getrlimit(limit_num)
print '%-23s %s / %s' % (desc, soft, hard)
```

The return value for each limit is a tuple containing the *soft* limit imposed by the current configuration and the *hard* limit imposed by the operating system.

```
$ python resource_getrlimit.py

Resource limits (soft/hard):
core file size          0 / 9223372036854775807
CPU time                9223372036854775807 / 9223372036854775807
file size               9223372036854775807 / 9223372036854775807
heap size               9223372036854775807 / 9223372036854775807
stack size              8388608 / 67104768
resident set size       9223372036854775807 / 9223372036854775807
number of processes     266 / 532
number of open files    7168 / 9223372036854775807
lockable memory address 9223372036854775807 / 9223372036854775807
```

The limits can be changed with `setrlimit()`.

```
import resource
import os

soft, hard = resource.getrlimit(resource.RLIMIT_NOFILE)
print 'Soft limit starts as  :', soft

resource.setrlimit(resource.RLIMIT_NOFILE, (4, hard))

soft, hard = resource.getrlimit(resource.RLIMIT_NOFILE)
print 'Soft limit changed to :', soft

random = open('/dev/random', 'r')
print 'random has fd =', random.fileno()
try:
    null = open('/dev/null', 'w')
except IOError, err:
    print err
else:
    print 'null has fd =', null.fileno()
```

This example uses RLIMIT_NOFILE to control the number of open files allowed, changing it to a smaller soft limit than the default.

```
$ python resource_setrlimit_nofile.py

Soft limit starts as   : 7168
Soft limit changed to : 4
random has fd = 3
[Errno 24] Too many open files: '/dev/null'
```

It can also be useful to limit the amount of CPU time a process should consume, to avoid using too much. When the process runs past the allotted amount of time, it is sent a SIGXCPU signal.

```python
import resource
import sys
import signal
import time

# Set up a signal handler to notify us
# when we run out of time.
def time_expired(n, stack):
    print 'EXPIRED :', time.ctime()
    raise SystemExit('(time ran out)')

signal.signal(signal.SIGXCPU, time_expired)

# Adjust the CPU time limit
soft, hard = resource.getrlimit(resource.RLIMIT_CPU)
print 'Soft limit starts as  :', soft

resource.setrlimit(resource.RLIMIT_CPU, (1, hard))

soft, hard = resource.getrlimit(resource.RLIMIT_CPU)
print 'Soft limit changed to :', soft
print

# Consume some CPU time in a pointless exercise
print 'Starting:', time.ctime()
for i in range(200000):
    for i in range(200000):
        v = i * i
```

```
# We should never make it this far
print 'Exiting :', time.ctime()
```

Normally, the signal handler should flush all open files and close them, but in this case, it just prints a message and exits.

```
$ python resource_setrlimit_cpu.py

Soft limit starts as   : 9223372036854775807
Soft limit changed to : 1

Starting: Sat Dec  4 15:02:57 2010
EXPIRED : Sat Dec  4 15:02:58 2010
(time ran out)
```

See Also:

resource (http://docs.python.org/library/resource.html) The standard library documentation for this module.

signal (page 497) Provides details on registering signal handlers.

17.6   gc—Garbage Collector

> **Purpose** Manages memory used by Python objects.
> **Python Version** 2.1 and later

gc exposes the underlying memory-management mechanism of Python, the automatic garbage collector. The module includes functions to control how the collector operates and to examine the objects known to the system, either pending collection or stuck in reference cycles and unable to be freed.

17.6.1   Tracing References

With gc, the incoming and outgoing references between objects can be used to find cycles in complex data structures. If a data structure is known to have a cycle, custom code can be used to examine its properties. If the cycle is in unknown code, the get_referents() and get_referrers() functions can be used to build generic debugging tools.

For example, get_referents() shows the objects *referred to* by the input arguments.

```python
import gc
import pprint

class Graph(object):
    def __init__(self, name):
        self.name = name
        self.next = None
    def set_next(self, next):
        print 'Linking nodes %s.next = %s' % (self, next)
        self.next = next
    def __repr__(self):
        return '%s(%s)' % (self.__class__.__name__, self.name)

# Construct a graph cycle
one = Graph('one')
two = Graph('two')
three = Graph('three')
one.set_next(two)
two.set_next(three)
three.set_next(one)

print
print 'three refers to:'
for r in gc.get_referents(three):
    pprint.pprint(r)
```

In this case, the `Graph` instance `three` holds references to its instance dictionary (in the `__dict__` attribute) and its class.

```
$ python gc_get_referents.py

Linking nodes Graph(one).next = Graph(two)
Linking nodes Graph(two).next = Graph(three)
Linking nodes Graph(three).next = Graph(one)

three refers to:
{'name': 'three', 'next': Graph(one)}
<class '__main__.Graph'>
```

The next example uses a `Queue` to perform a breadth-first traversal of all the object references looking for cycles. The items inserted into the queue are tuples containing the reference chain so far and the next object to examine. It starts with `three` and looks at everything it refers to. Skipping classes avoids looking at methods, modules, etc.

```python
import gc
import pprint
import Queue

class Graph(object):
    def __init__(self, name):
        self.name = name
        self.next = None
    def set_next(self, next):
        print 'Linking nodes %s.next = %s' % (self, next)
        self.next = next
    def __repr__(self):
        return '%s(%s)' % (self.__class__.__name__, self.name)

# Construct a graph cycle
one = Graph('one')
two = Graph('two')
three = Graph('three')
one.set_next(two)
two.set_next(three)
three.set_next(one)

print

seen = set()
to_process = Queue.Queue()

# Start with an empty object chain and Graph three.
to_process.put( ([], three) )

# Look for cycles, building the object chain for each object found
# in the queue so the full cycle can be printed at the end.
while not to_process.empty():
    chain, next = to_process.get()
    chain = chain[:]
    chain.append(next)
    print 'Examining:', repr(next)
    seen.add(id(next))
    for r in gc.get_referents(next):
        if isinstance(r, basestring) or isinstance(r, type):
```

```
            # Ignore strings and classes
            pass
    elif id(r) in seen:
        print
        print 'Found a cycle to %s:' % r
        for i, link in enumerate(chain):
            print '   %d: ' % i,
            pprint.pprint(link)
    else:
        to_process.put( (chain, r) )
```

The cycle in the nodes is easily found by watching for objects that have already been processed. To avoid holding references to those objects, their id() values are cached in a set. The dictionary objects found in the cycle are the __dict__ values for the Graph instances and hold their instance attributes.

```
$ python gc_get_referents_cycles.py

Linking nodes Graph(one).next = Graph(two)
Linking nodes Graph(two).next = Graph(three)
Linking nodes Graph(three).next = Graph(one)

Examining: Graph(three)
Examining: {'name': 'three', 'next': Graph(one)}
Examining: Graph(one)
Examining: {'name': 'one', 'next': Graph(two)}
Examining: Graph(two)
Examining: {'name': 'two', 'next': Graph(three)}

Found a cycle to Graph(three):
   0: Graph(three)
   1: {'name': 'three', 'next': Graph(one)}
   2: Graph(one)
   3: {'name': 'one', 'next': Graph(two)}
   4: Graph(two)
   5: {'name': 'two', 'next': Graph(three)}
```

17.6.2 Forcing Garbage Collection

Although the garbage collector runs automatically as the interpreter executes a program, it can be triggered to run at a specific time when there are a lot of objects to free or there is not much work happening and the collector will not hurt application performance. Trigger collection using `collect()`.

```
import gc
import pprint

class Graph(object):
    def __init__(self, name):
        self.name = name
        self.next = None
    def set_next(self, next):
        print 'Linking nodes %s.next = %s' % (self, next)
        self.next = next
    def __repr__(self):
        return '%s(%s)' % (self.__class__.__name__, self.name)

# Construct a graph cycle
one = Graph('one')
two = Graph('two')
three = Graph('three')
one.set_next(two)
two.set_next(three)
three.set_next(one)

print

# Remove references to the graph nodes in this module's namespace
one = two = three = None

# Show the effect of garbage collection
for i in range(2):
    print 'Collecting %d ...' % i
    n = gc.collect()
    print 'Unreachable objects:', n
    print 'Remaining Garbage:',
    pprint.pprint(gc.garbage)
    print
```

In this example, the cycle is cleared as soon as collection runs the first time, since nothing refers to the `Graph` nodes except themselves. `collect()` returns the number of "unreachable" objects it found. In this case, the value is 6 because there are three objects with their instance attribute dictionaries.

```
$ python gc_collect.py

Linking nodes Graph(one).next = Graph(two)
Linking nodes Graph(two).next = Graph(three)
Linking nodes Graph(three).next = Graph(one)

Collecting 0 ...
Unreachable objects: 6
Remaining Garbage:[]

Collecting 1 ...
Unreachable objects: 0
Remaining Garbage:[]
```

If Graph has a __del__() method, however, the garbage collector cannot break the cycle.

```
import gc
import pprint

class Graph(object):
    def __init__(self, name):
        self.name = name
        self.next = None
    def set_next(self, next):
        print '%s.next = %s' % (self, next)
        self.next = next
    def __repr__(self):
        return '%s(%s)' % (self.__class__.__name__, self.name)
    def __del__(self):
        print '%s.__del__()' % self

# Construct a graph cycle
one = Graph('one')
two = Graph('two')
three = Graph('three')
one.set_next(two)
two.set_next(three)
three.set_next(one)

# Remove references to the graph nodes in this module's namespace
one = two = three = None
```

```
# Show the effect of garbage collection
print 'Collecting...'
n = gc.collect()
print 'Unreachable objects:', n
print 'Remaining Garbage:',
pprint.pprint(gc.garbage)
```

Because more than one object in the cycle has a finalizer method, the order in which the objects need to be finalized and then garbage collected cannot be determined. The garbage collector plays it safe and keeps the objects.

```
$ python gc_collect_with_del.py

Graph(one).next = Graph(two)
Graph(two).next = Graph(three)
Graph(three).next = Graph(one)
Collecting...
Unreachable objects: 6
Remaining Garbage:[Graph(one), Graph(two), Graph(three)]
```

When the cycle is broken, the `Graph` instances can be collected.

```
import gc
import pprint

class Graph(object):
    def __init__(self, name):
        self.name = name
        self.next = None
    def set_next(self, next):
        print 'Linking nodes %s.next = %s' % (self, next)
        self.next = next
    def __repr__(self):
        return '%s(%s)' % (self.__class__.__name__, self.name)
    def __del__(self):
        print '%s.__del__()' % self

# Construct a graph cycle
one = Graph('one')
two = Graph('two')
three = Graph('three')
one.set_next(two)
```

```
two.set_next(three)
three.set_next(one)

# Remove references to the graph nodes in this module's namespace
one = two = three = None

# Collecting now keeps the objects as uncollectable
print
print 'Collecting...'
n = gc.collect()
print 'Unreachable objects:', n
print 'Remaining Garbage:',
pprint.pprint(gc.garbage)

# Break the cycle
print
print 'Breaking the cycle'
gc.garbage[0].set_next(None)
print 'Removing references in gc.garbage'
del gc.garbage[:]

# Now the objects are removed
print
print 'Collecting...'
n = gc.collect()
print 'Unreachable objects:', n
print 'Remaining Garbage:',
pprint.pprint(gc.garbage)
```

Because `gc.garbage` holds a reference to the objects from the previous garbage collection run, it needs to be cleared out after the cycle is broken to reduce the reference counts so they can be finalized and freed.

```
$ python gc_collect_break_cycle.py

Linking nodes Graph(one).next = Graph(two)
Linking nodes Graph(two).next = Graph(three)
Linking nodes Graph(three).next = Graph(one)

Collecting...
Unreachable objects: 6
Remaining Garbage:[Graph(one), Graph(two), Graph(three)]
```

```
Breaking the cycle
Linking nodes Graph(one).next = None
Removing references in gc.garbage
Graph(two).__del__()
Graph(three).__del__()
Graph(one).__del__()

Collecting...
Unreachable objects: 0
Remaining Garbage:[]
```

17.6.3   Finding References to Objects that Cannot Be Collected

Looking for the object holding a reference to something in the garbage list is a little trickier than seeing what an object references. Because the code asking about the reference needs to hold a reference itself, some of the referrers need to be ignored. This example creates a graph cycle and then works through the Graph instances and removes the reference in the "parent" node.

```python
import gc
import pprint
import Queue

class Graph(object):
    def __init__(self, name):
        self.name = name
        self.next = None
    def set_next(self, next):
        print 'Linking nodes %s.next = %s' % (self, next)
        self.next = next
    def __repr__(self):
        return '%s(%s)' % (self.__class__.__name__, self.name)
    def __del__(self):
        print '%s.__del__()' % self

# Construct two graph cycles
one = Graph('one')
two = Graph('two')
three = Graph('three')
one.set_next(two)
two.set_next(three)
three.set_next(one)
```

```
# Remove references to the graph nodes in this module's namespace
one = two = three = None

# Collecting now keeps the objects as uncollectable
print
print 'Collecting...'
n = gc.collect()
print 'Unreachable objects:', n
print 'Remaining Garbage:',
pprint.pprint(gc.garbage)

REFERRERS_TO_IGNORE = [ locals(), globals(), gc.garbage ]

def find_referring_graphs(obj):
    print 'Looking for references to %s' % repr(obj)
    referrers = (r for r in gc.get_referrers(obj)
                    if r not in REFERRERS_TO_IGNORE)
    for ref in referrers:
        if isinstance(ref, Graph):
            # A graph node
            yield ref
        elif isinstance(ref, dict):
            # An instance or other namespace dictionary
            for parent in find_referring_graphs(ref):
                yield parent

# Look for objects that refer to the objects that remain in
# gc.garbage.
print
print 'Clearing referrers:'
for obj in gc.garbage:
    for ref in find_referring_graphs(obj):
        ref.set_next(None)
        del ref # remove local reference so the node can be deleted
    del obj # remove local reference so the node can be deleted

# Clear references held by gc.garbage
print
print 'Clearing gc.garbage:'
del gc.garbage[:]

# Everything should have been freed this time
print
```

```
print 'Collecting...'
n = gc.collect()
print 'Unreachable objects:', n
print 'Remaining Garbage:',
pprint.pprint(gc.garbage)
```

This sort of logic is overkill if the cycles are understood, but for an unexplained cycle in data, using `get_referrers()` can expose the unexpected relationship.

```
$ python gc_get_referrers.py

Linking nodes Graph(one).next = Graph(two)
Linking nodes Graph(two).next = Graph(three)
Linking nodes Graph(three).next = Graph(one)

Collecting...
Unreachable objects: 6
Remaining Garbage:[Graph(one), Graph(two), Graph(three)]

Clearing referrers:
Looking for references to Graph(one)
Looking for references to {'name': 'three', 'next': Graph(one)}
Linking nodes Graph(three).next = None
Looking for references to Graph(two)
Looking for references to {'name': 'one', 'next': Graph(two)}
Linking nodes Graph(one).next = None
Looking for references to Graph(three)
Looking for references to {'name': 'two', 'next': Graph(three)}
Linking nodes Graph(two).next = None

Clearing gc.garbage:
Graph(three).__del__()
Graph(two).__del__()
Graph(one).__del__()

Collecting...
Unreachable objects: 0
Remaining Garbage:[]
```

17.6.4 Collection Thresholds and Generations

The garbage collector maintains three lists of objects it sees as it runs, one for each "generation" the collector tracks. As objects are examined in each generation, they are either collected or they age into subsequent generations until they finally reach the stage where they are kept permanently.

The collector routines can be tuned to occur at different frequencies based on the difference between the number of object allocations and deallocations between runs. When the number of allocations, minus the number of deallocations, is greater than the threshold for the generation, the garbage collector is run. The current thresholds can be examined with get_threshold().

```
import gc

print gc.get_threshold()
```

The return value is a tuple with the threshold for each generation.

```
$ python gc_get_threshold.py

(700, 10, 10)
```

The thresholds can be changed with set_threshold(). This example program reads the threshold for generation 0 from the command line, adjusts the gc settings, and then allocates a series of objects.

```
import gc
import pprint
import sys

try:
    threshold = int(sys.argv[1])
except (IndexError, ValueError, TypeError):
    print 'Missing or invalid threshold, using default'
    threshold = 5

class MyObj(object):
    def __init__(self, name):
        self.name = name
        print 'Created', self.name

gc.set_debug(gc.DEBUG_STATS)

gc.set_threshold(threshold, 1, 1)
print 'Thresholds:', gc.get_threshold()
```

```
print 'Clear the collector by forcing a run'
gc.collect()
print

print 'Creating objects'
objs = []
for i in range(10):
    objs.append(MyObj(i))
```

Different threshold values introduce the garbage collection sweeps at different times, shown here because debugging is enabled.

```
$ python -u gc_threshold.py 5

Thresholds: (5, 1, 1)
Clear the collector by forcing a run
gc: collecting generation 2...
gc: objects in each generation: 218 2683 0
gc: done, 0.0008s elapsed.

Creating objects
gc: collecting generation 0...
gc: objects in each generation: 7 0 2819
gc: done, 0.0000s elapsed.
Created 0
Created 1
Created 2
Created 3
Created 4
gc: collecting generation 0...
gc: objects in each generation: 6 4 2819
gc: done, 0.0000s elapsed.
Created 5
Created 6
Created 7
Created 8
Created 9
gc: collecting generation 2...
gc: objects in each generation: 5 6 2817
gc: done, 0.0007s elapsed.
```

A smaller threshold causes the sweeps to run more frequently.

```
$ python -u gc_threshold.py 2
```

```
Thresholds: (2, 1, 1)
Clear the collector by forcing a run
gc: collecting generation 2...
gc: objects in each generation: 218 2683 0
gc: done, 0.0008s elapsed.

Creating objects
gc: collecting generation 0...
gc: objects in each generation: 3 0 2819
gc: done, 0.0000s elapsed.
gc: collecting generation 0...
gc: objects in each generation: 4 3 2819
gc: done, 0.0000s elapsed.
Created 0
Created 1
gc: collecting generation 1...
gc: objects in each generation: 3 4 2819
gc: done, 0.0000s elapsed.
Created 2
Created 3
Created 4
gc: collecting generation 0...
gc: objects in each generation: 5 0 2824
gc: done, 0.0000s elapsed.
Created 5
Created 6
Created 7
gc: collecting generation 0...
gc: objects in each generation: 5 3 2824
gc: done, 0.0000s elapsed.
Created 8
Created 9
gc: collecting generation 2...
gc: objects in each generation: 2 6 2820
gc: done, 0.0008s elapsed.
```

17.6.5   Debugging

Debugging memory leaks can be challenging. gc includes several options to expose the inner workings to make the job easier. The options are bit-flags meant to be combined and passed to set_debug() to configure the garbage collector while the program is running. Debugging information is printed to sys.stderr.

The DEBUG_STATS flag turns on statistics reporting. This causes the garbage collector to report the number of objects tracked for each generation and the amount of time it took to perform the sweep.

```
import gc

gc.set_debug(gc.DEBUG_STATS)

gc.collect()
```

This example output shows two separate runs of the collector. It runs once when it is invoked explicitly and a second time when the interpreter exits.

```
$ python gc_debug_stats.py

gc: collecting generation 2...
gc: objects in each generation: 83 2683 0
gc: done, 0.0010s elapsed.
gc: collecting generation 2...
gc: objects in each generation: 0 0 2747
gc: done, 0.0008s elapsed.
```

Enabling DEBUG_COLLECTABLE and DEBUG_UNCOLLECTABLE causes the collector to report on whether each object it examines can or cannot be collected. These flags need to be combined with DEBUG_OBJECTS so gc will print information about the objects being held.

```
import gc

flags = (gc.DEBUG_COLLECTABLE |
         gc.DEBUG_UNCOLLECTABLE |
         gc.DEBUG_OBJECTS
         )
gc.set_debug(flags)

class Graph(object):
    def __init__(self, name):
        self.name = name
        self.next = None
        print 'Creating %s 0x%x (%s)' % \
```

```
            (self.__class__.__name__, id(self), name)
    def set_next(self, next):
        print 'Linking nodes %s.next = %s' % (self, next)
        self.next = next
    def __repr__(self):
        return '%s(%s)' % (self.__class__.__name__, self.name)

class CleanupGraph(Graph):
    def __del__(self):
        print '%s.__del__()' % self

# Construct a graph cycle
one = Graph('one')
two = Graph('two')
one.set_next(two)
two.set_next(one)

# Construct another node that stands on its own
three = CleanupGraph('three')

# Construct a graph cycle with a finalizer
four = CleanupGraph('four')
five = CleanupGraph('five')
four.set_next(five)
five.set_next(four)

# Remove references to the graph nodes in this module's namespace
one = two = three = four = five = None

print

# Force a sweep
print 'Collecting'
gc.collect()
print 'Done'
```

The two classes Graph and CleanupGraph are constructed so it is possible to create structures that can be collected automatically and structures where cycles need to be explicitly broken by the user.

The output shows that the Graph instances one and two create a cycle, but can still be collected because they do not have a finalizer and their only incoming references are from other objects that can be collected. Although CleanupGraph has a finalizer, three is reclaimed as soon as its reference count goes to zero. In contrast, four and five create a cycle and cannot be freed.

```
$ python -u gc_debug_collectable_objects.py

Creating Graph 0x100d99ad0 (one)
Creating Graph 0x100d99b10 (two)
Linking nodes Graph(one).next = Graph(two)
Linking nodes Graph(two).next = Graph(one)
Creating CleanupGraph 0x100d99b50 (three)
Creating CleanupGraph 0x100d99b90 (four)
Creating CleanupGraph 0x100d99bd0 (five)
Linking nodes CleanupGraph(four).next = CleanupGraph(five)
Linking nodes CleanupGraph(five).next = CleanupGraph(four)
CleanupGraph(three).__del__()

Collecting
gc: collectable <Graph 0x100d99ad0>
gc: collectable <Graph 0x100d99b10>
gc: collectable <dict 0x100c5b8e0>
gc: collectable <dict 0x100c5cb70>
gc: uncollectable <CleanupGraph 0x100d99b90>
gc: uncollectable <CleanupGraph 0x100d99bd0>
gc: uncollectable <dict 0x100c5cc90>
gc: uncollectable <dict 0x100c5cff0>
Done
```

The flag DEBUG_INSTANCES works much the same way for instances of old-style classes (not derived from object).

```
import gc

flags = (gc.DEBUG_COLLECTABLE |
         gc.DEBUG_UNCOLLECTABLE |
         gc.DEBUG_INSTANCES
         )
gc.set_debug(flags)

class Graph:
    def __init__(self, name):
        self.name = name
        self.next = None
```

```
        print 'Creating %s 0x%x (%s)' % \
            (self.__class__.__name__, id(self), name)
    def set_next(self, next):
        print 'Linking nodes %s.next = %s' % (self, next)
        self.next = next
    def __repr__(self):
        return '%s(%s)' % (self.__class__.__name__, self.name)

class CleanupGraph(Graph):
    def __del__(self):
        print '%s.__del__()' % self

# Construct a graph cycle
one = Graph('one')
two = Graph('two')
one.set_next(two)
two.set_next(one)

# Construct another node that stands on its own
three = CleanupGraph('three')

# Construct a graph cycle with a finalizer
four = CleanupGraph('four')
five = CleanupGraph('five')
four.set_next(five)
five.set_next(four)

# Remove references to the graph nodes in this module's namespace
one = two = three = four = five = None

print

# Force a sweep
print 'Collecting'
gc.collect()
print 'Done'
```

In this case, however, the `dict` objects holding the instance attributes are not included in the output.

```
$ python -u gc_debug_collectable_instances.py

Creating Graph 0x100da23f8 (one)
```

```
Creating Graph 0x100da2440 (two)
Linking nodes Graph(one).next = Graph(two)
Linking nodes Graph(two).next = Graph(one)
Creating CleanupGraph 0x100da24d0 (three)
Creating CleanupGraph 0x100da2518 (four)
Creating CleanupGraph 0x100da2560 (five)
Linking nodes CleanupGraph(four).next = CleanupGraph(five)
Linking nodes CleanupGraph(five).next = CleanupGraph(four)
CleanupGraph(three).__del__()

Collecting
gc: collectable <Graph instance at 0x100da23f8>
gc: collectable <Graph instance at 0x100da2440>
gc: uncollectable <CleanupGraph instance at 0x100da2518>
gc: uncollectable <CleanupGraph instance at 0x100da2560>
Done
```

If seeing the objects that cannot be collected is not enough information to understand where data is being retained, enable DEBUG_SAVEALL to cause gc to preserve all objects it finds without any references in the garbage list.

```python
import gc

flags = (gc.DEBUG_COLLECTABLE |
         gc.DEBUG_UNCOLLECTABLE |
         gc.DEBUG_OBJECTS |
         gc.DEBUG_SAVEALL
         )

gc.set_debug(flags)

class Graph(object):
    def __init__(self, name):
        self.name = name
        self.next = None
    def set_next(self, next):
        self.next = next
    def __repr__(self):
        return '%s(%s)' % (self.__class__.__name__, self.name)
```

```
class CleanupGraph(Graph):
    def __del__(self):
        print '%s.__del__()' % self

# Construct a graph cycle
one = Graph('one')
two = Graph('two')
one.set_next(two)
two.set_next(one)

# Construct another node that stands on its own
three = CleanupGraph('three')

# Construct a graph cycle with a finalizer
four = CleanupGraph('four')
five = CleanupGraph('five')
four.set_next(five)
five.set_next(four)

# Remove references to the graph nodes in this module's namespace
one = two = three = four = five = None

# Force a sweep
print 'Collecting'
gc.collect()
print 'Done'

# Report on what was left
for o in gc.garbage:
    if isinstance(o, Graph):
        print 'Retained: %s 0x%x' % (o, id(o))
```

This allows the objects to be examined after garbage collection, which is helpful if, for example, the constructor cannot be changed to print the object id when each object is created.

```
$ python -u gc_debug_saveall.py

CleanupGraph(three).__del__()
Collecting
gc: collectable <Graph 0x100d99b10>
gc: collectable <Graph 0x100d99b50>
```

```
gc: collectable <dict 0x100c5c740>
gc: collectable <dict 0x100c5cb60>
gc: uncollectable <CleanupGraph 0x100d99bd0>
gc: uncollectable <CleanupGraph 0x100d99c10>
gc: uncollectable <dict 0x100c5cc80>
gc: uncollectable <dict 0x100c5cfe0>
Done
Retained: Graph(one) 0x100d99b10
Retained: Graph(two) 0x100d99b50
Retained: CleanupGraph(four) 0x100d99bd0
Retained: CleanupGraph(five) 0x100d99c10
```

For simplicity, DEBUG_LEAK is defined as a combination of all the other options.

```python
import gc

flags = gc.DEBUG_LEAK

gc.set_debug(flags)

class Graph(object):
    def __init__(self, name):
        self.name = name
        self.next = None
    def set_next(self, next):
        self.next = next
    def __repr__(self):
        return '%s(%s)' % (self.__class__.__name__, self.name)

class CleanupGraph(Graph):
    def __del__(self):
        print '%s.__del__()' % self

# Construct a graph cycle
one = Graph('one')
two = Graph('two')
one.set_next(two)
two.set_next(one)

# Construct another node that stands on its own
three = CleanupGraph('three')

# Construct a graph cycle with a finalizer
four = CleanupGraph('four')
```

```
five = CleanupGraph('five')
four.set_next(five)
five.set_next(four)

# Remove references to the graph nodes in this module's namespace
one = two = three = four = five = None

# Force a sweep
print 'Collecting'
gc.collect()
print 'Done'

# Report on what was left
for o in gc.garbage:
    if isinstance(o, Graph):
        print 'Retained: %s 0x%x' % (o, id(o))
```

Keep in mind that because DEBUG_SAVEALL is enabled by DEBUG_LEAK, even the unreferenced objects that would normally have been collected and deleted are retained.

```
$ python -u gc_debug_leak.py

CleanupGraph(three).__del__()
Collecting
gc: collectable <Graph 0x100d99b10>
gc: collectable <Graph 0x100d99b50>
gc: collectable <dict 0x100c5b8d0>
gc: collectable <dict 0x100c5cad0>
gc: uncollectable <CleanupGraph 0x100d99bd0>
gc: uncollectable <CleanupGraph 0x100d99c10>
gc: uncollectable <dict 0x100c5cbf0>
gc: uncollectable <dict 0x100c5cf50>
Done
Retained: Graph(one) 0x100d99b10
Retained: Graph(two) 0x100d99b50
Retained: CleanupGraph(four) 0x100d99bd0
Retained: CleanupGraph(five) 0x100d99c10
```

See Also:

gc (http://docs.python.org/library/gc.html) The standard library documentation for this module.

weakref (page 106) The `weakref` module provides a way to create references to objects without increasing their reference count so they can still be garbage collected.

Supporting Cyclic Garbage Collection (http://docs.python.org/c-api/gcsupport.html) Background material from Python's C API documentation.

How does Python manage memory? (http://effbot.org/pyfaq/how-does-python-manage-memory.htm) An article on Python memory management by Fredrik Lundh.

17.7 sysconfig—Interpreter Compile-Time Configuration

Purpose Access the configuration settings used to build Python.
Python Version 2.7 and later

In Python 2.7, `sysconfig` has been extracted from `distutils` to become a stand-alone module. It includes functions for determining the settings used to compile and install the current interpreter.

17.7.1 Configuration Variables

Access to the build-time configuration settings is provided through two functions. `get_config_vars()` returns a dictionary mapping the configuration variable names to values.

```
import sysconfig

config_values = sysconfig.get_config_vars()
print 'Found %d configuration settings' % len(config_values.keys())
print


print 'Some highlights:'

print
print '  Installation prefixes:'
print '    prefix={prefix}'.format(**config_values)
print '    exec_prefix={exec_prefix}'.format(**config_values)

print
print '  Version info:'
print '    py_version={py_version}'.format(**config_values)
```

```
print '    py_version_short={py_version_short}'.format(**config_values)
print '    py_version_nodot={py_version_nodot}'.format(**config_values)

print
print ' Base directories:'
print '    base={base}'.format(**config_values)
print '    platbase={platbase}'.format(**config_values)
print '    userbase={userbase}'.format(**config_values)
print '    srcdir={srcdir}'.format(**config_values)

print
print ' Compiler and linker flags:'
print '    LDFLAGS={LDFLAGS}'.format(**config_values)
print '    BASECFLAGS={BASECFLAGS}'.format(**config_values)
print '    Py_ENABLE_SHARED={Py_ENABLE_SHARED}'.format(**config_values)
```

The level of detail available through the sysconfig API depends on the platform where a program is running. On POSIX systems, such as Linux and OS X, the Makefile used to build the interpreter and config.h header file generated for the build are parsed and all the variables found within are available. On non-POSIX systems, such as Windows, the settings are limited to a few paths, filename extensions, and version details.

```
$ python sysconfig_get_config_vars.py

Found 511 configuration settings

Some highlights:

  Installation prefixes:
    prefix=/Library/Frameworks/Python.framework/Versions/2.7
    exec_prefix=/Library/Frameworks/Python.framework/Versions/2.7

  Version info:
    py_version=2.7
    py_version_short=2.7
    py_version_nodot=27

  Base directories:
    base=/Users/dhellmann/.virtualenvs/pymotw
    platbase=/Users/dhellmann/.virtualenvs/pymotw
    userbase=/Users/dhellmann/Library/Python/2.7
    srcdir=/Users/sysadmin/X/r27
```

```
Compiler and linker flags:
  LDFLAGS=-arch i386 -arch ppc -arch x86_64 -isysroot / -g
  BASECFLAGS=-fno-strict-aliasing -fno-common -dynamic
  Py_ENABLE_SHARED=0
```

Passing variable names to `get_config_vars()` changes the return value to a `list` created by appending all the values for those variables together.

```
import sysconfig

bases = sysconfig.get_config_vars('base', 'platbase', 'userbase')
print 'Base directories:'
for b in bases:
    print '  ', b
```

This example builds a list of all the installation base directories where modules can be found on the current system.

```
$ python sysconfig_get_config_vars_by_name.py

Base directories:
  /Users/dhellmann/.virtualenvs/pymotw
  /Users/dhellmann/.virtualenvs/pymotw
  /Users/dhellmann/Library/Python/2.7
```

When only a single configuration value is needed, use `get_config_var()` to retrieve it.

```
import sysconfig

print 'User base directory:', sysconfig.get_config_var('userbase')
print 'Unknown variable   :', sysconfig.get_config_var('NoSuchVariable')
```

If the variable is not found, `get_config_var()` returns `None` instead of raising an exception.

```
$ python sysconfig_get_config_var.py

User base directory: /Users/dhellmann/Library/Python/2.7
Unknown variable    : None
```

17.7.2 Installation Paths

sysconfig is primarily meant to be used by installation and packaging tools. As a result, while it provides access to general configuration settings, such as the interpreter version, it is focused on the information needed to locate parts of the Python distribution currently installed on a system. The locations used for installing a package depend on the *scheme* used.

A scheme is a set of platform-specific default directories organized based on the platform's packaging standards and guidelines. There are different schemes for installing into a site-wide location or a private directory owned by the user. The full set of schemes can be accessed with get_scheme_names().

```
import sysconfig

for name in sysconfig.get_scheme_names():
    print name
```

There is no concept of a "current scheme" per se. The default scheme depends on the platform, and the actual scheme used depends on options given to the installation program. If the current system is running a POSIX-compliant operating system, the default is posix_prefix. Otherwise, the default is the operating system name, as defined by os.name.

```
$ python sysconfig_get_scheme_names.py

nt
nt_user
os2
os2_home
osx_framework_user
posix_home
posix_prefix
posix_user
```

Each scheme defines a set of paths used for installing packages. For a list of the path names, use get_path_names().

```
import sysconfig

for name in sysconfig.get_path_names():
    print name
```

Some of the paths may be the same for a given scheme, but installers should not make any assumptions about what the actual paths are. Each name has a particular semantic meaning, so the correct name should be used to find the path for a given file during installation. Refer to Table 17.4 for a complete list of the path names and their meaning.

Table 17.4. Path Names Used in sysconfig

Name	Description
stdlib	Standard Python library files, not platform-specific
platstdlib	Standard Python library files, platform-specific
platlib	Site-specific, platform-specific files
purelib	Site-specific, nonplatform-specific files
include	Header files, not platform-specific
platinclude	Header files, platform-specific
scripts	Executable script files
data	Data files

```
$ python sysconfig_get_path_names.py

stdlib
platstdlib
purelib
platlib
include
scripts
data
```

Use get_paths() to retrieve the actual directories associated with a scheme.

```
import sysconfig
import pprint
import os
for scheme in ['posix_prefix', 'posix_user']:
```

```
print scheme
print '=' * len(scheme)
paths = sysconfig.get_paths(scheme=scheme)
prefix = os.path.commonprefix(paths.values())
print 'prefix = %s\n' % prefix
for name, path in sorted(paths.items()):
    print '%s\n   .%s' % (name, path[len(prefix):])
print
```

This example shows the difference between the system-wide paths used for `posix_prefix` under a framework build on Mac OS X and the user-specific values for `posix_user`.

```
$ python sysconfig_get_paths.py

posix_prefix
============
prefix = /Library/Frameworks/Python.framework/Versions/2.7

data
  .
include
  ./include/python2.7
platinclude
  ./include/python2.7
platlib
  ./lib/python2.7/site-packages
platstdlib
  ./lib/python2.7
purelib
  ./lib/python2.7/site-packages
scripts
  ./bin
stdlib
  ./lib/python2.7

posix_user
==========
prefix = /Users/dhellmann/Library/Python/2.7

data
  .
```

```
include
  ./include/python2.7
platlib
  ./lib/python2.7/site-packages
platstdlib
  ./lib/python2.7
purelib
  ./lib/python2.7/site-packages
scripts
  ./bin
stdlib
  ./lib/python2.7
```

For an individual path, call get_path().

```
import sysconfig
import pprint

for scheme in ['posix_prefix', 'posix_user']:
    print scheme
    print '=' * len(scheme)
    print 'purelib =', sysconfig.get_path(name='purelib',
                                          scheme=scheme)
    print
```

Using get_path() is equivalent to saving the value of get_paths() and looking up the individual key in the dictionary. If several paths are needed, get_paths() is more efficient because it does not recompute all the paths each time.

```
$ python sysconfig_get_path.py

posix_prefix
============
purelib = /Library/Frameworks/Python.framework/Versions/2.7/site-\
packages

posix_user
==========
purelib = /Users/dhellmann/Library/Python/2.7/lib/python2.7/site-\
packages
```

17.7.3 Python Version and Platform

While `sys` includes some basic platform identification (see *Build-Time Version Information*), it is not specific enough to be used for installing binary packages because `sys.platform` does not always include information about hardware architecture, instruction size, or other values that affect the compatibility of binary libraries. For a more precise platform specifier, use `get_platform()`.

```
import sysconfig

print sysconfig.get_platform()
```

Although this sample output was prepared on an OS X 10.6 system, the interpreter is compiled for 10.5 compatibility, so that is the version number included in the platform string.

```
$ python sysconfig_get_platform.py

macosx-10.5-fat3
```

As a convenience, the interpreter version from `sys.version_info` is also available through `get_python_version()` in `sysconfig`.

```
import sysconfig
import sys

print 'sysconfig.get_python_version():', sysconfig.get_python_version()
print '\nsys.version_info:'
print '  major       :', sys.version_info.major
print '  minor       :', sys.version_info.minor
print '  micro       :', sys.version_info.micro
print '  releaselevel:', sys.version_info.releaselevel
print '  serial      :', sys.version_info.serial
```

`get_python_version()` returns a string suitable for use when building a version-specific path.

```
$ python sysconfig_get_python_version.py

sysconfig.get_python_version(): 2.7
```

```
sys.version_info:
  major      : 2
  minor      : 7
  micro      : 0
  releaselevel: final
  serial     : 0
```

See Also:

sysconfig (http://docs.python.org/library/sysconfig.html) The standard library documentation for this module.

distutils `sysconfig` used to be part of the `distutils` package.

distutils2 (http://hg.python.org/distutils2/) Updates to `distutils`, managed by Tarek Ziadé.

site (page 1046) The `site` module describes the paths searched when importing in more detail.

os (page 1108) Includes `os.name`, the name of the current operating system.

sys (page 1055) Includes other build-time information, such as the platform.

Chapter 18

LANGUAGE TOOLS

In addition to the developer tools covered in an earlier chapter, Python also includes modules that provide access to its internal features. This chapter covers some tools for working in Python, regardless of the application area.

The `warnings` module is used to report nonfatal conditions or recoverable errors. A common example of a warning is the `DeprecationWarning` generated when a feature of the standard library has been superseded by a new class, interface, or module. Use `warnings` to report conditions that may need user attention, but are not fatal.

Defining a set of classes that conform to a common API can be a challenge when the API is defined by someone else or uses a lot of methods. A common way to work around this problem is to derive all the new classes from a common base class. However, it is not always obvious which methods should be overridden and which can fall back on the default behavior. Abstract base classes from the `abc` module formalize an API by explicitly marking the methods a class must provide in a way that prevents the class from being instantiated if it is not completely implemented. For example, many of Python's container types have abstract base classes defined in `abc` or `collections`.

The `dis` module can be used to disassemble the byte-code version of a program to understand the steps the interpreter takes to run it. Looking at disassembled code can be useful when debugging performance or concurrency issues, since it exposes the atomic operations executed by the interpreter for each statement in a program.

The `inspect` module provides introspection support for all objects in the current process. That includes imported modules, class and function definitions, and the "live" objects instantiated from them. Introspection can be used to generate documentation for source code, adapt behavior at runtime dynamically, or examine the execution environment for a program.

The `exceptions` module defines common exceptions used throughout the standard library and third-party modules. Becoming familiar with the class hierarchy for exceptions will make it easier to understand error messages and create robust code that handles exceptions properly.

18.1 warnings—Nonfatal Alerts

Purpose Deliver nonfatal alerts to the user about issues encountered when running a program.
Python Version 2.1 and later

The `warnings` module was introduced by PEP 230 as a way to warn programmers about changes in language or library features in anticipation of backwards-incompatible changes coming with Python 3.0. It can also be used to report recoverable configuration errors or feature degradation from missing libraries. It is better to deliver user-facing messages via the `logging` module, though, because warnings sent to the console may be lost.

Since warnings are not fatal, a program may encounter the same warn-able situation many times in the course of running. The `warnings` module suppresses repeated messages from the same source to cut down on the annoyance of seeing the same warning over and over. The output can be controlled on a case-by-case basis, using the command-line options to the interpreter or by calling functions found in `warnings`.

18.1.1 Categories and Filtering

Warnings are categorized using subclasses of the built-in exception class `Warning`. Several standard values are described in the online documentation for the `exceptions` module, and custom warnings can be added by subclassing from `Warning`.

Warnings are processed based on *filter* settings. A filter consists of five parts: the *action, message, category, module,* and *line number*. The *message* portion of the filter is a regular expression that is used to match the warning text. The *category* is a name of an exception class. The *module* contains a regular expression to be matched against the module name generating the warning. And the *line number* can be used to change the handling on specific occurrences of a warning.

When a warning is generated, it is compared against all the registered filters. The first filter that matches controls the action taken for the warning. If no filter matches, the default action is taken. The actions understood by the filtering mechanism are listed in Table 18.1.

Table 18.1. Warning Filter Actions

Action	Meaning
error	Turn the warning into an exception.
ignore	Discard the warning.
always	Always emit a warning.
default	Print the warning the first time it is generated from each location.
module	Print the warning the first time it is generated from each module.
once	Print the warning the first time it is generated.

18.1.2 Generating Warnings

The simplest way to emit a warning is to call `warn()` with the message as an argument.

```
import warnings

print 'Before the warning'
warnings.warn('This is a warning message')
print 'After the warning'
```

Then, when the program runs, the message is printed.

```
$ python -u warnings_warn.py

Before the warning
warnings_warn.py:13: UserWarning: This is a warning message
  warnings.warn('This is a warning message')
After the warning
```

Even though the warning is printed, the default behavior is to continue past that point and run the rest of the program. That behavior can be changed with a filter.

```
import warnings

warnings.simplefilter('error', UserWarning)

print 'Before the warning'
warnings.warn('This is a warning message')
print 'After the warning'
```

In this example, the `simplefilter()` function adds an entry to the internal filter list to tell the `warnings` module to raise an exception when a `UserWarning` warning is issued.

```
$ python -u warnings_warn_raise.py

Before the warning
Traceback (most recent call last):
  File "warnings_warn_raise.py", line 15, in <module>
    warnings.warn('This is a warning message')
UserWarning: This is a warning message
```

The filter behavior can also be controlled from the command line by using the –W option to the interpreter. Specify the filter properties as a string with the five parts (action, message, category, module, and line number) separated by colons (:). For example, if `warnings_warn.py` is run with a filter set to raise an error on User-Warning, an exception is produced.

```
$ python -u -W "error::UserWarning::0" warnings_warn.py

Before the warning
Traceback (most recent call last):
  File "warnings_warn.py", line 13, in <module>
    warnings.warn('This is a warning message')
UserWarning: This is a warning message
```

Since the fields for *message* and *module* were left blank, they were interpreted as matching anything.

18.1.3   Filtering with Patterns

To filter on more complex rules programmatically, use `filterwarnings()`. For example, to filter based on the content of the message text, give a regular expression pattern as the *message* argument.

```
import warnings

warnings.filterwarnings('ignore', '.*do not.*',)

warnings.warn('Show this message')
warnings.warn('Do not show this message')
```

The pattern contains "`do not`", but the actual message uses "`Do not`". The pattern matches because the regular expression is always compiled to look for case-insensitive matches.

```
$ python warnings_filterwarnings_message.py

warnings_filterwarnings_message.py:14: UserWarning: Show this message
  warnings.warn('Show this message')
```

The example program `warnings_filtering.py` generates two warnings.

```
import warnings

warnings.warn('Show this message')
warnings.warn('Do not show this message')
```

One of the warnings can be ignored using the filter argument on the command line.

```
$ python -W "ignore:do not:UserWarning::0" warnings_filtering.py

warnings_filtering.py:12: UserWarning: Show this message
  warnings.warn('Show this message')
```

The same pattern-matching rules apply to the name of the source module containing the call generating the warning. Suppress all messages from the `warnings_filtering` module by passing the module name as the pattern to the *module* argument.

```
import warnings

warnings.filterwarnings('ignore',
                        '.*',
                        UserWarning,
                        'warnings_filtering',
                        )

import warnings_filtering
```

Since the filter is in place, no warnings are emitted when `warnings_filtering` is imported.

```
$ python warnings_filterwarnings_module.py
```

To suppress only the message on line 13 of `warnings_filtering`, include the line number as the last argument to `filterwarnings()`. Use the actual line number from the source file to limit the filter, or use 0 to have the filter apply to all occurrences of the message.

```
import warnings

warnings.filterwarnings('ignore',
                        '.*',
                        UserWarning,
                        'warnings_filtering',
                        13)

import warnings_filtering
```

The pattern matches any message, so the important arguments are the module name and line number.

```
$ python warnings_filterwarnings_lineno.py

/Users/dhellmann/Documents/PyMOTW/book/PyMOTW/warnings/warnings_filter
ing.py:12: UserWarning: Show this message
  warnings.warn('Show this message')
```

18.1.4 Repeated Warnings

By default, most types of warnings are only printed the first time they occur in a given location, with "location" defined by the combination of module and line number where the warning is generated.

```
import warnings

def function_with_warning():
    warnings.warn('This is a warning!')

function_with_warning()
function_with_warning()
function_with_warning()
```

This example calls the same function several times, but only produces a single warning.

```
$ python warnings_repeated.py

warnings_repeated.py:13: UserWarning: This is a warning!
  warnings.warn('This is a warning!')
```

The `"once"` action can be used to suppress instances of the same message from different locations.

```
import warnings

warnings.simplefilter('once', UserWarning)

warnings.warn('This is a warning!')
warnings.warn('This is a warning!')
warnings.warn('This is a warning!')
```

The message text for all warnings is saved, and only unique messages are printed.

```
$ python warnings_once.py

warnings_once.py:14: UserWarning: This is a warning!
  warnings.warn('This is a warning!')
```

Similarly, `"module"` will suppress repeated messages from the same module, no matter what line number.

18.1.5 Alternate Message Delivery Functions

Normally, warnings are printed to `sys.stderr`. Change that behavior by replacing the `showwarning()` function inside the `warnings` module. For example, to send warnings to a log file instead of standard error, replace `showwarning()` with a function that logs the warning.

```
import warnings
import logging
```

```
logging.basicConfig(level=logging.INFO)

def send_warnings_to_log(message, category, filename, lineno, file=None):
    logging.warning(
        '%s:%s: %s:%s' %
        (filename, lineno, category.__name__, message))
    return

old_showwarning = warnings.showwarning
warnings.showwarning = send_warnings_to_log

warnings.warn('message')
```

The warnings are emitted with the rest of the log messages when `warn()` is called.

```
$ python warnings_showwarning.py

WARNING:root:warnings_showwarning.py:24: UserWarning:message
```

18.1.6   Formatting

If warnings should go to standard error, but they need to be reformatted, replace `formatwarning()`.

```
import warnings

def warning_on_one_line(message, category, filename, lineno,
                        file=None, line=None):
    return '-> %s:%s: %s:%s' % \
        (filename, lineno, category.__name__, message)

warnings.warn('Warning message, before')
warnings.formatwarning = warning_on_one_line
warnings.warn('Warning message, after')
```

The format function must return a single string containing the representation of the warning to be displayed to the user.

```
$ python -u warnings_formatwarning.py

warnings_formatwarning.py:17: UserWarning: Warning message, before
  warnings.warn('Warning message, before')
-> warnings_formatwarning.py:19: UserWarning:Warning message, after
```

18.1.7 Stack Level in Warnings

By default, the warning message includes the source line that generated it, when available. It is not always useful to see the line of code with the actual warning message, though. Instead, `warn()` can be told how far up the stack it has to go to find the line that called the function containing the warning. That way, users of a deprecated function can see where the function is called, instead of the implementation of the function.

```python
#!/usr/bin/env python
# encoding: utf-8

import warnings

def old_function():
    warnings.warn(
        'old_function() is deprecated, use new_function() instead',
        stacklevel=2)

def caller_of_old_function():
    old_function()

caller_of_old_function()
```

In this example, `warn()` needs to go up the stack two levels, one for itself and one for `old_function()`.

```
$ python warnings_warn_stacklevel.py

warnings_warn_stacklevel.py:12: UserWarning: old_function() is
 deprecated, use new_function() instead
   old_function()
```

See Also:

warnings (http://docs.python.org/lib/module-warnings.html) The standard library documentation for this module.

PEP 230 (www.python.org/dev/peps/pep-0230) Warning Framework.

exceptions (page 1216) Base classes for exceptions and warnings.

logging (page 878) An alternative mechanism for delivering warnings is to write to the log.

18.2   abc—Abstract Base Classes

Purpose Define and use abstract base classes for interface verification.
Python Version 2.6 and later

18.2.1   Why Use Abstract Base Classes?

Abstract base classes are a form of interface checking more strict than individual `hasattr()` checks for particular methods. By defining an abstract base class, a common API can be established for a set of subclasses. This capability is especially useful in situations where someone less familiar with the source for an application is going to provide plug-in extensions, but they can also help when working on a large team or with a large code base where keeping track of all the classes at the same time is difficult or not possible.

18.2.2   How Abstract Base Classes Work

`abc` works by marking methods of the base class as abstract and then registering concrete classes as implementations of the abstract base. If an application or library requires a particular API, `issubclass()` or `isinstance()` can be used to check an object against the abstract class.

To start, define an abstract base class to represent the API of a set of plug-ins for saving and loading data. Set the __metaclass__ for the new base class to `ABCMeta`, and use the `abstractmethod()` decorator to establish the public API for the class. The following examples use `abc_base.py`, which contains a base class for a set of application plug-ins.

```
import abc

class PluginBase(object):
    __metaclass__ = abc.ABCMeta

    @abc.abstractmethod
    def load(self, input):
        """Retrieve data from the input source
        and return an object.
        """

    @abc.abstractmethod
    def save(self, output, data):
        """Save the data object to the output."""
```

18.2.3 Registering a Concrete Class

There are two ways to indicate that a concrete class implements an abstract API: either explicitly register the class or create a new subclass directly from the abstract base. Use the `register()` class method to add a concrete class explicitly when the class provides the required API, but it is not part of the inheritance tree of the abstract base class.

```
import abc
from abc_base import PluginBase

class LocalBaseClass(object):
    pass

class RegisteredImplementation(LocalBaseClass):

    def load(self, input):
        return input.read()

    def save(self, output, data):
        return output.write(data)

PluginBase.register(RegisteredImplementation)

if __name__ == '__main__':
    print 'Subclass:', issubclass(RegisteredImplementation,
                                  PluginBase)
    print 'Instance:', isinstance(RegisteredImplementation(),
                                  PluginBase)
```

In this example, the `RegisteredImplementation` is derived from `Local-BaseClass`, but it is registered as implementing the `PluginBase` API. That means `issubclass()` and `isinstance()` treat it as though it is derived from `PluginBase`.

```
$ python abc_register.py

Subclass: True
Instance: True
```

18.2.4 Implementation through Subclassing

Subclassing directly from the base avoids the need to register the class explicitly.

```
import abc
from abc_base import PluginBase

class SubclassImplementation(PluginBase):

    def load(self, input):
        return input.read()
    def save(self, output, data):
        return output.write(data)

if __name__ == '__main__':
    print 'Subclass:', issubclass(SubclassImplementation, PluginBase)
    print 'Instance:', isinstance(SubclassImplementation(), PluginBase)
```

In this case, normal Python class management features are used to recognize `PluginImplementation` as implementing the abstract `PluginBase`.

```
$ python abc_subclass.py

Subclass: True
Instance: True
```

A side effect of using direct subclassing is that it is possible to find all the implementations of a plug-in by asking the base class for the list of known classes derived from it (this is not an `abc` feature, all classes can do this).

```
import abc
from abc_base import PluginBase
import abc_subclass
import abc_register

for sc in PluginBase.__subclasses__():
    print sc.__name__
```

Even though `abc_register()` is imported, `RegisteredImplementation` is not among the list of subclasses because it is not actually derived from the base.

```
$ python abc_find_subclasses.py

SubclassImplementation
```

Incomplete Implementations

Another benefit of subclassing directly from the abstract base class is that the subclass cannot be instantiated unless it fully implements the abstract portion of the API.

```
import abc
from abc_base import PluginBase
class IncompleteImplementation(PluginBase):

    def save(self, output, data):
        return output.write(data)


PluginBase.register(IncompleteImplementation)


if __name__ == '__main__':
    print 'Subclass:', issubclass(IncompleteImplementation,
                                  PluginBase)
    print 'Instance:', isinstance(IncompleteImplementation(),
                                  PluginBase)
```

This keeps incomplete implementations from triggering unexpected errors at runtime.

```
$ python abc_incomplete.py

Subclass: True
Instance:
Traceback (most recent call last):
  File "abc_incomplete.py", line 23, in <module>
    print 'Instance:', isinstance(IncompleteImplementation(),
TypeError: Can't instantiate abstract class
IncompleteImplementation with abstract methods load
```

18.2.5 Concrete Methods in ABCs

Although a concrete class must provide implementations of all abstract methods, the abstract base class can also provide implementations that can be invoked via `super()`. This allows common logic to be reused by placing it in the base class, but forces subclasses to provide an overriding method with (potentially) custom logic.

```
import abc
from cStringIO import StringIO

class ABCWithConcreteImplementation(object):
    __metaclass__ = abc.ABCMeta

    @abc.abstractmethod
    def retrieve_values(self, input):
        print 'base class reading data'
        return input.read()
```

```
class ConcreteOverride(ABCWithConcreteImplementation):

    def retrieve_values(self, input):
        base_data = super(ConcreteOverride,
                          self).retrieve_values(input)
        print 'subclass sorting data'
        response = sorted(base_data.splitlines())
        return response

input = StringIO("""line one
line two
line three
""")

reader = ConcreteOverride()
print reader.retrieve_values(input)
print
```

Since `ABCWithConcreteImplementation()` is an abstract base class, it is not possible to instantiate it to use it directly. Subclasses *must* provide an override for `retrieve_values()`, and in this case, the concrete class massages the data before returning it at all.

```
$ python abc_concrete_method.py

base class reading data
subclass sorting data
['line one', 'line three', 'line two']
```

18.2.6   Abstract Properties

If an API specification includes attributes in addition to methods, it can require the attributes in concrete classes by defining them with `@abstractproperty`.

```
import abc

class Base(object):
    __metaclass__ = abc.ABCMeta

    @abc.abstractproperty
    def value(self):
        return 'Should never get here'
```

```
    @abc.abstractproperty
    def constant(self):
        return 'Should never get here'

class Implementation(Base):
    @property
    def value(self):
        return 'concrete property'

    constant = 'set by a class attribute'

try:
    b = Base()
    print 'Base.value:', b.value
except Exception, err:
    print 'ERROR:', str(err)

i = Implementation()
print 'Implementation.value    :', i.value
print 'Implementation.constant:', i.constant
```

The `Base` class in the example cannot be instantiated because it has only an abstract version of the property getter methods for `value` and `constant`. The `value` property is given a concrete getter in `Implementation`, and `constant` is defined using a class attribute.

```
$ python abc_abstractproperty.py

ERROR: Can't instantiate abstract class Base with abstract
methods constant, value
Implementation.value    : concrete property
Implementation.constant: set by a class attribute
```

Abstract read-write properties can also be defined.

```
import abc

class Base(object):
    __metaclass__ = abc.ABCMeta

    def value_getter(self):
        return 'Should never see this'
```

```
    def value_setter(self, newvalue):
        return

    value = abc.abstractproperty(value_getter, value_setter)

class PartialImplementation(Base):
    @abc.abstractproperty
    def value(self):
        return 'Read-only'

class Implementation(Base):

    _value = 'Default value'

    def value_getter(self):
        return self._value

    def value_setter(self, newvalue):
        self._value = newvalue

    value = property(value_getter, value_setter)

try:
    b = Base()
    print 'Base.value:', b.value
except Exception, err:
    print 'ERROR:', str(err)

try:
    p = PartialImplementation()
    print 'PartialImplementation.value:', p.value
except Exception, err:
    print 'ERROR:', str(err)

i = Implementation()
print 'Implementation.value:', i.value

i.value = 'New value'
print 'Changed value:', i.value
```

The concrete property must be defined the same way as the abstract property. Trying to override a read-write property in `PartialImplementation` with one that is read-only does not work.

```
$ python abc_abstractproperty_rw.py

ERROR: Can't instantiate abstract class Base with abstract
methods value
ERROR: Can't instantiate abstract class PartialImplementation
with abstract methods value
Implementation.value: Default value
Changed value: New value
```

To use the decorator syntax with read-write abstract properties, the methods to get and set the value must be named the same.

```python
import abc

class Base(object):
    __metaclass__ = abc.ABCMeta

    @abc.abstractproperty
    def value(self):
        return 'Should never see this'

    @value.setter
    def value(self, newvalue):
        return

class Implementation(Base):

    _value = 'Default value'

    @property
    def value(self):
        return self._value

    @value.setter
    def value(self, newvalue):
        self._value = newvalue

i = Implementation()
print 'Implementation.value:', i.value

i.value = 'New value'
print 'Changed value:', i.value
```

Both methods in the `Base` and `Implementation` classes are named `value()`, although they have different signatures.

```
$ python abc_abstractproperty_rw_deco.py

Implementation.value: Default value
Changed value: New value
```

See Also:
abc (http://docs.python.org/library/abc.html) The standard library documentation for this module.
PEP 3119 (www.python.org/dev/peps/pep-3119) Introducing abstract base classes.
collections (page 70) The collections module includes abstract base classes for several collection types.
PEP 3141 (www.python.org/dev/peps/pep-3141) A type hierarchy for numbers.
Strategy pattern (http://en.wikipedia.org/wiki/Strategy_pattern) Description and examples of the strategy pattern, a common plug-in implementation pattern.
Plugins and monkeypatching (http://us.pycon.org/2009/conference/schedule/event/47/) PyCon 2009 presentation by Dr. André Roberge.

18.3 dis—Python Bytecode Disassembler

Purpose Convert code objects to a human-readable representation of the bytecodes for analysis.
Python Version 1.4 and later

The `dis` module includes functions for working with Python bytecode by "disassembling" it into a more human-readable form. Reviewing the bytecodes being executed by the interpreter is a good way to hand-tune tight loops and perform other kinds of optimizations. It is also useful for finding race conditions in multithreaded applications, since it can be used to estimate the point in the code where thread control may switch.

Warning: The use of bytecodes is a version-specific implementation detail of the CPython interpreter. Refer to `Include/opcode.h` in the source code for the version of the interpreter you are using to find the canonical list of bytecodes.

18.3.1   Basic Disassembly

The function `dis()` prints the disassembled representation of a Python code source (module, class, method, function, or code object). A module such as `dis_simple.py` can be disassembled by running `dis` from the command line.

```
1  #!/usr/bin/env python
2  # encoding: utf-8
3
4  my_dict = { 'a':1 }
```

The output is organized into columns with the original source line number, the instruction "address" within the code object, the opcode name, and any arguments passed to the opcode.

```
$ python -m dis dis_simple.py

    4           0 BUILD_MAP               1
                3 LOAD_CONST              0 (1)
                6 LOAD_CONST              1 ('a')
                9 STORE_MAP
               10 STORE_NAME              0 (my_dict)
               13 LOAD_CONST              2 (None)
               16 RETURN_VALUE
```

In this case, the source translates to five different operations to create and populate the dictionary, and then save the results to a local variable. Since the Python interpreter is stack-based, the first steps are to put the constants onto the stack in the correct order with `LOAD_CONST` and then use `STORE_MAP` to pop off the new key and value to be added to the dictionary. The resulting object is bound to the name "my_dict" with `STORE_NAME`.

18.3.2   Disassembling Functions

Unfortunately, disassembling an entire module does not recurse into functions automatically.

```
1  #!/usr/bin/env python
2  # encoding: utf-8
```

```
3
4  def f(*args):
5      nargs = len(args)
6      print nargs, args
7
8  if __name__ == '__main__':
9      import dis
10     dis.dis(f)
```

The results of disassembling `dis_function.py` show the operations for loading the function's code object onto the stack and then turning it into a function (LOAD_CONST, MAKE_FUNCTION), but *not* the body of the function.

```
$ python -m dis dis_function.py


  4           0 LOAD_CONST               0 (<code object f at 0x1
00479030, file "dis_function.py", line 4>)
              3 MAKE_FUNCTION            0
              6 STORE_NAME               0 (f)

  8           9 LOAD_NAME                1 (__name__)
             12 LOAD_CONST               1 ('__main__')
             15 COMPARE_OP               2 (==)
             18 POP_JUMP_IF_FALSE       49

  9          21 LOAD_CONST               2 (-1)
             24 LOAD_CONST               3 (None)
             27 IMPORT_NAME              2 (dis)
             30 STORE_NAME               2 (dis)

 10          33 LOAD_NAME                2 (dis)
             36 LOAD_ATTR                2 (dis)
             39 LOAD_NAME                0 (f)
             42 CALL_FUNCTION            1
             45 POP_TOP
             46 JUMP_FORWARD             0 (to 49)
        >>   49 LOAD_CONST               3 (None)
             52 RETURN_VALUE
```

To see inside the function, it must be passed to `dis()`.

```
$ python dis_function.py
```

```
5                  0 LOAD_GLOBAL              0 (len)
                   3 LOAD_FAST                0 (args)
                   6 CALL_FUNCTION            1
                   9 STORE_FAST               1 (nargs)

6                 12 LOAD_FAST                1 (nargs)
                  15 PRINT_ITEM
                  16 LOAD_FAST                0 (args)
                  19 PRINT_ITEM
                  20 PRINT_NEWLINE
                  21 LOAD_CONST               0 (None)
                  24 RETURN_VALUE
```

18.3.3 Classes

Classes can be passed to dis(), in which case all the methods are disassembled in turn.

```
1  #!/usr/bin/env python
2  # encoding: utf-8
3
4  import dis
5
6  class MyObject(object):
7      """Example for dis."""
8
9      CLASS_ATTRIBUTE = 'some value'
10
11     def __str__(self):
12         return 'MyObject(%s)' % self.name
13
14     def __init__(self, name):
15         self.name = name
16
17  dis.dis(MyObject)
```

The methods are listed in alphabetical order, not the order they appear in the file.

```
$ python dis_class.py
```

```
Disassembly of __init__:
 15                0 LOAD_FAST                1 (name)
                   3 LOAD_FAST                0 (self)
```

```
               6 STORE_ATTR                0 (name)
               9 LOAD_CONST                0 (None)
              12 RETURN_VALUE

Disassembly of __str__:
  12             0 LOAD_CONST                1 ('MyObject(%s)')
                 3 LOAD_FAST                 0 (self)
                 6 LOAD_ATTR                 0 (name)
                 9 BINARY_MODULO
                10 RETURN_VALUE
```

18.3.4   Using Disassembly to Debug

Sometimes when debugging an exception, it can be useful to see which bytecode caused a problem. There are a couple of ways to disassemble the code around an error. The first is by using `dis()` in the interactive interpreter to report about the last exception. If no argument is passed to `dis()`, then it looks for an exception and shows the disassembly of the top of the stack that caused it.

```
$ python

Python 2.6.2 (r262:71600, Apr 16 2009, 09:17:39)
[GCC 4.0.1 (Apple Computer, Inc. build 5250)] on darwin
Type "help", "copyright", "credits" or "license" for more information.
>>> import dis
>>> j = 4
>>> i = i + 4
Traceback (most recent call last):
  File "<stdin>", line 1, in <module>
NameError: name 'i' is not defined
>>> dis.distb()
  1 -->          0 LOAD_NAME                 0 (i)
                 3 LOAD_CONST                0 (4)
                 6 BINARY_ADD
                 7 STORE_NAME                0 (i)
                10 LOAD_CONST                1 (None)
                13 RETURN_VALUE
>>>
```

The `-->` after the line number indicates the opcode that caused the error. There is no `i` variable defined, so the value associated with the name cannot be loaded onto the stack.

A program can also print the information about an active traceback by passing it to `distb()` directly. In this example, there is a `DivideByZero` exception; but since the formula has two divisions, it is not clear which part is zero.

```python
1  #!/usr/bin/env python
2  # encoding: utf-8
3
4  i = 1
5  j = 0
6  k = 3
7
8  # ... many lines removed ...
9
10 try:
11     result = k * (i / j) + (i / k)
12 except:
13     import dis
14     import sys
15     exc_type, exc_value, exc_tb = sys.exc_info()
16     dis.distb(exc_tb)
```

The bad value is easy to spot when it is loaded onto the stack in the disassembled version. The bad operation is highlighted with the `-->`, and the previous line pushes the value for `j` onto the stack.

```
$ python dis_traceback.py

   4           0 LOAD_CONST            0 (1)
               3 STORE_NAME           0 (i)

   5           6 LOAD_CONST            1 (0)
               9 STORE_NAME           1 (j)

   6          12 LOAD_CONST            2 (3)
              15 STORE_NAME           2 (k)

  10          18 SETUP_EXCEPT        26 (to 47)

  11          21 LOAD_NAME            2 (k)
              24 LOAD_NAME            0 (i)
              27 LOAD_NAME            1 (j)
     -->      30 BINARY_DIVIDE
```

```
        31 BINARY_MULTIPLY
        32 LOAD_NAME              0 (i)
        35 LOAD_NAME              2 (k)
        38 BINARY_DIVIDE
        39 BINARY_ADD
        40 STORE_NAME             3 (result)
```

...trimmed...

18.3.5   Performance Analysis of Loops

Besides debugging errors, `dis` can also help identify performance issues. Examining the disassembled code is especially useful with tight loops where the number of Python instructions is low, but they translate to an inefficient set of bytecodes. The helpfulness of the disassembly can be seen by examining a few different implementations of a class, `Dictionary`, that reads a list of words and groups them by their first letter.

```python
import dis
import sys
import timeit

module_name = sys.argv[1]
module = __import__(module_name)
Dictionary = module.Dictionary

dis.dis(Dictionary.load_data)
print
t = timeit.Timer(
    'd = Dictionary(words)',
    """from %(module_name)s import Dictionary
words = [l.strip() for l in open('/usr/share/dict/words', 'rt')]
    """ % locals()
    )
iterations = 10
print 'TIME: %0.4f' % (t.timeit(iterations)/iterations)
```

The test driver application `dis_test_loop.py` can be used to run each incarnation of the `Dictionary` class.

A straightforward, but slow, implementation of `Dictionary` starts out like this.

```python
#!/usr/bin/env python
# encoding: utf-8

```

```
4   class Dictionary(object):
5
6       def __init__(self, words):
7           self.by_letter = {}
8           self.load_data(words)
9
10      def load_data(self, words):
11          for word in words:
12              try:
13                  self.by_letter[word[0]].append(word)
14              except KeyError:
15                  self.by_letter[word[0]] = [word]
```

Running the test program with this version shows the disassembled program and the amount of time it takes to run.

```
$ python dis_test_loop.py dis_slow_loop

11              0 SETUP_LOOP            84 (to 87)
                3 LOAD_FAST             1 (words)
                6 GET_ITER
        >>      7 FOR_ITER             76 (to 86)
               10 STORE_FAST            2 (word)

12             13 SETUP_EXCEPT         28 (to 44)

13             16 LOAD_FAST             0 (self)
               19 LOAD_ATTR             0 (by_letter)
               22 LOAD_FAST             2 (word)
               25 LOAD_CONST            1 (0)
               28 BINARY_SUBSCR
               29 BINARY_SUBSCR
               30 LOAD_ATTR             1 (append)
               33 LOAD_FAST             2 (word)
               36 CALL_FUNCTION         1
               39 POP_TOP
               40 POP_BLOCK
               41 JUMP_ABSOLUTE         7

14      >>     44 DUP_TOP
               45 LOAD_GLOBAL           2 (KeyError)
               48 COMPARE_OP           10 (exception match)
               51 JUMP_IF_FALSE        27 (to 81)
```

```
         54 POP_TOP
         55 POP_TOP
         56 POP_TOP
         57 POP_TOP

15       58 LOAD_FAST            2 (word)
         61 BUILD_LIST           1
         64 LOAD_FAST            0 (self)
         67 LOAD_ATTR            0 (by_letter)
         70 LOAD_FAST            2 (word)
         73 LOAD_CONST           1 (0)
         76 BINARY_SUBSCR
         77 STORE_SUBSCR
         78 JUMP_ABSOLUTE        7
    >>   81 POP_TOP
         82 END_FINALLY
         83 JUMP_ABSOLUTE        7
    >>   86 POP_BLOCK
    >>   87 LOAD_CONST           0 (None)
         90 RETURN_VALUE
```

```
TIME: 0.1074
```

The previous output shows `dis_slow_loop.py` taking 0.1074 seconds to load the 234,936 words in the copy of `/usr/share/dict/words` on OS X. That is not too bad, but the accompanying disassembly shows that the loop is doing more work than it needs to do. As it enters the loop in opcode 13, it sets up an exception context (`SETUP_EXCEPT`). Then it takes six opcodes to find `self.by_letter[word[0]]` before appending `word` to the list. If there is an exception because `word[0]` is not in the dictionary yet, the exception handler does all the same work to determine `word[0]` (three opcodes) and sets `self.by_letter[word[0]]` to a new list containing the word.

One technique to eliminate the exception setup is to prepopulate the dictionary `self.by_letter` with one list for each letter of the alphabet. That means the list for the new word should always be found, and the value can be saved after the lookup.

```
1  #!/usr/bin/env python
2  # encoding: utf-8
3
4  import string
5
```

```
6  class Dictionary(object):
7
8      def __init__(self, words):
9          self.by_letter = dict( (letter, [])
10                                 for letter in string.letters)
11         self.load_data(words)
12
13     def load_data(self, words):
14         for word in words:
15             self.by_letter[word[0]].append(word)
```

The change cuts the number of opcodes in half, but only shaves the time down to 0.0984 seconds. Obviously, the exception handling had some overhead, but not a huge amount.

```
$ python dis_test_loop.py dis_faster_loop

14           0 SETUP_LOOP          38 (to 41)
             3 LOAD_FAST            1 (words)
             6 GET_ITER
       >>    7 FOR_ITER            30 (to 40)
            10 STORE_FAST           2 (word)

15          13 LOAD_FAST            0 (self)
            16 LOAD_ATTR            0 (by_letter)
            19 LOAD_FAST            2 (word)
            22 LOAD_CONST           1 (0)
            25 BINARY_SUBSCR
            26 BINARY_SUBSCR
            27 LOAD_ATTR            1 (append)
            30 LOAD_FAST            2 (word)
            33 CALL_FUNCTION        1
            36 POP_TOP
            37 JUMP_ABSOLUTE        7
       >>   40 POP_BLOCK
       >>   41 LOAD_CONST           0 (None)
            44 RETURN_VALUE

TIME: 0.0984
```

The performance can be improved further by moving the lookup for self.by_letter outside of the loop (the value does not change, after all).

```
1   #!/usr/bin/env python
2   # encoding: utf-8
3
4   import collections
5
6   class Dictionary(object):
7
8       def __init__(self, words):
9           self.by_letter = collections.defaultdict(list)
10          self.load_data(words)
11
12      def load_data(self, words):
13          by_letter = self.by_letter
14          for word in words:
15              by_letter[word[0]].append(word)
```

Opcodes 0-6 now find the value of `self.by_letter` and save it as a local variable `by_letter`. Using a local variable only takes a single opcode, instead of two (statement 22 uses `LOAD_FAST` to place the dictionary onto the stack). After this change, the runtime is down to 0.0842 seconds.

```
$ python dis_test_loop.py dis_fastest_loop

13              0 LOAD_FAST               0 (self)
                3 LOAD_ATTR               0 (by_letter)
                6 STORE_FAST              2 (by_letter)

14              9 SETUP_LOOP             35 (to 47)
               12 LOAD_FAST               1 (words)
               15 GET_ITER
        >>     16 FOR_ITER               27 (to 46)
               19 STORE_FAST              3 (word)

15             22 LOAD_FAST               2 (by_letter)
               25 LOAD_FAST               3 (word)
               28 LOAD_CONST              1 (0)
               31 BINARY_SUBSCR
               32 BINARY_SUBSCR
               33 LOAD_ATTR               1 (append)
               36 LOAD_FAST               3 (word)
               39 CALL_FUNCTION           1
               42 POP_TOP
```

```
        43 JUMP_ABSOLUTE              16
    >>  46 POP_BLOCK
    >>  47 LOAD_CONST                 0 (None)
        50 RETURN_VALUE
```

TIME: 0.0842

A further optimization, suggested by Brandon Rhodes, is to eliminate the Python version of the `for` loop entirely. If `itertools.groupby()` is used to arrange the input, the iteration is moved to C. This method is safe because the inputs are known to be sorted. If that was not the case, the program would need to sort them first.

```
1  #!/usr/bin/env python
2  # encoding: utf-8
3
4  import operator
5  import itertools
6
7  class Dictionary(object):
8
9      def __init__(self, words):
10         self.by_letter = {}
11         self.load_data(words)
12
13     def load_data(self, words):
14         # Arrange by letter
15         grouped = itertools.groupby(words, key=operator.itemgetter(0))
16         # Save arranged sets of words
17         self.by_letter = dict((group[0][0], group) for group in grouped)
```

The `itertools` version takes only 0.0543 seconds to run, just over half of the original time.

```
$ python dis_test_loop.py dis_eliminate_loop

    15              0 LOAD_GLOBAL      0 (itertools)
                    3 LOAD_ATTR        1 (groupby)
                    6 LOAD_FAST        1 (words)
                    9 LOAD_CONST       1 ('key')
                   12 LOAD_GLOBAL      2 (operator)
                   15 LOAD_ATTR        3 (itemgetter)
                   18 LOAD_CONST       2 (0)
```

```
                    21 CALL_FUNCTION              1
                    24 CALL_FUNCTION            257
                    27 STORE_FAST                2 (grouped)

        17          30 LOAD_GLOBAL               4 (dict)
                    33 LOAD_CONST                3 (<code object
<genexpr> at 0x7e7b8, file "dis_eliminate_loop.py", line 17>)
                    36 MAKE_FUNCTION             0
                    39 LOAD_FAST                 2 (grouped)
                    42 GET_ITER
                    43 CALL_FUNCTION             1
                    46 CALL_FUNCTION             1
                    49 LOAD_FAST                 0 (self)
                    52 STORE_ATTR                5 (by_letter)
                    55 LOAD_CONST                0 (None)
                    58 RETURN_VALUE

    TIME: 0.0543
```

18.3.6   Compiler Optimizations

Disassembling compiled source also exposes some of the optimizations made by the compiler. For example, literal expressions are folded during compilation, when possible.

```
 1   #!/usr/bin/env python
 2   # encoding: utf-8
 3
 4   # Folded
 5   i = 1 + 2
 6   f = 3.4 * 5.6
 7   s = 'Hello,' + ' World!'
 8
 9   # Not folded
10   I = i * 3 * 4
11   F = f / 2 / 3
12   S = s + '\n' + 'Fantastic!'
```

None of the values in the expressions on lines 5–7 can change the way the operation is performed, so the result of the expressions can be computed at compilation time and collapsed into single LOAD_CONST instructions. That is not true about lines 10–12.

Because a variable is involved in those expressions, and the variable might refer to an object that overloads the operator involved, the evaluation has to be delayed to runtime.

```
$ python -m dis dis_constant_folding.py

  5           0 LOAD_CONST              11 (3)
              3 STORE_NAME               0 (i)

  6           6 LOAD_CONST              12 (19.04)
              9 STORE_NAME               1 (f)

  7          12 LOAD_CONST              13 ('Hello, World!')
             15 STORE_NAME               2 (s)

 10          18 LOAD_NAME                0 (i)
             21 LOAD_CONST               6 (3)
             24 BINARY_MULTIPLY
             25 LOAD_CONST               7 (4)
             28 BINARY_MULTIPLY
             29 STORE_NAME               3 (I)

 11          32 LOAD_NAME                1 (f)
             35 LOAD_CONST               1 (2)
             38 BINARY_DIVIDE
             39 LOAD_CONST               6 (3)
             42 BINARY_DIVIDE
             43 STORE_NAME               4 (F)

 12          46 LOAD_NAME                2 (s)
             49 LOAD_CONST               8 ('\n')
             52 BINARY_ADD
             53 LOAD_CONST               9 ('Fantastic!')
             56 BINARY_ADD
             57 STORE_NAME               5 (S)
             60 LOAD_CONST              10 (None)
             63 RETURN_VALUE
```

See Also:

dis (http://docs.python.org/library/dis.html) The standard library documentation for this module, including the list of bytecode instructions (http://docs.python.org/library/dis.html#python-bytecode-instructions).

`Include/opcode.h` The source code for the CPython interpreter defines the byte codes in `opcode.h`.

***Python Essential Reference*, 4th Edition, David M. Beazley**
(www.informit.com/store/product.aspx?isbn=0672329786)

Python disassembly (http://thomas.apestaart.org/log/?p=927) A short discussion of the difference between storing values in a dictionary between Python 2.5 and 2.6.

Why is looping over range() in Python faster than using a while loop? (http://stackoverflow.com/questions/869229/why-is-looping-over-range-in-python-faster-than-using-a-while-loop) A discussion on StackOverflow.com comparing two looping examples via their disassembled bytecodes.

Decorator for binding constants at compile time (http://code.activestate.com/recipes/277940/) Python Cookbook recipe by Raymond Hettinger and Skip Montanaro with a function decorator that rewrites the bytecodes for a function to insert global constants to avoid runtime name lookups.

18.4 inspect—Inspect Live Objects

Purpose The inspect module provides functions for introspecting on live objects and their source code.

Python Version 2.1 and later

The `inspect` module provides functions for learning about live objects, including modules, classes, instances, functions, and methods. The functions in this module can be used to retrieve the original source code for a function, look at the arguments to a method on the stack, and extract the sort of information useful for producing library documentation for source code.

18.4.1 Example Module

The rest of the examples for this section use this example file, `example.py`.

```
#!/usr/bin/env python

# This comment appears first
# and spans 2 lines.

# This comment does not show up in the output of getcomments().

"""Sample file to serve as the basis for inspect examples.
"""
```

```
def module_level_function(arg1, arg2='default', *args, **kwargs):
    """This function is declared in the module."""
    local_variable = arg1


class A(object):
    """The A class."""
    def __init__(self, name):
        self.name = name

    def get_name(self):
        "Returns the name of the instance."
        return self.name

instance_of_a = A('sample_instance')

class B(A):
    """This is the B class.
    It is derived from A.
    """

    # This method is not part of A.
    def do_something(self):
        """Does some work"""

    def get_name(self):
        "Overrides version from A"
        return 'B(' + self.name + ')'
```

18.4.2 Module Information

The first kind of introspection probes live objects to learn about them. For example, it is possible to discover the classes and functions in a module, the methods of a class, etc.

To determine how the interpreter will treat and load a file as a module, use getmoduleinfo(). Pass a filename as the only argument, and the return value is a tuple including the module base name, the suffix of the file, the mode that will be used for reading the file, and the module type as defined in the imp module. It is important to note that the function looks only at the file's name and does not actually check if the file exists or try to read the file.

```
import imp
import inspect
import sys
```

```
if len(sys.argv) >= 2:
    filename = sys.argv[1]
else:
    filename = 'example.py'

try:
    (name, suffix, mode, mtype)   = inspect.getmoduleinfo(filename)
except TypeError:
    print 'Could not determine module type of %s' % filename
else:
    mtype_name = { imp.PY_SOURCE:'source',
                   imp.PY_COMPILED:'compiled',
                   }.get(mtype, mtype)

    mode_description = { 'rb':'(read-binary)',
                        'U':'(universal newline)',
                        }.get(mode, '')

    print 'NAME    :', name
    print 'SUFFIX :', suffix
    print 'MODE    :', mode, mode_description
    print 'MTYPE   :', mtype_name
```

Here are a few sample runs.

```
$ python inspect_getmoduleinfo.py example.py

NAME    : example
SUFFIX : .py
MODE    : U (universal newline)
MTYPE   : source

$ python inspect_getmoduleinfo.py readme.txt

Could not determine module type of readme.txt

$ python inspect_getmoduleinfo.py notthere.pyc

NAME    : notthere
SUFFIX : .pyc
```

```
MODE    : rb (read-binary)
MTYPE   : compiled
```

18.4.3   Inspecting Modules

It is possible to probe live objects to determine their components using `getmembers()`. The arguments are an object to scan (a module, class, or instance) and an optional predicate function that is used to filter the objects returned. The return value is a list of tuples with two values: the name of the member, and the type of the member. The `inspect` module includes several such predicate functions with names like `ismodule()`, `isclass()`, etc.

The types of members that might be returned depend on the type of object scanned. Modules can contain classes and functions; classes can contain methods and attributes; and so on.

```
import inspect

import example

for name, data in inspect.getmembers(example):
    if name.startswith('__'):
        continue
    print '%s : %r' % (name, data)
```

This sample prints the members of the `example` module. Modules have several private attributes that are used as part of the import implementation, as well as a set of `__builtins__`. All these are ignored in the output for this example because they are not actually part of the module and the list is long.

```
$ python inspect_getmembers_module.py

A : <class 'example.A'>
B : <class 'example.B'>
instance_of_a : <example.A object at 0x1004ddd10>
module_level_function : <function module_level_function at
0x1004cd050>
```

The *predicate* argument can be used to filter the types of objects returned.

```
import inspect

import example

for name, data in inspect.getmembers(example, inspect.isclass):
    print '%s :' % name, repr(data)
```

Only classes are included in the output now.

```
$ python inspect_getmembers_module_class.py

A : <class 'example.A'>
B : <class 'example.B'>
```

18.4.4   Inspecting Classes

Classes are scanned using `getmembers()` in the same way as modules, though the types of members are different.

```
import inspect
from pprint import pprint

import example

pprint(inspect.getmembers(example.A), width=65)
```

Because no filtering is applied, the output shows the attributes, methods, slots, and other members of the class.

```
$ python inspect_getmembers_class.py

[('__class__', <type 'type'>),
 ('__delattr__',
  <slot wrapper '__delattr__' of 'object' objects>),
 ('__dict__', <dictproxy object at 0x1004d0da8>),
 ('__doc__', 'The A class.'),
 ('__format__', <method '__format__' of 'object' objects>),
 ('__getattribute__',
  <slot wrapper '__getattribute__' of 'object' objects>),
 ('__hash__', <slot wrapper '__hash__' of 'object' objects>),
 ('__init__', <unbound method A.__init__>),
 ('__module__', 'example'),
```

```
('__new__',
 <built-in method __new__ of type object at 0x100187800>),
('__reduce__', <method '__reduce__' of 'object' objects>),
('__reduce_ex__',
 <method '__reduce_ex__' of 'object' objects>),
('__repr__', <slot wrapper '__repr__' of 'object' objects>),
('__setattr__',
 <slot wrapper '__setattr__' of 'object' objects>),
('__sizeof__', <method '__sizeof__' of 'object' objects>),
('__str__', <slot wrapper '__str__' of 'object' objects>),
('__subclasshook__',
 <built-in method __subclasshook__ of type object at 0x100385a10>),
('__weakref__', <attribute '__weakref__' of 'A' objects>),
('get_name', <unbound method A.get_name>)]
```

To find the methods of a class, use the `ismethod()` predicate.

```
import inspect
from pprint import pprint

import example

pprint(inspect.getmembers(example.A, inspect.ismethod))
```

Only unbound methods are returned now.

```
$ python inspect_getmembers_class_methods.py

[('__init__', <unbound method A.__init__>),
 ('get_name', <unbound method A.get_name>)]
```

The output for B includes the override for `get_name()`, as well as the new method, and the inherited `__init__()` method implemented in A.

```
import inspect
from pprint import pprint

import example

pprint(inspect.getmembers(example.B, inspect.ismethod))
```

Methods inherited from A, such as `__init__()`, are identified as being methods of B.

```
$ python inspect_getmembers_class_methods_b.py

[('__init__', <unbound method B.__init__>),
 ('do_something', <unbound method B.do_something>),
 ('get_name', <unbound method B.get_name>)]
```

18.4.5 Documentation Strings

The docstring for an object can be retrieved with `getdoc()`. The return value is the `__doc__` attribute with tabs expanded to spaces and with indentation made uniform.

```
import inspect
import example


print 'B.__doc__:'
print example.B.__doc__
print
print 'getdoc(B):'
print inspect.getdoc(example.B)
```

The second line of the docstring is indented when it is retrieved through the attribute directly, but it is moved to the left margin by `getdoc()`.

```
$ python inspect_getdoc.py

B.__doc__:
This is the B class.
    It is derived from A.


getdoc(B):
This is the B class.
It is derived from A.
```

In addition to the actual docstring, it is possible to retrieve the comments from the source file where an object is implemented, if the source is available. The `getcomments()` function looks at the source of the object and finds comments on lines preceding the implementation.

```
import inspect
import example


print inspect.getcomments(example.B.do_something)
```

The lines returned include the comment prefix with any whitespace prefix stripped off.

```
$ python inspect_getcomments_method.py

# This method is not part of A.
```

When a module is passed to getcomments(), the return value is always the first comment in the module.

```
import inspect
import example

print inspect.getcomments(example)
```

Contiguous lines from the example file are included as a single comment, but as soon as a blank line appears, the comment is stopped.

```
$ python inspect_getcomments_module.py

# This comment appears first
# and spans 2 lines.
```

18.4.6   Retrieving Source

If the .py file is available for a module, the original source code for the class or method can be retrieved using getsource() and getsourcelines().

```
import inspect
import example

print inspect.getsource(example.A)
```

When a class is passed in, all the methods for the class are included in the output.

```
$ python inspect_getsource_class.py

class A(object):
    """The A class."""
    def __init__(self, name):
        self.name = name
```

```
    def get_name(self):
        "Returns the name of the instance."
        return self.name
```

To retrieve the source for a single method, pass the method reference to get-source().

```
import inspect
import example

print inspect.getsource(example.A.get_name)
```

The original indent level is retained in this case.

```
$ python inspect_getsource_method.py

    def get_name(self):
        "Returns the name of the instance."
        return self.name
```

Use getsourcelines() instead of getsource() to retrieve the lines of source split into individual strings.

```
import inspect
import pprint
import example

pprint.pprint(inspect.getsourcelines(example.A.get_name))
```

The return value from getsourcelines() is a tuple containing a list of strings (the lines from the source file) and a starting line number in the file where the source appears.

```
$ python inspect_getsourcelines_method.py

(['    def get_name(self):\n',
  '        "Returns the name of the instance."\n',
  '        return self.name\n'],
 20)
```

If the source file is not available, getsource() and getsourcelines() raise an IOError.

18.4.7   Method and Function Arguments

In addition to the documentation for a function or method, it is possible to ask for a complete specification of the arguments the callable takes, including default values. The `getargspec()` function returns a tuple containing the list of positional argument names, the name of any variable positional arguments (e.g., `*args`), the name of any variable named arguments (e.g., `**kwds`), and default values for the arguments. If there are default values, they match up with the end of the positional argument list.

```
import inspect
import example

arg_spec = inspect.getargspec(example.module_level_function)
print 'NAMES   :', arg_spec[0]
print '*       :', arg_spec[1]
print '**      :', arg_spec[2]
print 'defaults:', arg_spec[3]

args_with_defaults = arg_spec[0][-len(arg_spec[3]):]
print 'args & defaults:', zip(args_with_defaults, arg_spec[3])
```

In this example, the first argument to the function, *arg1*, does not have a default value. The single default, therefore, is matched up with *arg2*.

```
$ python inspect_getargspec_function.py

NAMES    : ['arg1', 'arg2']
*        : args
**       : kwargs
defaults: ('default',)
args & defaults: [('arg2', 'default')]
```

The argspec for a function can be used by decorators or other functions to validate inputs, provide different defaults, etc. Writing a suitably generic and reusable validation decorator has one special challenge, though, because it can be complicated to match up incoming arguments with their names for functions that accept a combination of named and positional arguments. `getcallargs()` provides the necessary logic to handle the mapping. It returns a dictionary populated with its arguments associated with the names of the arguments of a specified function.

```
import inspect
import example
import pprint
```

```
for args, kwds in [
    (('a',), {'unknown_name':'value'}),
    (('a',), {'arg2':'value'}),
    (('a', 'b', 'c', 'd'), {}),
    ((), {'arg1':'a'}),
    ]:
    print args, kwds
    callargs = inspect.getcallargs(example.module_level_function,
                                   *args, **kwds)
    pprint.pprint(callargs, width=74)
    example.module_level_function(**callargs)
    print
```

The keys of the dictionary are the argument names of the function, so the function can be called using the $**$ syntax to expand the dictionary onto the stack as the arguments.

```
$ python inspect_getcallargs.py

('a',) {'unknown_name': 'value'}
{'arg1': 'a',
 'arg2': 'default',
 'args': (),
 'kwargs': {'unknown_name': 'value'}}

('a',) {'arg2': 'value'}
{'arg1': 'a', 'arg2': 'value', 'args': (), 'kwargs': {}}

('a', 'b', 'c', 'd') {}
{'arg1': 'a', 'arg2': 'b', 'args': ('c', 'd'), 'kwargs': {}}

() {'arg1': 'a'}
{'arg1': 'a', 'arg2': 'default', 'args': (), 'kwargs': {}}
```

18.4.8   Class Hierarchies

inspect includes two methods for working directly with class hierarchies. The first, getclasstree(), creates a tree-like data structure based on the classes it is given and their base classes. Each element in the list returned is either a tuple with a class and its base classes or another list containing tuples for subclasses.

```
import inspect
import example
```

```
class C(example.B):
    pass

class D(C, example.A):
    pass

def print_class_tree(tree, indent=-1):
    if isinstance(tree, list):
        for node in tree:
            print_class_tree(node, indent+1)
    else:
        print '   ' * indent, tree[0].__name__
    return

if __name__ == '__main__':
    print 'A, B, C, D:'
    print_class_tree(inspect.getclasstree([example.A, example.B, C, D]))
```

The output from this example is the "tree" of inheritance for the A, B, C, and D classes. D appears twice, since it inherits from both C and A.

```
$ python inspect_getclasstree.py

A, B, C, D:
 object
    A
       D
    B
       C
          D
```

If `getclasstree()` is called with *unique* set to a true value, the output is different.

```
import inspect
import example
from inspect_getclasstree import *

print_class_tree(inspect.getclasstree([example.A, example.B, C, D],
                                       unique=True,
                                       ))
```

This time, D only appears in the output once.

```
$ python inspect_getclasstree_unique.py

 object
    A
       B
          C
             D
```

18.4.9   Method Resolution Order

The other function for working with class hierarchies is getmro(), which returns a tuple of classes in the order they should be scanned when resolving an attribute that might be inherited from a base class using the *Method Resolution Order* (MRO). Each class in the sequence appears only once.

```python
import inspect
import example

class C(object):
    pass

class C_First(C, example.B):
    pass

class B_First(example.B, C):
    pass

print 'B_First:'
for c in inspect.getmro(B_First):
    print '\t', c.__name__
print
print 'C_First:'
for c in inspect.getmro(C_First):
    print '\t', c.__name__
```

This output demonstrates the "depth-first" nature of the MRO search. For B_First, A also comes before C in the search order, because B is derived from A.

```
$ python inspect_getmro.py

B_First:
        B_First
```

```
        B
        A
        C
        object

C_First:
        C_First
        C
        B
        A
        object
```

18.4.10 The Stack and Frames

In addition to introspection of code objects, `inspect` includes functions for inspecting the runtime environment while a program is being executed. Most of these functions work with the call stack and operate on "call frames." Each frame record in the stack is a six-element tuple containing the frame object, the filename where the code exists, the line number in that file for the current line being run, the function name being called, a list of lines of context from the source file, and the index into that list of the current line. Typically, such information is used to build tracebacks when exceptions are raised. It can also be useful for logging or when debugging programs, since the stack frames can be interrogated to discover the argument values passed into the functions.

`currentframe()` returns the frame at the top of the stack (for the current function). `getargvalues()` returns a tuple with argument names, the names of the variable arguments, and a dictionary with local values from the frame. Combining them shows the arguments to functions and local variables at different points in the call stack.

```python
import inspect


def recurse(limit):
    local_variable = '.' * limit
    print limit, inspect.getargvalues(inspect.currentframe())
    if limit <= 0:
        return
    recurse(limit - 1)
    return


if __name__ == '__main__':
    recurse(2)
```

The value for `local_variable` is included in the frame's local variables, even though it is not an argument to the function.

```
$ python inspect_getargvalues.py

2 ArgInfo(args=['limit'], varargs=None, keywords=None,
locals={'local_variable': '..', 'limit': 2})
1 ArgInfo(args=['limit'], varargs=None, keywords=None,
locals={'local_variable': '.', 'limit': 1})
0 ArgInfo(args=['limit'], varargs=None, keywords=None,
locals={'local_variable': '', 'limit': 0})
```

Using `stack()`, it is also possible to access all the stack frames from the current frame to the first caller. This example is similar to the one shown earlier, except it waits until reaching the end of the recursion to print the stack information.

```python
import inspect


def show_stack():
    for level in inspect.stack():
        frame, filename, line_num, func, src_code, src_index = level
        print '%s[%d]\n    -> %s' % (filename,
                                     line_num,
                                     src_code[src_index].strip(),
                                     )
        print inspect.getargvalues(frame)
        print


def recurse(limit):
    local_variable = '.' * limit
    if limit <= 0:
        show_stack()
        return
    recurse(limit - 1)
    return


if __name__ == '__main__':
    recurse(2)
```

The last part of the output represents the main program, outside of the `recurse()` function.

```
$ python inspect_stack.py

inspect_stack.py[9]
  -> for level in inspect.stack():
ArgInfo(args=[], varargs=None, keywords=None,
locals={'src_index': 0, 'line_num': 9, 'frame': <frame object at
0x100360750>, 'level': (<frame object at 0x100360750>,
'inspect_stack.py', 9, 'show_stack', ['    for level in
inspect.stack():\n'], 0), 'src_code': ['    for level in
inspect.stack():\n'], 'filename': 'inspect_stack.py', 'func':
'show_stack'})

inspect_stack.py[21]
  -> show_stack()
ArgInfo(args=['limit'], varargs=None, keywords=None,
locals={'local_variable': '', 'limit': 0})

inspect_stack.py[23]
  -> recurse(limit - 1)
ArgInfo(args=['limit'], varargs=None, keywords=None,
locals={'local_variable': '.', 'limit': 1})

inspect_stack.py[23]
  -> recurse(limit - 1)
ArgInfo(args=['limit'], varargs=None, keywords=None,
locals={'local_variable': '..', 'limit': 2})

inspect_stack.py[27]
  -> recurse(2)
ArgInfo(args=[], varargs=None, keywords=None,
locals={'__builtins__': <module '__builtin__' (built-in)>,
'__file__': 'inspect_stack.py', 'inspect': <module 'inspect' from
'/Library/Frameworks/Python.framework/Versions/2.7/lib/python2.7/
inspect.pyc'>, 'recurse': <function recurse at 0x1004cd050>,
'__package__': None, '__name__': '__main__', 'show_stack':
<function show_stack at 0x1004def50>, '__doc__': 'Inspecting the
call stack.\n'})
```

There are other functions for building lists of frames in different contexts, such as when an exception is being processed. See the documentation for `trace()`, `getouterframes()`, and `getinnerframes()` for more details.

See Also:

inspect (http://docs.python.org/library/inspect.html) The standard library documentation for this module.

Python 2.3 Method Resolution Order (www.python.org/download/releases/2.3/ mro/) Documentation for the C3 Method Resolution order used by Python 2.3 and later.

pyclbr (page 1039) The `pyclbr` module provides access to some of the same information as `inspect` by parsing the module without importing it.

18.5   exceptions—Built-in Exception Classes

Purpose The exceptions module defines the built-in errors used throughout the standard library and by the interpreter.

Python Version 1.5 and later

In the past, Python has supported simple string messages as exceptions as well as classes. Since version 1.5, all the standard library modules use classes for exceptions. Starting with Python 2.5, string exceptions result in a `DeprecationWarning`. Support for string exceptions will be removed in the future.

18.5.1   Base Classes

The exception classes are defined in a hierarchy, described in the standard library documentation. In addition to the obvious organizational benefits, exception inheritance is useful because related exceptions can be caught by catching their base class. In most cases, these base classes are not intended to be raised directly.

BaseException

Base class for all exceptions. Implements logic for creating a string representation of the exception using `str()` from the arguments passed to the constructor.

Exception

Base class for exceptions that do not result in quitting the running application. All user-defined exceptions should use `Exception` as a base class.

StandardError

Base class for built-in exceptions used in the standard library.

ArithmeticError

Base class for math-related errors.

LookupError

Base class for errors raised when something cannot be found.

EnvironmentError

Base class for errors that come from outside of Python (the operating system, file system, etc.).

18.5.2   Raised Exceptions

AssertionError

An `AssertionError` is raised by a failed `assert` statement.

```
assert False, 'The assertion failed'
```

Assertions are commonly in libraries to enforce constraints with incoming arguments.

```
$ python exceptions_AssertionError_assert.py

Traceback (most recent call last):
  File "exceptions_AssertionError_assert.py", line 12, in <module>
    assert False, 'The assertion failed'
AssertionError: The assertion failed
```

`AssertionError` is also used in automated tests created with the `unittest` module, via methods like `failIf()`.

```
import unittest

class AssertionExample(unittest.TestCase):

    def test(self):
        self.failUnless(False)

unittest.main()
```

Programs that run automated test suites watch for `AssertionError` exceptions as a special indication that a test has failed.

```
$ python exceptions_AssertionError_unittest.py

F
=======================================================================
FAIL: test (__main__.AssertionExample)
-----------------------------------------------------------------------
Traceback (most recent call last):
  File "exceptions_AssertionError_unittest.py", line 17, in test
    self.failUnless(False)
AssertionError: False is not True


-----------------------------------------------------------------------
Ran 1 test in 0.000s

FAILED (failures=1)
```

AttributeError

When an attribute reference or assignment fails, `AttributeError` is raised.

```
class NoAttributes(object):
    pass


o = NoAttributes()
print o.attribute
```

This example demonstrates what happens when trying to reference an attribute that does not exist.

```
$ python exceptions_AttributeError.py

Traceback (most recent call last):
  File "exceptions_AttributeError.py", line 16, in <module>
    print o.attribute
AttributeError: 'NoAttributes' object has no attribute 'attribute'
```

Most Python classes accept arbitrary attributes. Classes can define a fixed set of attributes using `__slots__` to save memory and improve performance.

```
class MyClass(object):
    __slots__ = ( 'attribute', )

o = MyClass()
o.attribute = 'known attribute'
o.not_a_slot = 'new attribute'
```

Setting an unknown attribute on a class that defines __slots__ causes an AttributeError.

```
$ python exceptions_AttributeError_slot.py

Traceback (most recent call last):
  File "exceptions_AttributeError_slot.py", line 15, in <module>
    o.not_a_slot = 'new attribute'
AttributeError: 'MyClass' object has no attribute 'not_a_slot'
```

An AttributeError is also raised when a program tries to modify a read-only attribute.

```
class MyClass(object):

    @property
    def attribute(self):
        return 'This is the attribute value'

o = MyClass()
print o.attribute
o.attribute = 'New value'
```

Read-only attributes can be created by using the @property decorator without providing a setter function.

```
$ python exceptions_AttributeError_assignment.py

This is the attribute value
Traceback (most recent call last):
  File "exceptions_AttributeError_assignment.py", line 20, in
<module>
    o.attribute = 'New value'
AttributeError: can't set attribute
```

EOFError

An `EOFError` is raised when a built-in function like `input()` or `raw_input()` does not read any data before encountering the end of the input stream.

```python
while True:
    data = raw_input('prompt:')
    print 'READ:', data
```

Instead of raising an exception, the file method `read()` returns an empty string at the end of the file.

```
$ echo hello | python exceptions_EOFError.py

prompt:READ: hello
prompt:Traceback (most recent call last):
  File "exceptions_EOFError.py", line 13, in <module>
    data = raw_input('prompt:')
EOFError: EOF when reading a line
```

FloatingPointError

This error is raised by floating-point operations that result in errors, when floating-point exception control (`fpectl`) is turned on. Enabling `fpectl` requires an interpreter compiled with the `--with-fpectl` flag. However, using `fpectl` is discouraged in the standard library documentation.

```python
import math
import fpectl

print 'Control off:', math.exp(1000)
fpectl.turnon_sigfpe()
print 'Control on:', math.exp(1000)
```

GeneratorExit

A `GeneratorExit` is raised inside a generator when its `close()` method is called.

```python
def my_generator():
    try:
        for i in range(5):
            print 'Yielding', i
            yield i
```

```
    except GeneratorExit:
        print 'Exiting early'

g = my_generator()
print g.next()
g.close()
```

Generators should catch `GeneratorExit` and use it as a signal to clean up when they are terminated early.

```
$ python exceptions_GeneratorExit.py

Yielding 0
0
Exiting early
```

IOError

This error is raised when input or output fails, for example, if a disk fills up or an input file does not exist.

```
try:
    f = open('/does/not/exist', 'r')
except IOError as err:
    print 'Formatted    :', str(err)
    print 'Filename     :', err.filename
    print 'Errno        :', err.errno
    print 'String error:', err.strerror
```

The `filename` attribute holds the name of the file for which the error occurred. The `errno` attribute is the system error number, defined by the platform's C library. A string error message corresponding to `errno` is saved in `strerror`.

```
$ python exceptions_IOError.py

Formatted    : [Errno 2] No such file or directory: '/does/not/exist'
Filename     : /does/not/exist
Errno        : 2
String error: No such file or directory
```

ImportError

This exception is raised when a module, or a member of a module, cannot be imported. There are a few conditions where an `ImportError` is raised.

```
import module_does_not_exist
```

If a module does not exist, the import system raises `ImportError`.

```
$ python exceptions_ImportError_nomodule.py

Traceback (most recent call last):
  File "exceptions_ImportError_nomodule.py", line 12, in <module>
    import module_does_not_exist
ImportError: No module named module_does_not_exist
```

If `from X import Y` is used and Y cannot be found inside the module X, an `ImportError` is raised.

```
from exceptions import MadeUpName
```

The error message only includes the missing name, not the module or package from which it was being loaded.

```
$ python exceptions_ImportError_missingname.py

Traceback (most recent call last):
  File "exceptions_ImportError_missingname.py", line 12, in
<module>
    from exceptions import MadeUpName
ImportError: cannot import name MadeUpName
```

IndexError

An `IndexError` is raised when a sequence reference is out of range.

```
my_seq = [ 0, 1, 2 ]
print my_seq[3]
```

References beyond either end of a list cause an error.

```
$ python exceptions_IndexError.py

Traceback (most recent call last):
  File "exceptions_IndexError.py", line 13, in <module>
```

```
    print my_seq[3]
IndexError: list index out of range
```

KeyError

Similarly, a `KeyError` is raised when a value is not found as a key of a dictionary.

```
d = { 'a':1, 'b':2 }
print d['c']
```

The text of the error message is the key being sought.

```
$ python exceptions_KeyError.py

Traceback (most recent call last):
  File "exceptions_KeyError.py", line 13, in <module>
    print d['c']
KeyError: 'c'
```

KeyboardInterrupt

A `KeyboardInterrupt` occurs whenever the user presses `Ctrl-C` (or `Delete`) to stop a running program. Unlike most of the other exceptions, `KeyboardInterrupt` inherits directly from `BaseException` to avoid being caught by global exception handlers that catch `Exception`.

```
try:
    print 'Press Return or Ctrl-C:',
    ignored = raw_input()
except Exception, err:
    print 'Caught exception:', err
except KeyboardInterrupt, err:
    print 'Caught KeyboardInterrupt'
else:
    print 'No exception'
```

Pressing `Ctrl-C` at the prompt causes a `KeyboardInterrupt` exception.

```
$ python exceptions_KeyboardInterrupt.py

Press Return or Ctrl-C: ^CCaught KeyboardInterrupt
```

MemoryError

If a program runs out of memory and it is possible to recover (by deleting some objects, for example), a `MemoryError` is raised.

```python
import itertools

# Try to create a MemoryError by allocating a lot of memory
l = []
for i in range(3):
    try:
        for j in itertools.count(1):
            print i, j
            l.append('*' * (2**30))
    except MemoryError:
        print '(error, discarding existing list)'
        l = []
```

When a program starts running out of memory, behavior after the error can be unpredictable. The ability to even construct an error message is questionable, since that also requires new memory allocations to create the string buffer.

```
$ python exceptions_MemoryError.py

python(49670) malloc: *** mmap(size=1073745920) failed
(error code=12)
*** error: can't allocate region
*** set a breakpoint in malloc_error_break to debug
python(49670) malloc: *** mmap(size=1073745920) failed
(error code=12)
*** error: can't allocate region
*** set a breakpoint in malloc_error_break to debug
python(49670) malloc: *** mmap(size=1073745920) failed
(error code=12)
*** error: can't allocate region
*** set a breakpoint in malloc_error_break to debug
0 1
0 2
0 3
(error, discarding existing list)
1 1
1 2
1 3
```

```
(error, discarding existing list)
2 1
2 2
2 3
(error, discarding existing list)
```

NameError

`NameError` exceptions are raised when code refers to a name that does not exist in the current scope. An example is an unqualified variable name.

```python
def func():
    print unknown_name

func()
```

The error message says "global name" because the name lookup starts from the local scope and goes up to the global scope before failing.

```
$ python exceptions_NameError.py

Traceback (most recent call last):
  File "exceptions_NameError.py", line 15, in <module>
    func()
  File "exceptions_NameError.py", line 13, in func
    print unknown_name
NameError: global name 'unknown_name' is not defined
```

NotImplementedError

User-defined base classes can raise `NotImplementedError` to indicate that a method or behavior needs to be defined by a subclass, simulating an interface.

```python
class BaseClass(object):
    """Defines the interface"""
    def __init__(self):
        super(BaseClass, self).__init__()
    def do_something(self):
        """The interface, not implemented"""
        raise NotImplementedError(
            self.__class__.__name__ + '.do_something'
            )
```

```
class SubClass(BaseClass):
    """Implementes the interface"""
    def do_something(self):
        """really does something"""
        print self.__class__.__name__ + ' doing something!'

SubClass().do_something()
BaseClass().do_something()
```

Another way to enforce an interface is to use the abc module to create an *abstract base class*.

```
$ python exceptions_NotImplementedError.py

SubClass doing something!
Traceback (most recent call last):
  File "exceptions_NotImplementedError.py", line 29, in <module>
    BaseClass().do_something()
  File "exceptions_NotImplementedError.py", line 19, in do_something
    self.__class__.__name__ + '.do_something'
NotImplementedError: BaseClass.do_something
```

OSError

OSError is raised when an error comes back from an operating-system-level function. It serves as the primary error class used in the os module and is also used by subprocess and other modules that provide an interface to the operating system.

```
import os

for i in range(10):
    try:
        print i, os.ttyname(i)
    except OSError as err:
        print
        print '  Formatted    :', str(err)
        print '  Errno        :', err.errno
        print '  String error:', err.strerror
        break
```

The errno and strerror attributes are filled in with system-specific values, as for IOError. The filename attribute is set to None.

```
$ python exceptions_OSError.py

0 /dev/ttyp0
1
  Formatted    : [Errno 25] Inappropriate ioctl for device
  Errno        : 25
  String error: Inappropriate ioctl for device
```

OverflowError

When an arithmetic operation exceeds the limits of the variable type, an `Overflow-Error` is raised. Long integers allocate more memory as values grow, so they end up raising `MemoryError`. Regular integers are converted to long values, as needed.

```python
import sys

print 'Regular integer: (maxint=%s)' % sys.maxint
try:
    i = sys.maxint * 3
    print 'No overflow for ', type(i), 'i =', i
except OverflowError, err:
    print 'Overflowed at ', i, err

print
print 'Long integer:'
for i in range(0, 100, 10):
    print '%2d' % i, 2L ** i

print
print 'Floating point values:'
try:
    f = 2.0**i
    for i in range(100):
        print i, f
        f = f ** 2
except OverflowError, err:
    print 'Overflowed after ', f, err
```

If a multiplied integer no longer fits in a regular integer size, it is converted to a long integer object. The exponential formula using floating-point values in the example overflows when the value can no longer be represented by a double-precision float.

```
$ python exceptions_OverflowError.py

Regular integer: (maxint=9223372036854775807)
No overflow for  <type 'long'> i = 27670116110564327421

Long integer:
 0 1
10 1024
20 1048576
30 1073741824
40 1099511627776
50 1125899906842624
60 1152921504606846976
70 1180591620717411303424
80 1208925819614629174706176
90 1237940039285380274899124224

Floating-point values:
0 1.23794003929e+27
1 1.53249554087e+54
2 2.34854258277e+108
3 5.5156522631e+216
Overflowed after  5.5156522631e+216 (34, 'Result too large')
```

ReferenceError

When a `weakref` proxy is used to access an object that has already been garbage collected, a `ReferenceError` occurs.

```python
import gc
import weakref

class ExpensiveObject(object):
    def __init__(self, name):
        self.name = name
    def __del__(self):
        print '(Deleting %s)' % self

obj = ExpensiveObject('obj')
p = weakref.proxy(obj)

print 'BEFORE:', p.name
obj = None
print 'AFTER:', p.name
```

This example causes the original object, `obj`, to be deleted by removing the only strong reference to the value.

```
$ python exceptions_ReferenceError.py

BEFORE: obj
(Deleting <__main__.ExpensiveObject object at 0x1004667d0>)
AFTER:
Traceback (most recent call last):
  File "exceptions_ReferenceError.py", line 26, in <module>
    print 'AFTER:', p.name
ReferenceError: weakly-referenced object no longer exists
```

RuntimeError

A `RuntimeError` exception is used when no other more specific exception applies. The interpreter does not raise this exception itself very often, but some user code does.

StopIteration

When an iterator is done, its `next()` method raises `StopIteration`. This exception is not considered an error.

```
l=[0,1,2]
i=iter(l)

print i
print i.next()
print i.next()
print i.next()
print i.next()
```

A normal **for** loop catches the `StopIteration` exception and breaks out of the loop.

```
$ python exceptions_StopIteration.py

<listiterator object at 0x100459850>
0
1
2
```

```
Traceback (most recent call last):
  File "exceptions_StopIteration.py", line 19, in <module>
    print i.next()
StopIteration
```

SyntaxError

A `SyntaxError` occurs any time the parser finds source code it does not understand. This can be while importing a module, invoking `exec`, or calling `eval()`.

```
try:
    print eval('five times three')
except SyntaxError, err:
    print 'Syntax error %s (%s-%s): %s' % \
        (err.filename, err.lineno, err.offset, err.text)
    print err
```

Attributes of the exception can be used to find exactly what part of the input text caused the exception.

```
$ python exceptions_SyntaxError.py

Syntax error <string> (1-10): five times three
invalid syntax (<string>, line 1)
```

SystemError

When an error occurs in the interpreter itself and there is some chance of continuing to run successfully, it raises a `SystemError`. System errors usually indicate a bug in the interpreter and should be reported to the maintainers.

SystemExit

When `sys.exit()` is called, it raises `SystemExit` instead of exiting immediately. This allows cleanup code in **try:finally** blocks to run and special environments (like debuggers and test frameworks) to catch the exception and avoid exiting.

TypeError

A `TypeError` is caused by combining the wrong type of objects or calling a function with the wrong type of object.

```
result = 5 + 'string'
```

TypeError and ValueError exceptions are often confused. A ValueError usually means that a value is of the correct type, but out of a valid range. TypeError means that the wrong type of object is being used (i.e., an integer instead of a string).

```
$ python exceptions_TypeError.py

Traceback (most recent call last):
  File "exceptions_TypeError.py", line 12, in <module>
    result = 5 + 'string'
TypeError: unsupported operand type(s) for +: 'int' and 'str'
```

UnboundLocalError

An UnboundLocalError is a type of NameError specific to local variable names.

```
def throws_global_name_error():
    print unknown_global_name

def throws_unbound_local():
    local_val = local_val + 1
    print local_val

try:
    throws_global_name_error()
except NameError, err:
    print 'Global name error:', err

try:
    throws_unbound_local()
except UnboundLocalError, err:
    print 'Local name error:', err
```

The difference between the global NameError and the UnboundLocal is the way the name is used. Because the name "local_val" appears on the left side of an expression, it is interpreted as a local variable name.

```
$ python exceptions_UnboundLocalError.py

Global name error: global name 'unknown_global_name' is not
defined
```

```
Local name error: local variable 'local_val' referenced before
assignment
```

UnicodeError

UnicodeError is a subclass of ValueError and is raised when a Unicode problem occurs. There are separate subclasses for UnicodeEncodeError, UnicodeDecodeError, and UnicodeTranslateError.

ValueError

A ValueError is used when a function receives a value that has the correct type, but an invalid value.

```
print chr(1024)
```

The ValueError exception is a general-purpose error, used in a lot of third-party libraries to signal an invalid argument to a function.

```
$ python exceptions_ValueError.py

Traceback (most recent call last):
  File "exceptions_ValueError.py", line 12, in <module>
    print chr(1024)
ValueError: chr() arg not in range(256)
```

ZeroDivisionError

When zero is used in the denominator of a division operation, a ZeroDivisionError is raised.

```
print 'Division:',
try:
    print 1 / 0
except ZeroDivisionError as err:
    print err

print 'Modulo   :',
try:
    print 1 % 0
except ZeroDivisionError as err:
    print err
```

The modulo operator also raises `ZeroDivisionError` when the denominator is zero.

```
$ python exceptions_ZeroDivisionError.py

Division: integer division or modulo by zero
Modulo  : integer division or modulo by zero
```

18.5.3   Warning Categories

There are also several exceptions defined for use with the `warnings` module.

Warning The base class for all warnings.

UserWarning Base class for warnings coming from user code.

DeprecationWarning Used for features no longer being maintained.

PendingDeprecationWarning Used for features that are soon going to be deprecated.

SyntaxWarning Used for questionable syntax.

RuntimeWarning Used for events that happen at runtime that might cause problems.

FutureWarning Warning about changes to the language or library that are coming at a later time.

ImportWarning Warning about problems importing a module.

UnicodeWarning Warning about problems with Unicode text.

See Also:

exceptions (http://docs.python.org/library/exceptions.html) The standard library documentation for this module.

warnings (page 1170) Nonerror warning messages.

slots Python Language Reference documentation for using `__slots__` to reduce memory consumption.

abc (page 1178) Abstract base classes.

math (page 223) The `math` module has special functions for performing floating-point calculations safely.

weakref (page 106) The `weakref` module allows a program to hold references to objects without preventing garbage collection.

Chapter 19

MODULES AND PACKAGES

Python's primary extension mechanism uses source code saved to modules and incorporated into a program through the **import** statement. The features that most developers think of as "Python" are actually implemented as the collection of modules called the standard library, the subject of this book. Although the import feature is built into the interpreter itself, there are several modules in the library related to the import process.

The `imp` module exposes the underlying implementation of the import mechanism used by the interpreter. It can be used to import modules dynamically at runtime, instead of using the **import** statement to load them during start-up. Dynamically loading modules is useful when the name of a module that needs to be imported is not known in advance, such as for plug-ins or extensions to an application.

`zipimport` provides a custom importer for modules and packages saved to ZIP archives. It is used to load Python EGG files, for example, and can also be used as a convenient way to package and distribute an application.

Python packages can include supporting resource files such as templates, default configuration files, images, and other data, along with source code. The interface for accessing resource files in a portable way is implemented in the `pkgutil` module. It also includes support for modifying the import path for a package, so that the contents can be installed into multiple directories but appear as part of the same package.

19.1 imp—Python's Import Mechanism

Purpose The imp module exposes the implementation of Python's import statement.

Python Version 2.2.1 and later

The `imp` module includes functions that expose part of the underlying implementation of Python's import mechanism for loading code in packages and modules. It is one access point to importing modules dynamically and is useful in some cases where the name of the module that needs to be imported is unknown when the code is written (e.g., for plug-ins or extensions to an application).

19.1.1 Example Package

The examples in this section use a package called `example` with `__init__.py`.

```
print 'Importing example package'
```

They also use a module called `submodule` containing the following:

```
print 'Importing submodule'
```

Watch for the text from the **print** statements in the sample output when the package or module is imported.

19.1.2 Module Types

Python supports several styles of modules. Each requires its own handling when opening the module and adding it to the namespace, and support for the formats varies by platform. For example, under Microsoft Windows, shared libraries are loaded from files with extensions `.dll` or `.pyd`, instead of `.so`. The extensions for C modules may also change when using a debug build of the interpreter instead of a normal release build, since they can be compiled with debug information included as well. If a C extension library or other module is not loading as expected, use `get_suffixes()` to print a list of the supported types for the current platform and the parameters for loading them.

```
import imp

module_types = { imp.PY_SOURCE:    'source',
                 imp.PY_COMPILED:  'compiled',
                 imp.C_EXTENSION:  'extension',
                 imp.PY_RESOURCE:  'resource',
                 imp.PKG_DIRECTORY: 'package',
                 }

def main():
    fmt = '%10s %10s %10s'
```

```
    print fmt % ('Extension', 'Mode', 'Type')
    print '-' * 32
    for extension, mode, module_type in imp.get_suffixes():
        print fmt % (extension, mode, module_types[module_type])

if __name__ == '__main__':
    main()
```

The return value is a sequence of tuples containing the file extension, the mode to use for opening the file containing the module, and a type code from a constant defined in the module. This table is incomplete, because some of the importable module or package types do not correspond to single files.

```
$ python imp_get_suffixes.py

Extension          Mode       Type
--------------------------------
        .so          rb    extension
module.so            rb    extension
        .py           U       source
       .pyc          rb     compiled
```

19.1.3   Finding Modules

The first step to loading a module is finding it. `find_module()` scans the import search path looking for a package or module with the given name. It returns an open file handle (if appropriate for the type), the filename where the module was found, and a "description" (a tuple such as those returned by `get_suffixes()`).

```
import imp
from imp_get_suffixes import module_types
import os

# Get the full name of the directory containing this module
base_dir = os.path.dirname(__file__) or os.getcwd()

print 'Package:'
f, pkg_fname, description = imp.find_module('example')
print module_types[description[2]], pkg_fname.replace(base_dir, '.')
print

print 'Submodule:'
```

```
f, mod_fname, description = imp.find_module('submodule', [pkg_fname])
print module_types[description[2]], mod_fname.replace(base_dir, '.')
if f: f.close()
```

find_module() does not process dotted names (example.submodule), so the caller has to take care to pass the correct path for any nested modules. That means that when importing the nested module from the package, give a path that points to the package directory for find_module() to locate a module within the package.

```
$ python imp_find_module.py

Package:
package ./example

Submodule:
source ./example/submodule.py
```

If find_module() cannot locate the module, it raises an ImportError.

```
import imp

try:
    imp.find_module('no_such_module')
except ImportError, err:
    print 'ImportError:', err
```

The error message includes the name of the missing module.

```
$ python imp_find_module_error.py

ImportError: No module named no_such_module
```

19.1.4 Loading Modules

After the module is found, use load_module() to actually import it. load_module() takes the full dotted-path module name and the values returned by find_module() (the open file handle, filename, and description tuple).

```
import imp

f, filename, description = imp.find_module('example')
try:
```

```
    example_package = imp.load_module('example', f,
                                      filename, description)
    print 'Package:', example_package
finally:
    if f:
        f.close()

f, filename, description = imp.find_module(
    'submodule', example_package.__path__)
try:
    submodule = imp.load_module('example.submodule', f,
                                filename, description)
    print 'Submodule:', submodule
finally:
    if f:
        f.close()
```

`load_module()` creates a new module object with the name given, loads the code for it, and adds it to `sys.modules`.

```
$ python imp_load_module.py

Importing example package
Package: <module 'example' from '/Users/dhellmann/Documents/
PyMOTW/book/PyMOTW/imp/example/__init__.pyc'>
Importing submodule
Submodule: <module 'example.submodule' from '/Users/dhellmann/
Documents/PyMOTW/book/PyMOTW/imp/example/submodule.pyc'>
```

If `load_module()` is called for a module that has already been imported, the effect is like calling `reload()` on the existing module object.

```
import imp
import sys

for i in range(2):
    print i,
    try:
        m = sys.modules['example']
    except KeyError:
        print '(not in sys.modules)',
    else:
        print '(have in sys.modules)',
```

```
    f, filename, description = imp.find_module('example')
    example_package = imp.load_module('example', f, filename,
                                          description)
```

Instead of a creating a new module, the contents of the existing module are replaced.

```
$ python imp_load_module_reload.py

0 (not in sys.modules) Importing example package
1 (have in sys.modules) Importing example package
```

See Also:

imp (http://docs.python.org/library/imp.html) The standard library documentation for this module.

***Modules and Imports* (page 1080)** Import hooks, the module search path, and other related machinery in the `sys` (page 1055) module.

`inspect` (page 1200) Load information from a module programmatically.

PEP 302 (www.python.org/dev/peps/pep-0302) New import hooks.

PEP 369 (www.python.org/dev/peps/pep-0369) Post import hooks.

19.2 zipimport—Load Python Code from ZIP Archives

Purpose Import Python modules saved as members of ZIP archives.
Python Version 2.3 and later

The `zipimport` module implements the `zipimporter` class, which can be used to find and load Python modules inside ZIP archives. The `zipimporter` supports the "import hooks" API specified in PEP 302; this is how Python Eggs work.

It is not usually necessary to use the `zipimport` module directly, since it is possible to import directly from a ZIP archive as long as that archive appears in `sys.path`. However, it is instructive to study how the importer API can be used to learn the features available, and understand how module importing works. Knowing how the ZIP importer works will also help debug issues that may come up when distributing applications packaged as ZIP archives created with `zipfile.PyZipFile`.

19.2.1 Example

These examples reuse some of the code from the discussion of `zipfile` to create an example ZIP archive containing a few Python modules.

```python
import sys
import zipfile

if __name__ == '__main__':
    zf = zipfile.PyZipFile('zipimport_example.zip', mode='w')
    try:
        zf.writepy('.')
        zf.write('zipimport_get_source.py')
        zf.write('example_package/README.txt')
    finally:
        zf.close()
    for name in zf.namelist():
        print name
```

Run `zipimport_make_example.py` before any of the rest of the examples to create a ZIP archive containing all the modules in the example directory, along with some test data needed for the examples in this section.

```
$ python zipimport_make_example.py

__init__.pyc
example_package/__init__.pyc
zipimport_find_module.pyc
zipimport_get_code.pyc
zipimport_get_data.pyc
zipimport_get_data_nozip.pyc
zipimport_get_data_zip.pyc
zipimport_get_source.pyc
zipimport_is_package.pyc
zipimport_load_module.pyc
zipimport_make_example.pyc
zipimport_get_source.py
example_package/README.txt
```

19.2.2 Finding a Module

Given the full name of a module, `find_module()` will try to locate that module inside the ZIP archive.

```python
import zipimport

importer = zipimport.zipimporter('zipimport_example.zip')

for module_name in [ 'zipimport_find_module', 'not_there' ]:
    print module_name, ':', importer.find_module(module_name)
```

If the module is found, the `zipimporter` instance is returned. Otherwise, `None` is returned.

```
$ python zipimport_find_module.py

zipimport_find_module : <zipimporter object "zipimport_example.zip">
not_there : None
```

19.2.3 Accessing Code

The `get_code()` method loads the code object for a module from the archive.

```
import zipimport

importer = zipimport.zipimporter('zipimport_example.zip')
code = importer.get_code('zipimport_get_code')
print code
```

The code object is not the same as a `module` object, but it is used to create one.

```
$ python zipimport_get_code.py

<code object <module> at 0x1002cb130, file
"./zipimport_get_code.py", line 7>
```

To load the code as a usable module, use `load_module()` instead.

```
import zipimport

importer = zipimport.zipimporter('zipimport_example.zip')
module = importer.load_module('zipimport_get_code')
print 'Name    :', module.__name__
print 'Loader :', module.__loader__
print 'Code    :', module.code
```

The result is a module object configured as though the code had been loaded from a regular import.

```
$ python zipimport_load_module.py

<code object <module> at 0x100431d30, file
```

```
"./zipimport_get_code.py", line 7>
Name    : zipimport_get_code
Loader : <zipimporter object "zipimport_example.zip">
Code    : <code object <module> at 0x100431d30, file
"./zipimport_get_code.py", line 7>
```

19.2.4 Source

As with the `inspect` module, it is possible to retrieve the source code for a module from the ZIP archive, if the archive includes the source. In the case of the example, only `zipimport_get_source.py` is added to `zipimport_example.zip` (the rest of the modules are just added as the `.pyc` files).

```
import zipimport

importer = zipimport.zipimporter('zipimport_example.zip')
for module_name in ['zipimport_get_code', 'zipimport_get_source']:
    source = importer.get_source(module_name)
    print '=' * 80
    print module_name
    print '=' * 80
    print source
    print
```

If the source for a module is not available, `get_source()` returns `None`.

```
$ python zipimport_get_source.py


================================================================
zipimport_get_code
================================================================
None


================================================================
zipimport_get_source
================================================================
#!/usr/bin/env python
#
# Copyright 2007 Doug Hellmann.
#
"""Retrieving the source code for a module within a zip archive.
```

```
"""
#end_pymotw_header

import zipimport

importer = zipimport.zipimporter('zipimport_example.zip')
for module_name in ['zipimport_get_code', 'zipimport_get_source']
    source = importer.get_source(module_name)
    print '=' * 80
    print module_name
    print '=' * 80
    print source
    print
```

19.2.5   Packages

To determine if a name refers to a package instead of a regular module, use
`is_package()`.

```
import zipimport

importer = zipimport.zipimporter('zipimport_example.zip')
for name in ['zipimport_is_package', 'example_package']:
    print name, importer.is_package(name)
```

In this case, `zipimport_is_package` came from a module and the
`example_package` is a package.

```
$ python zipimport_is_package.py

zipimport_is_package False
example_package True
```

19.2.6   Data

There are times when source modules or packages need to be distributed with noncode
data. Images, configuration files, default data, and test fixtures are just a few examples.
Frequently, the module `__path__` or `__file__` attributes are used to find these data
files relative to where the code is installed.

For example, with a "normal" module, the file system path can be constructed from
the `__file__` attribute of the imported package as follows.

```
import os
import example_package

# Find the directory containing the imported
# package and build the data filename from it.
pkg_dir = os.path.dirname(example_package.__file__)
data_filename = os.path.join(pkg_dir, 'README.txt')

# Find the prefix of pkg_dir that represents
# the portion of the path that does not need
# to be displayed.
dir_prefix = os.path.abspath(os.path.dirname(__file__) or os.getcwd())
if data_filename.startswith(dir_prefix):
    display_filename = data_filename[len(dir_prefix)+1:]
else:
    display_filename = data_filename

# Read the file and show its contents.
print display_filename, ':'
print open(data_filename, 'r').read()
```

The output will depend on where the sample code is located on the file system.

```
$ python zipimport_get_data_nozip.py

example_package/README.txt :
This file represents sample data which could be embedded in the ZIP
archive.  You could include a configuration file, images, or any other
sort of noncode data.
```

If the `example_package` is imported from the ZIP archive instead of the file system, using `__file__` does not work.

```
import sys
sys.path.insert(0, 'zipimport_example.zip')

import os
import example_package
print example_package.__file__
data_filename = os.path.join(os.path.dirname(example_package.__file__),
                             'README.txt')
```

```
print data_filename, ':'
print open(data_filename, 'rt').read()
```

The __file__ of the package refers to the ZIP archive, and not a directory, so building up the path to the README.txt file gives the wrong value.

```
$ python zipimport_get_data_zip.py

zipimport_example.zip/example_package/__init__.pyc
zipimport_example.zip/example_package/README.txt :
Traceback (most recent call last):
  File "zipimport_get_data_zip.py", line 40, in <module>
    print open(data_filename, 'rt').read()
IOError: [Errno 20] Not a directory:
'zipimport_example.zip/example_package/README.txt'
```

A more reliable way to retrieve the file is to use the get_data() method. The zipimporter instance that loaded the module can be accessed through the __loader__ attribute of the imported module.

```
import sys
sys.path.insert(0, 'zipimport_example.zip')

import os
import example_package
print example_package.__file__
print example_package.__loader__.get_data('example_package/README.txt')
```

pkgutil.get_data() uses this interface to access data from within a package.

```
$ python zipimport_get_data.py

zipimport_example.zip/example_package/__init__.pyc
This file represents sample data which could be embedded in the ZIP
archive.  You could include a configuration file, images, or any other
sort of noncode data.
```

The __loader__ is not set for modules not imported via zipimport.

See Also:

zipimport (http://docs.python.org/lib/module-zipimport.html) The standard library documentation for this module.

imp (page 1235) Other import-related functions.

PEP 302 (www.python.org/dev/peps/pep-0302) New Import Hooks.

pkgutil (page 1247) Provides a more generic interface to `get_data()`.

19.3 pkgutil—Package Utilities

> **Purpose** Add to the module search path for a specific package and work
> with resources included in a package.
>
> **Python Version** 2.3 and later

The `pkgutil` module includes functions for changing the import rules for Python packages and for loading noncode resources from files distributed within a package.

19.3.1 Package Import Paths

The `extend_path()` function is used to modify the search path and change the way submodules are imported from within a package so that several different directories can be combined as though they are one. This can be used to override installed versions of packages with development versions or to combine platform-specific and shared modules into a single-package namespace.

The most common way to call `extend_path()` is by adding these two lines to the __init__.py inside the package.

```
import pkgutil
__path__ = pkgutil.extend_path(__path__, __name__)
```

`extend_path()` scans `sys.path` for directories that include a subdirectory named for the package given as the second argument. The list of directories is combined with the path value passed as the first argument and returned as a single list, suitable for use as the package import path.

An example package called `demopkg` includes these files.

```
$ find demopkg1 -name '*.py'

demopkg1/__init__.py
demopkg1/shared.py
```

The __init__.py file in `demopkg1` contains **print** statements to show the search path before and after it is modified, to highlight the difference.

```
import pkgutil
import pprint

print 'demopkg1.__path__ before:'
pprint.pprint(__path__)
print

__path__ = pkgutil.extend_path(__path__, __name__)

print 'demopkg1.__path__ after:'
pprint.pprint(__path__)
print
```

The `extension` directory, with add-on features for `demopkg`, contains three more source files.

```
$ find extension -name '*.py'

extension/__init__.py
extension/demopkg1/__init__.py
extension/demopkg1/not_shared.py
```

This simple test program imports the `demopkg1` package.

```
import demopkg1
print 'demopkg1                :', demopkg1.__file__

try:
    import demopkg1.shared
except Exception, err:
    print 'demopkg1.shared     : Not found (%s)' % err
else:
    print 'demopkg1.shared     :', demopkg1.shared.__file__

try:
    import demopkg1.not_shared
except Exception, err:
    print 'demopkg1.not_shared: Not found (%s)' % err
else:
    print 'demopkg1.not_shared:', demopkg1.not_shared.__file__
```

When this test program is run directly from the command line, the `not_shared` module is not found.

> **Note:** The full file system paths in these examples have been shortened to empha-
> size the parts that change.

```
$ python pkgutil_extend_path.py

demopkg1.__path__ before:
['.../PyMOTW/pkgutil/demopkg1']

demopkg1.__path__ after:
['.../PyMOTW/pkgutil/demopkg1']

demopkg1              : .../PyMOTW/pkgutil/demopkg1/__init__.py
demopkg1.shared    : .../PyMOTW/pkgutil/demopkg1/shared.py
demopkg1.not_shared: Not found (No module named not_shared)
```

However, if the `extension` directory is added to the `PYTHONPATH` and the program is run again, different results are produced.

```
$ export PYTHONPATH=extension
$ python pkgutil_extend_path.py

demopkg1.__path__ before:
['.../PyMOTW/pkgutil/demopkg1']

demopkg1.__path__ after:
['.../PyMOTW/pkgutil/demopkg1',
 '.../PyMOTW/pkgutil/extension/demopkg1']

demopkg1              : .../PyMOTW/pkgutil/demopkg1/__init__.pyc
demopkg1.shared    : .../PyMOTW/pkgutil/demopkg1/shared.pyc
demopkg1.not_shared: .../PyMOTW/pkgutil/extension/demopkg1/not_
shared.py
```

The version of `demopkg1` inside the `extension` directory has been added to the
search path, so the `not_shared` module is found there.

Extending the path in this manner is useful for combining platform-specific versions of packages with common packages, especially if the platform-specific versions
include C extension modules.

19.3.2   Development Versions of Packages

While developing enhancements to a project, it is common to need to test changes to
an installed package. Replacing the installed copy with a development version may be

a bad idea, since it is not necessarily correct and other tools on the system are likely to depend on the installed package.

A completely separate copy of the package could be configured in a development environment using **virtualenv**, but for small modifications, the overhead of setting up a virtual environment with all the dependencies may be excessive.

Another option is to use `pkgutil` to modify the module search path for modules that belong to the package under development. In this case, however, the path must be reversed so the development version overrides the installed version.

Given a package `demopkg2` such as

```
$ find demopkg2 -name '*.py'

demopkg2/__init__.py
demopkg2/overloaded.py
```

with the function under development located in `demopkg2/overloaded.py`, the installed version contains

```
def func():
    print 'This is the installed version of func().'
```

and `demopkg2/__init__.py` contains

```
import pkgutil

__path__ = pkgutil.extend_path(__path__, __name__)
__path__.reverse()
```

`reverse()` is used to ensure that any directories added to the search path by `pkgutil` are scanned for imports *before* the default location.

This program imports `demopkg2.overloaded` and calls `func()`.

```
import demopkg2
print 'demopkg2                :', demopkg2.__file__

import demopkg2.overloaded
print 'demopkg2.overloaded:', demopkg2.overloaded.__file__
```

```
print
demopkg2.overloaded.func()
```

Running it without any special path treatment produces output from the installed version of `func()`.

```
$ python pkgutil_devel.py

demopkg2            : .../PyMOTW/pkgutil/demopkg2/__init__.py
demopkg2.overloaded: .../PyMOTW/pkgutil/demopkg2/overloaded.py
```

A development directory containing

```
$ find develop -name '*.py'

develop/demopkg2/__init__.py
develop/demopkg2/overloaded.py
```

and a modified version of `overloaded`

```
def func():
    print 'This is the development version of func().'
```

will be loaded when the test program is run with the `develop` directory in the search path.

```
$ export PYTHONPATH=develop
$ python pkgutil_devel.py

demopkg2            :.../PyMOTW/pkgutil/demopkg2/__init__.pyc
demopkg2.overloaded:.../PyMOTW/pkgutil/develop/demopkg2/overloaded.pyc
```

19.3.3 Managing Paths with PKG Files

The first example illustrated how to extend the search path using extra directories included in the `PYTHONPATH`. It is also possible to add to the search path using `*.pkg` files containing directory names. PKG files are similar to the PTH files used by the site module. They can contain directory names, one per line, to be added to the search path for the package.

Another way to structure the platform-specific portions of the application from the first example is to use a separate directory for each operating system and include a `.pkg` file to extend the search path.

This example uses the same demopkg1 files and also includes the following files.

```
$ find os_* -type f

os_one/demopkg1/__init__.py
os_one/demopkg1/not_shared.py
os_one/demopkg1.pkg
os_two/demopkg1/__init__.py
os_two/demopkg1/not_shared.py
os_two/demopkg1.pkg
```

The PKG files are named demopkg1.pkg to match the package being extended. They both contain the following.

```
demopkg
```

This demo program shows the version of the module being imported.

```
import demopkg1
print 'demopkg1:', demopkg1.__file__

import demopkg1.shared
print 'demopkg1.shared:', demopkg1.shared.__file__

import demopkg1.not_shared
print 'demopkg1.not_shared:', demopkg1.not_shared.__file__
```

A simple wrapper script can be used to switch between the two packages.

```
#!/bin/sh

export PYTHONPATH=os_${1}
echo "PYTHONPATH=$PYTHONPATH"
echo

python pkgutil_os_specific.py
```

And when run with `"one"` or `"two"` as the arguments, the path is adjusted.

```
$ ./with_os.sh one

PYTHONPATH=os_one

demopkg1.__path__ before:
['.../PyMOTW/pkgutil/demopkg1']

demopkg1.__path__ after:
['.../PyMOTW/pkgutil/demopkg1',
 '.../PyMOTW/pkgutil/os_one/demopkg1',
 'demopkg']

demopkg1           : .../PyMOTW/pkgutil/demopkg1/__init__.pyc
demopkg1.shared    : .../PyMOTW/pkgutil/demopkg1/shared.pyc
demopkg1.not_shared: .../PyMOTW/pkgutil/os_one/demopkg1/not_shared.pyc

$ ./with_os.sh two

PYTHONPATH=os_two

demopkg1.__path__ before:
['.../PyMOTW/pkgutil/demopkg1']

demopkg1.__path__ after:
['.../PyMOTW/pkgutil/demopkg1',
 '.../PyMOTW/pkgutil/os_two/demopkg1',
 'demopkg']

demopkg1           : .../PyMOTW/pkgutil/demopkg1/__init__.pyc
demopkg1.shared    : .../PyMOTW/pkgutil/demopkg1/shared.pyc
demopkg1.not_shared: .../PyMOTW/pkgutil/os_two/demopkg1/not_shared.pyc
```

PKG files can appear anywhere in the normal search path, so a single PKG file in the current working directory could also be used to include a development tree.

19.3.4   Nested Packages

For nested packages, it is only necessary to modify the path of the top-level package. For example, with the following directory structure

```
$ find nested -name '*.py'

nested/__init__.py
nested/second/__init__.py
nested/second/deep.py
nested/shallow.py
```

where `nested/__init__.py` contains

```
import pkgutil

__path__ = pkgutil.extend_path(__path__, __name__)
__path__.reverse()
```

and a development tree like

```
$ find develop/nested -name '*.py'

develop/nested/__init__.py
develop/nested/second/__init__.py
develop/nested/second/deep.py
develop/nested/shallow.py
```

both the `shallow` and `deep` modules contain a simple function to print out a message indicating whether or not they come from the installed or development version.

This test program exercises the new packages.

```
import nested

import nested.shallow
print 'nested.shallow:', nested.shallow.__file__
nested.shallow.func()

print
import nested.second.deep
print 'nested.second.deep:', nested.second.deep.__file__
nested.second.deep.func()
```

When `pkgutil_nested.py` is run without any path manipulation, the installed version of both modules is used.

```
$ python pkgutil_nested.py

nested.shallow: .../PyMOTW/pkgutil/nested/shallow.pyc
This func() comes from the installed version of nested.shallow

nested.second.deep: .../PyMOTW/pkgutil/nested/second/deep.pyc
This func() comes from the installed version of nested.second.deep
```

When the `develop` directory is added to the path, the development version of both functions override the installed versions.

```
$ export PYTHONPATH=develop
$ python pkgutil_nested.py

nested.shallow: .../PyMOTW/pkgutil/develop/nested/shallow.pyc
This func() comes from the development version of nested.shallow

nested.second.deep: .../PyMOTW/pkgutil/develop/nested/second/deep.pyc
This func() comes from the development version of nested.second.deep
```

19.3.5   Package Data

In addition to code, Python packages can contain data files, such as templates, default configuration files, images, and other supporting files used by the code in the package. The `get_data()` function gives access to the data in the files in a format-agnostic way, so it does not matter if the package is distributed as an EGG, as part of a frozen binary, or as regular files on the file system.

With a package `pkgwithdata` containing a `templates` directory,

```
$ find pkgwithdata -type f

pkgwithdata/__init__.py
pkgwithdata/templates/base.html
```

the file `pkgwithdata/templates/base.html` contains a simple HTML template.

```
<!DOCTYPE HTML PUBLIC "-//IETF//DTD HTML//EN">
<html> <head>
<title>PyMOTW Template</title>
```

```
</head>

<body>
<h1>Example Template</h1>

<p>This is a sample data file.</p>

</body>
</html>
```

This program uses `get_data()` to retrieve the template contents and print them out.

```
import pkgutil

template = pkgutil.get_data('pkgwithdata', 'templates/base.html')
print template.encode('utf-8')
```

The arguments to `get_data()` are the dotted name of the package and a filename relative to the top of the package. The return value is a byte sequence, so it is encoded as UTF-8 before being printed.

```
$ python pkgutil_get_data.py

<!DOCTYPE HTML PUBLIC "-//IETF//DTD HTML//EN">
<html> <head>
<title>PyMOTW Template</title>
</head>

<body>
<h1>Example Template</h1>

<p>This is a sample data file.</p>

</body>
</html>
```

`get_data()` is distribution format-agnostic because it uses the import hooks defined in PEP 302 to access the package contents. Any loader that provides the hooks can be used, including the ZIP archive importer in `zipfile`.

```
import pkgutil
import zipfile
```

```python
import sys
# Create a ZIP file with code from the current directory
# and the template using a name that does not appear on the
# local filesystem.
with zipfile.PyZipFile('pkgwithdatainzip.zip', mode='w') as zf:
    zf.writepy('.')
    zf.write('pkgwithdata/templates/base.html',
             'pkgwithdata/templates/fromzip.html',
             )

# Add the ZIP file to the import path.
sys.path.insert(0, 'pkgwithdatainzip.zip')

# Import pkgwithdata to show that it comes from the ZIP archive.
import pkgwithdata
print 'Loading pkgwithdata from', pkgwithdata.__file__

# Print the template body
print '\nTemplate:'
data = pkgutil.get_data('pkgwithdata', 'templates/fromzip.html')
print data.encode('utf-8')
```

This example uses `PyZipFile.writepy()` to create a ZIP archive containing a copy of the `pkgwithdata` package, including a renamed version of the template file. It then adds the ZIP archive to the import path before using `pkgutil` to load the template and print it. Refer to the discussion of `zipfile` for more details about using `writepy()`.

```
$ python pkgutil_get_data_zip.py

Loading pkgwithdata from pkgwithdatainzip.zip/pkgwithdata/__init__.pyc

Template:
<!DOCTYPE HTML PUBLIC "-//IETF//DTD HTML//EN">
<html> <head>
<title>PyMOTW Template</title>
</head>

<body>
<h1>Example Template</h1>

<p>This is a sample data file.</p>
```

```
</body>
</html>
```

See Also:

pkgutil (http://docs.python.org/lib/module-pkgutil.html) The standard library documentation for this module.

virtualenv (http://pypi.python.org/pypi/virtualenv) Ian Bicking's virtual environment script.

`distutils` Packaging tools from the Python standard library.

Distribute (http://packages.python.org/distribute/) Next-generation packaging tools.

PEP 302 (www.python.org/dev/peps/pep-0302) New Import Hooks.

`zipfile` **(page 457)** Create importable ZIP archives.

`zipimport` **(page 1240)** Importer for packages in ZIP archives.

INDEX OF PYTHON MODULES

INDEX

H

handle() method, SocketServer, 610

handle_close() method, asyncore, 621, 623–625

handle_connect() hook, asyncore, 621

Handler, implementing with asynchat, 632–634

handle_read() method, asyncore, 623, 628–629

handle_request(), SocketServer, 609

Handles, closing open, 169–170

handle_write() method, asyncore, 623

Hanging indents, textwrap, 12–13

Hard limits, resource, 1136

has_extn(), SMTP encryption, 730

hashlib module
creating hash by name, 471–472
incremental updates, 472–473
MD5 example, 470
purpose of, 469
reference guide, 473
sample data, 470
SHA1 example, 470–471

has_key() function, timeit, 1034–1035

has_option(), ConfigParser, 866–867

has_section(), ConfigParser, 865–866

Headers
adding to outgoing request in urllib2, 661–662
creating and setting Cookie, 678
encoding Cookie, 680–681
receiving and parsing Cookie, 681–682
setting in BaseHTTPServer, 650–651

"Heads," picking random items, 216

Heap sort algorithm. *See* heapq module

heapify() method, heapq, 90–92

heappop() method, heapq, 90–91

heapq module
accessing contents of heap, 90–92

creating heap, 89–90
data extremes from heap, 92–93
defined, 69
example data, 88
purpose of, 87–88
reference guide, 92–93

heapreplace() method, heapq, 91–92

Heaps, defined, 88

Help command, cmd, 840, 842–843

Help for modules, pydoc, 920–921

help() function, pydoc, 921

Help messages, argparse, 805–807

Help messages, optparse
application settings, 793–795
organizing options, 791–793
overview of, 790–791

hexdigest() method
calculating MD5 hash, hashlib, 470–471
digest() method vs., 475–476
HMAC message signatures, 474
SHA vs. MD5, 474–475

HistoryCompleter class, readline, 832–834

hmac module
binary digests, 475–476
message signature applications, 476–479
purpose of, 473
reference guide, 479
SHA vs. MD5, 474–475
signing messages, 474

Hooks, triggering actions in readline, 834–835

Hostname
parsing URLs, 639
socket functions to look up, 563–565

Hosts
multicast receiver running on different, 590–591
using dynamic values with queries, 359–362

hour attribute, time class, 181

HTML help for modules, pydoc, 920–921

HTML output, cgitb, 972

HTMLCalendar, formatting, 192

HTTP

BaseHTTPServer. *See* BaseHTTPServer module

cookies. *See* Cookie module

HTTP GET, 644, 657–660

HTTP POST, 646–647, 661

Human-consumable results, JSON, 692–694

Hyperbolic functions, math, 243–244

hypot() function, math, 242–243

Hypotenuse, math, 240–243

I

I/O operations
asynchronous network. *See* asyncore module
codecs, 287–289, 295–298
waiting for I/O efficiently. *See* select module

id() values, pickle, 342–343

idpattern class attribute, string.Template, 7–9

ifilter() function, itertools, 150

ifilterfalse() function, itertools, 150–151

ignore command, breakpoints in pdb, 999–1001

ignore mode, codec error handling, 292–293, 295

IGNORECASE regular expression flag
abbreviation, 45
creating back-references in re, 53
searching text, 37–38

Ignoring breakpoints, 999–1001

Ignoring signals, 502

Illegal jumps, execution flow in pdb, 1005–1008

imap() function, itertools, 145–146, 148

IMAP (Internet Message Access Protocol). *See also* imaplib module, 738–739

IMAP4_SSL. *See* imaplib module

IMAP4_stream, 739

imaplib module
connecting to server, 739–741
defined, 727
deleting messages, 756–758
example configuration, 741
fetching messages, 749–752

Developer's Library

ESSENTIAL REFERENCES FOR PROGRAMMING PROFESSIONALS

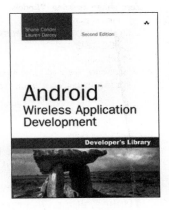

Python Essential Reference, Fourth Edition

David M. Beazley

ISBN-13: 9780672329784

Programming in Python 3: A Complete Introduction to the Python Language, Second Edition

Mark Summerfield

ISBN-13: 9780321680563

Android™ Wireless Application Development, Second Edition

Shane Conder
Lauren Darcey

ISBN-13: 9780321743015

Other Developer's Library Titles

TITLE	AUTHOR	ISBN-13
The Android™ Developer's Cookbook	James Steele / Nelson To	9780321741233
Drupal's Building Blocks	Earl Miles / Lynette Miles	9780321591319
Multicore Application Programming	Darryl Gove	9780321711373
Test-Driven JavaScript Development	Christian Johansen	9780321683915

Developer's Library books are available at most retail and online bookstores. For more information or to order direct, visit our online bookstore at **informit.com/devlibrary**.

Online editions of all Developer's Library titles are available by subscription from Safari Books Online at **safari.informit.com**.

Addison
Wesley

Developer's Library

informit.com/devlibrary

FREE Online Edition

Your purchase of **The Python Standard Library by Example** includes access to a free online edition for 45 days through the Safari Books Online subscription service. Nearly every Addison-Wesley Professional book is available online through Safari Books Online, along with more than 5,000 other technical books and videos from publishers such as Cisco Press, Exam Cram, IBM Press, O'Reilly, Prentice Hall, Que, and Sams.

SAFARI BOOKS ONLINE allows you to search for a specific answer, cut and paste code, download chapters, and stay current with emerging technologies.

Activate your FREE Online Edition at www.informit.com/safarifree

> **STEP 1:** Enter the coupon code: WGZEHBI.

> **STEP 2:** New Safari users, complete the brief registration form.
> Safari subscribers, just log in.

If you have difficulty registering on Safari or accessing the online edition, please e-mail customer-service@safaribooksonline.com